HUMAN RIGHTS AT WORK

Conc... the
'cred... their
labou... it to
reduc... is as
the a... both
natio... ights
are fu... ether
this i...

Th... urse
into l... The
rema... and
is div... nber
of na... d as
huma... can,
Amer... sists
of es... tems
for h... eat-
ment... oters
which... ghts
law. ... tory
appro...

EMPL
Fen
Std

Oñati International Series in Law and Society

A SERIES PUBLISHED FOR THE OÑATI INSTITUTE
FOR THE SOCIOLOGY OF LAW

General Editors

Judy Fudge   David Nelken

Founding Editors

William LF Felstiner   Eve Darian-Smith

Board of General Editors

Rosemary Hunter, University of Kent, United Kingdom
Carlos Lugo, Hostos Law School, Puerto Rico
Jacek Kurczewski, Warsaw University, Poland
Marie-Claire Foblets, Leuven University, Belgium
Roderick Macdonald, McGill University, Canada

Titles in this Series

Social Dynamics of Crime and Control: New Theories for a World in
Transition *edited by Susanne Karstedt and Kai Bussmann*

Criminal Policy in Transition *edited by Andrew Rutherford
and Penny Green*

Making Law for Families *edited by Mavis Maclean*

Poverty and the Law *edited by Peter Robson and Asbjørn Kjønstad*

Adapting Legal Cultures *edited by Johannes Feest and David Nelken*

Rethinking Law, Society and Governance: Foucault's Bequest
edited by Gary Wickham and George Pavlich

Rules and Networks *edited by Richard Appelbaum, Bill Felstiner
and Volkmar Gessner*

Women in the World's Legal Professions *edited by Ulrike Schultz
and Gisela Shaw*

Healing the Wounds *edited by Marie-Claire Foblets and Trutz von Trotha*

Imaginary Boundaries of Justice *edited by Ronnie Lippens*

Family Law and Family Values *edited by Mavis Maclean*

Contemporary Issues in the Semiotics of Law *edited by Anne Wagner, Tracey Summerfield and Farid Benavides Vanegas*

The Geography of Law: Landscapes, Identity and Regulation *edited by Bill Taylor*

Theory and Method in Socio-Legal Research *edited by Reza Banakar and Max Travers*

Luhmann on Law and Politics *edited by Michael King and Chris Thornhill*

Precarious Work, Women and the New Economy: The Challenge to Legal Norms *edited by Judy Fudge and Rosemary Owens*

Juvenile Law Violators, Human Rights, and the Development of New Juvenile Justice Systems *edited by Eric L Jensen and Jørgen Jepsen*

The Language Question in Europe and Diverse Societies: Political, Legal and Social Perspectives *edited by Dario Castiglione and Chris Longman*

European Ways of Law: Towards A European Sociology of Law *edited by Volkmar Gessner and David Nelken*

Crafting Transnational Policing: Police Capacity-Building and Global Policing Reform *edited by Andrew Goldsmith and James Sheptycki*

Constitutional Politics in the Middle East: With special reference to Turkey, Iraq, Iran and Afghanistan *edited by Saïd Amir Arjomand*

Parenting after Partnering: Containing Conflict after Separation *edited by Mavis Maclean*

Responsible Business: Self-Governance and Law in Transnational Economic Transactions *edited by Olaf Dilling, Martin Herberg and Gerd Winter*

Rethinking Equality Projects in Law *edited by Rosemary Hunter*

Regulating Deviance: The Redirection of Criminalisation and the Futures of Criminal Law *edited by Bernadette McSherry, Alan Norrie and Simon Bronitt*

Living Law: Reconsidering Eugen Ehrlich *edited by Marc Hertogh*

Multicultural Jurisprudence: Comparative Perspectives on the Cultural Defense *edited Marie-Claire Foblets and Alison Dundes Renteln*

Legal Institutions and Collective Memories *edited by Susanne Karstedt*

The Legal Tender of Gender: Welfare Law and the Regulation of Women's Poverty *edited by Shelley Gavigan and Dorothy Chunn*

Human Rights at Work

Perspectives on Law and Regulation

Edited by
Colin Fenwick
and
Tonia Novitz

Oñati International Series in Law and Society

A SERIES PUBLISHED FOR THE OÑATI INSTITUTE
FOR THE SOCIOLOGY OF LAW

·HART·
PUBLISHING
OXFORD AND PORTLAND, OREGON
2010

Published in the United Kingdom by Hart Publishing Ltd
16C Worcester Place, Oxford, OX1 2JW
Telephone: +44 (0)1865 517530
Fax: +44 (0)1865 510710
E-mail: mail@hartpub.co.uk
Website: http://www.hartpub.co.uk

Published in North America (US and Canada) by
Hart Publishing
c/o International Specialized Book Services
920 NE 58th Avenue, Suite 300
Portland, OR 97213-3786
USA
Tel: +1 503 287 3093 or toll-free: (1) 800 944 6190
Fax: +1 503 280 8832
E-mail: orders@isbs.com
Website: http://www.isbs.com

British Library Cataloguing in Publication Data
Data Available

ISBN: (PBK) 978-1-84113-998-2
(HBK) 978-1-84113-999-9

Typeset by Compuscript Ltd, Shannon
Printed and bound in Great Britain by
TJ International Ltd, Padstow, Cornwall

Foreword

The International Labour Organisation (ILO) Constitution declares that 'labour is not a commodity'. But what was once a bold claim has again become a cruel solecism in a world of rampant global capitalism, characterised by deregulation, privatisation and competitiveness. Alongside product markets and financial markets, we now have labour markets (a term used without either irony or shame), characterised in turn by insecurity, inequality and unfairness, in which people have again become 'neither more nor less than sugar'. In this world in which workers have become objects conspicuously bought and sold, labour law has become the servant of free market economists, with little scope for either humanity or empathy, and even less for equality and social justice.

In this new orthodoxy (which continues to endure), everything must be justified in terms of a 'business case'. The choice is thus presented sometimes as a choice between (i) no regulation (regulation is unnecessary and will impede wealth creation from which everyone benefits), or (ii) regulation for efficiency (smart regulation) whereby businesses can be required to accept (or may even desire) certain forms of regulation because they require a more efficient use of labour than the market might otherwise dictate (as in the case of race and gender discrimination), or (iii) regulation for market failure (regulation is desirable in order to alleviate the worst excesses of free market capitalism, and desirable as a result to safeguard the reputation of the latter).

THE FALSE PROSPECTUS

Yet despite these contemporary concerns, the relationship between labour law and economics is by no means new, though it no doubt finds expression in different ways in different countries. Labour law has always been subordinate to prevailing economic orthodoxy; it is just that many labour lawyers approved the prevailing orthodoxy until it changed in 1976 or thereabouts. So although labour lawyers tend to highlight great pieces of legislation as the key events in the development of their discipline, this obscures the truth that it is economics not politics that has been crucial: in the British case, for example, the seminal events in the development of labour law were not the great statutes of 1906 or 1974, but the ignominious events of 1929–1931 and 1976–1979.

The events of 1929–1931 led, in 1934, to the beginning of the end of the period of state regulatory inactivity since 1921, and to the end of the process of trade union decline. In the fall-out from the Great Depression, a Conservative government engineered a major revision of policy when it re-invested in the Whitley Council system, with the then Minister of Labour announcing to the House of Commons in 1938 that it was now government policy to 'foster and encourage the establishment of [collective bargaining] machinery over an ever-widening field' (House of Commons Debates, 11 May 1938). The reasons now seem obvious: even the Conservatives saw the wisdom of a virtuous circle which would raise wages, equalise incomes, stimulate demand, reduce unemployment, and promote social stability.

The latter events of 1974–1979 were crucial because a new economic crisis led to a rejection of the assumptions that had inspired the response to the last, and set in train a strategy for labour law that is well known, and with which we continue to live, subject only to a few mild adjustments since Labour came to power in 1997. That crisis helped to create a new economic orthodoxy which saw no room for trade unions and little room for employment standards determined by the state. So we have seen a massive programme of deconstruction and deregulation, in order to increase the supply of cheap labour, in order to release managerial prerogative, and in order to enhance the competitiveness of firms. Although commentators will point to the volume of 'progressive' legislation since 1997 and poke fun at the sceptics, that post-1997 legislation is to be judged by its regulatory impact, not by the number of pages it consumes in the statute book.

Despite the increase in the volume of labour law in recent years, at best this can be said to have moderated the harsh effects of the market rather than to have subordinated the latter to the needs of people. For all the achievements of initiatives like the national minimum wage, social inequality in the United Kingdom is at its highest levels since the early 1960s; there is a growing army of unregulated labour in the shape of agency workers; and trade unions (the instruments of social justice) operate under tight legal controls, with statutory bargaining rights that have been shown by experience to have been largely ineffective to prevent the continuing decline in collective bargaining coverage, which now stands proudly—or shamefully— at 33 per cent of the workforce. It is one of the great disappointments that the most recent global financial crisis has left this orthodoxy unshaken.

LABOUR LAW AND HUMAN RIGHTS

Which brings us eventually to the inspiring volume edited by Colin Fenwick and Tonia Novitz, and its frank assessment of an alternative vision for the study of labour law, a vision in which markets are subordinated to the interests of all people rather than one in which workers are sacrificed on the altar of free enterprise. It is a collection which in its different parts invites us to ask some very basic questions which have been notably absent in recent debates about the core and scope of labour law. Thus,

WHAT IS LABOUR LAW FOR?

Are labour lawyers merely handmaidens in the service of those who work in other disciplines, or does labour law have an identity of its own, separate from and beyond the interests of these other disciplines? If so,

WHAT ARE THE VALUES BY WHICH LABOUR LAW IS UNDERPINNED?

In making an important contribution to our understanding of the core values of labour law, this book invites us to cast aside old-fashioned and inappropriate private law concepts which have been a source of enduring restraint, and to put down roots in a new and different location. Human rights based in principles of public law provides the fertile soil for this new development, significant in the labour law context because of the growing global awareness of human rights treaties such as ILO Convention Nos 87 and 98, the International Covenant on Economic, Social and Cultural Rights, and the European Social Charters of 1961 and 1996. This is not to say that human rights discourse alone provides a convincing explanation of the core values of labour law in which equality and social justice also compete for attention. But at least for the time being, it is a convenient and convincing tool which is helpful (for some of the reasons addressed by Lance Compa in chapter ten) to overcome many of the problems encountered by labour lawyers schooled in private law techniques.

It is true that traditionally labour lawyers would have been sceptical of human rights as a defining framework for labour law, partly because—as pointed out in chapters one and twenty one—civil and political rights have traditionally been narrowly construed to exclude trade union rights or expansively construed to undermine these rights. But the mood has changed, not least because of the decision of the Strasbourg Court in *Demir and Baykara v Turkey* on 12 November 2008. There the Court repudiated more than three decades of case law and held that

> the right to bargain collectively with the employer has, in principle, become one of the essential elements of the 'right to form and to join trade unions for the protection of [one's] interests' set forth in Article 11 of the Convention, it being understood that States remain free to organise their system so as, if appropriate, to grant special status to representative trade unions.

Even more remarkable than the fact that the Court was prepared to change its mind so frankly, *and* that it was willing to do so by 17 votes to nil in the Grand Chamber, is that it held that in determining the substance of the new article 11 right to bargain collectively, it was necessary to have regard to core ILO conventions, the Council of Europe's Social Charter, and also the jurisprudence of the supervisory bodies of each.

Even more remarkable still is that this line of reasoning on the part of the Court opened the door to other 'essential' trade union rights, notably the right to strike which has been held to be a convention right, with no fewer than four cases on the right to strike (from Russia and Turkey) having been decided by the Court in the first 12 months following the landmark decision in *Demir and Baykara*. The applicants succeeded in all four cases. In the process, the Court considered a wide range of issues which tend to indicate (i) that the Convention right to strike follows a human rights rather than an industrial relations approach (the ILO model, which means that it is not confined to collective bargaining), (ii) that it is a right of the trade union as well as its members (with the victim in the first of the four cases being a Turkish trade union), and (iii) that various forms of penalty (from criminal sanctions to disciplinary warnings) imposed on individual workers constitute a breach of this right.

THE LIMITS OF HUMAN RIGHTS

The European Court of Human Rights is not alone in elevating the debate about labour standards beyond the horizons of economics and private law. Similar forces are at work in the Supreme Court of Canada, with Canadian labour law in a process of an unsteady transition, as we learn in chapter four. But as this book makes very clear, we should have a realistic sense of the capabilities of human rights—or more particularly human rights litigation—as a source of liberation. To a very large extent the reliance on human rights is a reflection of the failure of the promise of democracy, and of the capture of the democratic process by economic power, in a way which is now well documented by political sociologists (amongst whom the most notable is probably Ralph Miliband). It is a reflection of the claim attributed to Adam Smith by the great lawyer DN Pritt that 'whenever the legislature attempts to regulate the differences between masters and their workmen, its counsellors are always the masters' (DN Pritt, *Law, Class and Society, Book One: Employers, Workers and Trade Unions* (1970) 3).

In addressing the failure of democracy through law, we are faced with the most remarkable contradiction, at least for those of us schooled in the common law. It was the problem of law—notably in decisions such as the *Taff Vale* case in the United Kingdom and its equivalents elsewhere—that fuelled demands for more democratic participation and political institutions to enhance that participation. But it is the very failure of that democracy that has led trade unions in some jurisdictions to return to the very law by which they were initially oppressed. Instead of relying on 'counsellors who are "always the masters"', the need now is to rely on 'high priests' of the law—legal professionals and judges—despite the latter in the past having been nearly always unsympathetic to trade unions and their goals, and despite the fact that democracy is eclipsed by a process in which trade unions participate only as litigants with no opportunity, ever, to secure the reins of power in this particular forum.

Yet while the move from legislation to litigation as a trade union strategy may lead to significant advances, as this book reveals, it is one in which significant obstacles have to be overcome. So while helpful, human rights are no panacea and particular forms of human rights protections are no guarantee of respect for labour standards. In the pages that follow we learn from a number of national case studies that (i) in Brazil the acknowledgement of fundamental rights in the federal Constitution does not overcome 'difficulties in realizing these rights in practice' (chapter three); (ii) in China there is no system for the legal enforcement of constitutional rights (and indeed that labour law is a weak line of defence against the forces of economic reform) (chapter five); and (iii) in India the courts are falling into line behind new economic orthodoxy to reveal 'a shift in the approach of the court', particularly in areas where 'the interests of workers appear to be sharply pitted against those of the state and other employers' (chapter seven).

Apart from these problems of process (litigation rather than legislation) and substance (narrow rather than expansive reading of rights), there are other unexpected and mundane—but nevertheless real—problems of procedure that conspire to undermine the human rights approach. By a cruel irony these have been identified most powerfully in relation to South Africa, a jurisdiction that was a source of hope and optimism for progressives everywhere, and a jurisdiction with a constitution based on values 'including worker's rights' (chapter nine). These values find eloquent expression in the 1996 Constitution with its guarantees of 'fair labour standards' and core trade union rights (such as the right to bargain collectively and the right to strike). Yet as we also discover in the pages that follow, this 'constitutional-isation of workers' rights' has 'spawned unforeseen jurisdictional problems which to a certain extent, is leading the way to the de-compartmentalisation of labour law as an independent legal subject'.

THE LIMITS OF HUMAN RIGHTS INSTITUTIONS

Along with certain weaknesses of human rights law, this book also identifies a number of serious failings of political institutions and human rights instruments (chapters eleven to sixteen). Despite their rich formal content, the contribution of the United Nations (UN) covenants (the International Covenant on Civil and Political Rights (ICCPR) and the International Covenant on Economic, Social and Cultural Rights (ICESCR) has 'not been auspicious': many important labour rights (such as the right to bargain collectively) have not been 'meaningfully addressed', while others (such as the right to strike) have been the 'subject of unsatisfactory jurisprudence', revealing a failure to deal with the 'impact of globalisation upon labour rights ... coherently and strategically' (chapter eleven). The ILO has also been found wanting, with intervention to deal with freedom of association problems in specific jurisdictions having 'failed', and with the state of trade union rights in other parts of the world a testament to the fact that this is a global concern (chapter twelve).

While the application of international labour standards in national systems continues to be a problem caused in part by weak enforcement mechanisms, problems relating to the international agencies themselves are also nicely examined, especially in relation to the ILO (chapter twelve). The problems of the ILO are such, however, that its future role may have to be one in which it continues to work in what is an emerging and complex set of informal relationships with other political, judicial and non-governmental actors to implement and develop the standards it creates. The urge for institutional reform should not deflect attention from the real contemporary value of the supervisory bodies, which are now helping to inform the jurisprudence of international and national courts. Although there is a strong case for standards' modernisation in the context of globalisation, the contemporary importance of the ILO is not in standard-setting, but rather in the development of its existing standards.

As pointed out below in the treatment of regional human rights instruments, the value of developing ILO standards is to be seen specifically in the jurisprudence relating to the European Convention on Human Rights, where the European Court of Human Rights (ECtHR) is now making full use of ILO material of a wide and varied kind in the development of Convention rights. Nevertheless, there is a cautionary tale to be told here too, for while there has been a gradual and incremental extension of human rights (including workers' rights) protection under regional human rights instruments, there is a concern that 'this may not always be sufficient to ensure that the collective dimension of workers' rights is recognised as opposed to negative freedoms, such as that not to associate' (chapter fourteen), though as is also pointed out, 'the ECtHR (which has been the most active in developing the negative right) has not explored thoroughly the conditions in which union security clauses can be compatible with the ECHR' (chapter fifteen).

However, it is not only the problem of institutional failings: there is also the related problem of institutional danger, as in the case of the EU where there is an apparent attempt to reconcile fundamental social rights of workers with the economic freedoms of business under the one umbrella through various treaty mechanisms. As we discover, however, it is a case of giving with the one hand and taking with the other, with more being taken than being given (chapter sixteen). For as made very clear in the pages that follow, the economic rights of business have triumphed over the human rights of workers, much as they did under the common law in the nineteenth and twentieth centuries. It is not clear, however, whether this matter has been finally resolved, for as is also made clear in chapter one (and as has been suggested above), the dynamic nature of human rights instruments and their construction suggests that this matter will have to be revisited. Although it is impossible to predict what the outcome will be when this does eventually take place, some of the issues—to be canvassed in the shadow of the Lisbon Treaty—are carefully explored in chapter sixteen.

HUMAN RIGHTS AND CORPORATIONS

In addition to international and national laws promoting the human rights of workers, there are of course other instruments that can be used by regional bodies (such as the EU) or nations to encourage compliance with human rights obligations, whether in the form of trade preferences (chapter seventeen), supply-chain compliance (chapter twenty), or by other means (such as global framework agreements between multinationals and global union federations). The latter techniques raise questions too about the nature of the obligations that are or should be imposed on corporations by international or national law, and the scope for litigation against multi-nationals in the developed world that abuse workers' rights elsewhere. This is the subject of fierce debate within the UN, with the substance of the debate most recently captured by a helpful (if tepid) report of the Westminster Parliament's Joint Committee on Human Rights (HL Paper 5, HC 64, 2009–10).

Nevertheless, there remain important questions to be addressed about the capacity of human rights to tame the power of the global corporations based in the highly developed countries of the world. With the exception of the Organisation for Economic Co-operation and Development (OECD) Guidelines on Multinational Enterprises (under which some notable successes have been won (see HL Paper 5-II, HC 64-II, 2009–10, Ev 250 (ICTUR))), this is a regulation-free zone. The companies will tell us of course that they respect human rights through their highly developed codes of conduct and their corporate social responsibility programmes. Well, if the still naïve need any convincing about corporate social responsibility, take a look at the global financial crisis, caused by the corporate social irresponsibility of some of the biggest corporations in the world, now compounding their irresponsibility by insisting on paying their executives massive bonuses at the public's expense, after having been bailed out by taxpayers in what amounts to the biggest welfare scheme in history.

If global banks and other global corporations are to behave responsibly, it can only be because they are required to do so by law, by which they become accountable as a result of legal obligations to public institutions in the form of courts. This means regulation of all their activities, including the terms by which they or their agents or partners employ people. Here too the human rights framework cultivated by this book has an indispensable role to play in informing this debate, in the sense that companies ought to be subject to legally enforceable human rights norms wherever they operate, with accountability to the courts of the home country if necessary. The freedom of association guarantees of ILO Convention Nos 87 and 98 are directed to national governments rather than companies, and they require governments rather than companies to comply with minimum standards. If companies misbehave, it is governments which take the hit, being responsible for the law operating in their jurisdiction, even though they may be at the implicit or explicit mercy of the transnational corporations (TNCs).

So while the contemporary focus of the ILO is on the development of its existing standards, rather than on standard-setting, there nevertheless remains a compelling case for modernising ILO and other human rights standards to recognise these new realities, and to recognise the role of global union federations as well as the role of national trade unions. To this end, an important agenda of the labour rights is to expand the frontiers of existing standards so that:

— workers and trade unions have a right (as against TNCs) to organise in global union federations (GUFs);
— workers and trade unions have a right (through GUFs) to bargain collectively with TNCs with a view to negotiating global framework agreements (GFAs); and
— workers and trade unions (through GUFs and otherwise) have a right to organise and take part in transnational collective action.

Part of that reform agenda must involve creating a complaints mechanism that enables companies (as well as governments) to be held publicly to account for their failure to comply with these standards.

CONCLUSION

All of which is to say that this volume is a timely and extremely important contribution to the future shape of labour law, at a moment when the discipline is in crisis, bereft of function and lacking any coherence as to its core values or identity. While human rights may not necessarily provide an enduring framework, this book makes it very clear at various points that such a framework is useful at a number of levels, for the time being. Not the least of these is rhetorical, for as Compa points out in chapter ten below, the language of human rights is empowering for workers, while also putting employers on the defensive (though it is also a currency likely to be devalued by its over-use). At a more practical level, human rights instruments provide an opportunity for workers to fight back, at a time when democracy has failed them, and when human rights courts (if not yet common law courts) appear at the moment to be responsive to the claim that workers' rights are human rights. Indeed, it is all the more important that workers' organisations should be present in these forums, especially as they are now being used by employers alleging that labour law curtails their human rights.

Human rights thus provide trade unions with an opportunity to go on the offensive to reclaim lost rights, although a human rights strategy also needs to build in defence mechanisms to deal with complaints that trade union rights violate the human rights of others. A defensive human rights strategy is thus necessary to retain established rights from further erosion, with complaints being made in forums as diverse as the ECtHR and the European Court of Justice. But while using human rights as part of a strategy of advance, we should heed the advice of Compa and not 'overstate the case for human rights or exaggerate the effect of the human rights argument'. Recent decisions of the ECtHR may be only temporal victories which may not endure, and while there is a strong momentum driving them forward, it remains to be seen how well this jurisprudence operates outside of countries like Turkey, Russia and the United Kingdom. Nevertheless, the human rights dimension cannot be overlooked while it provides (i) litigation opportunities, as well as (ii) firmer political ground in which to root the discipline of labour law, (iii) quite apart from any need to have a highly visible presence in this arena for defensive reasons.

In provoking an argument about the future direction of their discipline, Fenwick and Novitz—along with each of the contributors to this impressive volume—have made an immense contribution, for which labour lawyers everywhere have reason to be deeply grateful. We must now engage with the debate that they have initiated.

KD Ewing
Institute of Employment Rights
18 December 2009

Contents

List of Contributors

Daniel Adler, Official at the World Bank.

Chioma Agomo, Professor of Law, University of Lagos.

Christian Brunelle, Assistant Dean, Faculty of Law, Université Laval, Québec, Canada; Researcher at the Interuniversity Research Centre on Globalisation and Work.

Liu Cheng, Professor, Shanghai Normal University.

Sean Cooney, Associate Professor, Associate Director (Taiwan), Asian Law Centre, Melbourne Law School.

Lance Compa, Senior Lecturer, Cornell University, ILR School.

ACL Davies, Reader in Public Law, Oxford University.

Ferdi de Ville, Graduate Student, Political and Social Sciences, Ghent University.

Stefan Van Eck, Professor of Law, University of Pretoria.

Colin Fenwick, Associate Professor, Centre for Employment and Labour Relations Law, Melbourne Law School.

Ramapriya Gopalakrishnan, Advocate, Madras High Court.

Sarah Joseph, Professor of Law and Director, Castan Centre for Human Rights Law, Monash University.

Virginia Mantouvalou, Lecturer in Law, School of Law, University of Leicester.

Shelley Marshall, Lecturer, Department of Business Law and Taxation, Monash University.

Deirdre McCann, Senior Lecturer in Law, University of Manchester.

Ana Virginia Moreira Gomes, International Labour Law Professor at the Santos Catholic University.

Jill Murray, Senior Lecturer, La Trobe University, Melbourne, Australia.

Tonia Novitz, Professor of Labour Law, University of Bristol.

Jan Orbie, Professor of European Union Politics at the Centre for EU Studies, Department of Political Sciences, Ghent University.

Lisa Tortell, Legal Officer, International Labour Standards Department, International Labour Office, Geneva. At the time of writing chapter thirteen, the author was a senior researcher at DINÂMIA—Centre for Studies in Socio-Economic Change, ISCTE, Lisbon, Portugal.

Phil Syrpis, Senior Lecturer in Law, School of Law, University of Bristol.

Michael Woolcock, Professor of Social Science and Development Policy at the University of Manchester, and Research Director of the Brooks World Poverty Institute.

1

The Application of Human Rights Discourse to Labour Relations: Translation of Theory into Practice

TONIA NOVITZ AND COLIN FENWICK

INTRODUCTION

THE EMERGENCE OF 'human rights' as an influential discourse nationally, regionally and internationally, has encouraged litigants and lobbyists to defend workers' interests in these terms. The reasons for their use of legal and other mechanisms associated with the protection of human rights are arguably manifold, but they have been linked in particular to the effects—whether actual or perceived—of market led globalisation.

A well-known narrative expresses concern that globalisation has placed pressure on employers to compete on the basis of wage costs, and that there are likely to be adverse effects for workers from (de)regulatory competition by states designed to attract investment.[1] It may be observed that these pressures are now made even more acute by the current 'credit crunch' which has contracted available credit and thereby the capacity of private capital to invest.[2] States are chasing fewer investors. Moreover, any recession leads to, at best, rationalisation and restructuring of both public and private

---

[1] See Deakin, S, 'Social Rights in a Globalized Economy' in P Alston (ed), *Labour Rights as Human Rights* (Oxford, Oxford University Press, 2005); Hepple, B, *Labour Laws and Global Trade* (Oxford, Hart Publishing, 2005) ch 10; and Fudge, J, 'The New Discourse of Labour Rights: From Social to Fundamental Rights?' (2007) 29 *Comparative Labor Law and Policy Journal* 29.

[2] For a brief overview of these developments, see Gray, J, 'Lessons from the BCCI Saga for the Current Accountability Debate Surrounding Northern Rock?' (2008) 23(2) *Journal of International Banking and Regulation* 37; Lamb, A, 'Weathering the Storm' (2008) 188 *Legal Business* 59; Ryder, N, 'The Credit Crunch—The Right Time for Credit Unions to Strike?' (2009) 29 *Legal Studies* 75. See also Aalbers, M, 'Geographies of the Financial Crisis' (2009) 41 *Area* 34.

enterprise and, at worst, lay-offs.[3] Access for newly qualified workers to the labour market is also obstructed, such that terms and conditions of employment have the potential to diminish considerably.[4] As one commentator has put it, 'rising worker insecurity is the flipside of money-manager capitalism'.[5]

We have yet to see whether the current economic climate will lead to further union decline,[6] or excite collective activism. What has, however, been evident for some considerable period of time is an attempt to seek protection of workers' interests through avenues that may be more effective than traditional labour legislation and collectively negotiated agreements. This may be all the more pressing in a context where economic interests are seen to take priority over the dignity and self-determination of working people.

The aim of our research project has been to assess efforts to promote the rights of workers and their organisations in terms of human rights. It began with a workshop held at the International Institute for the Sociology of Law in Oñati, at which first drafts of almost all of the contributions published here were first presented. We have, however, subsequently drawn on the expertise of others who work in this field, so as to provide as detailed and rich a basis of analysis as is possible within a single volume. In our view this project is timely, because while it is tempting to seek to prioritise workers' claims by reference to their status as human rights, and there have been numerous attempts both in academic and policy literature to promote such an approach,[7] there has been little comparative scrutiny of the outcomes of this endeavour.

Many of the essays included in this collection examine in detail the decisions of courts and other institutions applying hard law, particularly law whose purpose is the protection and promotion of human rights. Other essays are more concerned with the broader effects of the claim that workers' rights ought to be understood and respected as basic human rights, and alternative regulatory approaches that might be used to pursue

---

[3] Nixon, J, 'Managing the Credit Crunch' (2009) 159 *New Law Journal* 135; Bamforth, R, 'Pension Schemes: Contending with the Credit Crunch' (2009) 20(5) *Practical Law Companies* 43; Finch, V, 'Corporate Rescue in a World of Debt' (2008) *Journal of Business Law* 756.

[4] David, R, 'Riding Out the Storm: Graduates, Enterprise and Careers in Turbulent Economic Times' (2008) 50 *Education + Training* 748.

[5] Whalen, CJ, 'An Institutionalist Perspective on the Global Financial Crisis' (Visiting Fellow Working Papers, Cornell University ILR School, 2009) 27.

[6] The empirical evidence as to the decline of trade union membership and influence is in fact difficult to measure and offers mixed support for such a view. See for example International Labour Organization (ILO) and World Trade Organization (WTO), *Trade and Employment: Challenges for Policy Research* (Geneva, 2007). Nevertheless, it is a widely held view.

[7] Alston, *Labour Rights as Human Rights* (2005); Gross, JA (ed), *Workers' Rights as Human Rights* (Cornell, Cornell University Press, 2006). In a UK context, see Ewing, KD, 'Social Rights and Constitutional Law' [1999] *Public Law* 105; and Ewing, KD and Hendy, J (eds), *A Charter of Workers' Rights* (London, Institute of Employment Rights, 2002). For a recent contribution and anlaysis in the context of the United States, see K Kolben, 'Labor Rights as Human Rights' (2010) 50 *Virginia Journal of International Law* 449.

that objective. In sum, the contributions to this edited collection indicate that the discourse of human rights, generously understood, may offer significant potential to advance the rights of workers and their organisations, even while legal protection of rights appears to offer much less in practice than it may at first appear to promise. Our suggestion, then, is that reliance on human rights discourse has the potential to achieve certain advances in the protection of workers' interests, but that the degree of success may depend upon the regulatory mechanisms utilised for this purpose.

In this introductory chapter, we also acknowledge that the very assessment of the success of this strategy turns on one's conception of human rights. One straightforward (and positivist) sense in which workers' rights can be understood to constitute human rights is through their incorporation into specific international human rights treaties, as well as domestic constitutions and national legislation. In this respect, we consider worthy of note the United Nations (UN) Universal Declaration of Human Rights 1948, the UN Covenants of 1966, instruments adopted under the auspices of the International Labour Organization (ILO) and various regional human rights instruments. Conceptually, however, the view that workers' rights may be regarded as human rights dates back, well beyond international agreement to the terms of these legal instruments, to the identification of workers' rights as 'natural rights'. In this introduction we attempt to trace some of this history, as it is clear from the chapters in this volume that the terms of the debates that have characterised arguments about whether and how workers' rights ought to be understood as human rights continue to shape the outcomes of the application of contemporary human rights discourse to workers' claims.

No two commentators on the subject provide an identical version of the evolving treatment of labour rights as human rights. Our aim in this introductory chapter is not so much to provide a definitive account of the genealogy, as to identify tensions between different understandings of workers' entitlements. We consider religious, liberal, libertarian and socialist theories. It is our view that the tensions between (and within) these schools of thought have influenced the standard distinctions that we see today between civil and political rights, on the one hand, and social and economic rights on the other. They appear to have had a particular impact in establishing the basis for a distinction between individual and collective rights. In our view, when applied to workers' interests, these categorisations are often problematic, and, in many respects, misleading.[8] Nevertheless, these distinctions would seem to have had a significant and pervasive influence

---

[8] See also in support of this view, as regards positive duties associated with civil and political rights as well as socio-economic rights, Fredman, S, *Human Rights Transformed: Positive Rights and Positive Duties* (Oxford, Oxford University Press, 2008).

on legal culture, or at least on western liberal legal culture.[9] Further, we suggest that the contested economic entitlements of employers and workers, which were considered ripe for debate as early as the seventeenth century, are not squarely addressed within traditional human rights discourse, and that this poses particular problems for workers and their organisations that seek to pursue their interests collectively, especially through collective bargaining and industrial action. In our view, the evidence for these assertions may be found in the national case studies contained in the first part of this edited collection.

We also consider how the divisions between civil and political rights and other 'generations' of human rights, as well as the tension between individual and collective rights, have been reflected in and maintained by international and regional human rights instruments. We suggest that the political climate underlying the adoption of these instruments has had a lasting effect on the formulation of the workers' rights that they contain, as well as the supervisory mechanisms established for their enforcement. Finally, we consider the particular role played by the ILO in this context, insofar as it has asserted that workers' rights are civil, political *and* socio-economic in character, and how that role may be understood to have changed by virtue of a policy shift towards promotion of 'core labour standards'.

In our view, the transformation of the ILO's role seems also to follow from the increasing influence of two more recent theoretical developments, which have dominated international politics since the end of the Cold War. The first is 'capabilities' theory, as developed by Amartya Sen,[10] which, it has been suggested, could supplement traditional forms of human rights discourse in a way that reconciles economic and social demands. We examine here its potential to do so, while considering also the extent to which this theory allows scope for protection of both the individual and collective dimensions of workers' human rights. The second influence, which is more directly concerned with governance than with human rights per se, is deliberative theory, as found particularly in the work of Jürgen Habermas and others,[11] and which gives prominence to the role of dialogue in the resolution of social conflict. We suggest that each (to differing degrees)

---

[9] *Cf* Liu Cheng and Cooney in this volume below who offer a different perspective on the potential understanding and use of human rights in the context of industrial relations in a Chinese context.

[10] See, for example, Sen, A, *Development as Freedom* (Oxford, Oxford University Press, 1999); for further extension of and application of this approach, see Nussbaum, M, *Women and Development: The Capabilities Approach* (Cambridge, Cambridge University Press, 2000).

[11] Habermas, J, *Between Facts and Norms: Contributions to a Discourse Theory of Law and Society* trans by W Rehg (Boston, MIT, 1997); see also Nino, C, *The Constitution of Deliberative Democracy* (Yale, Yale University Press, 1998); and Young, IM, *Inclusion and Democracy* (Oxford, Oxford University Press, 2000).

supplements traditional forms of human rights discourse in interesting ways, and offers a potential normative foundation for some of the alternative regulatory devices for human rights protection that are outlined in Part III of this book. However, we also offer a critical perspective on their application. Specific issues relating to regulation are discussed further in our concluding chapter.

WORKERS' RIGHTS IN THEORY

Workers' Rights under Natural Law

The notion of 'natural rights' would appear to have been derived from the idea of 'natural law', initially an idea propagated by Greek theorists, such as Plato[12] and Aristotle.[13] Initially, adherence to a natural legal order did not so much imply recognition of the individual claims of particular persons, but rather that communities should be guided by ethical precepts, which led to them owing certain duties to themselves and each other.[14] The early Greek theorists did not so much conceive of workers possessing entitlements as making a potential positive contribution to their community. Thus, in Plato's *Republic*, the ideal society is divided into the workers, the soldiers, and the rulers. Workers are those who are best suited to perform a certain kind of labour and to follow obediently the instructions of the rulers who possess true wisdom.[15]

The notion of natural law was elaborated upon, in the Roman Catholic tradition, by the prominent theologians, Augustine and St Thomas of Aquinas.[16] The latter, in particular, developed an idea of the 'common good' which encompassed respect for the role played by workers in society, including the claim to a living wage, but within limits set by social responsibility.

[12] Plato, *The Laws*, trans by Saunders, TJ (Harmondsworth, Penguin Books, 1970); and *The Republic*, trans by Jowett, B (New York, Random House, Modern Library, 1960).

[13] For example, Aristotle, *The Politics*, trans by Sinclair, TA (Harmondsworth, Penguin Books, 1962); and *The Ethics of Aristotle*, trans by Thomson, JAK (Harmondsworth, Penguin Books, 1963).

[14] Morrison, W, *Jurisprudence: From the Greeks to the Post-Modernists* (London, Cavendish, 1997) 27.

[15] See Plato, *The Republic* (1960) at paras 433 and 443. As to Aristotle's pragmatic view of slavery, see Aristotle, *The Politics* (1962) 1253–1260, also discussed in Thalmann, WG, *The Swineherd and the Bow: Representations of Class in the Odyssey* (Ithaca, Cornell, University Press, 1998) 32–41.

[16] On which, see Finnis, J, *Aquinas: Moral, Political, and Legal Theory* (Oxford, Oxford University Press, 1998); and *Natural Law and Natural Rights* (Oxford, Oxford University Press, 1980).

Most often cited is the Thomist statement that it is legitimate for a worker to seek:

> to have external riches in so far as they are necessary ... to live in keeping with his [sic] condition of life. Wherefor it will be a sin for him to exceed this measure, by wishing to acquire or keep them immodestly.[17]

Ethical claims to the human dignity of workers continue to play a central role in the context of Roman Catholic social teaching on the nature of work, oriented towards recognition of both rights and obligations arising from employment, in respect of both workers and employers.[18]

The starting point for this teaching is Pope Leo XIII's encyclical *Rerum Novarum* of 1891, which states that the broad concept of a 'good society' should be pursued in the context of the workplace by people 'acting virtuously and justly towards one another'.[19] It has been suggested that the encyclical played a very significant role in leading many nations to move away from legal opposition to and repression of trade union organising, toward assuring respect for workers' freedom of association in law and in practice.[20] Later writings have identified a wide range of workers' rights, which are broadly similar to those expressed in article 23 of the Universal Declaration of Human Rights.[21] In addition to the entitlement to a 'just wage',[22] workers are said to have rights to adequate rest, to a safe working environment, to measures to protect security of employment, to recognition that many workers also have family responsibilities, and to social insurance and protection in times of need.[23] On the 90th anniversary of *Rerum Novarum*, the Roman Catholic

---

[17] St Thomas Aquinas, Summa Theologica vol II, II. Translated by The Fathers of the English Dominican Province (1947) available at: http://www.sacred-texts.com/chr/aquinas/summa/index.htm. See for contemporary discussion of the principles he proposed, Macdonald, JE, 'Just Prices and Fair Wages: An Ancient Idea Compared with a Modern One' (2006) Indian Journal *of Economics and Business* available at: http://findarticles.com/p/articles/mi_m1TSD/is_2006_March; Blackburn, K, 'The Living Wage in Australia: A Secularization of Catholic Ethics in Wages, 1891–1907' (1996) 20 *The Journal of Religious History* 93; and McGee, RW, 'Thomas Aquinas: A Pioneer in the Field of Law & Economics' (1990) 18 *Western State University Law Review* 471.

[18] See, for example, Abbott, K, 'Catholic Social Thought and Labouring Ideals in Australia's New Industrial Context' (2008) 50 *Journal of Industrial Relations* 157, especially at 159–162; and Australian Catholic Council for Employment Relations (ACCER), *Workplace Relations: A Catholic Perspective* (Australian Catholic Council for Employment Relations, 2007) (available at: www.accer.asn.au).

[19] Abbott, 'Catholic Social Thought' (2008) 159, referring to Rerum Novarum On the Condition of the Working Classes, Encyclical Letter of Pope Leo XIII issued on 15 May 1891, para 19. See also http://www.osjspm.org/majordoc_rerum_novarum_official.aspx.

[20] Bellace, J, 'The ILO Declaration on Fundamental Principles and Rights at Work' (2001) 17 *The International Journal of Comparative Labour Law and Industrial Relations* 269, 275.

[21] ACCER, *Workplace Relations: A Catholic Perspective* (2007) 22.

[22] Papal encyclical *Quadragesimo Anno* (Pius XI, 1931) *Quadresimo Anno* (1931) paras 198–202, referred to in Abbott (n 18) 160.

[23] Abbott (n 18) 160 and ACCER (n 18) 30–32.

church was explicit about the link between its conception of workers' rights and human rights:

> work is ... a source of rights on the part of the *worker*. These rights must be examined in the broad *context of human rights as a whole*, which are connatural with man, and many of which are proclaimed by various international organizations and increasingly guaranteed by the individual States for their citizens respect for this broad range of human rights constitute the fundamental condition for peace in the modern world ... .[24]

The Natural Right to Property in One's Labour

There remains active debate as to whether the work of the natural law theorist, John Locke, should be viewed as theological or secular, on the basis that his theory follows from what persons would consent to in a divinely created state of nature.[25] Of greater interest has been his view of the status of workers' rights as natural rights and, in particular, the entitlement of each individual worker to property in their labour. A key proposition in Locke's work was that in the original 'state of nature' all people were 'equal and independent'.[26] Locke provided an account 'of slavery' but in such terms that one cannot by contract enslave oneself.[27] According to Locke, in the state of nature, all things were originally given to all people, and they were given to be held and used in common.[28] This proposition, of course, raised the need for a justification within his theory of the origins and role of the institution of private property, which would otherwise need common consent.

[24] Laborem Exercens On Human Work, Encyclical of Pope John Paul II issued on 14 September 1981 (1981) at para 16 (original emphasis), referred to in ACCER (n 18) 26–27. See http://www.osjspm.org/majordoc_laborem_exercens_official_text.aspx.

[25] See Simmonds, AJ, *The Lockean Theory of Rights* (Princeton University Press, 1992) 36–45; and Mitchell, J, 'Locke's Muted Calvinism' (1995) 57(4) *The Review of Politics* 734; and Hasnas, J, 'Towards a Theory of Empirical Natural Rights' (2005) *Social Policy and Philosophy Foundation* 111, available at: http://journals.cambridge.org/download. php?file=%2FSOY%2FSOY22_01%2FS0265052505041051a.pdf&code=d375b2150882d4 6001f7ea49a2a202a6.

[26] Locke, J, *Second Treatise on Civil Government: An Essay Concerning the True Original, Extent and End of Civil Government* (1690) reprinted in G Cumberlege, *Social Contract: Essays by Locke, Hume and Rousseau* (London/New York/Toronto, Oxford University Press) para 6.

[27] Locke, *Second Treatise on Civil Government* (1690) ch 4. Notably, his treatment of the subject was cited both by those defending slavery and its opponents. See for commentary, Lott, TL, McGary, H and Cohen, J (eds), *Subjugation and Bondage: Critical Essays on Slavery and Social Philosophy* (Lanham, Rowman and Littlefield, 1998); and Loewenberg, RJ, 'John Locke and the Antebellum Defense of Slavery' (1985) 13 *Political Theory* 266.

[28] Locke (n 26) para 25: 'it is very clear, that God, as king David says ... has given the earth to the children of men; given it to mankind in common'.

The transformative power of human labour was the central plank in Locke's theory of private property. He argued that while everything was originally given to all in common, there must be 'a means to appropriate' things 'before they can be of any use'.[29] For Locke, that means was the application or exertion of labour:

> Whatsoever, then, he removes out of the state that nature hath provided and left it in, he hath mixed his labour with it, and joined to it *something that is his own* and thereby makes it his property. It being by him removed from the common state nature placed it in, it hath by this labour something annexed to it that excludes the common right of other men.[30]

An important part of the theory was the assertion that 'every man has a property in his own person'. From this it followed that '[t]he labour of his body, *and the work of his hands* ... are properly his'.[31]

Ownership of one's own labour provided the basis for Locke's argument that by applying labour to commonly held property, a man might then claim something as his own: 'this labour being the unquestionable property of the labourer, no man but he can have a right to what that is once joined to, at least where there is enough and as good, left in common for others'.[32] As Locke puts it in another passage: 'The labour that was mine, removing them out of that common state they were in, hath fixed my property in them.'[33]

Locke took this position for a variety of reasons, amongst these being that those who labour are industrious and merit the results of their labour. He also argued that 'labour makes the far greatest part of the value of things, we enjoy in this World'.[34] His writing has been linked to a labour theory of value, namely that the value of a commodity is related to the labour invested in its creation.[35]

Locke did concede that the property created by the application of a man's labour might belong to another:

> [t]hus the grass my horse has bit; the turfs my servant has cut and the ore I have dug in any place where I have a right to them in common with others, becomes my property ... [t]he labour that was mine ... hath fixed my property in them.[36]

This passage raises the question of the status of 'servants'.

---

[29] Ibid para 26.

[30] Ibid 24–25, para 27 (emphasis added).

[31] Ibid (emphasis added).

[32] Ibid.

[33] Ibid para 28.

[34] Ibid para 36. Shrader-Frechette, K, 'Locke and Limits on Land Ownership' (1993) 54 *Journal of the History of Ideas* 201, 204–05.

[35] Steiner, H, 'The Natural Right to the Means of Production' (1977) *The Philosophical Quarterly* 41.

[36] Locke (n 26) 25–26, para 28. See also Vaughn, KI, 'John Locke and the Labor Theory of Value' (1978) 2 *Journal of Libertarian Studies* 311, 319.

Locke largely saw the role of a servant as being to provide service to a master in exchange for wages, but as doing so giving their own labour, and temporarily, and subject to the terms of 'what is contained in the contract between "em"'.[37] The master could then make use of the labour provided and claim the property which arose as the result of that labour. Nevertheless, his acceptance of the possibility of exchange was not inconsistent with his general proposition, which was that each man had property in himself and in his own labour, the application of which to commonly held property might support it then being privately held: "though the things of nature are given in common, yet man, by being master of himself, and proprietor of his own person, and the action or labour of it, had still in himself the great foundation of property".[38]

While one school of thought has stressed John Locke's role as a defender of private property and therefore of capitalism,[39] what is interesting for our purposes is how Locke's theory of property was later developed by those arguing for recognition of workers' rights. While Locke argued that men owned their own labour, he accepted that they might alienate the value of that labour, through contract, in return for wages and/or other support. Others, however, considered the wage-work bargain insufficient, and went much further in their arguments about workers' entitlement to the value of their labour.

Concern with the role of wages as a cause of poverty emerged as a force in eighteenth century liberal, republican and socialist scholarship.[40] Thomas Paine and John Thelwall, for example, appealed to natural rights as a basis for the entitlements of working people. Paine's *Rights of Man* argued for a shift from soft, charitable assistance to the working poor, to 'hard' rights to justice enforceable by government.[41] Thelwall sought 'an equal participation of all the necessaries of life, which are the product of their labour'.[42] On this basis, he asserted that there was a duty 'not merely to protect, but to improve the physical, the moral, and intellectual enjoyments ... of the whole population of that state'.[43] Unjust contracts for the supply of labour 'extorted by the power of an oppressor' for inadequate wages were to be

---

[37] Locke (n 26) 70, para 85.

[38] Ibid para 44.

[39] For eg Macpherson, CB, *The Political Philosophy of Possessive Individualism* (Oxford, Oxford University Press, 1962).

[40] Claeys, G, 'The Origins of the Rights of Labor: Republicanism, Commerce, and the Construction of Modern Social Theory in Britain, 1796–1805' (1994) 66 *Journal of Modern History* 249, 255.

[41] Ibid. See also www.ushistory.org/paine/rights/ for the original text of 1791–92. Note also Hare, I, 'Social Rights as Fundamental Human Rights' in Hepple, B (ed), Social and Labour Rights in a Global Context (Cambridge, Cambridge University Press, 2002), 155–56.

[42] Claeys, 'The Origins of the Rights of Labor' (1994) 264; citing Thelwell, J, *The Tribune (1795–96)* vol 1, 13.

[43] Ibid 266, citing Thelwell, J, *The Rights of Nature* (London, 1796) pt 1:16.

regarded as void, since the genuine basis of property was not expediency but labour alone.[44] Indeed, he regarded employment as being governed by an original social contract which entitled labour to a proportionate share in the profits of capital as a 'partner'.[45] Thus, while Thelwall's emphasis on labour as the basis for the institution of property was very similar to Locke's, he went much further in his argument for the rights of workers.

Theories of natural rights, including civil liberties, were less significant in the work of Karl Marx, however, as he was sceptical of their value to working people. In his early essays, Marx saw rights as securing the 'right of self-interest' of the individual, and as capable of being reduced to protection of private property while, at the same time, creating an illusory notion of political freedom.[46] Nevertheless, a generous reading of Locke's connection between labour and property rights played a role in Marx's insistence that the ability of capital to make a profit at the expense of workers amounted to exploitation, alienation of the workers from the fruits of their labour, and even 'wage-slavery'.

As is well known, Marx argued that the owners of the means of production, the holders of capital, receive the profits that flow from the expenditure of labour in the production of commodities, but that the extent of their profits is illegitimate because the payment made by capitalists to workers does not adequately reflect the value of their labour.[47] In making this argument, Marx self-consciously drew on liberal economic theory, seeking deliberately to subvert their inferences from Locke's foundational propositions.[48] Moreover, he also took Thelwall's view of the broad duty owed to working people, observing that one should not view those who work 'only as workers' such that 'nothing more is seen in them, everything else being ignored'.[49] Instead, the satisfaction of all human aspects of individuality was required: 'from each according to his ability, to each according to his needs'.[50] His was an economic claim that was based on an ethical claim to the human dignity of workers. It is however arguable that the association of a labour theory of value with Marxism ultimately led to its demise, so that the economic claims of workers are neglected within contemporary human rights discourse.

[44] Ibid 268, citing Thelwell, *The Rights of Nature* (1796) 54–79, noting also 'there were echoes of Locke in particular in this account'.

[45] Ibid 270–73.

[46] Lukes, S, *Marxism and Morality* (Oxford, Clarendon Press, 1985) ch 4.

[47] Marx, K, *Capital: A Critique of Political Economy* (London, Lawrence and Wishart, 1977) vol 1, 477; Marx, K, *Theories of Surplus Value* (Moscow, Progress Publishers, 1963) 365–67.

[48] Husami, ZI, 'Marx on Distributive Justice' (1978) 8 *Philosophy and Public Affairs* 27, 40.

[49] Ibid at 45, citing Marx, K, 'Critique of the Gotha Program' in *Selected Works* (Moscow, Foreign Languages Publishing House, 1962) vol 2, 24.

[50] Ibid.

Civil, Political and Social Rights

The idea that essential human dignity operates as a basis from which to argue that workers have economic entitlements, would seem to have been subsumed by an accommodation reached by the mid-twentieth century. TH Marshall, examining the history of the welfare state, claimed that 'citizenship' had emerged through three stages, all three being essential to democratic governance. He sought to place the consequent rights of workers, as citizens, within this conceptual framework.

The first stage was said to be state endorsement of 'civil liberties',[51] being those rights necessary for individual freedom. These were the natural rights identified by theorists like Locke, which had sprung from resistance to feudalism and serfdom. Marshall acknowledged, in this context, the significance of individual economic freedom, which constituted a means of resisting feudal command.[52] However, he was far from asserting any extension of the right to property to workers' labour in the manner envisaged by Marx or early socialist theorists.[53] In this context, he identified rather the 'right to work, that is to say the right to follow the occupation of one's choice in the place of one's choice, subject only to legitimate demands for preliminary technical training'.[54] This was a shift 'from servile to free labour', which was foundational to the creation of citizenship.[55] Marshall was also interested in identifying (and defending) the role of the welfare state in promoting social justice for workers. He did so by identifying the development of 'political' rights in the nineteenth century and 'social' rights in the twentieth century.

'Political' rights consisted of the 'right to participate in the exercise of political power',[56] reflected by the achievement by working people of universal suffrage, a possibility not implemented or really conceived as a possibility at the time that Marx was writing. This had led in turn to social rights being introduced through the medium of a welfare state, which could cover:

> the whole range from the right to a modicum of economic welfare and security to the right to share to the full in the social heritage and to live the life of a civilised being according to the standards prevailing in society.[57]

---

[51] Marshall, TH, *Citizenship and Social Class* (Cambridge, Cambridge University Press, 1950) 10 et seq.

[52] Ibid 17.

[53] Klausen, J, 'Social Rights Advocacy and State Building: T.H. Marshall in the Hands of Social Reformers' (1995) 47(2) *World Politics* 244, 251–52.

[54] Marshall, *Citizenship and Social Class* (1950) 15–16.

[55] Ibid 18.

[56] Ibid 10–11.

[57] Ibid 10–11. The work of Locke and other writers referred to above also stresses rights to minimum levels of state support—see Claeys (n 40).

As Judy Fudge has observed, when commenting on Marshall's writings, 'a central feature of social rights is the decommodification of labour through the existence of a social safety net and labour standards that ameliorate the harshness of the market'.[58]

Marshall seems to have accepted that the legal form of social rights had to be differentiated from that of civil and political rights. He considered that civil and political rights were justiciable before the courts and indeed were 'in large measure the work of the courts'.[59] By contrast, because the implementation of social rights required collective decisions by the political machinery of the state as to allocation of available resources, the rights of the citizen could not be so 'precisely defined'. A 'modicum' of legally enforceable rights might be granted, but what mattered more were 'legitimate expectations'.[60] The question of the justiciability of (economic and) social rights remains a vexed one, although as the contributions in this volume on India and South Africa indicate, there have been important developments in this area since the date at which Marshall was writing.[61]

Notwithstanding later developments, Marshall's picture of a three tier classification of rights of 'citizenship' would seem on its own terms to offer a way to demonstrate the validity of workers' claims, without leading to the major economic disruption that would be entailed in recognising workers' property entitlement to the fruits of their labour in the ways that Marx and other writers had asserted. It offered different attractions instead. There were to be opportunities for workers to pursue other aspects of their self-fulfilment through the exercise of civil and political freedoms, such as freedom of speech, religious freedom, and universal suffrage. At the same time, the state would provide a social safety net to fulfil workers' welfare requirements.

Marshall also considered the role of civil society in providing for citizens' needs. Where workers are concerned, he saw scope for trade unions to assist in the provision of an acceptable standard of living. Indeed he acknowledged that trade unionism might create 'a secondary system of industrial citizenship parallel with and supplementary to the system of political citizenship'.[62] Marshall also acknowledged, however, that trade union activity could only function in this way insofar as it might be permitted by the state, and considered that responsibility for basic provision

---

[58] Fudge, 'The New Discourse of Labour Rights' (2007) 6.

[59] Marshall (n 51) 34.

[60] Ibid. See also Deakin, S and Browne, J, 'Social Rights and Market Order: Adapting the Capability Approach' in T Hervey and J Kenner (eds), *Economic and Social Rights under the EU Charter of Fundamental Rights: A Legal Perspective* (Oxford, Hart Publishing, 2003) 30.

[61] See Gopalakrishnan and van Eck below in this volume, in chapters seven and nine respectively.

[62] Marshall (n 51) 40.

lay primarily in the hands of the state.[63] That being so, the attachment of property rights to the exertion of labour would not arise. Indeed on that issue Marshall merely observed that 'the basic conflict between social rights and market value' had not been resolved.[64]

The theoretical framework presented by Marshall is by no means immune from criticism. For example, some question Marshall's account of the historical development of these rights, at least in other national contexts.[65] We do not wish here to delve into the complex arguments about whether liberal conceptions of human rights are universally applicable, much less the charge that to question whether liberal conceptions of human rights are of universal application is to indulge in moral relativism.[66] We do, however, take brief pause to note that Liu and Cooney argue in their chapter in this volume that conceptions of rights in China do not exhibit the same character as in liberal theory.[67]

Indeed, the categories of civil, political and social rights are not as distinct as Marshall suggests.[68] For example, the social right to health and safety in the workplace may be regarded as one of the many facets of the inalienable right to life, a minimum age of admission to employment can be viewed as an aspect of the inderogable right not to be subjected to forced labour, and rights to join a trade union, bargain collectively and strike may be regarded as implicit in the long-standing civil liberty, freedom of association.[69] Moreover, in recent years some courts have willingly mixed these categories, giving effect to social and economic rights as elements, or particular instances of broad civil and political rights, particularly the right to life.[70]

---

[63] Ibid 68–69.

[64] Ibid 42.

[65] Rees, AM, 'T.H. Marshall and the Progress of Citizenship' in M Bulmer and AM Rees (eds), *Citizenship Today: The Contemporary Relevance of T.H. Marshall* (London, UCL Press, 1996) at 14 et seq. See also Giddens, A, *Beyond Left and Right: The Future of Radical Politics* (London, Polity Press, 1994) 73–74.

[66] See Otto, D, 'Everything is Dangerous: Some Post-Structural Tools for Rethinking the Universal Claims of Human Rights Law' (1999) 5 *Australian Journal of Human Rights* 17; and 'Rethinking Universals: Opening Transformative Possibilities in International Human Rights Law' (1997) 18 *Australian Yearbook of International Law* 1; also Donnelly, J, *Universal Human Rights in Theory and Practice* (Ithaca and London, Cornell University Press, 1989).

[67] See Liu Cheng and Cooney in chapter five.

[68] As explained cogently by Van Hoof, GJH, 'The Legal Nature of Economic, Social and Cultural Rights: A Rebuttal of Some Traditional Views' in P Alston and K Tomasevski (eds), *The Right to Food* (Utrecht, Martinus Nijhoff, 1984).

[69] Novitz, T, *International and European Protection of the Right to Strike* (Oxford, Oxford University Press, 2003) 45–46. See judgments of the European Court of Human Rights (ECHR) in *Demir and Baykara v Turkey* (App no 34503/97) ECHR 12 November 2008 and *Enerji Yapi-Yol Sen v Turkey* (App no 68959/01) ECHR 21 April 2009.

[70] This strand of jurisprudence has been developed by the Supreme Court of India since *Maneka Gandhi v Union of India* [1978] 1 SCC 248 and *Francis Coralie v Union Territory of Delhi* AIR [1981] SC 746. See also *M C Mehta versus Union of India* 2004(12) SCC118 on the right of citizens to have access to water on grounds of protection of life and the right to liberty under article 21 of the Constitution.

From another perspective, it has been doubted whether labour rights have real potential to be 'genuinely universal', on the basis that they are 'confined to those members of the community who are economically active'.[71] This seems to us a peculiar exclusion, and one founded on a conflation of the nature of the right, on the one hand, and the separate question whether any individual might need or choose to avail themselves of it, on the other. The weakness of the point is evident from the fact that it is no less true of various civil and political rights. For example, not all persons will be in the circumstances of being imprisoned and in the position of claiming the right to a free and fair trial,[72] but this has not prevented this entitlement being understood as a fundamental human right.

A different line of opposition to social rights argues that they are an illegitimate addition to the family of human rights, which should be regarded as restricted to civil liberties and political rights, since it is these which truly reflect the universal desire of all persons to exercise their personal freedom.[73] This criticism encapsulates the view that civil and political rights are fundamentally individualistic, while social rights are essentially collective in nature. This is a critical issue in theory and, as the contributions in this volume show, in practice. In many ways, this distinction serves to explain much about the use of human rights law and discourse to promote workers' claims and interests. It therefore requires more detailed attention.

Individual versus Collective Rights

Liberal conceptions of civil and political rights—indeed human rights more broadly—have often been understood to create a sphere of freedom for each individual person from the control of the state. In this orthodox conception of civil and political rights, they are conceived of as 'negative' rights: they are rights not to be subject to state action that would interfere with their exercise. In that sense, they are said not to require positive action by states. According to this line of argument, social rights stand in contrast, being viewed as entitlements to state provision of social goods, and therefore requiring positive state action in order for them to be implemented. (As we have seen, so much perhaps flows from Marshall's work as well.) The perceived need for state action in order to realise social rights underpins the idea that they should be thought of as 'positive' rights. Isaiah Berlin,

---

[71] Hare, 'Social Rights as Fundamental Human Rights' (2005) 153.

[72] As for eg under article 10 of the Universal Declaration of Human Rights 1948 or article 6 of the European Convention on Human Rights 1950.

[73] See Cranston, M, *What Are Human Rights?* (London, Bodley Head, 1973) 65; and Dowell-Jones, M, *Contextualising the International Covenant on Economic, Social and Cultural Rights: Assessing the Economic Deficit* (Leiden, Martinus Nijhoff, 2004) 14.

for example, relied on this distinction during the Cold War period, when he argued that:

> Pluralism, with the measure of 'negative' liberty that it entails seems to me a truer and more humane ideal than the goals of those who seek, in the great, disciplined, authoritarian structures, the ideal of 'positive' self-mastery by classes or peoples, or the whole of mankind.[74]

There was no doubting where his preference lay.

In liberal theories about types of rights, particularly during the period in which Berlin was writing, there is a tendency to prioritise the exertion of freedom by the individual by reference to utilitarian theory. This is reflected in lexical priority of the two principles of justice identified by John Rawls. The first concern is to ensure a system of liberties. The second is to address social and economic inequalities, but to do so in such a way that this does not undermine the protection of liberty.[75] Indeed, despite the thought experiment offered by the original position, Rawls' use of 'reflective equilibrium'[76] led to a theory that largely reflected the accepted role of the Western liberal welfare state in the period after the Second World War, as opposed to systems of government in other states. A similar assumption seems to lie behind Ronald Dworkin's influential assertion that rights can be defined in terms of trumps over 'collective goals'.[77]

Rawls' *Theory of Justice* has been contested by libertarian thinkers who consider that even the restrictive forms of redistribution contemplated by Rawls would constitute an unacceptable form of coercion. Prominent amongst these was Robert Nozick who observed that: "The socialist society would have to forbid capitalist acts between consenting adults ... no end-state principle or distributional patterned principle of justice can be continuously realized without continuous interference with people's lives."[78]

Nozick, drawing on Locke's conceptions of natural rights,[79] went so far as to consider that 'taxation of earnings from labor' in the welfare state

---

[74] Berlin, I, 'Two Concepts of Liberty' (1958) in Berlin, I, *Four Essays on Liberty* (Oxford, Oxford University Press, 1969) 171.

[75] See Rawls, J, *A Theory of Justice*, revised edition, (Oxford, Oxford University Press, 1999) chs II, IV and V.

[76] Ibid 18.

[77] See Krouse, R and McPherson, M, 'Capitalism, "Property-Owning Democracy" and the Welfare State' in A Gutmann (ed), *Democracy and the Welfare State* (Princeton, Princeton University Press, 1988). *Cf* Dworkin, R, *Taking Rights Seriously* (London, Duckworth, 1977) 26. At 139, Dworkin adds on the same theme: 'A Man has a moral right against the State if for some reason that State would do wrong to treat him in a certain way, even though it would be in the general interest to do so.' See also more recently, Dworkin, R, *Freedom's Law: The Moral Reading of the American Constitution* (Cambridge, Massachusetts, Harvard Univesity Press, 1996) 21–35.

[78] Nozick, R, *Anarchy, State and Utopia* (New York, Basic Books, 1974) 163.

[79] Ibid 10–11 and 174–82.

'is on a par with forced labour'.[80] His argument was that redistribution of income to assist others should be a decision taken by each individual, being dependent on their charitable impulses. When one has to pay tax under state coercion for redistributive purposes, the labour during this period of earnings is forced upon you by the state. The only taxation that is defensible is that which is needed to enforce a criminal justice system and facilitate voluntary commercial transactions.

The concerns of these liberal and libertarian thinkers are not necessarily complete obstacles to the argument that workers have rights (whether civil and political, or economic and social), and that the state might therefore have obligations in relation to those rights. In the first place, much of what workers seek might fairly be thought of as civil and political, or 'negative' rights. The primary claim that workers make, and which the trade union movement makes on behalf of workers, is for the freedom to associate and to act in association when bargaining with employers without interference from the state. Thus, a key claim is usually for a sphere of freedom of action, such as immunity from liability for criminal conspiracy or civil liability for organising and participating in industrial action. This is a call for state action in the form of legislation, but one which limits the scope of the state to control the actions of trade unions.

It might also be observed that workers and their organisations commonly seek what have been described by various labour law commentators as 'procedural rights',[81] or what have been described as 'process rights'.[82] These are rights to participate in decision-making whether through trade union engagement in collective bargaining or other forms of workplace representation. In other words, the state can:

> by extending participation rights from the public to the private sphere ... thereby ensure not only the social accountability of those who exercise private power, but also the right of individuals to participate in making those decisions which affect them, where these decisions are taken outside the narrow confines of what might traditionally be regarded as the political process.[83]

---

[80] Ibid 169.

[81] Deakin, S and Wilkinson, F, 'Rights vs Efficiency? The Economic Case for Transnational Labour Standards' (1994) 23 *Industrial Law Journal* 289; and Ewing, 'Social Rights and Constitutional Law' (1999).

[82] This description has been used in discussion of prioritisation of 'core labour standards' within the ILO by commentators, in respect of which see Langille, B, 'Core Labour Standards— The True Story (Reply to Alston) (2005) 16 *European Journal of International Law* 409; Maupain, F, 'Revitalization Not Retreat: The Real Potential of the 1998 ILO Declaration for the Universal Protection of Workers' Rights' (2005) 16 *European Journal of International Law* 439; and Alston, P, 'Facing Up to the Complexities of the ILO's Core Labour Standards Agenda' (2005) 16 *European Journal of International Law* 467. See below.

[83] Ewing (n 7) 105.

Such measures do not impose direct costs on the state in the same manner as provision for such social rights as housing or healthcare might do; they are more comparable to deliberative processes which the state might choose to establish when determining the best ways in which to improve delivery of such entitlements.

Workers do, however, seek intervention from the state to constrain the actions of employers. Some of the areas in which they seek intervention are work-specific, such as constraints on wages and working time. Others concern issues that may arise in a workplace setting, but which are also matters of broader concern, such as invasions of privacy, and arbitrary discrimination. These might be seen as the more substantive aspect of the rights that workers seek, but fall a long way short of a broad redistributive policy, which even Marshall seems to contemplate would be the improper subject of determination by courts rather than democratically elected political organs, and to which Nozick objects so stridently. Moreover, while workers are asking that the state restrict the liberty of the employer, in so doing it is arguable that what they seek is no more than the creation of 'an equal right to the most extensive scheme of equal basic liberties compatible with a similar scheme of liberties for others'.[84]

There is one more important point that must be made in considering the argument that social, or collective claims ought not to be conceived of or protected as rights, because they entail positive obligations upon the state. As we noted above, and as Sarah Joseph explains in her chapter in this volume, a strict distinction between negative and positive rights is fallacious: 'all rights have positive and negative aspects'.[85] Joseph illustrates her point with reference to the well-recognised triptych of obligations to which legal protection of fundamental human rights gives rise: to respect, to protect and to fulfil. The obligation to 'respect' human rights expresses the state's negative duty not to interfere with a person's legitimate exercise of their freedoms. The obligation of 'protection' is linked to the state's duty to prevent human rights violations and, if necessary, non-state actors who are responsible for them. These obligations are in turn fulfilled through the enactment and enforcement of legislation and other appropriate policy-based measures, including resource (re-)allocation where appropriate. Just as freedom from torture cannot be guaranteed without state respect for the dignity of the individual, protection of that individual from the actions of its officials or other private persons, and fulfilment of these obligations by the provision of systems of training, deterrence, inspection and enforcement; so too does this threefold understanding of states' obligations come into play in respect of a myriad rights which workers claim.

---

[84] Rawls, *A Theory of Justice* (1999) 53.
[85] See Joseph in chapter eleven.

What then is the problem with protecting workers' rights as human rights? Here, the objections raised by Frederich von Hayek are particularly important, not only because of their intellectual content, but also because of their influence on some governments in recent decades. Hayek objected specifically to legislation that is designed to protect collective action by workers to protect their interests. Simply put, Hayek considered such laws to be distortions of the market in a way that impinges unacceptably on individual freedom. Nozick's understanding of state coercion and resistance to any but the most 'minimal state' is broadly akin to Hayek's theory of spontaneous order as reflected in his grand three-volume work on *Law, Legislation and Liberty*.[86] For Hayek, it is the private legal order— the common law (of contract, tort, restitution, property)—which is spontaneous. This is to be contrasted with imposed order as represented by public law, which is order imposed by government. Private law is thereby the precondition for human freedom, since the use of coercion within this framework is only 'necessary to secure the private domain of the individual against interference by others'.[87]

Hayek was prepared to contemplate state legislation which was corrective of the market, for example in respect of discrimination by employers and other dominant social groups.[88] He resisted, however, 'a third kind of "social" legislation', whose aim is to 'direct private activity towards particular ends and to the benefit of particular groups'. He cited trade union legislation as an example of this coercive interference with market freedom.[89] This is a position reminiscent of Nozick's opposition to end-state or patterned distributions.[90] It can however be differentiated from Nozick's position in terms of Hayek's particular hostility to the actions of trade unions as monopolistic forces which hinder market freedom, and which should not be given the legal 'privileges' to do so. His position can be illustrated by the stance he took on industrial action, namely that there is a right to strike, but that each worker should bear the consequences under private law of withdrawal of their labour, namely breach of contract and liability in tort.[91]

Hayek emphasised a restrictive, and one might add formalistic, understanding of the nature of human freedom as inherently individualistic.

[86] Hayek, F, *Law, Legislation and Liberty: A New Statement of the Liberal Principles of Justice and Political Economy* (London, Routledge, 1980).

[87] Hayek, F, *Rules and Order* (London, Routledge, 1973) 57.

[88] Ibid 141.

[89] Ibid 142–43. Deakin, 'Social Rights in a Globalized Economy' (2005) 54–55.

[90] Nozick, *Anarchy, State and Utopia* (1974) 153–82.

[91] Hayek, FA, *1980s Unemployment and the Unions: Essays on the Impotent Price Structure of Britain and Monopoly in the Labour Market*, 2nd edn (London, Institute of Economic Affairs, 1984) 51; and for an elaboration on the implications of this position, see Shenfield, A, *What Right to Strike? With Commentaries by Cyril Grunfeld and Sir Leonard Neal* (London, Institute of Economic Affairs, 1986).

As such, he regarded freedom as incapable of being legitimately exercised in conjunction with others, unless within commercial corporate structures which allow a single legal personality to be formed. As Lord Wedderburn observed, in commenting on the potential influence of this stance, when considering the scope of freedom of association, 'those propounding individualist philosophies interpret this freedom with emphasis, like Hayek, upon the right to *disassociate*'.[92] It is with this in mind, that at least one commentator has observed:

> rights talk tends to foster a libertarian dialogue, where capital's liberty of movement and employers' 'rights to manage' are tacitly affirmed rather than challenged. Arguing in a rights oriented framework forces workers to demand no more than that *their* rights be respected alongside their employers' rights.[93]

WORKERS' RIGHTS IN PRACTICE

There has not been wholesale endorsement of Hayek's position by any government.[94] Nevertheless, the formal parity of treatment of workers' and employers' claims appears to be evident in many of the contributions to this volume, as does a degree of resistance to the use of human rights mechanisms to protect collective action by workers and their organisations. Moreover, in both national and international legal institutions, there would seem to be a marked hesitance to protect the 'human rights' claimed by workers where these would have appreciable cost implications for states or significantly affect the property rights of capital.

National Case Studies

In the national studies provided in Part I of this collection, it is possible to identify a variety of ways in which key political actors and national courts have imbibed (and resisted) features of human rights discourse in their

---

[92] See Lord Wedderburn, 'Freedom of Association and Philosophies of Labour Law' (1989) 18 *Industrial Law Journal* 1, 17; also the concerns expressed by Ewing (n 7), in respect of the decision of the UK Government to incorporate only the European Convention on Human Rights and not also the European Social Charter into UK law, leaving determination of freedom of association to the ECtHR, which did not consider that this freedom necessarily included a right to collective bargaining, but placed considerable emphasis on the individual right of a worker to disassociate from a trade union in the context of a 'closed shop' agreement. This issue is discussed further by Davies and Mantouvalou in chapters six and fifteen respectively.

[93] McCartin, J, 'Democratizing the Demand for Workers' Rights: Toward a Re-framing of Labor's Argument' (Winter 2005) *Dissent*, cited by Compa in this volume below.

[94] Although Lord Wedderburn did detect some evidence of his influence on policies of UK Conservative governments from 1979 onwards. Wedderburn, 'Freedom of Association and Philosophies of Labour Law' (1989) 8–17.

treatment of workers and their organisations. They concern the treatment of human rights in what has been conventionally described as 'hard law', including specific legislation relating to workers, human rights legislation and constitutional mechanisms. Each reveals the powerful legacy of past distinctions between civil, political and social rights and between individual and collective rights. Some offer more hope than others as to the possibility to transcend the conventional limitations of these distinctions, and the consequences of doing so.

The collection begins with the example of Australia, where state and federal governments have both been reluctant to include human rights in legislation or, indeed, to treat workers' rights as human rights at all. From early 1996 to late 2007, Australia's (then) Liberal/National coalition federal government put reform of national labour laws at the heart of its economic and social policies. A key plank of that government's ideological approach was the signal importance it placed on workers' *individual* freedoms. Major reforms in 1996, and again in 2006 strongly promoted the rights of individual workers over, and in some cases against, the interests of workers collectively. Among other things, the law was changed to outlaw closed shops, to give individual agreements priority over collectively-agreed conditions, and to limit the scope for collectively-agreed conditions to include measures to promote trade union security (as for example by requiring union representation in dispute settlement procedures). As it has transpired, the rhetorical strength (and the political value) of emphasising individual rights have been demonstrated by the fact that the current Australian Labour Party Government has opted to retain many of the reforms introduced by the previous government. Thus, for example, the Fair Work Act 2009 continues to provide explicit protection of the right not to join an association.

The changes to Australia's labour laws have been implemented in a context in which there is no constitutional or national statutory protection of basic human rights, and where there is no regional human rights law machinery at all. At the time of writing, there are laws protecting basic human rights in two sub-national jurisdictions, the Australian Capital Territory and the state of Victoria. In neither case does the law extend to coverage of more than standard civil and political rights; neither, for example, makes specific provision for workers' entitlements to collective bargaining or industrial action. The September 2009 final report of the federal government's National Human Rights Consultation Committee essentially recommended a similarly limited approach. In the result, a limited version of that limited approach was adopted.

Chapter three by Ana Virgínia Moreira Gomes observes that Brazil's 1988 Constitution ostensibly protects a large number of labour rights, but that they are frequently not observed in practice. Women, in particular, experience discrimination in the labour market. There is also an ongoing problem with certain forms of forced labour, particularly in rural areas. Moreover, the constitutional provisions are in tension with both long-standing traditions in Brazilian labour law, and current policy proposals. Constitutional recognition of freedom of association, for example, stands in contrast to Brazil's historical approach to the regulation of trade unions. From the 1930s, Brazil implemented a corporatist model of industrial relations built around the policy of *unicidade*: certain unions recognised by the government have monopoly representation rights, and workers must pay a trade union tax. Thus far, efforts in the Brazilian congress to legislate and/or to amend the constitution as may be needed to overturn this approach are incomplete. At the same time, constitutional rights to basic employment conditions have come to be seen as potential obstacles to making the Brazilian labour market sufficiently flexible to facilitate competition in the global economy. While protected in the Constitution, some of these rights remain dead letters in practice, not least because of a lack of national legislation to provide for their implementation in practice.

By contrast, Canada has a significant track record of legal protection for workers' rights, some of which are protected in the terms of the Canadian Charter of Rights and Freedoms that has formed part of the Canadian Constitution since 1982. Christian Brunelle observes, however, that the approach of its drafters was 'rather classical and ... strongly in keeping with the tradition of liberal individualism, which may explain why the Canadian Charter mainly consecrates civil and political rights rather than social, economic and cultural rights'.[95] The recent decision of the Canadian Supreme Court in the *Health Services and Support-Facilities Subsector Bargaining Association v British Columbia* case,[96] building on the Court's earlier decision in *Dunmore v Ontario (AG)*,[97] has provided some cause for optimism about the scope of the labour rights protected in the Charter, although without altering the fundamental character of the instrument. Brunelle offers an opportunity to transcend the apparent dichotomy in the Charter. While trade unions are being held to account in Canada to respect, for example, claims of individual workers to protection from discrimination, he also points to ways in which trade unions can offer a way to prevent systemic discrimination against disadvantaged workers through the medium of collective bargaining. He rightly points out that discrimination has a collective or 'group' dimension as does collective bargaining.

In China, we see a somewhat paradoxical approach to and use of human rights concepts. Observers of Chinese industrial relations will be aware of complaints made to the ILO Governing Body Committee on Freedom of

[95] See Brunelle in chapter four below.

[96] *Health Services and Support-Facilities Subsector Bargaining Association v British Columbia* [2007] SCC 27. See also Fudge, J, 'The Supreme Court of Canada and the Right to Bargain Collectively: The Implications of the *Health Services and Support* case in Canada and Beyond' (2008) 37 *Industrial Law Journal* 25.

[97] *Dunmore v Ontario (AG)* [2001] 3 SCR 1016.

Association which allege that there has been state detention and 're-education through labour' in forced labour camps of trade union activists and members in response to peaceful trade union activities.[98] Also, serious concerns have been raised relating to the use of child labour: first, in the Lagoi camps (reform through labour) and Laojiao camps (re-education through labour and juvenile criminal camps), in which all prisoners, including those under 18, are subject to hard labour; secondly, under the programme of 'Diligent Work and Economical Study' (qingong jianxue), in which children are detained at school-run factories without communication with family without due process of law.[99]

Nevertheless, Liu Cheng and Cooney demonstrate that in Chinese labour law, both the constitution and the various statutes that regulate work, there is a strong emphasis on rights. The conception of rights that is used, however, is rather different from that which characterises the liberal notion of individual rights. They also demonstrate that, while Chinese citizens are not able to organise trade unions independently of the state, it is possible to utilise federal union structures to achieve unionisation in multinational corporations, such as Walmart, which resist union representation elsewhere. Whereas Moreira Gomes in chapter three is critical of corporatist approaches in Brazil, which centralise worker representation and potentially place trade unions under state control, Liu and Cooney suggest that this mode of trade union organisation can have potential benefits.

It would appear that the Chinese conception of rights, which Liu Cheng and Cooney trace in some respect to much longer-standing traditions of politics and governance in China, emphasises the obligation of the state to its citizens, so that laws are enacted and applied with reference to a set of principles. However, an alleged departure from such principles is not subject to legal challenge by the individuals affected and rights are not understood as the basis upon which to resist state intrusion into private life. Rather, rights discourse has the potential to play a significant role in debates relating to future reforms to Chinese labour law.

In England, human rights gain recognition through a relatively recent piece of legislation, the Human Rights Act 1998, which does not have constitutional force but which enables courts to interpret domestic law in

[98] *(China) (Case No 2189)* Report No 337: Complaint against the Government of China presented by the International Confederation of Free Trade Unions (ICFTU) and the International Metalworkers' Federation (IMF) (Vol LXXXVIII 2005 Series B No 2) para 488; *(Case No 2031)* Report No 321: Complaint Against the Government of China presented by the ICFTU (Vol LXXXIII 2000 Series B No 2) para 176.

[99] ILO Committee of Experts on the Application of Conventions and Recommendations (CEACR): Individual Observation concerning Worst Forms of Child Labour Convention 1999 (No 182) China (ratification 2002), published 2007, available at www.ilo.org/ilolex. See also views of the Conference Committee, Doc 132007CHN182: 'The Committee emphasized the seriousness of such violations of Convention No. 182 and urged the Government to take measures, as a matter of urgency.'

accordance with its provisions and to issue 'declarations of incompatibility' where English legislation violates the rights set out therein. In chapter
six, Anne Davies rejects the view that the Act's focus on the individual
necessarily poses a problem for labour law, considering that English law
is individualistic in any case, and that early indications are that this has
not been exacerbated by the 1998 Act. Rather, her concern is in some
ways akin to that of Fenwick, that the legislation has been transplanted
into a setting where there is a 'lack of a human rights culture' and limited enthusiasm on the part of judges for intervention in the exercise of
political discretion by government. Finally, she points to concerns that
the legislation is unbalanced, in that it does not include social and economic rights to act as a balance against the civil and political rights there
incorporated.

In chapter seven, Ramapriya Gopalakrishnan acknowledges the creative
efforts of the Supreme Court of India to extend the remit of its constitutional jurisprudence to protect workers from such hardships as forced
labour, child labour and forms of gender discrimination. However, she
also observes that on questions of worker participation in the making of
economic policy decisions that could affect their rights and interests, there
has been more reluctance, which she observes may be linked to the clash
of these rights with 'the new economic policy of the country'. Notably, she
does not consider that there is a straightforward distinction, in this respect,
between individual and collective rights. She also notes that the Court has
treated with caution the entitlement of contract workers and temporary
workers to permanent contracts, again because of the economic impact that
their claims might have.

In chapter eight, Chioma Agomo, by way of contrast, points to the continued poor treatment of trade unions and collective bargaining in Nigeria,
both through economic policies of structural adjustment and the legislative
framework which has supported such change. The constitution does make
provision for protection of freedom of association, and international instruments have potential effect once 'domesticated'. At the same time, however,
recent reforms have reduced the number of trade unions, weakening the
more vocal industrial associations of workers, and also criminalising the
right to strike. While Agomo voices hope that ILO programmes will prompt
change, and acknowledges the potential role of the new National Industrial
Court on promoting protection of individual and collective workers' rights,
particular those of women, the picture looks rather bleak.

There seems to be an underlying assumption in some of these jurisdictions that civil and political rights are justiciable, whereas the social claims
of workers are not readily so, given their ability to constrain the policies
pursued by the elected legislature. Stefan van Eck's contribution in chapter nine therefore offers valuable observations from the South African
situation, in which social rights have been deemed capable of constraining

legislative economic policy.[100] However, van Eck considers that the outlook is not as rosy as it might appear, given the complexities that the application of constitutional law adds to existing labour law. He is also reluctant to abandon specialist labour courts, apparently for some of the reasons that Agomo applauded their introduction in Nigeria, namely their appreciation of the industrial context of disputes.

The last national case study is Lance Compa's analysis of the position in the United States of America in chapter ten. In Compa's view, human rights discourse has not entered the mainstream of American labour law. He does, however, offer hope that academic commentators and activists are now putting compliance with international human rights norms on the agenda. He also notes increased use of ILO complaints procedures by US unions. His prediction is that there may be change, but that it is likely to be 'slow in coming and incremental'. He also sees such a cultural shift as potentially changing 'the climate for workers' organizing and bargaining by framing them as a human rights mission, not as a test of economic power ...' He adds that it also offers trade unions the opportunity to build alliances with human rights non-governmental organisations (NGOs).

Certainly, understanding the protection of workers' interests as human rights is likely to broaden their appeal at a time of marginalisation of trade unions as antiquated and outdated organisations. What may be problematic, though, in the wholesale adoption of such an approach, as Compa also observes, is that one may implicitly denigrate the status of workers' claims where it is more difficult to phrase them in terms of human rights. Deirdre McCann in chapter eighteen makes the same point in relation to working time. A related concern is that it may reduce the capacity of workers to stake their economic demands or insist on rights which, as Gopalakrishnan observes, impose economic costs on the employer and/or government.

In writing about Cambodia, presenting an alternative regulatory strategy, Adler and Woolcock in chapter nineteen argue that 'law can be used to support the development of rights even at the periphery of the global economy'. They consider as case studies the examples of Cambodia's Arbitration Council and the (high-profile) involvement of the ILO and other international actors in the monitoring of conditions in the garment industry, as part of a trade-related mechanism. In short, Adler and Woolcock indicate the need to be flexible about the purpose and function of law as a means of securing and promoting rights.

Overall, it would seem that the national case studies presented in this volume illustrate the discomfort of some domestic courts with protection of aspects of collective bargaining (and the economic interests of workers) in human rights terms. It would seem to be protection of individual

---

[100] *Government of South Africa v Grootboom* 2001 (1) SA 46 (CC).

workers, for example from discrimination, which thrives in such a context. While we can point to innovative attempts to seek to combine the collective and individual interests of workers within a human rights discourse, for example in the Canadian context, these creative solutions seem to be the exception rather than the rule. This, in turn, raises certain interesting regulatory questions. For example, are we, as Agomo and van Eck suggest, seeking to protect labour rights as human rights through the wrong regulatory mechanisms? For instance, would labour courts be better at this task than constitutional courts? Or ought we to have resort to litigation in those jurisdictions where the opportunity presents itself to seek redress for human rights violations, and to do so in the understanding that litigation is but one of a number of strategies that might be deployed? These are questions which we do not examine here, but to which we intend to return in our concluding chapter. What is apparent is that where workers or their organisations are making economic claims (which impede on fiscal planning by regional or national government), or claims which have significant economic costs for employers, these are less likely to receive protection through a human rights prism. What is also interesting is the influence that the ILO now has in certain jurisdictions and this merits further examination.

International and Regional Human Rights Mechanisms

On the international stage, three 'generations' of human rights have come to be recognised, which to some extent reflect the categorisation offered by Marshall. The first constitutes civil liberties and political rights. The second consists of social rights, which include matters considered suitable for provision by a welfare state, such as the right to education, the right to food, the right to housing and the right to healthcare, and the regulation of specific labour standards. More recently, in the era of decolonisation, a third generation of human rights has been identified. These encompass rights that often have a civil, political and social aspect but which are best understood as the rights of 'peoples', such as, for example, the rights to self-determination and to development.[101]

In this chapter, we have contended that a case can be made for workers' rights to be treated as human rights in a manner that does not adhere to such rigid and problematic categorisations. In this respect, the Universal Declaration of Human Rights (UDHR) of 1948 can be seen as setting an important precedent.[102] However, the UDHR was understood to have only declaratory effect at the time of its adoption, and the precedent it set was

---

[101] Crawford, J, *The Rights of Peoples* (Oxford, Oxford University Press, 1988); Jones, P, 'Human Rights, Group Rights, and Peoples' Rights' (1999) 21 *Human Rights Quarterly* 80.
[102] Universal Declaration of Human Rights (UDHR) 1948 arts 22–26 addressed what are now regarded as typical socio-economic rights. Also, see art 28 which states that: 'Everyone

not followed swiftly either at the international or regional level. Moreover, while apparently unifying treatment of civil, political and social rights, as Ivan Hare has observed, the instrument 'reads like two distinct documents which have been rather inelegantly stuck together'.[103]

It is apparent that political pressures during the Cold War period led to distinctions being drawn between the treatment of 'individual' civil and political rights and 'collective' social, economic and cultural rights. As Joseph observes, civil and political rights have received distinctive and privileged treatment in the United Nations (UN) context under the International Covenant on Civil and Political Rights (ICCPR) 1966, as opposed to its sister instrument adopted in the same year, the International Covenant on Economic, Social and Cultural Rights (ICESCR). This follows the precedent set within the Council of Europe, whereby the European Convention on Human Rights (ECHR) 1950, has pre-eminence rather than the less well-known, European Social Charter (ESC). While the ICCPR and the ECHR 1950 may be the subject of individual petitions, to the Human Rights Committee and the European Court of Human Rights respectively, the Optional Protocol to the ICESCR designed to achieve this was only adopted by the UN General Assembly in 2008 and opened for signature in 2009. Moreover, only a *collective* complaints procedure is available in respect of the ESC and, even then, only in respect of the few countries which have ratified the 1995 Protocol.[104] There is official recognition in the international arena that there is considerable overlap between these species of rights and of their indivisibility,[105] but this has yet to be fully reflected in international legal practice.

There is some hope of an 'integrated approach' emerging in the case law of the European Court of Human Rights, as Virginia Mantouvalou argues in chapter fifteen, but this has yet to be reflected in the political will of states to redraft these key human rights instruments with this premise in mind.

is entitled to a social and international order in which the rights and freedoms set out in this declaration can fully be realized.'

[103] Hare, 'Social Rights as Fundamental Human Rights' (2005) 154.

[104] For criticism of this method, see Novitz, T, 'Finding a Remedy for Violation of Social Rights within the Council of Europe: The Significance of Access to a Court' in C Kilpatrick, T Novitz, and P Skidmore (eds), *The Future of Remedies in Europe* (Oxford, Hart Publishing, 2000); Novitz, T, 'Are Social Rights Necessarily Collective Rights? A Critical Analysis of the Collective Complaints Protocol to the European Social Charter' (2002) 1 *European Human Rights Law Review* 50; and Churchill, R and Khaliq, U, 'The Collective Complaints System of the European Social Charter—An Effective Mechanism for Ensuring Compliance with Economic and Social Rights?' (2004) 15(3) *European Journal of International Law* 417.

[105] See the Vienna Declaration on Human Rights (1993) UN Doc A/CONF.157/24. Another example commonly cited is the Declaration on the Occasion of the 50th Anniversary of the Universal Declaration of Human Rights, adopted by the Council of Europe Committee of Ministers on 10 December 1998, para 4: civil, political and socio-economic rights are 'universal, indivisible, interdependent and interrelated'.

Moreover, there are, in this context, indications of the formalistic obsession with *negative* freedom of association, which Lord Wedderburn pointed to almost 30 years ago. It may be a comfort to some to know that trade unions have the same right not to associate with those who might be their members that their possible members have not to associate with them,[106] but many will see this as missing the point that a positive right to engage in collective bargaining remains absent from the jurisprudence of the European Court of Human Rights on freedom of association, despite some tentative steps taken in this direction in *Wilson and the NUJ v UK*.[107] Indeed, in the context of the European Union, when an employer's economic freedoms are pitted against the right to take collective action, the latter suffers by comparison.[108]

What is perhaps even more significant is that, as both Joseph and Novitz observe in chapters eleven and fourteen respectively, workers' rights are rarely considered within the remit of mainstream human rights mechanisms. It appears that they are considered more properly the province of the ILO, where a very different set of assumptions prevail. In the ILO setting, freedom of association is viewed as a civil and political right, *as well as* a socio-economic right, insofar as it extends to the requirement of protection of trade union organisation, those participating in collective bargaining and industrial action. Indeed, the ILO's supervisory system works broadly across the whole spectrum of internationally protected human rights, emphasising their inter-relationship at every juncture.[109] The ILO's unique blend of jurisprudence is well illustrated in this volume, in chapter thirteen, by Lisa Tortell's analysis of how that organisation has addressed the difficult case of Belarus, which is apparently reluctant to comply with its obligations to respect workers' freedom of association. The circumstances of Belarus also illustrate the ways in which trade union protections can be linked to the general protection of civil liberties.

More recently, the international community has placed emphasis on an identifiable group of 'core labour standards'. These are understood to be the freedoms of association and the related right to engage in collective bargaining, elimination of discrimination in respect of employment and occupation, elimination of all forms of forced or compulsory labour, and

---

[106] *ASLEF v United Kingdom* (Application no 11002/05) [2007] IRLR 361. See Ewing, KD, 'The Implications of the *ASLEF* Case' (2007) 36 *Industrial Law Journal* 425.

[107] *Wilson and the NUJ v UK* (2002) 35 EHRR 20.

[108] Case C-438/05 *International Transport Workers' Federation (ITF) and Finnish Seamen's Union (FSU) v Viking Line* [2007] ECR I-10779; [2008] All E.R. (EC) 127; [2008] IRLR 143; and Case C-341/05 *Laval un Partneri v Svenska Byggnadsarbetareförbundet* [2007] ECR I-11767; [2008] All E.R. (EC) 166; [2008] I.R.L.R. 160. Discussed by Novitz and Syrpis in chapter sixteen.

[109] Fenwick, C, 'The International Labour Organisation: An Integrated Approach to Economic and Social Rights' in M Langford and S Liebenberg (eds), *Socio-Economic Rights Jurisprudence: Emerging Trends in Comparative and International Law* (Cambridge, Cambridge University Press, 2008).

effective abolition of child labour. They are most prominently so listed in the ILO's 1998 Declaration of Fundamental Principles and Rights at Work, but most accounts of their origins trace them back at least as far as the 1995 Social Summit in Copenhagen.[110] Compliance with these norms has been pursued in the ILO, through a persuasive soft law 'follow-up' procedure, and also a series of programmatic funding initiatives.[111] The core labour standards have also proved to be a basis on which institutions such as the International Finance Corporation and the European Bank for Reconstruction and Development have granted funding in recent years.[112] This list of labour standards has also proved a key point of reference for forms of trade conditionality, as Orbie and De Ville show in their analysis of the European Union Generalised System of Preferences (GSP) regime, even though they question whether such conditionality is efficacious in practice.[113]

The very idea of a core of labour standards has come in for sustained criticism, even attack, particularly in the work of Philip Alston[114] and Bob Hepple.[115] By way of contrast, Brian Langille[116] and Francis Maupain,[117] have defended their selection, by reference to their role as 'process' or 'participation' rights. The issues in the debate are many, and include some that

---

[110] See, for example, Langille, B, 'The ILO and the New Economy: Recent Developments' (1999) 15 *International Journal of Comparative Labour Law and Industrial Relations* 229; and Bellace, J, 'The ILO Declaration on Fundamental Principles and Rights at Work' (2001).

[111] For some analysis of the outcomes of the programmes that have been carried out under the auspices of the Declaration, see Fenwick, C and Kring, T, *Rights at Work: An Assessment of the Declaration's Technical Cooperation in Select Countries* (ILO, Geneva, September 2007).

[112] Since 1 May 2006, all International Finance Corporation (IFC) loans include the requirement that borrowers comply with ILO core labour standards under the IFC *Policy and Performance Standards on Social and Environmental Sustainability.* The IFC policies are available at www.ifc.org/ifcext/sustainability.nsf/AttachmentsByTitle/pol_PerformanceStandards2006_full/$FILE/IFC+Performance+Standards.pdf. See also Kaufmann, C, *Globalisation and Labour Rights: The Conflict Between Core Labour Standards and International Economic Law* (Oxford, Hart Publishing, 2007) 110. The *European Bank for Reconstruction and Development* (EBRD) has adopted new criteria in its 'Environmental and Social Policy' which came into effect in November 2008.

[113] See Orbie and De Ville in chapter seventeen. See also Kaufmann, *Globalisation and Labour Rights* (2007) 169–241, who argues for trade incentives connected to compliance with core labour standards.

[114] Alston, P and Heenan, J, 'Shrinking the International Labor Code: An Unintended Consequence of the 1998 ILO Declaration on Fundamental Principles and Rights at Work?' (2004) 36 *New York University Journal of International Law and Politics* 221 and Alston, P, 'Core Labour Standards and the Transformation of the International Labour Rights Regime' (2004) 15 *European Journal of International Law* 457.

[115] Hepple (n 1) 56–67; and Hepple, B, 'Does Law Matter? The Future of Binding Norms' in Politakis, G (ed), *Protecting Labour Rights as Human Rights: Present and Future of International Supervision* (Geneva, ILO, 2006) 229–30.

[116] See Langille 'Core Labour Standards' (2005).

[117] See Maupain, 'Revitalization Not Retreat' (2005).

go beyond the scope of our present inquiry, such as the proper analysis of the role and the impact of the United States of America in arguing for the acceptance and promotion of a core of labour standards. For our purposes there are three, related key elements to the debate.

First, there is the issue as to whether it is legitimate to isolate a group of core labour standards, when this necessarily chooses to exclude other social rights of workers. Even assuming that a core might legitimately be identified without traducing the fundamental principle of the indivisibility and interconnectedness of all human rights, there is the subsidiary issue of whether the chosen core is adequate to the task. This is the jumping off point for the second key element of the debate, which is whether, and if so, how the selection of core labour standards might be justified. The concern has been expressed that the core labour standards identified by the ILO are commonly linked to civil liberties and political rights, the first generation of rights, and thereby draw on their status in a manner detrimental to other legitimate concerns of labour.[118] The final issue is, if we accept the de facto status of core labour standards, how it is appropriate to promote their application. Is a soft law review mechanism suitable, which encourages cooperation rather than demanding action? And how does the introduction of such a mechanism affect the status and thereby the efficacy of established supervisory mechanisms?

These are the issues that Jill Murray seeks to address, in her analysis of the ILO's attempt to develop a 'third way' frame of reference after the Second World War in chapter twelve. She offers a perspective informed by the successes and failures of the European Union. Hers is also a regulatory analysis, suggesting new ways to achieve the ILO 'decent work' agenda, such that those labour standards which do not fit within a standard civil and political rights matrix are not marginalised.

There is evidence also that the ILO is seeking to address these challenges, so as to combine hard and soft law mechanisms in a mutually reinforcing and efficacious manner, as in the ILO Declaration on Social Justice for a Fair Globalization 2008. This instrument directly addresses the phenomenon of market-led globalisation,[119] and while reaffirming the principles set out in the 1998 Declaration goes beyond these by placing them in the context of 'Decent Work' within which they are one aspect of 'four equally important strategic objectives of the ILO'.[120] Member States are placed under a duty to formulate their own 'national or regional strategy'[121] to work towards these objectives, but the onus in the Follow-up to the Declaration is on the

---

[118] See, for example, McCrudden, C and Davies, ACL, 'A Perspective on Trade and Labour Rights' (2000) 21 *Journal of International Economic Law* 43.

[119] See (n 1).

[120] ILO Declaration on Social Justice for a Fair Globalization 2008 art I.A.

[121] ILO Declaration on Social Justice for a Fair Globalization 2008 art II.B.

ILO to streamline and reform its own procedures so as to best assist its members. There is likely to be considerable dispute as to how this should be done, such that Murray's claim that 'the ILO has not fully "constitutionalised" decent work' continues to ring true. That process may, however, now be underway and it is to be hoped that Murray's contribution to this book may contribute to debates concerning its implementation.

THEORETICAL SUPPLEMENTS TO CONTEMPORARY HUMAN RIGHTS DISCOURSE

Additionally, we consider that current debates concerning the selection of core labour standards and their enforcement through trade and aid beg further significant normative questions. First, the promotion of certain core labour standards has been stated to be compatible with the achievement of economic prosperity and development.[122] In this context, many commentators and policy-makers have had recourse to the theory of 'capabilities', as developed by Amartya Sen, who seeks to unite our understandings of economic and human functionings.[123] The relevance of this theoretical perspective is therefore considered further below. Secondly, there remains lively debate about the role of deliberation or dialogue in the identification, promotion and enforcement of workers' rights. For this reason, we also consider the influential notion of 'deliberative democracy', as espoused by Jürgen Habermas and others.[124]

Capabilities Theory

The human capability approach, first developed by Amartya Sen, has been influential in recent years in thinking about labour law, and more broadly about the role of law, regulation and rights in the pursuit of human development. As Judy Fudge has noted, this approach would appear subsequently to have had a profound impact in the work of Brian Langille, and also the work of Simon Deakin, Frank Wilkinson and Jude Brown.[125]

---

[122] See *Trade, Employment and Labour Standards: A Study of Core Workers' Rights and International Trade* (Paris, Organization for Economic Co-operation and Development (OECD), 1996); and *International Trade and Core Labour Standards* (Paris, OECD, 2000). For comment, also see Langille, B, 'Eight Ways to Think about International Labour Standards' (1997) 31 *Journal of World Trade* 28; and Hepple (n 1) ch 1.

[123] Sen, *Development as Freedom* (1999) and Sen, A, 'Work and Rights' (2000) 139 *International Labour Review* 139.

[124] Habermas, *Between Facts and Norms* (1997). See also Young, *Inclusion and Democracy* (2000).

[125] Fudge (n 1) 57, citing Langille (n 82) and Brown, J, Deakin, S, and Wilkinson, F, 'Capabilities, Social Rights and European Market Integration' in R Salais and R De Villenueve, *Europe and the Politics of Capabilities* (Cambridge, Cambridge University Press, 2004).

It has been adopted as an organising principle within which to approach labour market regulation in New Zealand.[126] Also, the Supiot Report on *The Transformation of Work and the Future of Labour Law in Europe* provided a series of policy prescriptions structured around the notion of 'capabilities'.[127]

The idea is that the economic functioning of individuals is determined by their capabilities. According to Sen:[128]

> the concept of 'functionings' ... reflects the various things a person may value doing or being. The valued functionings may vary from elementary ones, such as being adequately nourished and being free from avoidable disease, to very complex activities or personal states, such as being able to take part in the life of the community and having self-respect.

Within this context, 'capability' is a 'kind of freedom: the substantive freedom to achieve alternative functioning combinations'.[129] In the context of labour, we might think of capabilities as the skills, knowledge and attitudes of people, and how, in using these skills, they can take advantage of the labour market opportunities available to them to gain financial or personal reward.[130] Deakin and Wilkinson stress that capabilities are a consequence not only of the endowments and motivations of individuals, but also of the access they have to the process of socialisation, education and training, which enable them to exploit their resource endowments.[131] Differences in wealth, information and expectations between communities and families provide individuals with variable degrees of access to the processes which result in opportunities for more highly rewarded employment. Hence the attraction of capabilities theory and the idea of social rights as a new normative underpinning for labour law: it shows their compatibility with free markets, and transcends their traditional understanding as claims to resources from the state (yet without abandoning that as a possibility).[132]

---

[126] The Chief Executive of the Department of Labour, John Chetwin, requested his staff to 'begin a project to establish a framework for developing policies relating to the development of New Zealand's human capability', Department of Labour, Corporate Plan 1999–2000, 3, cited in Tipples, R, 'The Human Capability Framework—An Important and Useful Framework for Understanding the Labour Market' (2004) 29 *New Zealand Journal of Employment Relations* 3, 57.

[127] Supiot, A, *Au delà de l'emploi. Transformations du travail et devenir du droit du travail en Europe* (Paris, Flammarion, 1999); also published as Supiot, A, *Beyond Employment: Changes in Work and the Future of Labour Law in Europe* (Oxford, Oxford University Press, 2001). See also Deakin (n 1) 58.

[128] Sen (n 10) 75.

[129] Ibid 75.

[130] Tipples, 'The Human Capability Framework' (2004) 5.

[131] Deakin, S and Wilkinson, F, *The Law of the Labour Market: Industrialisation, Employment and Legal Evolution* (Oxford, Oxford University Press, 2005) 286.

[132] Fudge (n 1) 57.

The capabilities approach is potentially of great significance as a way to think about the function of social rights. Indeed, Deakin and Wilkinson have adopted the human capability approach to argue that 'social rights, far from being inimical to the effective functioning of the labour market, are actually at the core of a labour market order in which the resources available to society are fully realised'.[133] The crucial question is whether a capabilities approach only justifies policies aimed at the promotion of individual freedom or whether it has the potential to legitimate protection of collective action and mobilisation.

As we have noted, Brian Langille has also drawn explicitly on Sen as the inspiration for his 'spirited defense of the conceptual coherence and normative salience of core labour rights'.[134] From this basis, Langille argues for an understanding of labour law as divisible into procedural and substantive claims. There are nevertheless some important difficulties and *lacunae* in Langille's account. For example, his distinction between procedural and substantive claims is at least not dissimilar to the supposed separation of civil and political rights from social and economic rights. The claim that some types of fundamental protection, such as for women to be protected from discrimination in the labour market, is purely procedural might be contested, and, according to Fudge, he also avoids dealing with feminist and critical perspectives on the fundamental nature or 'grammar' of labour law.[135] Alston, in his response to Langille, suggests that Langille's emphasis on individual human freedom, albeit based on Sen's work, looks not unlike Hayek's understanding of the central significance of individual human liberty.[136]

Fudge contrasts Langille's 'thin conception of capabilities'[137] with the work of Brown, Deakin and Wilkinson, who emphasise the significance of the market-creating function of social rights and so provide a means to outflank the criticisms of Hayek, among others, such that their fundamental quality becomes apparent.[138] At the same time, she considers, rightly in our view, that capabilities theory 'needs to be supplemented by a theory of social choice, deliberative mechanisms, and a social theory about power in order to provide a full account of social justice and human rights'.[139] Deakin has also put this point forward cogently in his defence of a capabilities theory

---

[133] Deakin and Wilkinson, *The Law of the Labour Market* (2005) 277.
[134] See Langille (n 82); and Fudge (n 1) 58.
[135] Ibid 60–61. *Cf* Nussbaum, *Women and Development: The Capabilities Approach* (2000).
[136] See Alston, 'Facing Up to the Complexities of the ILO's Core Labour Standards Agenda' (2005) 477.
[137] Fudge (n 1) 58.
[138] Fudge (n 1) 65.
[139] Ibid.

which encompasses and respects collective rights, as well as individual rights.[140]

We have a further observation to make. Our national case studies would seem to demonstrate that there remains the potential, although not the necessity, for individual and collective rights to clash, not only with each other, but also with economically defined objectives that otherwise promote human functionings and capabilities. An example is that raised by Gopalakrishnan in chapter seven in respect of the claims of Indian workers to entitlement to permanent contracts, which would doubtless enhance their capacity to gain further training and experience in their chosen areas of expertise, as well as maintaining social stability for their families. This however conflicts with the desire of the local and federal government to enhance investment in India which would widen the job opportunities for workers and thereby, with the enhancement in income this brings to workers and government, the potential for human flourishing, in terms of education, health care, housing and other aspects of human and physical capital, and the choices which such development allows individuals. Ultimately, we doubt that capabilities theory has the capacity to explain which of these two competing considerations (that may both be phrased in terms of human capabilities) should be prioritised; nor are we convinced that a capabilities approach is the normative basis which should determine any prioritisation. Neither, for that matter, would it seem that Sen would think so. It is worth reminding ourselves that his work is aimed at promoting development in a manner consistent with the protection of human freedom, rather than reaching prescriptive views on the most desirable economic policies.[141] What he proposes in the event of such a genuine dispute is democratic participation and debate as to where priorities should lie. His most recent book on the *Idea of Justice* places considerable emphasis on the role of public reason in making such decisions.[142] The question, then, is what form such deliberations should take.

Deliberative Theory

Theories of deliberative democracy seek to address a 'legitimacy crisis' faced by domestic governments as well as regional and international organisations. Jürgen Habermas, the leading advocate of deliberative 'governance' as opposed to 'top down' government, has sought to ensure

---

[140] Deakin (n 1) 59–60.

[141] Sen (n 10) 283: 'It is not so much a matter of having exact rules about how precisely we should behave, as of recognizing our shared humanity in the social choices that we face'. See also 85.

[142] Sen, A, *The Idea of Justice* (London, Allen Lane/Penguin, 2009).

that key policy decisions do not become too distant from the lives of the persons that they affect (the 'lifeworld'), so that they are perceived as illegitimate and inappropriate.[143] He has argued that we need to find ways in which law can reflect the understandings and concerns of all persons within society. His suggestion is that groupings of interests will spontaneously emerge within 'civil society' and that we then need to find ways of ensuring that they inform the development of public policy.[144] This is a view which embraces both individual self-determination and collective means for its realisation.

In this context, Habermas posits the 'ideal speech situation', which is not always realisable, but is something towards which we might hope to aim. Its creation entails, as a minimum, the establishment of a framework of basic rights upon which citizens can rely. Protection of civil liberties and political entitlements is necessary if persons are to exchange their views freely. These private rights rely on public government for their existence, but also give legitimacy to that government. The two are, Habermas tells us, 'co-original'.[145] In this way, he also offers a construction of human rights which is foundational, in this way to democracy, as opposed to economic development. Habermas is however less clear on the function of socio-economic rights and workers' entitlements. Indeed, his theory has been criticised for this reason.[146] There is however an emergent consensus amongst scholars working in the field of judicial review that the courts may usefully play a significant role in deliberating on whether the state is taking sufficient steps to realise constitutionally or legislatively entrenched social entitlements, such as for example in the field of housing and healthcare.[147]

When engaged in the deliberative process, those participating are expected to leave behind their own vested interests and prejudices, and be persuaded potentially to act in opposition to these. What is said to make this possible is the pragmatics of communication, which involves making a genuine effort to understand and relate to the words of another.[148]

---

[143] Habermas (n 11) 56.

[144] Ibid 367. Habermas describes 'civil society' as being 'composed of those more or less spontaneously emergent associations, organizations and movements that, attuned to how societal problems resonate in the private spheres, distil and transmit such reactions in an amplified form to the public sphere'.

[145] Ibid at 104. For further analysis of this relationship, see Cohen, J, 'Reflections on Habermas on Democracy' (1999) 12 *Ratio Juris* 385, 391 et seq.

[146] Noonan, J, 'Modernization, Rights and Democratic Society: The Limits of Habermas's Democratic Theory' (2005) 11 *Res Public* 101.

[147] See for comment on *Government of the Republic of South Africa v Grootboom and Others* (2000) (11) BCLR 1169 (CC); Dixon, R, 'Creating Dialogue about Socioeconomic Rights: Strong-Form versus Weak-form Judicial Review Revisited' (2007) 5 *International Journal of Constitutional Law* 391. See on healthcare, Syrett, K, *Law, Legitimacy and the Rationing of Healthcare* (Cambridge, Cambridge University Press, 2007).

[148] Habermas, J, *Communication and the Evolution of Society*, trans by Lawrence, FG (Boston, Beacon Press, 1979) 1–68.

Each person should be able and willing to question critically and evaluate the assertions of another. The aim is a consensus-led decision-making.[149] It is this consensus, emerging from a transparent and accessible process, which is understood to be constitutive of just solutions. The outcome remains open to future challenge on rational grounds, but until it is so challenged, it remains a workable basis of policy-making and law-making.[150]

In this way, deliberative governance would seem to challenge some of the long-held assumptions of collectivism in the context of labour relations. For example, this theoretical approach suggests that 'civil society' as a whole should have a voice, thereby challenging the privilege traditionally given to management and labour, such as the corporatist practices identified by Moreira Gomes in chapter three as operating in Brazil. Secondly, the aim of a deliberative framework is to transcend the particular interests of particular factions and reach, not a trade-off or a bargain between vested interests as is familiar in collective bargaining,[151] but a rational consensus that is in the interests of all, which everyone can understand, and to which everyone can commit themselves. If this ideal form of governance is given practical application, bargaining between employer and worker representatives according to their perception of their own vested interests, may come to be seen as an inappropriate basis for the generation of legal norms, which should be defensible on the grounds of 'public reasons' acceptable to all.

Habermas does recognise that there could be a need for 'bargaining' between opposing factions, such as workers and employers, which would not be objectionable insofar as any bargain is made according to fair procedures under which the rights of all persons are respected, but he does not contemplate that there will ever be so radical a conflict of value-systems or beliefs that there will be no scope for bargaining (or compromise) and no view of an appropriate shared procedure to settle the matter.[152] Given industrial relations literature, which acknowledges the capacity for conflict

---

[149] For a discussion of Habermas' work placed in this context, see Rosenfeld, M, 'Law as Discourse: Bridging the Gap Between Democracy and Rights' (1995) 108 *Harvard Law Review* 1163.

[150] Habermas, J, 'Struggles for Recognition in Constitutional States' (1993) 1 *Eur. J. Phil* 128.

[151] See the recent description of collective bargaining by Bercusson, B, 'The Trade Union Movement and the European Union: Judgment Day' (2007) 13 *European Law Journal* 279, 304.

[152] See McCarthy, T, 'Legitimacy and Diversity: Dialectical Reflections on Analytical Distinctions' (1996) 17 *Cardozo Law Review* 1083, who identifies this as a flaw in Habermas' theoretical framework. For a reply to such concerns, see Habermas, J, 'On Law and Disagreement: Some Comments on Interpretative Pluralism' (2003) 16(2) *Ratio Juris* 187. On this attempt to tame civil society, encompassing diversity, rather than recognising the challenges posed to the legal order, see Christodoulidis, E, 'Constitutional Irresolution: Law and the Framing of Civil Society' (2003) 9 *European Law Journal* 401.

or even which is pluralist in its orientation, this may prove a problematic assumption.[153]

Moreover, Habermas seeks generally to prevent dialogue being dominated by perlocutionary acts, so that it is illegitimate to seek to influence others by the way in which one speaks, rather than the content of one's arguments.[154] Yet, this restriction may in itself prove problematic, for as Iris Marion Young has observed, rhetoric is fundamental to communication of the emotional aspect of arguments, while dispassionate speech styles tend to correlate with social privilege, so that Habermas' proposed method to prevent verbal bullying may actually privilege the most powerful.[155] Such concerns may lay at the root of warnings that deliberative democracy, 'by strengthening the conceptual tools of the dominant paradigm ... encourages existing hierarchies'.[156] These are likely to remain a source of apprehension to trade unions when engaging in dialogue within the ILO (or other international and regional organisations) or within a national setting. Much depends on the scope given to workers and their organisations to voice differences and genuinely to influence policy outcomes.[157] It should be acknowledged that advocates of associative democracy consider that there are ways in which this can be achieved. Alan Bogg, in his recent book on *The Democratic Aspects of Trade Union Recognition,* draws on their work and seeks to offer a richer deliberative account of justification for collective action than is provided elsewhere. He suggests that 'direct action, while non-deliberative in form, can itself promote deliberative ends'.[158] In so doing, he offers the hope that deliberative theory could overcome its standard neglect of differentials of power, which as Fudge and others have warned, requires attention.[159]

[153] Kessler, I and Purcell, J, 'Individualism and Collectivism in Industrial Relations' in P Edwards, *Industrial Relations: Theory and Practice,* 2nd edn (Oxford, Blackwell, 2003); and the classic article, Korpi, W and Dhalev, M, 'Strikes, Industrial Relations and Class Conflict in Capitalist Societies' (1979) 30 *The British Journal of Sociology* 164.

[154] Habermas, *Communication and the Evolution of Society* (1979) ch 3; see also Bohman, J, 'Emancipation and Rhetoric: The Perlocutions and Illocutions of the Social Critic' (1988) 21(3) *Philosophy and Rhetoric* 185.

[155] Young (n 11) 39–40 and 63–77.

[156] Kohn, M, 'Language, Power and Persuasion: Toward a Critique of Deliberative Democracy' (2000) 7 *Constellations* 408, 426.

[157] For an analysis from an EU perspective, see Fredman, S, 'Transformation or Dilution: Fundamental Rights in the EU Social Space' (2006) 12 *European Law Journal* 40, who voices concern at EU social dialogue and policy-making undertaken in the context of a 'partnership' agenda, which under a 'third way' model seeks to diminish conflict and fails to acknowledge differences between the views of management and labour.

[158] Bogg, A, *The Democratic Aspects of Trade Union Recognition* (Oxford, Hart Publishing, 2009) 256.

[159] See Fudge (n 1) 68. See also Novitz, T and Syrpis, P, 'Assessing Legitimate Structures for the Making of Transnational Labour Law: The Durability of Corporatism' (2006) 35 *Industrial Law Journal* 367.

CONCLUSION

We have examined the early treatment of workers' rights as natural (or human) rights in theological, liberal, socialist and Marxist scholarship, and in particular the entitlement of workers to claim property in (and resulting from the exercise of) their own labour. By the mid-twentieth century, in Western liberal thought, this economic aspect of the construction of workers' rights as human rights seems to have been lost. The assumption is that the welfare state will provide for workers in the West, providing minimum standards for employment, a social safety net, and a space for trade union negotiation. In this way, workers' claims are subsumed under the newly established typology of human rights as civil, political (first generation), economic social and cultural (second generation) and rights of peoples (third generation). There is also resistance to the 'collective' dimension of workers' action which is regarded as inherently more coercive than 'individual' action by an employer. In this context, the economic claims of workers are also implicitly diminished and tamed by the priority given to individual liberty. The role that liberal and libertarian theories have played is relevant here, as is the role of Cold War politics, especially in the terms of the drafting of international human rights instruments. The result is that it would seem to be employers' economic liberties which have taken precedence over workers' attempts to organise to protect their economic interests.

From the perspective of protection of workers' interests, it seems that the strategy of protecting workers' rights as human rights is only feasible if legal scope is made for workers and their organisations to reassert workers' economic claims, namely that in certain circumstances they are entitled to impose 'costs' on employers and contest their property rights. In the current ideological climate this does not seem likely, especially if a formalistic approach is taken to the parity of exercise of rights, such as in the application of negative freedom of association.[160]

There remains, however, the possibility that recent theoretical developments, concerning capabilities and deliberative democracy, might be of service in this context. Capabilities theory, for example, has the potential to allow workers and their organisations to make both procedural and substantive economic claims, derived from the value of human freedom.[161] Such an approach may also be welcomed for its potential to overcome the artificial division between the traditional three 'generations' of human rights.

However, while capabilities theory seeks to reconcile economic and social claims, in doing so there remains a risk that any clash between the two

---

[160] See n 106.
[161] Deakin (n 1) 59–60.

will be obscured and ultimately neglected. In this chapter, for example, we have highlighted disagreement as to the most appropriate way to achieve human capabilities in India, and whether it could necessitate the perpetuation of insecure employment. We do not see how capabilities theory can provide a straightforward resolution of this dispute. Nor are we confident that a capabilities approach can readily resolve conflict between workers' economic claims and those of their employers, for it does not and is not designed to assist in determining priorities in such instances.

The other projected supplementary strategy, that of deliberative democratic dialogue, seems to provide a role for workers' organisations to become engaged in debates over prioritisation, as representatives of civil society, but the exercise of such a role raises crucial issues relating to imbalances of power which may arise in the context of industrial relations. These have yet to be resolved.

We offer more thorough consideration of the regulatory possibilities for the protection of workers' rights as human rights in our concluding chapter. At this stage, we merely make the point that the viability of any regulatory technique turns on the conception of human rights embraced as an objective by workers and their organisations. By identifying the variety of conceptions available, and the translation of these within capabilities and deliberative theory, we hope to offer workers, their representatives, and policy-makers a basis for choice between regulatory options and opportunities. This is not a choice of 'all or nothing'. In our view, a combination of regulatory mechanisms at various different levels of governance (both legal and non-legal) may be effective. However, their promise cannot be evaluated without a clear understanding of the envisaged objective (or objectives) that they serve. At present, such clarity appears to be lacking, but we hope that does not mean that it is unachievable.

Part I

National Perspectives

Part I

National Perspectives

2

Workers' Human Rights in Australia

COLIN FENWICK

INTRODUCTION

THIS CHAPTER IS about the legal protection of the human rights of workers in Australia.* I focus in particular on aspects of the protection of freedom of association, and on how aspects of Australian federal labour law act to eliminate discrimination in employment and occupation. This approach necessarily overlooks important human rights issues for workers. These include Australia's obligations as a state party to the International Covenant on Economic, Social and Cultural Rights (ICESCR), in particular as concerns the rights to work, to just and favourable conditions of work, and to social security.[1] The topics chosen do however serve to illustrate more fully some of the significant limitations of

---

* I thank Ingrid Landau for her research assistance in the preparation of this work; any remaining errors or omissions are my responsibility alone.

[1] International Covenant on Economic, Social and Cultural Rights (ICESCR) arts 6, 7 and 9. For some brief observations, see Fenwick, C and Landau, I, 'Work Choices in International Perspective' (2006) 19 *Australian Journal of Labour Law* 127. There is a substantial literature on the relationship between Australian labour market regulation and social security laws, although little of it appears to address the question of compliance with international human rights obligations or norms. See, eg, Carney, T, Ramia, G and Chapman, A, 'Which Law is Laggard? Gaps Between Labour Law and Social Security Law in Work Regulation' and O'Donnell, A, 'Reinventing Unemployment: Welfare Reform as Labour Market Regulation', both in C Arup et al (eds), *Labour Law and Labour Market Regulation: Essays on the Construction and Regulation of Labour Markets and Work Relationships* (Sydney, Federation Press, 2006) 454–69 and 344–63 (respectively); Ramia, G, Chapman, A and Michelotti, M, 'How Well do Industrial Relations and Social Policy Interact? Labour Law and Social Security Law in the Social Protection of Sole Parents' (2005) 21 *The International Journal of Comparative Labour Law and Industrial Relations* 249; Carney, T, 'Welfare to Work: Or Work Discipline Revisited?' (2006) 41 *Australian Journal of Social Issues* 27; Rider, C, 'Using Tax and Social Security to Reconstruct the Part-Time Labour Market: A Note on "Welfare to Work"' (2005) 18 *Australian Journal of Labour Law* 302; and Carney, T and Ramia, G, *From Rights to Management: Contract, New Public Management and Employment Services* (The Hague, Kluwer, 2002). The same is generally true of the extensive literature on occupational health and safety law in Australia, in which the issues are not generally cast in terms of a right to just and favourable conditions of work. See, eg, Johnstone, R, *Occupational Health and Safety Law and Policy: Text and Materials*, 2nd edn (Australia, Law Book Company, 2004).

Australian law as a means of protecting workers' human rights.[2] Moreover, in each case there are rich literatures on which to draw.

The defining feature of Australian human rights law is that it is almost entirely confined to legislative and administrative action by Australian governments. There are few if any human rights protections in either the federal or the state constitutions. Moreover, Australia neither belongs, nor could belong to any regional group of states that may have instruments and institutions that protect human rights. The protection of workers' human rights in Australia, therefore, depends almost entirely on the extent to which Australian governments have legislated for their protection and exercise, and on the extent to which workers are able to assert and protect their rights through the exercise of collective strength. Of course, the latter is significantly shaped by the former.

In this chapter I give a brief overview of economic and social conditions in Australia today, as a way to think about the human rights issues that arise for Australia's workers. Then I outline the legal structure for the protection of human rights in Australia, emphasising the lack of entrenched protection for human rights at any level of government. Following this, I examine aspects of how Australian law protects freedom of association for trade union purposes, from the point of view of how those laws compare with Australia's international legal obligations. I then consider legal measures in federal labour law to eliminate discrimination in employment and occupation. In the conclusion, I draw the themes together. I argue that the absence of a solid legal framework to protect human rights, combined with an Australian reluctance to embrace the discourse of human rights, leaves workers vulnerable to the whims of governments from time to time.

THE AUSTRALIAN LABOUR MARKET AND WORKERS' HUMAN RIGHTS

Australia has been experiencing a period of extraordinary prosperity, more or less since the early to mid 1990s. Unemployment fell from a peak of 10.7 per cent in 1992, to 5.2 per cent in February 2006,[3] and then still further to

---

[2] For an earlier contribution on this topic that is similarly focused, see MacDermott, T, 'Labour Law and Human Rights' in D Kinley (ed), *Human Rights in Australian Law* (The Federation Press, Leichardt, NSW, 1998) at 194. On child labour, see Creighton, B, 'ILO Convention No 138 and Australian Law and Practice Relating to Child Labour' (1996) 2 *Australian Journal of Human Rights* 293; and Creighton, B, 'Australian Law and Practice Relating to Child Labour and ILO Convention No 138' in M Jones and L Basser Marks (eds), *Children on the Agenda: the Rights of Australia's Children* (St Leonards, New South Wales, Prospect Media, 2000).

[3] Australian Bureau of Statistics, 'Australian Labour Market Statistics February 2006' (Cat No 6105.0, 2006); Barrett, S, Burgess, J and Campbell, I, 'The Australian Labour Market

4.2 per cent in August and September 2007.[4] Average weekly earnings increased in the decade May 1997 to May 2007 by 56 per cent for both women and men.[5] Disposable wealth and property values have also increased significantly. As is common, however, these sorts of indicators do mask important evidence of economic and social exclusion and inequality.[6] It is often argued, for example, that the official unemployment rate fails to acknowledge the large numbers of underemployed and hidden unemployed.[7] In addition, casual and other non-standard forms of employment are rising: casual employment among males rose from 13 per cent to 25 per cent from 1990 to 2004,[8] and in 2003 over a quarter of the Australian workforce was casually employed.[9] Various studies have suggested that as many as 20 per cent of Australia's employees work as 'permanent casuals'—that is, they are continuously engaged, but on an insecure basis and without the right to paid leave.[10]

Wage inequality persists,[11] as does the gender pay gap: women's average weekly earnings continue to be less than their male counterparts, in all industries.[12] A large proportion of women rely on part-time work in an effort to balance work and family life, leading to a higher proportion of women in precarious forms of employment and among the low-paid.[13] Australia is also distinguished by having had, in recent years, some of the longest full-time working hours per week among members of the Organisation for Economic Co-operation and Development (OECD).[14]

in 2004' (2005) 47 *Journal of Industrial Relations* 133; Australian Bureau of Statistics, 'Yearbook Australia 2006: Chapter 6: Labour' (Cat No 1301.0, 2006).

[4] Australian Bureau of Statistics, 'Labour Force, Australia, September 2007' (Cat No 6202.0). Even with the effects of the global financial crisis, unemployment in Australia appears to have gone no higher than 5.9% in July 2009: Australian Bureau of Statistics, 'Labour Force, Australia, July 2009' (Cat No 6202.0).

[5] Australian Bureau of Statistics, 'Yearbook Australia 2008' (Cat No 1301.0, 2008). For detailed recent figures on earnings, see Australian Bureau of Statistics, 'Average Weekly Earnings, Australia' (Cat No 6302.0).

[6] For a recent overview of changes in the Australian labour market see Campbell, I, 'Australia: Institutional Changes and Workforce Fragmentation' in S Lee and F Eyraud (eds), *Globalization, Flexibilization and Working Conditions in Asia and the Pacific* (ILO/Chandos, 2008) 115–52.

[7] Barrett, Burgess and Campbell, 'The Australian Labour Market in 2004' (2005).

[8] Australian Bureau of Statistics, 'Measures of Australia's Progress, 2006' (Cat No 1370.0, 2006).

[9] Australian Bureau of Statistics, 'Australian Social Trends 2005' (Cat No 4102.0, 2005).

[10] O'Donnell, A, '"Non-Standard" Workers in Australia: Counts and Controversies' (2004) 17 *Australian Journal of Labour Law* 89.

[11] See Saunders, P, 'Reviewing Recent Trends in Wage Income Inequality in Australia' (Social Policy Research Centre, University of New South Wales, February 2005).

[12] Australian Bureau of Statistics, 'Yearbook Australia 2008: Labour' (Cat No 1301.0, 2006).

[13] Pocock, B and Masterman-Smith, H, 'Work Choices and Women Workers' (2006) 56 *Journal of Australian Political Economy* 126.

[14] Campbell, I and Burgess, J, 'Casual Employment in Australia and Temporary Work in Europe: Developing a Cross-National Comparison' (2001) 15 *Work, Employment and Society* 171.

The incidence of full-time employees working extended hours has increased considerably over the past two decades.[15] Research suggests that much of this work is unpaid, and is the result of employer pressure and a weak regulatory framework.[16]

All of these working conditions, and the question whether a human rights approach might be useful in seeking to improve them, were thrown into sharp focus by federal labour laws that came into effect in March 2006. The Workplace Relations Amendment (Work Choices) Act 2005 (Cth) (Work Choices) implemented the greatest single change to Australian federal labour law since the turn of the twentieth century.[17] In particular, it marked the virtual abandonment of the use of arbitration by an independent tribunal, the Australian Industrial Relations Commission (AIRC), as a means of establishing minimum working conditions. The role of arbitrated awards to underpin both collective and individual bargaining was replaced by a set of five legislated minimum working conditions,[18] the Australian Fair Pay and Conditions Standard (AFPCS). Responsibility for determining wage rates was taken from the AIRC, and given to an Australian Fair Pay Commission (AFPC). Among the many ironies of the Work Choices system was that the AFPC was not by legislation directed to do anything that was 'fair' for Australian workers.[19]

At the time the changes were introduced, it appeared inevitable that the reforms would have a significant negative impact on the labour standards that many Australian workers enjoyed, particularly women and those in precarious or low-paid employment.[20] Many commentators argued that Work Choices would drastically undermine the scope and strength of the safety net of minimum employment conditions afforded to the Australian workforce; further promote individual employment contracts over collective arrangements; severely restrict the role of trade unions; and lead to reductions in real minimum wages as they were to be set under the legislative guidance given to the AFPC. All of these adverse effects were thought likely to be more significant than may otherwise have been the case because the new laws had the potential to control working conditions and how they were negotiated or determined for over 80 per cent of the Australian workforce.

---

[15]   Barrett, Burgess and Campbell (n 3) 142–43.

[16]   See discussion in Barrett, Burgess and Campbell (n 3) 139–45.

[17]   For commentary on the legal changes, see in particular the special issues of the *Australian Journal of Labour Law, Australian Journal of Political Economy, Deakin University Law Review, Economic and Labour Relations Review* and the *University of New South Wales Law Journal.*

[18]   The conditions were wages, hours, annual leave, parental leave, and personal/carer's leave.

[19]   Fenwick, C, 'How Low Can You Go? Minimum Standards Under Australia's New Labour Laws' (2006) 16 *Economic and Labour Relations Review* 85.

[20]   See generally the special issue of the *Journal of Australian Political Economy* (2006).

In the result, a recent meta-analysis of studies on the effects of legal changes during the period 1996 to 2007 concluded that there was a continuing trend toward greater workplace flexibility, and that this had been achieved at the cost of 'less employment security, reduced wages, longer working hours, less access to training, and less control generally over working lives and family life'.[21] The authors found it difficult to determine, on the basis of the studies examined, how to isolate the impact of legal changes from other relevant influences, including changes in the structure of the economy and of product markets. Nevertheless, they concluded that 'the legislative programme of the Coalition government after 1996 undoubtedly contributed to the shifting balance of power and interests away from workers and their institutions and towards employers throughout the 1996–2007 period, and beyond.'[22]

From the point of view of this book, the changes clearly raised issues about the human rights of Australia's workers. This includes, of course, not only the particular working conditions and how they might be set, but also the legal framework regulating workers' ability to combine and to take direct action in their own interests. During the period in office of the Coalition government led by Prime Minister John Howard (March 1996 to November 2007), successive waves of law reform significantly reduced the level of legal protection given to workers, and to trade unions as their representatives. Many of these changes were the subject of adverse comment from the supervisory bodies of the International Labour Organization (ILO). But in the absence of a solid legal framework for the protection of fundamental human rights in Australia, legal challenge to the Work Choices reforms had to be mounted on grounds concerning the allocation of legislative powers between the Commonwealth and state governments.[23] The challenge failed, by a majority of five judges to two. No serious argument was made about whether the new laws contravened the human rights of Australian workers. As I explain further in the following section, it would have been all but impossible to do so in any event. Accordingly, it is not surprising that there is little or nothing in any of the judgments in the case that tends to argument based on protection of human rights.

The two dissenting justices (Kirby and Callinan JJ) each relied upon the federal structure of the Australian constitution as a reason why the challenge should have succeeded. In a broad sense, their view of the need for checks and balances in the allocation of legislative powers is one that

---

[21] Arup, C et al, 'Assessing the Impact of Employment Legislation: The Coalition Government's Labour Law Programme 1996–2007 and the Challenge of Research' (Research Report, Monash University, October 2009) 39.

[22] Ibid.

[23] *New South Wales v Commonwealth (Work Choices Case)* (2006) 229 CLR 1. For analysis, see Evans, S, Fenwick, C, Saunders, C, Tham, J-C, and Donaldson, M, *Work Choices: The High Court Challenge* (Melbourne, Australia, Law Book Co. Thomson, 2007).

is founded on an interest in the protection of the individual liberties of the citizenry. Kirby J also made reference in his decision to the historical significance of Australia's federal system for conciliation and arbitration of industrial disputes, and to section 51 (xxxv) of the Constitution, which provides specifically for commonwealth legislative capacity to enact laws for this purpose. His Honour argued, among other things, that independent conciliation and arbitration of industrial disputes might tend to 'promote collective agreements between parties and the protection of economic fairness to all those involved in industrial disputes'.[24] But these are more or less the limits, and even the dissentients fell far short of engaging directly in anything like human rights discourse.

THE LEGAL FRAMEWORK FOR HUMAN RIGHTS PROTECTION

The Australian Constitution protects very few human rights; it has nothing like a Bill of Rights protecting individual liberties. Perhaps not surprisingly, the High Court of Australia has done relatively little to develop a settled constitutional jurisprudence of basic human rights. Neither are human rights in Australia generally protected by any entrenched legislative guarantee. The lack of constitutional or other entrenched protection for human rights, both at the federal and state levels, has fuelled persistent debates over the adoption of a Bill of Rights.[25] To date, however, only the (self-governing) Australian Capital Territory and the state of Victoria have adopted statutory Bills of Rights.[26] The state Government of New South Wales has considered taking steps toward similar ends.[27] More recently, the Federal Government announced its response to the final report of its National Human Rights Consultation process (the Brennan Report). Broadly speaking, that report recommended that the Government adopt a Bill of Rights on the same model as in the Australian Capital Territory (ACT) and Victoria.[28] As appears below, that model is broadly similar to the one that operates in the United Kingdom.

Australia has ratified a wide range of international instruments that include protection for workers' human rights. These include the International Covenant on Civil and Political Rights (ICCPR) and its First Optional Protocol, the ICESCR, and 54 ILO Conventions (of which it has denounced

---

[24] *Work Choices Case* (2006) 229 CLR 1 [446].

[25] See, eg, Alston, P (ed), *Towards an Australian Bill of Rights* (Australia, National Capital Printing, 1994). For a more recent contribution, see Robertson, G, The statute of liberty: How Australians can take back their rights (Sydney, Vintage Books, 2009).

[26] Human Rights Act 2004 (ACT). For comment and analysis see Evans, C, 'Responsibility for Rights: The ACT *Human Rights Act*' (2004) 32 *Federal Law Review* 291.

[27] Pearlman, J, 'Charter of Rights Plan to be Put to Cabinet', *The Sydney Morning Herald* (Sydney 20 March 2006).

[28] The report is available at: www.humanrightsconsultation.gov.au/.

seven). Australia has ratified seven of the 'core' ILO Conventions; it has not ratified Convention 138 (minimum age for employment).[29]

As a matter of Australian constitutional law, however, these instruments do not have direct effect: it is necessary for domestic legislation to create binding obligations in Australian law with respect to particular international obligations.[30] While it is possible that the rule may be different for obligations derived from customary international law,[31] this is in any case likely to be of little effect in practice: very few human rights obligations are widely accepted as having force at customary international law. Of those few, the prohibition on slavery bears most directly on workers, but Australian law and practice in this respect present few difficulties. Furthermore, Australian courts have no jurisdiction to compel the Government to respects its obligations arising from international treaties.[32]

In general, therefore, the principal source of legal protection for human rights in Australia is the content of domestic legislation, whether enacted by the Federal Government, or by the government of a state or a territory. To this might be added the body of principles developed in recent years concerning the interpretation of the Australian Constitution and of domestic statutes, the exercise of administrative power, and the development of the common law more generally. As we will see, these offer at best limited and problematic protection.

In the area of workers' human rights, the key instrument is now the Fair Work Act 2009 (Cth) (FW Act), which fully replaced the Workplace Relations Act 1996 (Cth) (WR Act) by January 2010. The FW Act is therefore the main federal statute regulating employment and labour relations in Australia. It is also the source of much of the legislative protection that exists for the exercise of freedom of association for trade union purposes. As did the Work Choices reforms, the FW Act relies predominantly on the Commonwealth power to legislate with respect to corporations.[33] By this means, it is able to regulate the working conditions of between 80 and 85 per cent of the Australian workforce. While the FW Act is so based,

---

[29] See www.ilo.org/ilolex/english/newcountryframeE.htm (accessed 29 October 2009).

[30] See, eg, Mitchell, A, 'Genocide, Human Rights Implementation and The Relationship between International and Domestic Law: *Nulyarimma v Thompson*' (2000) 24 *Melbourne University Law Review* 15, and Walker, K, 'Treaties and the Internationalisation of Australian Law' in C Saunders (ed), *Courts of Final Jurisdiction* (Sydney, Federation Press, 1996).

[31] Walker, K, 'International Law as a Tool of Constitutional Interpretation' (2002) 28 *Monash University Law Review* 85, 87. The author also argues that customary international law has a greater claim to being a legitimate influence on constitutional interpretation than do treaties: at 100.

[32] *Horta v Commonwealth* (1994) 181 CLR 183.

[33] See the definition of a 'National System Employer' in s 14 of the FW Act. The relevant power of the Commonwealth is to legislate with respect to 'foreign corporations, and trading or financial corporations formed within the limits of the Commonwealth': s 51 (xx) of the Commonwealth Constitution.

the current Government has also sought to negotiate with the states to establish a uniform system, at least for all workers in the private sector.[34] Discrimination in employment and occupation is regulated both by specific procedures within the WR Act, and by commonwealth, state and territory legislation dealing with discrimination more generally. I deal with these laws separately below.

It follows that there is relatively little entrenched protection for workers' human rights in Australia. The only real limitation on a government's ability to fail to protect those rights, or intentionally to trammel them, is the limitation presented by the political risk to which a government may expose itself when next it seeks to be elected. As Australia's recent experience of labour law change has shown, in a country where there is a culture of 'reluctance' about human rights,[35] this may be too slight a risk to be of great concern to a government. When it enacted its Work Choices reforms, the Howard Government continued—and indeed extended—a number of its policies, despite international criticism of them as being inconsistent with human rights obligations. As is so often the case, the unwillingness to be bound by human rights standards, or to draw on that rhetoric as a source of policy, seems to extend to governments of different political persuasions. As will appear presently, the FW Act continues many of the provisions of the former WR Act which were found wanting from the point of view of workers' human rights.

Limited Constitutional Protections for Human Rights

The Australian Constitution was drafted with little intention of guaranteeing the liberties of the people of the Commonwealth that it was to create; the rights that were uppermost in the minds of the drafters were those of the various colonies which, after federation, were to become Australian states. Indeed, while there was some attention to the matter of fundamental rights, and consideration of the model provided by the Constitution of the United States of America, the constitutional conventions that produced the various drafts of the text of the Australian Constitution preferred for the most part to leave the protection of individual rights to the system of responsible government that the Constitution was intended to entrench. Thus, for example,

---

[34] This would likely require the states to refer some of their legislative powers to the Commonwealth to achieve this. Under s 51 (xxxvii), the Commonwealth may legislate in areas where states refer their legislative competence. At the time of this writing, the Commonwealth had enacted the legislation required for its part, and the states of Queensland, South Australia, Tasmania and Victoria had each either introduced legislation for their part, or committed to doing so.

[35] Charlesworth, H, 'The Australian Reluctance about Rights' (1993) 31 *Osgoode Hall Law Journal* 195.

the Constitution was drafted with the express purpose of allowing the continued operation of certain laws that entrenched rights only for a few, being expressly discriminatory on the grounds of race.[36]

The Australian Constitution contains explicit protection for very few civil liberties.[37] There is some debate about how to constitute the list of rights that are protected in the Australian Constitution, but it might be said that it includes the right to vote;[38] the right to just compensation if property is acquired compulsorily by the Commonwealth;[39] the right to trial by jury for an indictable offence against federal law;[40] a right to participate in free trade and commerce between the States;[41] freedom of religion;[42] and freedom from discrimination or disability on the basis of residence in a particular state.[43]

In addition to the few express guarantees in the Constitution, the High Court held in a pair of cases decided in 1992 that, as the Constitution establishes and entrenches a system of representative government, people must be able to communicate with each about the election of their representatives and associated matters.[44] In other words, there is an implied freedom of political communication. This led the Court to invalidate a Commonwealth statutory provision that purported to protect members of the AIRC from being brought into disrepute,[45] and a Commonwealth legislative scheme for regulating the use of free broadcast time during federal election campaigns.[46] Although the Court has since revised its analysis of the juridical

[36] See generally Williams, G, *Human Rights under the Australian Constitution* (Melbourne, Oxford University Press, 1999) 25–45.
[37] The same is true of the various state constitutions, for an overview, see ibid 8–10.
[38] Commonwealth of Australia Constitution Act 1900 (Cth)) s 41 ('Commonwealth Constitution').
[39] Commonwealth Constitution s 51(xxxi).
[40] Commonwealth Constitution s 80.
[41] Commonwealth Constitution s 92.
[42] Commonwealth Constitution s 116.
[43] Commonwealth Constitution s 117. Some commentators have gone further, identifying other provisions as having a role in protecting freedoms or liberties, including, for example, those preventing the Commonwealth from discriminating between states in respect to taxation (Commonwealth Constitution s 51(ii)), and protecting the accrued entitlements of public servants transferred from a state to the Commonwealth (Commonwealth Constitution s 84): see generally Williams, *Human Rights under the Australian Constitution* (1999) 47–48. On the scope and interpretation of these express constitutional rights see, eg, ibid 96–128 (civil and political rights) and 129–54 (economic rights).
[44] *Nationwide News Pty Ltd v Wills* (1992) 177 CLR 1; *Australian Capital Television Pty Ltd v Commonwealth* (1992) 177 CLR 106.
[45] *Nationwide News Pty Ltd v Wills* (1992) 177 CLR 1, which considered the application of s 299(1)(d)(ii) of the Industrial Relations Act 1988 (Cth).
[46] *Australian Capital Television Pty Ltd v Commonwealth* (1992) 177 CLR 106, which considered the validity of pt IIID of the Broadcasting Act 1942 (Cth), which had been inserted by the Political Broadcasts and Political Disclosures Act 1991 (Cth). In subsequent cases, the High Court extended this principle so as to override certain principles of defamation law, whether embodied in state common law or statute: in essence it created a form of 'public figure' defence to an action for defamation: *Theophanous v Herald & Weekly Times Ltd* (1994)

basis from which the implied freedom of political communication may be said to arise, it has also confirmed the general principle that the implied freedom is an entrenched part of Australian constitutional law.[47]

Self-evidently, an implied freedom of political communication is not directly relevant to the promotion and protection of the human rights of workers in Australia, other than as an aspect of a broader freedom of expression. It has been suggested that the idea of representative government may also require the recognition of an implied freedom of association, and that some of the High Court's other decisions on the point may support this view.[48] It has also been suggested that those aspects of the High Court's reasoning that might limit the application of the implied freedom to industrial relations is flawed. Rachel Doyle has argued that it is not coherent to try to identify what counts as 'communication' for these purposes by seeking to distinguish between speech and action, and that there is no clear general distinction between communication about 'political' and 'industrial' matters.[49] As yet, however, these ideas have not been tested in the courts.

Another idea that has not yet been accepted in Australian constitutional jurisprudence is the notion that where there is ambiguity, the Constitution should be interpreted consistently with Australia's international legal obligations. While (the now-retired) Kirby J consistently expressed this view, it has not been adopted by any other member of the Court.[50] Indeed, a number of other judges have explicitly rejected the notion that international law has a necessary role to play in constitutional interpretation,[51] notwithstanding the limited nature of the principle for which Kirby J has contended.[52]

---

182 CLR 104; *Stephens v West Australian Newspapers Ltd* (1994) 182 CLR 211. The Court has also accepted that the freedom of political communication may extend to the advice given by a migration agent to their client, but in the circumstances of that case the Court upheld the statutory regime that was under challenge as being a reasonable limitation in light of its intended purpose: *Cunliffe v Commonwealth* (1994) 182 CLR 272.

[47] *Lange v Australian Broadcasting Corporation* (1997) 189 CLR 520.

[48] Gageler, S and Glass, A, 'Constitutional Law and Human Rights' in D Kinley (ed), *Human Rights in Australian Law* (Sydney, The Federation Press, 1998) 47, 51. The authors refer in particular to aspects of the judgments in *McGinty v Western Australia* (1996) 186 CLR 140 and *Kruger v Commonwealth* (1997) 190 CLR 1.

[49] Doyle, R, 'The Industrial/Political Dichotomy: The Impact of the Freedom of Communication Cases on Industrial Law' (1995) 8 *Australian Journal of Labour Law* 91, 99–101.

[50] See, in particular, Kirby J's judgments in *Newcrest Mining (WA) v The Commonwealth* (1997) 190 CLR 513, 657 and in *Kartinyeri v The Commonwealth* (1998) 195 CLR 337, 417–18. For analysis of the nature and function of any such interpretive principle, and of Kirby's judgments on the point, see Walker, 'International Law as a Tool of Constitutional Interpretation' (2002).

[51] See the joint judgment of Gummow and Hayne JJ in *Kartinyeri v The Commonwealth* (1998) 195 CLR 337, 384 and the joint judgment of Gleeson CJ, McHugh and Gummow JJ in *AMS v AIF* (1999) 199 CLR 170.

[52] His Honour has emphasised that in his view international law may be used to interpret the Constitution only where it is otherwise ambiguous. Where it is clear, its words must be

Human Rights Protection through Parliamentary Sovereignty

The Australian Capital Territory was the first Australian jurisdiction to enact 'comprehensive' human rights protection, with the Human Rights Act 2004 (ACT).[53] It was followed by Victoria with its Charter of Human Rights and Responsibilities Act 2006 (Vic).[54] As noted, the Brennan Report recommended that the Commonwealth follow suit.

The two laws that exist, and the one recommended in the Brennan Report, have much in common. The ACT and Victorian laws protect the wide range of rights that are found in the ICCPR. As enacted, in neither case is there any protection for economic, social and cultural rights. Nor did the Brennan Report recommend that a commonwealth law should protect these rights. In the case of the ACT, the Attorney-General was obliged to report to the ACT Legislative Assembly one year after the Act's entry into force on whether it should be expanded to include these rights.[55] In any event, the ACT Human Rights Act 2004 does recognise several fundamental workers' rights, including the right to protection against discrimination, freedom of association, and freedom from forced labour.[56] So too does the Victorian Charter of Human Rights and Responsibilities Act 2006. It includes a protection from forced work (section 11), and a right of association that specifically includes a right to form and join trade unions (section 16). For its part, the Brennan Report recommended that the list of rights that might be included in a federal bill of rights should be drawn from among well-known civil and political rights. Of these, there are many that might pertain to the interests of workers, including in particular the rights to freedom from forced work, to freedom of movement, to freedom of thought, conscience and belief, to freedom of expression, peaceful assembly, and association, to liberty and security of the person, and the right of children to be protected by family, society and state.[57]

given full effect even if they run counter to relevant provisions of international law. See generally Walker (n 31) 92–96.

[53] For detailed analysis of the ACT Act, see Evans 'Responsibility for Rights: The ACT *Human Rights Act*' (2004).

[54] On both Victoria and the ACT, see Evans, C and Evans, S, *Australian Bills of Rights: The Law of the Victorian Charter and the ACT Human Rights Act* (Melbourne, Australia, LexisNexis, 2008).

[55] Human Rights Act 2004 (ACT) s 43(2)(a). The Report, delivered in 2006, recommended that the ACT Government explore 'direct enforceability' of specified economic, social and cultural rights, but that the law not be amended to include them. It also recommended a further review after another five years: ACT Department of Justice and Community Safety, 'Human Rights Act 2004—Twelve Month Review—Report' (Department of Justice and Community Safety, ACT, Australia, June 2006) 49.

[56] Human Rights Act 2004 (ACT) ss 8, 15, 26.

[57] Brennan Report Recommendation 25 xxxvi and xxxvii.

The protection that is offered in both the ACT and Victoria, and recommended by the Brennan Report, is however rather limited, and closely tied to the political process. This is because the current laws (and the one recommended) closely follow the approach taken in the Human Rights Act 1998 (United Kingdom). The key limitation is that this type of law gives no judicial power to invalidate either legislative or administrative action that is inconsistent with the rights that are protected. Rather, court must interpret legislation (where possible) consistently with the rights that are protected, and where unable to do so, may only issue a declaration of incompatibility, which will have no effect on the operation of the legislation so declared incompatible.

This type of protection is tied to the political process because it creates important roles for the legislature and for the executive in promoting the rights that are protected. Legislatures are empowered to report on whether bills comply with the content of the Bill of Rights. Executives are required to report to the legislature on whether, in their view, proposed legislation is consistent with the Bill of Rights. The executive must report to the legislature in cases where the courts make a declaration of incompatibility. The executive is also entitled to appear and be heard in proceedings in which a declaration of incompatibility may be made. Ultimately, however, the protection of human rights on this model is political, for the executive is empowered to declare that legislation should be passed notwithstanding incompatibility with the Bill of Rights in question.

Many of these weaknesses, and few of the strengths (such as limited judicial scrutiny) will form part of Australian national law going forward. The Commonwealth's response to the Brennan report declined to implement many of it recommendations. The government expressed its intention to legislate to establish a Parliamentary Joint Committee on Human rights. It will scrutinise laws in terms of their compliance with UN human rights treaties binding on Australia. (But not, apparently, ILO Conventions). It will legislate to require that proposed laws be accompanied by a statement of compatability with those treaties. It will not establish any new scope for judical scrutiny of legislation. Neither will it enact a Bill or Charter of Rights.[58]

The Commonwealth Parliament's Legislative Powers with Respect to Human Rights

The Commonwealth Constitution allocates legislative powers between the Commonwealth and the state governments by explicitly identifying the topics about which the Federal Parliament can make laws.[59] No such limits

[58] Commonwealth of Australia, Australia's Human Rights Framework, April 2010, available at www.ag.gov.au/humanrightsframework.
[59] Commonwealth Constitution s 51.

exist on state or territory legislative powers. State governments have plenary legislative power, subject usually only to a requirement that any law
be for the 'peace, order and good government' of the jurisdiction in question.[60] However, a state law that covers the same topic as a Commonwealth
law will be invalid to the extent of any inconsistency between them: that
is, the Commonwealth law will prevail.[61] Although the territories are
self-governing, the Commonwealth has plenary legislative power that can
be used to override territorial legislation. The Commonwealth's exercise
of that power can have significant human rights implications: it legislated
in 1997 to override legislation in the Northern Territory that had created a
system for legal, voluntary euthanasia.[62]

The Commonwealth Government does not have an identifiable legislative power for human rights generally, for labour relations, or
for the employment relationship. There are however several heads of
Commonwealth legislative power that could be used to promote and protect workers' human rights. Given the provision for federal supremacy,
the Commonwealth has in practice used many of its legislative powers to
assume a substantial regulatory responsibility for much of the Australian
labour law system. Some key areas have generally been left to the states,
particularly regulation of occupational health and safety, and workers'
compensation.[63]

As noted, the key Commonwealth legislative power that was traditionally used to regulate working conditions was the power to make laws with
respect to 'conciliation and arbitration for the prevention and settlement of
industrial disputes extending beyond the limits of any one State'.[64] Other
powers that have been used include those concerning the federal public service;[65] constitutional corporations;[66] and 'external affairs'.[67] It is the last of
these that has the greatest potential as a source of power to create human
rights protection in Australia.

---

[60] See, eg, Constitution Act 1902 (New South Wales (NSW) s 5; Constitution Act 1975
(Victoria (Vic)) s 16 and Constitution Act 1889 (Western Australia (WA) s 2.

[61] Commonwealth Constitution s 109.

[62] Euthanasia Laws Act 1997 (Cth). The federal law was not government action, but a
private member's bill, sponsored by the Honourable Kevin Andrews MP. From October 2003,
Mr Andrews was the Minister for Workplace Relations, responsible among other things for
Work Choices.

[63] See generally FW Act ss 26, 27.

[64] Commonwealth Constitution s 51(xxxv). This source of power has traditionally underpinned the vast majority of Commonwealth labour law. An indication of the scope of this
power (when taken together with others), is that the High Court held that legislation to establish and regulate trade unions was properly 'incidental' to those made in the exercise of identified heads of legislative power. That is, regulation of trade unions was properly 'incidental' to
the system of resolving industrial disputes by means of conciliation and arbitration: *Jumbunna
Coal Mine, No Liability v Victorian Coal Miners Association* (1908) CLR 309.

[65] Commonwealth Constitution s 52(2).

[66] Commonwealth Constitution s 51(xx).

[67] Commonwealth Constitution s 51(xxix).

Since the 1980s, the Commonwealth Government has used its legislative power with respect to 'external affairs' to implement a number of obligations arising under international treaties. This has been possible because the High Court has held that the external affairs power will support Commonwealth legislation to give effect to Australia's international legal obligations, even in areas where the Commonwealth otherwise lacks legislative competence. Although the Court's landmark decisions on this provision date from the early 1980s,[68] the reasoning can be traced to the 1920s[69] and 1930s.[70] Indeed, in the 1930s, two members of the Court suggested that the external affairs power would support legislation to give effect to ILO Conventions.[71] As will be discussed below, Australian federal labour law has been significantly influenced by ILO Conventions since the early 1990s. Indeed, it was in the course of its decision to uphold the validity of Commonwealth legislation purporting to give effect to ILO Conventions that the High Court formulated the present test that controls the use of the external affairs power. The law must be 'reasonably capable of being considered appropriate and adapted to implementing the treaty'.[72]

The Commonwealth has relied on the external affairs power to promote human rights by enacting several statutes concerning discrimination based on race, sex, disability and age.[73] The Australian Human Rights Commission Act 1986 (Cth) creates the Australian Human Rights Commission (AHRC).

---

[68] The High Court gave its imprimatur to this use of the external affairs power in *Koowarta v Bjelke-Petersen* (1982) 153 CLR 168 and *Commonwealth v Tasmania* (1983) 158 CLR 1. The Federal Government, however, has not exploited the full potential of its legislative powers under the external affairs power. This reluctance has, in the past, been attributed to political considerations: that is, the concerns by the states over infringement of their legislative spheres: Charlesworth, 'The Australian Reluctance about Rights' (1993) 212. This reasoning, however, is less convincing in light of the Federal Government's recent attempts to take over labour relations through an extensive use of its corporations power.

[69] *Roche v Kronheimer* (1921) 29 CLR 329 (Higgins J) (note that the other judges upheld the legislation in question on the basis of other Commonwealth legislative powers). This case concerned implementation of the Treaty of Versailles.

[70] *R v Burgess, ex p Henry* (1936) 55 CLR 608. This case concerned implementation of the International Convention for the Regulation of Aerial Navigation.

[71] *R v Burgess, ex p Henry* (1936) 55 CLR 608, 681–82, 687 (Evatt and McTiernan JJ).

[72] *Victoria v Commonwealth (Industrial Relations Act Case)* (1996) 187 CLR 416, 487 (Brennan CJ, Toohey, Gaudron, McHugh and Gummow JJ). Compare, however, *Horta v Commonwealth* (1994) 181 CLR 183, where the Court held that a Commonwealth statute will not be invalid merely because it is inconsistent with an international legal obligation binding on Australia.

[73] At the federal level, a separate officer, the Privacy Commissioner, has responsibility for the protection and promotion of those rights that are conferred by the Privacy Act 1988 (Cth). At the state and territory level there is legislation in each jurisdiction with respect to non-discrimination. See Discrimination Act 1991 (ACT); Anti-Discrimination Act 1977 (NSW); Anti-Discrimination Act 1992 (Northern Territory (NT)); Anti-Discrimination Act 1991 (Queensland (Qld); Equal Opportunity Act 1984 (South Australia (SA)); Anti-Discrimination Act 1998 (Tasmania (Tas)); Equal Opportunity Act 1995 (Vic); and Equal Opportunity Act 1984 (WA).

It is responsible for promoting and protecting the rights that are recognised in the Racial Discrimination Act 1975 (Cth), the Sex Discrimination Act 1984 (Cth), the Disability Discrimination Act 1991 (Cth), and the Age Discrimination Act 2004 (Cth). The AHRC also has functions under the Native Title Act 1992 (Cth), and the FW Act.

These regimes have been criticised as inadequate in the protection that they offer. Hilary Charlesworth, for example, has argued that they suffer from several important limitations.[74] First, they offer protection that is limited in scope: to action in the public realm; to individual complaints and remedies; and to the unnecessarily narrow legislative definitions of 'equality'. Secondly, there are certain exemptions for action by states, although the Commonwealth Constitution's supremacy clause would enable a wider scope. Thirdly, various areas of activity are exempted from the operation of the statutes.[75] Fourthly, the legislation may only be indirectly enforced.[76] Finally, they do little to protect economic, social and cultural rights.[77]

The Role of the Common Law and the Courts in Protecting Human Rights

The common law is at best a limited source of protection for human rights in Australia; indeed it has been referred to as 'the least significant source of human rights law'.[78] Unlike courts in the United States of America, the United Kingdom, Canada and New Zealand, the Australian High Court has generally

---

[74] Charlesworth (n 35) 213–18.

[75] Common exemptions relate to superannuation, insurance, credit, migration and taxation. For exemption provisions, see Racial Discrimination Act 1975 (Cth) s 18D; Sex Discrimination Act 1984 (Cth) div 4; Disability Discrimination Act 1991 (Cth) div 5; and the Age Discrimination Act 2004 (Cth) divs 4 and 5.

[76] It might be noted that the decision of the High Court in *Brandy v Human Rights and Equal Opportunity Commission* (1995) 183 CLR 245, handed down after Charlesworth's observation on indirect enforcement, in fact requires a mechanism of indirect enforcement. The Court held that limitations in the Constitution on the ability of the Commonwealth to invest non-judicial power in a court created under c III of the Commonwealth Constitution had the effect of also limiting the Commonwealth's ability to invest judicial power in a non-judicial body, such as the Human Rights and Equal Opportunity Commission (HREOC). Thus, enforcement remains indirect and multi-staged, with a complainant required to take their complaint for mediation/conciliation to the HREOC, but to the federal courts for enforcement.

[77] This is also true of the Human Rights Act 2004 (ACT), even though the report of the Consultative Committee that recommended the implementation of that Act (which was chaired by Professor Charlesworth) recommended that economic, social and cultural rights be protected: O'Neill, N, Rice, S, and Douglas, R, *Retreat for Injustice: Human Rights in Australian Law*, 2nd edn (Sydney, Federation Press, 2004) 180. Economic and social rights, including the right to strike and equal pay for work of equal value, are to some extent protected by the FW Act; these topics are dealt with (respectively) in Parts IV and V below.

[78] O'Neill, Rice and Douglas, *Retreat for Injustice: Human Rights in Australian Law* (2004) 76, 106.

been reluctant to identify human rights in the Commonwealth Constitution and, when it has done so, has adopted a limited and very cautious approach.[79] The Court has hardly been less reluctant about human rights and the use of international law in its approach to the development of the common law.

The most important statement of judicial support for the use of international human rights law as a means of developing the common law is found in the judgment of Brennan J in *Mabo (No 2)*, where he said:

> The common law does not necessarily conform with international law, but international law is a legitimate and important influence on the development of the common law, especially when international law declares the existence of universal human rights.[80]

Even in making this statement, however, Brennan J was careful to emphasise that the courts should not rely upon international law to develop the common law where to do so would 'fracture the skeleton of principle which gives the body of our law its shape and internal consistency'.[81] The role of international human rights law, if any, in contributing to the development of the common law arose again in *Dietrich v R*,[82] where the High Court considered the question whether international law on the right to a fair trial gave rise to a right to state-provided legal representation. The Court decided that it did not.

In *Minister for Immigration and Ethnic Affairs v Teoh*,[83] the High Court held that as Australia had signed a treaty (the Convention on the Rights of the Child), a person might thereby have a legitimate expectation that an administrative decision-maker would exercise their administrative discretion consistently with the terms of such a treaty. The Court held that the expectation arose notwithstanding that Australia had not at the relevant time *ratified* the instrument in question. Although this principle is applied without difficulty in courts and tribunals,[84] it appears that the High Court may be prepared to overturn its decision in *Teoh*.[85]

---

[79] Charlesworth (n 35); Mason, A, 'The Role of the Judiciary in Developing Human Rights in Australian Law' in D Kinley (ed), *Human Rights in Australian Law* (Sydney, Federation Press, 1998) 26.

[80] *Mabo (No 2)* (1992) 175 CLR 1, 42 (Brennan J) (Mason CJ and McHugh J agreeing).

[81] *Mabo (No 2)* (1992) 175 CLR 1, 43 (Brennan J) (Mason CJ and McHugh J agreeing).

[82] *Dietrich v R* (1992) 177 CLR 292. See also the decision of the Full Federal Court in *Nulyarimma v Thompson* (1999) 96 FCR 153 (Australian common law does not include a crime of genocide absent specific action to create one, regardless of whether genocide is recognised as a peremptory norm of international law). See generally Mitchell, 'Genocide, Human Rights' (2000).

[83] *Minister for Immigration and Ethnic Affairs v Teoh* (1995) 183 CLR 273.

[84] Charlesworth, H et al, 'Deep Anxieties: Australia and the International Legal Order' (2003) 25 *Sydney Law Review* 423, 438.

[85] The High Court has recently indicated that the decision in *Teoh* might not withstand further scrutiny: *Re Minister for Immigration and Multicultural and Indigenous Affairs, ex p Lam* (2003) 214 CLR 1. See Charlesworth et al, 'Deep Anxieties' (2003) 450, Lacey, W, 'Judicial Discretion and Human Rights: Expanding the Role of International Law in the Domestic Sphere' (2004) 5 *Melbourne Journal of International Law* 108, 114 and particularly

Much of both the commentary and the case law in Australia dealing with how international human rights law influences judicial decisions is concerned with criminal law and justice.[86] Thus, the courts have done little to develop the common law, by use of international human rights law, in ways that are directly relevant to workers' rights.[87] As appears directly, ILO Conventions and other international instruments have been used to develop Australia's federal labour laws, and were used to interpret the WR Act. Perhaps for that reason, these instruments have had little impact on the development of the common law. In *National Workforce v Australian Manufacturing Workers' Union*,[88] for example, the Court held that while there may be a right to strike in international law, there was no such right in the WR Act—and neither was there one in the Australian common law.[89]

FREEDOM OF ASSOCIATION FOR TRADE UNION PURPOSES

Australia's obligations to protect freedom of association for trade union purposes derive from several international sources, including the ICCPR, the ICESCR, and key ILO instruments by which it is bound. These include ILO Conventions 87 (freedom of association and right to organise) and 98 (right to organise and collective bargaining), and the Declaration on Fundamental Principles and Rights at Work 1998. Broadly speaking, however, these instruments have had relatively little influence on the content of Australian labour law over time, even though in the last 15 years the implementation of Australia's international legal obligations has become a greater focus of federal labour law.

With the introduction of the Industrial Relations Reform Act 1993 (Cth) (IRR Act) it became a principal object of the Industrial Relations Act 1988 (Cth) (1988 Act) that it should assist in giving effect to Australia's international obligations. As we will see, however, Australia's interest in complying with those obligations does appear to have waned as time has passed. When the IRR Act was introduced, the legislative object was expressed as being to provide 'the means for ... ensuring that labour standards meet Australia's international obligations'.[90] With the transition to the WR Act from the beginning

the sources to which Lacey refers in fn 43 on that page. In any event it should be noted that following the decision in *Teoh* governments of both political persuasions adopted non-binding parliamentary declarations to the effect that no such expectation arises; they have also attempted to legislate to this effect.

[86] Lacey, 'Judicial Discretion and Human Rights' (2004) 116.

[87] Ibid 29–30.

[88] *National Workforce v Australian Manufacturing Workers' Union* [1998] 3 VR 265.

[89] *National Workforce v Australian Manufacturing Workers' Union* [1998] 3 VR 265, 275–76.

[90] Industrial Relations Act 1988 (Cth) s 3(b)(ii), as amended by the Industrial Relations Reform Act 1993 (Cth)(IRR Act) s 4.

of 1997, that commitment was changed to 'assisting in giving effect to Australia's international legal obligations in relation to labour standards'.[91]

This form of words was retained with the transition to Work Choices.[92] However, another object was added, which significantly affected the extent to which the WR Act could or should give effect to Australia's obligations in relation to freedom of association. The principal objects of the WR Act then included that it should:

> provide a framework for cooperative workplace relations which promotes the economic prosperity and welfare of the people of Australia by ... balancing the right to take industrial action for the purposes of collective bargaining at the workplace level with the need to protect the public interest and appropriately deal with illegitimate and unprotected industrial action.[93]

Since the further change to the FW Act, the legislative objects now include 'providing workplace relations laws that ... take into account Australia's international labour obligations' and

> enabling fairness and representation at work and the prevention of discrimination by recognising the right to freedom of association and the right to be represented, protecting against unfair treatment and discrimination, providing accessible and effective procedures to resolve grievances and disputes and providing effective compliance mechanisms.[94]

The current formulation of the legislative object that refers to freedom of association has the advantage over its predecessor in that it no longer includes a reference to illegitimate industrial action, which rather carried the implication that the phenomenon was so common and threatening as to warrant identification as such at the outset of the principal federal labour law. Nevertheless, within that part of the FW Act that includes the provisions protecting freedom of association, the legislative protection of the negative right of disassociation is continued. Moreover, the objects of that part of the FW Act specifically include 'ensuring that persons area ... free to become, or not become, members'. The provision also indicates that the new legislation would equally intend to protect the right not to be represented by an industrial association and the right not to participate in lawful industrial activities.[95]

This is in keeping with the fact that although the WR Act included from 1997 a specific object of protecting freedom of association, this was mainly for the purpose of protecting the negative right not to belong to an association. The legislation did continue to provide support for the exercise

---

[91] WR Act s 3(k) (pre-Work Choices).

[92] It is now s 3(n).

[93] WR Act s 3(i).

[94] FW Act s 3(a) and s 3(e). Note that s 722(b) also refers specifically to the ILO's Termination of Employment Convention No 158.

[95] FW Act s 336.

of trade union rights. At the same time, however (and indeed by the same provisions), it set out to ensure that those who do not wish to participate in trade union activity may decline to do so. All of this is continued in the FW Act. Moreover, under the Howard Government the power of federal agencies to enforce Australian labour law was significantly enhanced. Under the WR Act this started with the Office of the Employment Advocate, which ultimately became the Workplace Ombudsman. Under the FW Act it is now the Fair Work Ombudsman. The role of this office (however called over time) has always included enforcement of the legislative provisions protecting the right not to associate. In addition, from 2005 there has been an Australian Building and Construction Commission (ABCC), with specific enforcement powers for the building industry. The ABCC in particular has proved most assiduous at bringing proceedings to enforce the law protecting the right not to associate.[96] As Breen Creighton has pointed out, under international law it is *permissible* for domestic labour law to protect this negative right, but it is not *necessary* that it do so.[97]

What this all underscores is that the protection of fundamental rights in Australia, including the freedom of association, can shift significantly with changes in government, in the absence of a fixed point of reference such as an agreed bill of human rights. Secondly, it highlights Australia's somewhat ambiguous approach to the freedom of association, which is open to the interpretation that promoting the right has never been high on the list of priorities. This view is supported by consideration of the international instruments that various federal governments have chosen to annex to the federal Act from time to time. They have included those concerning termination of employment, workers' with family responsibilities, and equal pay for work of equal value,[98] but not those dealing with freedom of association.[99]

---

[96] See, for example, Hardy, T, 'A Changing of the Guard: Enforcement of the Laws Since Work Choices and Beyond' and also Fenwick, C and Howe, J, 'Union Security After Work Choices', both in A Forsyth and A Stewart (eds), *Fair Work: The New Workplace Laws and the Work Choices Legacy* (Sydney, Federation Press, 2009) 75–98 and 164–185 respectively.

[97] ILO, *General Survey of the Reports on the Freedom of Association and Protection of the Right to Organise Convention 1948 and the Right to Organise and Collective Bargaining Convention 1949* (81st session, ILC, 1994) Report III (pt 4B) at paras 100–103 and 205 (ILO, '*General Survey*' (1994)). An exception to this that might be noted is art 20(2) of the Universal Declaration of Human Rights (UDHR), which does refer to the negative right—although this of course is not a binding instrument. On the development of the protection of the negative right in Australia, see Forsyth, A and Sutherland, C, 'From "Uncharted Seas" to "Stormy Waters": How Will Trade Unions Fare under the Work Choices Legislation?' (2006) *Economic and Labour Relations Review* 215; Naughton, R, 'Sailing into Uncharted Seas: The Role of Unions Under the Workplace Relations Act 1996 (Cth)' (1997) 10 *Australian Journal of Labour Law* 112, and Quinn, D, 'To Be or Not to Be a Member—Is That the Only Question? Freedom of Association under the Workplace Relations Act' (2004) 17 *Australian Journal of Labour Law* 1.

[98] Pittard, M, 'International Labour Standards in Australia: Wages, Equal Pay, Leave and Termination of Employment' (1994) 7 *Australian Journal of Labour Law* 170.

[99] It is ironic then that the Commonwealth successfully argued before the High Court that the IRR Act provisions protecting a form of 'right to strike' were a valid exercise of

Trade Unions and Australian Conciliation and Arbitration

Australia not only has a general reluctance about rights,[100] it has a specific reluctance about freedom of association for trade union purposes. Broadly speaking, what are colloquially known as 'trade unions' in Australia are, for the most part, 'registered organisations' that are created and regulated by the operation of legislation to deal with the settlement of collective labour disputes. At the federal level, this is now done under the Fair Work (Registered Organisations) Act 2009 (Cth) (FWRO Act). Since the enactment of the Conciliation and Arbitration Act 1904 (Cth), the Australian model of conciliation and arbitration has always depended for its operation on the existence and operation of trade unions. That model had three elements: (1) a permanent publicly-funded tribunal for resolution of disputes that was obliged to take into account the public interest; (2) organisations of employers and employees as part of the system itself; and (3) compulsion to appear before the tribunal once it was seized with jurisdiction.[101]

The origins of federal (and state) regulation of labour organisations lay in the needs of the conciliation and arbitration system itself, rather than in any conception of the need for or the desirability of protecting the rights of workers. While that may have been an incidental consequence of creating a means of forming a registered organisation, the real purpose of these organisations was to serve as vehicles by which industrial disputes might be brought before the tribunals to be settled if bargaining failed to do so. The central role of trade unions necessitated significant ancillary protection of their organisational rights, and was accompanied by protection of the rights of individuals who might belong to those associations, once they became registered as organisations. Nevertheless, the focus was not on the rights of the individual, other than to the extent that this was necessary for or conducive to the proper functioning of the registered organisation. It was intended that these organisations would assist the functioning of the system of labour dispute resolution, the principal purpose of which was to protect society and the economy from the harmful effects of industrial disputation.[102]

---

its' legislative power over external affairs, to implement art 8 of the ICESCR. *Victoria v Commonwealth* (1996) 187 CLR 416. Somewhat curiously, in the same decision the High Court held that ILO Conventions 87 and 98 did not enable the Commonwealth to legislate to implement a right to strike, as the right to strike is not referred to in the text of either instrument. In so holding, the Court declined to be guided by the many years' interpretation of these instruments by the ILO's supervisory bodies: at 544–46.

[100] Charlesworth (n 35).

[101] See, broadly, Mitchell, R and Stern, E, 'The Compulsory Arbitration Model of Industrial Dispute Settlement: An Outline of Legal Developments' in S Macintyre and R Mitchell (eds), *Foundations of Arbitration: The Origins and Effects of State Compulsory Arbitration, 1890–1914* (Melbourne, Oxford University Press, 1989) 104.

[102] Broadly speaking, the Australian approach to conciliation and arbitration of industrial disputes was significantly influenced in its origins and purposes by a series of crippling strikes

In order to bolster the role of registered organisations, the legislation created several important mechanisms of trade union security.[103] These included powers to require that trade unionists be preferred in hiring, and also protection against acts of anti-union discrimination. But whatever was done in the legislation was always done *for the purposes of the system*, and not directly in the interests of the individuals that might have joined the organisations concerned:

> Within the federal conciliation and arbitration system the primary purpose or functional role played by the anti-victimisation and freedom of association provisions has always been to provide protection for the legislative system itself by protecting its constituent elements—the awards of the tribunal and the unions without which the system could not function.[104]

In short, it was never a goal of the system to promote and protect the rights of individuals, other than to the extent that this might have been necessary to support the operation of the organisations to which they might belong.

It is perhaps not surprising therefore that the Federal Government was able, in 1996, to re-align the legislative objectives with so much emphasis on the negative freedom of association. Where the legislation had previously emphasised the importance of registered organisations—that is, collectivities of individual workers—it thereby provided the opportunity for the then newly-elected Coalition Government to take the opportunity to break down (perceived) union power.[105] Given the usual understanding of freedom of association, it is somewhat counter-intuitive that the Government chose this key principle as the means by which to break down support for collective organisation. It is all the more ironic that, in the result, the provisions proved to be particularly useful to trade unions in their efforts to protect their members (and themselves) from the attacks on their position facilitated by the WR Act.

Freedom of Association under Australian Federal Labour Law

The shift to the WR Act wrought significant changes in the legal landscape. First, it removed a number of the supports that had previously been in place to provide trade union security. The WR Act removed the power of

across several colonies during the 1890s. Conciliation and arbitration systems were established to limit the chances of similar social and economic dislocation being repeated after Federation. See generally Macintyre and Mitchell, *Foundations of Arbitration* (1989) and Creighton, B and Stewart, A, *Labour Law*, 4th edn (Federation Press, Leichardt, NSW, 2005) 45–46.

[103] See generally Weeks, P, *Trade Union Security Law* (Sydney, Federation Press, 1995).
[104] Quinn, 'To Be or Not to Be a Member' (2004) 5.
[105] See, eg, Forsyth, A, 'Re-Regulatory Tendencies in Australian and New Zealand Labour Law' (Working Paper No 21, Centre for Employment and Labour Relations Law, University of Melbourne, March 2001) and Naughton, 'Sailing into Uncharted Seas' (1997).

the AIRC to grant preference to trade union members, specifically outlawed closed shops,[106] and forbade the AIRC from granting any provision in an industrial award that provided a trade union with a right of entry to an employer's premises, creating instead a more regulated statutory scheme for these purposes.[107] Secondly, it significantly altered the regulation of trade unions once registered in the system. It attempted to facilitate greater competition between trade unions for membership: the WR Act loosened the criteria for registration of unions; provided for registration of enterprise-based unions; and introduced provisions to facilitate disamalgamation of unions that had elected to amalgamate under the IRR Act regime.[108] Thirdly, it introduced a specific right not to belong to an association, and provisions aimed at protecting that right.

The significance of the negative right of association for the WR Act was reflected in the fact that it became a principal object of the legislation that it should 'ensur[e] freedom of association, including the rights of employees and employers to join an organisation or association of their choice, *or not to join an organisation or association*'.[109] As noted, while this is no longer a principal object of the legislation that is now the FW Act, protection of this right remains a feature of the system. So too do most other features of the system for registration and regulation of registered organisations that was introduced by the Howard government.

The Right to Form and Join Organisations

The need for unions as vehicles to resolve industrial disputes meant that conciliation and arbitration systems from their inception included provisions for the registration and regulation of organisations of employees and employers. Among other things, registration generally brought with it corporate status,[110] as well as the ability to enliven the compulsory and

---

[106] Although these had arguably been beyond the power of the federal tribunal, regardless of award provisions closed shops had long been a significant feature of Australian industrial regulation in practice: Creighton and Stewart, *Labour Law* (2005) 524–25.

[107] For an overview of the evolution of these provisions, see Forsyth and Sutherland, 'From "Uncharted Seas" to "Stormy Waters"' (2006). On the shift in these provisions under the FW Act regime, see Fenwick and Howe, 'Union Security After Work Choices' (2009). It is still the case that an award may not longer include provisions for right of entry of union officials: FW Act s 152.

[108] See Naughton (n 97) and MacDermott, 'Labour Law and Human Rights' (1998) 209–10; on enterprise unions see Creighton and Stewart (n 102) 509–10, and Forsyth, A, 'Ministerial Discussion Paper—Accountability and Democratic Control of Registered Industrial Organisations' (1999) 12 *Australian Journal of Labour Law* 193. On encouragement of competition between unions see *Re CPSU* (2000) 100 IR 296, 341–42.

[109] WR Act s 3(f) (pre-Work Choices) (emphasis added). This provision was retained in the same terms after Work Choices: see WR Act s 3(j).

[110] Except in Tasmania and Victoria, where the systems were slightly different; in any event there is no longer a Victorian system.

of … organisations'.[129] The latter of these has been removed with the shift to the FWRO Act, but the former provision remains.[130] A number of other more straightforward ones have been retained, concerning financial accountability and democratic functioning within organisations.[131] A major change under the provisions after Work Choices was that they attempted to regulate a broader range of organisations, in particular by seeking to absorb into the federal system what had formerly been state unions.[132] This aspect is also continued under the FWRO Act.[133]

Protection against Acts of Anti-Union Victimisation

Australian labour law has long included anti-victimisation provisions, even if their main purpose was traditionally to provide a measure of trade union security.[134] These provisions, which in recent years have come to be referred to as the freedom of association provisions, are now found in Part 3–1 of the FW Act, among provisions that are intended to establish a set of 'General Protections'. The FW Act has introduced a new concept, of taking 'adverse action' against a person, as broadly defined in s 342, on the grounds that they have the benefit of a 'workplace right', or because of the exercise or non-exercise of such a right (div 3). They similarly protect a person against adverse action in the event that they have engaged in 'industrial activities' (div 4).

The FW Act continues most of the protections that have existed in the federal system for many years, and has removed some of the limits on the protections that were introduced in the Work Choices reforms.[135] The concept of 'adverse action' covers a wide range of retaliatory conduct, up to and including termination of an employee's employment, or refusal to engage or continue to engage an independent contractor. The concepts of 'workplace rights' generally ensures that a person is entitled to the benefit of statutory protections, and to exercise certain related rights, including, for example, the right to participate in certain types of proceedings.[136] The concept of 'industrial activities' includes membership of a representative organisation and participation in its activities, including holding office, and participating in lawful industrial action.[137] (These last provisions, in

---

[129] RAOS r 5(4).
[130] FWRO Act s 5(3)(e).
[131] FWRO Act ss 5(3)(a) to (d).
[132] For comment see Forsyth and Sutherland (n 97).
[133] FWRO Act sch 1 and 2.
[134] *AMIEU v Belandra Pty Ltd* (2003) 126 IR 165 contains something of a history of these provisions.
[135] The relevant provisions were, in particular, the former ss 792 and 793 of the WR Act.
[136] FW Act s 341.
[137] FW Act s 347.

particular, are largely directed at the sort of objectives required by art 1 of ILO Convention 98: they protect individuals against acts of anti-union discrimination or victimisation.) The provisions have for many years included a reverse onus of proof, effectively obliging an employer to disprove an allegation that they engaged in prohibited conduct for a prohibited reason.[138]

The freedom of association provisions went through a major reworking as part of the changes leading to the WR Act. This was an important part of the then government's overall policy of removing legislative support for trade unions. Ironically, trade unions found the provisions very effective as a means of promoting and protecting their members' interests, especially in the face of business restructuring and outsourcing. The provisions were used to good effect in resisting a major corporate restructure and outsourcing of work in the course of a very public and damaging industrial dispute in the stevedoring (longshore) industry;[139] the outsourcing of homecare functions by a local government;[140] and various attempts by the Commonwealth Bank to move its employees from collective to individual forms of employment regulation.[141]

The cases involving the maritime industry and the local government illustrate the inter-relationship of individual protection and support for the integrity of the system's outcomes. Both involved the operation of the antecedents of what is now section 341(1)(a), which includes as a 'workplace right' that a person is entitled to the benefit of a 'workplace instrument'.[142] Under the Work Choices reforms, it was necessary for an applicant relying on this provision to establish that the respondent had retaliated against them on the ground of this benefit, and that this was the 'sole and dominant

---

[138] See now FW Act s 361. On the operation of these provisions in former versions of the Act, see especially Jessup, C, 'The Onus of Proof in Proceedings under Part XA of the Workplace Relations Act 1996' (2002) 15 *Australian Journal of Labour Law* 198.

[139] *Patrick Stevedores Operations No. 2 Ltd v Maritime Union of Australia* (1998) 195 CLR 1. For comment, see Orr, G, 'Conspiracy on the Waterfront' (1998) 11 *Australian Journal of Labour Law* 159. This dispute was the subject of a complaint to the ILO Committee on Freedom of Association, which was critical, among other things, of the role of the government in seeking to break the Maritime Union of Australia's 'virtual monopoly' of representation, and limitations on the capacity to take lawful strike action where it was having harmful economic effects. See Murray, J, 'Australian in the Dock: The ILO's Decision on the Waterfront Dispute' (2000) 13 *Australian Journal of Labour Law* 167.

[140] *Greater Dandenong City Council v Australian Services Union* (2001) 112 FCR 232.

[141] *Finance Sector Union of Australia v Commonwealth Bank of Australia* (2000) 106 IR 139; *Finance Sector Union of Australia v Commonwealth Bank of Australia* (2005) 223 ALR 6 and (2005) 224 ALR 467.

[142] Most recently the relevant provision was s 793(1)(i), and before that s 298L(1)(h) of the WR Act. For another successful use of these provisions, see *AMIEU v Belandra* (2003) 126 IR 165, in which the Court held that an employer had breached the Act when it decided to restructure its business by using labour hire workers, instead of re-hiring its former employees, as it had originally indicated it intended to do.

reason' for the retaliation.[143] Under the FW Act, this requirement has now been removed, which raises the possibility of further use of the provision to resist business restructuring, among other things.[144]

Another section that proved to be important in recent years in a number of high profile cases was the provision which protected workers against retaliation on the ground of them being 'an officer, delegate or member of an industrial association'.[145] The meaning of this protection for trade union membership was tested—and found wanting—in *AWU v BHPIO*.[146] The case involved a company's refusal to bargain with its employees' union, because it preferred instead to offer better conditions under individual agreements.[147] This is one of the few cases in Australian labour law to address the hybrid nature of the freedom of association: it is an individual human right, the efficacy of which requires that the collectivities that are formed in its exercise should also have particular rights.

The union's case was based on evidence that its members who had accepted individual agreements in other situations had tended subsequently to resign their union membership. The union argued that the company was pursuing a strategy that would reduce union membership, thereby diluting union bargaining strength. This in turn, it was alleged, harmed each individual who was a member of the union, and was therefore contrary to the former s 298L(1)(a) of the WR Act. In the result, the union failed in its application, as the trial judge held that any diminution of union strength would be a result of each individual's decision to resign their membership, not a consequence of the employer's action. Neither was the Court satisfied that there was sufficient evidence that the company *intended* to bring about the consequence of reduced union bargaining strength. The most troubling aspect of the decision, however, was that the Court held that the protection of the right to be a member did not extend to any of the incidents of membership of a trade union. In effect, the right to be a member of a trade union meant, therefore, only the right to purchase and to retain a membership ticket. This aspect of the decision has been criticised academically for the principle that it adopted,[148] and judicially as inconsistent with prior authority.[149]

---

[143] WR Act s 792(4).

[144] Fenwick and Howe (n 96).

[145] Most recently, WR Act s 793(1)(a), and before that, s 298L(1)(a). See now FW Act s 347(a).

[146] (2001) 106 Federal Court Reports 482.

[147] The instruments in question were creatures of the West Australian State industrial relations system.

[148] See Quinn (n 97), especially 27–31.

[149] *AMIEU v Belandra Pty Ltd* (2003) 126 IR 165, especially [135]–[150]. This decision is of some note also for the fact that the Court drew on a wide range of international law to assist in determining the proper meaning to be given the provisions: at [151]–[215]. As the issue was not determinative, the decision of course remains only persuasive authority.

In the absence of further cases, the decision in *AWU v BHPIO* appears however to be the law at the time of this writing. What remains to be seen is whether the new provisions in the FW Act lead to any shift in this important area of jurisprudence. Section 347(a) of the FW Act is slightly differently-worded than its predecessors. It indicates that it is an industrial activity if a person 'becomes or does not become, or remains or ceases to be, an officer or member of an industrial association'.

The Promotion of Free and Voluntary Collective Bargaining

This is an area in which the changes to the FW Act have taken some important steps toward better compliance with key international obligations. Under the WR Act, particularly as amended by Work Choices, Australian law was frequently found wanting in this area by the ILO's supervisory bodies. One problem was the aggressive promotion of individual statutory agreements, known as Australian Workplace Agreements (AWAs), in preference to collectively-determined working conditions. Another was the failure of collective bargaining provisions to establish or protect a legally enforceable *right* to engage in collective bargaining. Yet another was the emphasis on collective bargaining at the level of the 'single business', with limitations in the law on the right to bargain freely at other levels.

AWAs were inconsistent with the promotion of voluntary collective bargaining (under article 4 of ILO Convention No 98) in a number of ways. First, they were given legal priority over collectively-determined conditions. After Work Choices, an employer could offer an employee an AWA immediately after concluding collectively-determined conditions, and the AWA would take precedence. Secondly, too little was done to ensure that workers had a free choice not to enter into an AWA. Among other things, the law provided (first by judicial decision, and after Work Choices, in the WR Act itself) that there was no breach of the prohibition on using duress to conclude an AWA if the employer made signing an AWA a condition of employment.[150] All of these issues should now be in the past: AWAs were abolished even before the FW Act came into existence, by the Workplace Relations Amendment (Transition to Forward With Fairness) Act 2008 (Cth). While AWAs, that were in existence at the time that law came into effect continue to operate, since its coming into force it is no longer possible to make an AWA.[151]

The legislative framework for collective bargaining in Australia has generally not included any *right* to engage in collective bargaining. Neither did the AIRC have power to *compel* an employer to engage in collective

---

[150] On the inconsistencies of AWAs with Australia's obligations under ILO Convention 98, see Fenwick and Landau, 'Work Choices in International Perspective' (2006).

[151] See Sutherland, C, 'First Steps Forward (with Fairness): A Preliminary Examination of the Transition Legislation' (2008) 21 *Australian Journal of Labour Law* 137.

bargaining. This of course has contributed to it being lawful for an employer to offer its workforce individual arrangements and simply to elect not to engage in bargaining with the workers' chosen trade union bargaining agent.[152] For the most part, neither has there been any explicit obligation to bargain in good faith: the AIRC has only been able to exercise limited powers while parties were engaged in a 'bargaining period'.[153]

The FW Act has wrought significant changes in this respect. First, it has abolished the concept of the 'bargaining period', which under the WR Act it was necessary to initiate formally, in order to be able to commence negotiations, and subsequently to be able to make application to take lawful industrial action. Under the new provisions, bargaining will begin when an employer agrees to bargain or initiates bargaining. Where an employer does not wish to bargain, employee representatives may seek from Fair Work Australia a 'majority-support determination'.[154] Any of these events will trigger an obligation for the employer to notify their employees of their right to be represented in the course of bargaining.[155] Unions are automatically considered to be representatives for these purposes, but an employee or employees might elect to be represented in bargaining by someone else, or to represent themselves.[156]

All bargaining representatives must comply with good faith bargaining requirements.[157] These include attending and participating in meetings, recognising the appointed representatives of their bargaining counterpart, and refraining from acting capriciously or unfairly. It should be noted that there is a specific provision that no bargaining representative is required to make concessions or to reach agreement on proposed terms.[158] Failure to comply with the obligation to bargain in good faith means that the other bargaining party may seek a 'bargaining order' from Fair Work Australia. An application may also be made where a bargaining representative is concerned that the bargaining process is 'not proceeding efficiently or fairly because there are multiple bargaining representatives'.[159] A number of the

---

[152] See eg, *Australian Workers' Union v BHP Iron Ore Pty Ltd (No 3)* (2001) 106 FCR 482.

[153] See *CPSU v Sensis Pty Ltd* (2003) 128 IR 92. For a discussion of good faith bargaining under earlier legislation, see, eg, Naughton, R, 'Bargaining in Good Faith' in P Ronfeldt and R McCallum (eds), *Enterprise Bargaining, Trade Unions and the Law* (Sydney, Federation Press, 1995) 84; and Shaw, J, 'Observations on Trade Union Recognition in Britain and Australia' (2001) 24 *University of NSW Law Journal* 214. For a more recent discussion, see McCallum, R, 'Trade Union Recognition and Australia's Neo-Liberal Voluntary Bargaining Laws' (2002) 57 *Industrial Relations* 225.

[154] FW Act s 237. A bargaining representative may also seek a 'scope order' from Fair Work Australia to clarify which employees and parts of a business are to be covered by negotiations for an agreement: FW Act s 238.

[155] FW Act pt 2–4 div 3.

[156] FW Act s 176.

[157] FW Act s 228.

[158] FW Act s 228(2).

[159] FW Act s 229(4)(a)(ii).

early decisions under the FW Act suggest that whether a party is bargaining in good faith may be relevant to (although not determinative of) the question whether they are genuinely trying to reach agreement.[160] As appears below, this is important as a threshold requirement for being able to take lawful industrial action.

In addition to introducing a general concept of good faith bargaining, the FW Act includes new arrangements for collective bargaining by 'low-paid' workers.[161] Under these provisions, a representative of workers—usually a union—may seek approval from Fair Work Australia to negotiate an agreement with more than one employer. Grant of the approval—called a 'low-paid authorisation'—will be determined by criteria that include whether the authorisation would assist 'low-paid employees who have not had access to collective bargaining or who face substantial difficulty bargaining at the enterprise level'.[162] One of the reasons for the requirement to have approval is that it is necessary if a bargaining representative later wishes to apply for orders to compel good faith bargaining. These would otherwise not be available in negotiations for a collective agreement with more than one employer.[163] Another reason for the authorisation is that, where the parties do not already have an agreement and are unable to reach one, Fair Work Australia is empowered to arbitrate an outcome, called a 'low-paid workplace determination'.[164]

Thus, the FW Act has clearly moved forward in terms of establishing a framework to facilitate and promote bargaining. Nevertheless, the emphasis in Australian labour law on bargaining at the level of the single business remains. This is not surprising: it has been a feature of labour market policy for both sides of politics at least since the changes that introduced the Industrial Relations Act 1988 (Cth). Under the most recent provisions of the WR Act, the AIRC was required to give specific authorisation for certification of an agreement reached with more than one business.[165] The ILO Committee of Experts had suggested that these provisions violated the principle of autonomy of the bargaining parties, by restricting their ability to choose the level at which to bargain.[166] The Committee observed that

---

[160] See, eg, *MUA v Total Marine Services* [2009] FWA 187 and *TWU v CRT Group* [2009] FWA 425.

[161] FW Act pt 2–4 div 9.

[162] FW Act s 243.

[163] FW Act s 229(2).

[164] FW Act pt 2–5 div 2.

[165] Under s 170LC(4) of the WR Act, the AIRC could not certify a multiple-business agreement unless it were satisfied that it were in the public interest to do so, considering (a) whether the matters dealt with therein could be more appropriately dealt with by agreement other than at that level; and (b) any other matter that the AIRC considered relevant.

[166] Report of the Committee of Experts on the Application of Conventions and Recommendations, ILO, Geneva, 37. This principle is articulated in ILO, *'General Survey'* (1994) para 251.

the role of the AIRC in this respect effectively 'allow[ed] the authorities full discretion to deny approval ... or stipulate that the approval must be based on criteria such as compatibility with general or economic policy ...'.[167] The Committee has noted that, while procedural restrictions on multiple-business agreements may be legitimate, requiring prior approval on the basis of wider considerations is not.

Under the FW Act, the requirement to seek approval for an agreement with more than one employer has been removed,[168] other than in relation to low-paid bargaining. However, there are still important ways in which single-enterprise agreements are privileged within the bargaining system. First, Fair Work Australia has no power to issue a good faith bargaining order in the course of negotiations for an agreement with more than one employer.[169] Secondly, it is still not possible to take lawful industrial action (called 'protected action') in support of claims and negotiations for an agreement with more than one employer.[170]

The FW Act has introduced some changes to the rules concerning the permissible content of collective agreements. While these improve on the situation as it had been, it would appear that uncertainty remains in some respects. Despite criticism from the ILO's supervisory bodies, the WR Act contained many provisions that restricted the parties from reaching agreement on specified matters. Under the former s 170LI of the WR Act, parties could only reach agreement concerning those matters 'pertaining to the relationship of employer and employee'. This expression was given a restrictive interpretation by the High Court of Australia in *Electrolux Home Products Pty Ltd v AWU*.[171] The result was that important issues could no longer appear in a certified agreement, including the deduction of trade union membership dues, and the payment of a bargaining agent's fee by those persons covered by an agreement that do not belong to the trade union that has negotiated it.[172]

In the case of bargaining agent fees, the Howard government subsequently legislated in any event to prevent these from being permissible subjects in a certified agreement under the WR Act.[173] This legislative

---

[167] CEACR Report 2005 36.

[168] FW Act s 172. See also Forsyth, A, '"Exit Stage Left", now "Centre Stage": Collective Bargaining under Work Choices and Fair Work' in A Forsyth and A Stewart (eds), *Fair Work: The New Workplace Laws and the Work Choices Legacy* (Sydney, Federation Press, 2009).

[169] FW Act s 229.

[170] FW Act s 413(2). Note that this requirement applies to employer industrial action as well, although employers may only take 'responsive' industrial action in any event: FW Act s 411.

[171] *Electrolux Home Products Pty Ltd v AWU* (2004) 78 ALJR 1231.

[172] For comment on the Electrolux decision see Johns, L, 'The Answer Is: Not to Certify' (2004) 17 *Australian Journal of Labour Law* 317.

[173] Workplace Relations Amendment (Prohibition of Compulsory Union Fees) Act 2003 (Cth).

prohibition joined a number of others, including payment of strike pay,[174] and a clause in an agreement that would require an employer to offer preference in employment to members of a trade union, or oblige a worker to join a trade union upon commencing their employment.[175] The Committee of Experts criticised these provisions as constituting an unacceptable interference with the rights of the parties to bargain freely.[176]

Work Choices did not improve the situation: indeed it introduced rules that were highly prescriptive as to the content of collective agreements, including the concept of 'prohibited content'. An employer was forbidden, on pain of penalty, from lodging an agreement with such content.[177] The Workplace Relations Regulations 2006 (Cth) included a long list of matters that may not be included in a workplace agreement.[178] Many of these related to forms of support for the operation of trade unions, including deduction of union dues, and bargaining fees.[179] The list of prohibited content also included any term that provided for right of entry for union officials. The effect of these rules was great complexity in practice, as often employers and employees sought to conclude separate, or 'side' agreements under the common law, containing those matters upon which they wished to bargain, but were prevented by the WR Act from including in a collective agreement under its terms.[180]

Under the FW Act, complications remain; indeed it has been said that the notion of prohibited content, while modified in important ways, has been 'effectively retained'.[181] Under the FW Act an agreement may contain terms relating to the following things:

— Matters pertaining to the relations between each employer that will be covered by the agreement, and their employees.
— Matters pertaining to the relations between each employer and any unions that are covered by the agreement.
— Deductions from wages for any purpose authorised by an employee covered by the agreement.
— Matters relating to how the agreement will operate.[182]

---

[174] Former WR Act ss 166, 187AA and AB.

[175] Former WR Act ss 170LU(2A) and 298Y(1).

[176] See the CEACR's 'Individual Observations Concerning Convention No 98: Australia' in 1998, 2000, 2001 and 2005.

[177] WR Act ss 357 and 365.

[178] Workplace Relations Regulations 2006 (Cth) rr 8.5–8.8.

[179] In addition to prohibited content, Work Choices also deems a range of terms to be included in a workplace agreement. See further Forsyth and Sutherland (n 97).

[180] See Stewart, A and Riley, J, 'Working around Work Choices: Collective Bargaining and the Common law' (2007) 31 *Melbourne University Law Review* 903.

[181] Stewart, A, 'A Question of Balance: Labor's New Vision for Workplace Regulation' (2009) 22 *Australian Journal of Labour Law* 1, 28.

[182] FW Act s 172(1).

This means first of all that it will still be necessary to refer to the 'complex and often confusing body of case law' on what is a matter that 'pertains to the relationship of employer and employee'.[183] The second and third types of content that are permitted will certainly improve on the situation as it had been under the WR Act. These clearly provide for agreement on matters that may tend to support the activities of trade unions as institutions—the types of subjects, that is, which were directly prohibited under the WR Act. Moreover, an agreement may now (again) be able to regulate the terms upon which independent contractors are engaged—if not the question *whether* they should be engaged.[184]

The Right to Strike

Under the common law in Australia, all strike action is actionable as a breach of contract and/or a tort.[185] To the extent that there is any protection of workers' ability to exercise this fundamental human right in Australia, it has had to be found in statutory schemes. As the origins of Australia's industrial relations system lie in the reaction of legislators to the adverse social and economic effects of the outbreak of strike action, it is not surprising that the system has long featured strict regulation of industrial action.[186]

In its origins and purpose, the system of conciliation and arbitration was supposed to *replace* 'the rude and barbarous process of strike and lockout' with a 'new province for law and order'.[187] To this end, the system originally purported to require trade unions (and employer organisations) to relinquish their right to take industrial action, in return for the right to have access to the jurisdiction of the tribunal, with its compulsive powers. Penal provisions were included in the Conciliation and Arbitration Act 1904 (Cth) to support this system, but they were little used in practice and repealed in 1930.

However, the system soon developed a different method of legal constraint on industrial action, based on the inclusion in an arbitrated award

---

[183] Stewart, 'A Question of Balance' (2009) 29. The Full Federal Court reconfirmed in October 2009 the binding nature of the various High Court authorities on the question. While it did not lay down a firm rule, in the circumstances of the case the Court held that a clause providing for an employer to pay for income protection insurance was a matter pertaining in the relevant sense: *Australian Maritime Offices Union v Sydney Ferries Corporation* [2009] FCAFC 145.

[184] Stewart (n 180) 29.

[185] See, eg, *National Workforce v Australian Manufacturers Workers' Union* [1998] 3 VR 265. For an overview, see Creighton and Stewart (n 102) 553–72.

[186] Creighton, B, 'Enforcement in the Federal Industrial Relations System: An Australian Paradox' (1991) 4 *Australian Journal of Labour Law* 197.

[187] Higgins, HB, 'A New Province for Law and Order' (1915) 29 *Harvard Law Review* 13, 14.

of a 'bans' clause, that is, a clause that prohibited the imposition of bans or restrictions on work under the terms of the award. Where industrial action occurred, the employer needed only to seek an order to enforce obedience to the terms of the award, including by the use of injunctions. The technique was especially common during the 1950s and 1960s. Frequently, however, unions and their officials refused to comply with the injunctions, or to pay the fines that were imposed as a penalty for the contempt of court constituted by this refusal to comply. After an incident in which a union official was jailed for refusal to pay such a fine, leading to widespread public outrage, these procedures fell into disuse.[188]

From the late 1980s, government labour relations policy began to shift its emphasis from reliance on conciliation and arbitration by the public tribunal, to collective bargaining at the level of the workplace. From the early 1990s the federal statute included a regime that allows workers to engage in 'protected' industrial action (as defined)[189] during the course of a properly initiated 'bargaining period'. The 'protection' in question is protection from the disabilities under the common law that would otherwise apply to strike action. Although governments of both political persuasions have referred to this as a system for protection of workers' 'right' to strike, in truth it provides at best a (closely regulated) *freedom* to strike.

The industrial action regime in the WR Act was the subject of significant criticism by the ILO's supervisory bodies, as being inconsistent with Australia's obligations under ILO Conventions 87 and 98. One difficulty was that the system only permitted protected industrial action in support of identified claims for working conditions that might later be legally capable of being included in a single business collective agreement.[190] The ILO's supervisory bodies repeatedly emphasised that the right to strike should not be limited to industrial disputes that are likely to be resolved through the signing of a collective agreement.[191] Rather, the right to strike extends to enabling workers to express their dissatisfaction through industrial action with economic and social policy matters that affect their interests.[192] Moreover, the ILO's supervisory bodies were critical of the emphasis in

---

[188] See Creighton and Stewart (n 102) 539–41.

[189] The definition of 'industrial action' in s 4 of the WR Act was interpreted as not including picketing as a form of industrial action that might be capable of enjoying the limited protection that was otherwise available: *Davids Distribution v NUW* (1999) 91 FCR 436, 491.

[190] See in particular the *Electrolux* litigation, concerning the interpretation of the former s 170LI of the WR Act, which required that a certified agreement only include terms that were about 'matters pertaining to the relationship of employer and employee': *Electrolux Home Products Pty Ltd v AWU* (2004) 78 ALJR 1231.

[191] Gernigon, B, Odero, A, and Guido, H, 'ILO Principles Concerning the Right to Strike' (1998) 137 *International Labour Review* 441, 445.

[192] ILO, *Freedom of Association: Digest of Decisions and Principles of the Freedom of Association Committee of the Governing Body of the ILO*, 4th edn (ILO, Geneva, 1996) para 484.

the WR Act on negotiation of agreements that apply to a 'single business'. As noted, it has not been possible to take protected industrial action in support of such an agreement, which the ILO has considered an inappropriate limitation on the ability of workers to take strike action.[193] As also noted, and as appears further below, this limitation continues under the FW Act.

The ILO bodies have also criticised the prohibitions in Australian law on sympathy action, secondary boycotts, and the ability of the Government to make industrial action criminal by proclamation under sections 30J and K of the Crimes Act 1914 (Cth).[194] Neither has the ILO considered it appropriate that Australian law has imposed a blanket prohibition on workers receiving pay for the period during which they are engaged in industrial action: this is something over which the parties ought to be allowed to bargain, and to strike.[195]

Another major issue was the power of the former AIRC to suspend or to terminate a bargaining period (the former section 170MW). It follows from the nature of the regime that suspension or termination of a bargaining period was an abrogation of the limited freedom to strike that was otherwise conferred. The AIRC had power to suspend or to terminate a bargaining period if industrial action was threatening 'to cause significant damage to the Australian economy or to an important part of it' (the former section 170MW(3)(b)).[196] The ILO emphasised that the AIRC's powers in this respect went well beyond permissible limitations on the right to strike in the case of essential services, as the ILO has defined them.[197]

Work Choices did not improve the situation.[198] The WR Act thereafter included a requirement that workers authorise any industrial action through a secret ballot (section 445), which had first to be authorised by the AIRC (section 451). The ballot itself was subject to a difficult quorum requirement: at least 50 per cent of workers eligible to vote had to participate, and the action had to be approved by more than 50 per cent of the votes cast (section 478). Furthermore, the authorisation was only valid for the following 30 days.

Work Choices retained the AIRC's power to suspend or to terminate a bargaining period (section 430), and conferred a similar power directly on

---

[193] See CEACR, 'Individual Observation Concerning Convention No 87, Freedom of Association and Protection of the Right to Organise, 1948, Australia, 1999'.

[194] See, eg, CEACR, 'Individual Observation Concerning Convention No 87, Freedom of Association and Protection of the Right to Organise, 1948, Australia, 2004'.

[195] Ibid.

[196] See CEACR, 'Individual Observation Concerning Convention No 87, Freedom of Association and Protection of the Right to Organise, 1948, Australia, 1999'.

[197] They are 'services whose interruption would endanger the life, personal safety or health of the whole or part of the population', ILO, *General Survey* (n 97) para 164.

[198] For a fuller analysis of the industrial action provisions after Work Choices, see McCrystal, S, 'Smothering the Right to Strike: Work Choices and Industrial Action' (2006) 19 *Australian Journal of Labour Law* 198.

the Minister (section 498). A third party (that is, not a negotiating party) was empowered to apply to the AIRC for suspension of a bargaining period where industrial action was threatening them with significant harm (section 433). If industrial action involved persons who were not protected for the purposes of that industrial action, then *all* of the industrial action would be invalidated, rendering even those negotiating parties whose actions would otherwise have been lawful vulnerable to sanction under the common law (section 438). Finally, Work Choices made it clear that industrial action was not protected if it were undertaken in support of 'pattern bargaining' claims (section 439).

As it turns out, much of the Work Choices architecture remains in place following the advent of the FW Act.[199] It is true that the concept of the formal bargaining period has been abolished. Nevertheless, protected industrial action must still be authorised by a secret ballot,[200] and only upon the order of Fair Work Australia, which must be satisfied that the applicant has been 'genuinely trying to reach an agreement'.[201] Protected action may not be taken during the course of a current agreement, and must be preceded by three days' notice.[202] It is still unlawful to take industrial action in pursuit of terms in an agreement that would be unlawful, or if it arises out of a demarcation dispute.[203] However, the absolute prohibition on taking industrial action in support of claims that *may not* be permissible in a collective agreement has been relaxed: action will remain lawful provided those taking it reasonably believe it to be about permitted matters.[204]

There have been some other relaxations. Employers will no longer be permitted to take proactive lockout action.[205] Moreover, all employees who are to be covered by a proposed agreement will be able to take part in protected industrial action in support of the agreement—rather than only union members, as had previously been the case.[206] The provisions concerning compulsory deductions from pay for employees who engage in industrial action have been enhanced, to introduce some flexibility that was lacking under the previous system.[207] And employers will no longer

---

[199] For discussion of the evolution of the industrial action provisions, see McCrystal, S, 'A New Consensus: The Coalition, the ALP and the Regulation of Industrial Action', in Forsyth and Stewart, (n 96) 141–163.

[200] FW Act s 409.

[201] FW Act ss 413 and 443.

[202] FW Act s 414.

[203] FW Act s 409.

[204] FW Act s 409.

[205] FW Act s 411.

[206] FW Act ss 409(1)(b)(ii) and 437.

[207] FW Act ss 470, 471. Whereas formerly it was compulsory for an employer to make a minimum deduction equivalent to four hours' pay, that rule applies now predominantly in the case of unprotected (unlawful) industrial action. See Stewart (n 180) 36.

have an automatic right to appear in an application for a secret ballot order.[208]

On the other hand, the institutional power to limit or prevent the taking of industrial action has been retained in much the same form as previously: most of the powers of the former AIRC in this respect have simply been transferred to Fair Work Australia.[209] Thus, Fair Work Australia is empowered to make orders to suspend protected action on the application of a party to the bargaining, or on the basis of substantial harm to a third party that is not a party to the negotiations. Fair Work Australia retains the power to determine that protected action must stop because it is doing harm to the economy, or a part of it.[210] It is also still possible for the Minister to make a determination to terminate protected industrial action, on similar grounds.[211] Fair Work Australia retains the power to make orders to stop unprotected (unlawful) industrial action.[212] In cases where an employer argues that industrial action is being taken in pursuit of pattern-bargaining (as defined), an employer may go directly to the courts for an order to terminate the action.[213]

NON-DISCRIMINATION IN EMPLOYMENT AND OCCUPATION

Direct and indirect discrimination in employment (and other areas of life) is prohibited by several legislative schemes. The grounds on which discrimination is prohibited include: that the employee was involved with a trade union; and for reasons of the employee's race, colour, sex, sexual preference, age, physical or mental disability, marital status, family responsibilities, pregnancy, religion, political opinion, national extraction or social origin. Federal anti-discrimination statutes[214] are augmented by state and territory anti-discrimination legislation.[215] There are also important provisions in the FW Act, which protect employees against termination of employment on these grounds.[216] Legislation at both federal and state

---

[208] McCrystal, 'A New Consensus: The Coalition, the ALP and the Regulation of Industrial Action'.

[209] FW Act pt 3-3 div 6.

[210] FW Act s 424.

[211] FW Act s 431.

[212] FW Act s 418–22.

[213] FW Act s 422.

[214] The relevant federal anti-discrimination legislation is Disability Discrimination Act 1992 (Cth); Racial Discrimination Act 1975 (Cth); Sex Discrimination Act 1984 (Cth); Age Discrimination Act 2004 (Cth).

[215] Discrimination Act 1991 (ACT); Anti-Discrimination Act 1977 (NSW); Anti-Discrimination Act 1992 (NT); Anti-Discrimination Act 1991 (Qld); Equal Opportunity Act 1984 (SA); Anti-Discrimination Act 1998 (Tas); Equal Opportunity Act 1995 (Vic); Equal Opportunity Act 1984 (WA).

[216] FW Act s 351. Under the FW Act, this is one of the provisions on 'general protections', so that they protect employees against 'adverse action', as defined. See discussion above

levels also requires many public and some private sector organisations to formulate equal employment opportunity policies.[217]

As noted, however, these legislative schemes have been criticised in important respects. A key criticism for some time was that industrial tribunals and instruments were constituted as operating in a separate field from anti-discrimination concerns. Indeed for many decades the predecessors of the AIRC played a major role in entrenching gender inequality in the workplace, especially in the area of wages. They did so first by setting wages on the assumption that a wage-earner was a full-time male worker with responsibility to provide for a wife and children.[218] Although by the early 1970s the then Commonwealth Conciliation and Arbitration Commission acknowledged the principle of equal pay for work of equal value (which had appeared in the original constitution of the ILO!),[219] it nevertheless declined to apply that principle on the basis of equal pay for work of comparable worth.[220]

From 1992, government policy shifted dramatically: whereas previously the AIRC had been explicitly quarantined from the need to consider anti-discrimination principles, it was now obliged to engage with those ideas as an active participant in the process of overcoming impermissible discrimination in the workplace.[221] Broadly speaking, it was obliged to take into account discrimination concerns in the exercise of its functions, to review awards or agreements alleged to contravene certain anti-discrimination statutes, and to make orders for equal remuneration. Notwithstanding the shift in government policy, these provisions have more or less been a dead

---

nn 133 to 137 and accompanying text. Formerly, this protection appeared among a separate set of protections against 'unlawful termination', as opposed to 'unfair dismissal', that is, grounds related to the employee's (mis)conduct, or the apparent needs of the undertaking. On the changes to the termination of employment regime under Work Choices, see Chapman, A, 'Unfair Dismissal Law and Work Choices: From Safety Net Standard to Legal Privilege' (2006) 16 *Economic and Labour Relations Review* 237, and on the subsequent shift under the FW Act, see Chapman, A, 'The Decline and Restoration of Unfair Dismissal Rights' in Forsyth and Stewart (n 96) 207–28.

[217] See Anti-Discrimination Act 1977 (NSW) pt 9A; Public Service Act 1999 (Cth) s 10; Equal Employment Opportunity (Commonwealth Authorities) Act 1987 (Cth); Equal Opportunity in Public Employment Act 1992 (Qld); Equal Opportunity Act 1984 (WA) pt IX; Public Sector Management Act 1995 (SA) s 67; Equal Opportunity for Women in the Workplace Act 1999 (Cth).

[218] *Ex p H V McKay* (1907) 2 CAR 1.

[219] *Equal Pay Case* (1969) 127 CAR 1142; *Equal Pay Case* (1972) 147 CAR 172.

[220] For a succinct overview, see Creighton and Stewart (n 102) 185. On the situation in the years leading to the key legislative amendments see, eg, Hunter, R, 'Women Workers and Federal Industrial Law: From Harvester to Comparable Worth' (1988) 1 *Australian Journal of Labour Law* 147, and Bennett, L, 'Equal Pay and Comparable Worth in the Australian Industrial Relations Commission' (1988) 30 *Journal of Industrial Relations* 533.

[221] Creighton and Stewart (n 102) 184. Notably though, awards and industrial instruments are still not able to be challenged directly by an employee or a trade union under federal anti-discrimination legislation. See Sex Discrimination Act 1984 (Cth) s 40.

letter in practice since their introduction in 1993.[222] A notable exception is the application, in May 2010, by the Australian Services Union, for an equal remuneration order by Fair Work Australia.

When first given a role in combating discrimination in employment and occupation, the AIRC was required to review all awards and to remedy certain deficiencies, including any discriminatory provisions in awards.[223] Under the WR Act, it was required, when performing its functions, to take into account the need to apply the principle of equal pay for work of equal value; and the need to 'prevent and eliminate discrimination because of, or for reasons including, race, colour, sex, sexual preference, age, physical or mental disability, marital status, family responsibilities, pregnancy, religion, political opinion, national extraction or social origin'.[224] While there are specific provisions, identified below, that give Fair Work Australia an ongoing role in addressing discrimination in employment and occupation, there is no direct analogue to this general obligation. This primarily reflects the continuing move in Australian labour law away from a significant role for the federal tribunal, rather than a change in the level of commitment to the principles of anti-discrimination.

The general power of the AIRC to ensure that awards and agreements did not contain discriminatory provisions gave it, at least in theory, a significant role in preventing and eliminating employment-related discrimination. In particular, the AIRC's central role in making awards and in certifying enterprise agreements meant it had the opportunity to ensure that these instruments did not contain discriminatory provisions. It appears, however, that in practice the AIRC fulfilled this responsibility in a cursory way at best. In reviewing agreements under the former WR Act, for example, the AIRC appears to have accepted agreements 'at face value with little further investigation' of their potentially sexually discriminatory content.[225]

The scope for the AIRC to play an important role was significantly reduced by Work Choices. The AIRC was no longer permitted to make new awards,[226] and it was required to focus on rationalising and simplifying the awards that were already in place. The AIRC also lost its responsibility

---

[222] Stewart (n 180) 26.

[223] Industrial Relations Act 1988 (Cth) s 150A. This provision became operative on 22 June 1994, and provided that all awards were to be reviewed by 22 June 1997.

[224] WR Act s 104. The AIRC was specifically instructed to take into account the principles embodied in the Racial Discrimination Act 1975, the Sex Discrimination Act 1984, the Disability Discrimination Act 1992 and the Age Discrimination Act 2004 relating to discrimination in employment: s 105. The AIRC was also, in performing its functions, to take into account the principles embodied in the Family Responsibilities Convention: s 106.

[225] Charlesworth, S, 'Enterprise Bargaining and Women Workers: The Seven Perils of Flexibility' (1997) 8 *Labour & Industry* 101, 108. See also Halliday, S, Sex Discrimination Commissioner, 'Discrimination Law and the Industrial Relations Agenda' (Speech to the Australian Mines and Minerals Association National Conference, Hobart, 26 March 1999).

[226] The only new awards the AIRC is permitted to make are those made as part of the award rationalisation process: WR Act ss 539–40.

for certifying workplace agreements: they became valid merely upon lodgement with the (former) Employment Advocate.[227] While the Advocate was also required to prevent and eliminate discrimination,[228] the WR Act did not specifically require that the Advocate examine lodged workplace agreements for compliance with anti-discrimination principles. Subsequently, the responsibility for registering agreements was given to a (short-lived) agency called the Workplace Authority, the Director of which was similarly obliged to prevent and eliminate discrimination.[229] In practice, a major facet of the Workplace Authority's task was to vet agreements to determine whether they passed a so-called 'fairness' test.[230] Moreover, the Authority was soon overwhelmed with a backlog of agreements to approve, significantly reducing the likelihood of it dealing with discriminatory provisions.[231] Taken together, the various changes significantly reduced the likelihood that the AIRC would have many opportunities to 'prevent and eliminate' discrimination in awards or workplace agreements.

In principle, Fair Work Australia continues with the role of ensuring that collective agreements do not contain discriminatory terms. It must approve an agreement which meets specified requirements; these include that the agreement contains no 'unlawful' terms.[232] These in turn are defined so as to include a 'discriminatory term'.[233] Fair Work Australia must also be satisfied that the agreement passes the 'better off

---

[227] The Employment Advocate was also directed under the WR Act to prevent and eliminate discrimination on prohibited grounds: s 151(3). However, there was no mechanism in the WR Act by which the Employment Advocate was required to examine lodged workplace agreements for compliance with anti-discrimination principles.

[228] WR Act s 151(3)(b) directed that, in performing his or her functions, the Employment Advocate must have particular regard to the need to prevent and eliminate discrimination because of, or for reasons including, race, colour, sex, sexual preference, age, physical or mental disability, marital status, family responsibilities, pregnancy, religion, political opinion, national extraction or social origin.

[229] WR Act, former s 150B(2)(d).

[230] One of the major changes under Work Choices was the abolition of the former 'no-disadvantage test', which had been applied to all individual and collective agreements, to ensure that, viewed globally, they did not reduce working conditions that would otherwise apply. The introduction of the 'fairness' test was a major change of direction for the Howard government. Under the current Government, the 'fairness' test was quickly replaced by a new 'no-disadvantage test'; under the FW Act the test is whether the workers are 'better off overall'. See Sutherland, C, 'Making the BOOT fit: Reforms to Agreement-Making from Work Choices to Fair Work' in Forsyth and Stewart (n 96) 99–119.

[231] The Workplace Authority (and also the Workplace Ombudsman) were created by the Workplace Relations Amendment (Stronger Safety Net) Act 2007 (Cth). For comment, see Sutherland, C, 'All Stitched Up? The 2007 Amendments to the Safety Net' (2007) 20 *Australian Journal of Labour Law* 245.

[232] FW Act s 186.

[233] FW Act s 195. A term will be discriminatory 'to the extent that it discriminates against an employee covered by the agreement because of, or for reasons including, the employee's race, colour, sex, sexual preference, age, physical or mental disability, marital status, family or carer's responsibility, pregnancy, religion, political opinion, national extraction or social origin'.

overall test'.[234] According to the procedures for approval of an agreement published on the Fair Work Australia website, an agreement will be vetted against some, but not all of these tests. In particular, the information makes no mention of checking an agreement to determine whether it contains a discriminatory term—even though the information clearly states the obligation not to include such a term.[235]

Fair Work Australia will have an ongoing obligation in relation to the award system, including ensuring that awards do not contain terms that discriminate. One of the key developments of the FW Act system was the introduction of a process of 'award modernisation'—in effect a continuation of the Work Choices process of award 'rationalisation' and 'simplification'. (Although in fact those processes never went very far.) In essence, all state and federal awards are to be replaced, so far as possible, by a streamlined set of federal 'modern' awards. The process was due to be completed by 31 December 2009, in accordance with an instruction to Fair Work Australia from the Minister. In its terms, Fair Work Australia is directed, while modernising awards, to take into account 'the need to help prevent and eliminate discrimination ...' on a wide range of grounds.[236] Indeed, the FW Act prohibits Fair Work Australia from including such a term in a modern award.[237]

The award modernisation process will certainly reduce the number of awards, and this alone is likely to reduce the chance of discrimination through award terms. Nevertheless, the FW Act continues in operation a mechanism whereby the AHRC is empowered to initiate a process under which Fair Work Australia must review an award or workplace agreement that is alleged to be discriminatory on the basis of sex.[238] The provisions in their current form are simpler than their predecessors, giving very little instruction in how the exercise should be carried out. Under the legislation establishing the AHRC, a person may lodge a complaint in writing alleging that a person has 'done a discriminatory act under an industrial instrument', as defined.[239] If it appears to the President of the Human Rights and Equal Opportunity Commission (HREOC) that the act is discriminatory, they must refer the industrial instrument to Fair Work Australia. For their part, the Sex Discrimination Commissioner may make submissions in a proceeding to review a modern award[240] or an agreement.[241]

---

[234] FW Act s 186(2).
[235] See www.fwa.gov.au/index.cfm?pagename=agreementsapproval (last visited on 29 October 2009).
[236] *Award Modernisation Request—Consolidated Version*, [3(e)].
[237] FW Act s 153.
[238] FW Act s 161 (awards) and s 218 (agreements).
[239] Australian Human Rights Commission Act 1986 (Cth) s 46PW.
[240] FW Act s 161(b).
[241] FW Act s 218(2). Under this provision, the Australian Human Rights Commission might make submissions if there is an allegation of discrimination contrary to the Age Discrimination Act 2004 (Cth), and the Disability Discrimination Commissioner might

Under the WR Act, an employee, a relevant trade union or the Sex Discrimination Commissioner was able to apply to the AIRC for an order securing equal remuneration for work of equal value.[242] These provisions were originally introduced in 1993, to give effect to the Anti-Discrimination Conventions; the ILO's Equal Remuneration Recommendation 1951 (No 50); and the ILO's Discrimination (Employment and Occupation) Recommendation 1958 (No 111).[243] While the AIRC had applied principles relating to equal pay for work of equal value since the early 1970s, this had been as a result of its own jurisprudence rather than of any legislative direction.[244]

In practice, these provisions were limited in important ways. In particular, the AIRC could not proceed with an application if the relevant employee(s) had access to 'an adequate alternative remedy', such as under state and federal anti-discrimination legislation.[245] In 2005, the forerunner to the AHRC described the equal remuneration provisions in the WR Act as 'singularly unsuccessful in achieving pay equity'.[246] According to a then member of the AIRC, the provisions were 'complex and uncertain in their application' and the process 'could hardly be described as user friendly'.[247] This mechanism for obtaining equal remuneration in the WR Act was rarely used, and no successful orders were obtained. Since the 1990s, efforts by state industrial tribunals have been relatively more successful in advancing pay equity.[248]

It is to be hoped that they continue to be so, for the provisions in their current form in the FW Act more or less suffer from the same defects as their predecessors. The order may be sought by an employee, a relevant trade union, or the Sex Discrimination Commissioner. In one change that could have some potential for impact, the test for the order to be made now refers to 'equal remuneration for men and women workers for work of equal or comparable

make submissions in respect of an allegation of discrimination contrary to the Disability Discrimination Act 1992 (Cth).

[242] WR Act pt 12 div 3.

[243] WR Act s 620.

[244] Pittard, M, 'International Labour Standards in Australia: Wages, Equal Pay, Leave and Termination of Employment' (1994) 7 Australian Journal of Labour Law 170, 192. The AIRC's principles on equal pay were developed in the Equal Pay Case (1969) 127 CAR 1142 and the Equal Pay Case 1972 (1972) 147 CAR 172.

[245] Creighton and Stewart (n 102) 186 note that, in the only case on this issue, the AIRC concluded that, as such legislation focuses on individual complaints, they cannot offer a 'remedy of general application' like the AIRC can. See AMWU v Gunn and Taylor Pty Ltd (2002) 115 IR 353.

[246] Goward, P, Sex Discrimination Commissioner, on behalf of Human Rights and Equal Opportunity Commission, Submission to the Senate Employment, Workplace Relations and Education Legislation Committee's Inquiry into the Workplace Relations Amendment (Work Choices) Act 2005 (2005). The submission referred to the provisions as they stood before the Work Choices reforms, however, the point remained valid of the provisions thereafter.

[247] Commissioner Dominica Whelan, Paper presented 'The Gender Pay Gap: Assessing Possible Futures in the Post-Inquiries Era' to a Conference, University of Western Australia, Perth, 29 April 2005 at 1.

[248] See, eg, ibid and Creighton and Stewart (n 102) 186–91.

value'.[249] In this, the FW Act is moving away from the former adherence to the terminology of the ILO's Equal Remuneration Convention No 100[250], but potentially widening the scope for such orders. Fair Work Australia must not deal with an application for an equal pay order where the applicant has access to another jurisdiction, and proceedings are on foot.[251] As noted, the first even application for an equal remuneration order was lodged in May 2010.

In light of the limitations of the anti-discrimination mechanisms in Australia's federal labour laws, it is perhaps not surprising that gender inequity continues unabated: in 2005, for example, women earned 85 per cent of male full-time adult ordinary earnings. Taking into account total earnings, which include overtime, allowances and bonuses, in that year women earned only 80.9 per cent of men's earnings.[252] By early 2009, women's average full-time weekly earnings were still 17.4 per cent lower than men's. Taking into account part-time and casual work, the total earnings gap between men and women was some 35 per cent.[253] Gender pay inequity is exacerbated by the fact that women occupy a predominant position among those in precarious employment and the low-paid: the incidence of low pay for all female workers is 41 per cent, in contrast to 29 per cent for all workers.[254] Of course, this focus on the gender pay gap does not take into account wider issues pertaining to women workers of increasing concern in Australia, particularly the absence of a federal regulatory framework conducive to women achieving a balance between work and non-work commitments.[255]

The advent of Work Choices raised serious concerns in relation to pay equity. Far from improving the legislative mechanisms for reducing pay inequity, it was likely to make the problem worse. Moreover, the extension of federal laws over state systems ran the risk of curtailing the achievements of state industrial systems in furthering pay equity.[256] The reforms also had the effect of reducing the proportion of Australian workers whose working

[249] FW Act s 302(2).
[250] WR Act s 620 formerly referred to the instrument specifically and repeated its definition of equal remuneration, which does not include the word 'comparable'.
[251] FW Act s 724.
[252] Australian Bureau of Statistics, 'Average Weekly Earnings, February 2006' (Cat No 6302.0, 2006).
[253] Australian Bureau of Statistics, 'Average Weekly Earnings, May 2009' (Cat No 6302.0, 2009).
[254] Australian Bureau of Statistics, 'Employee Earnings, Benefits and Trade Union Membership, Australia', August 2005' (Cat No 6310.0, 2005).
[255] Australia is notorious for its inferior industrial relations policies on work and family balance. See, eg, Pocock and Masterman-Smith, 'Work Choices and Women Workers' (2006); and Baird, M and Todd, P, 'Government Policy, Women and the New Workplace Regime: A Contradiction in Terms and Policies' (Paper presented to the Workshop on the Federal Government's Proposed Industrial Relations Policy, University of Sydney, 20–21 June, 2005).
[256] See Whelan, 'The Gender Pay Gap' (2005) 2. In her speech, the Commissioner urged the industrial relations ministers to support a review of the equal remuneration provisions in the WR Act. See also Baird and Todd, 'Government Policy, Women and the New Workplace Regime' (20–21 June, 2005).

conditions are regulated by awards. As women are much more likely to be dependent on awards than males,[257] this reduction in the safety net of minimum working conditions for workers in Australia is likely to have had a disproportionately adverse effect on women workers. At the same time, more workers would have their working conditions regulated by collective or individual workplace agreements. This was only likely to exacerbate gender inequities: the gender pay gap is wider in enterprise agreements, and greater again in individual workplace agreements.[258]

CONCLUSION

Australia has less legal protection of fundamental human rights than any other industrialised democracy. The Commonwealth Constitution protects few individual liberties, and has rarely been interpreted in ways that give rise to human rights protections. Neither the few express nor the implied protections are particularly relevant to workers' human rights. The various state constitutions do even less, although there is movement toward the adoption of Bills of Rights at the territory and state level. At the Commonwealth level it presently appear there is little likelihood of a Bill of Rights being adopted. Moreover, further such laws are unlikely to offer much protection for economic, social and cultural rights, and will almost inevitably follow the model of the United Kingdom that has been adopted in the Australian Capital Territory and in Victoria. They will rely most heavily on parliamentary sovereignty and responsible government as the means to protect human rights.

Australia is a party to many international human rights instruments that offer important protections for workers' human rights. These instruments, however, are of no effect within Australia without domestic legal action to that end. Australians are heavily dependent on the actions of governments to protect their fundamental human rights. Thus far, however, governments have proved relatively unreliable in this respect. For example, although the Commonwealth Government could use its power to legislate with respect to external affairs in order to implement domestically its international legal obligations, in the area of workers' rights it has only ever done so

[257] In 2004, 24.4% of women relied upon awards to set their rate of pay, in comparison to 15.7% of men: Australian Bureau of Statistics, 'Employee Earnings and Hours, May 2004' (Cat No 6306.0, 2004).

[258] A comparison of non-managerial employees' average hourly rates of pay in 2004 found a gap of zero per cent between men and women on award only wages; a gap of 10.36% between men and women on registered collective agreements; and a gap of 20.32% between men and women on registered individual agreements. See ibid and Peetz, D, 'The Impact on Workers of Australian Workplace Agreements and the Abolition of the "No Disadvantage Test"' (Department of Industrial Relations, Griffith University, Brisbane, 2005).

selectively. Indeed its most recent legislative efforts have relied upon the power to regulate the activities of commercial corporations.

The domestic legal framework for protection of freedom of association for trade union purposes has long failed to comply with important elements of Australia's international legal obligations. The Work Choices reforms only exacerbated the situation, and the shift to the Fair Work regime has only ameliorated some of the deficiencies. Neither do Australia's domestic statutory regimes, intended to promote equality of opportunity in employment, do as much as they could to comply with international law. For many years labour laws were constituted as operating outside the concerns of anti-discrimination law and policy. More recently, federal labour law has obliged relevant institutions to seek to overcome discrimination in employment, especially where sex discrimination is concerned. In the result, however, these mechanisms have proved to be relatively ineffective; among other things, Australia continues to have a persistent gender pay gap.

That pay gap is only one of the many indications that there is room for improvement in respect of workers' human rights in Australia, despite the many outward signs of wellbeing, including low unemployment and steady growth in real wages. Women are more reliant on safety net working conditions; women and others in low-paid and casualised employment do less well out of bargaining at the workplace. And all are dependent on the decisions of the government of the day. As the history recounted in this chapter shows, Australian governments have proved most assiduous at adjusting the regulatory framework that affects, even controls the ability of Australian workers to exercise their fundamental human rights. Perhaps if there were a clear and binding set of basic human rights principles in Australia, the changes would be fewer, less frequent, and more likely to promote workers' interests.

3

Legal Protection of Workers' Rights as Human Rights: Brazil

ANA VIRGINIA MOREIRA GOMES

IN 1998, THE International Labour Organization (ILO) adopted the Declaration on Fundamental Principles and Rights at Work, in response to criticisms about the ILO's lack of power to effectively address the challenges presented by globalisation. The Declaration affirmed the following fundamental rights and principles: the elimination of forced labour, the elimination of discrimination in the workplace, the abolition of child labour and the right to freedom of association and collective bargaining. The Declaration itself has a promotional character, which means that it does not establish new obligations, but commits Member States to respect and promote the fundamental rights and principles that it sets out.

The Declaration is significant because, among other reasons, it is the first time that the ILO has adopted the concept of fundamental rights at work.[1] Although there is some debate on the literature about the election of the labour rights guaranteed as fundamental, for most developing countries, the scope of the 1998 Declaration is well designed, since violations of these rights constitute the most serious problems affecting workers. These are such structural problems that, for instance, in Brazil, years of constant growth and political stability were not enough to resolve them. In such a context, the Government's commitment in prioritising the guarantee of

---

[1] The ILO's use of the concept of fundamental rights has considerable strategic importance, as stressed by Bellace, for three reasons: 'First it removed the issue from the arena of national partisan politics. On any given labour standard, one political party might support it and another opposed it. If, however, a right has been declared to be a fundamental human right that must be observed in the workplace, it becomes extremely difficult for any government or political party to oppose acknowledging this right. Second, the shift in terminology placed the ILO's initiative on high moral ground, which is particularly important as the ILO relies essentially on moral suasion …. Third, the shift from labour "standard" to fundamental "rights" was critical because it moved the issue out of the miasma of debate on the universality of application of labour standards in the face of varying economic conditions.' Bellace, JR, 'The ILO Declaration of Fundamental Principles and Rights at Work' (2001) 17(3) *The International Journal of Comparative Labour Law and Industrial Relations* 269, 272–73.

these rights is crucial, and the 1998 Declaration's approach aims to help countries in promoting these rights.

Taking again the example of Brazil, the ILO and the Government have collaborated within the scope of the 1998 Declaration. In 2002, they established the technical cooperation programme for the combat of forced labour. This programme resulted in the project 'Combat of forced labour in Brazil', that aims to fortify the actions of the national institutions to abolish forced labour, as well as the rehabilitation of rescued workers to prevent them from returning to slavery activities. Another significant outcome is the creation of the mobile groups formed by Labour Ministry auditors, the Labour Public Prosecution Service and Federal Policy. Their main activities are to develop inspections in the workplace, and take immediate necessary measures to release the workers and punish the employer.[2] The collaboration with the ILO has helped the Government to keep focusing on abolishing forced labour, by placing forced labour on the legal and political agenda and by disseminating the progresses and obstacles of the Brazilian case both inside and outside the country.[3]

Another important initiative in the collaboration between the ILO and Brazil was the memorandum of understanding for the establishment of a technical cooperation programme promoting a decent work agenda in 2003. This programme, announced in 2006, establishes three priorities: to produce more and better jobs, with equality of opportunities and treatment; to eradicate forced labour and child labour, especially the worst forms of child labour; and to make the tripartite actors and social dialogue stronger as instruments of democratic governance.[4] These programmes show the Government's will to collaborate with the ILO in the promotion of the fundamental rights, even though the country still deals with challenges to fully protect these rights as we will see bellow. In this context, this chapter proposes to consider the case of Brazil, as a means of furthering the international debate on the protection of fundamental labour rights.

Brazil is an example of a very complex labour relations situation that challenges the goals of the ILO, including the ones of the Declaration. Brazil

---

[2] Vilela, RBV, Cunha, RMA, 'A experiência do grupo especial de fiscalização móvel no combate ao combate ao trabalho escravo' in Comissão Pastoral da Terra, *Trabalho escravo no Brasil Contemporâneo* (São Paulo, Loyola, 1999) 35. See Santos, A, 'A Proibição Internacional do Trabalho Escravo e a Cooperação entre OIT e o Brasil's' (Dissertaçao de Mestrado, Universidade Católica da Santos, 2006).

[3] For an analysis of the Brazilian cooperation with the ILO to combat forced labour, see Fenwick, C and Kring, T, *Rights At Work. An Assessment of the Declaration's Technical Cooperation in Select Countries* (Geneva, ILO, 2007) 55–60.

[4] Memorando de Entendimento entre a República Federativa do Brasil e a Organização Internacional do Trabalho para o estabelecimento de um programa de cooperação técnica para a promoção de uma agenda de trabalho decente. Available at: www2.mre.gov/dai/b_oit_07_5110.htm. Unfortunately, with respect to the last priority, the programme does not foresee the ratification of the ILO Convention No 87 on Freedom of Association.

has ratified 79 of the 188 ILO conventions and of the eight fundamental conventions of the 1998 Declaration, only Convention No 87 on the Freedom of Association and Protection of the Right to Organise has yet to be ratified. Nevertheless, ratification is only the first step in the progression towards effective implementation of the core labour standards and despite the large number of ratified conventions, one can find examples of violations of all the fundamental rights. Also, although the adoption of the 1988 Constitution has given greater legal recognition to labour rights as fundamental human rights, there is some disparity between the recognition of these rights. On the one hand, the prohibition of forced labour, equality at work and prohibition of child labour are progressing towards greater recognition and consolidation. Although there is still a long way to go to their full implementation, they constitute the successful examples of the protection of labour human rights in Brazil, since there is a much broader consensus about their status as fundamental rights. In other words, there has been a greater measure of success in these areas, unfortunately not in fully preventing the violation of these rights, but more in terms of the public recognition of their existence and the formulation of strategies to protect them. On the other hand, the protection of freedom of association is lost in a myriad of debates about the reform of a corporativist trade union structure and about the modernisation and increasing flexibility of the Brazilian labour market.

In order to draw this contrast between the protection of fundamental rights, this chapter will concentrate on two particular areas in order to develop a deeper analysis of Brazilian labour law and a more comprehensive picture of the protection of core labour standards: first, freedom of association and secondly, gender discrimination. Part I of the chapter examines the social and economic aspects of Brazil's labour market and provides an overview of its labour law system. Part II analyses the trade union system, highlighting some of the problems and deficits concerning freedom of association. In part III, the chapter analyses gender discrimination in the labour market and the legal system. The conclusion suggests that more changes are needed in order to build an effective system of protection of labour human rights.

PART I: SOCIAL AND ECONOMIC ASPECTS
OF BRAZIL'S LABOUR MARKET

Like many developing countries, Brazil began to open up its economy in the 1990s, in the search for greater productivity and competitiveness.[5] This process was based on the strategy of import substitution, which demanded

---

[5] In the 1930s the country had begun the process of transformation from an agricultural economy to an industrialised one.

a protected domestic economic environment through tariffs and non-tariff barriers and subsidies, in order to allow domestic industries to grow by insulating them from foreign competition.[6] The closed internal market did not encourage those industries to make new investments in modernisation. In addition, it allowed them to be complacent about costs and risks, since the competition was controlled, and losses could always be passed on to the buyer through higher prices.[7] In the 1980s, the results of this policy and the exhaustion of the model were felt: there was hyperinflation and anemic economic growth.[8]

The answer to this crisis came in the 1990s with the liberalisation of trade, of financial markets, privatisation and deregulation, which were intended to increase the competitiveness of the domestic industry. The transformation came with no warnings. The domestic industry was not ready to compete, with the result that unemployment rose, incomes fell and the country faced a deep economic and political crisis.[9] The fight against hyperinflation became an essential step for the country to get back onto the path of economic development.[10] With the change in the economic policy model, not only industry, but agriculture as well, had to modernise, increase its productivity, adopt new technologies and become more competitive in the international market.[11] But it was the service sector which gained many of the jobs that were lost in the industrial sector. During the 1990s, the service sector was the one that grew the most in terms of its contribution to the gross domestic product (GDP).[12]

[6] Almeida, ES, 'Mudança institucional e estrutural na economia brasileira do início dos anos noventa' (1999) 17(31) *Análise Econômica* 4.

[7] Barros, JR and Goldenstein, L, 'Avaliação do processo de reestruturação industrial brasileiro' (1997) 17(2) *Revista de Economia Política* 12.

[8] The shifts in the international scenario were also important elements in the crisis during the 1980s. However, it is clear that the import substitution model did not lead to the development of new technologies, and thereby to a growth in the competitivity of national industry. When globalisation came, the country was not ready to take advantage of the opportunities. Almeida, 'Mudança institucional e estrutural na economia brasileira do início dos anos noventa' (1999) 14–15.

[9] The crisis resulted in the impeachment of the President, Fernando Collor de Mello, in 1992. He was accused of corruption, and the takeover of the Vice President Itamar Franco. See Klein, HS and Luna, FV, 'Mudanças econômicas e sociais no Brasil, 1980–2000: A transformação Incompleta revisitada' in E Gonzales, A Moreno, and R Sevilha (eds), *Reflexões en torno a 500 años de História de Brasil* (Madrid, Editorial Atriel, 2001) 56.

[10] Since 1986, with the Plano Cruzado, the governments had tried to develop economic plans to combat the inflation. In 1993, Fernando Henrique Cardoso, Ministry of Economy at the time, introduced the Plano Real, which brought the country back to a level of low inflation. Fernando Henrique Cardoso was elected President of Brazil in 1994 and re-elected in 1998.

[11] Klein and Luna, 'Mudanças econômicas e sociais no Brasil, 1980–2000' (2001) 56.

[12] Cardoso Jr, JC, 'Estrutura Setorial-Ocupacional do emprego no Brasil e evolução do perfil distributivo nos anos 90' (Rio de Janeiro: Institute of Applied Economic Research (IPEA) Texto para discussão n. 655, julho de 1999) 9.

The reorganisation of both the industrial and service sectors, aiming at a higher productivity that would bring more international competitiveness, caused a structural crisis in the labour market, leading to higher levels of unemployment, and compounding pre-globalisation problems of inequality, informality, low qualifications and job insecurity. Since this time, the country's economy has been in recovery mode, but, even though, in recent years, economic growth has increased, these problems still pose major challenges to poverty alleviation and greater equality. Now, the country's economic growth is being affected by the economic crisis that begun in 2008. Thus, even though in 2008 the average unemployment rate decreased in relation to 2007, from 9.3 per cent to 7.9 per cent, the crisis has already contributed to the rise in unemployment to 8.5 per cent in March 2009.[13]

Inequality in Brazil is among the highest in the world: the share of income of the richest one per cent of the population is the same as that of the lowest 50 per cent. Additionally, the richest 10 per cent account for more than 40 per cent of the total income, and the poorest 40 per cent for less than 10 per cent.[14] One piece of good news in this very problematic situation is that income inequality has declined modestly in recent years. As measured by the Gini coefficient, the degree of income inequality over the period 2001–05 decreased by 4.6 per cent, from 0.593 to 0.566.[15] Even though this improvement is modest, the fall in income inequality does nevertheless represent a big step towards reversing an unfair trend. One of the reasons for the decline in inequality has been the introduction of the Bolsa Família, introduced by the Brazilian Federal Government in 2003.[16] Another reason for this decline is a decrease in the level of labour market discrimination by sector and by geography.[17] The biggest exception to discrimination decrease

[13] Instituto Brasileiro de Geografia e Estatística (IBGE), *Pesquisa Mensal de Emprego*. *Available at:* www.ibge.gov.br/home/estatistica/indicadores/trabalhoerendimento/pme_nova/pme_200902tmcomentarios.pdf (last accessed 10 April 2009). Indicating the decrease in employment before 2008, the IBGE states: 'With the results observed in the last quarter of the year, the unemployment trend in 2007 was below the one of 2006.' It is important to notice that this figure of 7.4% represents a fall of 1% from December 2006. It is also the lowest number since March 2002, when the IBGE survey began. IBGE, *Pesquisa Mensal de Emprego (Monthly Research of Employment)* (IPEA, Economic Quarterly No 12, June 2007) 4.

[14] Barros, RP et al, 'A Queda Recente da Desigualdade de Renda no Brasil' in RP Barros et al (eds), *Desigualdade de Renda no Brasil: uma análise da queda recente* (Brasília, Ipea, 2006) vol II 110.

[15] Ibid 108.

[16] The Bolsa Família is a social welfare programme that has provided conditional cash transfers to more than 11 million people in the first five years of its operation. It is the first general welfare programme in Brazil that targets the poorest segments of the population. Senna, M et al, 'Programa bolsa família: nova institucionalidade no campo da política social brasileira?' (2007) 10(1) *Rev. katálysis* 3.

[17] 'With the exception of the segmentation between the formal and informal segments, all the other forms of discrimination and segmentation declined during the decade and, in particular, during the last quarter. This reduction in the labour market's imperfections, with its growing integration, had a fundamental part to explain the inequality drop of labour remuneration

trend is the formal/informal segmentation in the labour market. Although the rate of informal employment has declined over the last decade, the wage gap between formal and informal employees and between formal employees and self-employed workers has grown. In the period 2001–05, the wage gap between formal and informal employees grew by four per cent, while the gap between formal employees and the self-employed grew by almost 15 per cent.[18]

According to recent data from the Instituto Brasileiro de Geografia e Estatística (IBGE),[19] the growth of jobs, in almost all surveyed regions, has been mostly in the formal sector.[20] In 2008, the average rate of informality was 39.1 per cent of the workers in the labour market, representing a decrease of 1.7 per cent in relation to 2007.[21] Despite these positive indicators, informality remains a characteristic of the labour market. Taking into account the difficulties associated with statistics on the informal economy,[22] it is estimated that in 2003, 98 per cent of urban enterprises with up to 5 employees in Brazil were informal. Of these, 88 per cent were owned by self-employed workers, 12 per cent by employers, 95 per cent had only one owner and 80 per cent had only one person employed.[23] In 2005, the informal economy accounted for 8.4 per cent of Brazilian GDP.[24]

---

and *per capita* income.' Barros, RP, Carvalho, M, Franco, S, Mendoça, R, *Discriminação e segmentação no Mercado de trabalho e desigualdade de renda no Brasil* (Rio de Janeiro, IPEA, 2007) 1. See Barros, RP, 'Uma análise das principais causas da queda recente na desigualdade de renda brasileira' (2006) 8(1) *Econômica: revista do Programa de Pós-Graduação em Economia da UFF* 117–47.

[18] Barros et al, *Discriminação e segmentação no Mercado de trabalho e desigualdade de renda no Brasil* (2007) 17.

[19] Brazilian Institute of Geography and Statistics (IBGE).

[20] IPEA, Boletim Mercado de Trabalho—Conjuntura e Análise n° 38, Fevereiro 2009 at 8. Available at: www.ipea.gov.br/default.jsp. Analysing the period from 1992 to 2002, Fligenspan concluded that in July of 1992 formal employees made up 52.3% of the total of workers and the total of informal ones was equivalent to 43.1%. In December of 2002, these percentages were, respectively, 45.4% and 50.3%, inverting the situation. Fligenspan, FB, 'Ganhos e Perdas no Mercado de Trabalho no Real. Uma Revisão por Posição na Ocupação' (2005) 9(1) *R. Econ. Contemp* 187, 196.

[21] These numbers treat informal workers as unregistered employees. IPEA, Boletim Mercado de Trabalho—Conjuntura e Análise n° 38 (2009).

[22] According to Hirata and Machado, considering the heterogeneity among the categories of informal workers, it is more appropriate to talk about an informal economy formed by different categories of informal workers: irregular employees, self-employed workers, small informal enterprises employers, domestic workers. See Hirata, GI and Machado, AF, 'Conceito de informalidade/formalidade e uma proposta de tipologia' (2007) *Mercado de Trabalho* 34. For a conceptual analysis of informal work, see Cacciamali, MC, 'Globalização e processo de informalidade' (2000) 14 *Economia e Sociedade* 153–74.

[23] IBGE, *Economia Informal Urbana* (2003) at 2, on line: IBGE, http://www.ibge.gov.br/home/estatistica/economia/ecinf/2003/comentario.pdf. This survey did not consider the street workers.

[24] IBGE, Sistema de Contas Nacionais—Brasil 2004–2005. Available at: www.ibge.gov.br/home/estatistica/economia/contasnacionais/referencia2000/2004_2005/default.shtm.

In addition, besides the traditional types of informal work—in a small production unit, domestic work, and illegal work—there are newer types of informal work that have become more prominent in recent years. These jobs result from the adoption of more flexible work relations. Globalization and search for labour flexibility constitute the framework within which new types of informal work has grown. Formal employees were turned into consultants, cooperative members, outsourced workers or partners.[25] These new relations can be found not only in the more disadvantageous segment of the labour market, but also in the more qualified and traditional segments, for example, in the health, education, management and law service sectors. Outsourcing is also very common in the industrial sector. Therefore, informal work, today, does not limit itself to one specific sector of the economy or to one specific group in the labour market.[26]

Ramos notes that informality is sometimes seen as a solution to a lack of formal employment opportunities.[27] However, he argues that informality is generally 'a survival strategy'[28] when the labour market cannot produce enough jobs with acceptable standards.[29] Workers in the informal economy earn considerably less than their formal counterparts, as well as being exposed to greater financial risks resulting from the precariousness of their working arrangements.[30] It is not surprising then that it is in the informal market that we find the most excluded segments of the Brazilian population: '51.3 per cent of poor Brazilians belong to families headed by informal workers'.[31]

This picture indicates that informality is not a transitory problem. Even though it is unlikely to disappear any time soon, appropriate labour policies can promote formalisation and thereby reduce the size of the informal sector and provide protection to the most vulnerable workers. For example,

[25] Although outsourcing and cooperatives are allowed by law, they are often used as instruments to disguise a real employment relationship and to defraud the labour legislation. Therefore, there is a grey area in which even big enterprises can comfortably hire workers through those relations in a veil of legality. Only if the case goes to a labour court can the employment relation be recognised. This solution, however, is not effective, because often workers wait to be dismissed before deciding to sue the enterprise, and any legal question cannot be taken to court after five years, during the employment relationship, and after two years of the ending of the relationship.

[26] In Brazil, for example, informality has increased among workers with more than 11 years of study. Reis, MC and Ulyssea, G, 'Cunha Fiscal, Informalidade e Crescimento: algumas questões e propostas de políticas' (2005) 1068 *Texto para discussão* 6.

[27] Ramos, L, 'O Desempenho recente do mercado de trabalho brasileiro: tendências, fatos estilizados e padrões espaciais' in *Brasil, o estado de uma nação* (Rio de Janeiro, Ipea, 2006) 34.

[28] Ibid.

[29] Ibid.

[30] Ulyssea, G, 'Instituições e a Informalidade no Mercado de Trabalho' (2005) 1096 *IPEA texto para discussão* 1.

[31] Neri, M, 'Empregos e negócios informais: subsídios para políticas' *Mercado de Trabalho conjuntura e análise* 5.

laws can increase the cost of informality and the benefits of formalisation, since, in Brazil, previous research has found that the main reason for choice of informality is to avoid taxes and the cost of social security.[32]

Another element of the national scenario is the lack of training and education. Barros, Henriques and Mendonça relate the weak performance of the Brazilian educational system with the high level of income inequality.[33] Brazil has one of the worst levels of professional qualification in Latin America.[34] This makes it harder for workers to get better jobs in the labour market and to have the capacity to build strong and well organised trade unions. Universal education of good quality is not yet a priority, and this is one of the structural obstacles to a more sustainable development of the country.

Finally, particularly among less qualified workers, job insecurity is indicated by the high involuntary turnover, because of employer action. As observed by the Ministry of Labour, the longest average employment tenure is in the public services, where the average employment relationship lasts 51.61 months, followed by the public administration sector (34.69 months) and the mineral industry (32.03 months).[35] On the other hand, farming (9.80 months) and civil construction (9.85 months) are the sectors with the shortest employment relationships. There are three major reasons for the country's job insecurity: the legal ease of hiring and firing, an a bundant labour force and a lack of workplace organisation.[36]

In this context, labour law has, to a certain degree, been delegitimised, as it has been seen more as adding to the problems in the labour market than

[32] Neri, M, 'Decent Work and the Informal Sector in Brazil' (Graduate School of Economics, Getulio Vargas Foundation, Economics Working Papers *(Ensaios Economicos da EPGE)* No 461, Nov 2002) 4. According to Ulyssea, 'Instituições e a Informalidade no Mercado de Trabalho' (2005), workers associate formal employment with income tax and social security contributions, despite the fact that informal workers are deprived of the financial benefit of certain rights guaranteed by a formal relationship, such as paid holidays, severance pay or unemployment insurance.

[33] Barros, RP, Henriques, R, Mendonça, R, 'Pelo fim das décadas perdidas: educação e desenvolvimento sustentado no Brasil' (Rio de Janeiro: *IPEA Texto para Discussão No 857*, janeiro de 2002).

[34] Pesquisa Nacional por Amostra de Domicílio. Instituto Brasileiro de Geografia e Estatística. *Síntese de Indicadores 2004:* 'In the population of workers with 10 years or more in the labour force, the ratio of those who had reached at least 11 years of study was 26.0 per cent.(...) For the population of 25 years or more, the number average of year of study was of 6.4 year and for the people working in this group, 7.1 year' [Free translation].

[35] See online at www.mte.gov.br/Empregador/CAGED/Estatistica/texto1/2004.asp.

[36] Pochmann, M, *O trabalho sob fogo cruzado. Exclusão, desemprego e precarização no final do século* (São Paulo, Contexto, 1999) 151. Flexibility in firing workers became the rule under an earlier constitutional reform that led to an option between job security (requiring just cause for dismissal) and the severance-pay fund for work time (FGTS) (allowing dismissal but requiring severance pay from a mandatory reserve fund). With the end of job security and the affording of severance pay in case of arbitrary firing, assured by art 7 subpara I of the Federal Constitution of 1988 and art 10 subpara I of the Transitory Constitutional Dispositions Act, firing workers became routine. *Cf* Mattoso, J, *O Brasil Desempregado* (São Paulo, Fundação Perseu Abramo, 1996) 16.

as a solution to the challenges brought by globalisation. Nevertheless, no broad reform has been undertaken in the labour law field. The most important examples of flexibility to be found in the Brazilian market, outsourcing and employment cooperatives, did not come from legal reforms, they came from the uglier realities of the labour market, escaping from the field of influence of trade unions and the arena of fundamental rights.

Outsourcing (*terceirização*)[37] is allowed by the Superior Labour Court[38] in the case of intermediary services, when there is no direct subordination[39] and the work is performed by the designated contractor (*pessoalidade*).[40] These limitations have not been enough to effectively regulate this practice, which has been growing as a means to disguise the employment relationship by making a non-employment contractual arrangement in order to avoid the costs of an employment relationship. According to Pochmann, who examined the period between 1985 and 2005 in the state of São Paulo, the number of workers in these triangular relationships went from 60,400 to 423,900; indeed, 12.1 per cent of the formal jobs created during that period consisted of such relationships. Also, the number of enterprises that provided triangular services went from 257 in 1985 to 6,308 some 20 years later. In 2005, almost a third of these enterprises had no employees, only 'partners' in the enterprise (another way to disguise the employment relationship).[41]

The employment cooperatives also act as 'providers' of workers (*cooperativas de mão-de-obra*). In the case of the disguised cooperatives (those that only provide labour for employers), the workers lack any semblance of labour rights, since they are deemed to be full members of a cooperative and not eligible for the benefits that come with employee status.

Until now, only isolated reforms have been made, and these have focused on individual labour rights: the temporary contract,[42] suspension of the labour contract,[43] and time-off in exchange for excess hours worked.[44] These reforms have not affected the most serious problems of the labour market in Brazil, discussed above. Next, we will develop a brief analysis of the Brazilian labour law system.

---

[37] 'Triangular employment relationships occur when employees of an enterprise (the "provider") perform work for a third party (the "user enterprise") to whom their employer provides labour or services.' ILO, *The Scope of the Employment Relationship*, Report V, 91st Session (Geneva, ILO, 2003) 39.

[38] Enunciado 331, Superior Labour Court (TST).

[39] The law does not define what constitutes direct or indirect subordination.

[40] *Pessoalidade* could be translated as 'personhood', meaning that it is essential that the work is done by the individual specified in the labour contract.

[41] Pochmann, M, *SINDEEPRES 15 Anos—A superterceirização dos contratos de trabalho* (São Paulo, SINDEEPRES, 2007) 12–14.

[42] Law 9.601 of 1998.

[43] *Consolidação das Leis do Trabalho* (CLT), Decree-law nr. 5452 art 476 (promulgated 1 May 1943).

[44] Law 10.101 (enacted 19 December 2000).

Overview of the Brazilian Labour Law System

Brazil's early labour laws were based on a particular brand of Latin American social constitutionalism that placed particular emphasis on the positive role of the state in emphasising the welfare of its citizens. The origin of labour law had its roots in industrial development, which replaced an economy based mainly on coffee and agriculture and restricted the autonomy of the social actors. According to Wolkmer, 'the emergence of labour regulation was not spontaneous, but a strategy within an authoritarian process to propel industrial development and the integration of the Brazilian bourgeois society'.[45] This process took place in the 1930s, during the authoritarian regime of Getúlio Vargas, known as the *Estado Novo*.[46]

Regulation of labour issues began effectively during the Vargas era: in the short period from 1931 to 1934, national regulation on work was introduced; working hours in commerce and industry were regulated; the labour code on women and minors was amended; a new vacation law was approved; and collective bargaining was created.[47] However, this era of change was marked not by the development of an autonomous trade union movement, but rather by the control of trade unions and workers by Vargas' corporativist state through the concession of individual rights and close control of the trade unions. This symbolised a new path towards a policy of social rights for the emerging working class through paternalistic, corporativist and direct intervention by the state in the labour market.[48]

The pejorative meaning often accorded in Brazil to terms such as 'interventionism' or 'protectionism' results from this Government's authoritarian action in imposing a corporatist labour law that stifled collective bargaining. An extremely authoritarian trade union structure combined with the state guarantee of favorable conditions for individual workers became the hallmarks of our labour law. This carefully constructed system was based on competing interests: the state's interests in keeping social peace; business's interests in maintaining an anti-negotiation posture, since the state would at the end resolve all labour conflicts; and trade union's interests in enjoying the benefits of being an official trade union. The corporativist structure continues to the current day and has survived periods of both authoritarian and democratic government in the Brazilian history.

---

[45] Wolkmer, AC, *Constitucionalismo e Direitos Sociais no Brasil* (São Paulo, Acadêmica, 1989) 35.

[46] The authoritarian state, presided over by Getúlio Vargas, lasted from 1930 to 1945.

[47] Gomes, AM de C, 'Empresariado e Legislação Social na Década de 30' in *A Revolução de 30: seminário realizado pelo Centro de Pesquisa e Documentação de História Contemporânea do Brasil (CPDOC) da Fundação Getúlio Vargas* (Rio de Janeiro, September 1980) (Brasília, Editora Universidade de Brasília, 1983) (Coleção temas Brasileiros, 54) 286.

[48] Wolkmer, *Constitucionalismo e Direitos Sociais no Brasil* (1989) 43.

The defining characteristic of this structure is not only interventionism, but also rather the exclusion of the democracy in the labour relations system.[49] This corporativist structure is based on three institutions: the labour legislation, the labour courts and the trade union structure. While the labour legislation over regulates all aspects of the employment relationship, the labour courts have an extensive role in solving all labour conflicts. Finally, the trade union structure imposes mandatory representation by only one trade union that will receive mandatory dues from workers. Therefore, there is little space left for authentic trade union representation and workers' involvement in the trade union. Below, we will describe the two first institutions, and, in Part II, the trade union structure will be analysed.

Brazil's body of formal labour law is composed of the 1988 Federal Constitution, the 1943 Brazilian Labour Code (*Consolidação das Leis do Trabalho*—CLT),[50] special laws, regulations and the consolidated jurisprudential rulings of the Superior Labour Court (*Enunciados dos TST*).[51] The CLT is comprised of 922 articles and more than 2000 special laws[52] and covers the major aspects of individual and collective labour relations—apprenticeships, employment contracts, trade union organisation, collective agreements, mediation, conciliation and arbitration commissions, application and collection of administrative fines, labour courts, public labour prosecution, and the judicial process.[53]

The 1988 Federal Constitution was the first constitution to establish labour rights as fundamental rights, alongside the more traditional individual rights, in arts 7 to 11.[54] Article 7 sets out a series of fundamental rights for urban and rural workers, in relation to employment, wages, social protection and working conditions.[55] Article 8 recognises freedom of association and, in subpara I, prohibits state interference in trade union

---

[49] Vianna stresses that what marks Brazilian labour law is not an excess of law but instead its systematisation within a corporatist order. Vianna, LW, *Liberalismo e Sindicato no Brasi*, 4th edn, (Belo Horizonte, UFMG, 1999) 60.

[50] The CLT was promulgated by the Federal Decree-law No 5.542 on 1 May 1943.

[51] There are 363 *Enunciados*, which are subordinate to statutes and regulations and do not serve as precedents to other decisions, but in practice they are applied as law.

[52] Yeung, L, 'The Need for Modernization of Brazilian Labour Institutions' in IIRA, *Social Actors, Work Organization and the New Technologies in the 21st Century* (International Industrial Relations Association (IIRA) 14th World Congress) (Lima, Fondo Editorial, 2006) 126: 'There are, nowadays, over 2000 'complementary laws' specifically related to labour issues.'

[53] Ibid 126–27.

[54] Labour rights are set out in Title II—Fundamental Rights and Guarantees.

[55] The constitutional choice was to elaborate a rule-based article containing 34 subparagraphs, due to the tradition in applying broad principles. In art 7, the 34 lines guarantee worker's rights that express the follow principles: prohibition of unfair dismissal, fair labour conditions (regarding remuneration, working hours and rest), protection of children, prohibition of any kind of discrimination at work, protection of health and safety, free collective bargaining. Most of the rights guaranteed by art 7 are regulated by the CLT or by specific laws and have full enforceability. Nevertheless, some of those rights are still waiting for a law to be

organisation. However, subpara II establishes the unicity rule (*unicidade sindical*)[56] which creates a strong limitation on freedom of association, as it allows only one union to represent a particular professional or economic category in a given territorial area. The effect of this rule will be discussed in further detail in Part II. Articles 9, 10 and 11 deal with collective rights: the right to strike, workers' and employers' participation in collective public bodies and representation in the workplace.

The status of fundamental rights accorded to labour rights by the Constitution represents a rupture with the corporatist past, which means that today the CLT is not considered to be the same set of authoritarian rules from the time of Getúlio Vargas. The relation between the Constitution and the CLT opens a new space for discussion and reflection on constitutional principles, human rights and the very raison d'être of the CLT—not as an accessory to industrialisation, but rather as society's commitment to the dignity of workers.

Within Brazil's federal legal system, labour law is a federal competency—that is, the federal states have no power to make labour laws—and the judicial labour system is federal, with three tiers of courts. The Superior Labour Court (TST)[57] is the highest labour court and has jurisdiction over the whole of Brazil. The Regional Labour Courts (TRTs) have jurisdiction over the states, while local labour courts have local jurisdiction—one city or more—and only deal with individual labour disputes. The Supreme Federal Court (STF) has jurisdiction over labour issues involving constitutional matters.

The labour court system has a very broad jurisdiction. Labour courts hear not only all the usual employment-related disputes—encompassing both individual and collective issues—but also disputes involving independent contractors, non-competition covenants, professional services contracts (lawyer-client disputes, for example), as well as other matters involving parties' livelihoods, according to art 114 of the 1988 Federal Constitution.[58] In the case of management-union conflicts over the course of collective bargaining, the parties can turn to the Labour Court for resolution. The Court is empowered to set the terms of the collective agreement, effectively replacing the social actors.

---

made and while this law remains inexistent, they have no enforceability. For example: protection in face of the automation and participation in the management of the enterprise.

[56] The requirement of a single imposed trade union is called *unicidade sindical*. This phrase does not mean trade union unity, as some English speakers mistakenly assume. An approximate translation might be trade union 'unicity', but for the fact that the word does not exist in English. *Unicidade* means 'oneness' or 'uniqueness'. According to the unicity rule, 'It is forbidden to create more than one union, at any level, representing a professional or economic category, in the same territorial base, which shall be defined by the workers or employers concerned, and which may not cover less than the area of one municipality.'

[57] See www.tst.gov.br/.

[58] Federal Constitution Amendment 45, 2004.

PART II: FREEDOM OF ASSOCIATION IN BRAZIL

When examining the origins of Brazil's labour laws, we stressed their corporatist element, which remains a key feature of the current labour regulation. Although the recognition of freedom of association and collective bargaining in art 8 of the 1988 Constitution is an important evolution, the maintenance of the corporatist structure continues to prevent the progress of labour relations in Brazil.

The Brazilian debate about modernisation has generally focused on individual rights rather than collective rights, with little reference to the corporatist trade union system. The discussion tends to focus on costs associated with the Brazilian labour force and the inflexibility of labour law. This line of argument contends that labour laws must be changed to allow Brazilian enterprises to become more competitive, to adapt labour relations to new ways of production and to fight unemployment. The debate focuses on the need for a broader scope for collective bargaining, including the negotiation of conditions below those guaranteed by law.[59] However, there has been little reference to the subject on who will take part in the collective bargaining, that is, if the trade unions are really representative or still part of a corporativist structure.

The reform to the trade union system is the necessary foundation for the modernisation of Brazil's labour relations, allowing greater freedom of association and scope for more representative collective bargaining. Labour law reforms that do not address the current obstacles regarding freedom of association will be empowering the trade union movement to bargain away statutory rights on behalf of workers, within a structure that is authoritarian and lacking representativeness. At the same time, current flexible working practices have not resulted from legal debate or consultation with workers or trade unions, but have come about 'by stealth': flexible arrangements such as outsourcing and cooperatives, which offer alternatives to the traditional employment relationship. The maintenance of the corporatist structure perpetuates the inability of the corporatist trade union to participate effectively in social dialogue about the future of labour law in Brazil and the guarantee of core labour standards. Even though freedom of association is recognised by the Federal Constitution as a fundamental right, it is clear that the current system still does not protect this right as a fundamental human right.

We suggest that it is important not to overlook the steps that trade unions have taken towards modernisation; in particular, the movement initiated by the new unionism in the ABC[60] region of the State of São Paulo at the end of the 1970s, which resulted, for instance, in the creation of the *Central Única*

---

[59] In Brazil, this process is called 'negotiation over legislation' (*negociado sobre o legislado*).
[60] The cities of Santo André, São Bernardo do Campo and São Caetano.

dos Trabalhadores (CUT), the main Brazilian trade union confederation. However, this progress took place within a legal order with clear corporatist structures. The full acknowledgment of freedom of association as a fundamental right can only take place within a democratic labour legal order, free from the corporativist rules. Only then may workers, the beneficiaries of this right, fully exercise this fundamental freedom and only then will there be significant change to social dialogue in Brazil, through greater democratisation, worker participation, union representativeness and engagement with workers. This type of reform has the potential to create such substantial changes to the current system that those who have vested interests in the maintenance of the corporatist system have prevented any change to date.

For example, in 2003, the Federal Government created the National Labour Forum (NLF),[61] a forum for social dialogue on potential trade union and labour reforms. This was a tripartite body composed of trade unions, employer associations and the Ministry of Labour and Employment. Proposed trade union reforms were discussed and the forum approved a number of principles adopted by consensus. The end result was an agreement on a transitory system between the present corporatist order and a future system based on the principle of freedom of association. As a result of the consensus arising from the NLF consultation, the Federal Government developed a proposal for constitutional amendment and a draft bill which were presented to the National Congress in 2005. Unfortunately, the bill is still in Congress, without any sign of the necessary political momentum to move it through to approval. Unfortunately, this is a recurring pattern with respect to trade union reform: passionate debate and agreement about the need for change, unaccompanied by concrete outcomes.

Similar events unfolded in relation to the proposed ratification of ILO Convention No 87. The power to ratify treaties belongs to the President, once authorised by the National Congress. In the case of Convention No 87, the presidential request for referendum approval was sent to the Congress in 1949 (Message #256), a year after the adoption of the Convention by the International Labour Conference. Nearly six decades later, the request is still in Congress awaiting action: it has been approved by the House of Representatives but is awaiting approval from the Senate.[62]

---

[61] Fórum Nacional do Trabalho (FNT) www.mtb.gov.br/fnt/default.asp.

[62] The internalisation of the international acts initiates with an exposition of reasons of the Minister of the Foreign Affairs, requesting to the President the submission of the internalisation, for Message, to the National Congress. The process continues in the Congress, being evaluated by the pertinent commissions and led to the plenary assembly. If approved, a legislative decree, signed by the President of the Senate, is issued and published. The President of the Republic, then, has the authorisation to ratify the international act and to make it valid in Brazil by means of a Presidential Decree, which will be published. We should note that, despite the fact that our law demands as internalisation process, Brazil applies the treaty itself.

The debate about the ratification of Convention No 87 faces one major legal hurdle: the Convention is not compatible with subpara II art 8 of the 1988 Constitution, which sets out the unicity rule. The next section of this chapter will consider the principle of freedom of association, as guaranteed by Convention No 87, and the provisions of the Brazilian legislation, both from the perspective of the individual and collective freedom.

Right of Employees and Employers to Form and Join Organisations

Article 2 of Convention No 87 states that all workers and employers, without distinction or prior authorisation, are entitled to establish and join organisations of their own choosing, subject only to the rules of the organisations concerned. This section encompasses a number of rights and their application in Brazil is discussed below.

1. The Right to Organise Trade Unions without Prior Authorisation

Prior to the 1988 Constitution, the power to create trade unions was vested in the Ministry of Labour through the trade union framework committee (*Comitê de Enquadramento Sindical*). Article 8 subpara I of the Constitution, however, prohibits any state interference in trade union organisation, and the system of trade union registration was changed to a model that would be consistent with Convention No 87.[63] According to the Constitution, the Ministry of Labour and Employment is responsible for the registration of trade unions. In principle, this is an administrative function that does not limit the application of Convention No 87, since it does not interfere in their organisation. However, as we will see, the right to organise trade unions without prior authorisation is still restricted, because the act of registration actually serves to maintain the unicity of trade unions.

The 1988 Constitution[64] establishes the unicity rule, according to which only one trade union can represent a category of workers in a specific territorial basis,[65] in the case of an existing category. In order to guarantee this rule, the Ministry of Labour will make the application for the registration of the new trade union public. If there is already a trade union representing

---

After the treaty is validated in the national juridical order, it has direct effect in the Brazilian domestic law with no previous adaptation between the treaty and the national norms. This kind of internalisation process causes, at least in the labour field, certain ignorance about the ratified ILO conventions, as these lie outside the CLT.

[63] In this respect, art 7 of the Convention states that the legal status of trade unions, or trade union federations and confederations, cannot be subject to conditions which limit the application of the Convention's provisions.

[64] 1988 Constitution art 8 subpara II.

[65] The territorial basis cannot be smaller than a city.

that same category, the existing trade union can impugn the application to form a new trade union. There is then a possibility of conciliation between the old and the new trade unions under the supervision of the labour ministry. If this conciliation fails, the trade unions can take the case to the labour court to decide which trade union will hold the representation. The labour court will consider whether the trade unions have the same territorial base or represent the same category.[66] If this is the case, the courts will decide based on seniority, that is, the trade union that already holds the representation will keep it, and the new trade union cannot be registered. This ultimately means that the decision regarding which trade union will represent a specific professional category is usually not done by workers, but by the Labour Court.

Therefore, despite the fact that the Constitution guarantees the non-interference of the state in trade union organisation, a simple examination of the registration procedure demonstrates that this rule is not implemented in practice. Although the Ministry of Labour does not have the power to prevent the creation of a trade union, the registration procedures effectively uphold the unicity system, by allowing an existing trade union to appeal to the judiciary to block the creation of a new trade union, arguing the violation of the unicity rule. The result is that an issue that should be resolved by workers themselves is decided instead by a labour court.

Finally, it is important to stress that Convention No 87 does not mandate trade union pluralism; that is, the existence of more than one trade union per industry sector, profession, or company within the same territory. Rather, the Convention states only that trade union pluralism must be possible.[67] This differentiation between trade union unicity and single trade union causes some confusion in the debate on trade union reform in Brazil. The concept of unicity refers to a legal restriction on the formation of trade unions: there may be only one trade union representing a group of workers in a professional category; while the representation by a single trade union is achieved by the workers themselves. As noted by Mascaro, the state-imposed restriction of unicity detaches the trade union movement from the principle of democracy,[68] according to which freedom of association should enable the formation of trade unions. In contrast, unicity,

---

[66] The procedure is regulated by the Ministry of Labour Resolution No 186 2008.

[67] As stressed by the Union Freedom Committee: 'It is derived from this principle that, although the Convention does not aim to make trade union pluralism compulsory, pluralism must be possible in every case, even if trade union unity was once adopted by the trade union movement. Systems of trade union unity or monopoly must not therefore be imposed directly by the law.' ILO, *International Labour Standards: A Global Approach: 75th anniversary of the Committee of Experts on the Application of Conventions and Recommendations* (Geneva, International Labour Office, 2001) 37.

[68] Nascimento, Amauri Mascaro: *O Direito Coletivo no Atual Momento Brasileiro*, Revista LTr (São Paulo, 1993) vol 57 no 12 1422.

which allows the existence of trade unions without true representativeness, promotes the weakening and fragmentation of trade unionism, as is currently the situation in Brazil.

According to an IBGE survey, although the number of trade unions increased from 11,193 to 15,963 from 1991 to 2001 (including both registered and unregistered trade unions),[69] overall membership numbers:

> changed very little [over the same period]: with respect to the economically active population, it decreased to about 25 per cent in 1990, to 23 per cent, in 2001; with respect to workers in relevant occupations, it remained in the level of 26 per cent'[70]

Data from the Ministry of Labour and Employment show that there were 23,726 trade unions registered in 2005.[71]

2. *The Trade Union Law is Guaranteed with no Distinction of Class, as Regards Occupation, Sex, Colour, Race, Religion, Nationality and Political Opinion*

Article 9 of Convention No 87 provides for two exceptions to this rule: '[t]he extent to which the guarantees provided for in this Convention shall apply to the armed forces and the police shall be determined by national laws or regulations'. In this respect, Brazil's legislation complies with

---

[69] From this total, 11,347 are recorded as trade unions and 4,614 are not. IBGE, *Sindicatos: indicadores sociais* (Rio de Janeiro, IBGE, 2002) 93. In the period from 1987 to 1991 the annual average growth was of 4.2%, as compared to the rate of the period under analysis (1991 to 2001) of 3.3%, a decrease which may be justified if we consider that in the first period (1987–91), with the enactment of the new Constitution, the requirements for the organisation of new trade unions were made relative. IBGE, *Sindicatos: indicadores sociais* (2002) 21.

[70] IBGE (n 69) 28. IBGE data indicates that, 'in 2006, the workers included in the group encompassing other industrial activities had the largest rate of syndicated members (37.3 per cent). On the other side, we found the group of domestic services, which presented the smallest rate (1.9 per cent). The workers included in the groups of construction, lodging and food, other collective, social and personal services, and commerce and restoration had less than 12 per cent of their workers associated to trade unions. The other groups had between 22 per cent and 31 per cent of members associated. The participation of people syndicated in the working population increased 2 percentage points from 1996 to 2006 (from 16.6 per cent to 18.6 per cent). It is worthy to record the expressive increase of participation of the syndicated in the farming sector. This behavior may be associated, among other factors, to the implementation of the Brazilian Program of Strengthening of the Familiar Agriculture—PRONAF, in which the participation of the trade unions is essential for the access to the rural credit. In the industry and other groups, such as commerce and restoration, construction, etc., the participation of the syndicated has not changed substantially in ten years. In the group related to other activities, a decrease was observed (from 30.0 per cent to 23.6 per cent).' IBGE in the Brazilian Survey per Sampling of Residences (PNDA) (2006) 29, available at: <www.ibge.gov.br/home/estatistica/populacao/trabalhoerendimento/pnad2006/comentarios2006.pdf

[71] Ministry of Labour and Employment, available at www.mte.gov.br/Estudiosos Pesquisadores/fnt/conteudo/pdf/DIAGNOSTICO_DAS_RELACOES_DE_TRABALHO_NO_BRASIL.pdf

Convention No 87, since the 1988 Federal Constitution guarantees public servants the right to freedom of association.[72] However, the Constitution does not recognise the right to bargain collectively.

3. *Workers and Employers are Entitled to Establish Organisations of their Own Choosing*

According to this rule, the imposition of legal criteria limiting the free creation of trade unions violates the provisions of Convention No 87;[73] for example, when the law imposes the general structure of trade union activity, it does so in terms of 'category', 'company' or 'profession'.

In Brazil, as the current system is defined by the unicity rule, the notion of 'category' is essential to guarantee representation by a single trade union. In other words, in order for the state to ensure that only one trade union will represent a category of workers, the law provides that workers organising themselves in trade unions must do so according to categories. A category is comprised of workers or employers[74] who have shared interests as a result of their activity in a specific economic field. The use of categories is reasonable for the organisation of workers, but it is the imposition of a category as the only criterion that violates the workers' freedom to create trade unions.[75]

The workers' right to establish organisations of their own choosing also encompasses the issue of association with a trade union, which is manifest in three ways: freedom to join a trade union, freedom not to join a trade union and freedom to withdraw from a trade union.[76] An important issue related to this aspect of Convention No 87 is the payment of mandatory trade union dues by workers whether associated or not with a trade union. Since 1942, trade unions that hold workers' representation according to the unicity rule receive mandatory trade unions dues.[77] These dues guarantee

---

[72] 1988 Federal Constitution art 37 s VI.

[73] According to the ILO, '[t]he various restrictions to which this right is subjected in many countries give rise to several problems, in particular as regards the structure and composition of organizations, the question of trade union unity or plurality and clauses respecting trade union security'. ILO, *Libertad sindical y relaciones del trabajo*, CIT, 30th Meeting, 1947, Report VII 11, *apud* ILO: *Libertad Sindical y Negociacion Colectiva*, International Labour Conference, 81st Meeting, 1994 para 79.

[74] In Brazil employers are also represented by trade unions.

[75] As noted by Magano, within a system of freedom of association, the category does not constitute a prior requirement for trade union organisation. Workers may be organised in several forms: coalition, category, region, enterprise, or group of enterprises. Magano, OB, *Idéias para uma reforma estrutural da organização sindical brasileira in* AS Romita (ed), *Sindicalismo* (São Paulo, LTr, 1986) ch XXIII 233.

[76] Gomes, O et al, *Curso de Direito do Trabalho*, 7th edn (Rio de Janeiro, Forense, 1995) vol I 748.

[77] Decree No 4.298, from 14 May 1942. The mandatory dues (*contribuição sindical*) are paid once a year by every worker, equal to one working day's wages.

the economic survival of a trade union representative of a category, regardless of the number of affiliates, minimising the need for real representativeness and discouraging association to trade unions. This system does not encourage trade unions to be representative, because they are maintained as a result of their status in the corporativist law rather than by their membership, support or involvement in collective bargaining. Therefore, these dues are in violation of the principle of freedom of association, since they are charged to all members of a category, regardless of trade union membership, trade union support or trade union involvement in collective bargaining.[78]

Different from the unicity rule, established by the Constitution, the mandatory dues are established by law; therefore, they can be revoked by a legislative amendment, that is, there is no need to amend the Constitution. However, instead of taking steps to abolish these dues, a recent reform recognised the right of the central trade unions to receive the dues.

In 2007, the President sent a law proposal to the National Congress recognising the trade union centrals as associations with trade union legal status, that is to say, authorised to represent the rights and interests of workers.[79] The proposal also included provisions on the financing of the trade union centrals, allocating to them a share of the trade union compulsory dues. According to the proposal, 10 per cent of the dues shall be allocated to the centrals.[80] The proposal[81] was approved and the President vetoed one provision that would have obliged the trade unions to submit their accountancy to a public body for supervision.

The approval of the new law has two immediate results. First, it means that the trade union centrals become participants in the corporatist system, since they will benefit from the trade union mandatory dues. Secondly, as part of this system, they will be able to negotiate, albeit on behalf of trade unions which are constituted and work within the limits of the unicity rules. Therefore, this is a superficial reform that does not lead to a profound transformation of the corporativist trade union structure; instead the new

---

[78] In Brazil, there are four types of trade union contributions: trade union dues, confederative dues, assistance dues and voluntary dues. While confederative dues are constitutionally guaranteed 'for the costs of the confederative system of the trade union representation' (art 8, IV), and must be fixed in a general meeting of the trade union, assistance dues are agreed upon during collective bargaining and '... [are] intended to [go towards] the payment of expenses incurred during the stages of the collective bargaining and for the legal, medical and odontological assistance'. Filho, F, de Sousa, G, *Contribuições sindicais e liberdade sindical* in N Prado (ed), *Direito Sindical Brasileiro: estudos em homenagem ao prof. Arion Sayão Romita* (São Paulo, LTr, 1998) 148. With respect to these sources of defrayal, case law holds that it can only be collected from the affiliates of the trade union and non-affiliates are entitled to object to this payment. ED-ED-RODC 764581/2001. Ruling Precedent No 119.

[79] Bill / House of Representatives 1990/2007.

[80] Today, by law, the contribution is divided among the trade union (60%), the federation (15%), the confederation (5%) and the ministry of labour (20%).

[81] Bill 11648, from 31 March 2008.

law makes it stronger, since the law includes the centrals in this structure. The trade union centrals strongly supported this Bill, including the transfer of trade union dues, and the presidential veto on their supervision.

Right of the Worker and Employer Organisations to Draw up their Constitutions and Rules, to Elect their Representatives in Full Freedom, to Organise their Administration and Activities and to Formulate their Programmes

1. Article 3 of Convention No 87 Preserves the Right of Trade Unions to Establish and Maintain their Own Freely Chosen Internal Structures

In Brazil, this right is acknowledged by the 1988 Federal Constitution in art 8, which prevents any interference of the public administration in the trade union. According to the ILO, 'Any restrictions on this principle must have as their sole object to ensure the democratic operation of the organizations and the protection of the interests of their affiliates.'[82] These are the limits on legislation dealing with the internal management of trade unions.

2. Programme of Action of the Trade Unions

A trade union organisation may exercise many functions, including service provision (such as medical assistance, educational and leisure activities)[83] or tax collection (the collection of dues from all members of a category, regardless of membership, as discussed above). However, the ability to negotiate on behalf of workers is the core function of a trade union, facilitating the resolution of labour conflicts, based on the autonomy of the parties involved. Brazilian law places a limit on trade unions' ability to exercise this function. There is a restriction on the negotiating power of federations and confederations, which may only negotiate jointly with trade unions or in the absence of a trade union.[84]

---

[82] ILO. *Libertad sindical y relaciones del trabajo*, CIT, 30th meeting, 1947, Report VII, page 11, *apud* ILO: *Libertad Sindical y Negociacion Colectiva*, International Labour Conference, 81st Meeting, 1994, 63.

[83] Note that this can be an important tool for trade unions to attract new members.

[84] We highlight further, as one of the activities carried out by the trade union to achieve its objects, the right to strike, despite the fact that it is not directly mentioned in Convention No 87, or in any other international labour rule. The strike must, therefore, be analysed in association with the principle of freedom of association, as guaranteed by this Convention. The lack of regulation regarding public servants' right to strike is one of the more relevant problems concerning the right to strike in Brazil. The right of public servants, despite being set out in the Constitution, has been awaiting a complementary law since 1988. We share the understanding of Magano: up to the enactment of said complementary law, 'it is licit for public servants to exercise the right to strike within the limits within which private sector employees and the employees of the economic agencies of the State may use it'. Magano, OB, *Relações entre Estado e Sindicato*, Rev. LTr (São Paulo, February 1991) vol 55(2) 143.

Prohibition of Administrative Dissolution or Suspension of Worker or Employer Organisations

Convention No 87 prevents state interference in both the organisation of trade unions and their internal organisation, only requiring the respect for legality in the exercise of these rights. The administrative dissolution or suspension of a trade union is one of the most radical ways for a public authority to intervene in trade union organisation and, consequently, it is not allowed in any legal system which guarantees the right to freedom of association. It is worthwhile to stress that Convention No 87 does not prevent judicial intervention. Any act, therefore, that leads to the dissolution or suspension of a trade union must be characterised by all guarantees set forth for a court proceeding, as takes place, in Brazil, since the enactment of the 1988 Federal Constitution.

The Possibility of Brazil's Ratification of ILO Convention No 87

Whenever Convention No 87 is discussed in Brazil, its incompatibility with the unicity rule is mentioned as an insurmountable obstacle. As discussed above, at least at the constitutional level, the unicity rule is the sole impediment to freedom of association. However, as a result of an amendment to art 5 of the Constitution, ratification and internalisation of the Convention may be possible. At the same time, however, there remains the obstacle of it not being constitutional because of the conflict with subpara II article 8 of the Federal Constitution. This was the situation until Constitutional Amendment—EC 45 was made in 2004. EC 45 added paragraph 3 to article 5 of the 1988 Federal Constitution, which states that 'treaties and international conventions on human rights which are approved, in each House of the National Congress, in two rounds, by three fifths of the votes of the respective members, are equivalent to constitutional amendments'.

Paragraph 3 of article 5 applies to Convention No 87, as it is a treaty on human rights. The right to freedom of association is acknowledged in the Universal Declaration of Human Rights:[85] 'every person is entitled to form and to join trade unions for the protection of his/her rights'.[86] This is reaffirmed both by the International Covenant on Civil and Political Rights[87] and the International Covenant on Social, Cultural and Economic Rights.[88]

---

[85] Adopted by the United Nations General Assembly in 1948.

[86] Universal Statements of Human Rights art 23 no 4.

[87] Adopted by the United Nations General Assembly in 1966. International Covenant on Civil and Political Rights art 22 para 1.

[88] Adopted by the United Nations General Assembly in 1966. International Covenant on Social, Cultural and Economic Rights art 8 para 1.

In a clear reference to Convention No 87, the two treaties set out, with the same text, that no provision:

> shall allow the States Parties to the International Labour Organization Convention of 1948 concerning freedom of association and protection of the right to organize to take legislative measures which would prejudice, or apply the law in such a manner as would prejudice, the guarantees provided for in that Convention'.

This granted recognition to the ILO Convention which expresses the fundamental right of freedom of trade union organisation. It is worth stressing that both treaties have been ratified by Brazil.[89] At the regional level, the American Convention on Human Rights of 1969,[90] also ratified by Brazil, guarantees the right to freedom of association in article 16, as does article 8 of the Additional Protocol to the Inter-American Convention on Human Rights in the Area of Economical, Social and Cultural Rights, 'Protocol of San Salvador' (ratified by Brazil).[91] Finally, the right to freedom of association is further enshrined in the 1998 ILO Declaration.

The inclusion of the right to freedom of association in the main international treaties on human rights indicates the relationship between freedom of association and fundamental human freedoms, acknowledged in the ILO itself.[92] Its importance and also the obstacles for its full recognition result from its central role in the regulation of the labour relations, guaranteeing to the social actors the power to establish the conditions in which their relations will develop.

As it would be ratified according to paragraph 3 of article 5 of the Federal Constitution, Convention No 87 would have the same status as a constitutional amendment. As a result, the issue of Convention No 87's incompatibility with the unicity rule is one of conflict between two constitutional rules; the unicity rule having original constitutional power, and Convention No 87 having derivative constitutional power. Obviously, the constitutional amendment represented by ratification might be unconstitutional in view of the original text; however, would this necessarily be the case?

Convention No 87 guarantees the right to freedom of association, which is also recognised by the main section of article 8 of the Constitution. Subparagraph II of article 8 is a constitutional rule limiting the exercise of the freedom of association, but it is not a fundamental right (there is no fundamental right to unicity!) and it is rather a restriction of the fundamental right to freedom of association. Consequently, the constitutional unicity rule

---

[89] Both Covenants were ratified by Brazil on 24 January 1992 and enacted by Presidential Decree 592 of 6 July 1992.

[90] (Pact of San José, Costa Rica). Ratified by Brazil on 25 September 1992.

[91] Ratified by Brazil.

[92] For the ILO, 'freedom of professional association is solely an aspect of the freedom of association in general which must be integrated to a broad set of fundamental freedoms of man, interdependent and complementary one to another'. ILO, 1994, 14.

cannot be considered an immutable clause and could be changed through constitutional amendment. The internalisation of Convention No 87 in the Brazilian legal system with status of Constitutional Amendment would then have authority to revoke subparagraph II of article 8 of the Constitution.

For the purpose of normative clarity and legal security, however, it would be preferable to introduce a Constitutional Amendment to expressly change the wording of subparagraph II article 8. Otherwise, the Supreme Federal Court would have to make a ruling on this constitutional conflict, following the publication of a Presidential Decree enacting the internalisation. It must be stressed once again, however, that the unicity rule is a restriction of a fundamental freedom, and therefore may be changed by constitutional amendment or, in this case, through international treaty internalised with the same status as an amendment.

Thus, in case the legislature considers convenient the reform of the Brazilian trade union system, the ratification of Convention No 87 can be approved through this special procedure, allowing it to reach the status of constitutional rule. However, it would also be possible to revoke the rule of unicity of trade unions and then approve the Convention, through the ordinary process.

PART III: GENDER DISCRIMINATION IN THE LABOUR MARKET

In contrast to the right to freedom of association, the other rights in the ILO Declaration—prohibition of child labour, abolition of forced labour and the end of discrimination at work—are more widely recognised as fundamental rights. This does not mean that they are enjoyed universally; however, there has been considerable progress in these areas in Brazil. With respect to child labour and forced labour, the perspective of human rights violation was the cause for definitively placing the two issues in the field of labour law. National action to protect children's rights, including the 1988 Constitution, which expressly acknowledges the rights of children and adolescents,[93] was largely influenced by the United Nations (UN) Convention on the Rights of the Child of 1989.[94] In the case of forced labour, Brazil

---

[93] 1988 Constitution art 224.

[94] See Gomes, AVM, Romero, AM, Carvalho, HJA, Sprande, MA, Udry, TV, *Análise e recomendações para a melhor regulamentação e cumprimento da normativa nacional e internacional sobre o trabalho de crianças e adolescentes no Brasil* (Lima, ILO-IPEC/ SIRTI-Spanish Cooperation, 2003). 'In 2006, according to PNAD (National Household Survey), there were 5.1 million children and adolescents from 5 to 17 years working in Brazil, representing 5.7 per cent of the occupied population with 5 or more years. The reduction of the number of children and adolescents working contributed for the participation of this population in the occupied population decreased 0.5 percentage points as regards 2005. Among the regions, Northeast was the one presenting the greatest participation of children and adolescents from five to 17 years in the occupied population, however, there was where the greatest decrease

adopted an action plan in partnership with the ILO in 2000, as described in the introduction to this chapter.[95] However, the work done on gender discrimination in Brazil is worth considering in isolation, as it constitutes important progress towards the recognition of gender equality as a fundamental right.[96] Also, as occurs in the cases of child labour and forced labour, the violations are still current and serious.

One of the challenges in relation to gender discrimination in Brazil, as well as racial discrimination, is that the discrimination is against the majority of the Brazilian population: women and African-Brazilians. As a result, it constitutes one of the main parts of the Brazilian social injustice scenario.[97]

In Brazil, women still occupy a secondary place in the labour market. The idea that a woman's principal role in society is related to the needs of her family creates tension between her domestic responsibilities and professional needs. This effect is particularly profound for younger and more qualified women, who must make choices in order to try to balance their career and family responsibility; that is, it is an integral part of the image they have of themselves and of social expectations. This conflict explains the ongoing gender wage gap and the fact that women continue to dominate informal and precarious employment, despite women's higher levels of education and higher workforce participation rates. Even at the higher echelons of the workforce, women struggle to occupy senior positions, still confronted by a glass ceiling. This ongoing gender stereotyping continues to attribute a role to women that blocks their full participation in society, including their access to the labour market and economic resources. The possibility of changing this situation depends not only on social change, but also on legal reform.

For this purpose, there is a clear and abundant body of domestic and international law that clearly states that equality in the workplace is a fundamental right. This body of law is diverse in its methods of tackling

---

took place from 2005 to 2006 (from 9.4 per cent to 8.4 per cent).' (IBGE) in the Brazilian Survey per Sampling of Residences (PNDA) (2006) 25. Available at: www.ibge.gov.br/home/estatistica/populacao/trabalhoerendimento/pnad2006/comentarios2006.pdf.

[95] See ILO, *Normas e cooperação técnica. In Princípios e direitos fundamentais no trabalho-declaração e normas da OIT.* Brasília. ILO/ACTRAV, Ed. 01, 2000.

[96] As observed by Lavinas and Nicoll, 'Disregarding political representation, an area in which Brazil lacks gender equality, the fact is that, in little more than thirty years, the workforce participation rate of women in Brazil doubled, significantly reducing the hiatus of income and reverted definitively educational hiatus, not to mention the profound demographic changes promoted by the removal of barriers': 'Pobreza, transferências de renda e desigualdades de gênero: conexões diversas' (2006) 22 *Parcerias Estratégicas* 39.

[97] 'The situation of black women is specially subject of concern, because they are victims, at the same time, of two forms of interrelated discrimination, which intensify one another.' The Brazilian Supplement to the Global Report published by ILO-Brazil contains a statistical analysis based on the Brazilian Survey per Sampling of Residences (PNAD) 2001.

workplace discrimination: some laws simply prohibit discrimination, while others aim to discourage discrimination through affirmative action. In reviewing these rules, a clearer view emerges with respect to their effectiveness in bringing about change, both in terms of the current situation and in terms of popular ideas about women's role in society.

This chapter aims, therefore, to examine how gender discrimination at work is being addressed in Brazil from a legal perspective, with respect to both the adequacy of the legislation (including recent legislative reforms) and its enforcement. The paradigms to be observed are the two fundamental ILO Conventions—No 100 and No 111—both ratified by Brazil.

First, it is useful to highlight two distinctive features of women's participation in the Brazilian labour market. First, the number of women in the workforce has been gradually increasing over the past few years: in 2004, 43.1 per cent; in 2005, 43.5 per cent; and, in 2006, 43.7 per cent.[98] Secondly, women who are active in the labour market have, on average, spent more time studying than men.[99]

Greater participation and greater qualification does not mean, however, that evidence of discrimination does not appear in labour market statistics, particularly with respect to the gender wage gap. Taking into account the fact that women tend to occupy lower paid jobs, women's wages were equal to 65.6 per cent of men's wages in 2006. This represents a slight decrease in the differential compared to the two previous years (2005, 64.5 per cent; 2004, 63.5 per cent). The gender wage gap also remains firmly in place among more qualified workers.[100] This indicates that women, even the more qualified ones, are not reaching the higher, and better remunerated, positions in the workplace. That is to say that functional discrimination exists alongside wage discrimination.[101]

---

[98] In accordance with IBGE. Brazilian Survey per Sampling of Residences (PNDA) 2006.

[99] 'Among men in the workforce, 90.3 per cent had concluded at least one year of study, while for women the estimate percentage was higher (92.9 per cent). This difference between men and women increases when the higher levels of education are compared. Among women, 43.5 per cent completed high school or equivalent, while only 1/3 of men had this level of education.' IBGE in the Brazilian Survey per Sampling of Residences (PNDA) 2006 16. Available at: www.ibge.gov.br/home/estatistica/populacao/trabalhoerendimento/pnad2006/comentarios2006.pdf.

[100] RAIS 2000 and RAIS 2001—TEM/SPPE/DES/CGETIP (Chart Brazil—average compensation in real prices in May 2002, per education level, per gender).

[101] An analysis of Brazil's labour market still demonstrates a situation of wage inequality. A study by Cristina Bruschini showed that the women earn about 64% of the male wage on average. Despite the difficulty in establishing objective criteria to determine the value of the work, criteria include the exerted function, the time spent at the workplace, the amount of working hours and the requisite professional qualifications. In relation to this last point, it is interesting to note that 'two thirds of men with 15 and more years of study gain 10 minimum wages more than, only one third of women with the same qualification level have incomes equivalents'. (Free translation) Bruschini, C, 'Gênero e Trabalho no Brasil: novas conquistas ou persistência da discriminação? (Brazil, 1985795)' in da Rocha, MIB (ed),

The first laws related to the employment of women in Brazil were introduced in the 1930s.[102] The first rule appeared in 1932, Decree No 21417-A, which set out, inter alia, 'a prohibition on night work and work in underground mines, stone quarries, public works and in dangerous and unhealthy services' and gave a right to eight weeks' maternity pay at half pay. Prior to this, a number of bills had been debated and never approved, such as the discussions regarding a proposed Labour Law Code in 1917. This Bill proposed a prohibition on women working at night, and called for an eight-hour workday, statutory maternity pay, and the freedom for a woman to commence an employment relationship without requiring her husband's permission.[103] The reactions against these provisions were vehement, including that of a congressman, as cited by Segadas Vianna: 'A woman's salary shall never be a regular salary. It is solely a tip. That is why the most sensate writers are right when asserting that women's work, economically anti-social, is, from the moral point of view, profoundly immoral.'[104] The evolution of Brazilian law on gender discrimination follows a similar path to international law: moving from predominantly prohibitive and paternalistic rules towards a combination of protective and promotional rules, based on the principle of equality. This principle requires a reasonable difference to justify a differentiated treatment of men and women, so as not to make it more difficult for women to join the workforce. Unreasonable differences can limit the use of the female workforce by the employer and raise the cost for women's work, specifically as regards to certain work conditions, such as night work and unhealthy or risky activities.[105] Brazilian labour law has followed this trend since 1989, with Law No 7855, by revoking a series of prohibitive provisions related to women's work (as regards extra time, night work and unhealthy, hard

Trabalho e Gênero: mudanças, permanências e desafios (São Paulo, Campinas, ABEP, NEPO/ UNICAMP E CEDEPLAR/UFMG, 2000) 47.

[102] Süssekind, A et al, *Instituições de Direito do Trabalho*, 19th edn (São Paulo, LTr, 2000) vol 2 969.

[103] Ibid 967.

[104] *Documentos Parlamentares. Legislação Social*, v. 3 (Rio de Janeiro: Tipografia do 'Jornal do Comércio', 1919) at 244. Süssekind, A et al, *Instituições de Direito do Trabalho*, (Sao Paulo: LTr, 2000) 967.

[105] In the case of the ILO, the normative change (of prohibitive measures to promote equality in the workplace) took place in 1975, upon the adoption of the Declaration on Equality of Opportunity and Treatment for Women Workers: 'Convinced that the persistence of discrimination against women workers is incompatible with the interests of the economy and social justice, it states that the protection of women at work shall be an integral part of the efforts aimed at improving living and working conditions of all employees, and that women shall be protected from risks inherent in their employment and occupation on the same basis and with the same standards of protection as men. It also emphasizes that positive special treatment during a transitional period aimed at effective equality between the sexes shall not be regarded as discriminatory.'

and risky activities), which are now governed by the same rules related to men's work.[106]

The 1988 Constitution states broadly that 'men and women have equal rights and obligations' (article 5 subparagraph I). Article 7 sets out the fundamental rights of women workers, guaranteeing the rights to statutory maternity pay for 120 days, without any loss of employment or salary (sub-paragraph XVIII),[107] specific legislative incentives for women's protection in the labour market (subparagraph XX), and a prohibition on discrimination in relation to recruitment and employment on the grounds of sex, age, colour or civil status (subparagraph XXX).

However, despite these broad constitutional rights, gender inequality pervades many different stages of the employment relationship, as follows:

— At the recruitment stage, when preconceptions about child-bearing, domestic responsibilities, physical strengths and traditional gender roles may be taken into account regardless of their relevance to the objective requirements of the position.
— As the employment relationship develops, and men and women are subject to different working conditions, particularly regarding remuneration.
— As promotions are decided on, and women may be overlooked for managerial roles.
— As women are dismissed on the grounds of marital status or pregnancy.
— In vocational training, with the application of amounts intended for worker qualification.

Therefore, gender discrimination in the workplace entails not only unequal conditions of employment but also unequal access to opportunity in employment, including access to the workplace at the recruitment stage and promotions. As a result, certain legislative reforms have sought to address gender discrimination at different stages of the employment relationship.

In 1999, article 373-A[108] on the protection of women's work was included in chapter III of the CLT, with provisions to prohibit discrimination in recruitment, dismissal, vocational training, promotion and remuneration. Law No 9029 of 1995 made it a criminal offence to require a certificate regarding a woman's pregnancy or sterilisation, the provision of any inducement to genetic sterilisation and the promotion of birth control in the workplace (article 2). This prohibition is echoed by article 373-A

---

[106] See art 372 and c III of the CLT.
[107] In 2008, Law No 11770 was approved. According to the new law, employers can voluntarily extend paid maternity leave for 60 days. While during the mandatory 120 days leave, the Social Security pays for the woman's wage; the employer will pay the wages during these 60 days. However, this value can be discounted in the employer's taxes.
[108] Law No 9,799 of 26 May 1999.

subparagraph IV of the CLT, which prohibits the requirement of a certificate or an examination of any nature to determine sterility or pregnancy, prior to or during the employment relationship. According to article 4 of Law No 9029/95, if the employment relationship is terminated on the grounds of pregnancy, the employee may opt to be reinstated or to receive double the pay required for the notice period.

Regarding the criteria for recruitment, article 373-A prohibits job advertisements from including reference to sex, age, colour or family status, except where it relates to an inherent requirement of the job (subparagraph I). It also prohibits the dismissal or the denial of employment or promotion on the grounds of sex, age, colour or family status except where it relates to an inherent requirement of the job. An inherent requirement must be reasonable; for example, the requirement of the use of physical strength within the limits set out in the law. However, the effectiveness of this anti-discrimination law is hampered by a constitutional rule regarding arbitrary dismissal (subparagraph I of article 7 of the Federal Constitution). Article 10, subparagraph I of the Transitory Constitutional Provisions Act requires only compensation in the event of dismissal without cause, with no obligation on the employer to give a reason for the dismissal. This makes it more difficult to produce evidence of discrimination; however, it should be noted that discrimination does not depend on intention, and the case analysis is linked to its objective aspects.[109]

The legislation still needs to incorporate some key ILO conventions. For example, the ILO's Maternity Protection Convention No 183, which was approved in 2000 and has not been yet ratified by Brazil, applies to all workers, including those in atypical employment relationships.[110] Here I used the official language of the ILO. It is not a translation. Brazil is also yet to ratify Convention No 156 on Workers with Family Responsibilities, adopted in 1981. This Convention recognises that gender equality is only possible where family responsibilities are shared equally between men and women, and that men and women must not subjected to discrimination

---

[109] As noted by the ILO's Committee of Experts in relation to Convention No 111, 'as regards the few complaints related to discriminatory acts considering the important anti-discriminatory legal provision, the lecturer stressed that the labour law in Brazil is one of the most flexible in the world. For this reason, the employer has no obligation to indicate the reason to dismiss the employee. This one can only submit to the courts the request for indemnification for pain and suffering and losses suffered, which is difficult to prove.' Examination of the individual case related to Convention No 111, Discrimination (Employment and Occupation) 1958 Brazil (ratification in 1965), published in 2000.

[110] Convention No 183 of the ILO on Protection of Maternity 2000: 'Article 3—Each Member shall, after consulting the representative organizations of employers and workers, adopt appropriate measures to ensure that pregnant or breastfeeding women are not obliged to perform work which has been determined by the competent authority to be prejudicial to the health of the mother or the child, or where an assessment has established a significant risk to the mother's health or that of her child.'

on the grounds of family responsibilities. The preamble to this Convention refers specifically to paragraph XIV of the Preamble of the UN Convention on the Elimination of all Forms of Discrimination against Women, noting that 'a change in the traditional role of men as well as the role of women in society and in the family is needed to achieve full equality between men and women'.

Besides legislative intervention, collective bargaining is the most important mechanism for regulating labour relations and an essential instrument for implementing gender equality. As opposed to legislation, collective bargaining allows for the tailoring of rules to different industrial sectors or economic activities, where discrimination manifests in different ways. A 2001 report makes some interesting conclusions regarding the inclusion of gender issues in collective agreements, particularly in relation to women's specific needs in light of the changing nature of the workplace. For example, women's concerns and needs are often overlooked in discussions regarding overtime and absences as criteria for profit and results sharing.[111] In addition, other notable omissions include gender-specific issues regarding promotion, training and professional incentive programmes, clauses related to occupational and reproductive health, sexual harassment and precariousness of employment.[112] It should be emphasised that legislation alone cannot end gender discrimination and other aspects of labour law, such as collective agreements, and must also seek to implement gender equality, paying careful attention to existing and emerging issues for women in the workplace.

In summary, Brazil's legislative framework clearly prohibits discrimination on the grounds of gender, in accordance with the principles of international law; however, in practice, discrimination against women in the workplace continues. This is not to say that existing legislation, including the fundamental rights guaranteed by the 1988 Constitution, is without value. To the contrary, although it may not be as effective as is desirable, the evolution of Brazil's anti-discrimination laws is a basic and crucial step towards eliminating inequality.

Article 5 subparagraph I of the Constitution provides a broad guiding principle for equality between men and women, influencing the regulation of female participation in the labour market. As previously observed, this regulation is no longer characterised by a set of paternalistic rules imposing prohibitions and protections, but by rules which aim to equalise working conditions for men and women and to exclude discrimination.

---

[111] Fund for Equality of Genders, *Gênero no Mundo do Trabalho: I Encontro de Intercâmbio de Experiências do Fundo de Gênero no Brasil* (Brasília, Canadian Agency for the International Development, 2001) 162.
[112] Ibid at 162–63.

At the same time, the ongoing existence of gender discrimination is not overlooked, requiring public policy to promote gender equality in the workplace, including through affirmative action. Government policy should identify the main obstacles to women's participation in the labour market and the possibilities for realising the fundamental right to equality. This will require a new balance in the situation of men and women with regard to employment rights and opportunities, guaranteeing equal access to vocational training, secure employment, equal remuneration and fair conditions.[113]

CONCLUSIONS

This chapter has aimed to examine certain aspects of 'labour rights as human rights' in Brazil. Taking as a reference point those rights acknowledged by the ILO 1998 Declaration, we have reviewed the right to the freedom of association and the prohibition on gender discrimination at work. Both are equally important and equally problematic in practice. The acknowledgment and evolution of those rights, however, take place in very different ways.

In a strict legal sense, Brazilian workers benefit from a clearly expressed set of labour rights, acknowledged as fundamental rights by the Federal Constitution. However, a closer inspection reveals the difficulties of realising these rights in practice. The importance of fully respecting and applying these fundamental rights should be acknowledged both by the law and by society itself. This is the exemplar of freedom of association in Brazil.

---

[113] Analysing the compliance with Convention No 111 by Brazil, an Expert Committee of the ILO stresses the importance and profoundness which must characterise said policies. 'The reason for the bad results achieved by the official policies and the legislative measures has its origin in the adoption of policies purely "cosmetic", and this despite the dimension of the issue. The realization of domestic seminars attended by one hundred participants or the distribution of explanatory pamphlets is insignificant as regards a population of 160 million inhabitants. Although these actions are necessary, they are, at the same time, insufficient. The effective application of the Convention requires the adoption of active policies of integration of the black population, women, Indians, and sexual minorities, which would be, for instance, to reserve work positions in the public administration or the conditioning of the public assistance to private companies considering the respect for the anti-discriminatory rules. Despite the state-owned companies had to be the example, the first case of discrimination judged by the Higher Labour Court referred to a public company. Furthermore, the employers had to be persuaded by the Government to carry out an active policy of non-discrimination and, concretely, through a system of professional education managed by them. Said system had to finance the professional education aimed for the integration of people excluded as a result of race or sex.' Examination of the individual case related to Convention No 111, Discrimination (Employment and Occupation) 1958 Brazil (ratified in 1965) and published in 2000.

Starting our review with the freedom of association, currently in Brazil we cannot separate the recognition of this right from the transformations in our trade union structure and, in a broader way, from debates regarding the modernisation of labour law. In these debates, the central criticisms of labour law are that state intervention is excessive and that labour relations are overregulated, with no room left for collective autonomy. The argument is that overregulation results in legal uncertainty for workers and employers and further costs to the economy and, most importantly, means that the system is unable to deal with post-globalisation problems that afflict the labour market.

We agree that there is an expectation in Brazil that a new law can always solve a new problem. Thus, uncontrolled and unsystematic normative production by the state creates confusion and is not a very effective tool to protect workers. The size of Brazil's informal economy and high levels of litigation[114] confirm this assumption. However, we believe that the major reason for this is not the protective character of labour law. The solution is not to deregulate the protective labour law system, which is the only way for some workers to live with dignity. The intense regulation in Brazil is not the natural result of a protective labour law, but stems from the lack of freedom of association.

If the modernisation of labour law in Brazil allows increased scope for collective bargaining, how can collective bargaining be an effective means of labour regulation while the trade union structure is still lagging behind in the old corporatist order? Brazil needs trade union reform, or it runs the risk of getting left behind and remaining mired in the debate about unicity and the lack of freedom of association. While other countries are already exploring new forms of collective organisation and bargaining, including transnational negotiation,[115] we still remain attached to the imposition of category, unicity and mandatory trade union dues.

In the case of the prohibition on discrimination at work, gender discrimination remains a problem. Violations of the fundamental right to equality still persist as everyday practices. However, in contrast to the right to freedom of association, the prohibition on gender discrimination in the labour market is an interesting example of how the status of fundamental rights can be used by workers to achieve better opportunities and better labour conditions.

---

[114] Two million complaints are filed in the labour courts every year. News of the Higher Labour Court, *Vanutil acredita que medo do desemprego explica redução de ações* (26 December 2003) is available at: http://ext02.tst.gov.br/pls/no01/no_noticias.Exibe_Noticia?p_cod_noticia=3462&p_cod_area_noticia=ASCS.

[115] *Cf* Lévesque, C et al, 'Building International Union Alliances in the Americas: Prospects and Limits for Union Renewal' in *Social Actors, Work Organization and New Technologies* (Lima: Universidad de Lima, 2006) 507–23.

The rules adopted by the ILO have had an undeniable influence on Brazilian legislation. For example, it has led to the development of a perspective that equality can only be reached by improving social conditions for both men and women rather than through imposing prohibitive, restrictive or special measures in relation to women's employment. The argument that gender discrimination in the workplace is a violation of fundamental rights can be found in the decisions of the labour courts[116] and in justifications for public policies.

This chapter has analysed the recognition and guarantee of labour rights as human rights, using freedom of association and gender discrimination as case studies. This chapter suggests that legislative progress has been made in relation to gender discrimination, despite the persistence of the gender wage gap and discriminatory practices. This evolution also includes transformations that have taken place outside the workplace, such as educational and cultural changes, and has been supported by greater legal recognition of equality as a fundamental right. In particular, the Constitution guarantees the status of women as a subject whose fundamental rights must be respected. This is progress, in particular, when observing how recent this change is in the legal order. In the case of freedom of association, however, the restriction of a fundamental freedom remains. The fundamental right to freedom of association is not fully recognised either politically or legally. This is demonstrated by Brazil's ongoing failure to ratify ILO Convention No 87 and to reform its corporatist trade union structure.

The permanence of this corporatist order stopped serving the rationale for corporatism a long time ago and is maintained only by virtue of the interests of those participating in the system in limiting freedom of association. The adoption of legislation to allocate a percentage of mandatory trade union dues to the central trade unions without accompanying requirements for accountability is the most recent example of how this system is sustained. Historically, the central trade unions had supported greater freedom of association, in opposition to the unicity rule, but now they seem content to be part of this system. The modernisation and democratisation of Brazil's labour relations system depends on the end of the corporatist system and the recognition and application of the freedom of association as a worker's fundamental right. However, there is not enough consensus among the social partners to promote the necessary reforms.

---

[116] For instance, the decision by the 6th Panel of the Higher Labour Court: 'Considering the depositions above transcribed, the discriminatory character of the attitudes of the claimant, hierarchical superior was proven. It is incredible that in the threshold of the third millennium feelings of depreciation for a human being are found, resulting from sex, belief, race, color, civil status, social position or any other different trace within a group. Respect for the human being, regardless of said aspects, as well as the inviolability of honour and image, are constitutional rights raised as one of the grounds of the Democratic Legal State itself, that is to say, dignity (Art. 1, III, Federal Constitution)'. Case No AIRR—560/2005-013-10-40. Published in the Judiciary Gazette on 17 November 2006.

4

The Growing Impact of Human Rights on Canadian Labour Law*

CHRISTIAN BRUNELLE

IF THE DEFINING characteristic of Canadian labour law were to be summed up in a word, the term 'dualism' might be generally agreed upon. Moreover, the dualism that is predominant here appears to be multidimensional.

First, from a *political* point of view, Canada is a federation in which power is shared by the Federal Parliament, on the one hand, and the legislatures of each of its 10 provinces, on the other hand. According to the terms of Canada's Constitution, these provincial legislatures have exclusive power to govern 'Property and Civil Rights in the Province' and 'Generally all Matters of a merely local or private Nature in the Province'.[1] The Canadian provinces are thus recognised as having general jurisdiction in the area of labour.[2] However, the Federal Parliament has sole authority to govern the working conditions in institutions and companies that come under its fields of constitutional jurisdiction.[3] For example, federal government employees or employees of the postal service, banks, airlines, shipping companies or railways or those working for broadcasting and telecommunications firms are subject exclusively to federal labour laws.[4]

At a *cultural* level, in Canada, two distinct societies, in terms of language and tradition, live side by side. According to data compiled by Statistics Canada, English is the native language of 57.8 per cent of Canadians, while French is the mother tongue of 22.1 per cent. It should be noted that slightly

---

* This chapter refers to materials available as at 1 January 2009.

[1] The Constitution Act 1867 30 & 31 Victoria c 3 (UK) s 92(13) and (16).

[2] *Toronto Electric Commissioners v Snider* [1925] AC 396 (HL) at 403; *Reference in the matter of Legislative Jurisdiction over Hours of Labour* [1925] SCR 505; *AG for Canada v AG for Ontario* [1937] AC 326 (HL); *Construction Montcalm Inc v Minimum Wage Commission* [1979] 1 SCR 754 at 768.

[3] *Reference as to the Applicability of the Minimum Wage Act of Saskatchewan to an employee of a Revenue Post Office* [1948] SCR 248; *Bell Canada v Québec* (CSST) [1988] 1 SCR 749.

[4] Canada Labour Code RSC 1985 c L-2 s 2.

over 79 per cent of these Francophones are concentrated in the province of Quebec. However, it is now probably more accurate to describe Canada in terms of cultural diversity rather than cultural duality.

In the *legal* sphere, this Canadian duality is expressed through two different systems of law covering relations between parties under private law. While civil law, inspired by the French system, constitutes the *jus commune* in Quebec and, as such, governs 'personal rights, relations and property',[5] *common law*, of British origin, applies everywhere else in Canada. When it comes to relations between parties covered by public law, however, 'those *common law* rules that are public in nature' are applied even in Quebec.[6] This influence of British law moreover carries with it 'a dualist conception of domestic law and international law', considered by Canadian law to be 'two distinct legal orders that operate in their own spheres'.[7] Consequently, international treaties and conventions concluded by the Canadian Government will not be directly applied in domestic law, unless the Federal Parliament or a provincial legislative assembly—based on their respective jurisdictions—incorporates them and transposes them into law.[8]

While each of these dimensions of Canadian dualism contributes in its own way to shaping labour law in Canada, the dimension that exerts the greatest influence in the current context is, rather, of a *philosophical* nature. Indeed, two currents of thought run through Canadian law today, highlighting two different approaches to labour relations.

The first approach, which is rooted in history, postulates that employees, organised into unions, can, through autonomous collective bargaining of their working conditions, impose respect for their fundamental dignity (**A.**). The second approach, which is more contemporary, instead advocates state intervention in labour relations so as to ensure better protection, by operation of law, of the fundamental rights of employees (**B.**). While both of these approaches can contribute effectively to the recognition and exercise of rights and freedoms at work, it can be seen by the current state of law that the courts are experiencing considerable difficulty reconciling the different principles underlying them.

---

[5] Civil Code of Québec SQ 1991 c 64.

[6] *Prud'Homme v Prud'Homme* [2002] 4 SCR 663 (§ 46). See generally, Lemieux, D, 'The Role of the Civil Code of Québec in Administrative Law' (2005) 18 *Canadian Journal of Administrative Law & Practice* 143.

[7] Brun, H, Tremblay, G and Brouillet, E, *Droit constitutionnel*, 5th edn (Cowansville (Québec), Les éditions Yvon Blais inc, 2008) 650 (translation).

[8] *Baker v Canada (Minister of Citizenship and Immigration)* [1999] 2 RSC 817 (§ 69); *Suresh v Canada* [2002] 1 SCR 3, 38 (§ 60). See generally, LeBel, L and Chao, G, 'The Rise of International Law in Canadian Constitutional Litigation: Fugue or Fusion? Recent Developments and Challenges in Internalizing International Law' (2002) 16 *Supreme Court Law Review* 35; Trudeau, G, 'Les droits fondamentaux de l'Homme au travail: de la logique internationale à la logique canadienne' in I Daugareilh (ed), *Mondialisation, travail et droits fondamentaux* (Brussels, Bruylant, 2005) 317–18.

THE EVOLUTION OF FREEDOM OF ASSOCIATION

Canadian law has long recognised the right of employees to form unions and bargain collectively for their working conditions (1.). However, this system, which was inspired by the system in the United States, does not have the benefit of full constitutional protection (2.), and this makes it vulnerable in the face of the rising tide of individualism and the neo-liberal ideology.

From the Right to Organise to the Collective Agreement

A brief look at the history of labour relations in Canada reveals that the right to organise to bargain collectively for working conditions is the result of a long process of maturation, marked by three successive stages: repression, neutrality, and finally, state recognition.[9]

Initially, Canadian law saw unions in the same light as unlawful conspiracy, liable to penal and civil sanctions. The adoption of the Trade Unions Act 1872[10] brought workers a degree of immunity such that the exercise of their trade union rights was no longer viewed from the outset as an illegal hindrance to the freedom of trade. However, this did not prevent the courts from issuing injunctions to stop pressure tactics being used against employers.[11] This attitude on the part of Canadian judges gave them—and to some observers, still gives them—the reputation of being fundamentally anti-union.[12]

The Great Depression that hit North America at the end of the 1920s prompted the United States' political establishment to carry out several reforms. Thus began the era of the New Deal. Legislative recognition of employees' right to bargain collectively for their working conditions was one of the changes experimented with.

Confronted with a wave of strikes punctuated with violent confrontations, the United States Government created the National Labor

---

[9] Arthurs, HW, 'Labour Law Without the State' (1996) 46 *University of Toronto Law Journal* 1, 3; Fudge, J, 'Voluntarism, Compulsion and the Transformation of Canadian Labour Law during World War II' in G Kealey and G Patmore (eds), *Canadian and Australian Labour History: Towards a Comparative Perspective,* (St-John, Committee on Canadian Labour History, 1990) 83.

[10] Trade Unions Act 1872 35 Victoria c 30.

[11] Fudge, J and Tucker, E, *Labour before the Law: The Regulation of Workers' Collective Action in Canada, 1900–1948* (Toronto, Oxford University Press, 2001) 18–34; McCallum, M, 'Labour and the Liberal State: Regulating the Employment Relationship, 1867–1920' (1996) 23 *Manitoba Law Journal* 574, 577–79.

[12] Arthurs, HW, 'Developing Industrial Citizenship: A Challenge For Canada's Second Century' (1967) 45 *Canadian Bar Review* 786, 814 and 829; Fudge, J and Glasbeek, H, 'The Legacy of PC 1003' (1995) 3 *Canadian Labour & Employment Law Journal* 357, 395–96.

Commission, presided over by Senator Robert Ferdinand Wagner. Senator Wagner came up against the resistance of employers to his various attempts to improve labour relations.[13] He thus became aware of the need to create a legal framework around the negotiation process, while radically altering the balance of power between employers and employees, addressing its inequalities by extending greater powers to the unions. He believed that it was necessary to recognise the social role played by trade unionism.

On 5 July 1935, the National Labor Relations Act came into force.[14] The aim of this American law was, in particular, to promote industrial peace by establishing a more equitable bargaining relationship between the employer and the employees, thus contributing to the democratisation of the workplace.[15]

In order to accomplish this, the law explicitly recognised the right of association of employees. To this end, it provided for certification, a legal mechanism which allowed the union chosen by a majority of employees to obtain the *exclusive* right to negotiate the working conditions of these same employees.[16] By thus forcing the employer to recognise the right of employees to form or join an association to negotiate their working conditions through collective action, the American legislator granted the employee a powerful tool to combat arbitrary action on the part of the employer.[17]

It is precisely this model that was then imported into Canada. While the Second World War continued, Privy Council Order 1003, decreed under the authority of the War Measures Act,[18] came into force on 20 March 1944.[19] Like the Wagner Act in the United States, this Canadian federal decree guaranteed employees a genuine right to impose on the employer the collective bargaining of their working conditions by the union of their choice.[20] Up until this time, the Canadian policy had essentially rested on a consensus-based approach: the employer was free to recognise or not the union association chosen by employees for the purpose of negotiating their working conditions.

[13] Rayback, J, *A History of American Labor* (New York, Free Press, 1966) 330; Schlesinger Jr, A, *The Coming of the New Deal* (Boston, Riverside Press Cambridge, 1959) 146–47.

[14] National Labor Relations Act 49 Stat 499 (1935).

[15] Brudney, J, 'A Famous Victory: Collective Bargaining Protections and the Statutory Aging Process' (1996) 74 *North Carolina Law Review* 939, 950–51.

[16] *U.E.S., local 98 v Bibeault* [1988] 2 SCR 1048, 1099: 'Certification is a mechanism whereby an association which counts among its members an absolute majority of all an employer's employees, or of a separate group of an employer's employees, is recognized as the sole representative of those employees to this employer for collective bargaining purposes.'

[17] Hall, B, 'Collective Bargaining and Workers' Liberty' in G Ezorsky (ed), *Moral Rights in the Workplace* (New-York, State University of New York Press, 1987) 165.

[18] War Measures Act RSC 1927 vol IV c 206.

[19] Journals of the House of Commons of the Dominion of the Canada vol 84 1945 8 Geo. VI, 202.

[20] Fudge, 'Voluntarism, Compulsion and the Transformation of Canadian Labour Law during World War II' (1990) 81.

Emboldened by the gains made by their comrades in the United States—who were now governed by the Wagner Act—Canadian unions had stepped up the pressure on the Federal Government to begin imposing collective bargaining on employers. The population, a large part of which was working to support the war effort, had gradually taken sides with the workers' movement. Caught in the trap of its own logic, which consisted in arguing for a consensus-based system while imposing wage ceilings to contain inflation,[21] the Canadian Government finally gave in.

Although federal authorities considered the recognition of the principle sanctioned by PC 1003 as a temporary measure,[22] the Canadian Government was no longer able to challenge the legitimacy of the system of collective bargaining after the war had ended. PC 1003 thus paved the way for the Canada Labour Code,[23] which is still in force today.

Furthermore, each of the Canadian provinces also took inspiration from the US model in recognising the right to collectively negotiate working conditions. Thus, certified unions were granted a legal monopoly of representation, in all jurisdictions across Canada. What exclusive representation took away from employees in terms of their contractual freedom, it was presumed to give back by establishing, in their favour, a more equitable balance of power at the negotiating table.[24] That said, whether an employee reveres or despises the elected union, sides with or stands against its policies, and esteems or abhors its leaders, the employee must, by force of law, hand over to it the freedom to negotiate his or her own working conditions:[25]

> The collective agreement is implemented, first and foremost, between the union and the employer. Certification, followed by the collective agreement, takes away the employer's right to negotiate directly with its employees. Because of its exclusive representation function, the presence of the union erects a screen between the employer and the employees. The employer loses the option of negotiating different conditions of employment with individual employees.[26]

---

[21] Ibid 89.

[22] MacDowell, L, 'The Formation of the Canadian Industrial Relations System During World War Two' in L MacDowell and I Radforth (ed), *Canadian Working Class History; Selected Readings* (Toronto, Canadian Scholars' Press, 1992) 583 and 590.

[23] Mahoney, D, *Adjudication of Human Rights Disputes Under the Collective Agreement, Current Issues Series* (Kingston, Industrial Relations Centre, Queen's University, 1993) 4; Weiler, P, 'The National Labor Relations Act: 1935–1985' in W Gershenfeld (ed), *Arbitration 1985: Law and Practice, Proceedings of the 38th Annual Meeting, National Academy of Arbitrators* (Washington D.C., Bureau of National Affairs Inc, 1986) 40.

[24] Dulude, L, *Seniority and Employment Equity for Women* (Kingston, IRC Press, 1995) 54–55; Swinton, K, 'Accommodating Equality in the Unionized Workplace' (1996) 33 *Osgoode Hall Law Journal* 703, 725.

[25] *Syndicat catholique des employés de magasins de Québec Inc. v Compagnie Paquet Ltée* [1959] SCR 206, 212; *McGavin Toastmaster Ltd v Ainscough* [1976] 1 SCR 718, 724–725; *Hémond v Coopérative fédérée du Québec* [1989] 2 SCR 962, 975.

[26] *Noël v Société d'énergie de la Baie James* [2001] 2 SCR 207, 228 (§ 42). See also *Bisaillon v Concordia University* [2006] 1 SCR 666, 682–84 (§ 24 to 28). As mentioned

While the presence of a certified union in a particular company prevents the employer from negotiating for a decline in the working conditions of a given employee, neither does it allow an employee to negotiate with the employer, on an individual basis, for better working conditions. Thus, each employee remains *individually* tied to the working conditions negotiated by the union on behalf of all employees *collectively*.

In order to counterbalance this monopoly of representation and regulate the possible tensions between the rights of the majority and those of the minority, the law imposes on the certified union the duty of fair representation. Thus, the latter must not act in an arbitrary or discriminatory manner, or show bad faith toward an employee, whether or not he or she is a member of the union.[27]

Nevertheless, the role of the state in determining working conditions remains very modest. The content of the collective agreement is left up to the free play of negotiation between the parties who enjoy a high degree of autonomy in this regard. This is why the terms of collective agreements can vary considerably from one company to another. Generally speaking, the collective agreement can include provisions relating to pay, leave and benefits, working hours, job classifications and descriptions, the procedure involved in relocation, transfer or promotion within the company, technological changes, and discipline, among others. In fact, it can contain any provision concerning the conditions of employment and any related matter.[28]

In Canada, the use of pressure tactics, such as a strike or lock-out, is prohibited throughout the entire duration of the collective agreement. Should a conflict arise between the parties concerning the application or interpretation of the collective agreement, a grievance must be submitted to a specialised arbitration tribunal. Here also, the parties enjoy a high degree of autonomy. They must agree on the identity of the grievance arbitrator who will hear the dispute. The latter can be a lawyer but this is not always the case. Generally speaking, the rules governing proof and procedure which apply to arbitration hearings are drawn up in the collective agreement.

---

by the Supreme Court of Canada in *Isidore Garon ltée v Tremblay; Fillion et Frères (1976) inc v Syndicat national des employés de garage du Québec inc* [2006] 1 SCR 27, 44 (§ 27): 'During the term of the collective agreement, however, the individual contract of employment cannot be relied on as a source of rights.'

[27] *Canadian Merchant Service Guild v Gagnon* [1984] 1 SCR 509; *Centre hospitalier Regina ltée v Labour Court* [1990] 1 SCR 1330; *Noël v Société d'énergie de la Baie James* [2001] 2 SCR 207. See generally, Bentham, K, 'The Duty of Fair Representation in the Negotiation of Collective Agreements', School of Industrial Relations Research Essay Series No 38 (Kingston, Industrial Relations Centre, Queen's University, 1991); Christian, T, 'The Developing Duty of Fair Representation,' (1991) II Labour Arbitration Yearbook 3.

[28] Nadeau, D, 'Droit du travail du Québec; une transformation dans la diversité culturelle' in L Vogel (dir), *La globalisation du droit des affaires: mythe ou réalité?*, coll. Droit Global/ Global Law (Paris, Université Panthéon-Assas, 2001/2) 85.

It should be noted that the grievance arbitrator has *exclusive* jurisdiction in determining 'whether the conduct giving rise to the dispute between the parties arises either expressly or inferentially out of the collective agreement between them'.[29] That said, the intervention of the courts in this matter is clearly laid out in Canadian law. Unless the decision taken by the arbitrator, in applying the collective agreement, exceeds the powers assigned to him by law, defies procedural fairness[30] or is marked by an unreasonable error, the judges will give due consideration to the determinations of the arbitrator and refuse to intervene.[31]

As can be seen, the Canadian system of collective labour relations is highly decentralised. It provides the parties with considerable room for autonomy in negotiating the working conditions that will be applied company-wide. Subject to the limits imposed by the law or public order, the parties thus have the power to draw up a collective agreement which is fully adapted to life within the company and its particular realities.[32]

From Freedom of Association to Trade Union Rights

The Canadian Charter of Rights and Freedoms has been part of the Constitution of Canada since 1982. Although the Charter is relatively recent, its approach is rather classical and is strongly in keeping with the tradition of liberal individualism, which may explain why the Canadian Charter mainly consecrates civil and political rights rather than social, economic and cultural rights[33]:

> It is surprising to note that the *Canadian Charter*, which nevertheless dates from 1982, is practically silent on all economic, social and cultural rights which are, moreover, affirmed by international documents ... The *Canadian Charter* is above all focused on protection by the state, and especially from the state, of the rights and freedoms of the individual person. [...] In this respect, the *Canadian Charter* is more like a liberal declaration of the 18th and 19th centuries than a charter of the late 20th century.[34]

---

[29] *Weber v Ontario Hydro* [1995] 2 SCR 929, 963.

[30] *Université du Québec à Trois-Rivières v Larocque* [1993] 1 SCR 471.

[31] *Dunsmuir v New Brunswick* [2008] 1 SCR 190.

[32] Nadeau, 'Droit du travail du Québec; une transformation dans la diversité culturelle' (2001/2) 87.

[33] Arthurs, H, 'Labour and the "Real" Constitution' (2007) 48 *Cahiers de droit* 43; Coutu, M, *Les libertés syndicales dans le secteur public*, coll. Minerve, Cowansville (Québec), Les éditions Yvon Blais, 1989 120; Vandycke, R, 'La Charte constitutionnelle et les droits économiques, sociaux et culturels' (1989–90) 6 *Canadian Human Rights Yearbook* 170.

[34] Rocher, G, 'Les fondements de la société libérale, les relations industrielles et les Chartes' in R Blouin et al (ed), *Les Chartes des droits et les relations industrielles*, (Québec, Presses de l'Université Laval, 1988) 12–13 [translation]. See also Jackman, M, 'Constitutional Rhetoric and Social Justice: Reflections on Justiciability Debate' in J Bakan and D Schneiderman (eds),

Section 2(d) of the Charter recognises the 'freedom of association' of 'everyone'. During the debates preceding the adoption of the Charter, some elected officials suggested adding, at the end of this provision, the words 'including the freedom to organize and bargain collectively'.[35] This proposal was not accepted, however, essentially because it was considered that the concept of 'freedom of association' was broad enough to include trade union rights.[36] The courts, however, would not interpret it in the same way.

In order to define constitutional 'freedom of association', judges, from the outset, established a distinction between associational activity, on the one hand, and the goals of an association, on the other hand, such that 'freedom of association protects only the associational aspect of activities, not the activity itself'.[37] In fact, this freedom was reserved for 'the individual and not for the group formed through its exercise':[38]

> [...] freedom of association means the freedom to associate for the purposes of activities which are lawful when performed alone. But, since the fact of association will not by itself confer additional rights on individuals, the association does not acquire a constitutionally guaranteed freedom to do what is unlawful for the individual.[39]

Understood in this light, freedom of association essentially protected the 'freedom to work for the establishment of an association, to belong to an association, to maintain it, and to participate in its lawful activity without penalty or reprisal'[40] and without being exposed to any interference on the part of the employer in the formation of such an association.

Nevertheless, even though exercising the right to strike may have constituted the ultimate means for a union to attain its goals, this did not change the fact that a federal[41] or provincial[42] law could prohibit recourse to this

---

Social Justice and the Constitution: Perspectives on a Social Union for Canada (Ottawa (Canada), Carleton University Press, 1992) 26: 'It has often been remarked that the Canadian Charter of Rights and Freedoms is more reminiscent of a rights document from the nineteenth century than the twentieth century. This assessment is based on its failure to recognize the basic social rights [...] which are contained in most modern constitutions, and which are well established in international human rights law. To many, this is all the more surprising given Canada's ratification in 1978 of the International Covenant on Economic Social and Cultural Rights, and the country's longstanding social welfare traditions.'

[35] Minutes of Proceedings and Evidence of the Special Joint Committee of the Senate and of the House of Commons on the Constitution, Ottawa, 1st Session, 32nd Parliament, Issue No 43 (Thursday, 22 January 1981) 43:68 (Svend Robinson, New Democratic Party MP).

[36] Brunelle, C and Verge, P, 'L'inclusion de la liberté syndicale dans la liberté générale d'association: un pari constitutionnel perdu?' (2003) 82 *Canadian Bar Review* 711, 714.

[37] *Canadian Egg Marketing Agency v Richardson* [1998] 3 SCR 157 227 (§ 105).

[38] *Reference Re Public Service Employee Relations Act (Alberta)* [1987] 1 SCR 313, 397.

[39] Ibid 409.

[40] Ibid 391.

[41] *Public Service Alliance of Canada v Canada* [1987] 1 SCR 424.

[42] *Retail Wholesale and Department Store Union v Saskatchewan* [1987] 1 SCR 460.

pressure tactic, without the possibility of such a legislative decision being called into question on the basis of the Canadian Charter.

According to the same logic, a majority of judges concluded that although collective bargaining 'may be the essential purpose of the formation of trade unions', it 'is not an activity that is, without more, protected by the guarantee of freedom of association'. According to the Supreme Court of Canada, as collective bargaining was not 'an activity that may lawfully be performed by an individual',[43] the legislator could impose restrictions on it without infringing the freedom of association recognised by the Constitution.

It was not until the *Dunmore v Ontario (Attorney General)* ruling, delivered at the end of 2001,[44] that this interpretation, stamped entirely by individualism, was enriched with a more significant collective dimension.[45] Asked to rule on the validity of an Ontario law passed in 1995, which repealed another law, adopted two years earlier, in accordance with which agricultural workers in the province had obtained trade union rights, the Supreme Court of Canada declared the abrogative law inoperative on the basis of s 2(d) of the Canadian Charter.

The Court recognised for the very first time that freedom of association can protect activities which are inherently 'collective in nature', in other words, which cannot, for one reason or another, be understood as the lawful activities of individuals. Emphasising, aptly, that 'individuals associate not simply because there is strength in numbers, but because communities can embody objectives that individuals cannot',[46] the Court added:

> [...] because trade unions develop needs and priorities that are distinct from those of their members individually, they cannot function if the law protects exclusively what might be 'the lawful activities of individuals.' Rather, the law must recognize that certain union activities—making collective representations to an employer, adopting a majority political platform, federating with other unions—may be central to freedom of association even though they are inconceivable on the individual level. This is not to say that all such activities are protected by s. 2(*d*), nor that all collectivities are worthy of constitutional protection; indeed, this Court has repeatedly excluded the right to strike and collectively bargain from the protected ambit of s. 2(*d*) [...]. It is to say, simply, that certain collective activities must be recognized if the freedom to form and maintain an association is to have any meaning.[47]

---

[43] *Professional Institute of the Public Service of Canada v Northwest Territories (Commissioner)* [1990] 2 SCR 367, 404–05.

[44] *Dunmore v Ontario (Attorney General)* [2001] 3 SCR 1016.

[45] Cameron, J, 'The "Second Labour Trilogy": A Comment on *R.* v. *Advance Cutting*, *Dunmore* v. *Ontario*, and *R.W.D.S.U.* v. *Pepsi-Cola*' (2002) 16 *Supreme Court Law Review* (2d) 67, 83.

[46] *Dunmore v Ontario (Attorney General)* [2001] 3 SCR 1016, 1039 (§ 16).

[47] Ibid.

For the Court, the 'core' of freedom of association thus included:

> the statutory freedom to organise [...] along with protections judged essential to its meaningful exercise, such as freedom to assemble, to participate in the lawful activities of the association and to make representations, and the right to be free from interference, coercion and discrimination in the exercise of these freedoms.[48]

The Court reached this conclusion in favour of workers who were characterised by 'political impotence, their lack of resources to associate without state protection' and, all things considered, 'their vulnerability to reprisal by their employers'.[49] It must be said that this particular factual context did not necessarily spark enthusiasm with regard to whether the Court would subsequently widen this opening that had suddenly appeared in its jurisprudence or whether it was going to strive instead to close it.

Judging by the recent *Health Services and Support—Facilities Subsector Bargaining Assn. v British Columbia*[50] ruling, the first hypothesis seems to be confirmed. In this case, six unions and eight unionised workers invoked their constitutional freedom of association against a provincial law aimed at lowering the costs and facilitating the efficient management of employees in the healthcare sector by granting the employer greater latitude to set working conditions as it saw fit. This law, adopted as quickly as possible in response to, in the Government's words, a 'crisis of sustainability' in the healthcare system,[51] included, in particular, provisions aimed at facilitating recourse to contracting out. The law had, moreover, the effect of invalidating important clauses in collective agreements that were in force at the time and of precluding any real negotiation on specified matters.

It should be noted that, before the Court delivered its ruling, a complaint against the Province of British Columbia had been filed with the International Labour Office. The Freedom of Association Committee had concluded that the provincial law contravened freedom of association principles on collective bargaining and, in particular, requested 'the Government to refrain from having recourse in future to legislatively imposed settlements, and to respect the autonomy of bargaining partners in reaching negotiated agreements'.[52]

---

[48] Ibid 1078 (§ 67).

[49] Ibid 1060 (§ 41).

[50] *Health Services and Support—Facilities Subsector Bargaining Assn. v British Columbia* [2007] 2 SCR 391.

[51] Ibid 406 (§ 4).

[52] *Canada (Case No 2180 Report No 330)* Complaint against the Government of Canada concerning the Province of British Columbia presented by the Canadian Labour Congress (CLC), the National Union of Public and General Employees (NUPGE), the British Columbia Government and Service Employees' Union (BCGSEU), the Health Sciences Association of British Columbia (HSA), the International Confederation of Free Trade Unions (ICFTU) and Public Services International (PSI) (Vol LXXXVI 2003 Series B No 1) (§ 305c). Available at <www.ilo.org/ilolex/cgi-lex/single.pl?query=0320033302166@ref&chspec=03.

At the outset, the Supreme Court of Canada acknowledged that the 'narrow focus' of its earlier rulings on the matter, based on 'the notion that freedom of association applies only to activities capable of performance by individuals' was 'overtaken by *Dunmore*.'[53] In the opinion of the Court, the concept of freedom of association under the Charter now includes 'a procedural right to collective bargaining':[54]

> [...] The constitutional right to collective bargaining concerns the protection of the ability of workers to engage in associational activities, and their capacity to act in common to reach shared goals related to workplace issues and terms of employment.[55]

Thus, the freedom of association guaranteed by the Canadian Constitution includes 'the collective right to good faith negotiations and consultation'.[56] Nevertheless, this right 'is a limited right'. On the one hand, it essentially concerns a 'process': there is no constitutional protection for the attainment of union members' objectives or the possible outcome of collective bargaining. On the other hand, the guarantee of freedom of association does not entail the right to demand any particular model of labour relations or even a specific bargaining method. Therefore, the Canadian system of collective labour relations based on a monopoly of union representation does not necessarily have any constitutional basis. Finally, only a *substantial* infringement of the freedom of association can justify an examination by the courts of the legislative provisions at issue.[57]

In order for the court to conclude that a Government measure constitutes a substantial infringement of the freedom of association, two conditions must be met. First, the measure must concern a matter that is 'important to the process of collective bargaining'.[58] Secondly, this measure must have been imposed without respect for 'the fundamental precept of collective bargaining—the duty to consult and negotiate in good faith'.[59]

Thus, in the *Health Services and Support* ruling, the Court held that the legislative measures having the effect of:

> not allowing the unions to restrict, through collective bargaining, the power of the employer to resort to contracting out;
>
> voiding provisions in existing collective agreements that impose on the employer an obligation to consult the union before resorting to contracting out;

---

[53] *Health Services and Support* [2007] 2 SCR 391 (§ 28).
[54] Ibid 433 (§ 66).
[55] Ibid 442 (§ 89).
[56] Ibid 450–51 (§ 107).
[57] Ibid 443–44 (§ 91).
[58] Ibid 447 and 451 (§ 97 et 109).
[59] Ibid 447 (§ 97).

prohibiting provisions in collective agreements that restrict, on the one hand, the power of the employer to lay off employees and that limit, on the other hand, the bumping rights of employees that have been laid off;

'constitute[d] a significant interference with the right to bargain collectively'.[60] Such infringements, the Court concluded, are not justifiable in a free and democratic society.

This ruling, delivered by the highest court in the land, thus opened a door which had been believed to be closed, thereby creating an enormous potential for the legal challenge to various government measures aimed at restricting access to union representation or limiting the exercise of collective bargaining. Evidently, the unions have not failed to exploit the possibilities inherent in this sudden change in the case law.

For example, the Court of Appeal for Ontario ruled that the Agricultural Employees Protection Act (AEPA),[61] which was enacted following the *Dunmore* ruling[62] in order to allow agricultural workers in Ontario to benefit from the minimum conditions for recognition of the freedom of association and the right to exercise this freedom as established by the Supreme Court of Canada, was nevertheless inoperative in light of the Canadian Charter. According to the Court of Appeal, the particular legislative regime established by the AEPA did not allow for sufficient protection of the procedural right to bargain collectively inferred by the constitutional freedom of association in the *Health Services and Support* ruling:

> It is important to note what is missing from the AEPA. It does not impose an obligation on employers to bargain in good faith—or, indeed, to bargain at all—with an employees' association. The AEPA does not include mechanisms to resolve either bargaining impasses or disputes regarding the interpretation or administration of the collective agreement. Another notable omission from the legislation is that it does not preclude the formation of multiple employees' associations within a single workplace, purporting to simultaneously represent employees in that same workplace with similar job functions.[63]

In Quebec, in order to counter the steps towards unionisation taken by individuals who were responsible for home child care, on the one hand, and offering home-based intermediate care for children or adults facing difficulties, on the other hand, the legislator adopted two laws[64] under which it withdrew from these individuals the status of 'employee' as defined in the

---

[60] Ibid 461 (§ 136).

[61] Agricultural Employees Protection Act S.O. 2002 c 16.

[62] *Fraser v Ontario (Attorney General)* 2008 ONCA 760 (CanLII) (application for leave to appeal to the Supreme Court of Canada granted: SCC No 32968).

[63] Ibid (§ 28).

[64] An Act to amend the Act respecting health services and social services, S.Q. 2003 c 12; An Act to amend the Act respecting childcare center and childcare services, S.Q. 2003 c 13.

Labour Code.[65] This effectively cancelled the union certification that had already been granted and ended the process of collective bargaining promoted by the Code, replacing it instead by a process of representation that was mainly dependent on government policies.

On 31 October 2008, the Superior Court of Quebec declared these two Quebec laws to be unconstitutional, invalid and ineffective given that they contravened freedom of association.[66] The Court noted that there had been substantial 'legislative interference' which had 'compromised the essential integrity of the collective bargaining process', a process which 'involves more than the actual bargaining itself' and also 'includes the step preceding it' which is 'essential to it',[67] namely the certification of individuals deemed to be 'employees'.

In fact, to say the least, it is surprising to see judicial power suddenly defend freedom of union association, inferred against all expectations of the Canadian Charter, whereas history reveals, instead, judges' propensity to repress most demonstrations.[68] The fact nonetheless remains that the Canadian Charter definitely adds to the range of pressure tactics made available to unions. If public labour policies get tougher (or collapse) in favour of employers, the unions will be able not only to mobilise their members to try and soften government action, but also to mobilise the judges precisely for this purpose.[69]

The reversal of the Supreme Court of Canada's jurisprudence with regard to the scope of the constitutional freedom of association can, to a large extent, be attributed to the important role that the Court now seems inclined to accord to international law. Following a brief analysis of the three instruments that have been duly ratified by Canada—the International Covenant on Economic, Social and Cultural Rights, the International Covenant on Civil and Political Rights and the International Labour Organization's (ILO's) Convention (No 87) Concerning Freedom of Association and Protection of the Right to Organize—the Court identified an 'international consensus'[70] according to which the 'right to collective bargaining is part of freedom of association'.[71] Nevertheless, while the Court made no reference whatsoever to the recommendations made on this subject by the Freedom

---

[65] Labour Code R.S.Q c C-27.

[66] *Confédération des syndicats nationaux v Québec (Procureur général)* 2008 QCCS 5076 (CanLII).

[67] Ibid (§ 272) (our translation).

[68] Tucker, E, 'The Constitutional Right to Bargain Collectively: The Ironies of Labour History in the Supreme Court of Canada' (2008) 61 *Labour/Le travail* 151.

[69] See generally Brunelle, C, 'The Law as a Political Pressure Tactic: The Case of Collective Labour Relations' in Conseil de la magistrature du Québec, *Which Judge for Which Society* (Proceedings of the 2008 Judges' Conference, Quebec City, 5–7 November 2008) 83. Available at: www.cm.gouv.qc.ca/documents/documentUp/Colloque_2008_en.pdf.

[70] *Health Services and Support*, [2007] 2 SCR 391, 434 (§ 71).

[71] Ibid 434 (§ 72).

of Association Committee—judging them in all likelihood to be 'not binding'[72]—the Court did not hesitate to observe in 'Canada's *current* international law commitments and the current state of international thought [...] a persuasive source for interpreting the scope of the *Charter*.'[73]

What, however, of the international instruments that have not been ratified by Canada, such as, for example, Convention (No 98) Concerning the Application of the Principles of the Right to Organize and to Bargain Collectively? It is reasonable to assume that these instruments will exert less influence on the Canadian courts. Indeed, the predisposition of the Supreme Court of Canada to be guided by international law appears to be essentially inspired by its desire to avoid placing Canada in a situation of failing to respect its international obligations, either as a signatory to a treaty or as a member of the international community bound by customary or conventional international law.[74] It is most likely for this sole purpose that the Court complies with the presumption of conformity of domestic laws to international law:

> In interpreting the scope of application of the *Charter*, the courts should seek to ensure compliance with Canada's *binding obligations* under international law where the express words are capable of supporting such a construction.[75]

Nevertheless, to a large extent, international law is still called upon to play an essential role in the interpretation of constitutional rights.[76]

Since the right to strike is central to trade union freedom in international law,[77] should it be deduced that this right is also an integral part of freedom of association under the Charter? While the legal logic should call for an affirmative answer,[78] the Court, for its part, chose to maintain the mystery around this question, thus reserving for itself some leeway for the future. In fact, there is no other explanation that can justify the following statement, which is, however, quite obvious in light of the facts of the ruling: 'We note that the present case does not concern the right to strike, which

---

[72] Ibid 436 (§ 76).
[73] Ibid 438 (§ 78).
[74] *R v Hape* [2007] 2 SCR 292, 323 (§ 53).
[75] Ibid 324 (§ 56) (our italics).
[76] Coutu, M, Fontaine, L and Marceau, G, 'L'arrêt *Health Services and Support* de la Cour suprême du Canada: La constitutionnalisation du régime québécois des relations industrielles?' (2008) 13(2) *Lex Electronica* 24–25 (§ 18).
[77] Brunelle and Verge 'L'inclusion de la liberté syndicale dans la liberté générale d'association' (2003) 730–35.
[78] Coutu, Fontaine and Marceau, 'L'arrêt *Health Services and Support* de la Cour suprême du Canada' (2008) 39–40 (§ 33) and 42–43 (§ 35); Fudge, J, 'The Supreme Court of Canada and the Right to Bargain Collectively: The Implications of the Health and Services and Support case in Canada and Beyond' (2008) 37(1) *Industrial Law Journal* 25, 43; Norman, K, 'What's Right is Right: The Supreme Court Gets it' (2008) 12 *Just Labour* 16, 20–21; Verge, P, 'Inclusion du droit de grève dans la liberté générale et constitutionnelle d'association: justification et effets' (2009) 50 *C. de D.* 267.

was considered in earlier litigation on the scope of the guarantee of freedom of association ...'[79]

That said, while certain important union activities may still not be covered by the constitutional protection offered by freedom of association, they might, on the other hand, find refuge under the freedom of expression guaranteed by section 2(b) of the Canadian Charter.[80] In this way, the right to form picket lines[81] or distribute flyers which, for example, call on consumers to boycott the employer[82] are considered to be expressive activities which come, a priori, under the constitutional freedom of expression.

Finally, if one were to trace the path of collective labour relations in Canadian law, it would start with the formation of the union and end with the collective agreement duly negotiated, or, failing that, with the exercise of the right to strike in order to break a deadlock in the negotiations. There was a time when the protection provided by the constitutional freedom of association stopped so short of this that it was still miles away from trade union freedom in the sense intended under international law.[83] Recent jurisprudence, however, shows that Canadian judges seem more inclined to let themselves be guided by international law when interpreting section 2(d) of the Canadian Charter.

Furthermore, although the constitutional freedom of association is now recognised to include an undeniable collective dimension, it is still just as closely linked to the promotion of individual aspirations, such that it also includes the freedom not to associate.[84] The Supreme Court of Canada thus agreed to rule on the constitutional validity of a Quebec law which imposed on every employee the obligation to become a member of a union in order to be permitted to work in the construction sector.[85] However, the Court considered that there are intrinsic limitations within the freedom not to associate, such that only proof that a law imposes an 'ideological constraint' can lead to its being rescinded. In fact, the contested law was upheld because a slight majority of judges concluded that compulsory membership

---

[79] *Health Services and Support* [2007] 2 SCR 391412 (§ 19).

[80] Fudge, J, 'Lessons From Canada: The Impact of the Charter of Rights and Freedoms on Labour and Employment Law' in KD Ewing (ed), *Human Rights at Work* (London, Institute of Employment Rights, 2000) ch 7, 186.

[81] *Retail Wholesale and Department Store Union v Dolphin Delivery Ltd* [1986] 2 SCR 573 at 587–88; *BCGEU v British Columbia (Attorney General)* [1988] 2 SCR 214, 230; *RWDSU Local 558 v Pepsi-Cola Canada Beverages (West) Ltd* [2002] 1 SCR 156, 172–74 (§ 32 to 35).

[82] *UFCW Local 1518 v Kmart Canada Ltd* [1999] 2 SCR 1083, 1099 to 1107 (§ 21 to 33).

[83] Fudge, J, "Labour is Not a Commodity": The Supreme Court of Canada and the Freedom of Association' (2004) 67(2) *Saskatchewan Law Review* 425, 448; Norman, K, 'ILO Freedom of Association Principles as Basic Canadian Human Rights: Promises to Keep' (2004) 67(2) *Saskatchewan Law Review* 591.

[84] *Lavigne v Ontario Public Service Employees Union* [1991] 2 SCR 211, 317–318.

[85] *R v Advance Cutting & Coring Ltd* [2001] 3 SCR 209.

in the union did not have the effect of imposing an ideology on its members, nor unjustifiably infringing their individual freedom.

THE RIGHT TO EQUALITY REVOLUTION

While the freedom of association guaranteed by the Canadian Constitution has not really contributed to strengthening the collective rights of workers,[86] at least until very recently, legislative protection against discrimination has proven to be quite effective in terms of strengthening their individual rights. In fact, the very notion of equality has evolved remarkably since the 1980s. Thus, employers and trade unions have had to take on new obligations that restrict, to a certain extent, their contractual autonomy.

From Formal Equality to Substantive Equality

By its very nature, the system of collective labour relations put in place in Canada is 'specifically designed to overcome or compensate any imbalance in bargaining power'.[87] The strength in numbers of the group is meant to be a countervailing force to the economic power of the employer.[88] That said, however, this system presumes that the community of interests of employees transcends their differences.[89]

It should be said that at the time when the first labour codes were adopted, the labour force was highly homogenous. In fact, the Canadian system of collective labour relations was essentially designed on the basis of a set type of employee: a *man*, working *full-time* for the same company, mainly in the *manufacturing* sector, for his whole life, or most of it!

This situation brought about the entrenchment, in unionised work environments, of a particularly *formal* concept of equality.[90] Indeed, in order to put an end to employer practices that were arbitrary or marked by favouritism, trade unions at first demanded *identical treatment* for all employees, without distinction.

However, the gradual diversification of the labour force that began in the 1960s gradually changed this situation. The mass arrival of women

---

[86] Brun, H, 'The Canadian Charter of Rights and the Trade Unions' in F McArdle (ed), *The Cambridge Lectures 1987*, Canadian Institute for Advanced Legal Studies, (Cowansville (Québec), Les Éditions Yvon Blais inc, 1989) ch 1, 1.

[87] *Dickason v University of Alberta* [1992] 2 SCR 1103, 1130.

[88] *Bisaillon v Concordia University* [2006] 1 SCR 666, 683 (§ 26).

[89] Fried, C, 'Individual and Collective Rights in Work Relations: Reflections on the Current State of Labor Law and Its Prospects' (1984) 51 *University of Chicago Law Review* 1012, 1035.

[90] Legault, M-J, 'Droits de la personne, relations du travail et défis pour les syndicats contemporains' (2005) 60(4) *Relations industrielles/Industrial Relations* 683, 696–98.

and minorities on the labour market altered its make-up considerably. On the one hand, as many women as men now hold jobs. On the other hand, individuals whose colour, race, origin, age, religion, language, handicap or sexual orientation distinguishes them from the 'majority', now make up a larger proportion of the labour force than ever before in private companies and government institutions. Canadian trade unions have certainly taken note of these demographic changes but it took them a while to do so.[91]

Under pressure from women and minority groups, who were often victims of discrimination, provincial legislatures and the Federal Parliament eventually adopted human rights laws to promote equality, notably in the field of employment. It should be noted that, although trade unions took part in this movement, they were neither the initiators nor the main driving force behind it.[92]

The Canadian courts have assigned these laws a particular, 'quasi-constitutional'[93] status, which grants them primacy in principle over all other laws, including, incidentally, employment laws, individual labour contracts and collective agreements which apply in unionised workplaces.[94] Thus, unless a law contains a provision which expressly overrides the rights guaranteed by a human rights law, the latter will have precedence.

Moreover, these laws have created human rights commissions having the power to investigate the discriminatory practices of employers, of course, but also those of trade unions. Specialised tribunals, whose powers are derived from these same laws, are thus called on to define the notion of equality in the work context.

These tribunals, which specialise in the area of discrimination, have greatly contributed to the modernisation of Canadian law. In 1985, the Supreme Court of Canada confirmed the ruling of one such tribunal by deciding that the intention to establish a prejudicial distinction is not an essential factor in concluding that illegal discrimination exists. At the same time, the Court also recognised that equality is not necessarily synonymous with identical treatment.

In this case, a sales clerk who belonged to the Seventh-day Adventist Church asked to be exempt from working from sunset on Fridays until sunset on Saturdays, so that she could observe the Sabbath. Faced with the

---

[91] Yates, C, 'Segmented Labour, United Unions? How Unions in Canada Cope with Increased Diversity' (2005) 4 *Transfer* 617.

[92] Sims, A, 'Wagnerism in Canada: A Fifty-Year Check-Up' in A Giles, A Smith, and K Wetzel (eds), *Proceedings of the XXXIst Conference* (Canadian Industrial Relations Association, 1995) 11.

[93] *Québec (Commission des droits de la personne et des droits de la jeunesse) v Communauté urbaine de Montréal* [2004] 1 SCR 789, 799 (§ 15); *Tranchemontagne v Ontario (Director, Disability Support Program)* [2006] 1 SCR 513, 531 (§ 33).

[94] *Winnipeg School Division No 1 v Craton* [1985] 2 SCR 150.

employer's refusal to change her work schedule, she filed a complaint with the human rights commission, alleging that she was the victim of discrimination based on religion.

Breaking its own legal precedents, Canada's highest court concluded that all discrimination is a priori prohibited, whether it is intentional or unintentional, direct or indirect.[95] Consequently, it imposed on the employer an obligation to accommodate the religious beliefs of its employees:

> The duty in a case of adverse effect discrimination on the basis of religion or creed is to take reasonable steps to accommodate the complainant, short of undue hardship: in other words, to take such steps as may be reasonable to accommodate without undue interference in the operation of the employer's business and without undue expense to the employer.[96]

The message was therefore clear: a rule or labour standard, which may appear neutral at first sight, can nonetheless be discriminatory if it has the *effect* of imposing burdens, obligations or disadvantages on an employee— or a group of employees who share one of the personal characteristics cited in the human rights law—which are not imposed on other employees.[97] In such a case, the employer has the duty to accommodate this personal characteristic short of 'undue hardship'.

The factors allowing the tribunal to conclude whether or not there has been such hardship in a particular case have been gradually brought out by the tribunals. They can be grouped together under three broad categories, as follows:

i) The limits of financial and material resources.
   — The real cost of the accommodation requested.
   — External sources of funding (loans, grants, tax credits and deductions, government assistance or compensation programmes, personal contribution on the part of the victim of discrimination, etc).
   — The nature of the company or institution (size, make-up of the labour force, organisational structure, production structure, private or public character, etc).
   — The total operating budget of the company (including head office and subsidiaries) or the institution.
   — The financial strength of the company or institution.
   — The economic context.

---

[95] See generally, Tomei, M, 'Discrimination and Equality at Work: A Review of the Concepts' (2003) 142 *International Labour Review* 401; Loenen, T, 'Indirect discrimination: Oscillating Between Containment and Revolution' in T Loenen and P Rodrigues (eds), *Non-discrimination Law: Comparative Perspectives* (The Hague, Kluwer Law International, 1999) 195.

[96] *Ontario Human Rights Commission v Simpson-Sears* [1985] 2 SCR 536, 555.

[97] *Andrews v Law Society of British Columbia* [1989] 1 SCR 143, 174.

ii) The infringement of rights.
  — Risks to the health or safety of the employee, his or her colleagues or the general public.
  — The collective agreement.
  — The prejudicial effect of the accommodation on other employees.
  — Conflicting rights.
iii) The smooth operation of the company or institution.
  — The relative interchangeability of employees.
  — The adaptability of the work premises, facilities and equipment.
  — The effect on the company's productivity.
  — The number of employees affected by the accommodating step being considered.
  — The beneficial effect of the accommodation on the other employees.
  — The duration and scope of the accommodation.[98]

Thus, an employee who, because of his or her religious beliefs, state of pregnancy or disability—to cite a few examples—is no longer able to accomplish his or her work based on the conditions imposed by the employer, is entitled to an accommodation such that these conditions must be adapted to his or her personal situation. The employer cannot shirk from this duty to accommodate unless it can establish that the employee's request indeed exposes it to 'undue hardship' based on the factors mentioned above.

In this sense, the introduction in the workplace of the duty to take reasonable steps to accommodate has brought about an *increasing individualisation of working conditions*. This has led to at least two major consequences.

First, equality can no longer be confused with the fact of applying the same treatment to or imposing the same treatment on everyone without distinction. This is eloquently illustrated in a ruling delivered by the Supreme Court of Canada in 1999. For safety reasons, the Government of British Columbia had mandated a team of university researchers to design tests that could assess the fitness of forest firefighters. One of the tests involved running a distance of 2.5 km in less than 11 minutes. Tawney Meiorin, a female forest firefighter who had been working for the Government for three years, was dismissed following this test on the grounds that she was unable to complete this shuttle run in less than 11:49 minutes. However, as the aerobic standard had been established by the researchers based on tests given mostly to men, the Court judged it to be a priori discriminatory towards women. In its defence, the employer failed in its attempt to show

---

[98] Brunelle, C, *Discrimination et obligation d'accommodement raisonnable en milieu de travail syndiqué* (Cowansville (Québec), Les Éditions Yvon Blais inc, 2001) 248–51.

that safety reasons justified imposing such a high standard. In its ruling, the Court wrote:

> The Court of Appeal suggested that accommodating women by permitting them to meet a lower aerobic standard than men would constitute 'reverse discrimination.' I respectfully disagree. As this Court has repeatedly held, the essence of equality is to be treated according to one's own merit, capabilities and circumstances. True equality requires that differences be accommodated ... A different aerobic standard capable of identifying women who could perform the job safely and efficiently therefore does not necessarily imply discrimination against men. 'Reverse' discrimination would only result if, for example, an aerobic standard representing a minimum threshold for <u>all</u> forest firefighters was held to be inapplicable to men simply because they were men.[99]

Secondly, the motives behind a given distinction are not highly relevant; it is enough that the distinction have a *prejudicial effect* on an employee or a group of employees expressly protected by the human rights law for this distinction to appear a priori discriminatory.[100]

Incidentally, the constitutional guarantee of equality which flows from section 15 of the Canadian Charter of Rights and Freedoms essentially has the same effect because it requires governments, when acting as employers, to duly take into account the particular circumstances, needs, merits and capacities of employees.[101] In this sense, Canadian law appears to have truly renounced the *formal equality* model in favour of *substantive equality*:[102]

> Employers designing workplace standards owe an obligation to be aware of both the differences between individuals, and differences that characterize groups of individuals. They must build conceptions of equality into workplace standards. By enacting human rights statutes and providing that they are applicable to the workplace, the legislatures have determined that the standards governing the performance of work should be designed to reflect all members of society, in so far as this is reasonably possible. Courts and tribunals must bear this in mind when confronted with a claim of employment-related discrimination. To the extent that a standard unnecessarily fails to reflect the differences among individuals, it runs afoul of the prohibitions contained in the various human rights statutes and must be replaced. The standard <u>itself</u> is required to provide for individual accommodation, if reasonably possible.[103]

This revolution obviously has repercussions for employers and trade unions ...

---

[99] *British Columbia (Public Service Employee Relations Commission) v BCGSEU* [1999] 3 SCR 3, 44 (§ 81).

[100] *Commission Scolaire Régionale de Chambly v Bergevin* [1994] 2 SCR 525.

[101] *Law v Canada (Minister of Employment and Immigration)* [1999] 1 SCR 497, 530 (§ 53); *Lavoie v Canada* [2002] 1 SCR 769.

[102] See, generally, Hepple, B, 'Equality and Empowerment for Decent Work' (2000) 140 *International Labour Review* 5.

[103] *British Columbia v BCGSEU* [1999] 3 SCR 3, 38 (§ 68).

From the Collective Agreement to Human Rights Laws

In 1992, the Supreme Court of Canada decided that the duty to accommodate was enforccable not only against employers but also against trade unions.[104] A school board employee used his seniority to secure a Monday to Friday job, as guaranteed by the collective agreement, working as a custodian at an elementary school. The work schedule set up by the employer and included in the collective agreement, involved a custodian's shift between 3:00 pm and 11:00 pm on Fridays. Because he belonged to the Seventh-day Adventist Church, the new custodian was not able to work the full Friday evening shift. He therefore requested that the employer accommodate him so that he could observe the precepts of his faith.

Following a meeting between the employee and a representative of the employer, who proved to be quite receptive to the idea of creating a special Sunday to Thursday shift for the employee, it was agreed that they would seek the union's consent, given that such accommodation might involve an exception to the collective agreement.

During a meeting at which the question was discussed, the union passed a motion by which it not only rejected the employer's proposal, but also committed itself to filing a grievance in order to prevent its implementation in the event that the employer decided to go ahead with it anyway. Having then attempted without success to find a viable compromise that might satisfy all interested parties, the employer finally proceeded to terminate the custodian's employment as a result of his refusal to work on Friday evenings according to the prescribed schedule.

As the legal controversy was finally referred to Canada's highest court, this Court ruled that the employer and the union had both failed in their duty to accommodate. In the opinion of the Court, neither of the two parties to the collective agreement had pushed the limits of compromise to the point just short of 'undue hardship'. Outlining the duty to accommodate when such duty is enforceable against an association of employees, the Court expressed itself as follows:

> [...] The duty to accommodate only arises if a union is party to discrimination. It may become a party in two ways.

> First, it may cause or contribute to the discrimination in the first instance by participating in the formulation of the work rule that has the discriminatory effect on the complainant. This will generally be the case if the rule is a provision in the collective agreement. It has to be assumed that all provisions are formulated jointly by the parties and that they bear responsibility equally for their effect on employees. [...]

---

[104] See generally, Lynk, M and Ellis, R, 'Unions and the Duty to Accommodate' (1992) 1 *Canadian Labour Law Journal* 238.

Second, a union may be liable for failure to accommodate the religious beliefs of an employee notwithstanding that it did not participate in the formulation or application of a discriminatory rule or practice. This may occur if the union impedes the reasonable efforts of an employer to accommodate. In this situation it will be known that some condition of employment is operating in a manner that discriminates on religious grounds against an employee and the employer is seeking to remove or alleviate the discriminatory effect. If reasonable accommodation is only possible with the union's co-operation and the union blocks the employer's efforts to remove or alleviate the discriminatory effect, it becomes a party to the discrimination.[105]

Thus, although it is the employer's right to manage the company, the courts assume that there is legal equality between it and the union. Moreover, according to the Supreme Court of Canada, '[t]o say that an employee is isolated or vulnerable when he or she is represented by a union would be an affront to organized labour!'[106] The employer and the union can therefore be held jointly responsible if the collective agreement that they have negotiated impedes the introduction of reasonable accommodation in favour of an employee who is the victim of discrimination.

Having said that, it can be observed that employees are requesting such accommodation in increasing numbers. Indeed, the duty to accommodate is not limited solely to religious beliefs. It is open to application based on all the personal characteristics targeted by human rights laws, such as national or ethnic origin, age, gender, pregnancy, family status, sexual orientation or disability.[107]

A prohibited ground of discrimination related to disability, whether it be physical or intellectual, constitutes in itself the source of a considerable number of requests for accommodation.[108] Employers are known to appreciate healthy, hardworking employees. The Canadian courts, however, have given a very broad interpretation to the notion of 'disability', such that it is liable to include anything to do with a person's 'illness', or more generally, 'health'.[109] Now, every time an employer attempts to terminate the employment of an individual who, in its opinion, is not fit to provide regular and satisfactory work, it has the burden of proving that it is impossible

---

[105] *Central Okanagan School District No 23 v Renaud* [1992] 2 SCR 970, 990–91.
[106] *Isidore Garon ltée v Tremblay* [2006] 1 SCR 27, 54 (§ 59).
[107] Brunelle, *Discrimination et obligation d'accommodement raisonnable en milieu de travail syndiqué* (2001) 134.
[108] Lynk, M, 'Accommodating Disabilities in the Canadian Workplace' (1999) 7 *Canadian Labour & Employment Law Journal* 183; Malhotra, R, 'The Duty to Accommodate Unionized Workers with Disabilities in Canada and the United States: A Counter-Hegemonic Approach' (2003) 3 *Journal of Law & Equality* 92.
[109] *Québec (Commission des droits de la personne et des droits de la jeunesse) v Montréal (City); Québec (Commission des droits de la personne et des droits de la jeunesse) v Boisbriand (City)* [2000] 1 SCR 665; *McGill University Health Centre (Montreal General Hospital) v Syndicat des employés de l'Hôpital général de Montréal* [2007] 1 SCR 161, 165 and 169 (§ 1 and 11).

to accommodate this employee's physical or psychological state of health without undergoing undue hardship.[110] Given that the average number of workdays lost due to sickness or disability in Canada is slightly rising,[111] it is obvious that the trend for employees to request accommodation is not about to slow down.

Be that as it may, in such a context, the parties can no longer reasonably claim that they have full control over the rules to be applied in the work-place. In fact, since the 1980s, 'the centre of gravity in the creation of standards governing labour relations [...] has been gradually moving towards the legislative source',[112] so much so that the parties can no longer presume that the collective agreement is a full regime in and of itself.[113]

The *Parry Sound (District), Social Services Administration Board v OPSEU, Local 324*[114] ruling is revealing in this regard. A probationary employee who had been away on maternity leave was discharged several days after returning to work. According to the terms of the applicable collective agreement:

> a probationary employee may be discharged at the sole discretion of and for any reason satisfactory to the Employer and such action by the Employer is not subject to the grievance and arbitration procedures and does not constitute a difference between the parties.

Despite this clearly-stated provision in the collective agreement, the union nevertheless filed an arbitration grievance on the grounds that the employer's decision was 'arbitrary, discriminatory, in bad faith and unfair'. In doing so, the union argued that the right to equal treatment without discrimination as regards employment—a right which is expressly recog-nised, in this instance, by the Ontario Human Rights Code—was implicitly included in the collective agreement, thus making discriminatory discharge an arbitrable dispute. A majority of judges in the Supreme Court of Canada took up the union's argument in their own ruling and agreed that the arbitration tribunal did indeed have jurisdiction to hear the grievance:

> [T]he substantive rights and obligations of the parties to a collective agreement cannot be determined solely by reference to the mutual intentions of the contract-ing parties as expressed in that agreement. [...] [T]here are certain terms and

---

[110] Roux, D and Laflamme, A-M, 'Le droit de congédier un employé physiquement ou psychologiquement inapte: revu et corrigé par le droit à l'égalité et le droit au travail' (2007) 48 *Cahiers de droit* 189.

[111] Statistics Canada, *Days Lost per Worker due to Illness or Disability, by Sex, by Province (Both Sexes)* (2008) Available at: www40.statcan.gc.ca/l01/cst01/health47a-eng.htm.

[112] Nadeau, D, 'L'arrêt *Morin* et le monopole de représentation des syndicats: assises d'une fragmentation' (2004) 64 *Revue du Barreau* 161, 194 [translation].

[113] Trudeau, G, 'L'arbitrage des griefs au Canada: plaidoyer pour une réforme devenue nécessaire' (2005) 84 *Canadian Bar Review* 249, 255.

[114] *Parry Sound (District), Social Services Administration Board v OPSEU, Local 324* [2003] 2 SCR 157.

conditions that are *implicit* in the agreement, *irrespective of the mutual intentions of the contracting parties*. [...] The statutory rights of employees constitute a bundle of rights to which the parties can add but from which they cannot derogate.[115]

The *McGill University Health Centre (Montreal General Hospital) v Syndicat des employés de l'Hôpital général de Montréal*[116] ruling constitutes another enlightening example. On 24 March 2000, Alice Brady, a medical secretary who had been working full-time at the Montreal General Hospital for 15 years, was forced to take a leave of absence from her job on account of a nervous breakdown. Between 26 June 2000 and 1 November 2001, she managed, despite a few interruptions, to gradually return to work three days a week, but was never able to return full-time. Then, to make matters worse, she had an automobile accident on 28 July 2002. If it had not been for this unfortunate accident, which left her unable to work for an undetermined period of time because of a shoulder injury, Ms Brady would, according to her doctor, have been able to return to work on 9 September 2002.

On 12 March 2003, the employer notified the employee of its decision to terminate her employment as of 3 April 2003, in accordance with the following clause in the applicable collective agreement:

12.11 An employee shall lose his or her seniority rights and his or her employment in the following cases:

[...]

5. absence by reason of illness or of an accident other than an industrial accident or occupational disease, after the thirty-sixth (36th) month of absence.

The union claimed that this decision on the part of the employer constituted illegal discrimination based on Ms Brady's 'disability' and asked the hospital to negotiate a reasonable accommodation with her in accordance with the Quebec Charter of Human Rights and Freedoms.[117] The employer asserted that clause 12.11 of the collective agreement consisted, in itself, of a reasonable accommodation measure.

In the final analysis, the Supreme Court of Canada decided in favour of the employer, essentially because the medical evidence presented before the arbitrator did not make it possible to conclude that the employee was able to 'return to work in the foreseeable future'.[118]

While recognising that 'the collective agreement plays an important role in determining the scope of the employer's duty to accommodate',[119] that

---

[115] Ibid 176 (§ 29).
[116] *McGill University Health Centre (Montreal General Hospital) v Syndicat des employés de l'Hôpital général de Montréal* [2007] 1 SCR 161, 165 and 169 (§ 1 and 11).
[117] Quebec Charter of Human Rights and Freedoms R.S.Q. c C-12.
[118] *McGill University Health Centre* [2007] 1 SCR 161, 178 (§ 37).
[119] Ibid 165 (§ 1).

it is 'a factor to consider'.[120] The Court indicated clearly that the period negotiated by the parties is, nonetheless, not definitive:

> Neither the employer nor the union may impose a period shorter than the one to which a sick person is entitled under human rights legislation in light of the facts of and criteria applicable to his or her particular case. A clause purporting to do so would have no effect against an employee who is entitled to a longer period. Since the right to equality is a fundamental right, the parties to a collective agreement cannot agree to a level of protection that is lower than the one to which employees are entitled under human rights legislation, nor can they definitively establish the length of the period in advance, since the specific circumstances of a given case will not be known until they occur, that is, after the collective agreement has been signed.[121]

While these remarks confirm the importance of the right to equality, some passages in the ruling seem to open the door to new limits to the duty of reasonable accommodation when it is applied in a unionised workplace. On the one hand, there appears to be a new interpretation with regard to the factor of 'undue hardship' relating to the size of the company. Up to now, the larger the company, the greater the extent to which the employer had to be prepared to consent to significant accommodation.[122] It now appears that, in some cases, the clauses in a collective agreement could serve as proof of such 'undue hardship', '... especially in the case of a large organization, where proving undue hardship resulting from an employee's absence could be complex'.[123] On the other hand, while the burden to prove 'undue hardship' must fall to the employer,[124] it now appears to be up to the unionised employee, seeking a more generous accommodation measure than that provided for in the collective agreement, to prove his or her ability to return to work within a reasonable timeframe.[125] It goes

[120] Ibid 171 (§ 20).
[121] Ibid.
[122] *Commission scolaire régionale de Chambly v Bergevin* [1994] 2 SCR 525, 546: '[...] in a large concern, it may be a relatively easy matter to replace one employee with another. In a small operation, replacement may place an unreasonable or unacceptable burden on the employer.'
[123] *McGill University Health Centre* [2007] 1 SCR 161, 175 (§ 27). Moreover, in *Hydro-Québec v Syndicat des employé-e-s de techniques professionnelles et de bureau d'Hydro-Québec, section locale 2000 (SCFP-FTQ)* [2008] 2 SCR 561, the Supreme Court of Canada did not even allude to the size of the firm criterion even if Hydro-Quebec is among the largest crown corporations in the country.
[124] *British Columbia v BCGSEU* [1999] 3 SCR 3,38 (§ 68); Roux and Laflamme 'Le droit de congédier un employé physiquement ou psychologiquement inapte' (2007) 208.
[125] *McGill University Health Centre* [2007] 1 SCR 161, 178 (§ 38): 'The duty to accommodate is neither absolute nor unlimited. The employee has a role to play in the attempt to arrive at a reasonable compromise. If in Ms. Brady's view the accommodation provided for in the collective agreement in the instant case was insufficient, and if she felt that she would be able to return to work within a reasonable period of time, she had to provide the arbitrator with evidence on the basis of which he could find in her favour.'

without saying that this reversal of the burden of proof is not likely to make the employee's task any easier.

However, the logic that was central to the *Parry Sound* ruling nevertheless remains intact. In short, the 'law of the parties', which the collective agreement represents, is not only subject to provisions concerning public order in human rights laws, but is also supposed to implicitly include these very provisions in its text. This means that the content of the collective agreement is, to a certain extent, out of the hands of the parties.

This loss of control is borne out in the parties' decisions not only regarding the content of the collective agreement, but also regarding the forum which will have jurisdiction to hear disputes that arise between them.

In 1997, in a concerted effort to reach the goal of 'zero deficit', the Government of Quebec and the Fédération des syndicats de l'enseignement de la Centrale des syndicats du Québec agreed to amend the collective agreement that was in force in the school system at the time, such that the experience acquired by teachers during the 1996–97 school year would not be recognised and therefore would not count. In reality, this freeze in pay increases and seniority had relatively little effect on most teachers, who, having acquired many years of experience, were already at the top of their pay scales. However, younger teachers with little experience argued that the measure had a disproportionately prejudicial effect on their group.

Rather than relying on the duly certified union to defend their rights, a group of young teachers formed their own association and encouraged their colleagues to file a complaint of discrimination based on age with the Commission des droits de la personne et des droits de la jeunesse.[126] No fewer than 13,400 complaints were thus sent to the Commission, which, following an investigation, decided to bring the matter before the Human Rights Tribunal. Judging the case to be inadmissible, the Attorney General of Quebec, the school boards and the teachers' unions united together to fight against the claim on the grounds that the grievance arbitrator had exclusive jurisdiction to hear the dispute.

While the Human Rights Tribunal asserted that it had jurisdiction to hear the case, the Quebec Court of Appeal, in a majority decision, ruled that it did not. Then, in a divided decision, wherein a majority actually hung on the decision of a single judge, the Supreme Court of Canada restored the ruling of the Court of First Instance, and concluded that the grievance arbitrator did not have exclusive jurisdiction in this matter.[127]

---

[126] Brunelle, C, 'The Emergence of Parallel Identity-Based Associations in Collective Bargaining Relations' in Law Commission of Canada (ed), *New Perspectives on the Public-Private Divide*, (Vancouver (Canada), UBC Press, 2003) ch 6, 166.

[127] *Québec (Commission des droits de la personne et des droits de la jeunesse) v Québec (Attorney General)* [2004] 2 SCR 185.

To justify its conclusion, the Court drew a distinction between the pre-contractual phase, that is, the *process of negotiation* and *adoption* (or *inclusion*) in the collective agreement of a provision having a discriminatory effect, on the one hand, and the *implementation* phase, that is, the *interpretation* and *application* of this same provision, on the other hand.[128] Only this last phase would in fact fall under the exclusive jurisdiction of the grievance arbitrator.

Therefore, given the obligation now imposed on the parties to the collective agreement to integrate notions of equality into workplace standards, the question arises as to whether or not any employee wronged by a provision which fails to provide for accommodation in his or her favour will be able to maintain that the discrimination, to which he or she claims to be subject, results from the *negotiation* rather than the *agreement* that applies to him or her. If such a claim were to be received favourably in case law, the monopoly of representation identified with the union could in turn be undermined.[129] Certainly, the grievance arbitrator who was justifiably referred to by the union would still be empowered to deal with the allegation of discrimination but his jurisdiction in this regard would no longer be exclusive. Thus, the employee who claims to be the victim of discrimination would be free to resort to recourse other than the grievance procedure, thus bypassing the compensation avenue traditionally favoured by the parties to the collective agreement.[130]

To sum up, while the union has long claimed to be a defender of employees' dignity by implementing a system of private justice[131] in which the collective agreement served, so to speak, as the Constitution, the legislator has gradually intervened so as to impose pre-eminent standards in the workplace from which the parties can by no means escape.[132]

Does the increasing power of individual rights and freedoms constitute a threat to the vitality of the union movement by favouring the break-up of the collective cohesion of employees? This phenomenon certainly poses a formidable challenge to trade unions since it urges them to review their conception of democracy so as to integrate into it a better balance between the interests of the majority and those of the minority.[133] If they fail at this

---

[128] Ibid 197–98 (§ 23 to 25).

[129] Nadeau, 'L'arrêt *Morin* et le monopole de représentation des syndicats: assises d'une fragmentation' (2004).

[130] See, for example, *Hôpital général juif Sir Mortimer B Davis v Commission des droits de la personne et des droits de la jeunesse*, 2010 QCCA 172 (CanLII), Available at : www.canlii.org/fr/qc/qcca/doc/2010/2010qcca172/2010qcca172.html.

[131] Carter, D, 'The Duty to Accommodate: Its Growing Impact on the Grievance Arbitration Process' (1997) 52(1) *Relations Industrielles/Industrial Relations* 185; Trudeau, 'L'arbitrage des griefs au Canada: plaidoyer pour une réforme devenue nécessaire' (2005).

[132] *Newfoundland Association of Public Employees v Newfoundland (Green Bay Health Care Centre)* [1996] 2 SCR 3.

[133] Blackett, A and Sheppard, C, 'Collective Bargaining and Equality: Making Connections' (2003) 142 *International Labour Review* 419; Brunelle (n 98).

task, it is feared that they will be gradually marginalised in favour of more individualised pressure groups. On the other hand, if they successfully take up this great challenge, they will find in employee diversity the support and creativity needed to consolidate their legitimacy and continue defending employees for a long time to come. In fact, the *Meiorin* and *Parry Sound* decisions clearly show that trade unions can take advantage of human rights laws to strengthen the protection of employees' fundamental rights and restore justice and equity in the workplace.

Moreover, no matter how much their virtues have been praised, human rights laws do not contain all the progressive measures likely to redress the inequalities and improve the condition of workers vis-à-vis the employer. In fact, union protection continues to be worthwhile for the employees who benefit from it. For example, based on September 2009 data, the average hourly wage of employees who are members of a union and employees who are not union members but who are covered by a collective agreement ($25.37) is 18.25 per cent higher than that of employees who are not members of a union or not covered by a collective agreement ($20.74).[134]

Unfortunately, union coverage is still reserved for a relatively small proportion of workers. Indeed, access to unionisation remains difficult in Canada, especially in the private sector. Across Canada, the average unionisation rate was 31.2 per cent in 2008. Among the Canadian provinces, the highest rate is observed in Quebec (39.4 per cent) while Alberta ranks last (24 per cent).

Behind these figures looms an inequality against which human rights laws seem to be quite powerless. In Canada as, moreover, in all industrialised countries, the precariousness of employment status is on the increase. While the Canadian system of collective labour relations is built, to a great extent, on a set type of employee, holding a full-time job, 'non-standard' employment (part-time, freelance, on-call and casual work, self-employment, telework, and so on) is increasing considerably.[135] Yet, people in a non-traditional work situation in the new economy often do not have access to union representation.[136] It is therefore perhaps not surprising that, for example, the average hourly wage of part-time Canadian workers ($15.66) is less than two-thirds of the average hourly wage paid to full-time workers

[134] Statistics Canada, Average hourly wages of employees by selected characteristics and profession (unadjusted data, by province) (September 2009) (Canada). Available at: www40.statcan.ca/l01/cst01/labr69a-eng.htm.
[135] Lowe, G, 'Employment Relationships as the Centrepiece of a New Labour Policy Paradigm' (2002) 28(1) *Canadian Public Policy* 93; Trudeau, G, 'Changing Employment Relationships and the Unintentional Evolution of Canadian Labour Relations Policy' (2002) 28(1) *Canadian Public Policy* 149.
[136] Vallée, G, 'Towards Enhancing the Employment Conditions of Vulnerable Workers: A Public Policy Perspective' (Vulnerable Workers Series No 2, Work Network, Research Report, Canadian Policy Research Network, March 2005). Available at: www.cprn.com/documents/35588_en.pdf

($23.65).[137] Obviously, for these more vulnerable employees,[138] the 'equality revolution' has yet to be carried out.

CONCLUSION

Canadian labour law is currently going through a period of transition. For a long time, the legislator has given full opportunity to employers and trade unions to establish, through collective bargaining, the standards applicable to their workplaces. This highly decentralised model, which was self-sufficient and based on the parties' contractual autonomy, responded quite well to the realities of a rather homogenous labour force.

However, the gradual diversification of the labour force from the 1960s onwards gave rise to important changes at the legislative level. The provincial legislatures and the Federal Parliament alternately adopted laws to combat discrimination, in particular at work. These so-called 'quasi-constitutional' laws have precedence over any other standard applicable to the workplace, whether it be legislative or contractual in nature. They thus allow any employee, individually, to challenge the provisions of the collective agreement which have a discriminatory effect on him or her. The employer and the trade union then have a duty to accommodate which they cannot shirk, unless they can demonstrate that the request of the wronged employee actually exposes them to 'undue hardship'.

Thus, Canadian labour law is currently characterised by two currents of thought. The first advocates that the parties' will, as expressed in the collective agreement (the 'law of the shop'), prevails. The second advocates instead that human rights laws exert sovereign domination over the workplace. For many observers, the situation comes down to the eternal conflict between the collective rights of the majority, embodied in the collective agreement, and the individual rights of the minority, guaranteed by law. The reality is perhaps more complex:

> The potential conflict between majority interests and minority rights is sometimes seen as a parallel to that between collective and individual rights. Equality rights are perceived in terms of individual rights while collective bargaining is seen as a mechanism for the pursuit of collective or social goals. Collective struggles to end discrimination in the workplace have been hampered by this dichotomy, according to some scholars who consider that civil rights laws have focused on individual rights while labour laws have advanced group rights. The cogency of this distinction is questionable. As regards discrimination, in particular, it is the group aspect

[137] Statistics Canada, Average hourly wages of employees by selected characteristics and profession (unadjusted data, by province) (September 2009) (Canada).

[138] Chaykowski, R, *'Non-standard Work and Economic Vulnerability'* (Vulnerable Workers Series No 3, Work Network, Research Report, Canadian Policy Research Network, March 2005). Available at: <www.cprn.com/documents/35591_in.pdf>.

of the unfair treatment that brings it under the rubric of equal rights. Though equal rights are often evoked by individuals, they are closely linked to group rights.[139]

Nevertheless, although the inclusion of the Canadian Charter of Rights and Freedoms into the Constitution of Canada in 1982 significantly contributed to reviving human rights laws and the protection of the right to equality, its effect on workers' rights was not as significant. In fact, until very recently, the freedom of association enshrined in the Charter did not guarantee the right to collective bargaining or the right to strike. It now remains to be seen what scope the Canadian courts will reserve for the 'procedural right to collective bargaining' that the Supreme Court of Canada has just brought out from the constitutional text.

It should be pointed out that the restrictive interpretation of freedom of association which prevailed up to now stemmed perhaps from the fact that the Canadian Charter chooses to overlook economic, social and cultural rights found in the major international instruments. In its essence, the Charter is a classical liberal document which mainly guarantees civil and political rights. This might at least partly explain the reluctance of Canadian judges to fully guarantee freedom of association through constitutional enactment.[140]

Under these circumstances, since the Charter is one of the tools which guide the evolution of Canadian law,[141] should there be concern that the law will evolve in favour of an increasing individualisation of labour relations and a logical weakening of the union movement? The danger seems to be quite real.

To avoid this situation, trade unions will obviously not be able to rely on politicians. Currently, there is nothing to suggest that there is a will on the part of elected officials to reform the Canadian Charter so as to enrich it with social and economic rights, including trade union rights. Moreover, anyone who knows the slightest bit of Canadian history knows how politically risky undertaking constitutional reforms can be!

Indeed, it is, rather, an opportunity for trade unions to derive a new basis for collective cohesion in order to bring together within their ranks the greatest number of employees possible so as to escape from this dreaded danger. And no matter what is said on the subject, the unions will not be able to achieve this ambitious goal unless they undertake to respect, promote and defend everyone's right to substantive equality.

---

[139] Blackett and Sheppard, 'Collective Bargaining and Equality: Making Connections' (2003) at 434.

[140] Brunelle and Verge (n 36) 752–54.

[141] *RWDSU Local 558 v Pepsi-Cola Canada Beverages (West) Ltd* [2002] 1 SCR 156, 167 (§ 18).

5

China's Legal Protection of Workers' Human Rights

LIU CHENG AND SEAN COONEY

INTRODUCTION

HUMAN RIGHTS DISCOURSE has become increasingly prominent in the Chinese labour law context. However, the dominant Chinese conceptions of human rights, including workers' human rights, diverge considerably from corresponding ideas in liberal democratic societies. Moreover, the institutional framework for giving effect to human rights in China is markedly different from many Western countries. Accordingly, we begin our analysis of the relationship between human rights and labour law in the Chinese context by first considering the status of human rights discourse in China generally.

The analysis then turns to the specific interactions between human rights and labour law. We provide a brief account of the complex nature of work relations in China and of the legal response to that complexity, emphasising the striking pace of social and legal change. We then focus on the extent to which human rights play a role in the process of change. We stress that it is not the purpose of this chapter to critique the Chinese approach to labour rights from a Western or international perspective. Our goal is rather to explore how labour rights are understood *within the Chinese context*.

We draw three major conclusions. First, the Chinese approach to labour rights enables them to be viewed as an emanation of human rights, both for constitutional purposes, and with respect to international human rights conventions. This conclusion comes with the qualification that China recognises a narrower range of rights than does international human rights jurisprudence. Secondly, human rights discourse is very important in Chinese labour law, primarily as an organising principle for legislation (and rather than as a basis for judicial review). The fact that legislative provisions are closely linked to labour rights operates as a break on attempts to reduce labour rights by actors (both Chinese and international) working from an idealised neo-liberal script. Thirdly, the central problem for labour law policymakers and stakeholders in the People's Republic of China (PRC), at least in the short term, is the implementation and enforcement of those labour rights which are accepted in China. While some PRC citizens do generally enjoy the rights stipulated in the key labour laws, large numbers of workers do not.

THE PRC VIEW OF HUMAN RIGHTS

Human rights discourse is becoming increasingly significant in the PRC. This statement may appear surprising, given the extensive criticisms often levelled at China by international agencies, non-governmental organisations and sometimes other countries. However, the statement is clearly accurate from an historical perspective—even from a very recent historical perspective.

With very limited exceptions, human rights discourse as it has developed in liberal democratic societies, has had little or no place in mainland Chinese political and legal practice until the last two decades. In dynastic China, while there were constraints on governmental action,[1] these were not conceptualised in terms of individual rights which the state could not violate.[2]

After the founding of the Republic of China in 1912, there were sporadic attempts to create a constitutional order, with various provisional constitutional instruments adopted. These attempts culminated in the promulgation of a Constitution in 1947. This Constitution, which exhibited a certain degree of liberal democratic influence, contained an extensive chapter on rights and duties. These included freedom of association (*jieshe zhi ziyou*) a right to subsistence (*shengcunquan*) and a right to work (*gongzuoquan*). However, the rights provisions in this Constitution had little practical effect on mainland China (although they have proved to be very important in Taiwan, where they are partially justiciable).[3] Throughout the Republican period, China was subject to internal conflict and in the later part of the period was engaged in conflict with Japan.

The 1947 Constitution was abolished in 1949 after the victory on the Chinese mainland of the Chinese Communist Party (CCP). The new constitutional arrangements set in place after the CCP victory, formalised in the

---

[1] See eg, Turner, K, 'Rule of Law Ideals in Early China? (1992) 6 *Journal of Chinese Law* 1–44; Alford, W, 'The Inscrutable Occidental?: Implications of Roberto Unger's Uses and Abuses of the Chinese Past' (1986) 64 *Texas Law Review* 915. Some of the constraints included meritocratic appointments to the bureaucracy, a well organised appeal system for local decision-making; and the concept of the 'mandate of heaven', which linked the legitimacy of imperial rule to the well-being of the people.

[2] See eg, Zhiping Liang, 'Explicating Law: A Comparative Perspective of Chinese and Western Legal Culture' (1989) 3 *Journal of Chinese Law* 56.

[3] Cooney, S, 'The Effects of Rule of Law Principles in Taiwan' in R Peerenboom (ed), *Asian Discourses of Rule of Law* (London, Routledge, 2004).

Constitution of 1954, naturally rejected liberal democratic ideas in favour of socialist legality.[4] These arrangements were severely disrupted during the Cultural Revolution, which rendered the legal system inoperative between 1966 and 1976. The late 1970s saw a return to socialist legality in the context of a more pragmatically oriented approach to communism under the de facto leadership of Deng Xiao-ping. This led to the adoption of the current PRC Constitution in 1982.[5]

The 1982 Constitution establishes the basic structure of government in China, and contains extensive lists both of state policies and, in chapter II, of fundamental rights and duties of citizens. The Constitution contains several provisions pertaining to human rights in general, and to labour rights in particular.[6]

In 2004, article 33, which commences chapter II, was amended to include the sentence '[t]he State respects and preserves human rights'. The term 'human rights' is not defined in the Constitution. One likely referent for the phrase is the set of provisions in chapter II that deploy the term 'rights' or 'freedoms'.[7]

In relation to rights associated with labour, chapter II states that PRC citizens enjoy, inter alia, the freedoms of association, of procession and of demonstration.[8] They also have the right and duty to work[9] and the right to rest.[10] Women enjoy equal rights with men, including in the economic sphere.[11] Further, PRC citizens have the 'right to material assistance from the state and society when they are old, ill or disabled'.[12]

As the wording of article 33 indicates, the Constitution contemplates that the enumerated rights are to be given effect by state action. In most of

---

[4] Kam C Wong, 'Human Rights and Limitation of State Power: The Discovery of Constitutionalism in the People's Republic of China' (2006) 1 *Asia-Pacific Journal on Human Rights and the Law* 1.

[5] The Constitution of the People's Republic of China (PRC) 1982 has been amended on four occasions, most recently at the Second Session of the Tenth National People's Congress on 14 March 2004.

[6] Article 6 of the Constitution provides that 'The system of socialist public ownership supersedes the system of exploitation of man by man; it applies the principle of 'from each according to his ability, to each according to his work.' This does not have any direct significance for labour rights, but is relevant insofar that debates over labour issues often appeal to socialist principles.

[7] International treaties constitute a second possible referent for the phrase 'human rights' in art 33 of the Constitution. As explained below, China's ratification of the treaties has been subject to concordance with its approach to rights.

[8] Constitution of the PRC 1982 art 35.

[9] Ibid art 42.

[10] Ibid art 43.

[11] Ibid art 48. Note that the Constitution contains two further provisions pertaining to equality. Article 4 provides for equality of treatment as between various ethnic groups in China and for protection of the lawful interests of minorities. Article 33 provides that all citizens of the PRC are equal before the law.

[12] Ibid art 45.

the labour provisions, the nature of state action is specified. Thus, the right to work is amplified by the statement that the state 'creates conditions for employment, strengthens labour protection, improves working conditions and, on the basis of expanded production, increases remuneration for work and social benefits'. The provision on the right to rest provides that the state is to 'expand facilities for rest and recuperation of working people, and prescribe working hours and leave for workers'. Similarly, the provision on equal rights is elaborated with the assertion that 'the state protects the rights and interests of women [and] applies the principle of equal pay for equal work to men and women'. Again, the provision relating to material assistance to those who are old, ill or disabled is supplemented by references to measures such as social insurance, pensions, health benefits, and special working arrangements for persons with disabilities.[13]

This approach to labour rights is consistent with the predominant thinking about human rights in China, which sees the state as delivering, rather than potentially infringing on, individual rights.[14] In this, the Constitution reflects the considerable emphasis placed on 'positive rights' in Chinese legal discourse. These are conceived as rights to state assistance flowing from the right to subsistence (*shengcunquan*) and right to development (*fazhanquan*). In principle, both these rights could be understood as entailing 'negative' protection against deprivation by state action, of personal freedom, or the capacity to develop oneself as one chooses. However, in the Chinese context, this negative protection tends to be downplayed. According to Liu Cheng:

> The [distinct aspects of] the concept of the right to subsistence are confused; the notion that a person cannot be deprived of subsistence is subsumed into the idea that a person should receive assistance; the right to subsistence thereby becomes a right to economic development, and from there an individual right becomes a right to *national* economic development.[15]

Indeed, chapter II seems to fuse what in other constitutions[16] is sometimes treated as two conceptually distinct matters; rights and fundamental state policy principles. Indeed, article 44, dealing with retirement incomes, is not expressed as a right at all.

The distinction between rights and state policies is important in other jurisdictions because the former are frequently justiciable, whereas the latter are not. However, as we shall see, judicial remedies for breach of

---

[13] Ibid art 45.

[14] For an extensive account of human rights in China, see Peerenboom, R, 'Assessing Human Rights in China: Why the Double Standard?' (2005) 38 *Cornell International Law Journal* 71. In relation to China's ratification of international human rights instruments, see 78–84.

[15] Liu Cheng, *Shehui Baozhangfa Bijiao Yanjiu* [Comparative Research into Social Protection Law] (Beijing, Chinese Labour and Social Security Publishing, 2006) 32.

[16] Such as India's or the former Republic of China Constitution (in operation in Taiwan).

constitutional rights are not available in China. The integration of the two does not therefore have any important direct legal consequences.

Chinese Response to International Human Rights Instruments

The Chinese view of rights just outlined is in tension with that reflected in the key international human rights instruments. In recent times, China has attempted to resolve this tension not by rejecting these instruments but by adopting them in a modified form. China is now a signatory to a large number of human rights treaties and conventions. The PRC has ratified 22 international human rights treaties,[17] including the International Covenant on Economic, Social and Cultural Rights (ICESCR),[18] the Convention on the Elimination of All Forms of Discrimination Against Women (CEDAW),[19] and the Convention on the Rights of the Child.[20] It has signed the International Covenant on Civil and Political Rights, and has indicated it is conducting reform of several key laws with a view to 'creating conditions for ratification'.[21]

China has also ratified 22 active conventions of the International Labour Organization (ILO).[22] These include conventions on weekly rest,[23] minimum wage fixing[24] and occupational health and safety,[25] as well as four of the ILO's Fundamental Human Rights Conventions. Those four pertain to the elimination of discrimination in employment and occupation[26] and to the elimination of child labour.[27]

An important aspect of the international instruments is that they view some of the rights set out in them as *constituting a restriction on state action*. In the labour field, an important restriction in several of the international treaties, and in the ILO conventions, is that relating to a state's ability to regulate trade unions. Thus, the ICESCR provides that:

The States Parties to the present Covenant undertake to ensure:

(a) The right of everyone to form trade unions and join the trade union of his choice, subject only to the rules of the organization concerned, for the promotion

---

[17] See its 'Aide Memoire' presented in the context of the 2006 elections to the United Nations (UN) Human Rights Council, available at www.un.org/ga/60/elect/hrc/china.pdf.
[18] Ratified 27 October 1997.
[19] Ratified 17 July 1980.
[20] Ratified 29 August 1990.
[21] Signed 5 October 1998. See 'Aide Memoire'.
[22] As of March 2009. A further three have been denounced.
[23] Convention No 14.
[24] Convention No 26.
[25] Convention No 155.
[26] Convention Nos 100 and 111.
[27] Convention Nos 138 and 182.

and protection of his economic and social interests. No restrictions may be placed on the exercise of this right other than those prescribed by law and which are necessary in a democratic society in the interests of national security or public order or for the protection of the rights and freedoms of others.

The tenor of this provision conflicts with the nature of the PRC political system,[28] and also with the approach to rights reflected in the PRC Constitution. It is not surprising, therefore, that China stated at the time of ratifying this treaty that

the application of Article 8.1 (a) of the Covenant to the People's Republic of China shall be consistent with the relevant provisions of the *Constitution of the People's Republic of China, Trade Union Law of the People's Republic of China* and *Labour Law of the People's Republic of China.*

These laws and the Trade Union Law in particular, make clear that Chinese trade unions must 'insist on the leadership of the Chinese Communist Party'[29] and must be organised on the principle of democratic centralism. This means that higher level trade unions (the peak body of which is the All China Federation of Trade Unions (ACFTU)) must approve the establishment of lower level unions and guide their activities.[30] The ACFTU Charter binds it closely to the CCP.[31]

As any trade union organisation formed outside the parameters of the CCP-controlled ACFTU is illegal, China's conception of freedom of association is at odds with that in the ICESCR and other international human rights instruments. Consequently, China has been unable to ratify two of the ILO's core conventions pertaining to the rights to organise and bargaining collectively.[32] Analogous difficulties have prevented it from ratifying the conventions on forced labour.[33]

Returning to the Constitutional amendment providing that the Chinese state will 'respect and preserve human rights', it is clear that, regardless of whether the referent for 'human rights' is chapter II, or those international instruments as ratified by China (including their reservations), the obligation the Chinese state is undertaking is to uphold labour rights, but only to the extent that they do not (in their view) subvert the Chinese political and legal order.

---

[28] According to art 1 of the PRC Constitution, the 'People's Republic of China is a socialist state under the people's democratic dictatorship led by the working class and based on the alliance of workers and peasants.'

[29] Zhonghua Renmin Gongheguo Gonghui Fa [Trade Union Law of the People's Republic of China] (hereafter Trade Union Law), passed by the National People's Congress on 3 April 1992 and revised 27 October 2001, with effect from that date, art 4.

[30] Trade Union Law arts 9 and 11.

[31] *Zhongguo Gonghui Guicheng* [Charter of Chinese Unions], passed by the 14th National Congress of the ACFTU on 26 September 2003.

[32] Convention Nos 87 and 98. In contrast to the position under the ICESCR, reservations are not permitted to be made to ILO Conventions.

[33] Convention Nos 29 and 105.

The Role of the Judiciary in Implementing Human Rights

The mode of giving effect to human rights in the PRC (understood as those rights which are accepted by the Chinese state) also differs from that in many (but not all[34]) liberal democratic societies. Judicial review is not available to secure compliance with constitutional rights. This is a consequence of institutional arrangements in China for reviewing the meaning and validity of legislation and other legal instruments. Chinese courts do not have general authority to interpret legal rules or invalidate laws or regulations. Generally speaking, the power to interpret laws is vested in the body that formulated them,[35] although this power is partially delegated to the Supreme People's Court, which frequently issues interpretations of law, including in the area of labour and social security law.[36]

However, this delegated power to clarify the meaning of laws does not extend to conferring a power on the Supreme People's Court, let alone courts lower in the hierarchy, to invalidate laws and rules which conflict with superior instruments, such as the Constitution. That power lies with bodies exercising legislative or executive power, such as the Standing Committee of the National People's Congress and the State Council.[37] Courts may refuse to enforce rules if they are inconsistent with higher level laws only in relation to a specific case.[38]

If citizens wish to challenge a law or other legal instrument on the ground that it is inconsistent with the Constitution, they are able to petition the Standing Committee of the National People's Congress.[39]

---

[34] Note that Australia, for example, has very few constitutionally entrenched rights. See Fenwick in chapter two.

[35] The power to interpret laws is vested in the Standing Committee of the National People's Congress, Legislation Law arts 42–47. Administrative Regulations are interpreted by the State Council: Regulations on the Procedures for the Formulation of Administrative Regulations art 31. Other rules are likewise interpreted by the formulating agency: Regulations on the Procedures for the Formulation of Rules art 33. These provisions stipulate that interpretations have the same legal effect as the original instrument.

[36] Zuigao Renmin Fayuan guanyu Shenli Laodong Zhengyi Anjian Shiyong Falü Ruogan Wenti de Jieshi [Interpretation of the Supreme People's Court Concerning Several Issues Regarding the Application of Law to the Trial of Labour Disputes Cases] (hereafter Labour Dispute Interpretation) (*Fashi 2001 No 14*), issued by the Supreme People's Court 16 April 2001 with effect from 30 April 2001. Note that the regulation of labour disputes has been affected by the new Labour Disputes Mediation and Arbitration Law. See also Peerenboom, R, *China's Long March toward the Rule of Law,* (Cambridge University Press, Cambridge, 2002) 317–18.

[37] Legislation Law arts 85–88.

[38] Peeronboom, *China's Long March toward the Rule of Law,* (2002) 316–18, 420–24. Zhonghua Renmin Gongheguo Xingzheng Susong Fa [Administrative Litigation Law of the People's Republic of China] (hereafter Administrative Litigation Law), passed 4 April 1989 with effect from 1 October 1990 arts 12(2) 52–53.

[39] Legislation Law art 90.

However, this is not very fruitful as the Standing Committee rarely invalidates rules.[40]

In China then, we do not see the development of extensive constitutional jurisprudence on labour rights, or related public interest litigation, as can be found in, for example, India. While the Supreme People's Court has made a very important contribution to the implementation of labour and social security law, this has been by way of 'gap filling' in relation to labour litigation, and in particular, clarifying the range of workers who can access labour dispute resolution processes.[41] In a practical sense, this does much for enabling non-standard workers, in particular, to enforce legislated labour rights through arbitration processes or the courts. However, in issuing its interpretations, the Supreme People's Court is not seeking to give new meaning to labour rights in any direct way.

To examine which labour rights are recognised in China, and how they are interpreted and implemented, it is therefore necessary to examine labour and social security legislation.

THE FRAMEWORK OF LABOUR LAW

The conception of rights reflected in the Chinese Constitution and in its qualified ratification of international human rights instruments is highly significant for its labour legislation. This category of legislation law is conceived in China (as in many countries influenced by the Civil Law tradition) as an aspect of social law,[42] and social law is a major vehicle for giving effect to the rights of subsistence and development. The term 'rights' is frequently used in the major laws, which elaborate on the key constitutional provisions dealing with labour.

---

[40] Peerenboom (n 36) 259. Citizens are also able to request the State Council and other organs to deal with conflicts between certain rules: Regulations on the Procedures for the Formulation of Rules art 35.

[41] Zuigao Renmin Fayuan guanyu Shenli Laodong Zhengyi Anjian Shiyong Falü Ruogan Wenti de Jieshi [Interpretation of the Supreme People's Court Concerning Several Issues Regarding the Application of Law to the Trial of Labour Disputes Cases] Number I (*Fashi 2001 No 14*), issued by the Supreme People's Court 16 April 2001 with effect from 30 April 2001; and Number II (*Fashi 2006 No 6*) issued by the Supreme People's Court on 10 July 2006 with effect from 1 October 2006.

[42] 'Social law' is an ambiguous term in China. It has multiple meanings that do not always coincide with either common law or civil law concepts. First, it can refer to social security law. Secondly, it refers to a combination of labour law and social security law; this is the definition used by the National People's Congress. Thirdly, it can cover areas including economic law more generally. Other scholars use the term in different ways again (see, eg, Wang Quanxing, 'Social Law Scholarship Should Learn Lessons from Economic Law Scholarship' (2004) 1 *Zhejiang Academic Journal*. Aside from using the term to classify areas of law, the term can also be used to refer to legal phenomena (such as the socialisation of public law and private law) or to certain legal rules.

Before examining how the terminology of rights is used in Chinese labour legislation, we will first provide an overview of the development and current structure of the key laws. Comparatively speaking, Chinese labour laws are of very recent origin. They have been enacted over the last 15 years, following the implementation of provisional legislative instruments during the 1980s.[43]

This recent origin is a consequence of the need to reconstruct the legal system following the disorder of the Cultural Revolution. It also reflects the incremental reorganisation of the economy along 'socialist market' lines. Two significant consequences of the reorganisation have been the conversion of administrative ordering (characteristic of central planning) to contractual arrangements and the ever increasing share of the economic activity represented by the private sector. The new labour laws have been enacted to provide a regulatory framework for transactions under these changed economic conditions. The major goals of these laws are promoting employment, protecting employees' rights and interests, coordinating labour relations (and reducing conflict), raising people's incomes and improving social security.[44]

The Key Laws

Legislative efforts over the last two decades have led to the enactment of a number of major laws in the field of labour relations. It should be appreciated that from the Chinese point of view, these are laws dealing with labour and *social security*; these two fields, while clearly delineated in some jurisdictions, are closely intertwined in the PRC. Thus, the administering agency for most aspects of the law is the Ministry of Human Resources and Social Security (MOHRSS, formerly the Ministry of Labour and Social Security), and several aspects of social insurance are dealt with in the key labour laws. This integrated approach is consistent with the constitutional specification of labour rights, which, as we have seen, includes both individual and collective labour rights and social security rights, often in the same provision.

The first major labour law enacted by the National People's Congress (NPC)[45] in the post-1978 era was the Trade Union Law of 1992.[46] As its name suggests, this Law, extensively revised by the NPC in 2001, provides

---

[43] The history of China's labour legislation is discussed in Josephs, H, *Labor Law in China* (Huntington, Juris Press, 2003).

[44] See Information Office of the State Council of the People's Republic of China, *Labour and Social Security in China* (April 2002, Beijing).

[45] As distinct from temporary and sub-legislative measures.

[46] Zhonghua Renmin Gongheguo Gonghui Fa [Trade Union Law of the People's Republic of China] (hereafter Trade Union Law), passed by the National People's Congress on 3 April 1992 and revised 27 October 2001, with effect from that date.

the legal basis for the regulation of the right to organise in China. The Trade Union Law was followed in 1994 by the Labour Law.[47] This is the key law governing employment relations. It applies to most enterprises, whether in the state or private sector, and to most forms of employment. The content of the Law is very extensive, covering employment contracts, termination, minimum standards, occupational health and safety, vocational training, social insurance, dispute resolution and enforcement.

The Law goes some way towards giving effect to China's international obligations under those conventions it has ratified. Thus, in (partial) accordance with ILO Convention 111, the Law provides that workers shall not be discriminated against in employment due to their nationality, race, sex, or religious belief[48] (although not political opinion or social origin, which are specifically referred to in the Convention).[49] The Law also stipulates equal pay for equal work (although not specifically for work of equal *value,* as Convention 100 requires).[50] There is a broad prohibition on child labour,[51] reflecting Convention 138.

As with many Chinese statutes, the Labour Law is comparatively short[52] and expressed in general terms. Not surprisingly, given the increasing complexity and diversification of labour relations in the PRC, it has been necessary to complement the law with other more specific statutes, as well as with subordinate legislation (*fagui*) issued by bodies ranging from the State Council to the MOHRSS to local government legislative and executive bodies. This subordinate legislation is voluminous and sometimes contradictory, often apparently addressed to the labour bureaucracy rather than the parties to labour relationships.[53] It undermines coherence in the labour law framework, although the gradual enactment of higher level laws is improving the situation.

These complementing higher level laws (which themselves require further elaboration) include the Law on the Prevention and Treatment of Occupational Diseases of 2001,[54] the Work Safety Law of 2002,[55] the

[47] Zhonghua Renmin Gongheguo Laodong Fa [Labour Law of the People's Republic of China] (hereafter 'Labour Law'), passed by the National People's Congress 5 July 1994 with effect from 1 May 1995.

[48] Labour Law arts 3 and 12.

[49] Labour Law art 1. Article 13 contains further provisions about gender equality.

[50] Labour Law art 46.

[51] Labour Law art 15.

[52] The Labour Law comprises 107 articles.

[53] See Cooney, S, 'Making Chinese Labor Law Work: The Prospects for Regulatory Innovation in the People's Republic of China' (2007) 30 *Fordham International Law Journal* 1050.

[54] Zhonghua Renmin Gongheguo Zhiyebing Zhiliao Fa [Law of the People's Republic of China on the Prevention and Treatment of Occupational Diseases] passed by the Standing Committee of the National People's Congress 10 October 2001, with effect from 1 May 2002.

[55] Zhonghua Renmin Gongheguo Anquan Shengchan Fa [Law of the People's Republic of China on Work Safety] (hereafter Work Safety Law) passed by the Standing Committee of the National People's Congress 29 June 2002, with effect from 1 November 2002.

Labour Contract Law of 2007,[56] the Employment Promotion Law of 2007[57] and the Labour Disputes Mediation and Arbitration Law of 2007.[58]

As economic conditions in China are rapidly changing, the laws require regular significant amendment. For example, the shift to contractually based economic arrangements has been accompanied by a proliferation of contractual forms in work relationships. Labour hire arrangements (or *paiqian*—'labour dispatch' as they are termed in China) have greatly expanded.[59] In several industries, such as construction, a workplace can be structured around a complex web of subcontracting and employment arrangements, where it is often difficult to determine how to categorise a particular form of engagement. The enactment of the Labour Contract Law was a major legal response to this.

Similarly, there is ever greater diversity in the nature of Chinese firms. The earlier relatively straightforward classification of firms as either state-owned, collective or individual (the latter formerly of little consequence), has given way to a wide range of business forms including corporatised state entities, township and village enterprises run by local governments, private companies, joint ventures, wholly foreign owned firms and small unincorporated private businesses. Labour relations mechanisms such as arbitration committees, unions and workers' councils (*zhigong daibiao dahui*), which were designed to operate under the old enterprise forms, are often ill-adapted to the new enterprise forms. In particular, they are frequently unable to deal effectively with labour disputes in the new types of firm. The new Labour Disputes Mediation and Arbitration Law is, in part, a reaction to these changes.

---

[56] Zhonghua Renmin Gongheguo Laodong Hetong Fa [Law of the People's Republic of China on Labour Contracts] passed by the Standing Committee of the National People's Congress 29 June 2007 with effect from 1 January 2008. See Cooney, S, Biddulph, S, Li Kungang and Ying Zhu, 'China's New Labour Contract Law: Responding to the Growing Complexity of Labour Relations in the PRC' (2007) 30 *University of New South Wales Law Journal* 788.

[57] Zhonghua Renmin Gongheguo Jiuye Cujin Fa [Employment Promotion Law of the People's Republic of China], passed by the Standing Committee of the National People's Congress on 30 August 2007 with effect from 1 January 2008.

[58] Zhonghua Renmin Gongheguo Laodong Zhengyi Tiaojie Zhongcai Fa [Labour Disputes Mediation and Arbitration Law], passed by the Standing Committee of the National People's Congress on 29 December 2007 with effect from 1 May 2008. For important empirical studies of dispute resolution practices in China prior to the passage of this law, see eg,: Halegua, A, 'Getting Paid: Processing the Labor Disputes of China's Migrant Workers' (2008) 26 *Berkeley Journal of International Law* 26, 101; Gallagher, M, '"Use the Law as Your Weapon"—Institutional Change and Legal Mobilization in China' in N Diamant, S Lubman and K O'Brien (eds), *Engaging the Law in China: State, Society and Possibilities for Justice* (Stanford, Stanford University Press, 2005); See Ho, V, *Labor Dispute Resolution in China: Implications for Labor Rights and Legal Reform* (Berkeley, Institute of East Asian Studies, 2003); Brown, R, *Understanding Labor and Employment in China* (Cambridge, Cambridge University Press, 2009).

[59] See Zhou Changzheng, *Laodong Paiqian de Fazhan yu Falü Guizhi [The Development and Legal Regulation of Labour Dispatch]* (Beijing, Ministry of Labour and Social Security Press, 2007).

Some of the key non-statutory legal instruments include rules made by the State Council (such as the Working Hours Regulations),[60] the MOHRSS (such as the Provisions on Collective Contracts)[61] and the Supreme People's Court (such as the interpretations on labour dispute settlement referred to earlier[62]).

Aside from these legal materials directed specifically at labour issues, there are laws of general application which contain provisions regulating labour relations. Of most significance to labour rights are the 'protection' laws concerning vulnerable groups in society. These include the 1991 Law on the Protection of Minors,[63] and the 1992 Law on the Protection of Rights and Interests of Women.[64]

THE USE OF RIGHTS LANGUAGE IN THE LEGISLATION

The labour laws translate the abstract constitutional rights into a more specific form, although as we will see, this process does not always deliver legally enforceable entitlements. The Labour Law and the Trade Union Law are the most important legal instruments setting out labour rights. It is apparent that the concept of a 'right' is fundamental in both statutes; it is mentioned at least 30 times in each, even though the Labour Law has little over 100 articles, and the Trade Union Law only 57. Sometimes, the term 'right' is used simply to indicate a procedural entitlement, as in an expression such as *youquan tichu yijian* ('to have the right to give an opinion').[65] However, much more frequently, the words *youquan* (to have a right) *quanli* ('right') or *quanyi* ('rights and interests') are employed in the sense of civil and political or economic and social rights. Thus, article 3 of the Labour Law provides that:

> Workers enjoy equal rights to employment and to choose their occupation, the right to remuneration for labour, the rights to rest and to take leave, the right to

[60] Guowuyuan guanyu Zhigong Gonzuo Shijian de Guiding [State Council Regulation concerning Working Hours], promulgated by the State Council 25 March 1995, in effect from 1 May 1995.

[61] Jiti Hetong Guiding [Collective Contract Regulations], promulgated by the Ministry of Labour and Social Security, 20 January 2004.

[62] Zuigao Renmin Fayuan guanyu Shenli Laodong Zhengyi Anjian Shiyong Falü Ruogan Wenti de Jieshi [Interpretation of the Supreme People's Court Concerning Several Issues Regarding the Application of Law to the Trial of Labour Disputes Cases] Number I (*Fashi 2001 No 14*), issued by the Supreme People's Court 16 April 2001 with effect from 30 April 2001; and Number II (*Fashi 2006 No 6*) issued by the Supreme People's Court on 10 July 2006 with effect from 1 October 2006.

[63] Zhongguo Renmin Gongheguo Ertong Baohu Fa [PRC Law on the Protection of Minors], passed by the Standing Committee of the Seventh National People's Congress on 4 September 1991, and effective as of 1 January 1992. Amended 29 December 2006. See arts 38 and 68.

[64] Zhongguo Renmin Gongheguo Funü Quanli Baohu Fa [PRC Law on the Protection of Rights and Interests of Women], passed by National People's Congress on 3 April 1992 and amended by the National People's Congress Standing Committee on 28 August 2005. See chapter IV relating to work rights.

[65] See eg, Labour Law art 30.

protection of their health and safety, the right to receive training in vocational skills, the right to social insurance and social welfare, the right to submission of labour disputes for settlement, and other rights as stipulated by law.

This provision links the labour rights laid out in the Constitution to the structure of the Labour Law, and the more specific provisions to be found in the remainder of the Law or in other related legislation. For example, the right to rest, found in article 3 of the PRC Constitution, and again in article 3 of the Labour Law, is given specific content in articles 36 to 44 of the Labour Law. These provisions establish an eight hour day, a 44 hour average working week,[66] the requirement for at least one day of rest, and a system of penalty rates for work outside ordinary hours. The provisions are complemented by an extensive set of national and local government regulations which give effect to some of the opt-out arrangements permissible under the Law.[67]

Of course, as discussed later, in many workplaces these provisions are more honoured in the breach. Nonetheless, the point being made here is that, despite the contradictions found between *specific* provisions in various regulations, there is an underlying coherence to the fundamental *structure* of Chinese labour law, which links it closely to constitutional rights.

A similar coherence between constitutional and statutory rights is evidenced in the Trade Union Law. Article 3 provides that:

> Blue and white collar workers who rely on wage income as the primary means to meet their living expenses have *the right to* participate in, and to organise trade unions in accordance with law, regardless of their nationality, race, sex, occupation, religious beliefs or educational level. No organisation or individual can interfere or restrict the exercise of this right.

Again, this general provision links back to the Constitution, and is elaborated on in subsequent articles. In this instance the phrase 'in accordance with law' is an especially important qualification, as it refers to the processes stipulated in the Trade Union Law that subordinate grass-root unions to the CCP-controlled All China Federation of Trade Unions.

The use of labour rights terminology set out in labour legislation is not limited to those matters specifically enumerated in the PRC Constitution. Some labour rights are connected more closely to those parts of international human rights instruments which China has acceded to than to the Constitution. For example, the Constitution does not expressly restrict inappropriate forms of child labour; it contains only a prohibition on the

---

[66] Guowuyuan guanyu Zhigong Gonzuo Shijian de Guiding [State Council Regulation concerning Working Hours].
[67] Based on arts 39, 41 and 42.

'maltreatment' of children.[68] Child labour is, however, regulated directly by two of the 'core' ILO Conventions that China has ratified, as well as in the ICCPR and the ICESCR. As mentioned earlier, these have been reflected in Chinese labour law. The Labour Law prohibits juvenile labour in broad terms.[69] This is made more precise in the State Council's Provisions on the Prohibition of Using Child Labour, most recently revised in 2002, following China's ratification of ILO Convention 182.[70]

Labour Rights Language as a Bulwark against Neo-liberal Labour Market Reforms

The underlying conceptual coherence[71] of Chinese labour law, prominently involving rights discourse, has an important political function in debates over labour policy. It assists opponents of radical labour market reforms that are sometimes urged by neo-liberal policy entrepreneurs either in international agencies, such as the World Bank[72] or within Chinese government ministries. These policy entrepreneurs are often strongly supported by business interests, and advocate reduction or elimination of union rights and of protective labour entitlements. Some Chinese academics also take this position, although perhaps not to an extreme extent. These scholars have criticised traditional labour law, which emphasises workers protection[73] and labour rights standards,[74] from the standpoint of human resource management theory and economics,[75] and/or have promoted 'corporate social responsibility (CSR) measures' as a way of complementing or even replacing labour law. However, neo-liberal policy advocates find themselves

---

[68] Constitution of the PRC art 49.

[69] Labour Law art 15.

[70] Adopted at the 63rd Executive Meeting of the State Council on September 18, 2002, promulgated by Decree No 364 of the State Council of the People's Republic of China on October 1, 2002, and effective as of December 1, 2002. See also art 68 of the Law on the Protection of Minors.

[71] As opposed to internal systemic coherence—as indicated earlier, there are many inconsistencies in Chinese labour legislation, particular at the level of subordinate and regional laws.

[72] See eg, the World Bank's *Doing Business Report*, which is heavily influenced by the work of scholars suggesting the labour market should be radically deregulated.

[73] Dong Baohua, *Legal Mechnism of Labour Relations* (Shanghai, Shanghai Jiaotong University Press, 1997) 77–78; Wang Quanxing, *Labour Law* (Beijing, Higher Education Press, 2004) 69–70; Dong Baohua, Zheng Shaohua, 'Social Law: a Study on the Third Field of Law' (1999) 1 *Journal of the East China University of Politics & Law*.

[74] Chang Kai, 'Labour Rights Standard: Base and Core of Labour Relations Construction' (1997) 13 *Labour Movement Study*; Jia Junling, *Labour Law* (Beijing, Peking University Press, 2003) 19–22; Guan Huai, *Labour Law* (Beijing, Renmin University of China Press, 2001) 20–21; Wang Quanxing, *Labour Law* (Beijing, Higher Education Press, 2004) 75–77.

[75] See Dong Baohua, 'What Kind of Labour Contract We Should Have' *First Finance and Economics Daily* (31 March 2006).

in direct contradiction to the Chinese conception of labour rights embedded in the PRC Constitution.

Two recent sets of circumstances may illustrate this. One concerns the right to organise. As we have seen, Chinese citizens do not have the right to organise a union independent of, or in opposition to, the party-state, but they do have the right to organise a union that is affiliated to the All China Federation of Trade Unions. This right was put to the test when the American retail giant Walmart began expanding its operations in China. It is well known that Walmart is very strongly opposed to being organised by unions in the United States.[76] It was also resistant to attempts by the ACFTU to set up enterprise unions in Walmart stores in China. In the tussle which followed, the ACFTU, directly supported by the Chinese President Hu Jintao, was ultimately successful in forcing Walmart to accept its presence in many of its stores.[77] In its unionisation campaign, the ACFTU was able to deploy the language of labour rights effectively against the American corporation.

The second example concerns the controversy around the drafting of the Labour Contracts Law. When a draft law was released for public comment, several business organisations, the most aggressive being the American Chamber of Commerce in Shanghai, vociferously opposed it,[78] particular the provisions pertaining to employee rights relating to human resources policies, and to termination and severance.[79] This led to a sometimes acrimonious debate over the bill, with opposing views strongly and publicly expressed in a way which would not have occurred in China until recently. Again, supporters of the draft laws' labour protection provisions appealed to the language of labour rights. Although a number of revisions were made to the original draft, the initial orientation of the legislation largely remained in its enacted form.

GIVING EFFECT TO THE RIGHTS IN PRACTICE

Of course, while the language of labour rights is demonstrably powerful in China, this does not mean that those rights are generally respected.

[76] See, eg, Human Rights Watch, *Discounting Rights Wal-Mart's Violation of US Workers' Right to Freedom of Association* (May 2007).

[77] Chan, A, 'Made in China: Wal-Mart Unions, Success of Chinese unions could foreshadow unionization for Wal-Mart elsewhere in the world' *YaleGlobal* (12 October 2006).

[78] On 23–24 April 2006, Dong Baohua (law professor at Huadong Zhengfa Daxue) and one of the authors (Liu Cheng), co-sponsored a conference on the draft of Employment Contract Act. During the conference, some participants argued in favour of replacing labour law with CSR and human resource management theory. A representative of AmCham Shanghai, together with 20 human resource managers of US enterprises 'crashed' our conference room, threatening that they would withdraw capital if we didn't revise the draft according to their wishes.

[79] Cooney et al, 'China's New Labour Contract Law' (2007).

On the contrary, it is notorious that extremely serious violations occur. This section of the chapter briefly examines some reasons why, despite the apparent support for (qualified) labour rights, widespread non-compliance persists. There are, of course, a very wide range of factors contributing to non-compliance.[80] These include the close relationships between local governments (responsible for enforcing labour law) and employers; the low status of workers migrating from rural areas, who are the chief victims of labour abuses such as non-payment of wages, overtime or social insurance premiums; the increasing use of short-term employment contracts and/or labour hire arrangements (although this may be curbed by the Labour Contract Law); widespread lack of will/ability to implement proper safety schemes; and financial constraints on smaller enterprises.

Apart from these well known difficulties, there are five further legal problems preventing workers from realising their rights that we highlight here: the poor quality of legislation; the absence of a legal framework regulating union litigation on behalf of workers; the lack of a legislative process for direct election of trade unions at the grassroots level; the lack of sufficient suitable qualified legal professionals able to defend workers rights; and inadequate legal education.

Quality of Labour Legislation

The problems in this area extend to bad drafting and confusion between law and policy. These are evident throughout the Chinese legal system but have been a particular concern in relation to the law of work.[81] The worst aspect of this is a failure to adequately specify an effective way for enforcing many apparent legal entitlements. Many laws ostensibly conferring rights on workers are paper tigers, for there are few if any sanctions for non-compliance. This is the case with many legal rules pertaining to anti-discrimination, as the Law on the Protection of the Rights and Interests of Women demonstrates.[82] This problem is exacerbated because legislation disproportionately emphasises administrative enforcement of law, at the expense of private litigation. This ignores the fact that some local governments are reluctant to enforce laws.[83] And where penalties do exist, they are often of insufficient seriousness to deter employers from violating laws.

---

[80] For a more extensive discussion, see Cooney, 'Making Chinese Labor Law Work' (2007) and Halegua, 'Getting Paid: Processing the Labor Disputes of China's Migrant Workers' (2008).

[81] See Peerenboom (n 36); Cooney (n 53); Halegua (n 58).

[82] Even after significant amendments in 2005, this law is extremely vague on the precise remedies available for violations of women's rights.

[83] Some local governments discourage labour officers from inspection for the purpose of economic growth.

A further aspect of poor drafting—and specifically of gaps in the labour law framework—is the lack of legal *procedures* designed to deal with labour issues. Labour law procedure tends to fall between the stools of administrative law and civil law. Many labour law issues traverse both these fields, but the relationships between them all have not been adequately addressed. Unfortunately, scholars of administrative law and of civil law mostly show little interest in labour law. This lack of interest leads to a failure to appreciate how general civil law or administrative law procedures are ill-suited to labour cases.

For example, industrial injuries are dealt with in the court system through civil procedures. Despite the fact that injuries are widespread, there are no specific civil procedure rules dealing with such cases, such as might be found in accident compensation legislation in developed countries. It is true that there are regulations about industrial injuries proceedings promulgated by the Human Resources and Social Security Ministry. These regulations contain rules about evidence, for example, but they are not usually applied by the civil courts and some parts of them may in any case contradict the Legislation Law. Thus, industrial cases are often judged in light of the General Principles of the Civil Law and the Civil Procedure Law of the People's Republic of China. These laws require, for example, employees to prove fault on the part of the employer as though the case were a negligence claim.

The problems caused by the absence of specific labour procedures are exacerbated in China by the fact that there are no labour courts; labour disputes are settled by the general court system.[84] These courts do not ordinarily have special expertise in labour matters, especially outside the main urban centres.

Trade Unions' Litigation Rights on Behalf of Workers

One of the important amendments of the Trade Union Law in 2001 was that the legislation granted trade unions litigation rights. These rights include submitting a case to labour arbitration and, subsequently, to the courts where an employer violates a collective agreement[85] or a provision of the Trade Union Law.[86] Unions are also required to assist a worker maintaining an action before an arbitration tribunal or a court,[87] and

---

[84] The Chinese court system allows for an appeal, usually from local to immediate courts but in complex cases sometimes involving high courts or ultimately the Supreme People's Courts.

[85] Trade Union Law art 20.

[86] Ibid art 49.

[87] Ibid art 21.

are empowered to recover union property where it has been embezzled.[88] At first glance, this would see to give Chinese unions a very important role in protecting labour rights.

However, this has not led to extensive court litigation in practice by unions on behalf of workers. Again, the absence of any labour law-specific procedures may be one of the main culprits here. There are no rules of any detail concerning the procedure for trade unions to litigate. None are to be found in the Trade Union Law, the Labour Disputes Mediation and Arbitration Law,[89] the Civil Procedure Law, the Administrative Litigation Law or in any related legislation. While the Supreme People's Court has issued Interpretations on labour disputes,[90] they too do not address the litigation rights of unions. Nor is there yet a national level law on collective contracts that would indicate how unions can ensure such contracts are complied with. Collective contracts are dealt with briefly in the Labour Law and (a little more extensively) in the Labour Contract Law, and in regulations issued by the Ministry of Human Resources and Social Security. However, these do not deal adequately with the enforcement of legal rights protected in a collective agreement.

Direct Election of Trade Unions at Grassroots Level

Chinese unions have had difficulties adapting to an environment where there are sharp conflicts of interest between management and staff.[91] Union leaders often hold management positions and so their capacity to represent the interests of workers and to defend their rights is sometimes called into question. One response to this has been for some grassroots (enterprise) unions to conduct direct elections for leadership positions. However, while there have been widespread trials for many years, there is still no law or regulation institutionalising their use. Grassroots elections need to become the norm; not just to ensure that trade unions are representative, but also to realise trade unions' basic duties under the Trade Union Law and the

---

[88] Ibid art 54.

[89] Unions have a well established role in mediation and arbitration procedures, a role confirmed and clarified by the new Mediation and Arbitration Law. However, this Law does not deal with a union's role in litigation to any extent.

[90] Zuigao Renmin Fayuan guanyu Shenli Laodong Zhengyi Anjian Shiyong Falü Ruogan Wenti de Jieshi [Interpretation of the Supreme People's Court Concerning Several Issues Regarding the Application of Law to the Trial of Labour Disputes Cases] Number I (*Fashi 2001 No 14*), issued by the Supreme People's Court 16 April 2001 with effect from 30 April 2001; and Number II (*Fashi 2006 No 6*) issued by the Supreme People's Court on 10 July 2006 with effect from 1 October 2006.

[91] Taylor, B et al, *Industrial Relations in China* (Cheltenham, Edward Elgar Publishing, 2003); Chen, F, 'Between the State and Labour: The Conflict of Chinese Trade Unions' Double Identity in Market Reform' (2003) 76 *The China Quarterly* 1006, 1018–22.

Labour Law. The appropriate way to do this is through amendment of both these laws.

Lack of Sufficient Professionals in the Labour Law Area

Under the command economy, industrial disputes were very uncommon. Now, in pace with the shift to a market economy, with large scale private ownership, the number of disputes has greatly increased.[92] However, there has not as yet been a corresponding growth in the number of legal and industrial relations professionals experienced in the resolution of industrial disputes. While worker advice centres, often staffed by lawyers, are growing in number and sophistication,[93] they are still generally confined to major cities, and/or to universities. It remains the case that most lawyers, judges and prosecutors have little knowledge of Chinese labour law, let alone international labour law.

Inadequate Labour Law Education and Training

The paucity of labour law professionals is partly a consequence of the limited opportunities to study labour law. First, labour law is not in the list of 14 core subjects that are a mandatory part of the law curriculum. Most law students do not study labour law, which results in the lack of qualified professionals in the field. Secondly, labour law training outside universities is scarce. Both governments and enterprises are usually unwilling to fund such training, and the training organised by trade unions is limited to trade union law. Thirdly, college students who do not major in law do not have a sound grasp of labour law, even if they are in disciplines such as industrial relations. This means that, where students go on to work in unions, there are not enough trade union leaders who understand key legal entitlements.

Reworking Chinese Labour Law to Give Better Effect to Labour Rights

In order to solve these various legal problems inhibiting effective implementation of the labour rights recognised in China, the relationships between

[92] According to publicly available Ministry of Labour and Social Security statistics, the number of labour disputes coming before the courts increased every year from 1996 to 2004, from 41, 697 to 249, 335. Over the same period, the number of collective labour disputes brought to arbitration increased from 3,150 to 19,241: see Ministry of Labour and Social Security Statistical Yearbook 2005, Table 9-1.

[93] See Halegua (n 58).

labour law, administrative law and civil law need to be clarified, in theory and in practice. The situation in contemporary China is in some ways reminiscent of the court system in European countries in the nineteenth century, before the distinct nature of labour law and labour rights was properly recognised through dedicated labour dispute resolution procedures and/or dedicated labour dispute resolution institutions. China does already recognise labour rights but lacks effective enforcement institutions. To be sure, there is a labour arbitration system, but this is insufficient because it is essentially an arm of the labour administration. If labour law is to be better implemented there need to be wider institutional reforms. In short, there needs to be a comprehensive institutional framework dealing with industrial relations issues,[94] including the status of unions in litigation.

This should be complemented with a much improved system of labour law education and training. At university level, this could include raising the status of labour law in the curriculum and enabling students from other disciplines to take classes in labour law as part of their studies. More broadly, judges and lawyers need to receive training on labour issues and there should be more public education campaigns. The need for such education and training should be apparent if for no other reason than the huge increase in labour disputes.

Given China's lack of experience in dealing with industrial relations in a competitive market economy, one important way of providing training is through international cooperation. For example, it would assist judges, lawyers and unionists in dealing with industrial disputes (including those arising from the violation of labour rights) if they were more exposed to overseas institutions and practices. In the case of exchanges between Chinese and international trade unions, this would have the added advantage of reducing some of the animosity which has been known to exist at the international level.

Scholarly exchanges, too, are another important vehicle for assisting in the conceptual development of Chinese labour law, and in overcoming the failure to integrate adequately labour law into the wider frameworks of administrative and civil law.

CONCLUSION

Labour rights are a well recognised concept in Chinese law, from the Constitution down to the level of individual enactments. The Chinese understanding of rights differs, however, from that accepted in many Western countries, and also from that reflected in several international conventions.

---

[94] Jia Junling, *Labour Law* (Beijing, Peking University Press, 2003) 4.

Essentially, rights to subsistence and development are emphasised at the expense of many individual rights, such as freedom of association. Nonetheless, there is considerable overlap between Chinese and international labour rights, including in many areas of the ILO's 'decent work' agenda, such as anti-discrimination, child labour and the need for labour standards in areas such as pay, working hours and workplace safety.

China has, and has not, been successful in giving effect to the labour rights it recognises. Insofar as the realisation of rights to subsistence and development are dependent on economic progress, China has been very successful indeed. The opening-up and modernisation of the economy have created favourable conditions for solving problems such as unemployment and poverty. A market-oriented system of employment relations has now been consolidated in China; this has laid a sound foundation for the further promotion of the 'positive' labour and social security rights.[95]

At the same time, the pursuit of market solutions to many labour issues has not led the Chinese Government to take a laissez-faire approach to labour standards. Chinese legislation does in fact create a fairly comprehensive floor of rights and the fact that these reflect constitutional stipulations prevents their erosion at the hands of the more extreme neo-liberal policy entrepreneurs.

On the other hand, at the level of individual workplaces, China's record of giving effect to labour rights has been much less impressive. We have seen that constitutional labour rights cannot be enforced by individual workers directly through judicial review. Workers must rather resort to the remedies set out in labour legislation. Yet, although labour legislation is taken seriously by the Chinese authorities (as the ongoing attempts to update the law illustrate), its implementation is still very poor. Some of the factors we pointed to that contribute to this are the poor quality of labour legislation; the failure to realise the litigation rights of trade unions; the failure of legislation to entrench the direct election of trade unions at grassroots level; the paucity and poor quality of labour professionals; and inadequate education and training. These problems are not insoluble, and are widely admitted. The preparedness of many Chinese policy-makers, scholars and organisations to continue to look for positive incremental reforms to the nation's laws are likely to see further amendments to key labour laws in the near future.

---

[95] Nonetheless, problems remain at this macroeconomic level, and the problems of structural employment and an aging population will remain serious for a long time to come.

6

Workers' Human Rights in English Law*

ACL DAVIES

INTRODUCTION

IN COMPARISON WITH many other countries of the world, the human rights of workers in England[1] are relatively well-protected. Trade unionists do not risk death or imprisonment, and the vast majority of workers enjoy decent working conditions. There is a comprehensive and detailed code of labour/employment[2] legislation, covering topics such as discrimination, unfair dismissal, health and safety, wages and hours, and collective bargaining. The United Kingdom has been a member of the European Union (EU) for over 30 years, and much of our employment law reflects EU requirements. Historically, the United Kingdom played a key role in the creation and development of the International Labour Organization (ILO). The United Kingdom was a founding signatory of the European Convention on Human Rights (ECHR) and has permitted individuals to petition the Court in Strasbourg since 1966. The United Kingdom is also a signatory to the European Social Charter 1961 (ESC), another Council of Europe instrument, which relates specifically to protection of socio-economic rights, but has yet to ratify the protocol on collective complaints or the Revised Social Charter of 1996.

Although it is important not to forget that workers enjoy a relatively high level of protection in the United Kingdom, particularly when viewed in global terms, there is no room for complacency. A detailed analysis of English law reveals a number of shortcomings, some of which involve breaches of basic human rights. For example, the United Kingdom has been condemned by the ILO on numerous occasions for permitting certain

---

* The author is grateful to the editors for their comments on an earlier draft of this chapter, though the author retains responsibility for any errors or omissions. This chapter incorporates developments up to April 2009.
[1] The UK is made up of four jurisdictions: England, Wales, Scotland and Northern Ireland. For reasons of space, this chapter will concentrate on English law unless otherwise indicated.
[2] These terms tend to be used interchangeably by English lawyers.

forms of discrimination against trade unionists, and for restricting the right to strike.[3] Moreover, workers may find it difficult to enforce their rights through litigation because of the cost and inconvenience this entails.

Workers' ability to rely explicitly on human rights arguments in the courts has, until recently, been limited. The United Kingdom has no written constitution and, as a result, no constitutional human rights guarantees. But the position has changed somewhat since the enactment of the Human Rights Act 1998 (HRA). This statute (to be explained in detail below) allows claimants to invoke most of the rights contained in the ECHR (but not the ESC) in the English courts. A number of Convention rights have relevance to employment law. The most obvious is freedom of association, but there are others, including freedom of expression, the right to respect for private life, and the (limited) right not to be subjected to discrimination. As the United Kingdom's first attempt to afford explicit legislative protection to human rights, the HRA must be the focus of attention in any discussion of workers' human rights in English law.

The aim of this chapter is to assess the extent to which the HRA should be regarded as a beneficial development in labour law. Some commentators have expressed concern that the Act's focus on the individual as the bearer of rights may be out of place in labour law, given the subject's traditional emphasis on the collective. It will be argued that this view is incorrect. Two more significant critiques of the Act will be advanced in this chapter. First, the Act has not yet been accompanied by the development of a 'human rights culture' either in the courts or in government. The courts have been unduly deferential when faced with justifications for infringing human rights, and the Government has introduced new legislation without fully considering its human rights implications. Secondly, because the Act draws on the ECHR alone, and not on its companion instrument, the ESC, it ignores economic and social rights which would have had greater relevance to labour law. Any protection it affords to workers' human rights is inevitably incomplete.

LEGAL FRAMEWORK

This section will explain the basic structure of English labour law for the benefit of those readers who are not familiar with the system. It will describe the role of statute and case law, the HRA, EU law and ILO Conventions. It will then provide the reader with a brief overview of the historical development of English law in order to explain the context into which the HRA has been introduced.

---

[3] See eg, ILO Committee on Freedom of Association, Case Nos 1540, 1618 and 1730.

English Labour Law

The English legal system is a common law system. This means that there are two main sources of law: statutes passed by Parliament and judicial decisions. The vast majority of English labour law is in statutory form. The Employment Rights Act 1996 (ERA) is the main source of individual employment law, and the Trade Union and Labour Relations (Consolidation) Act 1992 (TULRCA) is the main source of collective labour law, though there are numerous other enactments on specific topics. There is a complex interaction between statute and common law. For example, the main beneficiaries of statutory employment rights are those employed under a contract of employment.[4] The contract of employment is a common law concept which has been developed and defined by the judges in their decisions.[5]

An individual seeking to enforce his or her employment rights would, in general, pursue a claim in the employment tribunal in the first instance. These tribunals consist of a legally-qualified chairperson and two lay members, one representing employer interests and one representing employee interests. From the employment tribunal, it is possible to appeal on a point of law to the similarly-constituted Employment Appeal Tribunal (EAT). From the EAT, appeals lie to the ordinary higher appellate courts, the Court of Appeal and the House of Lords. Employment tribunals are bound to follow the decisions of the EAT and the higher courts.

Many labour lawyers are suspicious of the courts. They argue that judicial decisions are often hostile to workers' interests, and particularly to workers' collective interests as trade union members. Many examples could be given. The courts' interpretation of the contract of employment has been relatively narrow, tending to deny protection to the growing number of casual workers in today's economy.[6] The courts' approach to trade unions' disciplinary powers has been to limit them as far as possible, using doctrines drawn from public law.[7] On the one hand, these decisions could be regarded as the application of technical legal requirements from other areas of law (contract law, public law and so on) which do not fit particularly well with the underlying purposes of labour law. On the other hand, they could be seen as the manifestation of a broader ideological hostility to workers' interests. Some commentators' scepticism about the value

---

[4] Employment Rights Act 1996 (ERA) s 230.

[5] See eg, *Market Investigations v Minister of Social Security* [1969] 2 QB 173.

[6] See eg, Anderman, S, 'The Interpretation of Protective Statutes and Contracts of Employment' (2000) 29 *Industrial Law Journal* 223.

[7] Elias, P and Ewing, KD, *Trade Union Democracy, Members' Rights and the Law* (London, Mansell, 1987) chs 6 and 7.

of human rights arguments in labour law reflects, to some extent at least, their scepticism about the courts.[8]

The United Kingdom ratified the ECHR in 1951, and has permitted individuals to petition the Strasbourg Court since 1966. However, the Convention (and the Court's decisions) had no formal status in English law until the HRA came into force in 2000. This reflects English law's 'dualist' approach to international law. For many years, the Government argued that there was no need to incorporate Convention rights explicitly into domestic law. It claimed that the rights were sufficiently protected through existing legislation and common law, and stated that it would amend the law when called upon to do so by the European Court of Human Rights (ECtHR). The enactment of the HRA reflects a desire to allow the domestic courts—not just the ECtHR—to adjudicate on human rights questions. The HRA represents a compromise between the desire to afford greater judicial protection to human rights and an attempt to preserve the sovereignty of Parliament, a fundamental principle of the British constitution. The HRA does not empower the courts to strike down Acts of Parliament if they infringe Convention rights. Instead, it requires them to follow a two-stage process. First, they must attempt to interpret the statute in question consistently with those rights.[9] Secondly, if this is impossible, the courts may issue a 'declaration of incompatibility'.[10] This is merely an expression of opinion and does not oblige Parliament to take steps to amend the offending legislation. The Act's framers assumed that political pressure would be sufficient to ensure that amendments would be passed in most cases. The courts are to 'take into account' Convention jurisprudence when deciding cases.[11] The Act brings about two further significant changes. One is that public bodies are now obliged to act in accordance with human rights when exercising their powers.[12] The courts can enforce this obligation through judicial review. The other is that the courts themselves may take the Convention rights into account when developing the common law, though the exact scope of their obligation to do so remains a matter of debate.[13] It should be noted that a human rights point may be taken in the Employment Tribunal or the EAT, not just in the higher appellate courts, though the power to make a declaration of incompatibility lies only with the High Court, Court of Appeal or House of Lords.[14]

---

[8] See eg, Ewing, KD, 'The Human Rights Act and Labour Law' (1998) 27 *Industrial Law Journal* 275, 280–82.
[9] Human Rights Act 1998 (HRA) s 3.
[10] Ibid s 4.
[11] Ibid s 2.
[12] Ibid s 6.
[13] This follows from the courts' own status as public bodies within HRA s 6.
[14] HRA s 4(5).

The United Kingdom has been a member of the EU since 1973. As is well-known, successive Treaty amendments have expanded the EU's competence in employment law and it now has power to legislate on many significant topics such as discrimination, health and safety, working conditions, termination of employment, and information and consultation.[15] Pay, freedom of association, and the right to strike are, however, specifically excluded.[16] Most EU legislation takes the form of directives. These identify the end to be achieved but allow each Member State a discretion as to the method of achieving that end.[17] The United Kingdom has a relatively good record of implementing directives, although it is notorious for its hostility towards new proposals in the employment field, a hostility which has to some extent continued despite the election of an apparently more pro-European Labour Government in 1997. The European Court of Justice (ECJ) has played a significant role in developing anti-discrimination law in particular.[18] Its decisions are binding on the English courts. The EU has become increasingly focused on human rights in recent years, as part of an attempt to appeal more to its sometimes rather sceptical citizens. This culminated in the proclamation of the EU Charter of Fundamental Rights in 2000. The Charter is a comprehensive statement of human rights. It contains civil and political rights (drawing heavily on the ECHR) but also includes a wide range of economic and social rights. This makes it potentially very significant in the employment sphere. However, the Charter's role is limited.[19] First, it is designed only to constrain the Community institutions (and the Member States when they are implementing Community law) rather than to create new competences.[20] Secondly, it has no formal legal status at present, though this will change when the Treaty of Lisbon is finally brought into force. The ECJ has developed some jurisprudence to protect fundamental human rights against infringement by the Community but as yet this has been of limited significance in labour law.[21]

Finally, it should be noted that the United Kingdom is a long-standing member of the ILO. It has ratified all of the so-called 'core' Conventions and numerous others besides.[22] However, there are a number of areas in which the United Kingdom falls short of its ILO obligations. The United Kingdom

---

[15] Article 137 EC.

[16] Article 137(5) EC.

[17] Article 249 EC.

[18] Under article 141 EC in particular.

[19] For a helpful critique, see Ashiagbor, D, 'Economic and Social Rights in the European Charter of Fundamental Rights' (2004) 1 EHRLR 62.

[20] *Charter of Fundamental Rights of the European Union* [2000] OJ C364/1 art 51.

[21] See generally, Craig, P and de Búrca, G, *EU Law*, 4th edn (Oxford, Oxford University Press, 2008) ch 11. On recent developments in labour rights, see Davies, ACL, 'One Step Forward, Two Steps Back? The *Viking* and *Laval* Cases in the ECJ' (2008) 37 *Industrial Law Journal* 126.

[22] A list is available at: www.ilo.org/ilolex/english/newratframeE.htm.

has repeatedly been condemned by the ILO's supervisory bodies for permitting certain types of discrimination by employers against trade union members.[23] Although the present Government has not taken the extreme step of denouncing any Conventions, it seems content to ignore the ILO's criticisms. ILO Conventions have no formal status in the English legal system and are rarely referred to in court.

A Brief History

Historically, English labour lawyers did not think about their subject in terms of legal rights.[24] They focused on trade unions as the main mechanism for protecting workers. In many countries, union activities would, of course, be facilitated through legal rights, often enshrined in the constitution. In English law, trade unions were protected by means of statutory immunities against tort liability. Kahn-Freund, a highly influential figure in the early development of English labour law, regarded the relative absence of legal rights as beneficial.[25] He believed that workers could achieve better protection through collective bargaining. However, there were difficulties with this view. As majoritarian organisations, trade unions were not always very good at protecting workers in minority groups. Moreover, many workers did not join a union and these workers were also left in a vulnerable position. In the 1970s, the legislature began to redress the balance in favour of individual employment rights by enacting protections against unfair dismissal[26] and against sex and race discrimination.[27] Those academics who continued to favour collectivism regarded this legislation as creating a 'floor of rights' on which collective bargaining could build.[28]

The 1980s and early 1990s saw a succession of Conservative governments that were hostile to the trade union movement. This hostility was partly ideological and partly pragmatic. Ideologically, these governments favoured individualism, and pragmatically, they were concerned to tackle the high levels of industrial action that had plagued the United Kingdom in the late 1970s.[29] Interestingly, these governments attacked the unions through

[23] See eg, ILO Committee on Freedom of Association, Case Nos 1618 and 1730.

[24] For a detailed history of English labour law, see Davies, P and Freedland, M, Labour Legislation and Public Policy (Oxford, Clarendon Press, 1993).

[25] See eg, Kahn-Freund, O, 'Legal Framework' in A Flanders and H Clegg, The System of Industrial Relations in Great Britain (Oxford, Blackwell, 1954).

[26] Industrial Relations Act 1971, ultimately consolidated in the Employment Protection (Consolidation) Act 1978.

[27] Equal Pay Act 1970; Sex Discrimination Act 1975; Race Relations Act 1968; Race Relations Act 1976.

[28] Wedderburn, KW, The Worker and the Law, 3rd edn (Harmondsworth, Penguin, 1986) 6.

[29] See eg, Department of Employment, Industrial Relations in the 1990s: Proposals for Further Reform of Industrial Relations and Trade Union Law (Cm 1602, 1991).

a strategy of promoting individual rights. Thus, rights for individuals such as the right to refuse to join a union and the right to refuse to participate in industrial action were used to undermine unions' ability to compel individuals to act collectively.[30] In individual employment law, Conservative governments favoured limiting individuals' protection so that firms would have a greater degree of flexibility.[31] A major recession which resulted in high levels of unemployment exacerbated the difficulties faced by workers and unions at this time. Although the legislation of this period reflected a distorted perception of workers' rights, many academics began to use human rights arguments as an alternative ideology to that propounded by the Government.[32] This allowed them to draw on the jurisprudence of international organisations, such as the ILO and ESC supervisory bodies, which were highly critical of the Conservatives' policies.

Since 1997, the United Kingdom has had a series of Labour governments. These governments are often thought of as being proponents of 'third way' policies. Such policies seek to occupy a middle ground between the traditional left and right in British policies. Thus, the Government would claim that statutory rights for workers will promote, not hinder, business competitiveness.[33] Although this has resulted in a substantial body of new worker-protective legislation, it is important to recognise that such legislation is explained and justified largely on economic, not rights, grounds. Moreover, much of the legislation has been in the area of individual employment law and there has been less interest in collective labour law.[34] Despite the historic relationship between the unions and the Labour party, many of the unions' demands have gone unmet. The Labour Government was responsible for the introduction of the HRA in 1998. Initially, academic labour lawyers were divided as to the potential utility of the Act in their subject.[35] Nowadays, there is a growing consensus that human rights arguments (and appeals to international human rights bodies) are a useful weapon but have significant limitations. It is to these limitations that this chapter will now turn.

THE INDIVIDUALISM/COLLECTIVISM DEBATE

As a statement of civil and political rights, the ECHR is focused on the individual. English labour law, by contrast, has traditionally focused on

---

[30] See Employment Act 1988 ss 3 and 11.

[31] Department of Employment, *Employment for the 1990s* (Cm 540, 1988).

[32] The establishment of the Institute for Employment Rights in 1989 acted as a focal point for this movement. A list of its publications is available at: www.ier.org.uk

[33] Department of Trade and Industry (DTI), *Fairness at Work* (Cm 3968, 1998).

[34] With the notable exception of the statutory recognition procedure in new sch A1, Trade Union and Labour Relations (Consolidation) Act 1992 (TULRCA).

[35] Compare Hepple, B, 'Human Rights and Employment Law' (1998) 8 *Amicus Curiae* 19, with Ewing, 'The Human Rights Act and Labour Law' (1998) 8.

protecting the ability of workers to act collectively through trade unions. In the light of 1980s policies, in which individual rights were used to undermine the trade union movement, it is not surprising that many English labour lawyers regarded the HRA with suspicion. They feared that it would entrench English law's individualistic approach and make collectivist reforms unattainable. This section will first analyse the collectivist critique in more detail. It will be argued that some versions of the collectivist critique are overstated. The section will then explore the outlook of the ECtHR. The discussion will demonstrate that the ECtHR is, in fact, attuned to the need to interpret rights with regard to the collective context.

The collectivist critique of individual rights can take at least two forms. A broad version of the critique is to the effect that any legal protection for individual rights might undermine trade unions. Kahn-Freund, the great advocate of collective *laissez-faire*, took the view that legal rights for individual workers would remove their incentive to join a trade union.[36] Although such rights might protect workers' immediate interests, their long-term wellbeing would best be served through strong collective bargaining. However, this argument is difficult to sustain. First, trade unions are unlikely ever to achieve universal coverage of the workforce, because some groups of workers are difficult to organise. Unless the law intervenes, these workers would be left without basic protections against discrimination, unfair dismissal and so on. Secondly, trade unions are democratic organisations and as such must focus on protecting the interests of the majority of their members. Members who are in the minority on a particular issue may find that their rights are ignored. Thus, a union with male-dominated membership might ignore women's equality concerns. Again, the law should step in to protect these workers. Thirdly, the presence of legal rights does not necessarily take away the value of being a union member. The union may be able to negotiate for protection above and beyond that granted by the law. It may also be able to help individuals with the daunting task of enforcing their legal rights. Thus, few, if any, modern labour lawyers would regard individual rights as inherently inappropriate.

There is, however, a less radical version of the collectivist critique of individual rights that does have some force in relation to English labour law as it stands at present. It is that the use of individual rights *in trade union law in particular* may undermine unions' ability to function effectively. On this view, the problem with individual rights is that they prioritise individuals' choices over the views of the majority. Rights are incompatible with successful trade unionism because this requires (with some exceptions) that individuals accept majority decisions and act in ways which express solidarity

---

[36] Kahn-Freund, 'Legal Framework' (1954) 66.

with their colleagues.[37] At every stage in the relationship, English law prioritises individual choice over trade unions' collective decisions. First, trade unions cannot enforce a closed shop. In other words, they have no power to compel reluctant individuals to join. This flows from the fact that it is unlawful for an employer to refuse to employ or to dismiss an individual on the grounds that he or she is not a member of a trade union.[38] Secondly, at present, trade unions have little scope to exclude individuals whom they do not want to admit as members.[39] In effect, they may only exclude applicants for membership where they do not fall within the job category or live within the region that the union wishes to represent. If the individual has a history of strike-breaking, he or she cannot lawfully be excluded. Thirdly, unions have little scope to discipline their members.[40] For example, it is unlawful to discipline an individual who refuses to take part in a strike. This array of individual rights makes it difficult for unions to achieve high levels of membership, to exclude those whose aim is to subvert their goals, and to encourage high levels of participation in their activities.

This version of the collectivist critique—that rights for individual trade union members can undermine trade unions—derives considerable support from the ILO. The ILO starts from the premise that unions should have autonomy from state interference and should therefore be able to determine their own internal rules, provided that they comply with the general law of the land.[41] Some state regulation is appropriate: to ensure that unions comply with sex and race discrimination law, for example. But detailed legislation on unions' membership and disciplinary rules is not acceptable. Indeed, the ILO supervisory bodies have condemned the United Kingdom's position on a number of occasions.[42] A similar approach is adopted under the ESC, which protects the right to organise in article 5.[43] The only area in which the United Kingdom's approach is acceptable is in relation to the closed shop. The ILO allows states to decide whether or not to permit unions and employers to agree to closed shops, so the United Kingdom is within its margin of appreciation on this issue.[44] The Council of Europe specialist supervisory body, the European Committee on Social Rights,

---

[37] Barbalet, JM, *Citizenship: Rights, Struggle and Class Inequality* (Milton Keynes, Open University Press, 1988) 26.

[38] TULRCA ss 137 and 152–53.

[39] Ibid s 174.

[40] Ibid ss 64–65.

[41] ILO, Freedom of Association and Protection of the Right to Organise Convention (Convention No 87, 1948) arts 2, 3 and 8. See also Committee on Freedom of Association, *Digest of Decisions* (1996) paras 331–32.

[42] See eg, ILO Committee on Freedom of Association, Case Nos 1618 and 1730.

[43] See ESC Secretariat, *Digest of the Case Law of the ECSR* (2005) at 28–31; European Committee on Social Rights, *Conclusions XVIII-1, United Kingdom* (2006) 10–11.

[44] International Labour Conference (43rd Session): Report of the Committee of Experts, Report III (Part IV) (1959) para 36.

has interpreted the ESC as prohibiting the closed shop altogether.[45] It is expressly prohibited in the Universal Declaration on Human Rights.[46]

The HRA brings article 11 of the ECHR into English law. This protects the right to form and join associations, including trade unions. Because it forms part of a civil and political rights instrument, there is a general expectation that it will be interpreted in an individualistic way: that it will not give much space to the principle of trade union autonomy. Thus, the fear is that the HRA will entrench the individualistic approach and prevent any possibility of reform. But the force of this argument depends on the ECtHR's approach to article 11: does the Court always favour the individual?

It is true that the ECtHR has been relatively individualistic in its approach to the closed shop, as Mantouvalou explains elsewhere in this volume. In the recent case of *Sorensen v Denmark*, although the Court said that 'compulsion to join a particular trade union may not always be contrary to the Convention',[47] it also noted that closed shops were 'not an indispensable tool for the effective enjoyment of trade union freedoms'.[48] This suggests that the Court would uphold a closed shop only in exceptional circumstances. However, this approach is not out of line with the international jurisprudence. As we saw above, the ILO grants states a margin of appreciation on this issue and therefore does not demand that closed shops be allowed. Other instruments explicitly protect the right not to join on an equal footing with the right to join. Thus, this is an area in which there is widespread acceptance that the state may prioritise the rights of the individual. It is not appropriate to conclude from the closed shop cases alone that the ECtHR is excessively individualistic in its outlook.

The validity of the collectivist critique of the ECHR must therefore turn on its treatment of issues of trade union membership other than the closed shop. Does it follow the ILO in respecting unions' autonomy, or is it likely to reinforce English law's approach of prioritising the rights of individuals? The recent *ASLEF v UK* case indicates that the ECtHR is in fact fully aware of the need to strike a balance between the rights of the individual and the rights of the trade union.[49]

ASLEF, a trade union, discovered that one of its members was also an active member of the far-right British National Party. The union's rules provided that members of organisations with aims and objectives opposed to those of the union could be excluded or expelled. The union sought to expel

---

[45] ESC Secretariat, *Digest of the Case Law of the ECSR* (2005) 30.
[46] Universal Declaration on Human Rights art 20(2).
[47] *Sorensen v Denmark* (2008) 46 EHRR 29 [54].
[48] Ibid [75].
[49] *ASLEF v UK* (11002/05) (2007) 45 EHRR 34. For an excellent discussion of the issues written prior to the ECtHR's decision, see Hendy, J and Ewing, KD, 'Trade Unions, Human Rights and the BNP' (2005) 34 *Industrial Law Journal* 197.

the member under this provision. In doing so, it fell foul of English legislation which prohibited unions from using membership of a political party as a ground of exclusion or expulsion.[50] The EAT mitigated the force of the legislation somewhat by holding that the union would not be liable where its decision was attributable solely to the individual's *activities* as a member of the political party.[51] However, it was found on the facts that ASLEF had expelled the individual because of his membership, not his activities, so the union was forced to readmit him as a member and was potentially liable to pay him compensation.[52] In response to these proceedings, the Government amended the legislation to confirm the distinction drawn by the EAT between membership and activities.[53] Nevertheless, it remained unlawful for a union to exclude or expel an individual solely for *membership* of a political party. ASLEF challenged this legislation in the ECtHR.

The Court began by pointing out that 'the right to form trade unions involves, for example, the right of trade unions to draw up their own rules and to administer their own affairs'.[54] It cited various sources for this proposition, including ILO Convention No 87.[55] It went on to note that since individuals can choose whether or not to join a union, unions should have the equivalent right to decide who to admit to membership: 'Article 11 cannot be interpreted as imposing an obligation on associations or organisations to admit whosoever wishes to join.'[56] This meant that the UK legislation was in breach of article 11 so it fell to the Government to justify its interference with the union's rights. The Court accepted that the Government was seeking to protect the individual's political freedoms. However, it concluded that the Government had failed to strike the correct balance between those freedoms and the rights of the trade union. The Court stated that trade unions 'are not bodies solely devoted to politically-neutral aspects of the well-being of their members, but are often ideological, with strongly held views on social and political issues'.[57] On this view, it was legitimate for the union to set membership rules with some political content. There was no evidence to suggest that the union had erred in its application of these rules to the individual's case. From the individual's perspective, there was no real hardship involved in the loss of his union membership. It did not inhibit his political activities or his freedom of expression. Since there was no closed shop, he did not stand to lose

---

[50] Then TULRCA s 174(4)(a)(iii).

[51] *ASLEF v Lee* UKEAT/0625/03/RN (2004) [28]–[30].

[52] *Lee v ASLEF* 7 October 2004.

[53] TULRCA s 174, as amended, Employment Relations Act 2004 s 33.

[54] *ASLEF v UK* (11002/05) 27 February 2007 [38].

[55] ILO, Freedom of Association and Protection of the Right to Organise Convention (Convention No 87, 1948).

[56] *ASLEF v UK* (11002/05) 27 February 2007 [39].

[57] Ibid [50].

his job as a result of the union's decision. Moreover, he would continue to benefit from collective bargaining because the results of ASLEF's bargaining efforts would be afforded to all workers, not just to its own members. Overall, the Court concluded that the union's right to choose its members was the most important consideration and that the union had suffered a violation of its article 11 rights.

The UK Government has recently amended s 174 to address the issues raised in the *ASLEF* decision.[58] The Government's initial proposal was to remove all references to political party membership from s 174, leaving unions free to adopt and enforce their own rules on this topic.[59] However, when the proposal was put before Parliament, concern was expressed that this approach would not afford sufficient safeguards to union members. As a result, s 174 as amended allows unions to exclude or expel an individual for membership of a political party, but only where a detailed set of conditions is met. The conditions are that: membership of the political party is contrary to a rule of the trade union, or membership of the political party is contrary to an objective of the trade union where it is reasonably practicable to ascertain that objective; the decision to exclude or expel is taken in accordance with the union's rules; the individual is given notice of the proposal to exclude or expel him or her and the reasons for this, he or she is given a fair opportunity to make representations and those representations are considered fairly by the union; and it must not be the case that the exclusion or expulsion would cause the individual to lose his or her livelihood or suffer exceptional hardship.[60] Although these various conditions reflect statements in the ECtHR's judgment in *ASLEF*, concern has been expressed that the new provision is unnecessarily restrictive.[61] The legislation appears to be premised on a concern that excluded or expelled individuals are particularly vulnerable, but since the closed shop is unlawful, it is not obvious that this is the case. Moreover, in exclusion cases, unions are already required at common law to act in accordance with their rules and to follow fair procedures.

Disappointingly, the Government also rejected claims that it ought to amend other aspects of the law on trade union membership in the light of *ASLEF*.[62] The decision should have been viewed as an opportunity to revisit English law on trade union membership and to bring it into line

---

[58] Employment Act 2008 s 19.

[59] Department for Business, Enterprise and Regulatory Reform, *ECHR Judgment in the* ASLEF v UK *Case—Implications for Trade Union Law, Government Response to Public Consultation* (2007).

[60] TULRCA s 174(4A)–(4H).

[61] Ewing, KD, 'Implementing the *ASLEF* decision—a victory for the BNP?' (2009) 38 *Industrial Law Journal* 50.

[62] Department of Trade and Industry, *ECHR Judgment in ASLEF v UK Case—Implications for Trade Union Law* (2007) 12.

with the principle of autonomy which underlies the *ASLEF* decision and other relevant instruments, such as ILO Convention No 87 and the ESC. As explained earlier, the starting presumption of English law is that unions are *only* permitted to set membership rules within certain statutory constraints. This presumption ought to be reversed to comply with the principle of autonomy: unions should be free to set their own membership rules unless there is a good reason for restricting that freedom within article 11(2). Such restrictions might include requirements to comply with anti-discrimination law and to apply union rules in a fair and objective manner. But the Government's refusal to adopt a collective focus cannot be blamed on the ECtHR. The Government's response illustrates its reluctance to adopt a 'human rights culture', an issue to be considered in the next section.

For present purposes, the important point is that in the *ASLEF* judgment, the ECtHR has seized the opportunity to locate article 11 in a collectivist framework. It has accepted the importance of trade union autonomy and has refused to give priority to the rights of individuals. Labour lawyers' fears that the Convention would reinforce English law's individualistic approach are, on this evidence at least, unfounded.

A 'HUMAN RIGHTS CULTURE?'

A second major theme of this chapter relates to the notion of a 'human rights culture'. This term is intended to denote an ideal situation in which key actors in the legal system regard compliance with human rights norms as an important goal which takes priority over other considerations and which should be pursued with vigour. It reflects the view, powerfully articulated by Fredman, that human rights should not simply be regarded as prohibiting certain types of conduct by the state, but rather as imposing a complex bundle of obligations on the state to assist citizens in the realisation of their rights in practice.[63] Since a human rights culture is an ideal, no real-world legal system is likely fully to realise it in practice. Nevertheless, it may be helpful to consider the degree to which any particular legal system tends in this direction.

For this purpose, the most important actors are the courts and the Government (acting through the legislature). A human rights culture in the courts would be evidenced by careful consideration to determine whether rights were relevant to any decision, a generous interpretation of what those rights required (drawing on international human rights jurisprudence) and, in appropriate cases, rigorous scrutiny of any interference with rights using the proportionality test. A human rights culture in the Government would involve not just seeking to comply with human rights requirements in the

---

[63] Fredman, S, *Human Rights Transformed* (Oxford, Oxford University Press, 2008).

sense of avoiding breaches, but also more active endeavours to promote rights.[64] Thus, for example, the Government would strive to ensure that criticisms by international human rights bodies were addressed promptly and would actively review new and existing legislation for its compatibility with human rights. It would protect individuals against violations of their rights by third parties and positively encourage respect for human rights generally.

Of course, the enactment of a statute such as the HRA is unlikely to be sufficient in itself to prompt the development of a human rights culture. Its emergence is likely to depend upon a variety of factors, including the judges' familiarity with human rights reasoning, the political ideology of the ruling party, the strength of pro-rights pressure groups, media coverage of rights issues and so on. It will be argued in this chapter that—at least in the labour law field—there is, as yet, little evidence of the emergence of a human rights culture in the United Kingdom since the enactment of the HRA. Human rights arguments are viewed with suspicion by the courts and the Government's attitude has been summed up as 'grudging and minimalist'.[65] This point will be illustrated with examples drawn from the rights to freedom of association (focusing in particular on union members' rights not to be discriminated against by their employers) and freedom of expression and privacy (in the law on unfair dismissal).

Freedom of Association

Article 11 of the ECHR clearly requires that trade union members should not suffer discrimination in the workplace. The simple ability to join a union would be rendered nugatory if union members could be threatened or intimidated by their employers. English law on this issue was heavily criticised by the ECtHR in *Wilson v UK*.[66] In the Employment Relations Act 2004, the Government amended the law in response to this decision. However, as commentators have pointed out, the amendments are not sufficient to meet the ECtHR's concerns.[67] This illustrates the Government's reluctance to give appropriate priority to human rights issues in legislation. This reluctance is also evident in relation to the *ASLEF* litigation discussed in the previous section.

---

[64] In international human rights law, the state's obligation is often explained as a duty to respect, protect and fulfil. See, eg, Committee on Economic, Social and Cultural Rights, 'General Comment No. 12' (1999) UN Doc E/C.12/1999/5.

[65] Bogg, AL, 'Employment Relations Act 2004—Another False Dawn For Collectivism?' (2005) 34 *Industrial Law Journal* 72, 73, in the context of freedom of association.

[66] *Wilson v UK* (2002) 35 EHRR 20.

[67] Bogg, 'Employment Relations Act 2004—Another False Dawn For Collectivism?' (2005) 72–75, and see also Ewing, KD, 'The Implications of *Wilson and Palmer*' (2003) 32 *Industrial Law Journal* 1.

In *Wilson*, the employer was conducting a derecognition campaign and offered a pay rise to those workers who were willing to accept a so-called 'personal contract' instead of a collectively-bargained contract. Mr Wilson, who was unwilling to give up collective bargaining and was thus denied the pay rise, claimed that he had been discriminated against on grounds of trade union membership. His claim failed in the House of Lords.[68] One of the main reasons for this was that the House of Lords adopted a narrow definition of membership which did not include obtaining the benefits of collective bargaining. The ECtHR held that the Government had not complied with its positive obligation to secure Mr Wilson's enjoyment of his article 11 rights. It said:

> It is of the essence of the right to join a trade union for the protection of their interests that employees should be free to instruct or permit the union to make representations to their employer or to take action in support of their interests on their behalf. If workers are prevented from so doing, their freedom to belong to a trade union, for the protection of their interests, becomes illusory. It is the role of the State to ensure that trade union members are not prevented or restrained from using their union to represent them in attempts to regulate their relations with their employers.[69]

One of the key points emerging from this decision is that the article 11 right protects more than just union membership per se. It also affords protection to the use of union services: in this case, asking the union to make representations to the employer.[70]

Under s 146 of TULRCA 1992, a worker has a right not to be subjected to any detriment (whether by action or deliberate omission) to: prevent or deter trade union membership, to prevent or deter participation in union activities, or to prevent or deter the use of union services. The last of these three elements, the protection for the use of union services, was added in 2004 in response to the *Wilson* decision.[71] At first glance, it appears to reflect the ECtHR's views. However, the definition of union services for this purpose explicitly excludes collective bargaining.[72] The employer can therefore lawfully subject individuals to detriment or dismissal if they are seeking to make use of their union to negotiate on their behalf in the collective bargaining process. This is clearly incompatible with the ECtHR's ruling in *Wilson*, which required states to protect individuals not just in respect of their union membership but also in respect of asking their union to represent them in negotiations with the employer.

---

[68] *Associated Newspapers v Wilson* [1995] 2 All ER 100.
[69] *Wilson v UK* (2002) 35 EHRR 20 [46].
[70] Ewing, 'The Implications of *Wilson and Palmer*' (2003) 7–9.
[71] Employment Relations Act 2004 ss 30–31.
[72] TULRCA s 145B(4). See Bogg (n 65) 74–75.

Also in response to *Wilson*, the Government brought in two new provisions to address the specific fact situation in which the employer offers inducements to the workforce. The new TULRCA s 145A gives a worker a right not to have an offer made to him or her to induce him or her to give up union membership, or to refrain from using union services or participating in union activities. The new s 145B gives a worker the right not to have an offer made to him or her which, in conjunction with offers made to other workers, would have the effect of stopping collective bargaining. Because of the exclusion of collective bargaining from the definition of union services in the other provisions already examined, this is in fact the only right English law gives workers in respect of collective bargaining. Commentators have, however, identified weaknesses in these provisions. As a result, they may not be a particularly effective practical tool for the protection of workers' article 11 rights. First, the employer's attack on trade unionism must be its 'sole or main' purpose. This allows employers to argue that their purpose was something else—business reorganisation, for example—with the anti-union purpose as a minor side-effect.[73] Secondly, the main remedy under sections 145A and B is an award of £2500 in compensation.[74] This relatively small sum may not deter employers from offering inducements. Some employees may be happy to give up union membership or collective bargaining in return for the inducements. Those who are unwilling to give up their rights may not find it worthwhile to take the employer to a tribunal for minimal compensation.

A final problem is that the Government did not accept the need to enact any rights for unions themselves as part of this programme of reform.[75] In *Wilson*, the ECtHR clearly stated that the unions' rights had been violated:

> [The Court] considers that, by permitting employers to use financial incentives to induce employees to surrender important union rights, the respondent State has failed in its positive obligation to secure the enjoyment of the rights under Article 11 of the Convention. This failure amounted to a violation of Article 11, as regards both the applicant trade unions and the individual applicants.[76]

Both Bogg and Ewing have argued that this required fundamental change to English law to give unions, as well as individuals, a remedy against employer strategies designed to bring about derecognition.[77] This point is of particular significance in practice. Although individual rights not to be discriminated against on trade union grounds are clearly necessary to

---

[73] See Bogg (n 65) 74.
[74] TULRCA s 145E.
[75] Department of Trade and Industry (DTI), *Review of the Employment Relations Act 1999* (2003) paras 3.16–3.17.
[76] *Wilson v UK* (2002) 35 EHRR 20 [48].
[77] Bogg (n 65) 73; Ewing (n 67) 11–13.

the existence of trade unions, they may not be sufficient. This is because individuals may be reluctant to enforce their rights, either because of the costs of litigation or because they fear the employer's reaction. A remedy of some kind for the union would considerably enhance the effectiveness of the statutory regime.

Thus, although English law does contain protections for workers against discrimination by their employers on trade union grounds, some aspects of the law are clearly in breach of article 11 and others are, arguably, weak in the protection they offer. The Government has failed to comply fully with the spirit, and sometimes even the letter, of the *Wilson* decision. This is a clear sign that the Government has failed to embrace a human rights culture in this area. The main reason for this seems to be that the *Wilson* decision does not fit with the Government's pro-business agenda. Since coming into office, the Government has had an ambivalent view of unions, regarding them as beneficial but only when they work in 'partnership' with employers.[78] One of the practical manifestations of the Government's attitude is a desire to prevent the unions from regaining significant power by maintaining as much 1980s legislation as possible. This includes allowing employers the freedom to derecognise a union and—most importantly—to have the freedom to use certain 'tactics' (such as detrimental treatment and inducements) to bring about that result.[79] It is possible that the courts may be able to remedy English law's current failures using their interpretative powers under section 3 of the HRA,[80] but as the next subsection will demonstrate, the courts themselves have not fully embraced the human rights culture either. It may therefore be necessary for unions to take more cases to the ECtHR in order to clarify the precise requirements of article 11.

Employee Privacy

For many years, commentators have expressed concern that English law allows employers too much scope to monitor employees' activities both within and outside the workplace.[81] The HRA might have the potential to improve employees' protection in this area, but so far, the signs are not encouraging. Unfortunately, the ECtHR has recently reinforced the domestic courts' cautious approach.

The ECHR protects the right to respect for private and family life (article 8) and freedom of expression (article 10). Employers may be tempted to infringe these rights in various ways, for example, through surveillance in

---

[78] DTI, *Fairness at Work* (Cm 3968, 1998) ch 4.

[79] See DTI, *Review of the Employment Relations Act 1999* (2003) paras 3.12–3.13.

[80] For scepticism on this point see Bogg (n 65) 75.

[81] Collins, H, *Justice in Dismissal* (Oxford, Clarendon Press, 1992) ch 6.

the workplace, or through attempts to prevent employees from engaging in certain activities outside work, such as political campaigning. Sometimes, these infringements might be justified. Alcohol testing might be appropriate where workers' jobs involve operating dangerous machinery; controls on political activities might be appropriate for certain public sector workers. The value of framing these issues in terms of Convention rights is that the employer must satisfy the proportionality test. In other words, the employer must show that it is pursuing a legitimate aim and that it has struck a balance between its needs and the employee's rights. The burden of justification under the HRA should be a heavy one.

The case of *Pay v Lancashire Probation Service* illustrates both the potential of the HRA in this area and the problems with the courts' current approach.[82] Mr Pay was a probation officer. His employers discovered that he performed in fetish clubs in his spare time, and ran a company selling products relating to bondage, domination and sado-masochism on the internet. Although there was no criticism of his work, he was dismissed on the grounds that these activities might harm the reputation of the Probation Service. Mr Pay brought a claim for unfair dismissal. English unfair dismissal law employs a two-stage approach.[83] First, the employer must demonstrate the reason for the dismissal. Secondly, the tribunal must apply a reasonableness test. This involves deciding whether or not the employer acted within a 'band of reasonable responses' in dismissing the employee for the stated reason.[84]

Under section 3 of the HRA, the courts are under a duty to interpret statutes so as to make them compatible with the Convention rights. In *Pay*, the EAT accepted that the reasonableness test should be construed in accordance with Convention rights. Thus, the dismissal would be found to be unreasonable and unfair if the employer had violated the employee's Convention rights.[85] Although the *Pay* case involved a public authority, the Probation Service, which was obliged to act in conformity with human rights under section 6 of the HRA, the section 3 obligation is applicable in all cases regardless of the public or private status of the defendant. Thus, private employers will also be expected to show respect for employees' Convention rights if they are to demonstrate that their dismissal decisions are fair. There is, as yet, no clear authority on this point, but it has been suggested in *Pay* and another case and is clearly correct in principle.[86]

---

[82] *Pay v Lancashire Probation Service* [2004] ICR 187 (EAT). For a useful discussion of the case, see Vickers, L, 'Unfair Dismissal and Human Rights' (2004) 33 *Industrial Law Journal* 52.
[83] ERA 1996 s 98.
[84] *Iceland Frozen Foods v Jones* [1983] ICR 17; *Foley v Post Office* [2000] ICR 1283.
[85] *Pay v Lancashire Probation Service* [2004] ICR 187 (EAT) [35].
[86] Ibid [31]–[35]; see also *X v Y* [2003] ICR 1138.

However, the outcome of the *Pay* case on the facts is disappointing and illustrates the courts' reluctance to apply the proportionality test at an appropriate level of intensity.[87] The tribunal found, and the EAT accepted, that the claimant's article 8 rights were not engaged because his activities took place in public.[88] The Probation Service accepted that his article 10 rights had been infringed, but argued that it was acting to maintain the reputation of the service (particularly with victims of sex offenders) and that dismissal was a proportionate sanction. Whilst it must be the case that an employer has a legitimate concern to maintain its reputation, the EAT failed to explore in any detail the various stages in the argument. In particular, the EAT did not question the employer's assertions that victims of crime would find out about Mr Pay's activities outside work, or that they would connect them with his work, or that the reputation of the Probation Service would be damaged if either of these things occurred. Thus, the application of the proportionality test on the facts of the case was highly deferential to the employer's perception of the situation.[89]

The ECtHR recently considered the *Pay* case and ruled that it was inadmissible.[90] Although it was prepared to assume that article 8 might be engaged as well as article 10, it found that the proportionality test was satisfied. The Court adopted a similarly deferential attitude:

> Given the sensitive nature of the applicant's work with sex offenders, the Court does not consider that the national authorities exceeded the margin of appreciation available to them in adopting a cautious approach as regards the extent to which public knowledge of the applicant's sexual activities could impair his ability effectively to carry out his duties.[91]

Thus, although the Court recognised that dismissal was a severe sanction, it found that it was not disproportionate on the facts.

These are disappointing results. In principle, the proportionality test requires the courts to consider the legitimacy of the employer's aim and to balance this against the individual's rights. There is no evidence of this in the EAT's decision in *Pay*, and indeed it would be no exaggeration to say that the invocation of the HRA did not advance the claimant's case beyond ordinary unfair dismissal.[92] Although the ECtHR did consider the proportionality test a little more fully, recognising that protecting the employer's reputation was a legitimate aim and then considering the relationship between the aim and the sanction, it did not subject the employer's arguments to detailed

---

[87] For a different view, see Vickers, 'Unfair Dismissal and Human Rights' (2004).
[88] *Pay v Lancashire Probation Service* [2004] ICR 187 (EAT) [36]–[38].
[89] Ibid [39]–[46].
[90] *Pay v UK* (2009) 48 EHRR SE2.
[91] Ibid 26.
[92] See also Mantouvalou, V and Collins, H, 'Private Life and Dismissal' (2009) 38 *Industrial Law Journal* 133.

critical scrutiny. In both courts, it appears that deference to the employer's expertise in the management of its own reputation was the deciding factor.

Conclusion

At least in labour law, the HRA has not had a major impact because it has not been accompanied by the development of a human rights culture. The Government regards compliance with human rights requirements as a relevant, but by no means overriding, goal in policy-making. The courts have been nervous about embracing the new powers they are given under the Act, and the ECtHR's cautious approach in *Pay* may reinforce this to some extent. The Lord Chancellor has recently accepted that there is a need to educate the public and other government departments about the role of the HRA and to dispel some of the media myths about its provisions.[93] Nevertheless, it may take some time to transform the HRA from an underused statute into a major part of the United Kingdom's constitutional fabric.

ECONOMIC AND SOCIAL RIGHTS

This chapter's third theme is the emergence in English law of a division between civil and political rights on the one hand, and economic and social rights on the other.[94] In the United Nations (UN) system, rights of these different types are regarded as indivisible and of equal status. When enacting the HRA, however, the Government chose only to incorporate rights from the ECHR, a statement of civil and political rights, into UK law. It did not choose to incorporate any rights from its 'sister' statement of social and economic rights, the ESC, largely because these rights were not thought to command sufficient social consensus.[95] The unfortunate consequences of this are particularly apparent in labour law because many of the rights which are most relevant to workers, such as rights relating to wages and hours of work, are in the ESC.[96] The problem is that whilst many aspects of labour law should be underpinned and guided by human rights considerations, only a few aspects of English labour law—those linked to ECHR rights—will develop in this way. This distorts the subject as a whole. The most severe distortion is likely to occur when a particular sub-topic

---

[93] Department for Constitutional Affairs, *Review of the Implementation of the Human Rights Act* (2006), especially ch 4.

[94] See, generally, Ewing, KD, 'Social Rights and Constitutional Law' [1999] PL 104.

[95] Home Office, *Rights Brought Home: The Human Rights Bill* (Cm 3782, 1997) para 1.3.

[96] European Social Charter 1961 (ESC) art 2.

within labour law is governed by a combination of ECHR and ESC rights, as is the case with trade union membership and activities.

The right to engage in collective bargaining and the right to take industrial action are widely regarded as essential to the functioning of trade unions. But they only feature in article 6 of the ESC, which has not been made a part of English law. To some extent, this problem could be overcome if the ECtHR and the domestic courts adopted a purposive construction of article 11 that acknowledged the importance of collective bargaining and industrial action as trade union activities. The ECtHR has taken some tentative steps in this direction. The Court has held that because the purpose of a trade union is to campaign on behalf of its members, states are under an obligation to ensure that unions have some means of campaigning. However, the Court has not so far specified what those means must be, regarding this as a matter for states to determine within the 'margin of appreciation'.[97] The state can therefore choose which mechanisms to offer and can argue that the availability of one mechanism compensates for the absence of another. A union cannot use article 11 to argue for the provision of a particular mechanism. In *Wilson*, for example, the Court rejected the union's arguments that the state should have afforded it protection against derecognition.[98]

However, the story does not end there. Once the state has chosen a mechanism for union campaigning, the ECtHR may be willing to examine the effectiveness of that mechanism and in particular, to scrutinise any restrictions placed on that mechanism by the state. In *UNISON v UK*, restrictions on the right to strike in English law were examined by the Court using the proportionality test.[99] As Ewing has argued, this gives the right to strike a 'twilight status' within article 11.[100] The use of this test in *UNISON* itself is instructive. The employer in that case was a hospital which had decided to enter into a contract with a private firm to provide certain public services. Some hospital workers would transfer to the private firm under the contract and their union, UNISON, was concerned that their terms and conditions of employment might suffer as a result. But the Court of Appeal granted an injunction to stop UNISON calling a strike because the strike related to the terms and conditions of workers in the future and did not therefore fall within the definition of a trade dispute under English law.[101] The ECtHR held that this restriction on the right to strike was proportionate. It accepted that the law pursued the legitimate aim of protecting the

---

[97] See eg, *Swedish Engine Drivers' Union v Sweden* [1976] 1 EHRR 617 [40].
[98] *Wilson v UK* (2002) 35 EHRR 20 [44].
[99] *UNISON v UK* [2002] IRLR 497 [37]–[43].
[100] Ewing [n 67] 18.
[101] TULRCA s 244; *University College London Hospital NHS Trust v UNISON* [1999] IRLR 31.

rights of others, in the form of the hospital's ability to function effectively and to place contracts as it saw fit. It then reasoned that the restriction did not inhibit UNISON's ability to call a strike if the terms and conditions of workers currently employed by the hospital were under immediate threat, nor did it inhibit UNISON's ability to organise workers at the private firm after the transfer. Thus, because the restriction did not impose any immediate harm on UNISON's members, it was found to be proportionate.

From a domestic perspective, the *UNISON* decision raises the possibility that a court could be called upon to examine the many restrictions English law places on the right to strike using the proportionality test. For example, in a strike situation, the union is required to give notice to the employer when it ballots its members on strike action and before the strike itself commences.[102] It is at least arguable that the former requirement serves no legitimate purpose and is therefore a disproportionate restriction on the right to strike.[103] The strike notice is sufficient on its own to enable the employer to make contingency plans. However, the potentially radical implications of the *UNISON* decision are limited by two factors: the domestic courts' reluctance to embrace the HRA, discussed earlier, and the relatively weak use of the proportionality test in the ECtHR. The test's focus on harm to the employer, which is always present in an industrial dispute,[104] suggests that unions will face an uphill struggle if they are to demonstrate that restrictions on their activities are disproportionate.

Would the position be improved if English law incorporated article 6 of the ESC? There are two possible benefits. First, article 6 explicitly protects the right to bargain collectively and the right to strike. There would be no element of discretion on the part of the state to decide which rights to protect, so trade unions and their members would have clearer minimum guarantees. Secondly, article 6 might result in a stricter application of the proportionality test. Proportionality involves balancing, so the weight afforded to the right in question is just as important as the strength of the arguments advanced in favour of restricting it. The ESC gives explicit protection to the right to strike, for example, whereas under the ECHR it is one mechanism among many for the protection of trade union activities. The former type of right clearly carries more weight in a proportionality enquiry than the latter. The courts might still be reluctant to intervene, but express rights must offer more hope of breaking down their resistance than implicit ones.

Of course, none of this should be taken to suggest that the HRA has been an undesirable development in English law. Explicit protection for some

---

[102] TULRCA ss 226A and 234A.

[103] European Committee on Social Rights, *Conclusions XVIII-1, United Kingdom* (2006) 14.

[104] Novitz, T, *International and European Protection of the Right to Strike* (Oxford, Clarendon Press, 2003) 75–77.

rights is better than for none at all. However, it would clearly have been preferable had the Government made use of the ESC as well, or drafted a home-grown bill of rights that incorporated economic and social rights as well as civil and political ones. Although the Government has recently expressed some interest in the latter option, it has focused on a small selection of economic and social rights that does not include any labour rights.[105]

CONCLUSION

This chapter has sought to analyse the role of human rights arguments in English labour law by focusing specifically on the HRA. For the first time, this Act requires the courts to decide cases in the light of Convention rights. It is a watershed in English legal history. In labour law, the ECHR has already had some impact and clearly has considerable potential for the future, but it cannot and should not be looked to as the solution to all our problems.

The discussion has shown that fears that the HRA would prove positively harmful in labour law are exaggerated. The most plausible version of this claim is that in the area of trade union membership in particular, individual rights might serve to undermine unions' ability to set and enforce their own rules. English law already suffers from this problem because it prioritises individual rights over unions' preferences in most aspects of admission, discipline and expulsion. The ECHR reinforces the individualistic approach to some extent in relation to the closed shop, but in doing so it is not inconsistent with other international instruments. However, in the *ASLEF* case, the ECtHR has provided an interpretation of article 11 which upholds the important collective value of trade union autonomy as against the claims of an individual.

In fact, the real problem with the HRA is the lack of commitment to the legislation demonstrated by the courts and by the Government. Although the present Government promoted its enactment, it does not seem to welcome challenges to existing legislation. This is reflected in its ill-thought-out amendments following on from the decision in *Wilson v UK*, and its unwillingness to consider the broader implications of *ASLEF v UK*. The courts also seem reluctant to engage with human rights issues unless it is absolutely necessary to do so. The decision in *Pay* involved a refusal to apply the proportionality test strictly in an unfair dismissal case, an approach which has now been upheld to some extent by the ECtHR. It is difficult to avoid the conclusion that the HRA has, so far at least, been something of a damp squib.

---

[105] Ministry of Justice, *Rights and Responsibilities: Developing our Constitutional Framework* (Cm 7577, 2009), especially ch 3.

The 'human rights culture', in which compliance with human rights is the first priority of public policy, has yet to develop.

But perhaps the most worrying feature of English law's greater emphasis on human rights is its exclusive focus on civil and political rights. Respect for economic and social rights is also important for the full protection of workers' interests. The Government adopted the Convention as its preferred instrument for incorporation largely on the grounds that it would be the least controversial of the available options. It can now assert that English law protects 'human rights' even though it has ignored the fundamental principle of the indivisibility of human rights. Such assertions are rarely challenged in the media, for example, because there is little awareness of economic and social rights instruments outside academic circles. Some elements of economic and social rights thinking may be brought into English law through the ECtHR's broad interpretation of the Convention rights. However, English law's conception of 'labour rights' is inevitably distorted, and it is essential that academics and campaigners challenge this conception at every opportunity.

7

Enforcing Labour Rights through Human Rights Norms: The Approach of the Supreme Court of India

RAMAPRIYA GOPALAKRISHNAN

'Human rights are never safe in the country unless an activist judiciary with pragmatic humanism becomes the sentinel on the qui vive.'[1]

INTRODUCTION

INDIA, THE LARGEST democracy in the world, ranked 128th in the United Nations Development Programme (UNDP) Human Development Index,[2] has a workforce of over 400 million.[3] Workers in the unorganised sector,[4] including agricultural workers, construction workers, quarry

---

[1] Krishna Iyer, J, *Human Rights and Inhuman Wrongs* (Delhi, B.R. Publishing Corporation, 1990) 79.

[2] India is ranked 128th among 177 countries in the Human Development Index contained in the 2007/2008 Human Development Report. The Human Development Index measures the state of human development on the basis on life expectancy, educational attainment and standard of living. United Nations Development Programme (UNDP), *Human Development Report 2007/2008* (New York, Palgrave Macmillan, 2007) 231, available at http://hdr.undp.org/en/.

[3] Estimates about the strength of India's workforce vary widely. According to the Government of India, 'Census of India' (2001) www.censusindia.net/t_00_008.html), India has a workforce of about 402.2 million. However, according to the Central Intelligence Agency, 'The World Factbook' (2007) www.cia.gov/library/publications/the world-factbook/geos.in.html), India has a workforce of 509.3 million.

[4] The organised sector is defined as all public sector establishments and all private non-agricultural establishments employing 10 or more workers. Roy Chowdhury, S, 'Globalisation and Labour' 39(1) *Economic and Political Weekly* (3 January 2004) 105. Workers who do not belong to the organised sector may broadly be categorised as those in the unorganised sector. The term 'unorganised sector' has been described as one that eludes easy definition considering the wide range of workers it includes and the difficulties of defining it on the basis of any

workers, salt workers, head loaders and household workers, are estimated to constitute over 92 per cent of India's total workforce.[5] The unorganised sector workers lack job security and are poorly paid.[6] Only about two per cent of the workforce of India is estimated to be unionised.[7] Workers in the unorganised sector are largely not unionised.[8] India also has the largest number of child workers in the world.[9]

India is a party to several key international human rights instruments including the International Covenant on Civil and Political Rights, the International Covenant on Economic, Social and Cultural Rights, the Convention on the Elimination of All Forms of Discrimination against Women and the Convention on the Rights of the Child. It has also ratified 41 Conventions of the International Labour Organisation, including four of the fundamental conventions, namely, the Forced Labour Convention 1930 (No 29); the Abolition of Forced Labour Convention 1957 (No 105); the Equal Remuneration Convention 1951 (No 100) and the Discrimination (Employment and Occupation) Convention 1958 (No 111). In addition, the Constitution of India protects several of the internationally recognised human rights. India also has a number of labour laws protecting the rights of its workers. India thus has an obligation both under international and domestic laws to protect and promote the human rights of its workers.

The effective protection of human rights in any society is intrinsically linked to the existence of a strong, independent and sensitive judiciary. The Supreme Court of India, the apex court of the land,[10] has been lauded for its innovative human rights jurisprudence particularly in the areas of criminal procedure, environmental protection and economic, social and cultural rights.[11] Its contribution to the development of the concept of

---

one single criterion, such as the nature of the work involved. Government of India, Ministry of Labour and Employment, 'Report of the Second National Commission on Labour' (New Delhi, 2002) para 7.26.

[5] Ibid para 7.396.

[6] Roy Chowdhury 'Globalisation and Labour' (2004) 106 and Government of India, 'Report of the Second National Commission on Labour' (2002) paras 7.12, 7.18 and 7.30.

[7] Saini, DS, 'Dynamics of New Industrial Relations and Postulates of Industrial Justice' (2003) 46 *Indian Journal of Labour Economics* 651, 656.

[8] 'Report of the Second National Commission on Labour' (n 4) para 7.396.

[9] Estimates about the number of child workers in India between the age of 5 and 14 years vary from 11.28 million to 44 million. 'Report of the Second National Commission on Labour' (n 4) 1018–19.

[10] India's judicial system consists of courts at the district level, high courts at the state level and one Supreme Court for the entire country. The Supreme Court exercises original, appellate and advisory jurisdiction. Article 141 of the Constitution of India makes the law declared by the Supreme Court binding on all the courts in the country.

[11] For example, see Anderson, MR, 'Individual Rights to Environmental Protection in India' in AE Boyle and MR Anderson (eds), *Human Rights Approaches to Environmental Protection* (Oxford, Clarendon Press, 1996) 199. *Cf* Hunter, D, Salzman, J and Zaelke, D, *International Environmental Law and Policy* (New York, Foundation Press, 1998) 1354.

public interest litigation for the advancement of the human rights of the disadvantaged and marginalised sections of society has been noteworthy.[12] The Supreme Court has also developed a rich body of jurisprudence in the field of labour rights and has creatively applied human rights principles to address labour issues.

This chapter examines the manner in which the Supreme Court of India has applied human rights principles to address labour issues. It begins with a discussion of the human rights principles enshrined in the Constitution of India and the manner in which the Supreme Court has interpreted these principles to address labour concerns. This is followed by a brief look at the statutory framework for the protection of labour rights in India and the status of labour law enforcement in the country. The chapter then goes on to discuss the constitutional remedies for the protection of labour rights. As the scope and breadth of the constitutional remedies and the manner of application of human rights principles by the Supreme Court to labour issues is best illustrated by its approach to public interest actions concerning labour issues, the chapter focuses on this aspect. The chapter finally examines the potential of the constitutional remedies, in particular, public interest actions to further labour rights in the current economic context of India. In conclusion, this chapter takes the view that the Supreme Court's application of human rights principles has significantly strengthened labour rights in the country. However, on account of the discernible shift in recent times in the approach of the Court to certain labour issues that assume added significance in the current economic context of the country, this chapter takes the view that the potential of actions founded on human rights norms to address such labour issues is limited.

PROTECTION OF LABOUR RIGHTS IN INDIA

Workers' rights in India are protected both under the Constitution and various labour-related enactments.

Constitutional Protection of Labour Rights

Fundamental Rights

The Indian Constitution incorporates, in parts III and IV, several of the internationally recognised human rights. Part III of the Constitution guarantees

---

[12] See Ashok, HD and Muralidhar, S, 'Public Interest Litigation: Potential and Problems' in BN Kirpal et al (eds), *Supreme but not Infallible-Essays in Honour of the Supreme Court of India* (New Delhi, Oxford University Press, 2000) 159.

the right to equality, right to life, freedom of speech and expression, freedom of association and freedom of assembly among other rights. The rights protected under part III are referred to as the 'fundamental rights'.[13] The fundamental rights that are particularly relevant in the context of protection of labour rights are articles 14 to 16, 19, 21, 23, 24 and 32.

Articles 14–16 of the Constitution protect the right to equality. Article 14 provides that 'the state shall not deny to any person equality before the law or the equal protection of the laws within the territory of India'. The provision thus requires persons to be treated alike under like circumstances and conditions.[14] The Supreme Court has held that article 14 however permits classification under legislation when two conditions are fulfilled: (a) the classification is founded on intelligible differentia which distinguishes persons or things grouped together from those that are left out of the group and (b) the differentia must have a rational relation to the object sought to be achieved by the statute in question.[15]

Apart from unfair discrimination, the guarantee of article 14 has also been interpreted as a safeguard against any arbitrary state action. In *EP Royappa v State of Tamil Nadu*,[16] the Supreme Court held that equality is antithetic to arbitrariness and when state action is arbitrary, it is violative of article 14. The principles of natural justice have also been held to be part of the guarantee under article 14 on the basis that violation of the principles of natural justice results in arbitrariness.[17] The Supreme Court's judgment in *Central Inland Water Transport Corporation Ltd v Brojo Nath Ganguly*[18] is an example of the application by the Court of all the aforesaid three facets of article 14. In that case, the Court had held a service regulation of a government-run company which allowed for the termination of the services of a permanent employee at any time without any prior notice, by making payment in lieu of notice, as arbitrary and discriminatory and also in violation of the *audi alteram partem* rule implicit in article 14.

Article 15 prohibits discrimination on the grounds of religion, race, caste, sex or place of birth. Clause 3 of article 15, however, enables the state to make any special provision for women and children. The Supreme Court has held that the power conferred by clause 3 of article 15 extends to the matter of employment under the state and that therefore, both reservation

---

[13] In *Pradeep Kumar Biswas v Indian Institute of Chemical Biology* (2002) 5 SCC 111, 124, the Supreme Court observed: 'The various Articles in Part III have placed responsibilities and obligations on the state vis-a-vis the individual to ensure constitutional protection of the individual's rights against the state.'

[14] *Motor General Traders v State of Andhra Pradesh* (1984) 1 SCC 222, 229.

[15] *Ram Krishna Dalmia v Justice SR Tendolkar* AIR 1958 SC 538, 547.

[16] *EP. Royappa v State of Tamil Nadu* (1974) 4 SCC 3, 38.

[17] *Union of India v Tulsiram Patel* (1985) 3 SCC 398, 476.

[18] *Central Inland Water Transport Corporation Ltd v Brojo Nath Ganguly* (1986) 3 SCC 156, 221–24; also see *Delhi Transport Corporation v DTC Mazdoor Congress* 1991 Supp (1) SCC 600, 705, 769.

and affirmative action for women, in the matter of public employment, are permissible under the clause.[19]

Article 16 guarantees equality of opportunity in matters of public employment.[20] It has been held that the guarantee of article 16 extends to all employment-related issues, ranging from appointment to termination from service and also retirement benefits such as pension and gratuity.[21] Clause 4 of article 16 provides for affirmative action by way of reservation in the matter of appointment and promotion in favour of any backward class of citizens not adequately represented in the services of the state. Similarly, clause 4-A of article 16 enables reservation in promotion to any post in services under the state for members of scheduled caste and scheduled tribe communities not adequately represented in the services of the state.

Article 19(1)(a) guarantees to all citizens the freedom of speech and expression. The right to information has been held to be a facet of the freedom of speech and expression protected by article 19(1)(a).[22] Article 19(1)(b) protects the right of citizens to assemble peacefully without arms. In *Kameshwar Prasad v State of Bihar*,[23] the Supreme Court held that the right of workers to participate in peaceful and orderly demonstrations flows from articles 19(1)(a) and (b). In that case, the Court ruled that rule 4-A of the Bihar Government Servants' Conduct Rules was in violation of articles 19(1)(a) and (b) as it imposed a blanket ban on the participation of government employees in demonstrations of all kinds including peaceful and orderly demonstrations.[24]

The Supreme Court has held that the right of citizens to take out public processions and hold public meetings flows from article 19(1)(b), guaranteeing the freedom of assembly read together with article 19(1)(d) guaranteeing the freedom of movement throughout the territory of India.[25]

Article 19(1)(c) guarantees the right to form associations or unions. In the *All India Bank Employees' Association v The National Industrial Tribunal (Bank Disputes), Bombay* case,[26] the issue of whether the right of workers to form trade unions guaranteed by article 19(1)(c) would be inclusive of the right to collective bargaining and the right to strike came up for the consideration of the Supreme Court. The Court was of the view

---

[19] *Government of Andhra Pradesh v PB Vijayakumar* (1995) 4 SCC 520, 525, 528.
[20] In *EP. Royappa v State of Tamil Nadu* (1974) 4 SCC 3, 38, the Supreme Court observed that art 16 is an instance of the application of the concept of equality enshrined in art 14 and that art 14 is the genus while art 16 is a species.
[21] *Ganga Ram v Union of India* (1970) 1 SCC 377 and *State of Kerala v NM Thomas* (1976) 2 SCC 310.
[22] *People's Union for Civil Liberties v Union of India* (2004) 2 SCC 476, 494.
[23] *Kameshwar Prasad v State of Bihar* AIR 1962 SC 1166, 1168.
[24] Ibid 1172.
[25] *Himatlal K Shah v Commissioner of Police* (1973) 1 SCC 227, 240.
[26] *All India Bank Employees' Association v The National Industrial Tribunal (Bank Disputes)*, Bombay AIR 1962 SC 171, 180–82.

that the rights guaranteed by part III could not be interpreted as including concomitant rights necessary to achieve the object which might be supposed to underlie the grant of each of these rights as such an interpretation would be contrary to the scheme of part III and particularly, articles 19(1)(a) to (g). On this basis, the Court held that even a very liberal interpretation of article 19(1)(c) cannot lead to the conclusion that trade unions have a guaranteed right to effective collective bargaining or to strike.

Article 19(1)(g) protects the right of citizens to practice any profession, or to carry on any occupation, trade or business. The Supreme Court has observed that article 19(1)(g) enshrines a broad and general right which is available to all persons to do any work of any particular kind and of their choice.[27] Article 19(1)(g) has been held to include the right to be continued in employment under the state, unless the tenure is validly terminated consistent with the scheme of the fundamental rights.[28]

The fundamental rights guaranteed under article 19(1)(a) to (g) are subject to the reasonable restrictions specified respectively in clauses (2) to (6) of article 19. Reasonable restrictions by law may be imposed on the rights contained in article 19(1) on grounds such as the interests of the security of the state, public order, decency or morality.

Article 21 provides that 'no person shall be deprived of his life or personal liberty except according to procedure established by law'. Although the provision is couched in negative language, the Supreme Court has stressed that it guarantees the right to life and liberty.[29] Furthermore, it has held that the right to life does not connote mere animal existence,[30] but includes the right to live with human dignity.[31] It has also held that the article not only imposes a duty on the state to protect human dignity but also to facilitate it by taking positive steps in that direction.[32] By such a process of expansive interpretation,[33] the right to life has been held to encompass a range

---

[27] *Fertilizer Corporation Kamgar Union v Union of India* (1981) 1 SCC 568, 576.

[28] *Delhi Transport Corporation v DTC Mazdoor Congress* (1991) Supp. (1) SCC 600, 754.

[29] *Maneka Gandhi v Union of India* (1978) 1 SCC 248, 278.

[30] *Board of Trustees of Port of Bombay v Dilipkumar Raghavendranath Nadkarni* (1983) 1 SCC 124, 134.

[31] *Francis Coralie Mullin v Administrator, Union Territory of Delhi* (1981) 1 SCC 608, 618–19.

[32] *M Nagaraj v Union of India* (2006) 8 SCC 212, 244.

[33] The Supreme Court in *Maneka Gandhi v Union of India* (1978) 1 SCC 248, 280 observed: 'When interpreting the provisions of the Constitution conferring fundamental rights, the attempt of the court should be to expand the reach and ambit of the fundamental rights rather than to attenuate their meaning and content by a process of judicial construction.' More recently in *M Nagaraj v Union of India* (2006) 8 SCC 212, 240–41, the Supreme Court observed: 'A constitutional provision must not be construed in a narrow and constricted sense but in a wide and liberal manner so as to anticipate and take account of changing conditions and purposes so that a constitutional provision does not get fossilised but remains flexible enough to meet the newly emerging problems and challenges. This principle of interpretation is particularly apposite to the interpretation of fundamental rights.'

of other rights such as the right to a speedy trial,[34] right to pollution-free water and air,[35] right to food, clothing and shelter,[36] right to education,[37] etc. It had also been held to include the right to livelihood.[38]

In *Maneka Gandhi v Union of India*,[39] the Supreme Court held that the procedure contemplated under article 21 for deprivation of either the right to life or the right to personal liberty should be just, fair and reasonable. By extension of this principle, it has been held that the procedure for deprivation of the right to livelihood which is included in the right to life should also be just, fair and reasonable.[40] The requirement of adoption of a fair procedure in disciplinary proceedings against an employee in the services of the state has thus been held to flow from article 21.[41] The right to payment of subsistence allowance during the pendency of disciplinary proceedings against an employee had also been held to flow from article 21.[42]

Article 23 prohibits traffic in human beings and forced labour. Article 24 prohibits the employment of children below the age of 14 years in any factory or mine or any other hazardous employment. The rights under articles 23 and 24 have been held to be enforceable not just against the state but also against any other person indulging in such practices.[43]

The right to move the Supreme Court for the enforcement of the fundamental rights is, in itself, a fundamental right guaranteed by article 32 of the Constitution.

Directive Principles of State Policy

Part IV of the Constitution contains certain principles that are 'fundamental in the governance of the country' and are required to be implemented by the state by making laws.[44] These guidelines are referred to as the 'directive principles of state policy'. The directive principles, together with the fundamental rights, have been described as the 'conscience'[45] and the 'life-force'[46] of the Constitution. The Supreme Court has observed that the directive

---

[34] *Hussainara Khatoon (I) v Home Secretary, State of Bihar* (1980) 1 SCC 81, 89.

[35] *Subhash Kumar v State of Bihar* (1991) 1 SCC 598, 604.

[36] *Shantistar Builders v Narayan Khindal Totame* (1990) 1 SCC 520, 527.

[37] *Unni Krishnan JP v State of Andhra Pradesh* (1993) 1 SCC 645, 737.

[38] *Olga Tellis v Bombay Municipal Corporation* (1983) 3 SCC 545, 572.

[39] *Maneka Gandhi v Union of India* (1978) 1 SCC 248, 281–84.

[40] *DK Yadav v JMA Industries Ltd* (1993) 3 SCC 259, 269; *Delhi Transport Corporation v DTC Mazdoor Congress* (1991) Supp. (1) SCC 600, 651.

[41] *Board of Trustees of Port of Bombay v Dilipkumar Raghavendranath Nadkarni* (1983) 1 SCC 124.

[42] *State of Maharashtra v Chandrabhan Tale* (1983) 3 SCC 387, 390; *Capt M Paul Anthony v Bharat Gold Mines Ltd* (1999) 3 SCC 679, 694.

[43] *People's Union for Democratic Rights v Union of India* (1982) 3 SCC 235, 260.

[44] *Constitution of India* pt IV art 37.

[45] *Kesavananda Bharati v State of Kerala* (1973) 4 SCC 225, 408.

[46] *Ajay Hasia v Khalid Mujib Sohrawadi* (1981) 1 SCC 722, 781.

principles enshrine the constitutional goal of a new socio-economic order.[47]

The directive principles emphasise the need for securing social, economic and political justice,[48] a goal spelt out in the preamble to the Constitution. Towards this end, the directive principles call upon the state to ensure that the ownership and control of material resources are distributed in a manner best to serve the common good[49] and that the operation of the economic system does not result in the concentration of wealth and the means of production.[50] The directive principles also call upon the state to secure just and humane conditions of work,[51] a living wage for all workers,[52] equal pay for equal work,[53] protection of the health of workers[54] and the participation of workers in the management of undertakings.[55] Article 39-A, one among the directive principles, requires the state to provide free legal aid to deserving persons.

While the rights guaranteed by part III are enforceable, the provisions of part IV are as such not enforceable.[56] The Supreme Court has however held that the provisions of parts III and IV are supplementary and complementary to each other and that the fundamental rights must be construed in the light of the directive principles.[57] On this basis, the Court has interpreted the fundamental rights on various occasions in the light of the directive principles thus expanding the content of the fundamental rights. For instance, in the *Randhir Singh v Union of India* case,[58] interpreting articles 14 and 16 which protect the right to equality in the light of article 39(d), one among the directive principles which proclaims the goal of 'equal pay for equal work', the Supreme Court held that the right to equal pay for equal work is deducible from a combined reading of these provisions.

The Court has also relied on the directive principles to test the validity of executive action and to interpret the provisions of the labour laws. This would be illustrated by the ruling in *Municipal Corporation of Delhi v Female Workers (Muster Roll)*.[59] The case concerned the claim of women workers of the corporation working on a daily wage basis to maternity

---

[47] *People's Union for Democratic Rights v Union of India* (1982) 3 SCC 235, 253.
[48] Constitution of India art 38.
[49] Ibid art 39(b).
[50] Ibid art 39(c).
[51] Ibid art 42.
[52] Ibid art 43.
[53] Ibid art 39(d).
[54] Ibid art 39(e).
[55] Ibid art 43A.
[56] Ibid art 37.
[57] *Kesavananda Bharati v State of Kerala* (1973) 4 SCC 225, 730.
[58] *Randhir Singh v Union of India* (1982) 1 SCC 618, 623.
[59] *Municipal Corporation of Delhi v Female Workers (Muster Roll)* (2000) 3 SCC 224, 234–38.

benefits under the Maternity Benefits Act 1961. The Court observed that the validity of executive action in denying maternity benefits to them would have to be tested on the anvil of article 42 of the Constitution, one of the directive principles that requires the state to make provision for maternity relief. Noting that the Act does not restrict the benefits to be provided only to regular women workers and construing its provisions in the light of articles 14, 15(3) and 42 of the Constitution and article 11 of the Convention on the Elimination of All Forms of Discrimination Against Women (CEDAW), the Court held that daily wage women workers would be entitled to all the benefits under the Maternity Benefits Act 1961.

Statutory Protection of Labour Rights

Under the Indian Constitution, both the central Government and the governments of the 28 states in the country are empowered to legislate on labour-related subjects.[60] Thus, India has central as well as state laws relating to labour-related issues. While central laws generally have application all over India, the application of state laws is confined to the territories of the respective states concerned.

Legislation on labour-related issues in India is fragmented. There are separate laws relating to subjects such as wages, occupational safety and health and social security benefits. While some of the labour laws are more general in their application, there are others that are applicable only to specific categories of workers, such as construction workers, handloom workers and *beedi* workers. Moreover, the coverage of the labour laws is generally based on the definitions of the terms 'workman/worker/person employed' and 'employer' under the legislation in question. The definitions of these terms often refer to employment of a description specified in the schedule to the statute. In such cases, the coverage of the statute would extend only to the kinds of employment enumerated in the schedule to the statute. As a result of such a piecemeal approach, a large segment of workers in the unorganised sector is not adequately protected by the existing labour laws.[61] The key central labour laws of India are briefly outlined below.

[60] They have concurrent legislative powers in respect of subjects such as trade unions, industrial and labour disputes, social security, labour welfare, workmen's compensation and maternity benefits. Apart from this, the central Government has exclusive legislative powers in respect of subjects such as the regulation of labour and safety in mines and oilfields and industrial disputes concerning employees of the union. In addition, the central Government may make any law for implementing any treaty, agreement or convention or any decision made at any international conference or association or other body.

[61] The Unorganised Workers Social Security Act 2008, passed in December 2008, aims at remedying this defect to some extent by providing for the formulation of a suitable welfare scheme for workers in the unorganised sector, with regard to life and disability cover, health and maternity benefits, old age protection and other benefits as may be determined by the

The Trade Unions Act 1926 provides for the registration of trade unions and prescribes the rights and liabilities of registered trade unions. The Industrial Disputes Act 1947 recognises the collective bargaining rights of workers and their right to strike. The Act also prevents and penalises the commission of acts of anti-union discrimination classified as unfair labour practices under the Act. In addition, it prescribes the conditions to be followed when employers resort to lay-off, retrenchment or closure of industries and requires any industry employing more than 100 workers to seek the permission of the Government before taking recourse to such measures. Furthermore, the Act prescribes procedures for the resolution of industrial disputes. The Industrial Employment (Standing Orders) Act 1946 requires employers in industrial establishments to regulate the conditions of employment of their workers by framing standing orders which need to be certified by the labour law enforcement authorities.

The Minimum Wages Act 1948 provides for the fixation of the minimum rates of wages in the kinds of employment covered by the Act. The Payment of Wages Act 1936 regulates the payment of wages. It requires the employer to pay wages to the persons employed by her within a prescribed time frame, without deductions of any kind except those authorised under the Act. The Equal Remuneration Act 1976 provides for the payment of equal wages to men and women workers performing the same or similar kind of work and prohibits discrimination against women workers. The Payment of Bonus Act 1965 prescribes the payment by employers of a minimum bonus of 8.33 per cent of the annual wages to their workers. The Employees' Provident Fund and Miscellaneous Provisions Act 1952 and the Payment of Gratuity Act 1972 provide for the payment of retirement benefits to workers.

The Factories Act 1948 prescribes measures to ensure the occupational safety and health of factory workers. The Employees' State Insurance Act 1948 provides for monetary assistance by way of periodical payments to workers or their dependants in the case of sickness, disablement or death caused due to an employment injury or occupational hazard. The Workmen's Compensation Act 1923 provides for the payment of compensation to workers who suffer employment injuries resulting in disablement or contract occupational diseases. The Maternity Benefits Act 1961 enables women workers to avail of maternity leave and entitles them to wages for that period.

The Contract Labour (Regulation and Abolition) Act 1970 empowers the Government to abolish the employment of contract labour in work of a perennial nature integral to the manufacturing process of an establishment.

central Government. The Act has, however, come in for much criticism. For example, see Goswami, P, 'A Critique of the Unorganised Workers' Social Security Act' (44) 11 *Economic and Political Weekly* (14 March 2009) 17.

It permits the engagement of contract labour for work in relation to which there is no such prohibition and stipulates the responsibilities of the principal employer and the contractor. The Inter-State Migrant Workmen (Regulation of Employment and Conditions of Service) Act 1979 regulates the employment of inter-state migrant workmen defined as persons recruited by or through contractors in one Indian state for employment in an establishment in another state. It requires the wages and other conditions of migrant workmen to be on par with that of other workmen in the establishment performing the same or similar kind of work.

The Bonded Labour System (Abolition) Act 1976 abolishes the bonded labour system, a system of forced labour whereby in consideration of an advance made in cash or in kind, a person renders service to the creditor either without wages or for nominal wages. In addition, a bonded labourer usually does not either have the freedom of movement or freedom to take up any other means of livelihood. The Act also requires measures to be taken for the economic and social rehabilitation of freed bonded labourers.

The Child Labour (Prohibition and Regulation) Act 1986 prohibits the employment of children below the age of 14 years in certain hazardous occupations and regulates the conditions of work of children in other kinds of work.

Protection of Labour Rights, in Practice

While India has a number of laws protecting the rights of its workers,[62] the state of implementation of the laws is far from encouraging.[63] With a view to ensuring effective implementation of the laws, most of the Indian labour statutes contain provisions relating to inspection of workplaces. However, effective labour inspection is deterred by several factors including lack of adequate human resources, lack of proper training,[64] lack of co-operation with trade unions[65] and the unethical conduct of inspectors.[66] In some

[62] There are over 150 such central and state laws. Gonsalves, C, Bhat, R and Lewis, F (eds), *Cases on Indian Labour Laws* (New Delhi: Friedrich Ebert Stiftung, 1995) Vol I, xiii.

[63] Ibid xv, Gonsalves states in this context that '... there exists a huge gap between the law and its implementation'.

[64] See George, E, 'Strengthening the Labour Inspection System in Kerala' in A Sivananthiran and CS Venkataraman (eds), *Prevention and Settlement of Disputes in India* (New Delhi, International Labour Organisation, 2003) 155.

[65] See observations of the Centre of Indian Trade Unions (CITU) referred to in the International Labour Organisation (ILO) Committee of Experts on the Application of Conventions and Recommendations: Individual Observation concerning Convention No. 81, Labour Inspection, 1947, India (ratification: 1949), (2005), available at www.ilo.org/ilolex/english/newcountryframeE.htm.

[66] Mathew, B, 'A Brief Note on Labour Legislation in India' (Jan–March 2003) 46 *Asian Labour Update*, available at www.amrc.org.uk/4605.htm.

states in India, the lack of free access for inspectors to workplaces presents an additional problem.[67]

Most Indian labour welfare statutes also provide for the prosecution of defaulting employers and the imposition of penalties, including that of imprisonment on employers found guilty of violation of the law. However, prosecution for infringement of the labour laws can generally be initiated only upon a complaint being made by or with the sanction of the Government or the concerned labour inspector. Such a requirement, in practice, results in a very low incidence of prosecutions for the violation of labour laws. Consequently, penalties are rarely imposed on defaulting employers. Furthermore, the monetary fines prescribed for the infringement of the laws are often low.[68] Speaking of the lack of an effective deterrent system both under the law and in practice, Babu Mathew has observed:

> Cases of non-implementation have to be specifically identified and complaints filed before magistrates after obtaining permission to file the complaint from one authority or the other. Very few cases are filed, very rarely is any violator found guilty and almost never will an employer be sent to prison. Consequently, these powers are used by corrupt officials only for collecting money from employers.[69]

Most of the Indian labour welfare statutes also enable aggrieved workers to seek compliance with the provisions of the laws by petitioning the concerned authorities and the courts. In practice, however, workers and trade unions doing so are often faced with a delay-ridden system and by the end of the long drawn out legal process, it is often that the 'concerned worker has disappeared from the scene'.[70]

In such a scenario, there is a widespread disregard of the law by employers and consequently, the infringement of various labour rights of the workers. Employers often resort to unfair labour practices to dissuade workers from membership of trade unions. Thus, workers in various establishments in the country are unable to even form and join trade unions of their choice and assert their rights under the law.[71] Moreover, employers often refuse to recognise and negotiate with trade unions representing the

---

[67] For example, in Uttar Pradesh, labour inspectors can carry out an inspection only after obtaining the prior consent of an officer of the rank of Labour Commissioner or District Magistrate. In Rajasthan and Andhra Pradesh, several establishments have been exempted from the purview of labour inspection. Sharma, AN, 'Flexibility, Employment and Labour Market Reforms in India' 41(21) *Economic and Political Weekly* (27 May 2006) 2078, 2083.

[68] 'Report of the Second National Labour Commission' (n 4) para 11.33.

[69] Mathew, 'A Brief Note on Labour Legislation in India' (2003).

[70] Shenoy, PD, 'Effective Labour Administration: Trends and Issues' in A Sivananthiran and CS Venkataraman (eds), *Prevention and Settlement of Disputes in India* (New Delhi, International Labour Organisation, 2003) 11.

[71] The International Confederation of Free Trade Unions (ICFTU), 'India: Annual Survey of Violations of Trade Union Rights' (2006) www.icftu.org/displaydocument.asp?Index=991 223945&Language=EN.

majority of the workers.[72] Employers also resort to exploitative practices, such as the engagement of workers on a temporary or contract basis for performing core production work with a view to cut wage costs and also deprive them of other benefits that permanent workers enjoy. On account of the lack of adequate and effective law enforcement, there is also a high incidence of workplace accidents and occupational diseases.[73]

The situation in respect of implementation of the laws is far worse in the unorganised sector.[74] Apart from inadequate inspection efforts, the lack of awareness of labour rights among workers in the unorganised sector and the extremely low extent of their unionisation also account for the poor implementation of labour laws in the unorganised sector.[75]

As a result of the ineffective system of law enforcement, workers in the unorganised sector are often not even paid minimum wages prescribed by the law and women workers are not paid the same wages as male workers performing the same work.[76]

Furthermore, practices such as that of the engagement of bonded labour,[77] the engagement of child labour in hazardous work[78] and the engagement of bonded child labour[79] continue to be prevalent to this day.

CONSTITUTIONAL REMEDIES FOR THE PROTECTION OF LABOUR RIGHTS

Articles 32 and 226

Articles 32 and 226 of the Constitution of India afford redress for persons whose fundamental rights are infringed. Article 32 empowers the Supreme Court to issue directions, orders or writs, including writs in the nature of *Habeas Corpus*, *Mandamus*, Prohibition, *Quo Warranto* and *Certiorari*

---

[72] Ibid.

[73] It is estimated that more than 100,000 workers lose their lives due to occupational diseases and accidents every year in India and that there are over two million new cases of occupational diseases every year. This information is on the website of the Centre for Education and Communication, available at: <www.cec-india.org/leftlinks/05. Also see the US Department of Labour, Bureau of International Labour Affairs, 'Foreign Labour Trends Report: India, 2006' www.state.gov/g/drl/rls/77593.htm.

[74] Mathew (n 66) and Gonsalves, Bhat, and Lewis, *Cases on Indian Labour Laws* (1995).

[75] Mathew (n 66).

[76] Roy Chowdhury, S, 'Labour Activism and Women in the Unorganised Sector' 40 (22&23) *Economic and Political Weekly* (May 23 2005) 2250.

[77] See ILO Committee of Experts on the Application of Conventions and Recommendations: Individual Observation concerning Convention No. 29, Forced Labour, 1930, India (ratification: 1954) (2005), available at: www.ilo.org/ilolex/english/newcountryframeE.htm.

[78] US Department of Labour, 'Foreign Labour Trends Report: India, 2006'.

[79] Human Rights Watch, 'Small Change: Bonded Child Labour in India's Silk Industry' (2003) www.hrw.org/reports/2003/india/India/0103.htm.

for the enforcement of fundamental rights.[80] Under article 32, a petition may be filed against the state and all local or other authorities within the meaning of article 12 of the Constitution. Besides constitutional and statutory authorities, instrumentalities and agencies of the Government, such as statutory corporations and government companies, have also been held to be authorities within the meaning of article 12.[81]

Article 226 endows the high courts with the power to issue the writs mentioned above and other appropriate orders or directions in relation to the territories over which they exercise jurisdiction. The jurisdiction of the high courts under article 226 is, however, wider as they may exercise such power not only for the enforcement of the fundamental rights but also for the enforcement of other legal rights.[82] Furthermore, a petition under article 226 may be filed not just against the state and its agencies or instrumentalities but even against private persons or bodies when 'the monstrosity of the situation' or exceptional circumstances warrant the exercise of such jurisdiction.[83] It has also held that the jurisdiction under article 226 may be invoked against a private person or body discharging a public function when the decision sought to be corrected or enforced is in the discharge of such public function.[84]

On account of the relative simplicity and speed of proceedings invoking the writ remedies afforded by articles 32 and 226, thousands of Writ Petitions are filed in the Supreme Court and the high courts every year.[85] Over the years, numerous Writ Petitions founded on the fundamental rights have been instituted by employees of the Government, government-run

[80] While the power under art 32 has been conferred explicitly for the enforcement of the fundamental rights, in certain cases relating to the enforcement of statutory rights, the Supreme Court has taken an expansive view of the power under art 32 by construing the violation of the statutory rights as a breach of the fundamental rights. For instance, in *People's Union for Democratic Rights v Union of India* (1982) 3 SCC 235, 251–53, the Court considered the non-observance of the provisions of the Equal Remuneration Act 1946 as a breach of the principle of equality enshrined in art 14 and the non-observance of the provisions of the Contract Labour (Regulation and Abolition) Act 1970 and Inter-State Migrant Workmen (Regulation of Employment and Conditions of Service) Act 1979, as a breach of art 21 on the ground that these statutes were intended to ensure the basic dignity of workers. On this basis, the Court held the case as maintainable under art 32.

[81] See *Ramana Dayaram Shetty v International Airport Authority of India* (1979) 3 SCC 489, 507–11; *Ajay Hasia v Khalid Mujib Sohrawadi* (1981) 1 SCC 722, 731, 734, 736–37.

[82] *Bandhua Mukti Morcha v Union of India* (1984) 3 SCC 161, 192. It needs to be pointed out though that while the power of the High Court under art 226 has been held to be plenary, the exercise of jurisdiction under art 226 is subject to certain 'self-imposed limitations', one of which is that the Court will not normally entertain a Writ Petition for the enforcement of legal rights when an efficacious, alternative remedy is available to the petitioner. See *Whirlpool Corporation v Registrar of Trade Marks* (1998) 8 SCC 1, 9–10 and *UP State Co-operative Land Development Bank v Chandra Bhan Dubey* (1999) 1 SCC 741, 758.

[83] *Rohtas Industries Ltd v Rohtas Industries Staff Union* (1976) 2 SCC 82, 88.

[84] *Binny Ltd v V Sadasivam* (2005) 6 SCC 657, 665.

[85] Divan, S and Rosencranz, A, *Environmental Law and Policy in India*, 2nd edn (New Delhi, Oxford University Press, 2001) 123.

companies and other instrumentalities of the state in respect of various employment-related issues such as recruitment, seniority, promotion, pay-scales, permanency, penalties imposed in disciplinary proceedings, termination of service, age of superannuation, pension, etc.

The constitutional remedies have also often been invoked by other workers and their organisations to ensure compliance with labour laws and to challenge the constitutional validity of laws and executive action affecting labour rights.

Labour-related issues are also brought up for the consideration of the Supreme Court by way of Special Leave Petitions filed under article 136 of the Constitution. Under article 136, the Supreme Court may exercise its appellate power in respect of any judgment, decree or order passed by any court or tribunal in the country. Thus, Special Leave Petitions may be filed against orders passed by the high courts in the exercise of their jurisdiction under article 226 as well. The jurisdiction of the high courts under article 226 is often invoked to challenge the decisions of the labour courts and industrial tribunals in respect of a wide range of issues, including that of wage fixation, termination from service and permanency and such issues in turn are often brought up for the consideration of the Supreme Court by way of Special Leave Petitions.

Public Interest Litigation

While both articles 32 and 226 do not contain any prescription in respect of *locus standi*, the traditional view was that judicial redress under the provisions was available only to a person aggrieved by reason of the actual or threatened violation of her rights. Beginning from the mid-seventies however, taking into consideration the socio-economic conditions of Indian society and the need to afford greater access to justice to socially and economically disadvantaged persons, the Supreme Court recognised the need to liberalise the *locus standi* requirement and adopt a new approach.[86] In *SP Gupta v Union of India*,[87] it observed that:

> The court has to innovate new methods and devise new strategies for the purpose of providing access to justice to large masses of people who are denied their basic human rights and to whom freedom and liberty have no meaning. The only way in which this can be done is by entertaining Writ Petitions and even letters from public spirited individuals seeking judicial redress for the benefit of persons who have suffered a legal wrong or legal injury or whose constitutional or legal right has been violated but who by reason of their poverty or socially or economically disadvantaged position are unable to approach the court for relief.

---

[86] Eg, *Mumbai Kamgar Sabha v Abdulbhai Fazulbhai* (1976) 3 SCC 832, 834–38; *Sunil Batra v Delhi Administration* (1978) 4 SCC 494, 508.

[87] *SP Gupta v Union of India* (1981) Supp. SCC 87, 210–11.

This new approach was further explained in the case of *Bandhua Mukti Morcha v Union of India*[88] in the following words:

> In the case of a person or class of persons whose fundamental right is violated but who cannot however resort to the court on account of their poverty or disability or socially or economically disadvantaged position, the court can allow any member of the public acting bona fide to espouse the cause of such person or class of persons and move the court for the judicial enforcement of the fundamental right of such persons or class of persons.

This paved the way for the institution of a number of public interest actions under articles 32 and 226 in respect of the protection of the rights of disadvantaged sections of society such as pavement dwellers,[89] children detained in prisons,[90] children of sex workers,[91] prisoners,[92] etc. Public interest actions also gradually came to be filed in respect of a range of other diverse causes,[93] including that of the protection of the environment,[94] fairness in the distribution of state largesse[95] and proper functioning of government agencies.[96]

Public interest actions instituted in the courts in India have come to be generally referred to as 'Public Interest Litigation' or PIL, for short. The Supreme Court has pointed out that:

> PIL is not in the nature of adversary litigation but is a challenge and an opportunity to the Government and its officers to make human rights meaningful to the deprived and vulnerable sections of the country and to ensure them social and economic justice.[97]

PILs have therefore been described as a collaborative effort between the petitioner, the state or public authorities and the court to secure observance of constitutional or legal rights.[98] Divan and Rosencranz have explained the distinct features of PIL in the following terms:

> First, since the litigation is not strictly adversarial, the scope of the controversy is flexible. Parties and official agencies may be joined (and even substituted) as the litigation unfolds; and new and unexpected issues may emerge to dominate the

---

[88] *Bandhua Mukti Morcha v Union of India* (1984) 3 SCC 161, 186.
[89] Eg, *Olga Tellis v Bombay Municipal Corporation* (1983) 3 SCC 545.
[90] Eg, *Sheela Barse v Union of India* (1986) 3 SCC 596.
[91] Eg, *Gaurav Jain v Union of India* (1997) 8 SCC 114.
[92] Eg, *RD Upadhyay v State of Andhra Pradesh* (2000) 10 SCC 255.
[93] Sarkar notes that public interest litigation in India has thus traversed beyond the original objective of providing access to the judicial process to the poor and disadvantaged sections of society. Sarkar, SR, *Public Interest Litigation* (Allahabad, Orient Publishing Company, 2004) 431.
[94] Eg, *Vellore Citizens' Welfare Forum v Union of India* (1996) 5 SCC 647.
[95] Eg, *Common Cause, A Registered Society v Union of India* (1996) 6 SCC 530.
[96] Eg, *Vineet Narain v Union of India* (1996) 2 SCC 199.
[97] *Bandhua Mukti Morcha v Union of India* (1984) 3 SCC 161, 182.
[98] *People's Union for Democratic Rights v Union of India* (1982) 3 SCC 235, 242.

lawsuit. Second, the orientation of the case is prospective. The petitioner seeks to prevent an egregious state of affairs or an illegitimate policy from continuing into the future. Third, because the relief sought is corrective rather than compensatory, it does not derive logically from the right asserted. Instead, it is fashioned for the special purpose of the case, sometimes by a quasi-negotiating process between the court and the responsible agencies. Fourth, it is difficult to delimit the duration and effect of this new kind of litigation. Prospective judicial relief implies continuing judicial involvement. The parties often return to the court for fresh directions and orders. Finally because the relief is sometimes directed against government policies, it may have impacts that extend far beyond the parties in the case. In view of these features, judges must play a large role in organising and shaping the litigation and in supervising the implementation of relief. This activist role of the PIL judge contrasts with the passive umpireship traditionally associated with judicial functions.[99]

PUBLIC INTEREST ACTIONS FOR THE PROTECTION OF LABOUR RIGHTS

A number of PILs have been instituted over the years in the Supreme Court for the protection of the rights of workers. These include PILs:

(i) for the identification, release and rehabilitation of bonded labourers;[100]

(ii) for the enforcement of the provisions of labour welfare statutes such as the Minimum Wages Act, the Equal Remuneration Act, the Contract Labour (Regulation and Abolition) Act and Inter-State Migrant Workmen (Regulation of Employment and Conditions of Service) Act;[101]

(iii) for the prohibition of the engagement of child labour in hazardous industries;[102]

(iv) for the prevention of the occupational health hazards faced by workers in asbestos industries;[103]

(v) for the regularisation of the services of temporary workers engaged by the Government;[104]

(vi) for the payment of equitable pensionary benefits to retired employees;[105]

---

[99] Divan and Rosencranz, *Environmental Law and Policy in India* (2001) 131–34. These remarks are based on the Supreme Court's observations in its judgment in *Sheela Barse v Union of India* (1988) 4 SCC 226, 234.

[100] Eg, *Bandhua Mukti Morcha v Union of India* (1984) 3 SCC 161.

[101] Eg, *People's Union for Democratic Rights v Union of India* (1982) 3 SCC 235.

[102] Eg, *MC Mehta v State of Tamil Nadu* (1991) 1 SCC 283.

[103] Eg, *Consumer Education and Research Centre v Union of India* (1995) 3 SCC 42.

[104] Eg, *Dharwad District PWD Literate Daily Wage Employees Association v State of Karnataka* (1990) 2 SCC 396.

[105] Eg, *DS Nakara v Union of India* (1983) 1 SCC 305.

(vii) for the payment of arrears of wages to employees of state-owned corporations;[106]

(viii) for the effective functioning of the dispute resolution mechanisms under the Industrial Disputes Act 1947;[107]

(ix) challenging the Government's decision in respect of disinvestment and transfer of shares in a government-owned company;[108]

(x) questioning the legality of sale of plant and machinery in a public sector enterprise;[109] and

(xi) for the prevention of sexual harassment of women workers.[110]

Labour-related PILs have been instituted not only by trade unions and affected workers but also by human rights organisations,[111] lawyers,[112] journalists,[113] etc. Several labour-related PILs were initiated on the basis of letters addressed to the court.[114]

Reliance on Human Rights Principles

In labour-related PILs, the protection afforded by the fundamental rights has been invoked in different ways. In some PILs, the validity of a statute or rule or notification has been called into question on the basis that it violates the fundamental rights of workers. For instance in the *Sanjit Roy v State of Rajasthan* case,[115] the constitutional validity of the Famine Relief Works (Exemption of Labour Laws) Act 1964, which excluded the applicability of certain laws including the Minimum Wages Act 1948 to persons engaged in famine relief work, was challenged as being violative of articles 14 and 23 of the Constitution.

In some cases, it has been contended that the employment practices of the Government or its agencies are violative of the fundamental rights of workers. For instance, in the *Dhirendra Chamoli v State of Uttar Pradesh* case,[116] it was contended that the practice of the Government in engaging daily wage workers for performing the same duties as permanent workers but in not paying them the same wages is violative of article 14. In the

---

[106] *Kapila Hingorani v State of Bihar* (2003) 6 SCC 1.
[107] *Hospital Employees Union v Union of India* (2002) 10 SCC 224.
[108] Eg, *BALCO Employees Union v Union of India* (2002) 2 SCC 333.
[109] *Fertilizer Corporation Kamgar Union v Union of India* (1981) 1 SCC 568.
[110] *Vishaka v State of Rajasthan* (1997) 6 SCC 241.
[111] Eg, *People's Union for Democratic Rights v Union of India* (1982) 3 SCC 235.
[112] Eg, *Mukesh Advani v State of Madhya Pradesh* (1985) 3 SCC 162.
[113] Eg, *Neeraja Chaudhury v State of Madhya Pradesh* (1984) 3 SCC 243.
[114] Eg, *People's Union for Democratic Rights v Union of India* (1982) 3 SCC 235, *Neeraja Chaudhury v State of Madhya Pradesh* (1984) 3 SCC 243 and *Mukesh Advani v State of Madhya Pradesh* (1985) 3 SCC 162.
[115] *Sanjit Roy v State of Rajasthan* (1983) 1 SCC 525.
[116] *Dhirendra Chamoli v State of Uttar Pradesh* (1986) 1 SCC 637.

Kapila Hingorani v State of Bihar case,[117] it was contended that the failure of the State of Bihar to pay wages to the employees of government-run undertakings for several months is violative of their fundamental rights under articles 21 and 23.

Certain cases have been founded on the basis that a particular governmental decision is arbitrary and that this is violative of the fundamental rights of workers. For instance, in the *Fertilizer Corporation Kamgar Union v Union of India* case,[118] the decision to sell certain plants and machinery of a government-run enterprise was challenged on the ground that it was arbitrary and would result in the violation of the fundamental rights of the workers of the enterprise under articles 14 and 19(1)(g).

Several PILs have been instituted on account of the failure of the executive to implement labour laws resulting in the prevalence of harsh conditions of labour which constitute a violation of the fundamental rights of the workers concerned. For instance, the *People's Union for Democratic Rights v Union of India* ('*Asiad workers*' case)[119] and the *Labourers, Salal Hydro Project v State of Jammu and Kashmir* case[120] were founded on the basis that the non-implementation of the provisions of the Minimum Wages Act 1948, the Inter-State Migrant Workmen (Regulation of Employment and Conditions of Service) Act 1970 and the Contract Labour (Regulation and Abolition) Act 1970 in relation to workers employed in projects undertaken by the Government resulted in the infringement of their fundamental rights. Similarly, several cases relating to the inhuman bonded labour system had been instituted on account of the failure of the concerned authorities to implement the provisions of the Bonded Labour System (Abolition) Act 1976.[121]

There are also instances where PILs have been instituted to remedy lacunae in the law resulting in the infringement of the fundamental rights. For instance, in the *Vishaka v State of Rajasthan* case,[122] a PIL was filed with a view to judicially fill the vacuum that exists in the laws of the country on the subject of prevention of sexual harassment of women workers, relying on the provisions of the CEDAW. The PIL was founded on the basis that sexual harassment results in the violation of women's fundamental rights under articles 14, 15, 19(1)(g) and 21.

---

[117] *Kapila Hingorani v State of Bihar* (2003) 6 SCC 1.
[118] *Fertilizer Corporation Kamgar Union v Union of India* (1981) 1 SCC 568.
[119] *People's Union for Democratic Rights v Union of India* (1982) 3 SCC 235. This case is generally referred to as the Asiad workers' case.
[120] *Labourers, Salal Hydro Project v State of Jammu and Kashmir* (1983) 2 SCC 181.
[121] Eg, *Neeraja Chaudhury v State of Madhya Pradesh* (1984) 3 SCC 243; *P Sivaswamy v State of Andhra Pradesh* (1988) 4 SCC 466.
[122] *Vishaka v State of Rajasthan* (1997) 6 SCC 241.

Flexible Procedures

In the light of the non-adversarial character of PIL, the courts have adopted a distinctly different approach while dealing with PIL cases, be it in the manner of securing the facts of the case or the manner of granting relief. The very fact that the courts have permitted PILs to be instituted, even on the basis of letters written to the court, indicates the extent of the flexibility of procedures in PIL cases.

Subject Matter of the Case

In several PIL cases related to labour issues, the Supreme Court has expanded the scope of the litigation far beyond the original subject matter of the case. For instance, the case of the *People's Union for Civil Liberties v State of Tamil Nadu*[123] originally concerned migrant workers from the state of Tamil Nadu subjected to exploitation as bonded labourers in the state of Madhya Pradesh. However, considering the widespread nature of the problem, the Court expanded the scope of the case so as to cover the problems related to bonded labourers in all the states and union territories in the country. Similarly, the case of *MC Mehta v State of Tamil Nadu*[124] originally concerned the employment of children in fire-cracker manufacturing units in Sivakasi. However, the Court was of the opinion that the problem needed to be viewed from a broader perspective and the scope of the case thus came to encompass the central Government and the governments of various states in India. Another such instance is a case concerning the violation of labour laws in three *beedi* manufacturing units in the state of Tamil Nadu, wherein the Court ordered notice of the proceedings to be given not just to the concerned three units but also to the other *beedi* manufacturing units in the state.[125]

Gathering of Facts

As PILs have been instituted even on the basis of letters and newspaper reports and as the information given by the petitioner is often not sufficient, the Supreme Court has adopted an innovative approach to gather the necessary facts and data. In several cases, the Court has either required court-appointed advocate commissioners or other officials or bodies to ascertain the relevant facts and submit reports to the Court. For instance, in the *Bandhua Mukti Morcha v Union of India* case,[126] the Court appointed

---

[123] *People's Union for Civil Liberties v State of Tamil Nadu* (2004) 12 SCC 381, 382.

[124] *MC Mehta v State of Tamil Nadu* (1996) 6 SCC 756, 765.

[125] *Rajangam, Secretary, District Beedi Workers Union v State of Tamil Nadu* (1992) 1 SCC 221, 222.

[126] *Bandhua Mukti Morcha v Union of India* (1984) 3 SCC 161, 178, 190.

two advocates as commissioners to visit the stone quarries where the practice of bonded labour was allegedly prevalent and interview the workers and enquire about the conditions in which they were working. In the *Salal Hydro Project* case,[127] the Court directed the Labour Commissioner of Jammu to visit the site of the project in issue and ascertain whether migrant labour was employed in the project and also the status of observance of labour laws in the project.

Application of the Fundamental Rights for the Protection of Labour Rights

As in other cases where the protection afforded by the fundamental rights has been invoked, in PILs concerning labour issues, the Supreme Court has applied the fundamental rights in the following three ways:[128]

(a) It has applied the existing guarantees of the fundamental rights to protect labour interests.
(b) It has creatively interpreted the fundamental rights so as to include labour concerns.
(c) It has created new labour rights founded on the fundamental rights.

Applying the Existing Guarantees of the Fundamental Rights

The ruling of the Supreme Court in *DS Nakara v Union of India*[129] is an illustration of the application of the existing guarantees of the fundamental rights to protect employees' rights. In that case, the Government had issued a memorandum introducing a more favourable method of computation of pension, but made it applicable only to employees who retired on or after 31 March 1979. Finding the classification of pensioners into two classes on the basis of the cut-off date as not based on any rational principle and having no nexus to the objective sought to be achieved by liberalising the relevant rule, the Court held that restricting the application of the new method to only those who retired after 31 March 1979 is violative of article 14 which guarantees equality and the equal protection of the laws.

---

[127] *Salal Hydro Project* (1983) 2 SCC 181, 183.
[128] Anderson speaks of such a three-pronged approach in the context of using human rights principles to achieve environmental ends. Anderson, MR, 'Human Rights Approaches to Environmental Protection: An Overview' in Boyle and Anderson (eds), *Human Rights Approaches to Environmental Protection* (Oxford, Clarendon Press, 1996 4–10). *Cf* Hunter et al, *International Environmental Law and Policy* (1998) 1314.
[129] *DS Nakara v Union of India* (1983) 1 SCC 305, 328–31.

Expansive Interpretation of the Fundamental Rights

The Supreme Court has, in several labour-related PILs, expansively inter-preted the fundamental rights in the light of the directive principles and other international human rights principles in order to effectively address labour concerns. This would be evident from the following examples.

In the *Bandhua Mukti Morcha v Union of India* case,[130] interpreting the right to life guaranteed by article 21 in the light of the directive principles contained in articles 39(e) and (f), 41 and 42, the Court held that the right to life includes the protection of the health and strength of workers, just and humane conditions of work, maternity relief, protection of men, women and children against abuse and opportunities and facilities for chil-dren to develop in a healthy manner. In *Consumer Education and Research Centre v Union of India*,[131] reading article 21 together with articles 39(e), 41 and 43 of the directive principles, the Supreme Court ruled that the right of industrial workers to health and medical care while in service or post-retirement is their fundamental right.

In the *Asiad workers* case,[132] with a view to prevent the exploitation of workers, the Supreme Court expansively interpreted article 23 by holding that the provision of labour or service by a person to another for remu-neration which is less than the prescribed minimum wage would amount to 'forced labour' which is prohibited under the provision. Furthermore, in the *Bandhua Mukti Morcha* case,[133] the Court observed that whenever it is shown that a labourer is made to provide forced labour, the Court would make the presumption that he is required to do so in consideration of an advance or other economic consideration received by him and that he is a bonded labourer to whom the Bonded Labour System (Abolition) Act 1976 would apply. In the *Neeraja Chaudhury* case,[134] the Court held that suit-able rehabilitation of bonded labourers on their release is a requirement of articles 21 and 23.

Creating New Rights on the Basis of the Fundamental Rights

As mentioned before, the Supreme Court has relied on international human rights principles in several PIL cases concerning workers' rights.[135] In *Vishaka v State of Rajasthan*,[136] the Court observed: 'Any international

---

[130] *Bandhua Mukti Morcha v Union of India* (1984) 3 SCC 161, 183.
[131] *Consumer Education and Research Centre v Union of India* (1995) 3 SCC 42, 76.
[132] *People's Union for Democratic Rights* (1982) 3 SCC 235, 259–60.
[133] *Bandhua Mukti Morcha* (1984) 3 SCC 161, 207.
[134] *Neeraja Chaudhury v State of Madhya Pradesh* (1984) 3 SCC 243, 255.
[135] Eg, *MC Mehta v State of Tamil Nadu* (1996) 6 SCC 756; *Kapila Hingorani v State of Bihar* (2003) 6 SCC 1.
[136] *Vishaka v State of Rajasthan* (1997) 6 SCC 241, 247, 251–54.

Convention not inconsistent with the fundamental rights and in harmony with its spirit must be read into these provisions to enlarge the content and meaning thereof ...'

On this basis, by reading articles 14, 15, 19(1)(g) and 21 of the Constitution in the light of the provisions of the CEDAW, the Court ruled that the sexual harassment of women workers results in the violation of their fundamental rights protected by these provisions.

In addition, noting that there was no domestic law operating in the field, it laid down guidelines for observance at all workplaces concerning the prevention of sexual harassment of women workers. It also directed the constitution of complaints mechanisms to deal with cases of sexual harassment. Thus, by the application of human rights norms, the Court created new rights for women workers in the country.

Relief Granted

The Supreme Court has issued a wide variety of directions in labour-related PILs, as would be evident from the following examples.

In several cases, the Court has emphasised the need for strict implementation of the labour laws.[137] It has called for more frequent inspections by the enforcing authorities.[138] It has also urged that the violation of labour laws be viewed seriously and dealt with severely by magistrates and other judges and that adequate penalties are imposed on erring employers.[139]

In order to ensure effective implementation of the provisions of the Bonded Labour System (Abolition) Act 1976, the Court has directed vigilance committees[140] to be set up in accordance with the provisions of the Act.[141] It has also called upon state governments to make arrangements to sensitise district magistrates and other statutory authorities of their duties under the Act. Furthermore, the Court has tasked the National Human Rights Commission with monitoring the implementation of the provisions of the Act.[142]

---

[137] Eg, *People's Union for Democratic Rights* (1982) 3 SCC 235, 261; *Rajangam, Secretary, District Beedi Workers Union v State of Tamil Nadu* (1992) 1 SCC 221, 223–24.

[138] Eg, ibid 261–62; *Salal Hydro Project* (1983) 2 SCC 181, 194.

[139] Eg, *Bandhua Mukti Morcha* (1984) 3 SCC 161, 218; *People's Union for Democratic Rights* (1982) 3 SCC 235, 248.

[140] Section 13 of the Bonded Labour System (Abolition) Act 1976 provides for the constitution of vigilance committees and s 14 enumerates their functions. Ensuring proper implementation of the Act and the rules framed there under and providing for the economic and social rehabilitation of freed bonded labourers are among the functions of the committees.

[141] Eg, *Bandhua Mukti Morcha* (1984) 3 SCC 161, 219; *People's Union for Civil Liberties v State of Tamil Nadu* (2004) 12 SCC 381, 384.

[142] *People's Union for Civil Liberties* (2004) 12 SCC 381, 382, 384.

With a view to effectively prevent the engagement of child labour in hazardous industries, the Court directed that every offending employer be asked to pay a compensation of Rs. 20,000/- for every child employed in contravention of the Child Labour (Prohibition and Regulation) Act 1986 and that the amount be deposited in a fund called the Child Labour Rehabilitation cum Welfare Fund. Furthermore, it suggested that state governments consider providing work to one adult member of every family whose child is employed in hazardous work. The Court also directed the creation of a separate cell in labour departments to oversee the work of inspectors concerned with the implementation of the Child Labour (Prohibition and Regulation) Act 1986.[143]

The Court has in various cases issued detailed directions to the Government to ensure the welfare of workers. For instance, in cases concerning bonded labour, it has issued detailed directions with regard to the rehabilitation of bonded labourers including directions to provide employment, land, food, shelter and rural credit facilities to the workers.[144] Similarly, in cases concerning child labour, it has issued detailed directions for improving the quality of life of the children, including the provision of facilities for education, recreation, food, medical care, insurance and the creation of a welfare fund for them.[145]

In certain cases, the Court has directed the Government to evolve suitable policies. For instance, in a case concerning the prohibition of child labour, favouring the progressive eradication of child labour through well planned policies on the basis that total banishment may drive the children to destitution, the Court directed the central Government to convene a meeting of the ministers concerned of the respective state governments to evolve principles and policies for the progressive elimination of the employment of children below the age of 14 years.[146]

The Court has on some occasions even recommended legislative reforms. For example, in the *Asiad workers'* case,[147] the Supreme Court directed the concerned state governments to amend the schedule to the Employment of Children Act 1938 then in force to include employment in the construction industry. In the *Hospital Employees Union v Union of India* case[148] concerning the dispute resolution machinery under the Industrial Disputes Act 1947, the Court suggested that the Government take appropriate steps to make a provision in the Act enabling a workman to approach the Court

---

[143] *MC Mehta v State of Tamil Nadu* (1996) 6 SCC 756, 771–74.
[144] Eg, *Bandhua Mukti Morcha* (1984) 3 SCC 161, 219; *People's Union for Civil Liberties* (2004) 12 SCC 381, 384.
[145] Eg, *Bandhua Mukti Morcha* (1997) 10 SCC 549, 557–58; *MC Mehta* (1991) 1 SCC 283, 285–86.
[146] *Bandhua Mukti Morcha* (1997) 10 SCC 549, 557.
[147] *People's Union for Democratic Rights* (1982) 3 SCC 235, 246.
[148] *Hospital Employees Union v Union of India* (2002) 10 SCC 224, 225.

directly without the requirement of a reference by the Government in the case of individual industrial disputes. In a case concerning the health of asbestos workers, the Court recommended a review of the standards of permissible exposure.[149]

Apart from issuing directions in respect of corrective action in the future, in certain cases, the Court has also issued directions with a view to ensure that the workers concerned with the case are suitably recompensed for the violation of their rights in the past. For instance in the *Sanjit Roy v State of Rajasthan* case,[150] the Court declared as invalid the provisions of the Famine Relief Works (Exemption of Labour Laws) Act 1964 insofar as it excludes the applicability of the Minimum Wages Act to workers engaged in famine relief work and directed the state to thereafter pay the prescribed minimum wage to workers engaged in any famine relief work. It also directed the respondent to pay each of the workers concerned in the case the arrears of the difference between the minimum wage and actual wage paid during the period when they had worked on the project in issue, within a period of two months.

In the asbestos workers' case referred to above, the Court directed the medical examination of the concerned workers by the National Institute of Occupational Health and the grant of compensation of Rs. 100,000/- to each of them within three months if it is certified that their health has been affected by reason of occupational exposure to asbestos. It also directed that the health records of the workers be maintained from the beginning of their employment and 10 years after the cessation of their employment and that the workers be insured.[151]

In certain PIL cases concerning claims that temporary workers in continuous service for several years ought to be treated on a par with permanent workers performing similar work, the Court had directed that they be accorded the same wages and service conditions as permanent workers performing similar work with effect from the date when their employment commenced.[152] The Court had also issued directions for the permanent absorption of temporary workers.[153]

Follow-Up of Orders

In several cases, the Court has issued directions for the supervision of the implementation of its orders. For example, in a case relating to the employment

---

[149] *Consumer Education and Research Centre v Union of India* (1995) 3 SCC 42, 73–74.

[150] *Sanjit Roy v State of Rajasthan* (1983) 1 SCC 525, 534–536.

[151] *Consumer Education and Research Centre v Union of India* (1995) 3 SCC 42, 73–74.

[152] Eg, *Dhirendra Chamoli v State of Uttar Pradesh* (1986) 1 SCC 637, 638–39.

[153] Eg, *Dharwad District PWD Literate Daily Wage Employees Association v State of Karnataka* (1990) 2 SCC 396, 407–09. The judgment in this case was recently overruled by the Supreme Court in *Secretary, State of Karnataka v Umadevi* (2006) 4 SCC 1, 26–27, 42.

of child labour, the Court appointed a Committee consisting of the district judge of the area, the district magistrate, a public activist operating in the area and the local labour officer to oversee the implementation of its directions.[154] In another case concerning *beedi* workers in Tamil Nadu, the Court directed the Tamil Nadu State Legal Aid and Advice Board to oversee the implementation of its directions.[155]

In certain cases, the Court has directed the respondent to indicate the manner in which its directions have been implemented. For instance, in *Sanjit Roy's* case[156] referred to earlier, the Court directed the respondent to submit a report to the Court within a stipulated time-frame, setting out particulars of the payment made and the names of the workers to whom such payments were made. Similarly, in another case, the Court directed the Secretary to Government, Ministry of Labour to apprise the Court within one year about the compliance of its directions.[157]

THE COURT'S APPROACH IN RECENT TIMES

The aforesaid discussion would indicate that the Indian Supreme Court has creatively addressed labour concerns by expansively interpreting the fundamental rights in the light of the directive principles and other international human rights principles and thus strengthened labour rights. It would also appear from the aforesaid discussion that writ remedies in general and PIL procedures in particular hold great promise to effectively address labour concerns in general, and issues concerning poor and marginalised workers in particular.

However, a note of caution needs to be sounded at this point in the wake of considerable criticism of the labour jurisprudence of the Supreme Court over the last decade. Labour activists speak of a distinct paradigm shift in the labour jurisprudence of the Court during this period following the country's adoption of the new economic policy.[158]

Prior to the country's adoption of the new economic policy, the apex court is credited with having built a strong edifice for the protection of labour rights by interpreting labour enactments in the light of the social philosophy of the Constitution and the directive principles of state policy.[159]

---

154 *MC Mehta* (1991) 1 SCC 283, 286.

155 *Rajangam, Secretary, District Beedi Workers Union v State of Tamil Nadu* (1992) 1 SCC 221, 225.

156 *Sanjit Roy* (1983) 1 SCC 525, 536.

157 *MC Mehta v State of Tamil Nadu* (1996) 6 SCC 756, 774.

158 For example, see Kumar, V, 'Co-opted by Globalisation' *Combat Law* (November–December 2008) 114, 116 and Prasad, NGR, 'Protect Thy Worker' *Combat Law* (November–December 2008) 86.

159 Singh, G, 'Judiciary Jettisons Working Class' *Combat Law* (November–December 2008) 24.

The Court's expansive interpretation of terms such as 'industry' and 'workman' extending the coverage of the labour laws and its rulings during that period in respect of a wide range of labour issues such as that of the entitlement of temporary workers to regularisation and permanency in state-run establishments, eligibility for payment of retrenchment compensation and unjust termination from service, have been hailed as progressive.

However, following the adoption of the new economic policy, concerns have been expressed about the Court abandoning its earlier approach and becoming a conservative court[160] with an 'anti-worker stance'.[161] The decisions of the apex court in respect of several labour issues have been criticised on the grounds of being contrary to precedent and the directive principles. This is ascribed to the Court's 'approval of the new economic policy'[162] and its being influenced by 'the values fostered by liberalization'.[163]

At this point therefore, it is necessary to take a quick look at the new economic policy of India and its implications for labour.

The New Economic Policy and its Implications for Labour

In 1991, in a marked departure from its earlier economic policy,[164] the Indian Government adopted the New Economic Policy (NEP) aimed at liberalising and deregulating the Indian economy. The key features of the NEP include globalisation and liberalisation of the economy and the privatisation of state-run industries and services.[165] The introduction of this policy paved the way for greater foreign investment in India and exposed Indian industries to greater competition.

Pursuant to the adoption of the policy, the Indian Government disinvested its shares in several state-run industries leading to their privatisation. The opening up of the economy also led to the closure of several industrial establishments, in particular, small scale establishments resulting in the loss of employment for hundreds of thousands of workers.[166] There have also been

---

[160] Karat, P, 'Supreme Court in Liberalized Times' 09/08/2003 www.countercurrents.org/hr-karat090803.htm.

[161] Sharma, 'Flexibility, Employment and Labour Market Reforms in India' 41(21) *Economic and Political Weekly* (27 May 2006) 2078, 2083.

[162] Bhushan, P, 'Supreme Court and Public Interest Litigation, Changing Perspectives under Liberalisation' (2004) 39(18) *Economic and Political Weekly* 1772.

[163] Karat, 'Supreme Court in Liberalized Times' 09/08/2003.

[164] During the first four decades since India became independent in 1947, import substitution and industrial licensing were important features of its economic policy. The public sector played a predominant role in the economy then and there was a mushrooming of state-run industries and services. Foreign investment in the country was restricted and the private sector was subject to licensing and controls. See 'Report of the Second National Commission on Labour' (n 4) paras 3.3–3.30.

[165] The salient features of the new economic policy have been discussed in ibid para 4.31.

[166] Ibid paras 4.127, 4.274.

significant changes in the employment structure in industrial establishments. There has been a considerable downsizing of the permanent workforce in previously state-run industries, as well as other private industries by the introduction of early separation schemes called voluntary retirement schemes. On the other hand, there is an increasing trend of the engagement of temporary workers, contract workers and trainees to do the work previously done by permanent workers. Employers have also resorted to tactics such as the redesignation of workers as managers so as to bring them out of the purview of labour laws. Furthermore, there is an increasing trend of subcontracting or outsourcing core production work.[167] Payment of wages has been increasingly linked to performance and workers are also compulsorily required to do overtime work without any extra payment.

Alongside, there have been strident calls from the industry for effecting reforms in the labour laws, giving employers greater flexibility in hiring and firing workers; in particular, for the removal of provisions in the Industrial Disputes Act 1947 relating to prior governmental permission for effecting closures and the lay-off and retrenchment of workers in industries employing a 100 or more workers. There have also been demands for the removal of the restrictions on the use of contract labour under the Contract Labour (Regulation and Abolition) Act 1970, in particular, the restrictions imposed by section 10 of the Act.[168]

The changes in the employment structure in the new economic climate and also the increasing use of unfair methods by employers to dissuade workers from joining trade unions[169] have affected the strength of trade unions and eroded their bargaining power.[170] In turn, there is a significant increase in the incidence of lockouts while the incidence of strikes has reduced.[171]

It would now be of interest to examine the response of the apex court to certain labour rights issues that assume particular significance in the post NEP era.

Landmark rulings in the post NEP era

The rulings of the Court in *Steel Authority of India Ltd v National Union Waterfront Workers* ('the *SAIL* case')[172] concerning the right of contract

---

[167] Sharma (n 67) 2083. Also see Roy Chowdhury, 'Globalisation and Labour' (2004) 106.
[168] 'Report of the Second National Commission on Labour' (n 4) paras 6.84 and 6.109.
[169] Singh 'Judiciary Jettisons Working Class' (2008) 29.
[170] Sharma (n 67) 2083; Roy Chowdhury (n 4) 108.
[171] 'Report of the Second National Commission on Labour' (n 4) para 4.280; Sharma (n 67) 2080.
[172] *Steel Authority of India Ltd (SAIL) v National Union Waterfront Workers* (2001) 7 SCC 1. This case is generally referred to as the '*SAIL case*'.

workers to permanent absorption, the *BALCO Employees Union v Union of India* case[173] concerning the privatisation of a previously state-run industry, *TK Rangarajan v Government of Tamil Nadu*[174] concerning the right to strike and *Secretary, State of Karnataka v Umadevi*[175] concerning the right of temporary workers employed by the state to regularisation and permanent absorption, are most often cited as exemplifying the new approach of the Court to labour issues in the post NEP era. It is therefore proposed to briefly discuss the rulings in these cases.

The SAIL Case

In the *SAIL* case,[176] the main issue that came up for the consideration of the Supreme Court was the entitlement of the contract labour employed in an establishment to absorption upon the issue of a notification under section 10 of the Contract Labour (Regulation and Abolition) Act 1970. Section 10 of the Act enables the Government to prohibit employment of contract labour in any process, operation or other work in any establishment, having regard to factors such as the nature of the work involved and its necessity for the establishment.

The implications of the issue of a notification under section 10 of the Act on the contract labour employed in the establishment have not been explicitly spelt out either in section 10 or elsewhere in the Act. In *Air India Statutory Corporation v United Labour Union*,[177] interpreting the provisions of the Act in the light of the directive principles, the Supreme Court was of the view that the Act did not intend to denude the contract labourers of their source of livelihood on the issue of such a notification under section 10(1). It therefore held that they would be entitled to be absorbed on a regular basis in the establishment upon the issue of a notification under section 10(1) when the work performed by them is of a perennial nature.

However, in the subsequent *SAIL* case, the Court was of the view that it could not read in some remedy not specified in the Act. In this context, the Court made the following observation:

> The principle that a beneficial legislation needs to be construed liberally in favour of the class for whose benefit it is intended does not extend to reading in the provisions of the Act what the legislature has not provided whether expressly or by necessary implication or substituting remedy or benefits for that provided by the legislature.

---

[173] *BALCO Employees Union v Union of India* (2002) 3 SCC 333.
[174] *TK Rangarajan v Government of Tamil Nadu* (2003) 6 SCC 581.
[175] *Secretary, State of Karnataka v Umadevi* (2006) 4 SCC 1.
[176] *Steel Authority of India Ltd v National Union Waterfront Workers* (2001) 7 SCC 1, 42–63.
[177] *Air India Statutory Corporation v United Labour Union* (1997) 9 SCC 377, 434–46.

The Court thus overruled its judgment in the *Air India* case and held that the contract labour employed in an establishment have no right to automatic absorption when a notification for abolition of contract labour in the establishment is issued by the Government under section 10(1) of the Act.

The BALCO Employees' Union *Case*

In the *BALCO Employees Union* case,[178] the trade unions of workers of a government-run aluminium manufacturing company challenged the decision of the central Government to disinvest the majority of its shares in the company in favour of a private company on the ground that it was arbitrary. They also contended that the decision being one that adversely affected the interests of the company's workers, they ought to have been heard both prior to and at different stages of the process of disinvestment. It was urged that the right of hearing should extend to vital issues such as the wisdom of going through the disinvestment process in the first place, the choice of the private party to whom the company's shares are to be transferred and the manner in which the bids of the competing private parties are to be evaluated.

On the facts of the case, the Court held that no case had been made out by the petitioners that the decision of the Government was in any way capricious, arbitrary, illegal or uninformed. More generally, the Court also spelt out its views on the scope of judicial review of such decisions. It held that it is not for the Courts to consider whether a particular public policy is wise or whether a better policy can be evolved and that such an economic policy decision could not be interfered with unless it was against any law or was established to be *mala fide*.

The Court also made a pronouncement in respect of the standing to question such economic policy decisions. Apart from the concerned trade unions, the aforesaid decision was also challenged by a citizen in the public interest. Noting that he was neither an employee nor a prospective bidder, the Court observed that 'PIL was not meant to be a weapon to challenge the financial or administrative decisions taken by the Government in exercise of their administrative power. A PIL at the behest of a stranger ought not to be entertained.'

On the aspect of the right of the workers to participate in the making of such decisions, the Court ruled that workers are not entitled to a right of hearing or consultation prior to the making of such decisions and cannot claim a right of continuous consultation at various stages of the disinvestment process.

---

[178] *BALCO Employees Union* (2002) 3 SCC 333, 362–82.

TK Rangarajan's *Case*

The case of *TK Rangarajan*[179] concerned the en masse summary dismissal of about 200,000 employees of the Government of Tamil Nadu. This was on the basis of the provisions of the Tamil Nadu Essential Services Maintenance Act 2002 that prohibited strikes in services declared as essential under the Act and Tamil Nadu Ordinance 3 of 2003 that allowed for the summary mass dismissal of government employees on strike. They were dismissed for their participation in a strike protesting against the withdrawal of pensionary and other benefits.

The employees filed Writ Petitions challenging the validity of the Tamil Nadu Essential Services Maintenance Act 2002 and Tamil Nadu Ordinance 3 of 2003 and their dismissals. The case thus centred on the issue of government employees' right to strike.

Following the earlier rulings of the Court in the *All India Bank Employees' Association v The National Industrial Tribunal (Bank Disputes), Bombay* case[180] and other cases,[181] the Supreme Court held that government employees have no fundamental right to strike. The Court also went one step further, holding that they have no legal, moral or equitable right to go on strike. On the basis that there is no statutory provision empowering the employees to go on a strike, while rule 22 of the Tamil Nadu Government Servants Conduct Rules 1973 prohibits government employees from engaging in strikes or incitements thereto or similar activities, the Court took the view that government employees do not have a legal or statutory right to strike. Expressing the opinion that strike as a weapon is mostly misused, resulting in chaos and total maladministration and that the employees could resort to the machinery provided under different statutory provisions for redressal of their grievances, the Court observed that there can be no moral or equitable justification to go on strike as well.

In the course of the proceedings before the Court, the state Government proposed to reinstate the majority of the dismissed government employees subject to an unconditional apology, as well as an undertaking by them to the effect that they would abide by rule 22 of the Conduct Rules. In the circumstances, the Court did not make any pronouncement in respect of the issue of the constitutional validity of the laws under challenge.

---

[179] *TK Rangarajan* (2003) 6 SCC 581, 589–94.

[180] *All India Bank Employees' Association v The National Industrial Tribunal (Bank Disputes), Bombay* AIR 1962 SC 171.

[181] *Radhey Shyam Sharma v Post Master General* AIR 1965 SC 311 concerning the validity of ss 3–5 of the Essential Services Maintenance Ordinance 1960; *Ex-Capt Harish Uppal v Union of India* (2003) 2 SCC 45 concerning lawyers' strikes and *Communist Party of India (M) v Bharat Kumar* (1998) 1 SCC 201 regarding the right to call or enforce a 'bandh'.

Umadevi's *case*

In *Umadevi's* case,[182] the Court considered the claim of temporary workers employed by the state for regularisation of their services and permanent absorption, based on the fact that they had continued in employment for a number of years.

Even while noting that there might be occasions when the state or its instrumentalities resort to employing persons on a temporary basis without following the required procedures to discharge the duties attached to sanctioned posts and that such engagement may be for a considerable length of time, the Court rejected the claim of the workers. Overruling its earlier decisions in cases such as the *Dharwad District PWD Literate Daily Wage Employees Association v State of Karnataka* case[183] wherein such claims had been allowed, the Court held that unless the appointment of such temporary workers was in terms of the relevant rules after a proper competition among qualified persons, it would not confer any right on them for regularisation and permanent absorption. Rejecting the contentions of the workers based on articles 14 and 16 of the Constitution of India, the Court held that their claim for equal treatment with regularly employed workers would fail as they had not been appointed in conformity with articles 14 and 16 of the Constitution of India and that the equities of those in such temporary employment need to be balanced with those consequently deprived of the opportunity for public employment. While the judgment lays emphasis on the need for adherence to the constitutional scheme of public employment, the financial implications for the state in the event of orders for such regularisation and permanent absorption being issued by the Court was also a factor taken into consideration.

An Assessment of the Court's Approach in Recent Times

The aforesaid rulings of the Court certainly seem to indicate that the Court has adopted a more restrictive approach to labour rights issues in recent times. A distinct shift from the Court's earlier approach is discernible in its interpretation of labour laws, as well as the manner in which it has viewed the application of the fundamental rights and directive principles to labour rights issues. The Court also appears to have adopted a narrower perspective in respect of issues involving the collective rights of workers such as that of the right of workers to participate in the making of economic policy decisions that could potentially have adverse implications for their rights

---

[182] *Umadevi* (2006) 4 SCC 1, 22–26, 36, 40–41.
[183] *Dharwad Disrict PWD Literate Daily Wage Employees Association v State of Karnataka* (1990) 2 SCC 396.

and interests, the right of workers to question such decisions and the right to strike.

An analysis of the Court's decisions in the recent past in respect of various other labour rights issues, such as that of the payment of back-wages to workers found to have been wrongfully dismissed from service and the application of the principles of natural justice to disciplinary proceedings, also indicate that the Court has indeed adopted a new approach. This has been confirmed even by the Court in some of its decisions. For instance, in *Hombe Gowda Educational Trust v State of Karnataka*,[184] the Court observed:

> The Supreme Court has come a long way from its earlier viewpoints. The recent trend in the decisions of the Supreme Court seek to strike a balance between the earlier approach to industrial relations where only the interest of the workmen was sought to be protected with the avowed object of fast industrial growth of the country.

Some of the Court's recent decisions also seem to emphasise the need for a more 'pragmatic' approach to labour rights issues.[185] For instance, in *UP State Brassware Corporation Ltd v Uday Narain Pandey*,[186] in respect of the issue of the payment of back-wages upon an order of dismissal being declared invalid, the Court observed:

> ... although a direction to pay full backwages used to be the usual result, now a pragmatic view of the matter is taken by the court realising that an industry may not be compelled to pay for the period during which he apparently contributed little or nothing at all to the industry, for a period that was spent unproductively, as a result whereof the employer would be compelled to go back to a situation which prevailed many years ago, namely, when the workman was retrenched.

While on the one hand, the Court has adopted a different approach in respect of issues such as the ones discussed above post the adoption of the NEP, on the other, its approach to issues, such as that of the entitlement of temporary women workers to maternity benefits[187] and the effective enforcement of the law prohibiting bonded labour[188] seem to indicate that the Court is continuing to act in its earlier progressive vein.

It may therefore be argued that the Court in recent times has adopted a narrower approach while dealing with labour rights issues that could have significant financial implications for the state and other employers, issues arising out of the current economic context where the interests of the

---

[184] *Hombe Gowda Educational Trust v State of Karnataka* (2006) 1 SCC 430, 441.
[185] See Sinha, J, 'Emerging Industrial Relations' (2004) 6 SCC (Jour) 1, available at www.ebc-india.com/lawyer/Articles/2004v6a1.htm.
[186] *UP State Brassware Corporation Ltd v Uday Narain Pandey* (2006) 1 SCC 479, 486.
[187] *Municipal Corporation of Delhi v Female Workers (Muster Roll)* (2000) 3 SCC 224.
[188] Eg, *People's Union for Civil Liberties* (2004) 12 SCC 381.

Government and other employers contrast starkly with those of workers, and issues concerning workers' collective rights as such. However, while dealing with issues concerning certain particularly disadvantaged groups of workers such as bonded labourers, there does not appear to be any discernible shift in its approach.

CONCLUSION

The Supreme Court of India has adopted a creative approach to address labour concerns, particularly through PIL procedures where it has made a radical departure from the procedural rigours that traditional litigation is associated with. Through its application of the constitutionally enshrined and other international human rights principles, it has made a significant contribution towards ensuring fair treatment of serving and retired workers by the Government and other employers, equal treatment of women workers, prevention of sexual harassment of women workers, prevention of forced labour and child labour, improvement of occupational safety and health, better enforcement of national labour standards, etc. The human rights approach of the Supreme Court has thus strengthened labour rights in the country.

The recent decisions of the Supreme Court in respect of issues such as that of the right of workers to participate in the making of economic policy decisions that could adversely affect their rights and interests, the right of workers to question such decisions and the entitlement of contract workers and temporary workers to permanent absorption, however, indicates a shift in its approach in as much as it has not applied human rights principles in such cases with a view to further the rights of the affected workers. It therefore appears that there has been a shift in the approach of the Court while considering labour rights issues where the interests of workers appear to be sharply pitted against those of the state, issues that could have significant financial implications for the state and other employers and issues involving the collective rights of workers. It therefore appears that the potential of the constitutional remedies to address such labour rights issues arising in the current economic context of India through cases founded on human rights principles is limited.[189]

On the other hand, the continued human rights approach of the Supreme Court on issues such as that of forced labour, enforcement of national labour standards, occupational safety and health and issues specific to women workers in the last decade and a half indicates that the constitutional remedies certainly afford an effective tool for the labour movement in the country in addressing these types of labour issues.

---

[189] The recent judgment of the Supreme Court in *Harjinder Singh v Punjab State Warehousing Corporation* (JT 2010 (1) SC 598) wherein a Division Bench of the Court has been critical of the Court's shift in approach and called for interpreting Labour enactments in keeping with the Constitution's philosophy, in particular, the Directive Principles has however raised hopes that the Courts would be more sensitive to such issues as well.

8

Legal Protection of Workers' Human Rights in Nigeria: Regulatory Changes and Challenges

CHIOMA AGOMO

INTRODUCTION

T HE WORLD OF work is in a state of flux. Globalisation has opened up domestic labour market conditions to international scrutiny, and has led to a demand for new paradigms for determining the nature, scope and content of employment relationships at both the individual and collective levels. In Nigeria, traditional common rules for determining the complex nature of employment relations have, against these developments, proved to be grossly inadequate. This is particularly so in the area of individual employment relations where the demand for the observance of human rights principles has become a crucial point of reference in the public sector of the Nigerian economy. Freedom of association, collective bargaining and the right to strike, all features of collective labour relations, constitute other areas where human rights principles and international human rights instruments have long been in use as measuring rods for determining the efficacy of national legislation. The courts, including the National Industrial Court, are playing significant roles in providing the parameters for determining the scope of these rights and the class of beneficiaries. These issues, including the rights of women as a vulnerable group, will be discussed here.

THE POLITICAL AND SOCIAL CONTEXT

Nigeria is a Federal Republic comprising 36 states and a federal capital territory, Abuja. The country occupies a land mass of about 923,768 square kilometers, extending from the Gulf of Guinea in the South to the Sahara desert in the North. It shares common boundaries with the Republic of Benin in the West, Cameroon and Chad in the East and the Niger Republic in the North. There are well over 350 different ethnic groupings in Nigeria. The predominant groups are the Hausas in the North, Igbos in the East and the Yorubas in the West. There are also significant minorities such as the Ijaws, the Urhobos, the Efiks and the Fulanis. The latest official census conducted in 2006 put the total population at 140,003,542. The gender breakdown shows 51 per cent male and 49 per cent female (71,709,859 male, 68,293,683 female).

Nigeria became one nation in 1914 following the amalgamation of the northern and southern protectorates by the British colonial government. The colony of Lagos had formally been annexed and declared a crown colony and protectorate in 1861.[1] Trade was the underlying reason for subsequent colonisation.[2] The trading activities and interest of the Royal Niger Company led to the opening up of the hinterland and the establishment of the northern and southern protectorates as autonomous administrative units. Both were fused together in 1914 into one entity called Nigeria as indicated earlier.[3]

Four Constitutions were passed for Nigeria by the colonial government between 1922 and 1957. While the 1922 Constitution established a legislative council for the whole country, the 1954 Constitution divided the country into three regions, namely, the Eastern region and Southern Cameroun, the Western region and the Northern region.[4] Nigeria became independent on 1 October 1960.

Nigeria's legal system is deeply rooted in the English common law.[5] The components of the received law are, the common law of England and the doctrines of equity, together with the statutes of general application that were in force in England on 1 January 1900.[6]

The aim of the colonial labour policy for Nigeria was to make its labour and social policy in the colonies conform as nearly as possible to British labour principles, and international labour standards. However, it has been said that the introduction of English law into Nigeria, was borne not out of goodwill for Nigeria and the workers, but rather as a means of facilitating 'the commercial and economic objectives and interests of the colonial

---

[1] The colony of Lagos was initially governed together with the Gold Coast colony (Ghana). Lagos had earlier been made a protectorate in 1852.

[2] Initially, it was trade in human cargo and subsequently trade in palm produce and other commodities.

[3] The decision to establish official presence in the West African coast did not happen overnight. See Udoma, U, *History and the Law of the Constitution of Nigeria* (Lagos, Malthouse Press Ltd, 1994) 2.

[4] A mid Western region was carved out of the Western region in 1962.

[5] See Adeogun, AA, 'From Contract to Status in Quest for Security' (Inaugural Lecture, University of Lagos, 1986).

[6] Courts Ordinance 1876, see also Ogunniyi, O, *Nigerian Labour and Employment Law in Perspective*, 2nd edn (Lagos, Folio Publishers Ltd, 2003) 6.

masters'.[7] Indeed, this assertion might have some element of truth, as there were evidences of hostile attitude towards indigenous workers.[8]

In 1966, the democratically elected government headed by the Prime Minister, Abubakar Tafawa Balewa, was overthrown in a bloody *coup d'etat* by some officers of the Nigerian Army.[9] The Constitution was replaced by Decree No 1 of 1966.[10] This marked a 30-year period of military rule by decrees and edicts in Nigeria.[11] Laws passed during these periods did not pass through democratic legislative processes,[12] because there were none. Indeed, all the relevant labour laws passed during this period[13] were promulgated as decrees. The peremptory language of the Trade Disputes Act and the Trade Unions Acts provide two very good examples of cavalier military attitude. The increased reliance on the use of force by Nigerian governments to ensure civil obedience and compliance with its policies, led to the organisation of civil society to counter the assault on civil and political organisational rights and mobilisation of the trade union movement.[14]

The Civil Liberties Organisation (CLO) was established in 1987 by a group of activist lawyers after receiving complaints from trade unionists and workers who had been victims of the military government. More human rights organisations slowly emerged, determined to promote the recognition of basic rights proclaimed by the Universal Declaration of Human Rights and the African Charter; and to put pressure on the government to recognise basic civil liberties.[15] These organisations raised public awareness about human rights abuses that were taking place at the hands of the state by issuing critical press statements and taking the government to court over arbitrary arrests and other government actions, but the state reacted by including ouster clauses in decrees, which excluded the jurisdiction of courts making it impossible for people to legally assert their international human rights.[16]

---

[7] Ibid.

[8] In 1945 coalminers agitating for better working conditions were gunned down and killed in Eva Valley Coal mine, Enugu.

[9] The Eastern Region declared itself the Republic of Biafra in May 1967, after failure of talks with the Federal Government of Lt Colonel Gowon. This led to a 30-month civil war, which ended in 1970 with the surrender of Biafra.

[10] See Udoma, *History and the Law of the Constitution of Nigeria* (1994) 231.

[11] There was brief period between 1979 and 1983 when a democratically elected government governed the country until overthrown by yet another coup.

[12] See Udoma (n 3) 239–42 for some of the numerous decrees churned out with seeming ease and rapidity.

[13] For example, the Trade Unions Act 1973, the Labour Act 1974, Wages Board and Industrial Councils Act 1973, Trade Disputes Act 1976 and Trade Disputes (Essential Services) Act 1976 among others.

[14] Aiyede, E Remi, 'United We Stand: Labour Unions and Human Rights NGOs in the Democratisation Process in Nigeria' (2004) 14 *Development in Practice* 224, 228.

[15] Ibid.

[16] Ibid 229.

After legal attempts at asserting human rights were frustrated by government decrees and increased force, human rights non-governmental organisations (NGOs) started advocating for wider democratic change, however, they needed to mobilise the public in order to put pressure on the government. This was realised through the formation of the Campaign for Democracy (CD), an umbrella body made up of a broad spectrum of activists including the labour union movement.[17] This is despite the fact that, during this period, workers' rights, particularly at the collective labour relations level, were neither recognised nor protected.[18] Strikes were (and still are) practically outlawed, while freedom of association and the right to form or to belong to a trade union of one's choice were severely curtailed. This will be discussed more fully subsequently.

ECONOMIC CONTEXT

Nigeria is richly endowed with vast agricultural, mineral, marine and forest resources.[19] Over 60 per cent of the population is involved in some form of agricultural production, mostly at subsistence level. In 2008, agriculture contributed 42.07 per cent of the Gross Domestic Product (GDP).[20] However, oil and gas products have continued to drive the Nigerian economy and account for about 95 per cent of the country's export earnings.[21] The link between workers' rights and a mono economy based on oil may be illustrated by the spate of industrial actions organised by labour unions from time to time, to protest unilateral changes in the pricing of petroleum products. Indeed, the situation in the Niger Delta region, the heartland of oil exploration and production, speaks eloquently of the nexus between oil, workers and the Nigerian economy.

In 1994, the National Union of Petroleum and Natural Gas Workers (NUPENG) National Executive Council formulated a number of demands, including workers conditions and reinstatement of democratic and political institutions, as well as the immediate release of all detained union officials and other activists.[22] The strike by the 150,000-strong membership of NUPENG crippled an already ailing economy which depended on oil for

---

[17] Ibid.

[18] See Eso, K, 'Nigerian Law and Human Rights' in *The Nigerian Judiciary: What Vision for the 21st Century* (Lagos, Faculty of Law, University of Lagos, J.I.C. Taylor lecture series, 1997), where he painstakingly explored the negative effect of military law making on law the judiciary, law and human rights.

[19] See www.nigeriaembassyusa.org/thisisnigeria.shtml.

[20] See www.nigeriastat.gov.ng/news.php.

[21] Report of the Vision 2010 Committee (1997) Main Report, iii.

[22] Ihonvbere, JO, 'Organized Labor and the Struggle for Democracy in Nigeria' (1997) 30(3) *African Studies Review* 77, 89–90.

over 90 per cent of its export earnings at that time[23] and consequently had a devastating effect on the lives of Nigerians including electricity outages, gas shortages and lack of clean water. However, despite this, the strike still received popular support from workers and citizens throughout Nigeria.[24] The 8,000-strong Petroleum and Natural Gas Senior Staff Association (PENGASSAN) also joined the strike, demanding the end of military rule and the release of prominent trade union officials.

The response of the Nigerian Military Government was roundly condemned by the international community, including the International Labour Organisation (ILO), which used its monitoring processes to put pressure on Nigeria to respect the right to freedom of association. The ILO Committee on Freedom of Association examined cases on violations of workers' rights in Nigeria brought before it. The first was in 1995. This concerned the arrests of prominent trade union activists for carrying out legitimate trade union activities.[25] The Committee urged the Government to release those who had been arrested, and repeal immediately the military decrees which legally empowered such arrests. It also urged the Government to restore the executive councils of the Nigeria Labour Congress (NLC), NUPENG and PENGASSAN which had been dissolved by Government.[26] The second case, in 1997,[27] concerned the continued detention of trade unionists without being charged. It also looked at the Government's violations of Convention No 87 through the enactment of decree which nullified existing affiliations to unapproved international trade union organisations and banned future affiliations without approval.[28]

After persistent refusal by the Government of Nigeria to conform to the requests of the Committee, the ILO Governing Body established a Commission of Inquiry under article 26(4) of the Constitution, to investigate Nigeria's alleged violations of workers' right to freedom of association and collective bargaining, on 26 March 1998.[29] The Commission's sitting

[23] Ibid.

[24] Ibid 95.

[25] Complaint against the Government of Nigeria presented by the International Confederation of Free Trade Unions (ICFTU), the Organization of African Trade Union Unity (OATUU) and the World Confederation of Labour (WCL) Report No 300, Case(s) No(s) 1793, Vol. LXXX, 1995, Series B, No 3.

[26] International Labour Organisation (ILO) Freedom of Association Committee Report No 315, Cases(s). No(s) 1793, 1935 Vol LXXXII, 1999, Series B, No.1.

[27] Complaints against the Government of Nigeria presented by the International Confederation of Free Trade Unions (ICFTU), the Organization of African Unity (OATUU), the World Confederation of Labour (WCL) and the International Federation of Chemical, Energy, Mine and General Workers' Union (ICEM) Report No.315, Case(s) No(s). 1793, 1935.

[28] ILO Freedom of Association Committee Report No 315.

[29] GB.273/15/1 available at www2.ilo.org/public/English/standards/relm/gb/docs/gb271/gb-18-5. See also ILO, 'Nigerian Labour Practices Under Scrutiny: ILO Governing Body Establishes Commission of Enquiry' (Press Release, 26 March 1998).

was however delayed for 60 days to allow a direct contacts mission to Nigeria in August 1998. This mission, headed by Justice Rajsoomer Lallah, Chair Designate of the appointed Commission of Inquiry, visited Nigeria from 17–21 August 1998.[30] It submitted a report of its findings.[31] This was however overshadowed, less than a year later, by the country's transition to democracy elections in 20 years, which brought Olusegun Obasanjo into power, as the executive President of the Federal Republic of Nigeria. The landmark transition raised expectations from all segments of society, including workers, of imminent dismantling of undemocratic policies and laws. It turned out to be short-lived.

Workers have had to contend with undemocratic practices within the workplace, engendered partly by the underlying common law philosophy of freedom of contract which gives an employer the right to hire and fire at will;[32] and partly by inconsistent labour policies.

It is perhaps pertinent to mention briefly two such policies which, in practical terms, failed to advance the rights of workers in any significant manner. One such policy is the indigenisation policy of government which attempted to localise ownership of businesses through equity transfers to individuals, in order to create both employment and entrepreneurial opportunities for Nigerians. It did not succeed.[33] Had it succeeded, it would have provided a model for worker participation in the governance of the workplace in the sense that those workers as joint equity holders would have a real voice in decision making organs, where issues affecting their rights, welfare and health and safety were decided.

The second policy worthy of mention here is the Structural Adjustment Programme (SAP) which was introduced by the General Babangida administration between 1985 and 1995. It was a major departure from public sector-led development process to a market-oriented development process. It promoted trade liberalisation, interest rates deregulation, public sector reforms and privatisation.[34] The impact of these policy changes on workers' rights and liberties has been drastic. One noticeable effect has been the

---

[30] ILO Freedom of Association Committee Report No 315.

[31] See ILO Report: 'Observance by Nigeria of the Freedom of Association and Protection of the Right to Organise Convention, 1948 (No. 87), and the Right to Organise and Collective Bargaining Convention, 1949 (No. 98): Report of the direct contacts mission to Nigeria (17–21 August 1998)'.

[32] This is the common law principle of freedom of contract where the question asked is: how was the termination effected? Not why the employment terminated.

[33] There were two indigenisation decrees in 1972 and 1977. See also Report of the Vision 2010 Committee 63.

[34] Report of the Vision 2010 Committee 63; Olukoshi, A, 'The Historical Significance of the Policy of Privatisation in Nigeria' in RO Olaniyan and CN Nworie (eds), *The Impact of SFEM (Second Tier Foreign Exchange Market) on the Economy* (Lagos, Nigerian Institute of International Affairs, 1990) 122. See also Quadri, TH, 'The Effect of Privatisation on Labour in Nigeria' (LL.B final year Research Project, 2004).

shrinking size of trade union membership as a result of the increase in the use of outsourcing as a means of hiring of labour. This practice has particularly affected unionisation in the financial and oil and gas sectors of the Nigerian economy. The right to freedom of association and the free exercise of workers' right to belong to trade unions of their choice are virtually non-existent in these establishments.

SOURCES OF LABOUR LAW

Sources of Nigerian labour law include the common law, made up of decisions of English courts and Nigerian courts,[35] statutes of general application in force in England on 1 January 1900,[36] and local legislation. Most of the labour laws were promulgated as military decrees between 1973 and 1999 by the various military governments. However, all statutes, whether enacted by a civilian government or promulgated by military government, are deemed to be Acts of the National Assembly in accordance with the Constitution.

The outbreak of the Nigerian civil war between 1967 and 1970 marked a turning point in the history of labour relations in Nigeria. The war provided the platform for a shift from the non-interventionist policy of government to an interventionist one. It was intended to be a temporary wartime measure; but unfortunately it became more and more entrenched into the system, and continued even after 1999, when Nigeria returned to a democratically elected government.[37] There have however, been some attempt since 2002 to effect fundamental changes, under the supervision of the ILO through a wholesale review of existing labour laws in conformity with international labour standards.[38] It is necessary to here to say something about this special collaboration between the ILO and the US Government (the donor).

---

[35] There is an academic debate concerning the binding force of decisions of English courts on Nigerian courts after 1960 when Nigeria became independent, and particularly after 1963 when the country became a Republic, and the Judicial Committee of the Privy Council ceased to be the highest court of appeal for Nigeria. I say academic, because the Nigerian courts continue to adopt decisions of English courts as binding, often without any explanation. There has, however, been a marked departure in some respects, this will be discussed in detail in the main body in subsequent paragraphs.

[36] See the Trade Unions Ordinance 1938; Workmen's Compensation Act 1941; Labour (Wage Fixing and Regulation) Ordinance 1943; Labour Code Ordinance 1945.

[37] Although the interventionist model has not been dismantled, there have been visible attempts since 2002 under the supervision of the ILO to review existing labour laws in conformity with International Labour Standards, see The NIGERIA DECLARATION PROJECT .NIR/00/50/USA.

[38] NIGERIA DECLARATION PROJECT (NIDEC) NIR/00/50/USA. The expert review committee submitted draft legislation for further processing, to the President Olusegun Obasanjo as an Executive Bill. It was not passed until he left office. There is some indication that the present National Assembly is working on the Labour Standards Bill.

The ILO, in collaboration with the US Department of Labour, executed the project known as the Nigerian Declaration Project (NIDEC), designed to promote the application of the ILO's Declaration on Fundamental Principles and Rights at Work between 2001 and 2005. One of the main aims of the Project was to provide support for the reform of existing labour laws in the country; the other was to build institutions and local capacity for dissolution of labour disputes through social dialogue.[39] Whatever else that may be said about the Project, it succeeded in producing a comprehensive draft of a labour standards bill to replace all existing labour laws.

The Constitution

The basic law is the Constitution of the Federal Republic of Nigeria 1999, which was promulgated by the Constitution of the Federal Republic of Nigeria (Promulgation) Decree 1999.[40] It came into force on 29 May 1999. Section 1 states that it is supreme and that its provisions shall have binding force on all authorities and persons throughout the Federal Republic of Nigeria.[41] Any law that is inconsistent with its provisions is declared void to the extent of the inconsistency.[42] The superiority of the constitution over military decrees had been the subject matter of judicial decisions in a number of cases and it seems settled beyond doubt that decrees took precedence over all other laws including the Constitution in times of military rule.[43]

Indeed, the inviolability of the Constitution was recently emphasised by the Supreme Court in *Governor of Kwara State & The Attorney-General &*

---

[39] See Evaluation Summaries International Labour Office: Evaluation; Promoting Democracy through Fundamental principles and rights at work and Tripartism in Nigeriia (NIDEC Project). June 2005(final Evaluation date). See n 38.

[40] Constitution of the Federal Republic of Nigeria (Promulgation) Decree 1999 No 24 of 1999. Before 1999, Nigeria had other constitutions, each regarded as the supreme law from which all laws derived their legitimacy.

[41] Ibid s 1 subs I; Mowoe, KM, *Constitutional Law in Nigeria,* (Lagos, Malthouse, 2003) vol I, 37, pointed out rightly that the concept of constitutional supremacy was always the first to be abrogated by the various military administrations in Nigeria. In times of military rule, decrees were supreme to the Constitution. Indeed, the first act by any military government on seizing power was to promulgate a decree suspending and modifying the Constitution, making decrees to prevail over the Constitution in cases of conflict between the two.

[42] Ibid s 1(3).

[43] See, for example, *Obaba v Military Government of Kwara State* (1994) 4 Nigeria Weekly Law Reports (part 26) 39; *Military Governor, Ondo State & Attorney General Ondo State v Victor Adegoke Adwunmi* (1988) 3 Nigeria Weekly Law Reports (part 82) 280, 306–07, the Supreme Court re-emphasised the superiority of military decrees over all other laws including the unsuspended parts of the constitution coexisting with it. See Eso 'Nigerian Law and Human Rights' (1997) 34.

Commissioner for Justice, Kwara State v Alhaji Issa Ojibara.[44] Oguntade, Justice of the Supreme Court, said:

> I have said this much in the hope that all players in the field of politics will imbibe the culture of paying due reverence and regard to the provisions of the Constitution. This has become necessary because in these times there is an unrestrained inclination to disregard the Constitution and treat its terms with irreverence and disrespect. The Constitution is the very foundation and structure upon which the existence of all organs of governance is hinged. It must be held inviolable.

Oguntade had earlier put it emphatically in these words:

> Courts cannot amend the Constitution. They cannot change the words. They must accept the words, and so far as they introduce change it can come only through their interpretation of the meaning of the words which change with the passage of time and change.[45]

The interpretation of the provision on freedom of association as it relates to trade unions should therefore be understood in this light.[46] This issue will be discussed in some detail in the next section.

HUMAN RIGHTS PROVISIONS

The Constitutional provisions for the legal protection of the human rights of workers in Nigeria can be found in chapters II and IV of the 1999 Constitution. Chapter II contains the Fundamental Objectives and Directive Principles of State Policy. Section 14 declares that the Federal Republic of Nigeria is a state based on the principles of democracy and social justice. Section 15 proscribes discrimination on the grounds of place of origin, sex, religion, status, ethnic or linguistic association; while section 16 articulates the responsibility of the state to promote national prosperity and an efficient, dynamic and self-reliant economy, by harnessing the resources of the nation.

Section 17 emphasises, among other things, the equality of rights, obligations and opportunities of every citizen before the law; recognition of the sanctity and dignity of the human person; the independence, impartiality and integrity of courts of law, as well as their easy accessibility. Section 17(3) is particularly relevant, because it enjoins the state to direct its policy towards ensuring equal opportunity for securing adequate means of livelihood, provision of suitable employment under just and humane conditions, with equal pay for equal work without discrimination on grounds of sex

---

[44] *Governor of Kwara State & The Attorney-General & Commissioner for Justice, Kwara State v Alhaji Issa Ojibara* [2006] 18 Nigeria Weekly Law Reports (part 1012) 645, 660.

[45] Ibid 659.

[46] *Osawe v Registrar of Trade Unions* [1985] 1 *Nigeria Weekly Law Report* (part 4) 553.

or any other ground. It also provides against exploitation of children and young persons.

The provisions in chapter II correspond with the economic, social and cultural rights found in international instruments. The issue, however, is that these provisions are not legally enforceable by virtue of section 6 (6)(c) of the 1999 Constitution, which provides:

> The judicial powers vested in accordance with the foregoing provisions of this section-
> (c) shall not, except as otherwise provided by this Constitution, extend to any issue or question as to whether any act or omission by any authority or person or as to whether any law or any judicial decision is in conformity with the Fundamental Objectives and Directive Principles of State Policy set out in Chapter II of this Constitution ...

Fundamental objectives were first introduced into the Constitution in 1979. In its report, the Constitutional Drafting Committee (CDC) explained that the rationale for such inclusion was to direct the attention of developing countries preoccupied with 'power and its material prerequisites' to the detriment of political ideals, to those ideals that show how society can be best governed.[47]

The CDC classified the fundamental objectives as the identification of the ultimate objectives of the nation, while the directive principles of state policy show the path which should lead to the objectives. The CDC was of the opinion that they did not create justiciable rights. Instead, it included item 61(a) in the Exclusive Legislative List of the 1979 Constitution to give the National Assembly power to make laws for their promotion and observance. This provision is now contained in item 60(a) of the 1999 Constitution.[48] It must be pointed out that this strict interpretation has come under increasing criticism, especially by civil society groups engaged in human rights advocacy. They feel that the judiciary ought to be liberal in its interpretation of the fundamental rights contained in chapter IV in such a way as to include chapter II rights. One fully shares this view and feels that the socio-economic rights in chapter II cannot in reality be separated from chapter IV.

Chapter IV contains the constitutionally guaranteed fundamental rights. These include: the right to life,[49] the right to the dignity of the human person,[50] the right to personal liberty,[51] the right to fair hearing,[52] the right to private

---

[47] Report of the Constitution Drafting Committee (1976) vol 1, para 3.1–3.2. See also Mowoe, KM, *Constitutional Law in Nigeria- Fundamental Rights* (Lagos, Goldwaters Communications Ltd, 2005) vol II, 7–13.

[48] Ibid.

[49] Constitution of the Federal Republic of Nigeria 1999 s 33.

[50] Ibid s 34.

[51] Ibid s 35.

[52] Ibid s 36.

and family life,[53] the right to freedom of thought, conscience and religion,[54] the right to freedom of expression and the press,[55] the right to peaceful assembly and association,[56] the right to freedom of movement,[57] and the right to freedom from discrimination.[58] Section 45 allows restrictions on some of these rights, including the right to freedom of association and the right to freedom from discrimination on various grounds, those of public health and public peace.

There is no doubt that the emergence of the newer generation of rights within the social-economic sphere has continued to call into question the exclusion of chapter II rights from the mainstream rights under chapter IV.

The Status of International Instruments

Section 12(1) of the Constitution provides that 'No treaty between the Federation and any other country shall have the force of law except to the extent to which any such treaty has been enacted into law by the National Assembly.'

This provision signifies that Nigeria operates the incorporation of treaties or dualist mode of adoption. This, therefore, means that it is not enough to sign or ratify a treaty or convention; it must be domesticated through an Act of the National Assembly for it to have a legally binding effect. Beside domestication, there is also another issue, namely that of its hierarchy vis-à-vis national legislation.

A very good example is the African Charter on Human and Peoples' Rights (Ratification and Enforcement) Act.[59] Articles 8, 9, 10 and 11 correspond broadly with the constitutional provisions on freedom of association and freedom of assembly. The status of the Charter was decided by the Supreme Court in *Gani Fawehinmi v Abacha*,[60] and it was held that the Charter is not inferior to locally enacted laws. Therefore, Charter provisions

---

[53] Ibid s 37.
[54] Ibid s 38.
[55] Ibid s 39.
[56] Ibid s 40.
[57] Ibid s 41.
[58] Ibid s 42.
[59] African Charter on Human and Peoples' Rights (Ratification and Enforcement) Act promulgated in 1983 as an Act to enable effect to be given in the Federal Republic of Nigeria to the African Charter on Human and Peoples' Rights.
[60] *Gani Fawehinmi v Abacha* (1990) 9 Nigeria Weekly Law Reports (part 475) 710. See also *Oshevire v British Caledonia Airways Ltd* (1990) 7 Nigeria Weekly Law Reports (part 163) 159; Popoola, AA, 'The Role of the Constitution in The Domestic Application of International Human Rights Norms and Standards with Particular Reference to Women' in A Akiyode-Afolabi (ed), *Gender Gaps in The 1999 Constitution of Nigeria* (Lagos, Women Advocates Research & Documentation Center (WARDC), 2003) 67.

on human rights such as a right to work[61] may be used to protect the human rights of workers in the workplace. This means that international human rights instruments once domesticated may be relied upon for the protection of the human rights of workers.

Chapter II of the Constitution can be said to represent an attempt to domesticate the provisions of the International Covenant on Economic, Social and Cultural Rights. The problem, however, is that these provisions are not legally enforceable because the Constitution so provides. The thinking as indicated earlier, however, is that a more liberal interpretation of the chapter IV rights, in line with the ever widening scope of human rights globally, will bring the socio-economic rights in chapter II of the Constitution within the ambit of enforceable human rights in Nigeria. The provision on the right to work is contained in chapter II.

Nigeria has ratified 38 ILO conventions, including Convention No 87 on Freedom of Association, No 98 on the Right to Organise and Collective Bargaining, No 100 on Equal Remuneration, No 111 on Employment Discrimination, No 138 on Minimum Age, No 155 on Occupational Safety and Health, and No 182 on Elimination of the Worst Forms of Child Labour. It is interesting to note that the provisions of many ILO conventions have become part of domestic legislation by the inclusion of the contents of these conventions into the text of the local legislation. The Labour Act[62] is a very good example of national legislation that incorporates various ILO provisions without explicitly saying so.

The Labour Act is the only comprehensive legislation with direct reference to individual employment law. It contains detailed provisions on wages, terms of employment of workers, medical examination, sickness and sickness pay, and holidays. It also has a section on special groups, namely apprentices, children and young persons and women, amongst others. The significant point about this legislation is that it has not received much attention either by way of statutory amendment or by judicial interpretation of its provisions since its promulgation in 1974.[63] It is therefore difficult to postulate the extent to which it has served as an instrument for the protection of the human rights of workers. But one significant point to note is that the various provisions of the Act are re-enactments of some of the ILO conventions ratified by Nigeria.[64]

---

[61] African Charter art 15 provides that every individual shall have the right to work under equitable and satisfactory conditions and shall receive equal pay for equal work.

[62] Labour Act No 21 of 1974 as amended and classified as chapter 198 Laws of the Federation of Nigeria 1990.

[63] See Aturu, Bamidele, commentary in Stiftung, FE, *A Handbook of Nigerian Labour Laws* (Lagos, Frankard Publishers, 2001) 188. See also www.ilo.org/dyn/natlex.

[64] Some of these are: ILO Convention No 29 on forced labour 1930 and ILO Convention No 105 on abolition of forced labour 1957; ILO Convention No 45 on underground work (women) 1935, ILO Convention No 59 on minimum age (industry) (revised) 1937, ILO Convention No 87 on freedom of association and ILO Convention No 98 on protection of the right to organize 1948, among others.

LABOUR LEGISLATION

The Constitution regulates, among other things, the distribution of legislative powers between the National Assembly and the various State Houses of Assemblies. The National Assembly, a bi-cameral legislative body, makes laws for the peace, order and good government of the Federation or any of its constituent parts (section 4). This power is both exclusive and concurrent.[65] Labour, including trade unions, industrial relations, conditions, safety and welfare of labour, industrial disputes, fixing of a national minimum wage for the federation; and industrial arbitrations, belong to the Exclusive Legislative List. Pensions, gratuities and similar benefits payable out of the consolidated revenue fund or any public fund of the federation also come under the Exclusive Legislative List.

The National Assembly has exclusive extensive powers to make laws and regulations affecting workers' rights. In addition, it also has concurrent power with State Houses of Assembly in respect of the matters on the Concurrent list. For example, it may make laws for the Federation or any part thereof with respect to the health, safety and welfare of persons employed to work in factories, offices and other premises or inter-state transportation and commerce including the training, supervision and qualification of such persons. State Houses of Assembly also have concurrent powers to make laws for their respective states with respect to the industrial, commercial or agricultural development of their respective states.[66]

All the relevant labour legislation, except the Pensions Reform Act 2004 and the Trade Unions (Amendment) Act 2005, were originally promulgated as decrees by successive military regimes. They did not go through the normal legislative processes. It should not be surprising, therefore, that in substance they are at variance with some of the basic international labour standards such as freedom of association, and the right to free collective bargaining, even though there is some semblance of conformity.[67]

STATUS OF FREEDOM OF ASSOCIATION

Freedom of association and the right to form or to belong to a trade union of one's choice is a fundamental right guaranteed by the Constitution, and the African Charter. The Trade Unions Act also provides that any person

---

[65] The second schedule to the Constitution contains two lists: the Exclusive Legislative List and the Concurrent List.

[66] See items 17 and 19 on the Concurrent List.

[67] Akanbi, one time president of the Court of Appeal, said that it would be idle to pretend that the law in a constitutional democracy spoke the same language as in a military regime.

who is otherwise eligible for membership of a particular trade shall not be refused admission to membership of the union because of his ethnic origin, religion or political opinion. Any union rules that are inconsistent with the provisions of the law, are void to the extent of the inconsistency.[68] The Labour Act equally makes it unlawful for any employer to make it a condition of employment that a worker shall or shall not join a trade union or shall not relinquish membership of a trade union; or cause a worker to be dismissed or in any way be prejudiced because of trade union membership, or trade union activities.[69]

It is necessary to examine the main legislation that, apart from the Constitution, provides the legal framework for collective labour relations. This is the Trade Unions Act, first promulgated in 1973 as a military decree, and subsequently amended over a period of 26 years. All the various amendments are incorporated in the main Act and will be treated as such, unless otherwise indicated.

The changes which took place between 1978 and 1996[70] were fundamental and far reaching. Not only did the Government unilaterally restructure the trade unions then in existence, it also made trade union dues payable by every worker who was eligible to belong to a trade union, whether or not the worker actually belonged to one. It has been argued that this provision is contrary to section 9(6) of the Labour Act which prohibits making membership of a trade union compulsory.[71]

Part of the rationale for some of the reforms that were effected in 1996 was said to be the need to remove 'overlapping and duplication in the objectives of the trade unions, which resulted in numerous court cases;— duplication, amorphous structures and overlapping jurisdiction'. That restructuring exercise which led to the reduction of the then existing 40 registered trade unions to 29 industrial unions did not go down well with the unions. Besides, it was a discriminatory reform which did not touch senior staff associations and employers associations, thus suggesting that the reforms were aimed at weakening the industrial unions that were more vocal, and always ready to challenge government actions perceived not to be in the interests of workers. However, the Trade Union (Amendment) Decree No 1 of 1999 removed the uncertainty surrounding the status of senior staff associations.[72]

---

[68] Section 12(3) of the Trade Unions Act c T14 Laws of the Federation of Nigeria 2004.

[69] Section 9(6) of the Labour Act c L1 Laws of the Federation of Nigeria 2004.

[70] The two notorious amendments are Trade Union (Amendment) Decree No 4 and Trade Union (Amendment) (No 2) Decree No 26, both of 1996.

[71] Agomo, CK, Oyewunmi, A and Abugu, JO, 'The Future of Law and Labour Relations in Nigeria' (Paper presented at the 1997 Annual Conference of the Nigerian Association of Law Teachers).

[72] Ibid.

The Trade Unions Act

The Trade Unions Act[73] contains comprehensive provisions for the formation, registration and organisation of trade unions. The registration requirements are stringent and largely inconsistent with the provisions of ILO Convention Nos 87 and 98. Indeed, this has been the subject matter of observations by the Committee of Experts on the Application of Conventions and Recommendations (CEACR). One of the provisions that have been rightly criticised is the requirement that an application for registration as a trade union of workers must be signed by at least 50 members of the trade union.[74]

The Registrar of Trade Unions has an unfettered discretion to refuse to register a proposed union, where in his/her opinion there is in existence another union sufficiently representative of the interests of the applicants. This provision is clearly contrary to article 2 of ILO Convention No 87. The question, however, is whether there is an unfettered right to freedom of association regardless of local circumstances. This issue came up for consideration in *Osawe v The Registrar of Trade Unions*.[75] The Supreme Court had this to say:

> One has to bear in mind that the rights guaranteed under sections, 34, 35, 36, 37 and 38 of the 1979 Constitution are 'qualified rights'. They are not absolute rights. They are subject to any law that is reasonably justifiable in a democratic society:
>
> in the interest of defence, public safety, public order, public morality or public health; or
>
> for the purpose of protecting the right and freedom of other people.
>
> Now the right to assemble freely, to associate with other people and to form political parties, or trade unions no doubt exists. But freedom to exercise that right is an entirely different thing. That freedom exists within and not outside all existing and relevant laws.[76]

---

[73] The original decree was promulgated in 1973, and has since been amended several times, twice in 1996 by the infamous decrees 4 and 26. The latest is the Trade Unions (Amendment) Act 2005. All the amendments up to 31st December 2002 have been revised the Law Revision Committee and published as Trade Unions Act c T 14. See also Stiftung, *A Handbook of Nigerian Labour Laws* (2001).

[74] The Committee of Experts on the Application of Conventions and Recommendations (CEACR), in Observation 2000 on Nigeria's compliance with Convention No 87, noted that 50 was an excessive number which offended against art 2 of Convention No 87. It must on the other hand be noted that the number was increased from the low figure of five under the Trade Unions Ordinance to 50, to avoid a proliferation of trade unions as was the case before 1973. Nevertheless, 50 is still considered excessive.

[75] *Osawe v The Registrar of Trade Unions* (1985) 1 Nigeria Weekly Law Reports (part 4) 755; [2004] 1 Nigerian Labour Law Reports 34, 49, 50, 53, 57.

[76] Oputa, Justice of the Supreme Court (JSC), 57. See also *Sea Trucks (Nigeria) Ltd v Pyne* [2004] 1 Nigeria Labour Law Report 58, 69.

In *Osawe*, the Registrar rejected the application of the plaintiffs for the registration of a trade union called 'Nigerian Unified Teaching Service Workers' Union'. The refusal was based on section 3(2) of the Trade Unions Act 1973 which gave the Registrar the absolute discretion to refuse to register a trade union 'where there already exists a trade union'. In an earlier case comment on that decision, I said:[77]

> The case raises a fundamental issue—that of balancing conflicting interests. Undoubtedly, the individual possesses a fundamental right to associate with whomsoever he likes, but in the case of trade unions it has been found, as a fact of history, that this unalloyed freedom led to proliferation of unions which in turn considerably affected, adversely, their power to bargain effectively with the employers. This was not good for the system of collective bargaining, hence the 1978 Amendment. The argument of the High Court Judge in this respect was therefore not farsighted enough.

One's view on that decision, based on those facts, has not changed. The Trade Unions (Amendment) Act 1978 was aimed at restoring sanity and order within the trade union movement in Nigeria. The Court of Appeal made this point, and Justice Kazeem emphasised it in his lead judgment in the Supreme Court. As one said then:

> The case therefore represents a situation where it is necessary and reasonable to curtail the freedom to exercise a right in order to save the claimants of that right from the adverse consequences that would emanate from an unrestricted exercise of the right.[78]

In 1995, the National Industrial Court[79] said in a case concerning the Nigeria Civil Service Union,[80] that

> a worker is not free to join any union that catches [his] fancy. While it is correct that the 1979 Constitution guarantees freedom of association, nonetheless, a worker is not entitled to join any union of his choice without any limitation whatsoever.

Although both the provision and the Supreme Court decision run counter to article 2 of Convention No 87, they are however justifiable in the larger interests of workers.[81] As the Court pointed out, before the restructuring

---

[77] See Agomo, CK, case comment on '*Erasmus Osawe & 2 Ors v The Registrar of Trade Unions*' (1985) 4 *Journal of Private and Property Law* 113–14.

[78] Ibid.

[79] The Court charged with exclusive responsibility for settlement of trade disputes in Nigeria.

[80] An association of senior servants of Nigeria.

[81] See s 45 of the Constitution of the Federal Republic of Nigeria 1999, which permits derogation in the interest of defence, public policy, public order, public morality or public health or for the purpose of protection of the right and freedom of other persons. See also Agomo, case comment on '*Erasmus Osawe & 2 Ors v The Registrar of Trade Unions*' (1985). The CEACR also observed that this provision ran counter to art 2 of Convention No 87.

exercise of 1978, the status of registered trade unions was precarious. They could not bargain effectively with employers. There were over 800 registered trade unions with weak foundations and unclear objectives. A restructuring exercise was carried out to strengthen the unions. On the other hand, one does admit that it is equally reasonable to argue that although valid at that time, such unfettered discretion has ceased to be justifiable under the country's current democratisation process.[82]

The Trade Unions Ordinance of 1938, undoubtedly encouraged the growth of trade unions in the country, but it also arguably set the tone for subsequent proliferation of weak and unstable unions which could not protect the interests of their members through collective bargaining.

It is pertinent to mention here that section 11 of the Trade Unions Act, which prohibits employees in specified establishments from organising or becoming members of a trade union, constitutes a direct infringement of the right to organise of some categories of workers. Whilst restrictions on the Nigerian Armed Forces, the Nigeria Police, the Prisons Department may be justified; there is no basis for putting restrictions on the Customs Preventive Service, the Nigeria Security Printing and Minting Company Limited, the Central Bank of Nigeria and every Federal or State Government establishment, the employees of which are authorised to bear arms in the same bracket. There is also an omnibus provision that gives the Minister of Employment, Labour and Productivity power to include other establishments from time to time.[83] This provision has also been criticised by the ILO from time to time.[84] The Nigeria Labour Congress (NLC) recently asked the President of the Federal Republic of Nigeria to heed the ILO's request that the Government should amend the section so that these categories of workers are granted the right to organise and bargain collectively. This is yet to happen.

Trade Unions (Amendment) Act 2005

The Trade Union (Amendment) Act 2005 was signed into law by President Obasanjo on 30 March 2005. The Act fundamentally amended the Trade Union Act by opening the door for more central unions to be recognised aside from the NLC. The CEACR noted this provision in its 2006 77th Session with interest. In principle, it upholds the constitutionally guaranteed right to freedom of association, in line with the spirit and intendment

---

[82] See criticism from the ILO in this regard, CEACR Observation 2000, discussed above at n 74.

[83] Uvieghara, EE, *Trade Union Law in Nigeria* (Lagos, Ethiope Publishing Corporation, 1976) 81–82.

[84] See www.ilo.org/ilolex/english/newcountryframeE.htm in respect of Nigeria.

of Convention No 87. It is, however, widely believed that the real target of the reform was the NLC. The reform though arguably carried out in bad faith can be said to have cast a shadow over the decision in *Osawe*.[85]

Section 3 of the Act is aimed at undoing the damage inflicted on the right to freedom of association of workers by Decree No 4 of 1996. This had introduced a compulsory check-off from the wages of 'every worker who is eligible to be a member of any of trade unions for the purpose of paying contributions to the trade union so registered;' and 'paying any sum so deducted directly to the registered office of the trade union after deducting what is due and payable to the Central Labour Organisation'. This provision thus made it compulsory for every worker to contribute to the funds of a trade union, whether or not a member.

Under the new provision, actual membership is the basis for deductions of membership dues. Secondly, the provision for automatic deduction for the benefit of the Central Labour Organisation has been removed. The new section 17(1) makes reference to the 'appropriate registered Federation of Trade Unions' and not the 'Central Labour Organisation'. Before 2005, there was only one Central Labour Organisation, the NLC, itself a creature of a decree, not a product of freedom of association. Another central labour union has since been recognised—the Trade Union Congress (TUC). This is an umbrella association of senior staff associations, while the NLC is an umbrella body for industrial unions. The 2005 Act has removed this dichotomy between junior and senior staff associations.

The Trade Unions (Amendment) Act 2005 is one of the most controversial pieces of legislation in recent memory, largely because it was seen by trade unions as an anti union legislation, even though on the face of it, it seems to have liberalised the process of trade union formation and organisation.[86]

Collective Bargaining

The Trade Disputes Act 1976 purports to recognise the principle of collective bargaining and voluntary settlement of trade disputes.[87] However, in reality, it entrenches compulsory processes that leave little room for the disputing parties to apply the normal checks and balances inherent in

---

[85] *Osawe* (1985) 1 Nigeria Weekly Law Reports (Part 4) 755; [2004] 1 Nigerian Labour Law Reports 34, 49, 50, 53, 57.

[86] Trade Unions (Amendment) Act 2005 s 2.

[87] See Trade Disputes Act 1976, cap 432 Lawa of the Federation of Nigeria, 1990 ss 2 and 3. Section 2 requires at least three copies of any collective agreement for settlement of a trade dispute to be deposited with the Minister of Employment Labour and Productivity. The section makes it imperative for the parties to attempt to settle their disputes using any agreed means. However, this is subject to the Minister's overriding discretion to prescribe a means once he or she apprehends a dispute.

a free collective bargaining environment of which the right to strike is a fundamental feature. The law notwithstanding, Nigerian workers have never hesitated to exercise their right to strike, even with the criminalisation of such conducts.[88] This is often the only way to get employers to the bargaining table, particularly in the public sector. The organised private sector is more amenable to the process of collective bargaining than the public sector. This has been one of the commonest causes of trade disputes and industrial action within the public sector. Indeed, the recent collective agreement reached between the Academic Staff Union of Universities (ASUU) and the Federal Government is yet to be implemented. There is already the feeling that the Government may not honour the collectively negotiated agreement.

Section 24 of the Trade Unions Act 1973 provides for automatic recognition of a trade union by an employer where persons in the employment of that employer are members of that union. It does not, however, state whether automatic recognition confers on the recognised union the right to represent its members in collective bargaining with the employer. This ambiguity did not prevent a recognised union from entering into collective bargaining on behalf of its members. The position now under the 2005 Act is that all registered unions in the employment of an employer are to constitute an electoral college to elect members to represent them in collective bargaining for negotiations with the employer.

This provision is a double-edged sword. On the one hand, it appears to have established a clear nexus between an employer's compulsory recognition of a trade union as required by section 24 of the Trade Unions Act 1973, and collective bargaining. On the other hand it talks of an electoral college of all registered unions within an establishment to elect representatives for collective bargaining with the employer. This seems to be a recipe for anarchy, especially since section 30 of the Trade Unions Act, as amended by section 6 of the 2005 Act, has paved the way for employees of one employer to join different federations of trade unions. It is unlikely that the interests of workers will be better served in the long run by this provision. This again raises the issue of the correctness or otherwise of the decision in *Osawe*,[89] and suggests that we cannot but recognise the relevance of peculiar local circumstances in determining the scope of the right to freedom of association. In one's opinion, peculiar circumstances must form part of the consideration in deciding whether or not a country has fulfilled its obligations.

---

[88] See Trade Disputes Act s 17(2) and s 37 (7) of the Trade Unions Act 1973, as amended by s 6 of the Trade Union (Amendment) Act 2005.

[89] *Osawe* (1985) 1 Nigeria Weekly Law Reports (Part 4) 755; [2004] 1 Nigerian Labour Law Reports 34, 49, 50, 53, 57.

The Right to Strike

The right to strike was described in *Crofter Hand Woven Harris Tweed v Veitch*[90] as an essential ingredient in the collective bargaining mechanism, and it is, but the question is: is there a right to strike in Nigeria? This question always elicits different responses. The answer however is to be found in section 17 of the Trade Disputes Act 1976 as amended. That provision makes it unlawful for workers and employers to engage in strikes and lockouts without first exhausting the laid-down procedure. In reality, it is almost impossible to engage in a lawful strike because the procedure that must be exhausted can be described as a merry go round. It is designed to prevent lawful exercise of the right to strike. Nevertheless, workers have not been deterred from exercising their right as they deem fit. Has the position of the law changed since 2005, with the passage of the Trade Union (Amendment) Act? Nothing has really changed.

Whilst section 6 of the Act would appear to have simplified the strike procedure, it did not repeal the law as contained in the Trade Disputes Act. It has therefore not changed the draconian nature of the law of strike in Nigeria, as it only allows workers to go on strike if they have fully exhausted the lengthy statutory procedures of the Trade Disputes Act.[91]

The position of workers in 'essential services' requires a special mention. The workers that fall within this group are required to give the employer at least 15 days' notice before going on strike. The issue is that the definition of 'essential service' is unjustifiably broad. It embraces employees of the federal, state and other establishments. The arbitrariness of the definition can be clearly seen by the inclusion of all categories of civil and public servants, including teachers at all levels. In practice, however, it has failed to have the desired impact, as workers in essential services do go on strike when the occasion demands, regardless of the threat of imprisonment or a fine on conviction.[92]

Under the provisions of the law (the Trade Unions Act), the Central Labour Organisation has no independent legal right to engage in any collective bargaining on behalf of any of its affiliates, except on invitation. Similarly, it cannot legally call out its members on strike. It is common knowledge, however, that from time to time, the NLC calls out its members on strike over issues that may or may not fall within the definition of trade dispute under the Trade Disputes Act. The case of *Federal Government of Nigeria & Attorney General of the Federation v Adams Oshiomhole &*

---

[90] *Crofter Hand Woven Harris Tweed v Veitch* [1942] Appeal Cases 435; [1942] 1 All England Law Reports 142.

[91] Laws of the Federation of Nigeria 1990 c 432.

[92] Section 41(4) Trade Disputes (Essential services) Act 1976, c 433 Laws of the Federation of Nigeria 1990.

Nigeria Labour Congress,[93] decided by the Federal High Court, articulated not only the role of the Central Labour Organisation, but also the relationship between it and trade unions affiliated to it in organising and prosecuting strikes. The Court made it clear that although the workers have fundamental rights guaranteed under section 40 of the 1999 Constitution, 'that right is not at large. It must relate or flow from an employment'.[94]

THE ROLE OF THE COURTS

Regular Courts

The regular courts,[95] particularly at the appellate level, have made considerable impact on the legal protection of the human rights of individual workers. However, as will be seen from the discussion that follows, there is a dichotomy between private sector employment and public sector employment. Protection of workers' human rights has been more pronounced in the public sector than in the private sector. The common law employment at will doctrine still holds sway.

The principle of law applicable to the private sector is the common law doctrine of employment at will, with the employer's right to hire and fire for a reason or for no reason. The attitude of the courts is that a willing employee will not be foisted on an unwilling employer. Termination remains valid even if wrong. Damages are the only remedy, and only in very rare circumstances will an order of specific performance be made.[96] The position is different in the public sector. Here, the position since 1981 is that employment with statutory backing must be terminated in the way and manner prescribed by the relevant statute. Any other manner of termination inconsistent with the particular provisions in question is null and void, and the remedy is reinstatement.[97]

The dichotomy is the product of judicial creativity in using the concept of natural justice to interpret the rights and obligations of workers and

---

[93] *Federal Government of Nigeria & Attorney General of the Federation v Adams Oshiomhole & Nigeria Labour Congress* [2004] 1 Nigerian Labour Law Reports (Part 3) 541.

[94] Ibid 581.

[95] Section 6(4) of the Constitution of the Federal Republic of Nigeria 1999 specifies the following as the superior courts of record: the Supreme Court, The Court of Appeal, the Federal High Court, the state high courts, among others. The National Industrial Court is not one of them. It comes under s 6(5)(j) of the Constitution which recognises such other courts as may be authorised by law to exercise jurisdiction on matters with respect to which the National Assembly may make laws.

[96] See eg *Union Bank of Nigeria v Ogboh* [1995] 2 Nigeria Weekly Law Reports (389) 649, 664; *Chukwuma v Shell Petroleum Co* [1993] 4 Nigeria Weekly Law Reports (part 289) 516, 560.

[97] *Isievwore v National Electric Power Authority* [2004] 1 Nigeria Labour Law Reports 99.

employers respectively within the public sector of the labour force. This development started with the landmark decisions of the Supreme Court in *Shitta Bey v Federal Public Service Commission* in 1981,[98] and *Olaniyan v University of Lagos* in 1985.[99] In *Shitta Bey*, the Supreme Court established the nexus between the Civil Service Rules that govern the conditions of service of civil servants and the Constitution. The Court pointed out that the Civil Service Rules of the Federal Republic which govern conditions of service of federal public servants derive their power and authority from the Constitution.

> These rules—have Constitutional force and they invest the public servant over whom they prevail, a legal status; which makes relationship with the respondent and the government although one of master and servant certainly beyond the ordinary or mere master and servant relationship.[100]

These two decisions remain the hallmarks of judicial protection of human rights of civil and public servants. The approach of the regular courts to the issue of termination of contract of employment has transformed public servants from workers without rights to workers with status and rights protected by the Constitution. The practical effect of this judicial activism is to expose the weakness of the common law and its failure to recognise that a worker has a legitimate interest in job security.[101]

Ordinarily, the courts are reluctant to lift the veil of procedure to inquire into the justice of a case. But in *Olaniyan*, the Court did go behind the veil to expose the real reason behind the decision of the University to terminate the employment of five professors and the registrar, even though it is the common right of an employer to hire and fire at will. Using the constitutional basis of the decision in *Shitta Bey*, the Supreme Court held that section 17 of the University of Lagos Act, which gives the University the right to dismiss, demands the observance of rules of natural justice in cases of alleged misconduct.[102] The affected employees were alleged to have been guilty of misconduct without being heard.

It has now become entrenched in the law that where misconduct is alleged by an employer of a worker with status, rules of natural justice must be observed. Before 1981, natural justice usually arose only in cases of breach of fundamental rights under the Constitution. Since 1981, the

---

[98] *Shitta Bey v Federal Public Service Commission* [1981] 1 Supreme Court Cases 40.
[99] *Olaniyan v University of Lagos* [1985] 2 Nigeria Weekly Law Reports 599; *Eperokun v University of Lagos* [1986] 4 Nigeria Weekly Reports 34.
[100] *Shitta Bey v Federal Public Service Commission* [1981] 1 Supreme Court 55–56.
[101] Elias, E, 'The Structure of the Contract of Employment' [1982] *Current Legal Problems* 95. Agomo, CK, 'Natural Justice and Individual Employment Law in Nigeria' in IO Agbede and EO Akanki (eds), *Current Themes in Nigerian Law* (Lagos, Faculty of Law University of Lagos, 1997) 95–117.
[102] [1985] 2 Nigerian Weekly Law Reports 599.

constitutional provision for fair hearing has featured prominently in cases of alleged wrongful termination of employment of public servants.[103] Sadly however, the position of workers in the private sector and workers in the public service who do not come within the concept of 'workers with status' are still subject to common rules that seem to be averse to honouring the human rights of workers.[104]

The National Industrial Court

The National Industrial Court (NIC)[105] was one of the two special institutions[106] established by the Trade Disputes Act 1976. Section 19 of the Trade Disputes Act described it as a Court 'with such jurisdiction and powers as are conferred on it by this or any other Act with respect to the settlement of trade disputes, the interpretation of collective agreements and matters connected therewith'. This provision conferred both original and appellate jurisdiction on the Court in matters of trade disputes. It, however, lacked the constitutional authority to carry out its mandate effectively, because it was not one of the courts of superior record under the Constitution. The lacuna was plugged in 1992 by the Trade Disputes (Amendment) Decree No 42 which expressly declared it a superior court of record, and enlarged its jurisdiction to include inter- and intra-union disputes. Again, this amendment created its own problem by failing to amend the definition of 'trade dispute' in the Trade Disputes Act 1976, The NIC consequently faced a fundamental jurisdictional problem,[107] which led to delays in hearing and disposal of cases. It also gave unions the opportunity to engage in forum shopping between the regular courts and the NIC. These problems have now been considerably addressed by the National Industrial Court Act 2006.

The Act expressly describes the Court as a superior court of record (but it still needs to be confirmed by constitutional amendment.[108] It is expected

---

[103] Agomo, 'Natural Justice and Individual Employment Law in Nigeria' (1997) 108, above n 101.

[104] There are numerous cases confirming the law as established in *Ajayi v Texaco Nig Ltd* (1987) 3 NWLR (Part 62) S. C. 577.

[105] Originally established by s 20 of the Trade Disputes Act 1976 c T8 Laws of the Federation of Nigeria 2004. Now see Federal Republic of Nigeria Official Gazette No 38 16th June, 2006, Volume 93.

[106] The other is the Industrial Arbitration Panel (IAP). The National Industrial Court (NIC) is now governed by the National Industrial Court Act 2005.

[107] See Kanyip, BB, 'Trade Unions and Industrial Harmony: The Role of the National Industrial Court and the Industrial Arbitration Panel' (presented at the 2001 Annual Conference of the Nigerian Bar Association, 27–31 August 2001).

[108] National Industrial Court Act 2006 s 6(3) needs to be amended to include the NIC as one of the superior courts of record.

that the National Assembly will be able to effect this much needed change before the end of its term). The Court now has exclusive jurisdiction in civil causes and matters relating to labour, trade unions, industrial relations, conditions, health, safety and welfare of employees and matters related to them. It also includes matters relating to the grant of any order to restrain any person or body from taking part in any strike, lock-out or any industrial action, or any conduct in contemplation or in furtherance of a strike, lock-out or any industrial action. The NIC is empowered under the same section to adjudicate on matters in respect of any alleged or threatened violation of any fundamental right entrenched in the Constitution as they relate to employment, labour or industrial relations. Finally, it has jurisdiction to determine any question as to the interpretation of (i) any collective agreement, (ii) any award made by an arbitral tribunal in respect of a labour dispute or an organisational dispute, among others.

The jurisdiction is now enlarged to cover both rights and issues disputes. It is worthy of note that the NIC is concerned with substantive justice and protection of human rights of workers in both public and private sectors. In *United Geophysical Nigeria Ltd/Integrated Data Services Ltd (UGN/IDSL) Joint Venture JV 165 v National Union of Petroleum and Gas Workers (NUPENG)*,[109] the Court pointed out that that it would not sacrifice the issue at hand on the altar of technicality. It also made it clear in that case that:

> It is wrong for an employer to raise in its defence, in a recognition and /or check-off dues dispute, the fact that employees do not want to join or remain as members of a union without attaching the individually signed letters by the employees to that effect. The right to join a union or having joined, to cease to continue as a member of a union, belongs to the individual employee, not to the employer.

There is no doubt that the NIC is set to change the face of labour law and labour relations, especially now that its jurisdictional scope has encroached on traditional common law areas within the jurisdiction of regular courts. The view expressed by the Court in the case between *Petroleum and Natural Gas Senior Staff Association of Nigeria and Schlumberger Anadrill Nigeria Ltd*[110] provides a good example of its readiness to apply international best practices as the need arises. It said:

> The respondent also argued that it has the right to terminate the employment of any of its employee for reason or no reason at all. While we do not have any problem with this at all, the point must be made that globally it is no longer

---

[109] *United Geophysical Nigeria Ltd/Integrated Data Services Ltd (UGN/IDSL) Joint Venture JV 165 v National Union of Petroleum and Gas Workers (NUPENG)* Suit no NIC/3/2006, decided by the NIC on 22 January 2008.

[110] *Petroleum and Natural Gas Senior Staff Association of Nigeria and Schlumberger Anadrill Nigeria Ltd* Suit no NIC/9/2004, decided on 18 September 2007. This case predated the 2006 Act, but was decided after it had come into effect.

fashionable in industrial relations law and practice to terminate an employment relationship without adducing any valid reason for such termination.

Indeed, the Court has, since its inception, adjudicated on various issues affecting the human rights of workers. Cases decided cover government establishments, private-sector employers of large labour forces, as well as the relatively small employers. Issues dealt with over the years cover wages and salaries, pensions and gratuity, and other fringe benefits, wrongful termination of employment, trade union recognition, victimisation and intimidation for trade union activities, refusal to operate the check-off system, negotiable and non-negotiable matters, and interpretation of collective agreements among others.

The Court's decision in *Printing and Publishing Workers' Union v Caxton Press (WA) Ltd*[111] concerned the meaning of 'without prejudice' contained in a notice which requested 'interested ex-employees' to apply for re-employment 'without prejudice' to the dispute before the Industrial Arbitration Panel (IAP). This was said by the Nigeria Employers' Consultative Association (NECA) to have 'raised as well as settled some issues of Law that are noteworthy not only from the point of view of industrial jurisprudence but also from the perspective of industrial relations'. The Court held that the attitude of the respondents was inconsistent with their notice. By so holding, the Court indicated what constitutes good industrial relations *practice*.

The Court's interpretation of specific statutory provisions, such as the redundancy provisions under the Labour Act, check-off system and the meaning of 'projection of management' are but a few examples of the issues that the Court has handled.[112] On industrial relations practice in the country, the decisions of the Court constitute a guide to management and unions in negotiating collective agreements in a more congenial atmosphere. However, it is not very clear how far they are in fact relied on by the parties in subsequent negotiations. In its Memorandum to the Joint Committee of the National Assembly on the Public Hearing of the National Industrial Court Bill, the Court asserted that the rate of compliance was as high as in the regular courts, and this, it claimed, showed the great impact the decisions of the Court have had on industrial relations practice in the country. Views from institutions, associations and individuals support the assertion that the Court has really contributed to industrial relations practice and jurisprudence.

One area in which the Court has had an impact on the law regulating and protecting workers' human rights, is in the area of damages for wrongful

---

[111] *Printing and Publishing Workers' Union v Caxton Press (WA) Ltd* (1982–83) NICLR 11.

[112] See nn 108 and 109; see also *NASCO Foods Nigeria Ltd v Food Beverages & Tobacco Senior Staff Association* Suit No NIC/6/2003 decided 16 July 2007.

termination of employment. The common law does not respect human rights of individual workers under the employment at will doctrine. Thus, termination of employment by an employer, whether right or wrong, effectively terminates the relationship. The only remedy is damages, and the attitude of the common law is that the damages payable should represent the period of notice that could have been given to lawfully terminate the relationship and is no way reflective of any recognition of existence of tenure in favour of the worker. The NIC introduced the concept of severance pay which is tied to the length of service of the aggrieved worker. This has served the interests of those workers, whose grievances were taken over by their unions as collective disputes, better. There are indications that the impact of the Court on employer/employee relations will become more pronounced with time by reason of its enlarged jurisdiction and change of status.

Industrial Arbitration Panel

The Industrial Arbitration Panel (IAP)[113] is another special institution that hears and makes awards on trade disputes,[114] as described by the Act. It was established in 1976 by the Trade Disputes Act. However, neither individuals nor trade unions have direct access to it. The Minister of Employment Labour and Productivity is the link between the IAP and unions. It does not hear individual cases. Even though it is an institution established by the same instrument that originally established the NIC, both institutions did not operate on an industrial court system. They were administered separately, and this had contributed to some of the problems that plagued the institutions. It is bound to be different now that the Industrial Court Act 2006 envisages an industrial court system. The problem, however, is that the IAP still derives its authority from the Trade Disputes Act, while the section which had established the Court under the Act has been repealed by the 2006 Act. These discrepancies need to be sorted out sooner or later.

There is no doubt that the IAP has acted as a bridge across the normally wide gap between labour and management in the articulation and enforcement of their rights and obligations towards each other. In this respect, the contribution of the IAP has been described as being more in the nature of conciliation than arbitration.[115]

[113] Established by s 8 of the Trade Disputes Act.
[114] Trade dispute means any dispute between employers and workers or between workers and workers, which is connected with the employment or non-employment, or the terms and physical conditions of work of any person. Section 47 of the Trade Disputes Act.
[115] See Agomo, CK, 'The Report on the Evaluation of the Performance of the Industrial Arbitration Panel and the National Court' (research paper commissioned by the Federal Ministry of Employment Labour and Productivity, October 1992).

USE OF NON-DISCRIMINATION PROVISIONS
TO PREVENT SOCIAL EXCLUSION

Nigeria has ratified the Convention on the Elimination of All Forms of Discrimination Against Women (CEDAW), but the process for domestication as required by the Constitution is still on. It also endorsed the Beijing Platform for Action. Yet women still suffer various forms of discrimination in the workplace, as well as in society. Apart from general provisions prohibiting discrimination under the Constitution, there is as yet, no gender specific legislation directed at implementation of CEDAW. The Bill for the domestication of CEDAW is still before the National Assembly.

The same Constitution that prohibits discrimination also, in itself, contains the seed of discrimination against women. Section 42 subsection 3 permits discrimination in the appointment of any person to any office under the state or as a member of the armed forces of the Federation or a member of the Nigerian Police Force or to an office in the service of a body corporate established by any law in force in Nigeria. This provision may provide the reason, but not the justification, for some of the glaring discriminatory practices against women in the armed forces and the police force.

The majority of the workforce is in the informal sector of the economy, either as wage-earners or the self-employed. This is an area marked by a total lack of protection. Women form a large part of this group and are the most discriminated against. There is no right to organise and no platform for collective bargaining, largely because of the insecurity of employment in the informal sector.[116] The labour legislation meant for the protection of workers does not cover vulnerable groups such as domestic workers.

There are specific provisions ostensibly for the protection of women workers in the Labour Act. There is maternity protection including right to maternity pay, protection against night work and protection against underground work. The provision on maternity is supposed to protect women workers from discriminatory policies in the workplace based on their reproductive functions. For example, every worker is entitled to annual leave with pay after 12 weeks' continuous period of service, but a pregnant woman who is granted maternity leave will lose either her leave pay or her annual leave. Another area is that of funding for the maternity pay. As the law stands, employers bear the entire cost. The consequence is that women of child bearing age face a harder time securing and remaining in employment, particularly in the private sector.

In 1919, when ILO Convention No 3 on maternity was passed at the first International Labour Conference of the ILO, it was stipulated that maternity pay should be provided either out of public funds or by means of

---

[116] International Conference on Organising the Informal Economy held in Ahmedabad, India, 3–6 December, 2003.

a system of insurance. The provision in the Labour Act does not meet this requirement, not to talk of the provisions of Convention No 183 of 2000. Nigeria's law in this area lags behind international standards in significant respects.[117]

Reproductive health and rights of workers, particularly women in the workplace, are not adequately protected. Sexual harassment is hardly reported because of cultural norms, and more importantly because of lack of defined workplace policies on it. It is therefore unlikely that affected workers will get any redress or protection under the law. There is also no specific legislation against discrimination on grounds of HIV/AIDS status at the national level. There is, however, a national policy on HIV/AIDS and a few employers do have some form of policy on HIV/AIDs.

The development of a solid jurisprudence on the concept of 'status' and natural justice has done much to sensitise workers on their human rights as workers, particularly in relation to the termination of the employment relationship. The level of awareness is still however low, for example, in respect of anti-discrimination law, except in the situations where the dispute becomes a labour dispute or where it becomes a matter for human rights advocacy by civil society groups.

CONCLUSIONS

It seems fairly clear from the issues treated here that there is a low level of practical realisation of the human rights provisions in the Constitution as they affect freedom of association. The Trade Unions Act, a specific legislation on freedom of association, which derives its authority from the Constitution, is restrictive in many respects. Whilst it may be justifiable on the ground of history and need, it is doubtful whether it is sustainable today. The equally restrictive provisions on the right to strike have however, not deterred unions from exercising their freedom to do so. This shows the futility of enacting laws restrictive of the exercise of workers' rights.

In the area of individual employment relations, one must commend the role of the courts, including the specialist labour court, the NIC. There are positive indications that the newly repositioned National Industrial Court Act will have far reaching effect, on both individual and collective labour relations law and practice in the country. The position of women as a vulnerable group is still precarious. It is hoped that the CEDAW and the Protocol to the African Charter on Human and Peoples Rights will soon be domesticated or ratified as appropriate.

[117] Agomo, CK, 'The Working Woman in a Changing World of Work' (Inaugural Lecture, University of Lagos (Lagos, University of Lagos Press, 2004) 29–34, 40–42.

There is no doubt that recognition of the rights of workers as human rights is not negotiable. The development of the use of principles of natural justice to enforce the contract of employment in the public sector is a very good example of what the recognition of the human rights of workers can do for the development of the law. Human rights in whatever context are inter-related and can benefit from the cross-fertilisation of ideas.

The 1998 ILO Declaration on Fundamental Principles and Rights at Work has become a catalyst for the reform of Nigeria's labour laws. It is reasonable to say that the adoption of the Declaration marked a turning point on the relevance of international labour standards to the shaping of national responses in the area of the human rights of workers in Nigeria.[118] There has been a greater awareness of the issues at stake. It is only hoped that the National Assembly will sooner, rather than later, pass the Labour Standards Bill before it, into law. The draft bill was submitted by the Committee that reviewed Nigeria's labour laws under the Declaration Project Nigeria. This comprehensive bill, when passed, will definitely have far reaching implications for adjudication and implementation of workers' rights and issues in Nigeria.

---

[118] Lawyers and unions appearing before the NIC now make reference to international conventions in support of their arguments. This is indeed a healthy development.

9

Constitutionalisation of South African Labour Law: An Experiment in the Making

STEFAN VAN ECK

POLITICAL AND SOCIO-ECONOMIC BACKGROUND

Introduction

A T THE OUTSET, two preliminary aspects must be put forward before proceeding with the rest of this chapter. First, although there is convincing evidence that workers' rights have fared poorly in an increasingly globalised economy, the opposite is true for employees in the formal sector of South Africa's economy. In terms of legal doctrine, at least, their position has improved in the recent past. Although this state of affairs may not necessarily be evident in practice, workers' human rights were for the first time entrenched in the South African Constitution[1] 16 years ago: a new set of labour laws that give effect to International Labour Organisation (ILO) principles were enacted between 1996 and 1998[2] and local labour law reforms during 2002 witnessed further strengthening of worker's rights in the statute books.[3] In theory also, workers' rights have been promoted on a regional level in the Southern African Development Community's (SADC) Charter on Fundamental Social Rights during 2003, under the heading,

---

[1] See s 27 of the Interim Constitution 200 of 1993, which came into force on 27 April 1994 and s 23 of the Final Constitution 108 of 1996 that became effective on 4 February 1997. It is to be noted that this contribution was updated up to December 2008.

[2] The so-called 'trilogy' of labour laws are as follows: the Labour Relations Act 66 of 1995; the Basic Conditions of Employment Act 75 of 1997; and the Employment Equity Act 55 of 1998.

[3] The most notable changes were as follows: s 200A of the Labour Relations Act 66 of 1995 introduced a presumption with the view of widening the scope of the term 'employee'; s 189A, for the first time provided employees with the right to strike in the prelude to operational requirements dismissals; and s 197 was amended to provide improved protection to employees when a business is transferred as a going concern.

'Basic Human Rights and Organisational Rights'.[4] Although this may not necessarily be evident in workers' day-to-day lives, these legislative and policy reforms serve as indicators that their rights have been enhanced in Southern Africa in a conceptual sense in the past two decades.

Secondly, the South African Constitution has had both astonishingly positive and niggling negative effects on the recent evolution of our labour law framework. It will be argued in this chapter that, added to the well-received human rights orientation provided by the supreme law, the inter-relationship of different types of constitutional protection has made the enforcement of workers' protection complex to the point that it may even threaten the effectiveness of some of these rights. Rather than seeing the development of a uniform labour law dispute resolution framework, an intricate and overlapping system of dispute resolution has emerged under the post-apartheid dispensation. The independence of labour law as an autonomous discipline, under which individual and collective rights may be developed into a coherent framework of principles by specialist judges, is in the process of being watered down. The future of South African labour courts is in the balance and draft legislation has been published that points in the direction of the abolition of these specialist institutions.[5] Should this happen, one of the consequences of the demise of the labour courts may be the fact that judges who do not fully appreciate the intricate nuances inherent to labour law, which include the balance between the common law contract of employment and the notion of fairness, and the rebalancing of social power, will be responsible to shape future developments in labour law.

Towards Democracy and Fundamental Labour Rights

Every country's historical and political context[6] plays a significant role in the evolution[7] of workers' rights. Some remarks about South Africa's past

---

[4] Article 3(1) of the Southern African Development Community's (SADC) Charter. As will be seen in the discussion below, the SADC Charter has no legally binding legal effect and it merely serves as policy statement which has the potential of guiding member countries in their domestic affairs.

[5] Superior Courts Bill [B 2003]; Van Eck, BPS, 'The Constitutionalisation of Labour Law: No Place for a Superior Labour Appeal Court in Labour Matters (Part 1)' (2005) *Obiter* 549. See also Van Eck, BPS, 'The Constitutionalisation of Labour Law: No Place for a Superior Labour Appeal Court in Labour Matters (Part 2)' (2006) *Obiter* 20, the discussion under the heading 'Specialist Labour Courts' below and the references in n 156.

[6] For a political overview, see Dugard, J, *Human Rights and the South African Legal Order* (Princeton, Princeton University Press, 1978).

[7] Hepple points out that the underlying nature of labour law is a 'process' rather than 'a relatively static and neutral set of rules ... which regulate employment'. See Hepple, B (ed), *The Making of Labour Law in Europe: A Comparative Study of Nine Countries up to 1945* (London and New York, Mansell Publishing Ltd, 1986) 1.

are deemed necessary to illustrate just how closely related the battle for basic political and human rights has been to the struggle for core workers' rights.

Nelson Mandela was released from confinement on 11 February 1990.[8] His freedom symbolised the birth of a democratic nation, breaking the restraints of colonialism and years of white minority rule at the southern tip of Africa. The international community witnessed the formation of long lines of voters during our first democratic elections on 27 April 1994. This was also the date for the coming into effect of South Africa's Interim Constitution,[9] which had a revolutionary effect on the South African legal system.[10] For the first time, equal civil, political and labour rights were afforded to all South Africans regardless of their race or origin.

Turning the clock back, a dramatic mineworkers' strike during 1922[11] was followed by South Africa's first comprehensive but primitive labour legislation: the Industrial Conciliation Act of 1924.[12] This Act introduced a framework for collective bargaining, but explicitly excluded black workers from the definition of 'employee'. This laid the foundation for a dual system of labour law for white and black workers. The Nationalist Government formalised job reservations for white workers after 1948[13] and black opposition resistance movements, including the African National Congress, were forced underground during 1961.[14] The trade union movement played a significant role in the liberation struggle that ensued.[15]

In an attempt to normalise the labour market that was spinning out of control,[16] the Government was forced to appoint the Wiehahn Commission

---

[8] See De Klerk, FW, 'Opening of the Ninth Parliament of the Republic of South Africa' (Cape Town, 2 February 1990) www.fwdklerk.org.za.

[9] This Interim Constitution 200 of 1993 set out the procedures for the negotiation of the Final Constitution. The Final Constitution 108 of 1996 was signed into law by Nelson Mandela on 10 December 1996 and came into effect on 4 February 1997.

[10] Currie, I and De Waal, J, *The Bill of Rights Handbook* (Cape Town, Juta and Co Ltd, 2005) 2.

[11] Myburgh, JF, '100 years of Strike Law' 2004 *ILJ (South Africa)* 962, 963; Du Toit, MA, *South African Trade Unions* (Johannesburg, McGraw-Hill Book Co, 1976) 13.

[12] Industrial Conciliation Act 11 of 1924. Du Toit, *South African Trade Unions* (1976) 13–14.

[13] Section 77(6)(a) of the Industrial Conciliation Act 28 of 1956. See GN 1066 in *Government Gazette* dated 25 July 1958 and GN 979 in *Government Gazette* dated 26 June 1959 for examples of job reservation determinations.

[14] For a discussion of the history of the 'black consciousness movement' see Davenport, TRH and Saunders, C, *South Africa: A Modern History* (London, MacMillan Press Ltd, 2000) 436–37.

[15] Du Toit, D, Bosch, D, Woolfrey, D, Godfrey, S, Cooper, C, Giles, G, Bosch, C and Rossouw, J, *Labour Relations Law: A Comprehensive Guide* (Durban, LexisNexus Butterworths, 2006) 13.

[16] Thompson, C, 'Twenty-five Years after Wiehahn—A Story of the Unexpected and the Not Quite Intended' (2004) *ILJ (South Africa)* iv.

of Enquiry[17] into labour matters during 1977. Recommendations made by the Commission provided the groundwork for equal labour rights for black and white workers and for the creation of a specialist labour tribunal, the so-called 'Industrial Court'. Since the early 1980s, this institution in effect crafted a 'new labour law' for South Africa.[18] During this period, black workers found a limited voice by participating in effective 'stay-away' action,[19] which was co-organised by the Congress of South African Trade Unions.[20] In *AZAPO v President of the Republic of South Africa*,[21] the Constitutional Court captured something of the scope of this pre-1994 labour revolution:

> For decades South African history has been dominated by a deep conflict between a minority which reserved for itself all control over the political instruments of state and a majority who sought to resist that domination. ... The result was a debilitating war of internal political dissention and confrontation, massive expressions of labour militancy, perennial student unrest [and] punishing international economic isolation.

As pointed out by Hlophe, the 'origins of our labour rights are to be found in the history of the struggle against apartheid'.[22] After FW de Klerk unbanned resistance movements during 1990, negotiations for a new constitutional model commenced. Generous labour rights were included in both the Interim and Final Constitutions and barely two years after the first elections in 1994 a new set of labour statutes were enacted giving effect to these fundamental rights.[23] The urgency with which the Government tackled the task of implementing a new set of labour laws 'can to a large extent be explained by the role of organised labour in the struggle against apartheid'.[24]

Social and Economic Concerns

In his annual 'State of the Nation' address in Parliament, on 3 February 2006, former President Thabo Mbeki stated that 'despite all its challenges,

---

[17] *The Complete Wiehahn Reports Parts 1–6 and the White Paper on Each Part with Notes by Prof NE Wiehahn* (Johannesburg, Lex Patria, 1982).

[18] Van Niekerk, A, 'In Search of Justification: The Origins of the Statutory Protection of Security of Employment in South Africa' (2004) *ILJ (South Africa)* 853.

[19] As pointed out by Hepple, B, 'The Role of Trade Unions in a Democratic Society' (1990) *ILJ (South Africa)* 645, 646, '[d]emocracy means participation' and it is 'not surprising that trade unions past and present have a crucial role in the fight for democracy'.

[20] Du Toit et al, *Labour Relations Law: A Comprehensive Guide* (2006) 14. See also Baskin, J, *Striking Back: A History of COSATU* (Johannesburg, Ravan Press, 1991) 287–89.

[21] *AZAPO v President of the Republic of South Africa* 1996 (4) SA 671 (CC) [1].

[22] Hlope, JM, 'Opening Address: Constitutionalisation of Labour Rights' (Institute of Development and Labour Law, Occasional Paper 1/2004, University of Cape Town) 1.

[23] The so-called 'trilogy' of labour laws are as follows: the Labour Relations Act 66 of 1995; the Basic Conditions of Employment Act 75 of 1997; and the Employment Equity Act 55 of 1998.

[24] Du Toit et al (n 15) 16.

South Africans are firmly convinced that our country has entered its Age of Hope'.[25] With reference to a December 2005 Gallup International Survey, he mentioned that optimism has doubled in South Africa since 2002.[26] He also referred to a local Markinor Survey indicating that South Africa is experiencing the longest sustained period of positive Gross Domestic Product (GDP) growth in our recorded economic history.[27]

At face value, these positive sentiments confirm a story of good fortune, but mask a picture of a developing country that is faced with immense socio-economic challenges. The present South African population is esti- mated at 47 million people.[28] The African (Black) population constitutes approximately 81 per cent, the White portion is estimated at nine per cent, the Coloured population at eight per cent and the Indian/Asian segment stands at two per cent.[29] Both ILO and World Bank country reviews[30] indi- cate that South Africa is one of the countries which has the most unequal distribution of income in the world and that poverty is overwhelmingly concentrated in the African and Coloured populations. Unemployment stands at an estimated 27 per cent[31] and the prevalence of HIV/AIDS is at approximately 9.8 per cent of the total population.[32] South Africa is a country with two economies, consisting of a modern first world economy and a third world informal sector economy.[33] A significant portion of the

---

[25] As quoted from Van der Merwe, J, 'Mbeki hails dawn of the Age of Hope' *Sunday Times* (5 February 2006) 22.

[26] Gallup International, 'Voice of the People Survey 2006' www.voice-of-the-people.net/ accessed 5 February 2006.

[27] A fourth quarter Markinor Survey indicates that Gross Domestic Product (GDP) growth reached 4.8%, accessed from www.jcci.co.za/newsflash-hong-kong-address.html on 5 February 2005.

[28] Statistics South Africa viewed at www.statssa.gov.za/publications/P0302/P03022005.pdf and accessed 26 January 2006.

[29] Ibid.

[30] Standing, G, Sender, J and Weeks, J, 'Restructuring the Labour Market: The South African Challenge' *An ILO Country Review* (International Labour Office (ILO), Geneva, 1996). This state of affairs is confirmed by a more recent World Bank Report Country Brief, updated in November 2005, which reports that 'South Africa's income aggregates hide extreme differences in incomes and wealth between the white (similar to OECD aver- age of GNI per capita of about US$26,000) and non-white populations (similar to many low-income African countries, with GNI per capita under US$825. Thirteen per cent of the population lives in "first world" conditions, while at the other extreme, about 22 million people live in "third world" conditions. In this latter group only one-quarter of households have access to electricity and running water; only half have a primary school education; and over a third of the children suffer from chronic malnutrition.' See http://web. worldbank.org/WBSITE/EXTERNAL/COUNTRIES/AFRICAEXT/SOUTHAFRICAEXTN/ 0,,menuPK:368086~pagePK:141132~piPK:141107~theSitePK:368057,00.html accessed 9 October 2006.

[31] Statistics South Africa viewed at www.southafrica.info/ess_info/sa_glance/demographics/ unemployment-10405.htm and accessed 28 February 2006.

[32] Ibid.

[33] See Mbeki, T, 'Two Worlds Two Economies' (2004) 28 *South African Labour Bulletin* 2, 10–11. See also the reference to the World Bank *Country Briefs* in n 30 above.

population makes a living in the latter sector. In modern cities individual food vendors, taxi owners, and people who usher parking to motorists are to be seen everywhere.

The South African Constitution does not only guarantee the traditional first generation liberal rights to equality, personal liberty, free speech and free assembly and association—it also contains a number of second generation, socio-economic rights. Rather than merely protecting citizens against the abuse of state power, the latter rights 'oblige the state to do as much as it can to secure for all members of society a basic set of social goods'.[34] The most notable of these rights entrench the rights of access to adequate housing, health care services, sufficient food and water and social security.[35] But, to what extent are the courts prepared to force the Government to assist the socially deprived portion of our population? In two key cases dealing with medical care and housing, we have received mixed signals from the Constitutional Court regarding this question.[36] In *Soobramoney v Minister of Health, Kwa Zulu Natal*,[37] the Court was approached by a 41-year-old unemployed man. He suffered from kidney failure and applied to have a policy, which excluded him from treatment reviewed. The Court accepted the hospital's policy that was designed to ensure that more patients would benefit from the availability of dialysis machines over the long-term and held that it would be 'slow to interfere with rational decisions taken in good faith' by medical authorities and political organs who deal with such matters.[38] However, in *Government of South Africa v Grootboom*,[39] the Court adopted a more proactive approach. This case involved more than 500 squatters who had been forcibly removed and claimed a violation of their constitutional right to access to housing. Here the Constitutional Court came to the assistance of the homeless. According to Fredman, the Court 'developed a more substantive notion of reasonableness, focussing not only on accountability but also on the value of equality' when the state was ordered to 'devise and implement ... a comprehensive and coordinated programme progressively to realise the right to access of adequate housing'.[40]

---

[34] Currie and De Waal, *The Bill of Rights Handbook* (2005) 567.

[35] Sections 26 and 27 of the Constitution of the Republic of South Africa 1996.

[36] For a useful discussion of the most significant Constitutional Court cases regarding the fundamental right to social security, see Fredman, S, *Human Rights Transformed* (Oxford, University Press 2008) 114–23 and Hare, I, 'Social Rights and Fundamental Human Rights' in B Hepple, *Social and Global Rights in a Global Context* (Cambridge, University Press, 2002) 177–80.

[37] *Soobramoney v Minister of Health, Kwa Zulu Natal* 1998 (1) SA 765 (CC).

[38] Ibid [25]. Fredman, *Human Rights Transformed* (2008) 116 argues that the 'legacy of *Soobramoney* has therefore been rightly criticized as requiring so little beyond transparency as to lose the thrust of a human rights duty at all. At most, the case could be read as endorsing the accountability parameter; but the equality and deliberative dimensions are missing.'

[39] *Government of South Africa v Grootboom* 2001 (1) SA 46 (CC).

[40] Fredman (n 36) 116 and *Grootboom* 2001 (1) SA 46 (CC) [99].

It is submitted that the Court in *Grootboom* played an important role in setting a tone of policy which will reinforce the goals of realising the rights contained in the Constitution. Although the Court would not go as far as to ignore the availability of resources, it would not shy away from placing positive duties on the Government in respect of its socio-economic responsibilities.

Although huge strides have been made by the state in respect of the provision of housing, electricity and running water to the underprivileged, labour law has largely failed in extending protection to members of the third economy. In the discussion that follows, it will become apparent that a number of constitutional cases have been decided involving labour law principles. However, it will also dawn on the reader that in these matters, the arguments did not extend in any depth into the social and economic nature of these rights in the application of labour and constitutional law principles.[41]

Kalula observes that South Africa has borrowed and transplanted principles from different Western countries in the formation of our post-1994 labour law.[42] These laws were developed to protect employees in the formal economy and they were not devised to extend beyond the traditional employer employee relationship. Despite our modern Constitution and progressive labour laws, the growing number of 'atypical workers bordering on unemployment and self-employment'[43] has not gained under the realm of labour law. Until such time as the definition of labour law is broadened to the extent that it is interwoven with socio-economic undertones so as to cover workers on the periphery of employment, it will continue to fail the socially deprived in the third economy.

LEGAL FRAMEWORK

Status of International Instruments Concerning Labour Standards

South Africa has pledged itself to the Constitution of the ILO on two occasions—first, as one of its founder members when it was established during

---

[41] There is an exception to this in cases dealing with affirmative action. The constitutional matter, *Minister of Finance v Van Heerden* 2004 *ILJ (South Africa)* 1593 (CC), serves as an example. At [145] Sachs J mentions that 'though some members of the advantaged group may be called upon to bear a larger portion of the burden of transformation than others, they, like all other members of society, benefit from the stability, social harmony and restoration of natural dignity that the achievement of equality brings'.

[42] Kalula, E, 'Labour Marker Regulation in Southern Africa' in C Barnard, S Deakin and GS Morris (eds), *The Future of Labour Law: Liber Amicorum Sir Bob Hepple QC* (Oxford and Portland, Oregon, Hart Publishing, 2004) 277. Hepple, B, 'Can Collective Labour Law Transplants Work? The South African Example' (1999) *ILJ (South Africa)* 1, 2 also observes that 'the debt which it owes to international labour standards and to comparative labour standards' is one of the most striking features of the South African Labour Relations Act 66 of 1995.

[43] Ibid 281.

1919, and secondly when it rejoined the ILO in 1994. In between, South Africa withdrew its membership in 1966 after persistent criticism of its internal policies from within the ILO.

Rubin observes that there is 'a self imposed modesty by the ... ILO which belies its importance ..., influence ... and significance for South Africa.'[44] It is not all that well-known that, even during its period of absence, South Africa continued to be influenced by ILO principles which it had accepted during its first period of membership. First, South Africa's reporting obligations under the ILO Constitution remained in place concerning ratified conventions that it had not denounced after its withdrawal.[45] Secondly, quite unexpectedly, South Africa witnessed a significant era of labour law development during operation of the Industrial Court between 1980 and our re-admittance to the ILO in 1994. Under an almost 'breathtakingly wide'[46] definition of 'unfair labour practice', at a time when there was a vacuum within which a body of labour rights had to be formulated, the members of this humble administrative tribunal[47] sought guidance from ILO conventions and international jurisprudence to fashion the right not to be unfairly dismissed, the rights to associate and negotiate, the duty to bargain and limited protection against unfair dismissal for participating in strike action.[48] In the opinion of Van Niekerk,[49] 'the ILO played a more significant role in the 28 years after South Africa left the organisation than it did in the almost 50 years' before it withdrew its membership.

Soon after South Africa's re-admittance to the ILO during 1994, it signed Conventions No 87 (freedom of association and protection of the right to organise) and No 98 (right to organise and collective bargaining). The 'Cheadle Task Team' fashioned a fresh set of labour laws under the new constitutional dispensation and gained valuable assistance from the ILO

---

[44] Rubin, N, 'International Labour Law and the Law of the New South Africa' (1998) *The South African Law Journal* 685.

[45] Ibid 687.

[46] Grogan, J, *Dismissal, Discrimination & Unfair Labour Practices* (Cape Town, Juta & Co Ltd, 2005) 37.

[47] In *SA Technical Officials' Association v President of the Industrial Court* 1985 *ILJ (South Africa)* 186 (A), the Civil Appeal Court held that the Industrial Court was not a court of law even when it performed judicial functions.

[48] A number of decisions were based on the view that ILO instruments formed part of international customary law. See, for example: *Metal & Allied Workers Union v Stobar Reinforcing* 1983 *ILJ (South Africa)* 84 (IC); *NAAWU v Pretoria Precision Castings* 1985 *ILJ (South Africa)* 369 (IC); and generally Thompson, C, 'Borrowing and Bending: The Development of South Africa's Unfair Labour Practice Jurisprudence' in R Blanpain and M Weis (eds), *The Changing Face of Labour Law and Industrial Relations: Liber Amicorum W Summers* (Baden-Baden, Nomos Verlagsgeschaft, 1993) 109.

[49] Van Niekerk, A, 'The International Labour Organisation and South African Labour Law' (1996) 5 *Contemporary Labour Law* 111, 112.

with the drafting of the newly codified labour law framework.[50] It is no wonder then, that in section 1 of the Labour Relations Act of 1995 (LRA) under the heading 'Purpose of this Act', it is stated that one of the objectives of this statute is 'to give effect to obligations incurred by the Republic as a member state of the International Labour Organisation'.[51] Added to this, the LRA stipulates that when interpreting the provisions of the Act, it must be interpreted in compliance with the South African Constitution and 'in compliance with the public international law obligations of the Republic'.[52] Within the South African Constitution, it is mentioned that when interpreting the Bill of Rights, a court 'must consider international law',[53] and it 'may consider foreign law'.[54]

Apart from its responsibilities as member to the ILO, South Africa is one of the members of SADC, established by treaty in Namibia during 1992.[55] In August 2003, the Heads of State and Government adopted the SADC Charter of Fundamental Social Rights in SADC. Article 3 of the Charter, under the heading, 'Basic Human Rights and Organisational Rights', declares that:

> This Charter embodies the recognition by governments, employers and work-ers in the Region of the universality and indivisibility of basic human rights proclaimed in instruments such as the United Nations Universal Declaration of Human Rights, the African Charter on Human and Peoples' Rights, the Constitution of the ILO, the Philadelphia Declaration and other relevant interna-tional instruments.

It is one of the stated purposes of the Charter of Fundamental Social Rights to harmonise policies in the Southern African region regarding: freedom of association and collective bargaining; equal treatment for men and woman; protection of children and young people; protection of elderly persons; protection of people with disabilities; social security schemes of

---

[50] In the 'Explanatory Memorandum to the Draft Labour Relations Bill', published in *Government Gazette* 16259 dated 10 February 1995 at 112, it is mentioned that: 'The Task Team was assisted throughout by the ILO which not only provided resources for the Team's 10-day stay at the ILO in Geneva but also three world-class experts to help the Team: Dr B Hepple, ...; Professor A Adeogun, ...; and Professor Manfred Weiss, ... The Task Team also consulted internationally renowned experts within the ILO itself.'

[51] Labour Relations Act of 1995 (LRA) s 1(b).

[52] Ibid s 3(b)–(c).

[53] Ibid s 39(1)(b).

[54] Ibid s 39(1)(c).

[55] The original treaty was signed on 17 August 1992 in Windhoek, Namibia. On 14 August 2001, Heads of State and Government signed an Agreement Amending the SADC Treaty. The current members of SADC are the Republic of Angola; the Republic of Botswana; the Democratic Republic of Congo; the Kingdom of Lesotho; the Republic of Malawi; the Republic of Mauritius; the Republic of Mozambique; the Republic of Namibia; the Republic of Seychelles; the Republic of South Africa; the Kingdom of Swaziland; the United Republic of Tanzania; the Republic of Zambia; the Republic of Zimbabwe.

Member States; and the promotion of workplace democracy.[56] Although all of these are noble intentions, there is unfortunately limited evidence of progress being made with regard to the harmonisation of labour policy and the improvement of the socially deprived in the region.[57] Only two draft codes have been published, the one dealing with freedom of movement of people, and the other with fundamental social rights.[58] It is patently clear that there are no enforcement mechanisms which go hand in hand with the ideals contained in the Charter and there have been no signs of member countries holding each other accountable to the noble ideals contained in it. However, despite the apparent lack of significant progress on a substantive level, there is at least hope that these policy statements may have indirect positive effect, by means of sensitising interest groups and possibly influencing individual governments, towards both the recognition and improvement of social justice in the region.

The Constitutional Framework

The Constitution is the 'supreme law' of the land[59] and the previous doctrine of parliamentary supremacy was replaced with a doctrine of constitutional supremacy. Courts have been given the power to declare any 'law or conduct' that is inconsistent with the Bill of Rights invalid. Apart from the more commonly accepted fundamental rights contained in the Constitution,[60] labour rights, social security rights and the right to just administrative action have also been enshrined therein. In Canada, organised labour opted not to have labour rights included into the Charter of Rights and Freedoms of 1982. According to Arthurs, the main reasons were that if labour sought to include labour rights, business would strive to include property rights and that, in any event, judges 'were unlikely to apply those rights in a useful way'.[61] But in South Africa things are different. The battle for political rights went hand-in-hand with the battle over

---

[56] See arts 4, 6, 7, 8, 9, 10 and 13 of the Charter of Fundamental Social Rights in SADC.

[57] Kalula, 'Labour Marker Regulation in Southern Africa' (2004) 277–81. See also Van Eck, BPS and Boraine, A, 'A Plea for the Development of Coherent Labour and Insolvency Principles on a Regional Basis in SADC Countries' in PJ Omar (ed), *International Insolvency Law* (Hampshire England, Ashgate Publishing Ltd, 2008) 267.

[58] Kalula (n 42) 283.

[59] The South African Constitution s 2.

[60] See the 'Bill of Rights', c II of the South African Constitution, in respect of the rights to equality, human dignity, property, freedom and security of person, privacy, freedom of religion and expression and political rights.

[61] Arthurs, H, 'The Constitutionalisation of Labour Rights' (Occasional Paper 1/2004 Development and Labour Monograph Series presented for the Institute of Development and Labour Law, University of Cape Town) 5.

labour rights. The Constitutional Assembly incorporated both labour and property rights in the Constitution.

Under the heading 'Labour Relations', it is specified that 'everyone has the right to fair labour practices' (section 23(1)); every 'worker' has the right 'to form and join a trade union' (section 23(2)(a)); every 'worker' has the right 'to strike' (section 23(2)(c)); 'every employer' has the right 'to form and join an employer's organisation' (section 23(3)(a); and 'every trade union, employer's organisation and employer has the right to engage in collective bargaining' (section 23(5)). But, what is the scope of application of our Constitution? Is it limited to indirect application or does it also find direct application between private individuals? The traditional role of a bill of rights is where it is intended to protect people against state power, by enshrining rights which may not be violated by means of law-making or through state conduct.[62] This entails an indirect application of the so-called 'vertical' relationship, namely between state and citizens. Under our Interim Constitution, the Constitutional Court in *Du Plessis v De Klerk*[63] confirmed that the Interim Constitution conformed to the conventional model. It had no direct application to 'horizontal' relationships emanating from the common law. This decision validated the 'two track' jurisdictional scheme in terms of which constitutional disputes were the preserve of the Constitutional Court and all other matters, including the development of the uncodified common law, was the preserve of the civil High Court and its appellate division.[64] Mindful of the limiting effects this could have on violations of private law rights, the Constitutional Assembly created a new scope of application and jurisdictional scheme in the Final Constitution. It now states that the Bill of Rights 'binds the legislature, the executive, the judiciary and all organs of state'.[65] It also applies to 'natural and juristic persons' and it states that courts must apply the rights contained in the Bill to develop the common law.[66] This changed the legal system to a unified jurisdictional scheme. Under the present system, the civil High Court shares jurisdiction with the Constitutional Court in disputes concerning constitutional principles. This has prompted the Constitutional Court, in the *Pharmaceutical Manufacturers Association of SA* case,[67] to hold that there 'is only one system of law. It is shaped by the Constitution which is the supreme law, and all law, including the common law, derives its force from the Constitution and is subject to constitutional control'.

---

[62] Curry and De Waal, (n 10) 33.
[63] *Du Plessis v De Klerk* 1996 (3) SA 850 (CC).
[64] Ibid [57].
[65] The South African Constitution s 8(1).
[66] The South African Constitution s 8(2)–(3).
[67] *Pharmaceutical Manufacturers Association of SA: In re: ex p President of the Republic of South Africa* 2000 (2) SA 674 (CC) [44].

Undoubtedly, there lies great potential for the protection of worker's rights under this constitutional framework—both due to its broad scope of coverage (the right to fair labour practices covers all conceivable labour practices for those in formal employment) and due to the fact of its direct horizontal application. In addition to public service employment relationships, the relationship between the private sector employer and its workers is directly covered by the application of the Constitution. It is quite often in the sphere of private entities where problems with the observance of labour rights may occur and this also falls under constitutional application. The protection does not only lie within this horizontal application itself, but also in the fortification of labour standards due to the fact that present and future governments may find it difficult to erode workers' rights (by means of individualisation thereof and incorporating more flexibility into it) without meeting constitutional challenge.[68]

However, apart from the potential protection of workers' rights inherent to the Constitution, problems have also been created with the enforcement of these rights. Initially, labour lawyers did not foresee the extent of the jurisdictional problems that this single system of law would create for labour dispute resolution. It has generally been accepted, on mistaken assumptions,[69] that disputes about labour matters remain the exclusive preserve of specialised labour dispute resolution forums. The effect of the constitutionalisation of labour law is only now becoming more apparent. Despite the fact that specialist labour fora have been established to determine labour matters, parties to labour disputes seek redress in the civil courts (in the form of the High Court and Supreme Court of Appeal) on the ticket of constitutional principle. This leads to forum shopping, costly arguments about which courts have the jurisdiction to entertain labour disputes and the undermining of sound reasons (as mentioned further along in the discussion) for the existence of a set of labour courts.

Relevant Legislative Enactments

Although South Africa has nine provinces, it does not have separate federal and state labour laws. Apart from the Constitution, there is one set

---

[68] Cheadle, H, 'Regulated Flexibility: Revisiting the LRA and the BCEA' (2006) *Industrial Law Journal (South Africa)* 663, 664 mentions that 'we live in a constitutional state that has entrenched ... a suit of labour rights ... [and this] means that labour market policy choices are constrained and the justification for any limitation of these rights is not simply a matter of economic choice.'

[69] Landman, AA, 'Your Petitioner Humbly Prays—Will the Supreme Court of Appeal Entertain Petitions from Aggrieved Labour Court Litigants' (2005) *Industrial Law Journal (South Africa)* 1901, 1902.

of national labour statutes finding application in all provinces making up the Republic.

As mentioned by Grogan, the Constitution 'now guarantees a sweeping guarantee of the right to fair labour practices' and a trilogy of labour statutes primarily gives effect to this constitutional right.[70] Essentially, the LRA concerns itself with the following number of significant aspects:[71] the right to freedom of association (which closely resembles ILO Conventions Nos 87 and 98);[72] the maintenance of a framework for voluntary collective bargaining, bolstered by organisational rights and protection of the right to strike;[73] the promotion of workplace democracy with the institution of workplace forums;[74] the regulation of unfair dismissal law (which follows the structure of ILO Convention No 158);[75] and the establishment of specialist labour dispute resolution fora, with the primary function of resolving 'labour matters'.[76] The Basic Conditions of Employment Equity Act,[77] the second of the trilogy, provides a floor of rights in respect of maximum hours of work, minimum leave provisions and it dictates within which boundaries those parties who are not covered by collective agreements may conclude contracts of employment. The third, the Employment Equity Act,[78] prohibits unfair discrimination and promotes the implementation of 'affirmative action'. In each of these enactments, the sentiment is expressed that effect should be given to the rights contained in the South African Constitution and to give effect to obligations incurred as member of the ILO.

The respective scopes of application of these laws are synchronised and relatively few categories of employers and employees are excluded from their reach. The ILO Fact Finding Mission during 1992, prior to its readmission, criticised South Africa for excluding domestic workers and farm workers from the LRA of 1956, on grounds that it infringed upon ILO Conventions Nos 87 and 98. Contrary to the position in Nigeria, where labour laws do not apply to the public sector as a whole, exclusions in South Africa are presently limited to members of the National Defence Force, the National Intelligence Agency and the South African

---

[70] Grogan, *Dismissal, Discrimination & Unfair Labour Practices* (2005) 38.
[71] See the discussion of the LRA in Hepple, 'Can Collective Labour Law Transplants Work? The South African Example' (1999) 1–3.
[72] LRA c II.
[73] Ibid c III. Hepple (n 42) 2 observes that 'the Italian model of strong organisational rights, and a right to strike has been preferred to an American model of a duty to bargain at plant level'.
[74] Ibid c V. This model, based on the German and Netherlands models, has sadly failed in South Africa.
[75] Ibid c VIII.
[76] Ibid c VII.
[77] Basic Conditions of Employment Equity Act 75 of 1997.
[78] Employment Equity Act 55 of 1998.

Secret Services.[79] Although fixed term and casual employees are covered, 'independent contractors' are excluded by virtue of the definition given to 'employee'. Similar to the situation in other jurisdictions,[80] it has been problematic for our courts to find the appropriate definition for 'employee' and the courts have devised a number of tests to distinguish between 'workers' and 'independent contractors'.[81] However, in an attempt to clarify the situation and to broaden the meaning of 'employee', the 2002 amendments have introduced a rebuttable presumption that a person is an employee, 'regardless of the form of the contract', if any one of a list of factors is present in the relationship.[82] In addition to this, the 'Code of Good Practice: Who is an Employee' was adopted in 2006, which incorporates the provisions of the ILO Employment Relations Recommendation 197. However, in practice this has not dramatically extended the reach of labour law to include atypical workers in the informal sector. The reason for this is probably universal in nature. Even though the worker who renders services to the informal food vender on the street corner may fall under the formal definition of employee, this does not necessarily present the informal worker with the required know-how and capacity to enforce his or her worker's rights. Generally speaking, the informal worker is likely to be illiterate and more concerned with the problems associated with eking out a day-to-day living rather than enforcing workers' protection in labour dispute resolution institutions. In addition to this, in the Southern African region, employers in this sector operate outside the formal legal framework. Most often they are not registered to pay taxes, they do not make contributions to unemployment and compensation funds and it could even be problematic to serve documents on these employers for purposes of legal processes.

[79] LRA s 2.

[80] For the view of the ILO, see ILO, 'Meeting of Experts on Workers in Situations needing Protection (The Employment Relationship Scope)' (Geneva May 2000), available at www.ilo.org/public/ english/dialogue/ifpdial/publ/mewnp/index.htm.

[81] For a clear discussion of these tests, see Brassey, M, 'The Nature of Employment' (1990) *Industrial Law Journal (South Africa)* 889; Benjamin, P, 'An Accident of History: Who Should and Who Should not be an Employee under South African Labour Law' (2004) *Industrial Law Journal (South Africa)* 787.

[82] See s 200A of the LRA and s 83A of the BCEA (fn 2 above), which include factors like: being under the control or direction of the other person; forming part of the organisation of the employer; being economically dependent on that other person; and being provided with the tools of trade by the other person. Also on 1 December 2006, a 'Code of Good Practice: Who is an Employee' was published in terms of s 200A of the LRA in *Government Gazette 29445*. This Code includes, in the form of an annexure, the 'ILO Recommendation Concerning the Employment Relationship' as accepted by the ILO Governing Body during its 95th session on 31 May 2006. It is submitted that this Code has unfortunately not broadened the pre-existing concept 'employee' that was in existence before the publication of the Code.

LABOUR RIGHTS AS HUMAN RIGHTS

The Right to Fair Labour Practices

The first section in the Constitution under the heading 'Labour Relations', states that '[e]veryone has the right to fair labour practices'.[83] Cheadle mentions that this right 'is an odd right to include in a Bill of Rights, and [it] is not found in other constitutions, bar one', namely Malawi which drew on the South African example.[84] The reason for this inclusion is not difficult to find. Against a background of the positive developments in the field of workers' rights that had occurred under the Industrial Court's unfair labour practice jurisdiction, 'the drafters of the Constitution were determined to constitutionalise the gains that had been made'.[85]

Although this fundamental right is bestowed upon 'everyone', it has been argued that the limitation of this right lies in the words 'labour practices'.[86] Cheadle opines that such practices go hand-in-hand with the broader relationship where one person is dependent on another by virtue of being paid for work rendered. It therefore does not apply to the genuine independent contractor working under the *locatio concuctio operis*, for example the builder who repairs the homeowner's garden wall on an ad hoc basis. Nor would it apply to the lawyer or doctor who works under the common law contract of mandate. However, despite this imbedded limitation alluded to by Cheadle, the word 'everyone' holds potential for the extension of worker rights to the atypically employed who may not fall within the limiting boundaries of the term 'employee' and the 'common law contract of employment'. Although the extension of this right to members of the informal economy has not been tested, the courts have on occasion, already indicated that it would be prepared to extend fundamental labour rights to relationships 'akin to an employer and employee' and to employees rendering services under unlawful contracts.[87]

Returning to the LRA and the term 'unfair labour practice', the open-ended notion of 'unfair labour practice' known to the Industrial Court (and as included in the Constitution) was abandoned with the adoption of the new set of labour laws. However, the term 'unfair labour practice' had regrettably been retained in the LRA. Having codified unfair dismissal law,

---

[83] South African Constitution s 23(1).
[84] Cheadle, H, 'Labour Relations' in Cheadle, MH, Davis, DM and Haysom, NRL, *South African Constitutional Law: The Bill of Rights* (Durban, LexisNexis Butterworths, 2005, updated July 2006) 18–8.
[85] Christianson, M, 'Labour Relations' in Currie and De Waal (n 10) 501.
[86] Cheadle 'Labour Relations' (2005) 18–3.
[87] *SA National Defence Force Union v Minister of Defence* 1999 *Industrial Law Journal (South Africa)* 2265 (CC). The issue of the inclusion of soldiers is discussed in the section below. See also *Discovery Health Ltd v CCMA* [2008] 7 BLLR 633 (LC) regarding the inclusion of employees rendering services under unlawful contracts.

the 'new' statutory definition of 'unfair labour practice' in the LRA now covers only a specified arbitrary list of remnant employer actions, notably in connection with the unfair promotion and demotion of employees and other disciplinary action short of dismissal against them.[88] These actions could just as well have been grouped in the LRA under a new concept, such as 'pre-dismissal unfair practices'. The retention of the term 'unfair labour practice' in both the LRA and the Constitution with their different meanings, create uncertainty about what exactly is covered by the term in the different acts. However, this does not mean that we have witnessed the end of the open-ended concept as contained in the Constitution. As stated by Landman,[89] the constitutionalisation of the term will keep the 'torch' of this open-ended concept 'burning brightly' in the new era under the Constitution.[90]

In *National Education Health and Allied Workers Union v University of Cape Town*,[91] the Constitutional Court confirmed this position by holding that:

> The [constitutional] concept of fair labour practice is incapable of precise definition. ... Indeed, what is fair depends upon the circumstances of a particular case and essentially involves a value judgment. ... The concept of fair labour practice must be given content by the legislature and thereafter left to gather meaning, in the first instance, from the specialist tribunals including the LAC [Labour Appeal Court] and the Labour Court. ... That is not to say that [the Constitutional Court] has no role in the determination of fair labour practices. Indeed, it has a crucial role in ensuring that the rights guaranteed in section 23(1) are honoured.

There are advantages and disadvantages to the inclusion of this abstract right into the Constitution. However, it is my view that the negative overshadows the positive. Commencing with the (not insignificant) positive elements, it guarantees protection for categories of persons excluded from labour legislation and holds potential for the extension of workers' rights to the economically active in the informal economy. It also inhibits present and future governments to bring flexibility into labour law by, for example, amending labour laws to exclude categories of small businesses from the coverage of labour legislation. As pointed out by Cheadle,[92] 'we live in a constitutional state that has entrenched ... a suit of labour rights' and this 'means that labour market policy choices are constrained and the justification for any limitation of these rights is not simply a matter of economic

---

[88] LRA s 186(2).
[89] Landman, AA, 'Fair Labour Practices—The Wiehahn Legacy' (2004) *Industrial Law Journal (South Africa)* 805.
[90] Ibid 807.
[91] *National Education Health and Allied Workers Union v University of Cape Town* (2003) 24 *ILJ* 95 (CC) [33]–[35].
[92] Cheadle, 'Regulated Flexibility: Revisiting the LRA and the BCEA' (2006) 664.

choice.' However, especially in respect of the extension of labour rights to the informal sector, it is submitted that the mere existence of such a possibility, without accompanying statutory measures directly addressing the issue of extending coverage to the atypically employed, would have no radical effects on such development.

Turning to the negative, the fact of the matter is that tailor made labour legislation now extensively regulates employer/ employee conduct through the extension of specific labour rights. Transgressions of these rights are to be adjudicated by carefully crafted labour dispute resolution institutions. These institutions focus on conciliatory process before adjudication, are constituted of labour law specialists, have been created to ensure expeditious and affordable dispute resolution, create an informal environment where trade union representatives feel at ease to represent their members and are more likely to steer the development of labour law in the appropriate direction in the modern world of work. The constitutional right to fair labour practices is wide enough to cover all labour-related matters already covered by labour legislation. The Constitution clothes the civil high courts with the jurisdiction to consider constitutional matters[93] and the LRA establishes the labour courts to entertain labour matters.[94] Due to the broad ambit of the right to fair labour practices, all labour matters can just as well be classified as constitutional matters and be heard by the civil High Court. This opens two potential channels of dispute resolution and creates fertile ground for forum shopping. It actually raises the question whether there is any justification for having specialist labour courts.[95]

To illustrate the problem, in *Fedlife Assurance v Wolfaardt*,[96] a matter dealing with the alleged premature breach of a fixed-term contract, the civil Supreme Court of Appeal held that the Interim Constitution, which also guaranteed the right to fair labour practices 'might [already] have imported into the common-law employment relationship' the right not to be unfairly dismissed even before the LRA was enacted. Even though the LRA presently specifically regulates unfair dismissal law, the Court was not prepared to hold that the civil Court's jurisdiction had been curtailed by the LRA, as had been argued in the matter, by virtue of the codification of unfair dismissal law. In two subsequent Supreme Court of Appeal cases,[97]

---

[93] South African Constitution s 169.
[94] LRA s 157(1)–(2).
[95] Van Eck (n 5, Pts 1 and 2) 549.
[96] *Fedlife Assurance v Wolfaardt* 2001 ILJ *(South Africa)* 2407 (SCA) [14].
[97] *Boxer Superstores Mthatha v Mbenya* [2007] 8 BLLR 693 (SCA); *Old Mutual Life Assurance Co SA Ltd v Gumbi* [2007] 8 BLLR 699 (SCA). See also the contrary view of the House of Lords in England in *Eastwood v Magnox Electric* [2004] UK HL 35 [12]–[13] where it is stated that '[a] common law obligation having the effect that an employer will not dismiss an employee in an unfair way would be much more than a major development of the common law of this country … Crucially, it would cover the same ground as the statutory right not to be dismissed unfairly.'

it has now indeed been confirmed that the civil courts may be approached, based on breach of contract on grounds that the common law contract of employment has under the Constitution now been developed to imply the right to a fair pre-dismissal hearing. This in effect establishes a dual dispute resolution system with the Commission for Conciliation Mediation and Arbitration (CCMA) and labour courts on the one hand and the civil courts on the other, which encourages the undesired practice of forum shopping.[98] The issue regarding the establishment of specialist dispute resolution forums and the problems that have been established by the Constitution in respect of the overlap of administrative law and labour law principles are discussed further along in the contribution.

Freedom of Association and the Right to Join Trade Unions

The Right to Join Trade Unions

The Constitution recognises the general principle that 'everyone has the right to freedom of association,[99] more specifically, in the employer employee context; it guarantees that 'every worker' has the right to 'form and join a trade union' and to 'participate in the activities and programmes of a trade union'.[100] Also included is the mirror right of 'every employer' to 'form and join an employer's organisation' and to join in their activities.[101]

As mentioned above, members of the South African National Defence Force are excluded from the scope of application of the LRA and they are consequently precluded from registering and joining trade unions in terms of the LRA. Apart from this, the provisions of the previous Defence Act[102] expressly prohibited soldiers from belonging to trade unions. The first in a sequence of South African National Defence Union (SANDU) cases,[103] serves as an excellent example of just how the inclusion of this collective labour right in the Constitution has been able to protect workers' rights. In the Defence Force Union's quest to have the limiting provisions of the Defence Act declared unconstitutional, the matter proceeded through the civil High Court to the Constitutional Court.

---

[98] The decision of the Supreme Court of Appeal in *Denel v Vorster* 2004 *ILJ (South Africa)* 659 (SCA) is a clear example of this phenomenon.

[99] South African Constitution s 18. The word 'everyone' denotes that this right is not limited to, for example, employees or citizens.

[100] Ibid s 23(2)(a)(b).

[101] Ibid s 23(3)(a)(b).

[102] Defence Act 44 of 1957 s 126B(1). This Act has since been replaced by the Defence Act of 2003.

[103] *South African National Defence Union v Minister of Defence* 1999 *ILJ (South Africa)* 2279 (CC).

The first question considered by the Court was whether members of the armed forces are 'workers', for if they were, the Court held, the restriction would undoubtedly be contrary to the constitutional right to form and join trade unions. The Court took account of article 2 of the ILO Freedom of Association Convention No 87[104] that reads, '[w]orkers and employers, without distinction whatsoever, shall have the right to establish and ... join organisations of their own choosing'. It also considered article 9(1) of the same Convention that provides that '[t]he extent to which the guarantees provided for in this convention shall apply to the armed forces and the police shall be determined by national laws and regulations'. Pointing out that the courts are constitutionally bound to consider 'international law',[105] it held that members of the South African National Defence Force are indeed 'workers' despite the fact that 'the relationship that they have with the defence force is unusual and not identical to an ordinary employment relationship'.[106]

The second issue to be considered was whether these rights may justifiably be limited under the Constitution's limitations clause that provides that the 'rights in the Bill may be limited ... to the extent that the limitation is reasonable and justifiable in an open and democratic society based on human dignity, equality and freedom'.[107] Implementing a generous and purposive interpretation to accord individuals full protection of their rights,[108] the Constitutional Court held that a total ban on trade unions in the SANDF was unreasonable and unjustifiable.[109]

The Constitutional Court directed that new regulations be drafted and enacted by Parliament that would provide for the registration of trade unions in the defence force and to make provision for procedures that have to be followed should deadlock be reached in the negotiation process. In this indirect role, the Constitution played a positive role in the protection of workers' rights without undermining labour law as self-supporting discipline.

Collective Bargaining: 'Freedom' or 'Duty'?

The Interim Constitution provided that '[w]orkers and employers shall have the right to organise and to bargain collectively'.[110] However, for reasons unknown to observers outside the Constitutional Assembly, the wording of the Final Constitution was changed. It presently reads that 'every trade

---

[104] Ibid [26].
[105] South African Constitution s 39.
[106] *SA National Defence Union* 1999 *ILJ (South Africa)* 2279 (CC) [27].
[107] South African Constitution s 36(1).
[108] *SA National Defence Union* 1999 *ILJ (South Africa)* 2279 (CC) [28].
[109] Ibid [36].
[110] Interim Constitution s 27(3).

union, employer's organisation and employer has the right to engage in collective bargaining'.[111] As will become evident from the discussion that follows, an inconclusive debate ensued amongst judges and academics on the point of whether this constitutional provision places a positive duty, such as to be found in the United States of America, on employers to participate in collective bargaining.

The Cheadle Task Team was unanimous in their decision not to introduce a legally enforceable duty to participate in collective bargaining into the then new LRA. In the Explanatory Memorandum to the Draft Labour Relations Bill, it was stated that 'the absence of a statutory duty to bargain' would be a notable feature of the LRA. In its deliberations, the Task Team considered three models: first, a system of statutory compulsion. Secondly, a more flexible model that relies on intervention by the judiciary to determine appropriate bargaining levels and topics. In the words of the Task Team:

> the third model, unanimously adopted ... is one which allows the parties, through the exercise of power, to determine their own arrangements. The exercise of power ... is given statutory impetus by the ... provision of organisational rights and a protected right to strike.[112]

This is how things turned out in terms of the LRA. It is silent about a duty to bargain, however, it is interwoven with employee and trade union rights, called 'organisational rights', which make organised labour's 'capacity to bargain more effective'.[113] These rights include the right of access to the workplace, the deduction of trade union dues, the appointment of trade union representatives and the right to relevant information. Apart from granting protection to employees participating in procedurally correct strike action regarding matters of 'mutual interest' (which would include disputes about organisational rights), these rights can be secured by means of statutory conciliation, followed by arbitration. But, what would the position be in respect of those categories of workers excluded from the ambit of the LRA, devoid of a right to strike and the opportunity to refer disputes to conciliation and arbitration in terms of the LRA?

In the second of the SANDU cases,[114] having registered their trade union under newly drafted regulations, the armed force trade union brought a matter before the High Court to enforce a positive duty to bargain on their employer. The Court noted that the Interim Constitution 'recognised a *right* to bargain collectively, with a correlative *duty* to bargain on the other side'. However, the Final Constitution now provides for a 'right to *engage*

---

[111] Final Constitution s 23(5).
[112] Explanatory Memorandum to the Draft Labour Relations Bill' (1995) 121.
[113] Grogan, J, *Workplace Law* (Cape Town, Juta, 2005) 359.
[114] *SA National Defence Force Union v Minister of Defence* 2003 ILJ *(South Africa)* 1495 (T).

in collective bargaining'. This, the Court held, only confers a 'freedom' to bargain collectively, and although this freedom of the initiating party may not be violated, it does not impose a duty on the opposing party to participate in the bargaining process.[115]

A reading of the decision makes it clear that the Court was sensitive to sentiments raised by the Task Team, by steering away from a court-induced duty to bargain. However, there are coherent arguments suggesting that it is an incorrect decision. First, the Task Team's arguments against a court-induced duty to bargain only apply in relation to a broader collective bargaining structure where employees have the right to strike and the option of enforcing organisational rights through conciliation and arbitration. Any particular 'freedom' to engage in collective bargaining rings hollow in the absence of a right to strike or a right to refer organisational rights disputes to conciliation and arbitration. Secondly, it is a flawed argument to consider sentiments emanating from a statute giving effect to the Constitution to interpret the provisions of the Constitution. Lastly, it is questionable whether the change in wording from 'the right to bargain' to 'the right to engage in bargaining' is sufficiently clear to justify the downgrading of a constitutional 'right' to a mere 'freedom'. Had the Constitutional Assembly contemplated such a significant change in emphasis, surely they would have exchanged the word 'right' with 'freedom'.[116]

In the third SANDU[117] case, the same division of the High Court in a separate matter came to a different conclusion. In this instance, the Court held that it could see no reason why a 'right to engage in collective bargaining' could not impose a correlative duty to bargain on the other party. In context of the constitutional right to fair labour practices, the Court accepted guidance from the pre-1994 dispensation, where both the Industrial Court[118] and the Appellate Division[119] placed a positive duty to bargain in good faith on employers covered by the old LRA.

The third SANDU case was followed by a decision of the Supreme Court of Appeal, and in the final instance by a decision of the Constitutional

---

[115] Vettori, S, 'A Judicially Enforceable Duty to Bargain?' (2005) *De Jure* 382 supports arguments in favour of this interpretation. See also Steenkamp, A, Stelzner, S and Badenhorts, N, 'The Right to Bargain Collectively' (2004) *Industrial Law Journal (South Africa)* 943.

[116] Some commentators support the interpretation of the Constitution to include a 'duty to bargain'. See Landman, AA, 'The Duty to Bargain—An Old Weapon Pressed into Service' 2004 *ILJ (South Africa)* 39 and Van Jaarsveld, SR, 'Die Reg op Kollektiewe Bedinging, Nog Enkele Kollektiewe Gedagtes' (2004) *De Jure* 349.

[117] *SA National Defence Force Union v Minister of Defence* 2003 ILJ 2101 (T).

[118] Ibid [2112G], the Court referred to *FAWU v Speckenham Supreme* 1988 ILJ 628 (IC) 636J, where it was held that 'in general it is unfair for an employer not to negotiate with a representative trade union'.

[119] In *NUM v East Rand Gold & Uranium Co Ltd* 1992 (1) SA 700 (A) 734E, the Court quoted with approval Brassey, M, Cameron, E, Cheadle, H and Olivier, M, *The New Labour Law* (Cape Town, Juta 1987), mentioning that 'there is nothing so subversive of collective bargaining, as to refuse to bargain entirely or to pretend to bargain without doing so'.

Court.[120] The Supreme Court of Appeal held that although the Constitution recognises the importance of collective bargaining, it does not impose in the absence of the right to strike an enforceable judicial duty on the employer to participate in collective bargaining with its collective bargaining adversaries. The Constitutional Court, in a final twist of the tail, overturned the decision of the Supreme Court of Appeal and held that the answer lies in the regulations which had been promulgated subsequent to the first SANDU case and which made provision for the registration of trade unions in the Defence Force. In terms of the regulations, the employer is compelled to negotiate with the trade unions on a broad range of issues and it may not elect to withdraw from the negotiation process without following the arbitration process prescribed by the regulations. This leaves us with the somewhat ironic situation which entails that although an enforceable duty to bargaining had not been included under the carefully crafted provisions of the Labour Relations Act, such duty had been imposed on the Defence Force by the Constitutional Court in terms of the regulations which had been implemented subsequent to the first SANDU case.

The Right to Strike

The Final Constitution confers on 'every worker' the 'right to strike',[121] but no mention is made of a right to lock-out. This represents a significant shift in emphasis from the Interim Constitution, which guaranteed the right to strike 'for purposes of collective bargaining' and which also recognised 'an employer's recourse to the lock-out for purposes of collective bargaining'.[122] Whereas the original protected a collective right, which co-existed with collective bargaining, the present provision protects the individual employee's right to strike. To what extent does this right protect workers' rights on the collective level?[123]

The exclusion from the Final Constitution of the right to lock-out was challenged in the certification process in the *Ex p Chairperson of the*

---

[120] *South African National Defence Union v Minister of Defence* 2007 (1) SA 402 (SCA) was followed by the Constitutional Court decision *South African National Defence Union v Minister of Defence* unreported case number CCT 65/06 decided on 30 May 2007.

[121] Final Constitution s 23(2)(c).

[122] Interim Constitution s 27.

[123] Hepple points out that at the time of the drafting of the South African Constitution he was concerned whether the inclusion of an individual right to strike would simultaneously 'reflect the "organic" character of collective worker's solidarity ... and, at the same, protect the individual worker from dismissal for participating in a strike'. See the excellent discussion of this issue in Hepple, B, 'The Right to Strike: A Case Study in Constitutionalisation' (Occasional Paper 1/2004 Development and Labour Monograph Series presented for the Institute of Development and Labour Law, University of Cape Town) 15. See also Welch, R, 'Collectivism versus Individualism in employee Relations: For Human Rights at the Workplace' 1996 *ILJ (South Africa)* 1041.

Constitutional Assembly: In Re Certification of the Constitution of the Republic of South Africa.[124] The argument raised by counsel on behalf of the employer was that in order to engage in effective collective bargaining, the right to exercise economic power by both parties to collective bargaining should expressly be recognised in the Constitution. The Court quite correctly rejected the challenge on grounds that strikes and lock-outs are not true equivalents. While the Court deemed it appropriate for the Constitution to protect employees' right to strike, the same did not apply to the right to lock-out because employers have greater social and economic power, including such economic weapons as to dismiss employees, to make use of replacement labour and to implement new terms and conditions of employment. The Court held that the recognition of the right of all employers to engage in collective bargaining already implies that parties to collective bargaining are entitled to exercise economic power (including to lock-out) against their partners in collective bargaining. The position in South Africa is thus similar to countries including Italy, France and Portugal, which have constitutional protection for the right to strike, but not for the right to lock-out.[125]

In *National Union of Metalworkers of South Africa (NUMSA) v Bader Bop (Pty) Ltd,*[126] the Constitutional Court had the opportunity to consider whether a minority trade union has the right to strike in order to secure organisational rights. NUMSA, only representing 26.6 per cent of Bader Bop's employees, notified the employer of a planned strike in their quest to secure recognition of their shop stewards. The LRA confers the right to recognition of elected shop stewards and the right to the disclosure of information to trade unions that represent the 'majority' of employees at a particular workplace.[127] The Labour Appeal Court[128] confirmed an interdict against the strike on grounds that the LRA prescribes that disputes about organisational rights should be referred to conciliation followed by arbitration for finalisation. Arguing that this was an infringement of their constitutional right to strike, the trade union appealed to the Constitutional Court.

---

[124] *Ex p Chairperson of the Constitutional Assembly: In Re Certification of the Constitution of the Republic of South Africa* 1996 ILJ *(South Africa)* 821 (CC) [64]–[68].

[125] Hepple, 'The Right to Strike: A Case Study in Constitutionalisation' (Occasional Paper 1/2004) 15.

[126] *National Union of Metalworkers of South Africa (NUMSA) v Bader Bop (Pty) Ltd* 2003 ILJ *(South Africa)* 305 (CC). See also Grogan, J, 'Organisational Rights and the Right to Strike' (2002) 11 *Contemporary Labour Law* 69.

[127] LRA ss 14 and 16. LRA ss 12 and 13 secure 'sufficiently representative' trade unions the right of access to the workplace and the right to the deduction of trade union dues. See Mischke, C, 'Getting a Foot in the Door: Organisational Rights and Collective Bargaining in terms of the LRA' (2004) 16 *Contemporary Labour Law* 51.

[128] *Bader Bop (Pty) Ltd v NUMSA* 2002 ILJ *(South Africa)* 104 (LAC).

The Court accepted that NUMSA was not a majority trade union and that it was seeking trade union rights analogous to the organisational rights contained in the LRA. The Court held that the LRA was open to different interpretations and there was nothing in the LRA that explicitly prevented minority unions from using industrial action to secure recognition of shop stewards. Traversing ILO Conventions Nos 87 and 98, the views of the ILO Committee of Experts and the Freedom of Association Committee, the Court accepted the view that 'a majoritarian system will not be incompatible with freedom of association, as long as minority unions are allowed to exist, to organise members ... and to seek to challenge majority unions from time to time.' Against this backdrop, the Court accepted that a generous interpretation should be given to the LRA, one that does not infringe upon the rights to freedom of association, the right to strike and to participate in collective bargaining. NUMSA therefore succeeded in its appeal against the interdict that curtailed its right to strike.

Despite the fact that the right to strike is coached in individual terms, the *Chairperson of the Constitutional Assembly* and *Bader Bop* cases point towards a correct application of constitutional principles in the collective labour law sense. Hepple mentions that, in the *Bader Bop* case, the Court used the Constitution 'to provide an interpretive principle', rather than granting an individual constitutional right that exists outside the general collective bargaining framework provided for in terms of the LRA.[129] From this the conclusion can be drawn that despite the individualistic wording contained in the Constitution, the Constitutional Court has thus far fared reasonably well in protecting collective labour rights in their interpretation of South Africa's fundamental labour rights.

Equality and Affirmative Action

In *Brink v Kitshoff*, the Constitutional Court highlighted the fact that the previous government 'systematically discriminated against black people', and amongst others, deprived the historically disadvantaged from, 'senior jobs and access to schools and universities'.[130] It is in this context that the first human right included in the Constitution reads that 'everyone is equal before the law'. Directly following this right, it is stated that, '[e]quality includes the full and equal enjoyment of all rights and freedoms' and 'to promote the achievement of equality, legislative ... measures designed

---

[129] However, Hepple's concerns as mentioned above, (n 123), have not been allayed in respect of the protection of an individual right not to be dismissed for participating in industrial action. See the critical analysis of *Xinwa v Volkswagen of SA (Pty) Ltd* 2003 ILJ *(South Africa)* 15–18 in Hepple (n 123) 15–18.

[130] *Brink v Kitshoff* 1996 (4) SA 197 (CC) [40].

legal practice which is steeped in common law tradition—where employer prerogative and sanctity of contract plays a more significant role than fairness in the determination of disputes.[171] It is submitted that, for these judges, it may be problematic to develop through their decisions an appropriate balance between individual employee welfare, collective labour rights and business interests in the prevailing era of the changing world of work.

Secondly, it is a pity that on constitutional principle, a protracted lineage of appeal has been opened in labour matters. Whereas initially, labour lawyers were of the view that there was only the option of taking CCMA awards on review to the Labour Court, followed by one level of appeal to the Labour Appeal Court, it has now become apparent that it is possible to take matters on two further levels of appeal, namely to the Supreme Court of Appeal, and then to the Constitutional Court. This inevitably departs from the worthy ideas of the expeditious and affordable resolution of labour disputes. This state of affairs favours corporations and successful businesses that can afford to incur substantial legal costs and to whittle down the opposition's resistance by means of relative financial strength.

Thirdly, trade union representatives, and even individuals who lodge matters in the absence of representation, have become accustomed to the relative informal and accessible environment of the CCMA and the labour courts. Whereas the civil High Court is notorious for its formalism in attire, form of address and the high standards which are required in respect of court documents and pleadings, CCMA commissioners and Labour Court judges have shown a tendency to allow for a measure of leniency towards non-qualified applicants and their representatives. This has led to the tendency of increased accessibility for workers who can ill afford lawyer's legal fees.

CONCLUSION

It is my thesis that the Constitution is an expression of the fact that South Africa is a country based on values, including workers' rights. Workers have played a significant role in the establishment of the present constitutional democracy. The Constitution, as a peoples' charter, generates a broad policy framework, or context, within which courts must interpret

---

[171] In *Denel v Vorster*, the Supreme Court of Appeal accorded more weight to the sanctity of contract than on fairness in the employment relationship despite the right to fair labour practices contained in the Constitution. In the as yet unreported *Rustenburg Platinum Mines Ltd (Rustenburg Section) v Commission for Conciliation, Mediation and Arbitration* Case no 598/05, 26 September 2006, the Supreme Court of Appeal reintroduced the 'reasonable employer' test in disciplinary enquiries which in effect strengthens the employer prerogative in the employer employee relationship.

and further develop social and labour principles. The Constitution directs that South African courts are enjoined, when interpreting any legislation, to prefer any explanation that is consistent with international law. This inextricably links the future development of domestic labour law to global workers' rights emanating from supranational norms. The Constitution also serves as fortification of labour standards due to the fact that present and future governments may find it difficult to bring flexibility into South African labour law without meeting constitutional challenge. It is my argument that the Constitutional Court has to a large extent been successful in applying some of these rights (most notably the right to join trade unions and the right to strike) to interpret the LRA in such a manner that it has been to the benefit of collective workers' rights.

However, the constitutionalisation of workers' rights has spawned unforeseen jurisdictional problems, which to a certain extent, is leading the way to the decompartmentalisation of labour law as independent legal subject. From a labour lawyer's perspective, this is unfortunately pointing towards the abolition of our labour courts. A number of factors are contributing to this process. The Constitution has direct, as opposed to mere indirect application, and all law, including the common law, derives its force from the supreme law of the land. As pointed out by the Constitutional Court, '[if] the effect of this requirement is that this court will have jurisdiction in all labour matters that is a consequence of our constitutional democracy'.[172]

The South African experience illustrates that other courts clothed with the jurisdiction to entertain constitutional disputes, such as the High Court and Supreme Court of Appeal, would not hesitate to decide labour matters (despite the existence of labour courts) as long as they comfortably fit under constitutional guarantees. This interrelationship between different types of constitutional protection (such as the right to fair labour practices and the right to rational administrative action), and the phenomenon of forum shopping, has made the enforcement of workers' protection complex to the point that it may undermine its effectiveness. The constitutional vision of having one coherent hierarchy of courts with the Supreme Court of Appeal and the Constitutional Court at the apex, overrides labour policy considerations that include expeditious, affordable and specialised labour dispute resolution. This is watering down the quest of developing labour law as an independent discipline within which specialised labour courts can co-exist and flourish besides the traditional courts. Amongst the consequences of the demise of the labour courts, may be the fact that judges who are not adequately equipped to deal with the nuances between the common law contract of employment, fairness and the rebalancing of social power, will

---

[172] See the *National Education Health and Allied Workers Union* (2003) 24 *ILJ* 95 (CC)[16].

become responsible to shape the future of labour law in South Africa. This could lead to an over emphasis of lawfulness, as derived from the contract of employment as yardstick in the determination of labour disputes. However, as pointed out above, possibly the most significant concern may be the fact that our labour courts with their specialist composition, are in the process of being abolished even though they are in all probability better suited than the civil courts to guide the future development of labour law in the prevailing era of globalisation.

10

Legal Protection of Workers' Human Rights: Regulatory Changes and Challenges The United States

LANCE COMPA

INTRODUCTION

Social and Economic Concerns

W ORKERS IN THE United States share the social and economic concerns of working people everywhere. Their plight is not the same as two-dollars-a-day poverty in the poorest developing countries, but even before the recession that began in 2008, millions of Americans saw poverty and social inequality increasing as wealth created by workers flowed to owners and investors.[1] Adjusted for inflation, real wages have fallen even while productivity rose. The federal minimum wage was stuck for 10 years at $5.15 per hour, the lowest level, relative to average wages, in 56 years before increasing to $6.55 per hour in 2006 and $7.25 per hour in 2009—a level still below that of decades earlier, relative to average wages.[2]

---

[1] See eg, Porter, E, 'After Years of Growth, What About Labor's Share?' *Sunday New York Times* (15 October 2006) s 3, 3; Greenhouse, S and Leonhardt, D, 'Real Wages Fail to Match a Rise in Productivity' *New York Times* (28 August 2006) A1; Johnson, JB, 'Making Ends Meet; The Well-off are Better Off, but the Ranks of the Poor are Growing, and Middle- and Low-income Workers Feel Pressure of High Prices' *San Francisco Chronicle* (28 September 2005) A1. For wide-ranging analysis and critique of problems faced by American workers, see Greenhouse, S, *The Big Squeeze: Tough Times for the American Worker* (New York, Knopf, 2008).

[2] See Bernstein, J, 'Nine Year of Neglect: Federal Minimum Wage Remains Unchanged for Ninth Straight Year; Falls to Lowest Level in More than Half a Century' (Economic Policy Institute (EPI) Issue Brief #227, 31 August 2006); Cannell, ME, 'New Floor Set for Wages; $6.55 an Hour: Latest Increase Revives Debate that Goes Back to Depression' *Atlanta Journal-Constitution* (24 July 2008) 1B.

Inequality between men and women is also an enduring problem. Women's annual earnings, relative to men's, have moved up more slowly since the early 1990s than previously, and still remain substantially below parity. Women who work full-time throughout the year made 79.9 per cent of men's earnings in 2008. If part-time workers were included, the ratio would be much worse because women are more likely than men to work part-time to meet childcare and other family responsibilities.[3]

Before the 2008 recession, many big manufacturing companies announced large-scale layoffs and plant closures, often linked to 'runaway' production shifts to developing countries.[4] High-technology and service companies are supposed to be a fount of future employment in an economy shifting away from a manufacturing base. However, these companies have begun 'outsourcing' jobs in massive numbers, ranging in skills from computer programmers to call centre operators.[5]

A special concern of American workers is health insurance. Without a national health insurance plan, as in most other countries, workers depend on employers for access to private health plans. However, employers are not required to provide health benefits, and many do not. As a result, nearly 50 million people in the United States lack health insurance.[6] In companies that provide insurance, employers are pushing more cost burdens onto employees. Health insurance costs are the biggest single cause of strikes and 'giveback' bargaining in the United States.[7]

The recession that began in 2009 worsened American workers' job security, social protection, and living standards. Official unemployment rose

[3] See Institute for Women's Policy Research, 'The Gender Wage Gap: 2008' (IWPR #C350, updated April 2009).

[4] See eg, Content, T, 'Delphi Veterans to be Gone by 2007; Cheaper, Temporary Workers Will Fill in Until Plants Shut Down' *Milwaukee Journal-Sentinel* (30 September 2006) D1; Williams, FO, 'Mexico Gets American Axle Work: Buffalo Plant Loses Out on Parts for New GM Car' *Buffalo News* (21 September 2006) A1. For book length treatment of the scope and effects of plant closings and layoffs, see Uchitelle, L, *The Disposable American: Layoffs and Their Consequences* (New York, Knopf, 2006).

[5] See eg, Godinez, V, 'EDS Embraces a World-wise Outlook: Company's CEO Says Outsourcing to Nations like India is "Fact of Life" ' *Dallas Morning News* (16 October 2006) 1D; Fillion, R, 'Teletech Expands in Pacific: Outsourcing Firm to Add 2 Call Centers in Philippines' *Denver Rocky Mountain News*, (1 November 2005) 6; Dhillon, A, 'From Hearts to Homes, Outsourcing Goes Upmarket, Today's Offshore Back Office is Filled with Lawyers, Doctors and Even Architects' *South China Morning Post* (15 November 2005) 7.

[6] See Yi, D, 'More US Workers Go Uninsured: Rising Health Premiums are Prompting Firms to Drop Coverage or Employees to Forego it, an Annual Survey Shows' *Los Angeles Times* (27 September 2006) C1.

[7] See eg, Snowbeck, C, 'Health Care's Bite: Push for Employees to Take on More Medical Costs at Root of Contract Disputes' *Pittsburgh Post-Gazette* (8 September 2006) C1; Paine, G, 'Health Insurance is Key to Labor Negotiations: Many Experts Argue it Cannot Be Resolved at the Bargaining Table' *San Francisco Chronicle* (3 September 2006) F1; D Lazarus, 'Health Costs Will Cause More Strikes' *San Francisco Chronicle* (23 December 2005) C1.

above nine per cent in March 2009 with expectations of more.[8] Beyond that, millions more unemployed and underemployed workers are not counted in the official statistics.[9] Many workers lost their homes,[10] and the health insurance crisis intensified.[11]

The Crisis in Freedom of Association

Like workers everywhere, Americans often seek to defend their jobs and wages by forming and joining trade unions. Polls indicate that some 60 million workers who are not union-represented would like to have a union in their workplace.[12] But in the United States, efforts to form trade unions and bargain collectively meet fierce employer resistance. Employers unlawfully fire workers for trying to form unions in more than one-fourth of union-organising campaigns.[13] Restrictive legislation, debilitating delays, and weak enforcement create high obstacles to workers' freedom of association in the United States.[14]

In 2008, union 'density' in the US labour force was 12.4 per cent of employed wage and salary earners, down from 35 per cent in the 1950s and 20 per cent in the early 1980s.[15] Most of the millions of unrepresented workers are considered 'at-will' employees under common law doctrine in many states (there is no federal common law of the employment relationship). This means that employers can dismiss them at any time for any reason not prohibited by law, such as anti-discrimination statutes. In sum, workers not covered by collective bargaining agreements do not have the

[8] See eg, Hagenbaugh, B and Hansen, B, 'The Future Holds More Job Losses, Survey Says; Unemployment Could Top Out Near 10%' *USA Today* (27 April 2009) 1B; Goodman, PS and Healy, J, 'Job Losses Hint At Vast Remaking of US Economy' *New York Times* (7 March 2009) A1; Norris, F, 'In This Recession, More Men Are Losing Jobs' *New York Times* (14 March 2009) B3; Goodman, PS and Healy, J, '660,000 More Jobs Lost; Total Surpasses 5 Million' *New York Times* (4 April 2009) A1; Luo, M, 'Longer Periods of Unemployment for Workers 45 and Older' *New York Times* (13 April 2009) A11.

[9] See eg, Posada, J, 'Who are the Jobless?; The Real Stories: If You Look Behind the Numbers, You Find the Discouraged, the Involuntary Part-Timers, People Who Don't Fit Neatly into Statistical Categories' *Hartford Courant* (19 April 2009) A1.

[10] Fagan, K, 'Ranks of Newly Homeless Soar as Prospects Plunge; The Economy in Turmoil' *San Francisco Chronicle* (6 April 2009) A1.

[11] Roan, S, 'In an Ailing Economy, the Doctor can Wait; More People, Even the Chronically Ill, Forgo Preventive Care' *Los Angeles Times* (8 April 2009) A1.

[12] See eg, Reich, RB, 'The Union Way Up: America, and its Faltering Economy, Need Unions to Restore Prosperity to the Middle Class' *Los Angeles Times* (26 January 2009).

[13] See eg, Schmitt, J and Zipperer, B, 'Dropping the Ax: Illegal Firings During Union Election Campaigns, 1951–2007' (Center for Economic and Policy Research, March 2009).

[14] For information on the systematic failure of US labour law to protect workers' organising and bargaining rights, see the website of American Rights at Work available at www.araw.org.

[15] United States Bureau of Labor Statistics, 'Union Members in 2008' (28 January 2009).

protection of a 'just cause' standard for discipline or dismissal, because 'at-will' is the default rule in the American employment law system.[16]

The reach of federal law prohibiting anti-union discrimination is limited. US labour law excludes millions of workers from statutory protection of the right to organise and collectively bargain. They include agricultural workers, household employees, employees of religious institutions, employees labelled 'supervisors' and 'managers' or 'independent contractors', and more. Under the at-will rule, they have no protection against dismissal for associational activity. If these 'excluded' workers protest abusive working conditions or try to organise a union, employers can fire them with impunity. If they seek to bargain collectively, employers can ignore them. They have no labour board or unfair labour practice mechanism for redress.

Millions of public employees face similar exclusions from labour law coverage. Many US states deny public employees the right to bargain collectively. For example, North Carolina specifically prohibits collective bargaining between any state, county or municipal agency and any organisation of employees. Texas declares it to be against public policy for any state, county or municipal officials to enter into a collective bargaining agreement with a labour organisation. Virginia holds collective bargaining 'contrary to the public policy of Virginia'.

In a 2002 study, the US Government Accountability Office reported that more than 32 million workers in the United States lack protection of the right to organise and to bargain collectively.[17] But since then, the situation has worsened. A series of decisions by the federal authorities under President George Bush has stripped many more workers of organising and bargaining rights. The administration took away bargaining rights for hundreds of thousands of employees in the new Department of Homeland Security and the Defense Department.[18] In the years before the 2009 change of administration, a controlling majority of the five-member National Labor Relations Board (NLRB), appointed by President Bush, denied protection to graduate student employees, disabled employees, temporary employees and other categories of workers.[19]

---

[16] For a discussion, see Stieber, J, 'Protection against Unfair Dismissal: A Comparative View' (1980) 3 *Comparative Labor Law Journal* 229, stating 'The United States stands almost alone among industrialized nations in not providing statutory protection against unfair dismissal for all employees.'

[17] See US General Accounting Office, 'Collective Bargaining Rights: Information on the Number of Workers with and without Bargaining Rights' (Report No GAO-02-835, September 2002).

[18] See LaBrecque, LC, 'DOD Unveils Final Personnel System Rule Covering 650,000 Workers; Unions Plan Suit' Bureau of National Affairs *Daily Labor Report* (28 October 2005) A-8; 'Homeland Security Announces Final Rule Changing Personnel System for Agency' Bureau of National Affairs *Daily Labor Report* (27 January 2005) A-9.

[19] See *Brown University*, 342 NLRB No. 42 (2004); *Oakwood Care Center*, 343 NLRB No. 76 (2004) (Note that this is not the same 'Oakwood' as that of the supervisor case in

An October 2006, a NLRB decision was especially alarming for labour advocates. The NLRB set out a new, expanded definition of 'supervisor' under the section of US labour law that excludes supervisors from protection of the right to organise and bargain collectively.[20] This exclusion has enormous repercussions for millions of workers who might now become 'supervisors' and lose protection of their organising and bargaining rights.[21] This case is discussed in more detail below in connection with a complaint to the International Labour Organisation (ILO) Committee on Freedom of Association.

The Human Rights Context

'American exceptionalism' to international law is deeply rooted in American legal discourse and culture.[22] Labour and employment law practitioners and jurists rarely invoke human rights instruments and standards on freedom of association, child labour, nondiscrimination, health and safety, wages and hours, migrant workers' rights or other subjects of international human rights law to address failures in US labour law and practice.

Outside a small cadre of specialists interested in comparative and international labour law, most actors in the US labour law system have no familiarity—if they are even aware of their existence—with labour provisions in the Universal Declaration of Human Rights, the International Covenant on Civil and Political Rights (ICCPR), the International Covenant on Economic, Social and Cultural Rights, ILO conventions and declarations, Organisation for Economic Co-operation and Development (OECD) guidelines, trade agreements and other international instruments.

---

n 20 below); *Brevard Achievement Center*, 342 NLRB No. 101 (2004). For a fuller description of these and other National Labor Relations Board (NLRB) decisions weakening workers' rights, see 'Workers Rights Under Attack by Bush Administration: President Bush's National Labor Relations Board Rolls Back Labor Protections' (Report by Congressman George Miller, Senior Democratic Member, Committee on Education and the Workforce, US House of Representatives, 13 July 2006), available at: http://edworkforce.house.gov/democrats/pdf/NLRBreport071306.pdf.

[20] See *Oakwood Healthcare, Inc*, 348 NLRB No. 37; *Croft Metal, Inc*, 348 NLRB No. 38; *Golden Crest Healthcare Center*, 348 NLRB No. 39 (October 2, 2006), called the *Oakwood* trilogy.

[21] See Eisenbrey, R and Mishel, L, 'Supervisors in Name Only: Union Rights of Eight Million Workers at Stake in Labor Board Ruling' *Economic Policy Institute* (12 July 2006) available at: www.epi.org/content.cfm/ib225; 'The Potential Impact of NLRB's Supervisor Cases '*Economic Policy Institute* (6 September 2006) available at: www.epi.org/content.cfm/pm115.

[22] For a collection of essays on this question, see M Ignatieff (ed), *American Exceptionalism and Human Rights* (Princeton, Princeton University Press, 2005). See also, Roth, K, 'The Charade of US Ratification of International Human Rights Treaties' (Fall 2000) 1 *Chicago Journal of International Law* 347.

The United States has ratified only 14 of the ILO's 186 conventions, and among these only two of the eight 'core' conventions.[23]

When the United States ratified the ICCPR in 1992, the then-Bush administration insisted that 'ratification of the Covenant has no bearing on and does not, and will not, require any alteration or amendment to existing Federal and State labor law' and that 'ratification of the Covenant would not obligate us in any way to ratify ILO Convention 87 or any other international agreement'.[24] In its most recent report on the ICCPR, the State Department supplied nothing more than a few desultory paragraphs suggesting 'general' compliance with article 22.[25] As one scholar concluded:

> The official American view is that international human rights are endangered elsewhere, and that American labor law is a model for the rest of the world. The rest of the world may not be convinced that American labor law, old and flawed as it is, is a model for the modern world. But more to the present point, American legal institutions and decision makers have thus far been deaf to the claim that international labor law provides a potential model for American labor law, or even a critical vantage point from which to view American labor law.[26]

Most lawyers, legislators and judges in the United States ignore international law and look instead to the US Constitution for fundamental rights. But even in this national context, ideas of fundamental rights for workers are often lacking. Labour law scholars and practitioners traditionally see regulating the employment relationship as a series of policy choices unrelated to constitutional rights, unless the Constitution speaks clearly. Some valuable constitutional safeguards for workers can still be found in the First Amendment's protection of speech, protecting peaceful picketing rights, for example. Public employees, in particular, rely on the First Amendment to protect their associational rights and right to petition legislators in states where collective bargaining is outlawed. In general, though, US labour and employment law reflects malleable policy choices, not fundamental rights.

---

[23] The United States has ratified Convention No 105 on forced labour and Convention No 182 on worst forms of child labour. The United States has not ratified Convention No 29 on forced labour, No 87 on freedom of association, No 98 on the right to organise, No 100 on equal pay, No 111 on nondiscrimination, and No 138 on child labour.

[24] See Appendix B, Senate Foreign Relations Committee, Senate Comm. on Foreign Relations, 'Report on the International Covenant on Civil and Political Rights (ICCPR)', S. Exec. Rep. No. 23, 102d Cong., 2d Sess. 25 (1992), reprinted in 31 I.L.M. 645, 660 (1992).

[25] See 'Second and Third Report of the United States of American to the UN Committee on Human Rights Concerning the International Covenant on Civil and Political Rights' (21 October 2005). The report did mention, without discussion, the Supreme Court's 2002 decision in *Hoffman Plastic Compounds v NLRB*, 535 US 137 (2002), discussed in detail below. A failure to mention *Hoffman Plastic* would have signalled either gross incompetence or deliberate omission.

[26] See Estlund, CL, 'The Ossification of American Labor Law' (2002) 102 *Columbia Law Review* 1527.

The Wagner Act: A Fateful Choice

US law protecting workers' organising and bargaining is not grounded in fundamental rights. It rests on the commerce clause of the Constitution empowering Congress to regulate interstate business. Congress could conceivably have grounded 'Labor's Magna Carta', as the 1935 Wagner Act has often been called, in fundamental rights provisions of the Constitution like the First Amendment's protection of speech and assembly, the Thirteenth Amendment's affirmation of free labour, and the Fourteenth Amendment's guarantee of equal protection. Such a fundamental rights foundation to labour law might have made it easier now to apply international human rights standards to domestic labour law.

But Wagner Act drafters worried that the Supreme Court would declare the new law unconstitutional. They opted for narrow economic grounds to justify passage, citing the commerce clause and Congress's need to address what the Act's findings called 'forms of industrial strife or unrest ... burdening or obstructing commerce ...' The Supreme Court upheld the Wagner Act based on commerce clause arguments that the Act reduced strikes, not that it advanced workers' rights.[27] Professor James Gray Pope has suggested that the Supreme Court was really responding to massive social pressures of workers' organising and strikes, including sit-down strikes, and that 'there is no a priori reason to believe that—had the justices been presented with an argument based on the Thirteenth Amendment instead of the Commerce Clause—they would not have chosen to uphold the Act on that ground'.[28]

The choice of a narrow economic base stressing free flow of commerce, rather than a broader rights-based framework, set US labour law on a path away from human rights as a guiding principle. Ironically, the only genuinely rights-based feature is the 'employer free speech' amendment in the 1947 Taft-Hartley Act, which allows employers to campaign openly and aggressively against workers' self-organisation.[29]

Trade union growth after the Wagner Act masked the implications of choosing economic rather than fundamental rights underpinning to US labour law. But when union membership fell and prevailing values shifted away from industrial democracy and social solidarity toward management control and global competitiveness, free market economic imperatives

---

[27] See *NLRB v Jones & Laughlin Steel Corp* (1937) 301 US 1.

[28] See Gray Pope, J, 'The Thirteenth Amendment Versus the Commerce Clause: Labor and the Shaping of American Constitutional Law, 1921–1957' (2002) 102 *Columbia Law Review* 1.

[29] See National Labor Relations Act s 8(c). It says, 'The expressing of any views, argument, or opinion, or the dissemination thereof, whether in written, printed, graphic, or visual form, shall not constitute or be evidence of an unfair labor practice under any of the provisions of this Act, if such expression contains no threat of reprisal or force or promise of benefit.'

trumped workers' fundamental rights. Strikebreaking with permanent replacements became widespread.[30]

Without a human rights foundation, employers could argue that workers' organising and bargaining were themselves 'burdens' on the free flow of commerce. Thus, in landmark labour law decisions, the US Supreme Court decided that workers have no right to bargain over an employer's decision to close their workplace because employers need 'unencumbered' power to make decisions speedily and in secret,[31] and that workers have no right to receive written information from trade union organisers in a publicly accessible shopping mall parking lot because the employer's private property rights outweigh workers' freedom of association.[32] As Professor Estlund observes:

> Even when it is operating within the bounds of existing precedent, the Board is hemmed in by Congress and particularly by the federal judiciary, both of which have grown unsympathetic to—even unfamiliar with—the collectivist premises of the New Deal labor law regime as it falls increasingly out of sync with the surrounding legal landscape.[33]

Despite the traditional and still prevalent reluctance of American legal actors to rely on international human rights law, an encouraging movement to do just that has begun taking shape. Labour advocates are more often raising human rights concepts and arguments both in legal arenas and in grass roots activism. For their part, human rights activists and organisations are bringing workers' rights in the United States higher on their own agendas, going beyond an earlier, narrower view that labour rights are distinct from human rights. More on the new human rights focus in US labour advocacy follows the discussion below on legal frameworks for workers' rights.

US LEGAL FRAMEWORKS OF LABOUR AND EMPLOYMENT LAW[34]

This brief section sketches US labour and employment legislation and enforcement as they appear 'on the books' as background for section III on

---

[30] See eg, Rosenblum, JD, *Copper Crucible: How the Arizona Miners' Strike of 1983 Recast Labor-Management Relations in America*, 2nd edn (Ithaca, New York, ILR Press of Cornell University Press, 1998).

[31] See *First National Maintenance Corp v NLRB* (1981) 452 US 666.

[32] See *Lechmere, Inc v NLRB* (1992) 502 US 527.

[33] See Estlund, 'The Ossification of American Labor Law' (2002).

[34] Note that US labour law scholars and practitioners distinguish 'labour law' and 'employment law' in their discourse. 'Labour law' is usually taken to mean law governing labour-management relations in the trade union context (what other countries often call 'collective labour law'). 'Employment law' usually means aspects of labour law outside the trade union organising and collective bargaining context—anti-discrimination laws, health and safety laws, minimum wage and overtime standards, etc—effectively 'individual labour law' in that it normally covers all workers as employees, whether or not they are union-represented.

how they work in practice. Some elements of US law on their face violate international standards—the exclusion of farm workers from protection of the right to organise, for example. Most US labour specialists will be familiar with this information, but it is offered here as a primer for foreign analysts.

Constitutional Underpinnings of US Labour and Employment Law

US labour and employment law is deeply rooted in a national legislative framework generated mainly (but not exclusively) by policy choices rather than human rights. The US Constitution makes no specific mention of workers' right to organise, to bargain collectively, or to strike, nor does it address economic and social rights. However, the commerce clause in article I section 8 of the United States Constitution empowers Congress to 'regulate commerce among the several states'. The commerce clause is the constitutional foundation of most labour and employment laws.

The Statutory Framework for Freedom of Association

Based on the commerce clause, twentieth century legislation set the framework for protection of workers' rights to organise, to bargain and to strike. The Wagner Act of 1935 and the Taft-Hartley Act of 1947 are the most important federal labour laws governing private sector labour-management relations. While they are separate statutes, they overlap and refer to one another in a complex legislative structure. For convenience, scholars and practitioners often call this bundle of statutes simply 'the Act'.

The Wagner Act has often been called the American workers' Magna Carta. Section 7 of the Wagner Act grants private sector workers 'the right to self-organisation, to form, join, or assist labor organisations, to bargain collectively through representatives of their own choosing, and to engage in other concerted activities for mutual aid or protection'.

These 'Section 7 rights' are protected by section 8 of the National Labor Relations Act (NLRA), which defines and prohibits unfair labour practices (ULPs) by employers that violate these rights. ULPs include interference with workers' organising activities (threats of workplace closure, for example); discrimination against workers for their organising or bargaining activity (firing leaders of an organising effort, for example), and refusal to bargain in good faith with a trade union chosen by a majority of workers in a defined 'bargaining unit' to represent them ('surface bargaining' with no intention of reaching an agreement, for example).

The Wagner Act was not without its own flaws. Section 2, for example, excluded agricultural workers from its protection, an exclusion that still stands. But the overall thrust of the Act was to promote trade union organising and collective bargaining. Mass organising drives in the 1930s and during World War II brought millions of workers into the US labour movement.[35]

The American business community struck back. In 1947, Congress adopted the Taft-Hartley Act in reaction to workers' organising success after the Wagner Act. Millions of workers joined unions between 1935 and 1947 in mass production industries and other economic sectors around the country. Since 1947, the Taft-Hartley Act has

— excluded independent contractors and supervisors from protection of the right to organising;
— made illegal any form of 'secondary' worker solidarity where workers in different enterprises can support each others' struggles;
— allowed individual states to enact so-called 'right to work' laws barring voluntary agreements between workers and employers to require payment of union dues by all represented employees; and
— established an 'employer free speech' clause permitting managers to openly and aggressively campaign against worker self-organisation in the workplace.

The Role of the NLRB

The NLRB is the government agency that enforces the NLRA, which covers most workers in the private sector labour force. The Board has many attributes of a 'labour court' found in other countries, though it is an independent executive agency, not part of the judiciary. Knowing how the NLRB works is especially needed for understanding how legal entanglements in the Board and the courts often frustrate workers' freedom of association rights.[36]

The NLRB has three independent branches: the five-member board in Washington, DC; a general counsel also based at NLRB headquarters, and a division of administrative law judges. A network of 33 regional offices carries out NLRB tasks around the country.

The five-member NLRB has two main functions. The first is to set up and oversee representation elections in which workers in a bargaining unit choose whether to bargain collectively with their employer. The second is to serve as an appeal panel reviewing written decisions by administrative law judges in cases involving unfair labour practices.

---

[35] See Bernstein, I, *The Turbulent Years: A History of the American Worker, 1933–1941* (Boston, Houghton-Mifflin Co, 1970).

[36] A comprehensive history of the NLRB is found in Gross, JA, *Broken Promise: The Subversion of US Labor Relations Policy, 1947–1994* (Philadelphia, Temple University Press, 1995).

Acting through the directors and staff in 33 regional offices, the NLRB general counsel conducts investigations of unfair labour practice charges filed by workers, unions or employers. Key steps in the investigation include gathering relevant documents, interviewing and taking statements from workers, employers, and others involved in a case, and evaluating the evidence to decide if charges have 'merit'. If the investigation finds merit in the charge that an unfair labour practice occurred, the general counsel issues a 'complaint' specifying the violations in detail and setting a date for hearing—that is, a trial on the evidence—before an administrative law judge.

Administrative law judges are independent of the Board and of the general counsel. A corps of experienced labour law experts, approximately 75 NLRB judges preside over unfair labour practice hearings in much the same way that civil and criminal court judges preside over non-jury trials (there are no juries in NLRB proceedings).

A party unhappy with an administrative law judge's decision can appeal it to the NLRB in Washington. The Board reviews the evidence, the transcript, and the judge's written decision and opts to uphold it, reverse it, or modify it. The NLRB's own written decision can adopt the judge's ruling without comment or offer the Board's separate reasoning based on its reading of the case record.

Remedies

The NLRB cannot penalise an employer for breaking the law. In a very early case, the Supreme Court rebuked the Board for imposing a penalty against an employer committing an unfair labour practice.[37] The NLRB can only order a 'make-whole' remedy restoring the status quo ante as the remedy for unfair labour practices. The standard remedy for an unfair labour practice is to have the employer post a notice at the workplace promising not to repeat the unlawful conduct.

Discriminatory discharge because of trade union activity is the most common unfair labour practice charge filed with the NLRB. Here the standard remedy includes an order to reinstate victimised workers with back pay. However, any interim earnings fired workers received during the period of discharge are subtracted from the employer's back-pay liability.

In practice, many discriminatory discharge cases are settled with a small back-pay payment and workers' agreement not to return to the workplace. At a modest cost and with whatever minor embarrassment comes with posting a notice, the employer is rid of the most active union supporters, and the organising campaign is stymied.

---

[37] *Consolidated Edison v NLRB* (1938) 305 US 197.

In the other most common unfair labour practice cases involving charges that employers refused to bargain in good faith with the workers' chosen representative, the remedy is an order to post a notice acknowledging the conduct and to return to the bargaining table and bargain in good faith. There is no further remedy, so the same cycle can repeat itself indefinitely without an agreement being reached.

Appeal to the Federal Courts

Occasionally, the NLRB makes decisions favourable to workers, finding employer violations and fashioning innovative remedies. For example, in the *First National Maintenance Corp v NLRB* and *Lechmere, Inc v NLRB* cases discussed in the Introduction above,[38] the Board ruled in favour of workers' right to bargain over workplace shutdown decisions, and in favour of union representatives' access to employees near the workplace. But the Supreme Court overruled the Board in these cases.

Doctrinally, courts are supposed to defer to the administrative expertise of the NLRB. In practice, however, appeals courts often make their own judgment on the merits of a case to overrule the NLRB. Professor Julius Getman has described the dynamic thus:

> [T]he courts are notoriously difficult to replace or control. The notion that courts would simultaneously defer and enforce was unrealistic. So long as the courts had the power to refuse enforcement, it was inevitable that they would use this power to require the Board to interpret the NLRA in accordance with their views of desirable policy.

> The NLRA was intended to replace judicial commitment to property rights and instead put the force of law behind the rights of employees to unionize, strike, and bargain collectively. But the common law, like judicial discretion, dies hard ... the judicial attitude towards collective bargaining has increasingly become one of suspicion, hostility, and indifference ...

> The reason for the courts' retreat from collective bargaining is difficult to identify, but it seems to rest on a shift in contemporary judicial thinking about economic issues. The NLRA, when originally passed, had a Keynesian justification. Collective bargaining, it was believed, would increase the wealth of employees, thereby stimulating the economy and reducing the likelihood of depression and recession. Today, courts are more likely to see collective bargaining as an interference with the benevolent working of the market, and, thus, inconsistent with economic efficiency most likely to be achieved by unencumbered management decision making.[39]

---

[38] See *First National Maintenance Corp* (1981) 452 US 666 and *Lechmere* (1992) 502 US 527.

[39] See Getman, J, 'The National Labor Relations Act: What Went Wrong; Can We Fix It?' (2003) 45 *Boston College Law Review* 125.

The Statutory Framework for Anti-Discrimination Legislation

Post-Civil War constitutional amendments eliminating slavery and requiring equal protection of the laws set the foundation for anti-discrimination policies in the United States. Congress immediately enacted a strong laws prohibiting race discrimination, the Civil Rights Acts of 1866 and 1870. But it took a century of civil rights struggle to bring anti-race discrimination principles into an enduring statutory framework. Similarly, organising efforts by women, older Americans, disabled Americans and other social movements achieved legal recognition of their claims for protection against discrimination based on their characteristics.

The Equal Pay Act of 1963 requires equal pay for men and women performing essentially the same job. The law does not require equal pay for work of equal value. This 'comparable worth' principle has been rejected by state and federal courts in cases where workers sought to win comparable worth through application of existing anti-discrimination laws,[40] and Congress has not acted to adopt comparable worth laws.[41]

Title VII of the Civil Rights Act of 1964 prohibits job discrimination based on race, colour, religion, sex, or national origin.

The Age Discrimination in Employment Act (ADEA) of 1967 prohibits discrimination against workers 40 years of age and older.

The Americans with Disabilities Act (ADA) of 1990 prohibits discrimination against persons with disabilities.

The Equal Employment Opportunity Commission

The Equal Employment Opportunity Commission (EEOC) is the federal agency charged with enforcing workplace anti-discrimination laws. The EEOC is similar to the NLRB in some respects. It has a five-member board appointed by the president and an independent general counsel. It receives complaints at one of many regional offices around the country, and investigates them to see whether they are 'meritorious' complaints.

However, the EEOC does not have its own enforcement power beyond investigation and conciliation. If the Commission finds merit to a complaint, it can only file a suit on the complainant's behalf in a federal district court. The court becomes the enforcement authority.

The EEOC files such cases rarely, usually when large numbers of employees are involved in a class action, or when a major legal issue is at stake.

---

[40] See eg, *County of Washington v Gunther* (1981) 452 US 161, 166. The Supreme Court found that female prison guards were victims of discrimination, but did not accept the comparable worth theory.

[41] For information on the pay equity movement, see the website of the National Committee on Pay Equity, available at: www.pay-equity.org/index.html.

More commonly, the Commission grants the complainant a 'right-to-sue' letter, whereupon the aggrieved employee must get his or her own attorney to file the case in federal court. In either case, this means that federal district courts and juries decide discrimination claims, subject to appeals to federal circuit courts and to the US Supreme Court.

The boundaries of workers' characteristics covered by federal anti-discrimination laws are those mentioned above: race, colour, religion, sex, national origin, age and disability. Some states and local governments have gone further, extending anti-discrimination protections against workers based on political beliefs, sexual orientation, genetic makeup, marital status, lawful off-work activities, gender identity and other attributes.[42]

This skeletal outline of anti-discrimination laws cannot begin to suggest the complexity of their application by administration agencies and courts, which has prompted an enormous legal literature in books and law review articles. For example, litigation has given rise to distinctions between 'disparate treatment' and 'disparate impact' discrimination; between 'quid pro quo' sexual harassment and 'hostile environment' sexual harassment; between 'reasonable accommodation' of employee rights and 'undue burden' on the employer's business; among standards of judicial review characterised as 'rational basis,' 'strict scrutiny' and an intermediate 'heightened scrutiny' or 'moderate scrutiny'; among shifting burdens of proof in litigation, and many other issues too detailed for treatment here.[43]

The Statutory Framework for Labour Standards Legislation

As noted above, the 'Commerce Clause' empowering Congress to regulate interstate commerce is the constitutional foundation for federal labour standards legislation in the United States. Contrary to a widely held view outside the United States that the American workplace is home to an unregulated *capitalisme sauvage* with no protection for workers, an extensive regulatory regime governs wages, hours and conditions in the workplace. Federal employment law sets nationwide minimum standards, but state governments are also important actors, since they can adopt state laws above federal minimum standards.

---

[42] See eg, Dishman, N, 'The Expanding Rights of Transsexuals in the Workplace' (2005) 21 *The Labor Law* (American Bar Association) 121.

[43] A useful overview and discussion of these issues can be found in Rutherglen, G, *Major Issues in the Federal Law of Employment Discrimination*, 4th edn (Federal Judicial Center, 2004), available at: www.fjc.gov/library/fjc_catalog.nsf/.

The Fair Labor Standards Act (FLSA) of 1938 provides for a federal minimum wage ($7.25 per hour as of July 2009), overtime pay requirements (150 per cent of pay after 40 hours in a week), and child labour laws (setting age 16 as the basic age for admission to employment, and age 18 for employment in industrial settings). The US Department of Labour and counterpart state agencies are the main enforcement bodies for wage, hour and child labour laws, first through an administrative procedure, then by recourse to federal courts when cases are not resolved administratively.

Almost 20 states and many municipalities have set minimum wage levels higher than the federal minimum wage.[44] In fact, a remarkable 'living wage movement' has taken shape around the United States pressing for state and local action to raise minimum wages, and can point to many successes.[45]

The Occupational Safety and Health Act (OSHA) of 1970 imposes a general duty on all employers to provide a safe and healthy workplace for workers. In addition to this 'general duty clause', specific standards are set for hazardous materials and safety rules. The US Occupational Safety and Health Administration (also called OSHA), an agency of the Labour Department, sets standards and enforces the Act through administrative action, backed up by federal court orders.

The Social Security Act of 1935 created a mandatory, universal retirement pension system that is now the mainstay of retired workers' income, with average benefits about $1500 per month. The Social Security Act also provides monthly income to workers of any age who become permanently disabled, and to the families of workers who die.

The Social Security Act also established the unemployment insurance system providing weekly unemployment benefits. Workers who lose employment 'through no fault of their own' can receive 50 per cent of their regular weekly pay for six months, up to a capped maximum amount (normally the average wage in the state).

Although not created by federal law, workers' compensation statutes in every state provide for medical care and wage replacement benefits (usually two-thirds of regular pay) for workers who become disabled from job-related injuries or illnesses, or benefits to the families of workers who die on the job. Administrative commissions in each state enforce workers' rights to unemployment insurance and to workers' compensation, subject to review by state courts.

---

[44] A list of higher minimum wage states and their minimum wages is available at: www. dol.gov/esa/minwage/america.htm. For information on municipal minimum wage laws, see Sonn, PK, 'Citywide Minimum Wage Laws: A New Policy Tool for Local Governments' (Policy Brief, Brennan Center for Social Justice, May 2006), available at: www.brennancenter. org/resources/books.html#aj.

[45] Information on the living wage movement is available at: www.livingwagecampaign.org/.

US LABOUR AND EMPLOYMENT LAW IN PRACTICE

Freedom of Association

Interference with Organising

The reality of US labour law enforcement falls far short of the Wagner Act's goals. A culture of near-impunity has taken shape in much of US labour law and practice. Any employer intent on resisting workers' self-organisation can drag out legal proceedings for years, fearing little more than an order to post a written notice in the workplace promising not to repeat unlawful conduct. Many employers have come to view remedies like back pay for workers fired because of union activity as a routine cost of doing business, well worth it to get rid of organising leaders and derail workers' organising efforts. Enervating delays and weak remedies invite continued violations.

Discrimination against Union Supporters

Firing or otherwise discriminating against a worker for trying to form a union is illegal but commonplace in the United States. In the 1950s, workers who suffered reprisals for exercising the right to freedom of association numbered in the hundreds each year. In the 1960s, the number climbed into the thousands, reaching slightly over 6,000 in 1969. By the 1990s and continuing today, more than 20,000 workers each year were victims of discrimination for union activity.[46]

An employer determined to get rid of a union activist knows that all that awaits, after years of litigation if the employer persists in appeals, is a reinstatement order the worker is likely to decline and a modest back-pay award. For many employers, it is a small price to pay to destroy a workers' organising effort by firing its leaders.

Employers can force workers to attend captive-audience meetings in work time. They can fire workers for not attending the meetings. They can impose a 'no questions or comments' rule at captive-audience meetings, and discipline any worker who speaks up.

Most often, these meetings include exhortations by top managers that are carefully scripted to fall within the wide latitude afforded employers under US law to deter workers from choosing union representation.

Under US law, employers and anti-union consultants they routinely hire to oppose workers' organising have refined methods of legally 'predicting'—as distinct from unlawfully threatening—workplace closures, firings, wage and benefit cuts, and other dire consequences if workers form

---

[46] See Annual Report of the National Labor Relations Board for relevant years, available at: www.nlrb.gov.

and join a trade union. A 'prediction' that the workplace will be closed if employees vote for union representation is legal if the prediction is carefully phrased and based on objective facts rather than on the employer's subjective bias.[47]

This fine distinction in the law is not always apparent to workers or, indeed, to anyone seeking common-sense guidance on what is allowed or prohibited. Unfortunately for workers' rights, federal courts have tended to give wide leeway to employers to 'predict' awful things if workers vote for a union.

Delays

Delays in the US labour law system arise first in the election procedure. NLRB elections take place at least several weeks after workers file a petition seeking an election. In many cases, the election can be held up for months by employers who challenge the composition of the 'appropriate bargaining unit'.

An employer can also file objections to an election after it takes place, arguing that the union used unfair tactics. It takes several months to resolve these objections. However, even when the NLRB rules in workers' favour and orders the company to bargain with the union, the employer can ignore the Board's order. This forces the NLRB to launch a new case on the refusal to bargain, often requiring years more to resolve in the courts. In many cases, workers who voted in favour of union representation years earlier must wait for bargaining to begin while employees' appeals are tied up in court.

Long delays also occur in unfair labour practice cases. Most cases involve alleged discrimination against union supporters or refusals to bargain in good faith. Several months pass before the cases are heard by an administrative law judge. Then several more months go by while the judge ponders a decision. The judge's decision can then be appealed to the NLRB, where often two or three years go by before a decision is issued. The NLRB's decision can then be appealed to the federal courts, where again up to three years pass before a final decision is rendered. Thus, many fired workers who win reinstatement orders from administrative judges and the NLRB still wait many years for clogged courts to rule on employers' appeals.

Surface Bargaining

Even after workers form a union and bargaining begins, employers can continue to thwart workers' choice by bargaining in bad faith—going through the motions of meeting with the workers and making proposals

---

[47] The distinction between threats and predictions was set out by the Supreme Court in *NLRB v Gissel Packing Co* (1969) 395 US 575.

and counterproposals without any intention of reaching an agreement. This tactic is called 'surface bargaining'. The problem is especially acute in newly organised workplaces where the employer has fiercely resisted workers' self-organisation and resents their success.[48]

Non-standard Workers

Many employers can use subcontracting arrangements and temporary employment agencies to avoid any obligation to recognise workers' rights of organisation and collective bargaining. This problem afflicts workers in the apparel manufacturing industry, in janitorial services, in high-technology computer services, and other sectors characterised by layers of subcontracting arrangements. Prime contractors often simply cancel the contracts of subcontractors whose employees form and join unions. The result is widespread denial of workers' freedom of association.[49]

Striker Replacements

Under US labour law, employers can hire new employees to permanently replace workers who exercise the right to strike. This doctrine runs counter to international standards recognising the right to strike as an essential element of freedom of association. Considering the US striker replacement rule, the ILO's Committee on Freedom of Association determined that the right to strike 'is not really guaranteed when a worker who exercises it legally runs the risk of seeing his or her job taken up permanently by another worker, just as legally' and that permanent replacement 'entails a risk of derogation from the right to strike which may affect the free exercise of trade union rights'.[50]

Employment Law Failures

Just as in the case of laws meant to protect freedom of association, the existence of a wide range of employment laws is no guarantee of their

---

[48] For discussion, see Dannin, E, 'From Dictator Game to Ultimatum Game ... and Back Again: The Judicial Impasse Amendments' (2004) 6 *University of Pennsylvania Journal of Labor & Employment Law* 241.

[49] For a discussion of this problem in the garment sector, see Lung, S, 'Exploiting the Joint Employer Doctrine: Providing a Break for Sweatshop Garment Workers' (2003) 34 *Loyola University Chicago Law Journal* 291.

[50] See International Labour Organisation (ILO), Committee on Freedom of Association: Complaint against the Government of the United States presented by the American Federation of Labor and Congress of Industrial Organizations (AFL-CIO) para 92, Report No 278, Case No 1543 (1991).

substantive protection or their effective enforcement.[51] An increasingly conservative federal judiciary has issued decisions vitiating many protections against discrimination under Title VII, ADEA, ADA and other statutes. Contrary to international standards, US law has never recognised the principle of equal pay for work of equal value. The law requires equal pay only for equal work, meaning substantially the same job.[52]

The federal minimum wage was frozen at $5.15 per hour for 10 years until Congress acted to raise it to $7.25 in 2009. Based on full-time work, the federal minimum wage yields a monthly income of $1,258 and an annual income of $15,080. This is substantially below the federal poverty level of $21,200 for a family of four. About 15 million workers labour at the minimum wage or slightly above the minimum wage, and about 30 million employees work for less than $10 per hour, still below the official poverty level.[53]

Minimum wage law violations are widespread. A leading non-governmental organisation that focuses on employment standards notes,

> growing numbers of employers routinely violate our nation's core workplace standards by not paying the minimum wage or overtime, calling workers 'independent contractors' to deny them basic protections … At the same time, workers' ability to respond is often constrained—by outdated government enforcement systems, fear of retaliation for speaking up, and lack of immigration status.[54]

A 2009 report by the US Government Accountability Office (GAO), a non-partisan congressional auditing authority, confirmed this analysis. The report found widespread enforcement failures by the Department of Labour's Wage and Hour Division, which is supposed to investigate and remedy violations of minimum wage, overtime and child labour standards.[55] Most analysts converge on estimates that between two and three million workers in the United States are actually paid less than the legal minimum wage, and more than three million are misclassified by their employers as independent contractors when they are really employees, allowing employers to avoid minimum wage and overtime pay requirements.[56]

---

[51] For a comprehensive analysis and critique of failures in effective enforcement of employment law, see Bernhardt, A, Boushey, H, Dresser, L and Tilly, C, *The Gloves-Off Economy: Workplace Standards at the Bottom of America's Labor Market* (Cornell University Press, 2008).

[52] See Mooney Cotter, A, *Gender Injustice: An International Comparative Analysis of Equality in Employment* (Ashgate Press, 2004).

[53] See 'Minimum Wage: Facts at a Glance' (Issue Brief, *Economic Policy Institute*, August 2008), available at www.epi.org/publications/category/wages_and_living_standards/P20/.

[54] See National Employment Law Project, 'Enforcement of Workplace Standards' at www.nelp.org/index.php/site/issues/category/enforcement_of_workplace_standards.

[55] Greenhouse, S, 'Labor agency is failing workers, report says' *New York Times* (24 March 2009) A16.

[56] See Bobo, K, *Wage Theft in America: Why Millions of Working Americans Are Not Getting Paid—and What We Can Do About It* (New York, New Press, 2009).

The universal term used by workers in the United States for overtime pay is 'time- and-a-half'. Time-and-a-half after 40 hours is the only substantive overtime requirement under US labour law. The United States is practically unique in the world in not having any legislated limits on overtime work (except in specialised occupations like airline pilots and long-distance truck drivers). Most other countries limit the amount of overtime that can be demanded of an employee without consent, but US employers are under no such constraints. Employers can terminate workers who refuse overtime in any amount—incidental, reasonable, excessive or intolerable. Only workers with a collective bargaining agreement can limit or condition overtime demands.[57]

Managers, supervisors, professionals, and other 'administrative' employees are exempt from overtime pay requirements, as are independent contractors.[58] In practice, many employers improperly place employees in these categories to extract unpaid labour from them.[59] Many employers, most notoriously Wal-Mart, the giant retail chain, pressure their 'non-exempt' employees (ie hourly employees who are clearly entitled to overtime pay) to work during unpaid lunch and rest breaks.[60] These abuses sometimes give rise to lawsuits for back overtime pay,[61] but many employers get away with such violations because workers are unaware of their rights or afraid of reprisals if they file wage claims with government authorities.

While it is not comparable to the situation in many developing countries, child labour is still a problem in some employment sectors in the United States. It is most acute in agriculture, especially where migrant workers bring their children into the fields to help with piecework production.[62] But the problem is also widespread in retail stores and fast food restaurants, where 14 and 15-year-old employees (who are legally permitted to work in

[57] For a comprehensive review of overtime regulation in the United States, see Linder, M, *Moments Are the Elements of Profit: Overtime and the Deregulation of Working Hours under the Fair Labor Standards Act* (Iowa City, Iowa, Fanpihua Press, 2000).

[58] See Camille Hebert, L, 'The Fair Labor Standards Act: Updating the "White-Collar" Employee Exemptions to the Fair Labor Standards Act' (2003) 7 *Employee Rights and Employment Policy Journal* 51.

[59] For comprehensive discussion and analysis, see Goldstein, B, Linder, M, Norton, LE, and Ruckelshaus, CK, 'Enforcing Fair Labor Standards in the Modern American Sweatshop: Rediscovering the Statutory Definition of Employment' (1999) 46 *UCLA Law Review* 983.

[60] See eg, Chang, A., 'Wal-Mart settles suits by workers: Dozens of class actions had accused the firm of violating rules on wages and breaks' Los Angeles Times (24 December 2008) C1; From Tribune News Services, "Wal-Mart settles suits in work-time dispute: Retail giant agrees to pay employees up to $640 million" Chicago Tribune (24 December 2008) C29.

[61] See eg, Waldmeir, P, 'US Workers Lose Faith in the Dogma that Overwork is Good for the Soul; Employers are Facing a Growing Number of Lawsuits over Pay and Hours' *Financial Times* (9 June 2006) 6.

[62] See the Human Rights Watch report, 'Fingers to the Bone: United States Failure to Protect Child Farmworkers' (1999), available at: www.hrw.org/reports/2000/frmwrkr/.

such establishments) often work past the maximum daily or weekly hours limit.[63]

Because of eligibility requirements for a sustained 'attachment' to the labour force, fewer than half of unemployed workers actually receive weekly unemployment insurance benefits.[64] Part-time, temporary, and other 'non-standard' workers rarely qualify for benefits.[65]

Many workers also fail to receive workers' compensation benefits for job-related injuries and illnesses because they have to prove the job-relatedness of their condition. This is difficult in cases where an injury is not obvious, as in back injuries and repetitive motion injuries, and in illnesses with long latency periods before symptoms occur. In most of these cases, employers challenge workers' claims, arguing that their conditions are not work-related. Many workers simply give up their claims rather than go through a long legal battle that might take years to resolve.[66]

A Special Note on Immigrant Workers

Millions of immigrant workers have entered the US labour force in recent years. In the 2000 census, about 12 per cent of the US population were foreign-born, more than 32 million people, compared with eight per cent of the population in 1990. More than half were from Latin America, and of these more than two-thirds came from Mexico and Central America.

Estimates put the number of undocumented workers in the United States at more than eight million, possibly as many as 12 million.[67] Nearly 60 per cent of them are migrant workers from Mexico. Many have been in the country for years working long hours for low pay in demanding, dirty and dangerous jobs.[68]

Many undocumented workers shrink from exercising rights of association or from seeking legal redress when their workplace rights are violated for fear of having their legal status discovered and being deported. Their uncertainty has been exacerbated in the aftermath of the 11 September 2001

[63] See eg, Greenhouse, S, 'Wal-Mart Agrees to Pay Fine in Child Labor Cases' *New York Times* (12 February 12 2005) A1.

[64] The Upjohn Institute maintains an ongoing research project on unemployment insurance in the United States, with information available at www.upjohninst.org/uicenter.html#wp.

[65] See National Employment Law Committee, 'Part-Time Workers and Unemployment Insurance' (Fact Sheet, March 2004), available at: www.nelp.org/ui/initiatives/part_time/parttimeui0304.cfm.

[66] For a comprehensive history and analysis, see Spieler, EA, 'Perpetuating Risk? Workers' Compensation and the Persistence of Occupational Injuries' (1994) 31 *Houston Law Review* 119.

[67] See Passel, JS, 'Size and Characteristics of the Unauthorised Migrant Population in the US: Estimates Based on the March 2005 Current Population Survey' (Pew Hispanic Center, 7 March 2006), available at: http://pewhispanic.org/reports/report.php?ReportID=61.

[68] See eg, Human Rights Watch, 'Blood, Sweat, and Fear: Workers' Rights in US Meat and Poultry Plants' (December 2004), available at: www.hrw.org/reports/2005/usa0105/.

events.[69] Fully aware of workers' fear and sure that they will not complain to labour law authorities or testify to back up a claim, employers have little incentive against violating their rights—sometimes with fatal consequences.[70]

A NEW OPENING TO INTERNATIONAL HUMAN RIGHTS STANDARDS

Freedom of Association

Confronted with the challenges outlined above, workers' rights supporters in the United States are starting to consider international human rights standards as a new source of protection for workers under US law. So far, this new turn in labour advocacy in the United States aims mainly at freedom of association standards. Advocates argue that the United States is obligated under international human rights law to respect workers' freedom of association in its labour laws and labour law enforcement, and to protect workers' freedom of association against violations by employers.

The United States has acknowledged its international responsibility to honour workers' freedom of association by signing the Universal Declaration of Human Rights and by ratifying important human rights instruments, in particular the ICCPR.[71] Although it has not ratified ILO Conventions Nos 87 and 98 on freedom of association, the United States acknowledges its responsibility, by virtue of ILO membership, to comply with those Conventions. These commitments are underscored by US support for the ILO's 1998 Declaration on Fundamental Principles and Rights at Work.[72]

US Commitments on Labour Rights and Trade

US trade laws and labour rights clauses in international trade agreements, promoted and signed by the United States, articulate workers' rights.

[69] See Garcia, RJ, 'Labor's Fragile Freedom of Association Post-9/11' (2006) 8 *University of Pennsylvania Journal of Labor & Employment Law* 283.

[70] See eg, Franklin, S, 'Illinois Study Finds Deaths, Serious Injuries Increase Even as Overall Workplace Fatalities Decline' *Chicago Tribune* (6 November 2005) C1.

[71] See Universal Declaration of Human Rights, General Assembly (GA) Res 217A (III) (1948) UN Doc A/810) 71; International Covenant on Civil and Political Rights, GA Res 2200A (XXI) (1966) UN GAOR Supp (No 16) 52, UN Doc A/6316.

[72] See ILO Convention No 87: Freedom of Association and Protection of the Right to Organise (1948); Convention No 98: Right to Organize and Collective Bargaining (1949). In 1975, the ILO's Committee on Freedom of Association determined that member countries are 'bound to respect a certain number of general rules which have been established for the common good ... among these principles, freedom of association has become *a customary rule above the Conventions*'. See Fact Finding and Conciliation Commission on Chile (Geneva, ILO, 1975) para 466.

The United States has affirmed obligations to honour workers' freedom of association in its preferential trade programmes and in laws governing US involvement in the World Bank, the International Monetary Fund, and other multilateral bodies. The same labour clauses also address certain economic and social rights, requiring prohibitions on child labour and 'acceptable conditions' on wages, hours, and workplace health and safety.[73]

US trade agreements with Jordan, Chile, Singapore, Morocco, Australia, and Central American nations incorporate ILO core labour standards declaration with a 'strive to ensure' obligation stating:[74]

> The Parties reaffirm their obligations as members of the International Labor Organisation ('ILO') and their commitments under the ILO Declaration on Fundamental Principles and Rights at Work and its Follow-up. The Parties shall strive to ensure that such labor principles and the internationally recognized labor rights ... are recognized and protected by domestic law.

These agreements further require parties, including the United States, to effectively enforce their national laws on 'internationally recognised worker rights', defined as:[75]

— the right of association;
— the right to organise and bargain collectively;
— prohibitions on forced labour and child labour; and
— acceptable conditions of work with respect to minimum wages, hours of work, and occupational safety and health.

'Internationally recognised' is in quotes because the US statutory definition of these rights is an idiosyncratic formulation resulting from legislative compromises, not grounded in United Nations (UN) or ILO instruments. Acting on its own, the US congress calls these five standards 'internationally recognised worker rights' in US trade laws and trade agreements.[76]

[73] See eg, the labour rights amendment in the US Generalised System of Preferences (GSP), 19 USC.A. § 2461 *et.seq*. The GSP programme permits a developing country to export goods to the United States on a preferential, duty-free basis as long as they meet the conditions for eligibility in the programme.

[74] These agreements and their labour chapters are all available on the website of the US Trade Representative at www.ustr.gov. Among them, only the US-Jordan Free Trade Agreement makes labour rights guarantees binding and enforceable through trade measures. The others lack an effective enforcement mechanism.

[75] Note that nondiscrimination is *not* included in the US statutory definition of 'IRWR'. For extended discussion, see Compa, L and Vogt, JS, 'Labor Rights in the Generalized System of Preferences: A 20-Year Review' (2001) 22 *Comparative Labor Law and Policy Journal* 199.

[76] For a stinging critique on this point, see Alston, P, 'Labor Rights Provisions in US Trade Law: Aggressive Unilateralism?' in L Compa and SF Diamond (eds), *Human Rights, Labor Rights, and International Trade* (University of Pennsylvania Press, 2001).

NAFTA and the NAALC

The most extensive subject matter treatment of workers' rights in trade agreements is contained in the North American Agreement on Labor Cooperation (NAALC), the supplemental labour accord to the North American Free Trade Agreement (NAFTA). Going beyond the ILO's core standards formulation, the NAALC sets forth 11 'Labour Principles' that the three signatory countries commit themselves to promote. The NAALC Labour Principles include:[77]

— freedom of association and the right to organise;
— the right to bargain collectively;
— the right to strike;
— prohibition of forced labour;
— prohibition of child labour;
— equal pay for men and women;
— non-discrimination;
— minimum wage and hour standards;
— occupational safety and health;
— workers' compensation; and
— migrant worker protection.

The NAALC signers pledged to effectively enforce their national labour laws in these subject areas, and adopted six 'Obligations' for effective labour law enforcement to fulfill the principles. These obligations include:[78]

— a general duty to provide high labour standards;
— effective enforcement of labour laws;
— access to administrative and judicial forums for workers whose rights are violated;
— due process, transparency, speed, and effective remedies in labour law proceedings;
— public availability of labour laws and regulations, and opportunity for 'interested persons' to comment on proposed changes; and
— promoting public awareness of labour law and workers' rights.

In sum, the United States has acknowledged its international responsibility to honour workers' rights by signing and ratifying human rights instruments, by accepting obligations under ILO standards in connection with instruments it has not ratified, and by committing itself in trade agreements with labour protections to effectively enforce US laws protecting workers' rights.

---

[77] North American Agreement on Labor Cooperation (NAALC) Annex 1, Labor Principles.
[78] Ibid art 2, Obligations.

International Human Rights Standards' Effect on US Law

There is still reason for hope. International human rights law is moving slowly into the ken of lawyers, legislators, and judges in the United States. The most significant positive development outside the labour context was the Supreme Court's decision in 2005 that the execution of minors (ie who committed capital crimes when they were below age 18) is unconstitutional under the 'cruel and unusual punishments' clause of the Eighth Amendment. The Court said:

> Our determination that the death penalty is disproportionate punishment for offenders under 18 finds confirmation in the stark reality that the United States is the only country in the world that continues to give official sanction to the juvenile death penalty. This reality does not become controlling, for the task of interpreting the Eighth Amendment remains our responsibility. Yet ... It is proper that we acknowledge the overwhelming weight of international opinion against the juvenile death penalty ... The opinion of the world community, while not controlling our outcome, does provide respected and significant confirmation for our own conclusions ....
>
> It does not lessen our fidelity to the Constitution or our pride in its origins to acknowledge that the express affirmation of certain fundamental rights by other nations and peoples simply underscores the centrality of those same rights within our own heritage of freedom.[79]

This element of the Court's opinion provoked a furious response by right-wing judges Antonin Scalia and Clarence Thomas. Thomas said the majority used international law sources to 'impose foreign moods, fads, or fashions on Americans'. Like-minded right-wing members of Congress have introduced legislation to prohibit federal courts from using any international law sources in considering US cases.[80]

In the labour context, international standards have some effect in US court cases filed on behalf of workers in countries outside the United States. Human rights strictures against forced labour and ILO findings on forced labour in Burma were central elements of a lawsuit brought against the California-based Unocal Corporation in federal court. The case ultimately was settled before going to trial with millions of dollars in recompense to victims of forced labour violations.[81]

In a case involving killings of union leaders at an American mining company's operations in Colombia, Professor Virginia Leary, a long-time

---

[79] See *Roper v Simmons* (2005) 543 US 551.
[80] See Cleveland, S, 'Is There Room for the World in Our Courts?' *The Washington Post* (20 March 2005) B4.
[81] See Lifsher, M, 'Unocal Settles Human Rights Lawsuit Over Alleged Abuses at Myanmar Pipeline; A Deal Ends a Landmark Case Brought by Villagers who said Soldiers Committed Atrocities,' *Los Angeles Times* (22 March 2005) C1.

advisor to the ILO, gave expert testimony on workers' freedom of association under international human rights standards. Her testimony helped convince a federal judge to move the case toward trial. The judge denied the US-based coal company's motion to dismiss the case, saying:[82]

> Although this court recognizes that the United States has not ratified ILO Conventions 87 and 98, the ratification of these conventions is not necessary to make the rights to associate and organize norms of customary international law. As stated above, norms of international law are established by general state practice and the understanding that the practice is required by law ....
>
> This court is cognizant that no federal court has specifically found that the rights to associate and organize are norms of international law for purposes of formulating a cause of action under the ATCA. However, this court must evaluate the status of international law at the time this lawsuit was brought under the ATCA. After analyzing 'international conventions, international customs, treatises, and judicial decisions rendered in this and other countries' to ascertain whether the rights to associate and organize are part of customary international law, this court finds, at this preliminary stage in the proceedings, that the rights to associate and organize are generally recognized as principles of international law sufficient to defeat defendants' motion to dismiss.

In a foreign lawsuit with potentially dramatic effect in the United States, US labour law faced examination under ILO standards in a Norwegian court. In 2002, the Norwegian oil workers union (NOPEF) sought judicial permission under Norwegian law to boycott the North Sea operations of Trico Corp, a Louisiana company that allegedly violated American workers' rights in an organising campaign in the Gulf Coast region. Trico's North Sea arm was the company's most profitable venture, and a boycott could have devastating economic effects.

A key issue in the case was whether US labour law and practice conform to ILO norms. NOPEF and Trico's Norwegian counsel each called expert witnesses from the United States to testify whether US law and practice violate ILO core standards on freedom of association. The Norwegian court's finding that US law failed to meet international standards would let the NOPEF boycott proceed.

Just before the US experts' testimony, NOPEF settled the case with Trico's promise to respect workers' organising rights in Louisiana.[83] The boycott trigger was deactivated. Still, the Trico case signalled a remarkable impact

---

[82] See *Rodriguez et al v Drummond Co.* (2003) 256 F. Supp. 1250. At trial, the jury found in favour of the defendant corporation, convinced by the company's arguments that it was not complicit in the murders. See Whitmire, K, 'Alabama Company Is Exonerated in Murders at Colombian Mine' *New York Times* (27 July 2007) C1. However, the jury's verdict does not vitiate the judge's finding that freedom of association is a paramount principle of international law.

[83] See Amber, M, 'US Company Agrees in Norwegian Court To Inform Employees of Organizing Rights' *BNA Daily Labor Report* (12 November 2002).

of ILO core standards within the United States. Similar cases could arise in the future as trade unions increase their cross-border solidarity work.[84]

A Changing Climate

The challenge now is to move the application of human rights standards from workers abroad whose rights are violated, to workers in the United States. We are still in an early stage of this process, where international human rights law appears to be having a nascent 'climate changing' affect on American labour law, bringing it closer to a human rights framework.

One signal came in the United States' 1999 report to the ILO under the 1998 Declaration's follow-up procedure. The United States, for the first time, acknowledged serious problems with US labour law and practice on workers' organising and bargaining rights under ILO standards. That was a move by the Clinton administration; the Bush administration later reverted to a standard formulation that US law and practice are 'generally in compliance' with ILO standards.

US labour law scholars are incorporating human rights norms and ILO core standards in their analyses, not just domestic discourse based on the commerce clause and other economic considerations. Professor James A Gross, for example, has developed a creative proposal to bring international human rights jurisprudence into US labour arbitration practice.[85] Professor Philip Harvey argues compellingly for application of the UN's economic, social and cultural rights covenant to the right to employment in the United States.[86] Social scientists are also adopting a human rights approach to labour issues.[87]

Human rights advocates give new prominence to international labour standards in analysing workers' rights in the United States. Human Rights Watch published two major studies in 2000 on US workers' freedom of association and on child labour in American agriculture. In 2005, the group followed with a major report on workers' rights violations in the US meat and poultry industry,[88] and in 2007 with another book-length report

---

[84] For extensive analysis of cross-border solidarity efforts, see Atleson, J, 'The Voyage of the Neptune Jade: The Perils and Promises of Transnational Labor Solidarity' (2004) 52 *Buffalo Law Review* 85.

[85] See Gross, JA, 'Incorporating Human Rights Principles into US Labor Arbitration: A Proposal for Fundamental Change' (2004) 8 *Employment Rights & Policy Journal* 1.

[86] See Harvey, P, 'Human Rights and Economic Policy Discourse: Taking Economic and Social Rights Seriously' (2002) 33 *Columbia Human Rights Law Review* 363.

[87] See eg, Swidorski, C, 'From the Wagner Act to the Human Rights Watch Report: Labor and Freedom of Expression and Association 1935–2000' (March 2003) 25 *New Political Science* 55.

[88] See Human Rights Watch, 'Unfair Advantage: Workers' Freedom of Association in the United States under International Human Rights Standards; Fingers to the Bone:

on violations of workers' organising rights by Wal-Mart.[89] A new student movement that began against sweatshops in overseas factories has adopted a human rights and labour rights approach to problems of workers in their own campuses and communities, often citing international labour rights norms for guidance.[90]

The American Federation of Labor and Congress of Industrial Organizations (AFL-CIO) has launched a broad-based 'Voice@ Work' campaign stressing international human rights in support of workers' organising campaigns around the country. Every 10 December, International Human Rights Day, Voice@ Work mobilises mass demonstrations around the county.[91] This movement has taken legislative shape in the proposed Employee Free Choice Act (EFCA), which has gained support from many members of Congress. Using Human Rights Watch's reports in its justification, the EFCA would incorporate international labour rights principles into US law on union organising.[92]

Some unions have begun issuing human rights reports on specific organising campaigns. They find that charging employers with violations of international human rights, not just violations of the NLRA, gives more force to their claims for support in the court of public opinion. The Teamsters union, for example, has launched a human rights campaign against Maersk-Sealand, the giant international shipping company, for violating rights of association among truck drivers who carry cargo containers from ports to inland distribution centres. The company has fired workers who protest low pay and dangerous conditions, and threatened retaliation against others if they continue an organising effort.[93]

Similar violations by a large Catholic hospital chain in Chicago prompted another report, explaining how the employer's actions violated both international human rights standards and principles of Catholic social

United States Failure to Protect Child Farmworkers; Blood, Sweat, and Fear: Workers' Rights in the US Meat and Poultry Industry'; all available at the Human Rights Watch website at www.hrw.org.

[89] See Human Rights Watch, 'Discounting Rights: Wal-Mart's Violations of US Workers' Right to Freedom of Association' at www.hrw.org.

[90] See eg, Bell, M, 'UM's Low-wage Workers to Get Pay Raise, Benefits' *Orlando Sentinel* (18 March 2006) B5; see also information on Harvard students' 'living wage' campaign for the university's low-wage employees available at: www.hcs.harvard.edu/~pslm/livingwage/portal.html.

[91] See eg, Greenhouse, S, 'Labor to Press for Workers' Right to Join Unions' *The New York Times* (9 December 2005) A18; Grant, A, 'Labor Supporters Take to Streets; Week of Demonstrations Meant to Rev Up US Union Movement' *Cleveland Plain Dealer* (10 December 2005) C2; Idell Hamilton, T, 'Labor Union Advocates Rally for Better Workers' Rights' *San Antonio Express-News* (11 December 2005) 5B.

[92] More information is available at: www.aflcio.org/joinaunion/voiceatwork/efca/.

[93] See 'Workers' Rights Violations at Maersk: Actions by US divisions of Maersk-Sealand in Light of International Human Rights and Labor Rights Standards' (3 September 2004), available at: www.teamster.org/divisions/port/pdfs.

doctrine.[94] The Teamsters union and the Service Employees International Union collaborated to present a human rights report at the May 2006 annual general meeting of First Group Plc, a multinational British firm. The report detailed workers rights violations by its US subsidiary, First Student, Inc, a school bus transportation company with a record of aggressive interference with workers' organising efforts.[95]

In 2004, trade unions and allied labour support groups created a new non-governmental organisation (NGO), 'American Rights at Work' (ARAW), with an ambitious programme to make human rights the centrepiece of a new civil society movement for workers' rights.[96] Less directly connected to organised labour, but with labour rights an important part of its agenda, the National Economic and Social Rights Initiative (NESRI) took shape the same year with the express mission of incorporating principles of the UN Covenant on Economic, Social and Cultural rights into US law and practice.[97] Many scholars and organisations are turning to international human rights arguments in defence of immigrant workers in the United States.[98]

Using the ILO

The American labour movement's new interest in international human rights law is also reflected in its increasing use of ILO complaints. While recognising that the ILO Committee on Freedom of Association (CFA) cannot 'enforce' its decisions against national labour law authorities and courts, US unions are turning to the Committee for its authoritative voice and moral standing in the international community. Committee decisions critical of US violations of workers' organising and bargaining rights can bolster movements for legislative reform to reverse anti-labour decisions by the NLRB and the courts.

This part reviews trade unionists' use of international human rights complaint mechanisms to put domestic labour disputes under international scrutiny. The American labour movement's new interest in international human rights law is reflected in its increasing use of ILO complaints and

---

[94] See 'Freedom of Association and Workers' Rights Violations at Resurrection Health Care: Report and Analysis under International Human Rights and Labor Rights Standards' (August 2004), available from AFSCME Council 31 at: www.afscme31.org.

[95] See 'Freedom of Association and Workers' Rights Violations at First Student, Inc' (May 2006).

[96] Available from the American Rights at Work (ARAW) website at:www.araw.org for detailed information on the group's programme and activities.

[97] See the National Economic and Social Rights Initiative (NESRI) website at: www.nesri.org.

[98] See eg, Alexander, LD, 'Fashioning a New Approach: The Role of International Human Rights Law in Enforcing Rights of Women Garment Workers in Los Angeles' (2003) 10 *Georgetown Journal of Poverty Law and Policy* 81.

international human rights mechanisms. Advocates understand that these mechanisms do not provide enforceable orders. The ILO does not have international labour marshals to compel compliance with decisions of the CFA, for example. But Committee decisions provide authoritative vindication of their claims to workers' rights as human rights.

Hoffman Plastic

In 2002, the AFL-CIO filed a complaint to the ILO CFA, challenging the Supreme Court's *Hoffman Plastic Compounds, Inc v NLRB* decision.[99] In *Hoffman*, the Supreme Court had held, in a 5-4 decision, that an undocumented worker, because of his immigration status, was not entitled to back pay for lost wages after he was illegally fired for union organising. The five-justice majority said that enforcing immigration law takes precedence over enforcing labour law.[100]

The union federations' ILO complaint argued that eliminating the back pay remedy for undocumented workers annuls protection of workers' right to organise, contrary to the requirement in Convention No 87 to provide adequate protection against acts of anti-union discrimination.[101]

The AFL-CIO's complaint was successful: in November 2003, the CFA announced that the *Hoffman* doctrine violates international legal obligations to protect workers' organising rights. The Committee concluded that 'the remedial measures left to the NLRB in cases of illegal dismissals of undocumented workers are inadequate to ensure effective protection against acts of anti-union discrimination'.[102]

The ILO Committee recommended congressional action to bring US law 'into conformity with freedom of association principles, in full consultation with the social partners concerned, with the aim of ensuring effective protection for all workers against acts of anti-union discrimination in the wake of the Hoffman decision'.[103]

Targeting the United Kingdom—on behalf of US workers

A similar reliance on international mechanisms is evident in a decision by the International Federation of Professional Technical Employees (IPFTE),

---

[99] *Hoffman Plastic Compounds* 535 US 137 (2002).

[100] The four dissenting justices said there was not such a conflict and that a 'backpay order will *not* interfere with the implementation of immigration policy. Rather, it reasonably helps to deter unlawful activity that *both* labor laws *and* immigration laws seek to prevent.'

[101] See 'Complaint presented by the AFL-CIO to the ILO Freedom of Association Committee' (AFL-CIO, October 2002).

[102] See *Complaint against the United States (Case No 2227)* (2003) Report of the Committee on Freedom of Association No 332.

[103] Ibid.

together with the AFL-CIO and the global union federation Public Services International (PSI), to file a CFA complaint on behalf of locally-engaged staff at the British Embassy in Washington, DC after embassy officials refused to bargain with employees' choice of IFPTE as their union representative.[104] The embassy said that it need not recognise the employees' choice because locally hired workers were 'engaged in the administration of the state', taking them outside protection of ILO standards based on earlier Committee decisions. IFPTE argued that locally engaged staff have the right to form and join a trade union for the defence of their interests under application of ILO principles and standards reflected in Conventions Nos 87 and 98, as well as in the Declaration on Fundamental Principles and Rights at Work.

Once again, the unions' reliance on CFA paid off: in March 2007, the CFA issued an opinion fully supporting the unions' position. The Committee said that 'all public service workers other than those engaged in the administration of the State should enjoy collective bargaining rights' and that 'the Embassy should negotiate with the [union] in respect of the terms and conditions of employment of the locally engaged staff'.[105] The UK Government accepted the ruling and entered into bargaining with the employees' chosen union.[106]

Supervisory Exclusion Case

In October 2006, the AFL-CIO filed another CFA complaint, this time against the NLRB's decision in the so-called *Oakwood Trilogy*. In *Oakwood*, the NLRB announced an expanded interpretation of the definition of 'supervisor' under the NLRA.[107] Under the new ruling, employers can classify as 'supervisors' employees with incidental oversight over co-workers, even when such oversight is far short of genuine managerial or supervisory authority.

In its complaint to the ILO, the AFL-CIO relied on the ILO Conventions, arguing that the NRLB's decision on the definition of supervisors contravened No 87's affirmation that 'Workers and employers, without distinction

---

[104] See 'Complaint against the Government of the United Kingdom presented by the Association of United States Engaged Staff (AUSES), the International Federation of Professional and Technical Employees (IFPTE), the American Federation of Labor and Congress of Industrial Organizations (AFL-CIO) and Public Services International (PSI)' (23 June 2005).

[105] See *Complaint against the United Kingdom (Case No 2437)* (March 2007) Report of the Committee on Freedom of Association No 344, *Report in which the Committee requests to be kept informed of developments.*

[106] Author email exchange with Julia Akins Clark, General Counsel, International Federation of Professional and Technical Engineers (18 March 2008).

[107] See *Oakwood Healthcare, Inc* 348 NLRB No. 37; *Croft Metal, Inc*, 348 NLRB No. 38; *Golden Crest Healthcare Center* 348 NLRB No. 39 (October 2, 2006), called the *Oakwood* trilogy.

whatsoever, shall have the right to establish and ... to join organizations of their own choosing without previous authorization.' In its March 2008 decision, the Committee found that the criteria for supervisory status laid out in the *Oakwood* trilogy 'appear to give rise to an overly wide definition of supervisory staff that would go beyond freedom of association principles' and urged the US Government 'to take all necessary steps, in consultation with the social partners, to ensure that the exclusion that may be made of supervisory staff under the NLRA is limited to those workers genuinely representing the interests of employers'.[108]

TSA Airport Screeners Case

In November 2006, the ILO CFA issued a decision in a complaint filed by the AFL-CIO and the American Federation of Government Employees (AFGE) against the Bush administration's denial of collective bargaining rights to airport screeners. The administration argued that the events of 11 September 2001 and concomitant security concerns made it necessary to strip Transportation Security Administration (TSA) employees of trade union rights accorded to other federal employees.

The Committee said that the Government's de-recognition violated employees' rights and urged it to bargain over terms and conditions of employment 'which are not directly related to national security issues with the screeners' freely chosen representative'.[109]

North Carolina Public Employees Case

In 2006, the United Electrical, Radio and Machine Workers of America (UE), an independent union known for its progressive politics and internal democracy,[110] followed the AFL-CIO's lead and filed a complaint with the ILO CFA. The complaint charged that North Carolina's ban on public worker bargaining, and the failure of the United States to take steps to protect workers' bargaining rights, violated Convention No 87's principle that 'all workers, without distinction' should enjoy organising and bargaining rights,

---

[108] See *Complaint against the United States (Case No 2524)* (March 2008) Report of the Committee on Freedom of Association No 349, *Report in which the Committee requests to be kept informed of developments.*

[109] See *Complaint against the United States (Case No 2292)* (November 2006) Report of the Committee on Freedom of Association No 343, *Report in which the Committee requests to be kept informed of developments.*

[110] Traditionally a manufacturing sector union, the United Electrical, Radio and Machine Workers of America (UE) began an innovative organising campaign among low-paid public sector workers in North Carolina, a state that prohibits collective bargaining by public employees. Using state and local civil service procedures, the union has won several grievances and wage increases for workers.

and Convention No 98's rule that only public employees who are high-level policymakers, not rank and file workers, should have the right to bargain.

In April 2007, the Committee ruled in the union's favour and urged the US Government

> to promote the establishment of a collective bargaining framework in the public sector in North Carolina ... and to take steps aimed at bringing the state legislation, in particular through the repeal of NCGS §95-98 [the statute prohibiting collective bargaining by public employees], into conformity with the freedom of association principles ...[111]

This decision prompted North Carolina state legislators to introduce, for the first time in decades, legislation that would grant collective bargaining rights to state and local employees.[112] The legislation is pending and advocates recognise that achieving it is difficult, but they count getting such a bill onto the legislative agenda as an important policy advance, and credit the international attention through the ILO case and other international mechanisms for reaching this point.[113]

CONCLUSION

The movement toward a human rights and labour rights approach to workers' rights in the United States does not mean changes in US law will follow quickly, even with the change of administration in January 2009. Decisions of the ILO and other international bodies have no binding effect in US labour law. Advocates can only use them to buttress legal arguments based in conventional law, or in campaigns for reform legislation.

Some labour supporters remain skeptical of a human rights argument for workers' organising in the United States. They maintain that a rights-based approach fosters individualism instead of collective worker power; that demands for 'workers' rights as human rights' interfere with calls for renewed industrial democracy; that channeling workers' activism through a legalistic rights-enhancing regime stifles militancy and direct action. Labour historian Joseph McCartin says:

> Because it puts freedom ahead of democracy, rights talk tends to foster a libertarian dialogue, where capital's liberty of movement and employers' 'rights to manage' are tacitly affirmed rather than challenged. Arguing in a rights-oriented framework forces workers to demand no more than that *their* rights be respected alongside their employers' rights ...

---

[111] See *Complaint against the United States (Case No 2460)* (2007) Report of the Committee on Freedom of Association No 344.

[112] See North Carolina General Assembly, House Bill No 1583 (April 2007).

[113] Author interview with Robin Alexander, Director of International Affairs, United Electrical Workers (20 March 2008).

I am not suggesting that today's labor advocates should abandon their rights-based arguments. These have undeniable power, speak to basic truths, and connect to important traditions—including labor's historic internationalism. Rather, I am arguing that the 'workers' rights are human rights' formulation alone will prove inadequate to the task of rebuilding workers' organisations in the United States unless we couple it with an equally passionate call for democracy in our workplaces, economy, and politics.[114]

Historian Nelson Lichtenstein argues:

> Two years ago HRW published '*Unfair Advantage: Workers' Freedom of Association in the United States Under Human Rights Standards,*' which is certainly one of the most devastating accounts of the hypocrisy and injustice under which trade unionists labor in one portion of North America.

> This new sensitivity to global human rights is undoubtedly a good thing for the cause of trade unionism, rights at work, and the democratic impulse ... [But] as deployed in American law and political culture, a discourse of rights has also subverted the very idea, and the institutional expression, of union solidarity ... Thus, in recent decades, employer anti-unionism has become increasingly oriented toward the ostensible protection of the individual rights of workers as against undemocratic unions and restrictive contracts that hamper the free choice of employees ... without a bold and society-shaping political and social program, human rights can devolve into something approximating libertarian individualism.[115]

Historian David Brody suggests that a human rights analysis too willingly accepts the view that collective bargaining is gained through a bureaucratic process of government certification rather than through workers' direct action. He writes, '[t]hat a formally democratic process might be at odds with workers' freedom of associationseems to fall below the screen of "human rights analysis".'[116]

Labour lawyer Jay Youngdahl insists that

> the replacement of solidarity and unity as the anchor for labor justice with 'individual human rights' will mean the end of the labor movement as we know it .... Elevating human rights to the dominant position within labor ideology will eviscerate support for the common concerns of all workers that is the keystone for labor solidarity.[117]

These are healthy cautions from serious, committed scholars and defenders of trade unions and workers' rights. They contribute to a needed debate about the role and effectiveness of human rights activism and human rights

---

[114] McCartin, J, 'Democratizing the Demand for Workers' Rights: Toward a Re-framing of Labor's Argument' (Winter 2005) *Dissent.*

[115] Lichtenstein, N, 'The Rights Revolution' (Spring 2003) *New Labor Forum.*

[116] Brody, D, 'Labor Rights as Human Rights: A Reality Check' (2001) 39 *British Journal of Industrial Relations* 601.

[117] Youngdahl, J, 'Solidarity First: Labor Rights Are Not the Same as Human Rights' (Winter 2009) *New Labor Forum.*

arguments in support of workers' rights. All three historians agree that human rights advocacy is important for advancing the cause of social justice; that one need not make an 'either-or' choice.

Conditions have ripened for raising the human rights platform to advance workers' rights in the United States. International labour law developments are fostering new ways of thinking and talking about labour law in the United States—a necessary condition for changing policy and practice.

Arguing from a human rights base, labour advocates can identify violations, name violators, demand remedies, and specify recommendations for change. Workers are empowered in organising and bargaining campaigns, convinced that they are vindicating their fundamental human rights, not just getting a wage increase. Employers are thrown more on the defensive by charges that they are violating workers' human rights. The larger society is more responsive to the notion of trade union organising as an exercise of human rights rather than economic strength.

This is not meant to overstate the case for human rights or to exaggerate the effects of the human rights argument. 'Human rights' is still an abstraction for most workers. Labour advocates cannot just cry 'human rights, human rights' and expect employers to change their behaviour or Congress to enact labour law reform.

Changes will be slow in coming and incremental. Labour and human rights advocates still confront general unawareness in the United States of international human rights standards and of the ILO's work in giving precise meaning to those standards. Advocates have an enormous educational challenge of making them more widely known and respected.

The new focus on workers' rights as human rights contributes to this educational effort. At the same time, it changes the climate for workers' organising and bargaining by framing them as a human rights mission, not a test of economic power between an employer and a 'third party' (employers' favourite characterisation of unions in organising campaigns).

A human rights emphasis also has alliance-building effects. Human rights supporters and human rights organisations are a major force in civil society, one that historically stood apart from labour struggles, seeing them not as human rights concerns but as institutional tests of strength. Human rights NGOs are an important addition to labour's traditional allies in civil rights, women's, and other organisations that help create a favourable stream where workers and their unions can swim more freely.

Part II

International and Regional Perspectives

11

UN Covenants and Labour Rights

SARAH JOSEPH

INTRODUCTION

LABOUR RIGHTS ARE at the vanguard of the modern human rights movement. Some of the earliest 'human rights' campaigns concerned labour issues, such as the anti-slavery movement, early campaigns against child labour, and the trade union movement. Such campaigns were necessitated by the excesses of colonialism and the Industrial Revolution. The International Labour Organisation (ILO), established in 1919, significantly predates most other international human rights machinery, which generally emerged after World War II.[1]

It is perhaps because international labour rights movements started earlier than other human rights movements that labour rights tend to have been separated, and arguably even marginalised, within the mainstream human rights bodies at the global level.[2] For example, a survey of the resolutions and decisions of the United Nations (UN) Human Rights Council in 2009 revealed that no resolutions directly concerned labour rights. It may be that labour rights are seen as properly within the province of the ILO, thus leaving the overstretched UN bodies to concentrate on other human rights issues. While most of the core UN human rights treaties recognise and protect labour rights, the contribution of the UN treaty bodies to the development of labour rights law has thus far been modest.

In this chapter, the relevant jurisprudence developed under the UN human rights covenants, that is the International Covenant on Civil and Political Rights (ICCPR), and the International Covenant on Economic Social and Cultural Rights (ICESCR), is analysed. The provisions in the ICCPR and especially the ICESCR offer the greatest labour rights coverage amongst the UN core human rights treaties, as they are not limited to

---

[1] See Drzewicki, K, 'The Right to Work and Rights in Work' in A Eide, C Krause and A Rosas (eds), *Economic Social and Cultural Rights: A Textbook*, 2nd edn (Dordrecht, Martinus Nijhoff, 2001) 223.
[2] See also Hepple, B, *Labour Laws and Global Trade* (Oxford, Hart Publishing, 2005) 21–23.

a particular group, such as those in the Convention on the Rights of the Child or the Convention on the Protection of the Rights of all Migrant Workers and their Families, nor is discrimination a prerequisite to their activation, as is the case with the relevant provisions in the International Convention on the Elimination of all forms of Racial Discrimination and the Convention on the Elimination of all forms of Discrimination Against Women.

The Relevant Covenant Provisions

Labour rights are protected by numerous provisions of the ICESCR. Article 6 guarantees the right to work. Article 7 recognises the right to just and favourable conditions of work. Article 8 recognises the right to join effective trade unions, which is necessary to guarantee workers' rights considering the common imbalance of power between individual workers and employers. Article 9 recognises a right to social security, which should include unemployment benefits and workers' compensation rights when necessary.[3] Article 10 generally guarantees protection and assistance for families and children; Article 10(2) recognises a right of paid maternal leave, and article 10(3) recognises that measures must be taken to protect against the exploitation of young people in an employment context. Finally, article 12, which generally concerns the right to the highest attainable standard of health, obliges states parties to take measures to improve industrial hygiene (paragraph 2(b)) and to combat occupational diseases (paragraph 2(c)).

The ICCPR addresses a much narrower range of labour rights than in the ICESCR. Articles 8(1) and 8(2) absolutely prohibit slavery and servitude. Article 8(3) prohibits forced labour, but does allow the imposition of 'hard labour' as a sentence, military conscription, as well other forms of national service designed to take account of conscientious objectors to military service, compulsory service designed to combat emergencies or calamities, and 'work or service which forms part of normal civic obligations'. Article 22 of the ICCPR guarantees freedom of association, including the right to form and join trade unions, and therefore overlaps in that respect with article 8 of the ICESCR. Finally, article 25(c) offers a very limited right of employment in the public sector.

Both Covenants also prohibit discrimination in relation to the enjoyment of labour rights.[4]

---

[3] Scheinin, M, 'The Right to Social Security' in A Eide, C Krause and A Rosas (eds), *Economic Social and Cultural Rights: A Textbook*, 2nd edn (Dordrecht, Martinus Nijhoff, 2001) 214–15.

[4] See eg, International Covenant on Economic Social and Cultural Rights (ICESCR) arts 2(2) and 3; International Covenant on Civil and Political Rights (ICCPR) arts 2(1), 3 and 26.

OVERVIEW OF THE NATURE OF LABOUR
RIGHTS IN THE COVENANTS

States parties to the ICCPR are required under article 2(1) to immediately guarantee the rights recognised therein. Thus, for example, states parties are required under article 8 to immediately combat slavery, servitude, and forced labour.

In contrast, the ICESCR, clearly the more important Covenant in relation to labour rights, has a weaker obligation provision in its article 2(1), which reads:

> Each State Party to the present Covenant undertakes to take steps, individually and through international assistance and co-operation, especially economic and technical, to the maximum of its available resources, with a view to achieving progressively the full realisation of the rights recognised in the present Covenant by all appropriate means, including particularly the adoption of legislative measures.

Thus, states are not required to immediately guarantee ICESCR rights, but are required to progressively increase enjoyment thereof to the extent that resources permit. States in effect are required to 'try hard' in protecting ICESCR rights. The soft obligation undoubtedly makes it easier for states to evade findings of violation of the ICESCR. It is much easier to determine whether a state has or has not protected a right, as is required for determinations under the ICCPR, than it is to determine whether a state has exercised sufficient endeavour in attempting to protect a right, as is the standard of obligation apparently dictated by the ICESCR. It is difficult to hold states accountable for obligations if it is difficult to determine whether they have in fact breached those obligations.

Why is the ICESCR so much weaker in terms of its obligation provisions than the ICCPR? Traditionally, economic social and cultural rights are felt to give rise to positive duties, while civil and political rights are felt to give rise to negative duties. Positive duties require the performance of affirmative actions for fulfilment, while negative duties require the mere refraining from certain actions. It is easier and cheaper to refrain from action, which is in effect to do nothing, than it is to undertake positive acts.[5]

A manifestation of the perceived dichotomy concerns the justiciability of, respectively, ICCPR rights and ICESCR rights. ICCPR rights have long been recognised as justiciable, as reflected by the existence of the Optional Protocol (OP) to the ICCPR, pursuant to which individuals can submit complaints against states parties to the monitoring body under the ICCPR,

---

[5] See Scott, C, 'The Interdependence and Permeability of Human Rights Norms: Towards a Partial Fusion of the International Covenants on Human Rights' (1989) 27 *Osgoode Hall Law Journal* 769, 832–33.

the Human Rights Committee (HRC). The HRC then decides whether, in the circumstances, the state party has breached the ICCPR. Until recently, no such individual complaints mechanism existed under the ICESCR. This absence reflected the commonly held idea that economic social and cultural rights are non-justiciable, as it is too difficult to identify violations. It was also prompted by the idea that economic social and cultural rights arise in policy areas that are inappropriate for judicial or quasi-judicial determination.[6]

On 10 December 2008, the UN General Assembly adopted an Optional Protocol to ICESCR, which will provide for an individual complaints system under that treaty. It will come into force once 10 states have ratified it. Its adoption by consensus signals an end to the previously orthodox presumption that economic social and cultural rights are inherently non-justiciable.[7]

In fact, the strict division of civil and political rights on the one hand, and economic social and cultural rights on the other into categories of 'negative' and 'positive', is misleading. All rights have positive and negative aspects. For example, freedom from torture (ICCPR article 7) cannot be guaranteed simply by the state undertaking to refrain from torture. Training programmes must be put in place to ensure that relevant personnel (eg prison officers, police interrogators) do not resort to torture in any circumstances. Legislation must be enacted to ensure that potential perpetrators are deterred, actual perpetrators are apprehended and punished, and victims are compensated. Systems must be devised to prevent the opportunity for torture, and to detect torture when it occurs.[8] Furthermore, certain civil and political rights seem inherently positive, such as the right to a fair trial in article 14 of the ICCPR, which requires the provision of courts, trained judges, and on occasion legal aid. On the other hand, article 8 of the ICESCR seems largely negative, as it requires states to refrain from interfering with the proper functioning of trade unions.

Indeed, all human rights entail obligations to respect, protect, and fulfil the enjoyment of relevant rights.[9] In this tripartite typology, the obligation

---

[6] See eg, Hunt, P, 'Reclaiming Economic Social and Cultural Rights' (1993) 1 *Waikato Law Review* 141 (discussing and then refuting the contention).

[7] Economic social and cultural rights have been justiciable in some national courts for some time: see generally, Langford M (ed), *Social Rights Jurisprudence: Emerging Trends in International and Comparative Law* (Cambridge University Press, Cambridge, 2008).

[8] See General Comment 20: Art 7 ICCPR, Forty-Fourth Session of the Human Rights Committee, 10/03/92. General Comments are consensus comments issued by the treaty bodies to all states parties. A General Comment normally expands upon the meaning of a particular right.

[9] See eg, 'Maastricht Guidelines on Violations of Economic Social and Cultural Rights' (1998) 20 *Human Rights Quarterly* 691. This document contains a set of guidelines devised by 30 human rights experts in January 1997. See also 'Civil and Political Rights: the Human

to 'respect' entails the state's negative obligations, while the obligations to protect and fulfil are positive. The 'protection' obligation corresponds with the state's obligations to prevent or punish human rights violations by non-state actors. Such obligations are discharged by the enactment and enforcement of legislation, and the taking of reasonable steps to appropriately control the actions of private entities. The latter obligations are important in the arena of labour rights, given the increasing dominance in most countries of the private sector over the availability of work.[10] The 'fulfilment' obligation requires appropriate resource allocation to ensure the enjoyment of rights, particularly those who lack the resources to provide for themselves.

While a progressive obligation may be softer than an immediate obligation, it is nevertheless an obligation which has 'meaningful content', that is 'to move as expeditiously and effectively as possible' towards fulfilment of the individual ICESCR rights.[11] It can sometimes be obvious if a state is simply doing nothing to improve its record on economic, social and cultural rights. Deliberately retrogressive measures for example are prima facie violations. While states might in some circumstances legitimately move backwards on one social right by reallocating resources to improve its observance of another social right, they bear the burden of proof in demonstrating why retrogressive measures are necessary.[12]

In any case, certain duties in the ICESCR are immediate. Article 2(2) of the ICESCR requires states parties to 'guarantee that the rights enunciated in the present Covenant will be exercised without arbitrary discrimination. This non-discrimination duty is not expressed in the language of progressiveness and the Committee on Economic Social and Cultural Rights (CESCR), the international body which monitors the ICESCR, has confirmed that the article 2(2) duty is in fact immediate.[13] States parties are therefore not permitted to implement economic social and cultural rights in a discriminatory manner. That is, a segment of society cannot be arbitrarily left behind in the process of progressively realising those rights.

Article 2(2) of the ICESCR mirrors article 26 of the ICCPR in this respect. Article 26 has been interpreted to require states parties to the ICCPR to refrain from any arbitrary or unreasonable discrimination against persons with regard to the enjoyment of any right, including economic social and cultural rights. Therefore, discrimination in regard to the enjoyment of economic social and cultural rights is actionable under the ICCPR and the

---

Rights Committee' (Fact Sheet 15, Geneva, Office of the High Commissoner for Human Rights (UNHCHR)) 3.

[10] Maastricht Principles para 2.

[11] General Comment 3: The Nature of States Parties Obligations (art 1, para 1) contained in UN doc E/1991/23, (14 December 1990) para 9.

[12] Ibid para 9.

[13] Ibid para 1.

OP. For example, on the labour rights front, article 26 cases have concerned non-discrimination in relation to employment[14] and unemployment benefit entitlements.[15]

In its General Comment 3 on 'The Nature of State Party Obligations', the CESCR identified that states parties have a presumptive immediate obligation to provide for the satisfaction of the 'minimum core', that is 'minimum essential levels', of each ICESCR right.[16] There is a presumption that states are capable of satisfying, and therefore may reasonably be obliged to provide for, 'minimum core' levels of ICESCR rights. States bear the burden of proof of demonstrating that they are genuinely unable, rather than unwilling, to fulfil their minimum core obligations.[17]

Finally, there is one area where the ICESCR apparently imposes superior obligations compared to the ICCPR. Article 2(1) of the ICESCR refers explicitly to 'international assistance and cooperation': the CESCR confirmed in General Comment 3 its view that 'cooperation for development and thus for the realisation of economic, social and cultural rights is an obligation of all States'.[18] This duty is most obviously incumbent upon the most wealthy and powerful nations.[19] At the least, states should not undermine economic social and cultural rights in other states, and may be required to take positive actions to improve enjoyment of those rights, particularly when a latter state is unable to provide for minimum core rights.

JURISPRUDENCE ON LABOUR RIGHTS

The following commentary focuses on the areas where the HRC and the CESCR have issued their most significant labour rights jurisprudence. Of course, the lack of individual communications under the ICESCR has hampered the development of jurisprudence under that treaty. The advent of the new Optional Protocol will facilitate the development of a greater understanding of the scope of the labour rights in the ICESCR, as the CESCR will be able to identify whether those rights have or have not been violated in concrete situations.

---

[14] *Bwalya v Zambia* (314/1988) CCPR/C/41/D/314/1988; *Wackenheim v France* (854/1999), CCPR/C/75/D/854/1999.

[15] See eg, *Broeks v Netherlands* CCPR/C/29/D/172/1984; *Zwaan-de-Vries v Netherlands* CCPR/C/29/D/182/1984.

[16] General Comment 3 (n 11) para 10.

[17] Ibid para 10.

[18] Ibid para 14.

[19] Ibid para 14. This aspect of art 2(1) reflects arts 55 and 56 of the UN Charter, which require states to take joint and separate action to realise human rights, as well as art 4 of the Declaration on the Right to Development 1986.

The Right to Work

On 24 November 2005, the CESCR issued General Comment 18 on 'The Right to Work' in article 6 of the ICESCR. In General Comment 18, the CESCR confirms that the right to work is not an unconditional right to be employed.[20] However, states are required to 'adopt, as quickly as possible, measures aiming at achieving full employment'.[21] The CESCR also stresses the undesirability of work in the informal sector, due, for example, to the almost inevitable lack of protection (eg union or legislative protection) for workers in that sector.[22] Minimisation of official unemployment should serve to reduce the incidence of informal work.

The right encompasses freedom from unfair dismissal.[23] In this regard, the General Comment identifies ILO Convention No 158 on Termination of Employment as the reference point for determining when dismissal is justified or unjustified and therefore in breach of article 6.[24]

States are also obliged to take steps to guarantee availability, decency of work, and accessibility. Regarding availability, states should assist people via specialised services to identify and obtain work.[25] Regarding decent work, that is 'acceptability and quality' of work, work must be reasonably remunerated, and should be conducted under reasonable and safe conditions.[26] Decent work does not necessarily imply interesting, stimulating or enjoyable work. Indeed, the General Comment does not mention whether job progression must be available, aside from stating that opportunities for promotion must be offered without discrimination. Regarding accessibility, states should guarantee that work be physically accessible to all, including disabled persons and, presumably, persons in remote areas.[27] Information on job opportunities should also be accessible, for example via 'data networks'.[28]

The CESCR goes on to identify examples of the duties of states to 'respect, protect and fulfil' the right to work.[29] Retrogressive measures are, as with all rights, prima facie violations of the duty to 'respect'.[30] States must only undertake such measures if they somehow enhance enjoyment of other ICESCR rights (by for example reallocating resources), and 'after

[20] General Comment 18: Art 6 of the ICESCR E/C.12/GC/18 para 6, 24 November 2005.
[21] Ibid para 19.
[22] Ibid para 10; see also Concluding Observations on Senegal (CESCR) (2001) UN Doc E/2002/22, 61 para 346.
[23] General Comment 18 (n 20) para 4.
[24] Ibid para 11.
[25] Ibid para 12(a).
[26] Ibid paras 7 and 12(c).
[27] Ibid para 12(b)(ii).
[28] Ibid para 12(b)(iii).
[29] Ibid para 22.
[30] Ibid para 33–34.

consideration of all alternatives'.[31] A failure to protect persons from third parties, as well as a failure to appropriately regulate such third parties, is a breach of the duty to 'protect' the right to work.[32]

Regarding the obligation to 'fulfil', the CESCR subdivides that duty into obligations to provide, facilitate and promote the right to work. *Provision* of the right to work entails the adoption of national policies, such as the creation of public and private employment services at national and local levels of government, aimed at achieving full employment, and in particular at assisting those 'unable, for reasons beyond their control, to realise the right themselves by the means at their disposal'.[33] Further, states must take steps to 'establish a compensation mechanism in the event of loss of employment'.[34] *Facilitation* of the right to work includes the enabling and assisting of individuals to get into a position to gain employment, and the implementation of appropriate 'technical and vocational education plans'.[35] *Promotion* of the right to work includes the implementation of 'educational and informational programmes to instil public awareness on the right to work'[36] in both the public and private sectors.[37] Blatant failure to implement appropriate programmes, as well as 'insufficient expenditure or misallocation of public funds' which harms the right to work, violate the 'fulfilment' obligation.[38] So too does a failure to attempt any monitoring or evaluation of relevant programmes, which is necessary to ensure that policies are progressively improving enjoyment of the right.[39]

As noted above, there is a presumption that states will be able to immediately implement minimum core obligations within each ICESCR right. The core of article 6 is identified as including the duty to ensure access to employment for vulnerable persons, the avoidance of discriminatory measures, a duty not to weaken existing protections for vulnerable persons, and a duty to 'adopt and implement a national employment strategy and plan of action'.[40] This plan should particularly target disadvantaged persons[41] and it should

---

[31] Ibid para 21.

[32] Ibid para 35.

[33] Ibid para 26.

[34] Ibid para 26.

[35] Ibid para 27. See, on technical and vocational education, General Comment 13: Right to Education E/C.12/1999/10 para 16; see also United Nations Educational, Scientific and Cultural Organisation (UNESCO) Convention on Technical and Vocational Training 1989 adopted on the Report of Commission II at the twenty-fifth session Paris, on 10 November 1989.

[36] General Comment 18 (n 20) para 28.

[37] Ibid para 43.

[38] Ibid para 36.

[39] Ibid para 36.

[40] Ibid para 31. See also Siegel, RL, 'The Right to Work: Core Minimum Obligations' in Chapman A and Sage R (eds), *Core Obligations: Building a Framework for Economic Social and Cultural Rights* (Antwerp, Intersentia, 2002) 34.

[41] General Comment 18 (n 20) para 44.

comprise 'indicators and benchmarks by which progress' regarding article 6 'can be measured and periodically reviewed'.[42]

The CESCR goes on to suggest appropriate content for these national plans of action. Efforts should be made to identify and locate the resources needed to achieve full employment.[43] Relevant groups from civil society, such as trade unions and employer groups, as well as international organisations (eg the ILO), should be involved in the design, execution, and monitoring of the plan.[44] The plans should contain 'numerical targets and a time frame for implementation',[45] so that implementation may be usefully measured and assessed.[46] Standard ILO indicators, such as unemployment rates, rates of part-time to full-time work, ratios of formal to informal work, should be used in this regard.[47] The 'right to work indicators', as well as appropriate national benchmarks and targets regarding those indicators adopted by a state party, will be monitored by the CESCR throughout the reporting process relating to that state.[48]

Victims of violations of their right to work are entitled to 'effective judicial and other appropriate remedies'.[49] In this regard, the CESCR affirms its belief that economic social and cultural rights are justiciable, and should be incorporated into the domestic legal framework of states parties.[50]

The General Comment is undoubtedly a valuable addition to the jurisprudence of the treaty bodies on labour rights. The most helpful aspect of the General Comment is where the CESCR outlines a process for monitoring the progressive development of 'right to work' indicators as part of the reporting process. The proposed process adds real 'teeth' to the progressive obligation.

However, the General Comment suffers from a number of flaws. It is occasionally badly organised and repetitive. It is not always legally sound. For example, the paragraphs on child labour seem contradictory. The CESCR confirms that children must be protected from 'economic exploitation',[51] though it initially falls short of labelling all forms of child labour as 'exploitative'. Rather, the CESCR seems only concerned with child labour which interferes with a child's development or health. Nine paragraphs

---

[42] Ibid para 31(c).
[43] Ibid para 41.
[44] Ibid para 38; see also paras 40 and 42.
[45] Ibid para 38.
[46] Ibid para 45.
[47] Ibid para 46.
[48] Ibid para 47; under the ICESCR (and the ICCPR), states are generally expected to report every five years to the Committee. Each report is then examined in a dialogue between the Committee and representatives of the state party.
[49] Ibid para 48.
[50] See also General Comment 9: The Domestic Application of the Covenant E/C.12/1998/24 paras 9–10.
[51] Ibid para 15.

later, the concern however has escalated so that any 'labour of children under the age of 16' is prohibited. It would be preferable for the CESCR to adhere to ILO standards in this regard, which prescribe a minimum age of 15,[52] and for it to clarify the meanings of 'exploitative' child labour, so as to distinguish that type of labour from those in which child work is generally permitted.[53]

The General Comment also contains too many generalised 'motherhood' statements, with little practical guidance for states on how to progress from a situation of mass underemployment to full employment, or overemphasis on aspects of the right that can be readily assumed from the text of the ICESCR.[54] More examples should be used to illustrate general recommendations.

The General Comment is promised to be the first of three General Comments on labour rights in the ICESCR. The next two will address article 7, the right to just conditions of work, and article 8, rights regarding trade unions.[55] Once those latter two General Comments are in place, outstanding 'gaps' in the understanding of ICESCR labour rights will hopefully be filled in. Indeed, it might have been more desirable for CESCR to deal with the more specific elements of the right to work in articles 7 and 8 before addressing the general background right in article 6.[56] It must be noted that, four years on from General Comment 18 on article 6, no General Comment has yet appeared on articles 7 or 8.[57]

In particular, it is hoped that those future General Comments address the perceived dissonance between article 6 rights and the rights in articles 7 and 8,[58] and the possible conflict between article 6 and other economic social and cultural rights.[59] For example, it is arguably easier for a state to provide for full employment if it lowers standards regarding labour conditions contrary to article 7; an employer can afford to hire more people if

---

[52] See ILO Convention No 138, 'the Minimum Age Convention', art 2(3). Under arts 2(4) and 2(5), some developing states may prescribe a minimum age of 14.

[53] According to the ILO, the following economic activity on the part of children is excluded from the notion of impermissible child labour: household chores, schooling, children over the age of 12 working for only a few hours a week in light work, or children over the age of 15 working in conditions that are not hazardous. Hazardous work is that which detrimentally affects a child's health, safety, and moral development. See ILO, *The End of Child Labour: Within Reach* (ILO, Geneva, 2006) 6.

[54] Note in this respect the continuing references to the fact that work must be freely chosen and accepted, which is explicitly mentioned in arts 6(1), without expansion of this concept beyond the self evident fact that forced labour is forbidden.

[55] General Comment 18 (n 20) para 8.

[56] See Drzewicki, 'The Right to Work and Rights in Work' (2001) 227, referring to the right to work as a 'complex normative aggregate, and not a single legal concept'.

[57] Indeed, General Comments have appeared instead on art 9 (see below, text at nn 108–112) and on art 2(2), the ICESCR guarantee against discrimination.

[58] See eg, Siegel, 'The Right to Work: Core Minimum Obligations' (2002) 24; Hepple, *Labour Laws and Global Trade* (2005) 11 and 16.

[59] Drzewicki (n 1) 236 refers to the 'economic inefficiency' of full employment policies, which might undermine a state's capacity to fulfil other ICESCR rights.

he or she has to pay each person less. As trade unions generally promote better labour conditions, similar arguments could indicate that article 6 and 8 rights occasionally contradict each other.[60]

Such arguments are particularly prevalent with ongoing increased trade liberalisation, which facilitates greater international competition in local markets, driving a perceived greater need for competitiveness in labour conditions within those local markets. For example, a state will arguably lose jobs to offshore competition if its labour market is too costly or inflexible.[61] These issues and arguments are not addressed at all in General Comment 18, with the CESCR simply asserting that articles 6, 7, and 8 are interdependent,[62] and that states must not only strive for full employment but also decent employment.[63] The CESCR cannot hope to maintain relevance regarding labour rights if it simply ignores such arguments rather than acknowledge or combat them.[64] General Comment 18 would have been more useful if the CESCR had given some guidance on how a state should balance the imperatives of full employment and decent employment (eg how 'low' can labour conditions go in order to facilitate job availability), or alternatively, if it had explained why those imperatives are utterly harmonious despite arguments to the contrary.[65] For example, the CESCR could have pointed out that poor working conditions can cause low productivity and consequent business failure, thus leading to more unemployment.[66]

Labour Rights and Globalisation

Siegel has argued that labour rights are more strongly affected by globalisation than any other sphere of social and economic (or human) rights.[67] Indeed, the CESCR has been a critic of globalisation. In a consensus statement issued in 1998 on 'Globalisation and its impact on economic social and cultural rights',[68] the CESCR stated, at paragraph 3:

> [G]lobalisation risks downgrading the central place accorded to human rights by the Charter of the United Nations in general and the International Bill of Human

---

[60] See eg, Department of Foreign Affairs and Trade, *Globalisation: Keeping the Gains* (Commonwealth of Australia, Canberra, 2003) 21.

[61] See eg, Hepple (n 2) 12.

[62] General Comment 18 (n 20) para 8.

[63] Ibid para 7.

[64] See also Drzewicki (n 1) 240.

[65] See eg, Deakin, S, 'Social Rights in a Globalised Economy' in P Alston (ed), *Labour Rights as Human Rights* (Oxford, Oxford University Press, 2004) 25–60.

[66] Hepple (n 2) 14.

[67] Siegel (n 40) 25.

[68] See CESCR, 'Globalisation and its impact on economic social and cultural rights' (1998) UN Doc E/1999/22 ch VI.

Rights[69] in particular. This is especially the case in relation to economic, social and cultural rights. Thus, for example, respect for the right to work and the right to just and favourable conditions of work is threatened where there is an excessive emphasis upon competitiveness to the detriment of respect for the labour rights contained in the Covenant.[70] The right to form and join trade unions may be threatened by restrictions upon freedom of association, restrictions claimed to be 'necessary' in a global economy, or by the effective exclusion of possibilities for collective bargaining or by the closing off of the right to strike for various occupational and other groups.

Economic globalisation generates greater global interdependence between states, so the policies of states are more likely to impact beyond their own borders on the economies of other states, and thus affect the capacity of those latter states to respect human rights, including labour rights. In that respect, the duties of states to other states, obliquely referenced in article 2(1) of the ICESCR, are important to delineate. On that issue, CESCR stated in General Comment 18 that states should be aware of and promote the right to work in their bilateral and multilateral negotiations, such as those within the World Trade Organisation (WTO).[71] Such duties would of course apply with regard to the right to work of a state's own people, but also the right to work of the people of other states. Furthermore, states parties should attempt to influence the policies of international institutions to which they are members, such as the International Monetary Fund (IMF) or the World Bank, to ensure compatibility between those policies (eg lending policies, credit agreements, and structural adjustment programmes) and the right to work.[72]

Non-state actors are influential participants in the process of globalisation, particularly multinational corporations and international organisations such as the WTO, IMF, and the World Bank. Indeed, one concern about globalisation is that the policy autonomy of states, and thus their ability to control aspects of labour rights within their territories, is significantly reduced.[73] Such a reduction undermines the effectiveness and potential impact of the ICESCR, as it only binds states.[74] In General Comment 18, the CESCR conceded 'that only States ... are ultimately accountable for compliance with' the ICESCR.[75] Nevertheless, the CESCR suggested that non-state actors should themselves observe the right to work, given their enormous influence in that area. For example, private

---

[69] The two Covenants and the Universal Declaration of Human Rights 1948 are commonly known as the International Bill of Rights.
[70] See also General Comment 18 (n 20) para 25.
[71] Ibid para 33.
[72] Ibid para 30.
[73] Siegel (n 40) 26.
[74] See also Drzewicki (n 1) 241.
[75] Ibid para 52.

sector employers should respect the right in their employment practices, and promote awareness of the right within their networks.[76] The CESCR also outlines proposed duties for international organisations, such as the WTO, IMF, and the World Bank; they 'should cooperate effectively with states parties to implement the right to work at the national level', within their spheres of competence.[77]

In General Comment 2, on 'International Technical Assistance Measures', the CESCR expressed concern that some development assistance activities had been 'ill conceived and even counterproductive in human rights terms', probably due to a lack of consideration by (or even knowledge of) the relevant development bodies (eg the IMF and the World Bank) of ICESCR norms.[78] In this regard, structural adjustment programmes were singled out as examples of such counterproductive measures.[79] While such programmes are in some circumstances unavoidable and 'will frequently involve a major element of austerity', the CESCR stresses that such circumstances only increase the need for state vigilance in upholding economic social and cultural rights.[80] General Comment 2 was adopted in 1990 at a time when structural adjustment programmes were characterised by demands for swift privatisation, reduction of government expenditure on social welfare, and trade liberalisation. While such measures were designed to spark and even shock underperforming economies into growth, and may have catalysed economic growth in the long term on some occasions, they also had a devastating effect on economic social and cultural rights, including labour rights, particularly in the short term.[81] These days, human rights have at least entered the agenda in tailoring structural adjustment programmes for needy states, with more account apparently taken of the impact of programmes on the most vulnerable. Nevertheless, legitimate concerns remain that human rights are too often sacrificed on the altar of economic efficiency in the structure of loan agreements between needy states and international financial institutions.[82]

Of course, the primary duty to protect the labour rights of the people of a state remains with that state. Therefore, when a state borrows from an

---

[76] Ibid para 52.

[77] Ibid para 53.

[78] General Comment 2: 'International Technical Assistance Measures (Art 22)', contained in UN doc. E/1990/23, 2 February 1990, para 7.

[79] Ibid para 9; see also 'Globalisation and Economic Social and Cultural Rights' Decision of CESCR contained in UN doc. E/1999/22, 31 May 1999, Chapter VI, at para 7.

[80] General Comment 2 (n 78) para 9.

[81] See eg, Dohnal, J, 'Structural Adjustment Programs: a Violation of Rights' (1994) 1 *Australian Journal of Human Rights* 57; Darrow, M, *Between Light and Shadow: The World Bank, The International Monetary Fund and International Human Rights Law* (Oxford, Hart Publishing, 2003) 68–72.

[82] Darrow, *Between Light and Shadow* (2003) 87–91.

international financial institution, such as the IMF and World Bank, and is therefore subjected to the loan conditions of such institutions, it should endeavour to minimise any adverse impact of those conditions on the right to work (and other labour rights), particularly for marginalised people.[83] For example, in Concluding Observations[84] on the Republic of Korea in 2001, the CESCR stated:

> [T]he State party did not take into account its Covenant obligations when nego-
> tiating with international financial institutions to overcome its financial crisis
> and restructure its economy. The over-reliance on macro-economic policies has
> had profound negative effects on the enjoyment of economic, social and cultural
> rights in that there have been large-scale employee dismissals and lay-offs, the
> significant deterioration in employment stability, growing income inequalities, an
> increasing number of broken families and marginalisation of a large number of
> persons.[85]

Furthermore, 'States parties should provide an environment [to facilitate] the discharge' of the obligations, regarding the right to work, of non-state actors within their jurisdiction.[86] Thus, a state must appropriately regulate the activities of corporations, including the local operations of a multinational corporation. In this regard the regulation of employers, normally multinational corporations, in 'export zones' has been a concern. For example, the CESCR noted, with regard to El Salvador, that:

> the working conditions in the duty-free zones have deteriorated and that
> difficulties have resulted from the inadequacy of resources available to enable
> the factory inspectorates to enforce legislation on the minimum wage, equal
> remuneration for men and women, industrial safety and hygiene, and wrongful
> dismissal.[87]

The CESCR has also condemned the 'virtual total impunity in enterprises located in duty-free zones of the rights contained in articles 7 and 8 [of the ICESCR]' in El Salvador,[88] and the 'extremely unsatisfactory working conditions in the free trade zones', including extreme discouragement of trade union activity in the Dominican Republic.[89] Regarding Mauritius, the CESCR has stated: 'The excessive overtime work in the Export Processing

---

[83] General Comment 18 (n 20) para 30.

[84] Concluding Observations are issued by both the CESCR and the Human Rights Committee (HRC) pursuant to the reporting processes under their respective treaties.

[85] CESCR, 'Concluding Observations on the Republic of Korea' (2001) UN Doc E/2002/22 45, para 222.

[86] General Comment 18 (n 20) para 52.

[87] CESCR, 'Concluding Observations on El Salvador' (1996) UN Doc E/1997/22 34, para 162.

[88] Ibid para 165.

[89] CESCR, 'Concluding Observations on the Dominican Republic' (1997) UN Doc E/1998/22 43, para 219; see also paras 230 and 236.

Zones is of concern. In these zones the Labour Act does not apply fully, which leaves more than 80,000 workers unprotected.'[90]

Working conditions in the *maquilas*, assembly line factories focused on export markets, which are found in a number of Latin American countries, have also been criticised.[91] The HRC has also noted deficiencies in the exercise of the right to join trade unions under article 22 of the ICCPR in free trade zones.[92]

A final issue of concern regarding globalisation that commonly arises, particularly in CESCR jurisprudence, concerns employment vulnerability arising from privatisation.[93] The CESCR has commented on the need in Hong Kong to 'retrain those who have lost employment or are underemployed as a result of economic restructuring'.[94] The CESCR also noted the loss of jobs and 'significant social repercussions' of the 'downsizing of the public sector' in the Solomon Islands, which had previously accounted 'for almost one third of wage employment'.[95] Similarly, regarding Benin, the CESCR was concerned with 'the dismissals resulting from privatisation or liquidation' of a number of national enterprises'.[96] Regarding Mongolia, the CESCR noted the extreme problems caused during its 'transition to a market economy', such as unemployment generated by the 'closure or downsizing of State enterprises'.[97] Regarding Bosnia and Herzegovina, the CESCR noted that 'following privatisation, employers frequently failed to respect their contractual obligations towards their employees'.[98]

The comments of the treaty bodies, especially the CESCR, regarding the labour rights impacts of globalisation have been largely negative. This conclusion only renders it more imperative for the treaty bodies, particularly the CESCR, to clarify how or whether labour rights can be meaningfully protected in the face of increased international economic interdependence

---

[90] CESCR, 'Concluding Observations on Mauritius' (1994) UN Doc E/1995/22 37, para 174. See also CESCR, 'Concluding Observations on India' (2008) E/C.12/IND/CO/5 para 63.

[91] See eg, CESCR, 'Concluding Observations on Honduras' (2001) UN Doc E/2002/22 33, para 122 (see also para 143); CESCR, 'Concluding Observations on Guatemala' (1996) UN Doc E/1997/22 29, para 131.

[92] See eg, CESCR, 'Concluding Observations on the Dominican Republic' (1993) UN Doc A/48/40 vol I 95, para 464 and CESCR, 'Concluding Observations on Sri Lanka' (1995) UN Doc A/50/40 vol I 75, para 458.

[93] General Comment 18 (n 20) para 25.

[94] CESCR, 'Concluding Observations on UK (Hong Kong)' (1996) UN Doc E/1997/22 58, para 356.

[95] CESCR, 'Concluding Observations on the Solomon Islands' (1999) UN Doc E/2000/22 40, para 201.

[96] CESCR, 'Concluding Observations on Benin' (2002) UN Doc E/2003/22 34, para 168.

[97] CESCR, 'Concluding Observations on Mongolia' (2000) UN Doc E/2001/22 53, para 267; see also CESCR, 'Concluding Observations on the Ukraine' (2001) UN Doc E/2002/22 78, para 490.

[98] CESCR, 'Concluding Observations on Bosnia and Herzegovina' UN Doc E/C.12/BIH/CO/1, para 15(c), 24 January 2006.

and linkage. More detailed guidance is needed, rather than continuous general exhortations for the protection of labour rights; such repetitive urgings risk being viewed as obsolete and irrelevant.[99]

Indeed, it may be that the titans of globalisation are now more receptive to ideas regarding the protection of labour and other social and economic rights in a globalised world. Globalisation in the 1990s was characterised by neo-liberal 'Washington Consensus' policies, such as privatisation, deregulation, and trade liberalisation.[100] Washington Consensus policies were trumpeted as the solutions to underdevelopment, economic stagnation and poverty in the developing world. However, those policies undoubtedly generated detrimental effects for the enjoyment of economic social and cultural rights. The Washington Consensus is now under sustained attack;[101] the expected benefits of such policies have simply not materialised in many parts of the world.[102] In a 2005 report, the World Bank explicitly rejected the 'one size fits all' approach of the Washington Consensus,[103] and instead recognised that a diverse range of economic policies are appropriate in different situations.[104] Furthermore, responses to the Global Financial Crisis of 2008–09 have involved policies, such as massive government spending coupled with increased regulation and quasi-nationalisation, which hardly conform to Washington Consensus strategies.[105] A move away from top-down rigid economic policy-making towards the allowance of greater local discretion should signal a reassertion of greater state control of their own economies,[106] which would open the door for a more meaningful role for CESCR and the other treaty bodies in the continuing debates about appropriate economic policies.[107]

---

[99] Siegel (n 40) 28. The CESCR itself acknowledged in 1994 that the social policies that it generally favoured were increasingly viewed as 'obsolete and invalid': see 'Extract from the Report of the Committee on Economic Social and Cultural Rights on its tenth session, held from 2 to 20 May 1994', UN Doc E/1994/L. 13, 16 June 1994, para 18.

[100] John Williamson coined the term in 'What Washington means by policy reform', in Williamson J (ed), *Latin American Adjustment: How much has happened?* (Washington DC, Institute of International Economics, 1990).

[101] Rodrik, D, 'Goodbye Washington Consensus, Hello Washington Confusion' (January 2006), available at: ksghome.harvard.edu/~drodrik/papers.html; see also Lamy P, Director General World Trade Organization, 'Making Trade work for Development: Time for a Geneva Consensus' (Emile Noel Lecture New York University Law School, 30 October 2006) paras 3–4, available at: www.wto.org/english/news_e/sppl_e/sppl45_e.htm.

[102] World Bank, *Economic Growth in the 1990s: Learning from a Decade of Reform* (Washington DC, World Bank, 2005) 3.

[103] Ibid 11.

[104] Ibid 11–14.

[105] The death of the Washington consensus has been proclaimed with particular vigour since the advent of the Global Financial Crisis in late 2008. For example, UK Prime Minister Gordon Brown declared the 'old Washington consensus over' on 2 April 2009 at the conclusion of the G20 summit: see www.number10.gov.uk/Page18934 (22 April 2009). Of course, it remains to be seen whether such proclamations are premature.

[106] World Bank, *Economic Growth in the 1990s* (2005) 14–16.

[107] See also Deakin, 'Social Rights in a Globalised Economy' (2004) 60.

Right to Social Security

The CESCR issued General Comment 19 on article 9, the right to social security, in 2008.[108] Although article 9 is not, strictly speaking, a labour right, it does address rights which arise due to a lack of labour-related income. General Comment 19 confirms that states should take steps to provide for social security for unemployed persons, for persons injured at work, and for dependents of persons killed in a workplace accident.[109] Under article 10(2) of the ICESCR, maternity benefits should be provided for working mothers. Furthermore, care must be taken to ensure that workers in unorthodox employment situations, namely part-timers, casual workers, the self-employed, homeworkers, and those in the informal sector are adequately covered by social security schemes.[110] The CESCR does not exhibit a particular preference for universal schemes, targeted schemes or contributory insurance schemes, to which employers and potential beneficiaries contribute, or even private schemes,[111] so long as the schemes adequately cover those in need of social security.

In the General Comment, the CESCR acknowledge that the right to formal social security is meaningfully enjoyed by only about 20 per cent of the world's population.[112] General Comment 19 will hopefully be used by states to develop strategies to redress this massive shortfall in human rights enjoyment. It is not proposed, however, to further analyse this Comment here due to its tangential relationship to labour rights.

Right to Work in the Public Sector

A narrow employment right is found in article 25(c) of the ICCPR, whereby all citizens have an equal right to work in the public service of their country. In that respect, 'the criteria and processes for appointment, promotion, suspension and dismissal must be objective and reasonable'.[113] Article 25(c) does not guarantee an actual public service job.[114] Nor is the Government required to ensure that many such jobs are available: no

---

[108] General Comment 19: The right to social security (4 February 2008) UN Doc E/C.12/GC/19.

[109] Ibid paras 16 and 17.

[110] Ibid paras 33–34.

[111] Ibid paras 4–5. CESCR notes that almost all states will require some form of non-contributory scheme in order to properly fulfil the right, as insurance based schemes are unlikely to cover everybody (para 4(b)).

[112] Ibid para 7.

[113] General Comment 25: The right to participate in public affairs, voting rights and the right of equal access to public service (1996) UN Doc CCPR/C/21/Rev.1/Add.7 para 23.

[114] *Kall v Poland* CCPR/C/60/D/552/1993, 29 September 1997 [13.2].

particular public/private divide is prescribed under the ICCPR.[115] Article 25(c) is therefore very different to article 6 of the ICESCR, where states should take steps to maximise gainful employment amongst its adult population in the public and private sectors. Rather, article 25(c) guarantees each adult citizen a right to be free from unfair exclusion or removal from an available government position.

Trade Union Rights

In the ICESCR, trade union rights are protected by article 8, which explicitly protects the right to strike 'provided that it is exercised in conformity with the laws of the particular country' in paragraph 1(d). This provision represents the only explicit recognition of the right to strike in a global international instrument.[116] It is possible that the qualifier in paragraph 1(d) serves to totally undercut the right to strike, as 'the laws' of a country might totally prohibit strikes. The CESCR has however interpreted the phrase so as to ensure that the right has substantive content. For example, the CESCR expressed concern that Mauritian laws operated in such a way as to render most strikes illegal,[117] and that strikes in Russia could only be authorised if approved by the majority of a quorum of union members, with the quorum requirement set at the unreasonably high rate of two thirds of union members.[118] These concerns indicate that the right to strike cannot, in the CESCR's interpretation of article 8(1)(d), be unreasonably constrained by a state's municipal law. It is probable that the qualifier refers

---

[115] Joseph, S, Schultz, J and Castan, M, *The International Covenant on Civil and Political Rights: Cases, Commentary and Materials*, 2nd edn (Oxford, Oxford University Press, 2004) 671–72. Of course, other human rights imply a duty upon a state to have adequate personnel in certain sectors. For example, the right to security of the person under art 9 of the ICCPR would require states to employ an adequate number of police to protect people from crime. The right to free primary education in art 13(2)(a) of the ICESCR implies that states have an adequate number of government-run primary schools, with appropriate numbers of employees. Indeed, art 6 of the ICESCR itself may imply a duty upon states not to privatise certain sectors if that will cause significant job loss: see text above at nn 93–98.

[116] Fenwick, C, 'Minimum Obligations with Respect to Art 8 of the International Covenant on Economic Social and Cultural Rights' in Chapman and Sage, *Core Obligations: Building a Framework for Economic Social and Cultural Rights* (Antwerp, Intersentia, 2002) 67. The right is also explicitly protected by regional treaties.

[117] CESCR, 'Concluding Observations on Mauritius' (1994) UN Doc E/1995/22 37, para175. See also CESCR, 'Concluding Observations on the United Kingdom' (1997) UN Doc E/1998/22 56, paras 294 and 306; CESCR, 'Concluding Observations on Egypt' (2000) UN Doc E/2001/22 38, para 160; CESCR, 'Concluding Observations on Australia' (2000) UN Doc E/2001/22 66, paras 382 and 394.

[118] CESCR, 'Concluding Observations' (2003) UN Doc E/2004/22 64, paras 463 and 491.

to reasonable restrictions upon strike action, such as prohibitions on acts which inflict bodily harm.[119]

In *JB et al v Canada*,[120] a number of trade unionists submitted an OP communication in respect of laws in Alberta that prohibited strike action. The ICCPR does not explicitly refer to the right to strike. Rather, article 22 of the ICCPR guarantees freedom of association, which explicitly applies in paragraph 1 to persons wishing to form or join trade unions. The HRC majority correctly observed that any right to strike would have to be implied from the words of article 22. They found that the *travaux preparatoires* of the ICCPR did not mention a right to strike as an aspect of article 22. They further noted that the explicit inclusion of the right in article 8 of the ICESCR, which concerns trade union rights, indicated that it was not a fundamental aspect of the right to join trade unions. Therefore, the majority found the communication to be inadmissible for failure to raise a substantive matter under the ICCPR.

A sizeable minority, which included Ms Roslyn Higgins, later the President of the International Court of Justice, dissented. The minority found it unsurprising, and therefore inconclusive, that a right to strike was textually absent from article 22 as well as the relevant *travaux preparatoires*, as the article concerned a general freedom of association, extending far beyond trade unions. The explicit inclusion of a right to strike in article 8 of the ICESCR did not imply its absence from article 22 when one took into account the differing nature of the provisions, that is the specificity of the former (confined to trade unions) and the generality of the latter (applying to all types of associations).

In the minority view, article 22 clearly extended beyond the bare right to associate to the right to engage in certain collective activities as associations. 'Which activities are essential to the exercise of this right cannot be listed *a priori* and must be examined in their social context in the light of the other paragraphs of this article'.[121] Therefore, the question of whether article 22 protects a right to strike was, in the view of the minority, certainly admissible, and could probably be answered in the affirmative.

The minority noted that the right to strike is protected under ILO Convention No 87 on Freedom of Association and the Right to Organise,[122] and that there was 'no reason [at least at the admissibility stage] to interpret article 22 in a manner different from ILO when addressing a comparable consideration' such as the extent of the right to associate of trade

---

[119] The HRC has interpreted 'lawful' in the text of some ICCPR rights in a broad way to prohibit states from adopting perverse laws to evade ICCPR duties: see eg, Joseph, Schultz and Castan, *The International Covenant on Civil and Political Rights* (2004) 340–45.

[120] *JB et al v Canada* CCPR/C/28/D/118/1982.

[121] Ibid, dissenting opinion [3].

[122] The ILO Committee on Freedom of Association had in fact deemed the relevant Alberta law to be in breach of ILO Convention No 87: see ibid, dissenting opinion [7].

unionists.[123] ILO Convention No 87 does not explicitly guarantee a right to strike, but the right has been deemed an activity that is an essential means by which workers can protect their occupations, which of course is a prime function of trade unions.[124]

The minority opinion is preferable to that of the majority. The majority arguably interpreted article 22 as encompassing a bare right to associate, rather than rights to join associations which are able to conduct those activities necessary to fulfil their purposes. It is surely doubtful that the minimal protection offered to trade union activities under article 22 by the majority decision applies to all associations. For example, a right to join a political party is completely undercut if that party is unable to engage in political campaigns. On the other hand, there is no reason to single out trade unions for special disadvantage, as has possibly been done by the majority.[125] Further, the majority interpretation unfortunately means that the interpretation of 'freedom of association' under the ICCPR differs from that of the ILO under ILO Convention No 87, thus generating normative dissonance in international law.

Despite the *JB* precedent, the HRC has expressed concern in several Concluding Observations over restrictions on the right to strike, and the compatibility of those restrictions with article 22.[126] For example, in 2004 the HRC stated that a new labour law in Lithuania that severely restricted the right to strike 'may amount to a violation of article 22'.[127] It must be noted that such statements have been sporadic; it cannot be confidently asserted that the HRC has departed from the *JB* precedent.[128]

Gauthier v Canada (633/95)[129] raised the issue of the freedom not to join associations, a topic of relevance to the issue of 'closed shops' that is compulsory union membership. The complaint concerned the exclusive access of members of the Parliamentary Press Gallery (PPG) to the federal Canadian Parliament. The complainant, a journalist, was denied full membership in the PPG, and was therefore unable under Parliamentary rules to gain full access to Parliamentary media facilities. A minority of seven HRC members found that the requirement for the complainant to join a particular group in order to function as a reporter of parliamentary issues

---

[123] *JB et al v Canada* CCPR/C/28/D/118/1982 [7].

[124] Ewing, K, 'Freedom of Association and Trade Union Rights' in Harris, D and Joseph, S (eds), *The International Covenant on Civil and Political Rights and United Kingdom Law* (Oxford, Oxford University Press, 1995) 484.

[125] Joseph, Schultz, and Castan (n 115) 581.

[126] See eg, HRC, 'Concluding Observations on Chile' (1999) UN Doc CCPR/C/79/Add. 104 para 25.

[127] See eg, HRC, 'Concluding Observations on Lithuania' (2004) UN Doc CCPR/CO/80/LTU para 17.

[128] The treaty bodies are not strictly bound by their own precedents, but they rarely depart from them.

[129] *Gauthier v Canada* CCPR/C/65/D/633/1995, 7 April 1999.

amounted to a breach of article 22. The majority, in an opaque decision, found that the complaint was not substantiated.

Compulsory membership of a union certainly restricts one's 'freedom' to associate, which necessarily includes the freedom not to associate.[130] On the other hand, such a restriction on freedom of association might plausibly be justified on the basis that it protects 'the rights of others' under article 22(2) as compulsory unionism provides strong protection for the rights to work and to fair working conditions.[131]

Most other OP cases relating to trade unions have concerned horrendous examples of persecution of unionists. In particular, numerous early complaints against Uruguay[132] involved allegations of incommunicado detention and torture of people because of their union affiliations. Such cases do not advance our understanding of the protections offered by the ICCPR to trade unionists because the facts clearly manifested blatant and egregious human rights breaches.

Of greater (legal) interest is *Sohn v Republic of Korea*.[133] The complainant was a trade union leader convicted of a crime for having supported a strike against a shipping company and having condemned the state party's use of troops to break that strike. The state party justified the law, which prohibited third party interference in labour disputes, on the basis that it preserved public order and national security, particularly because the labour movement in the state was 'politically motivated and ideologically influenced'.[134] Further, the state party alleged that the complainant's support for the shipyard strike was 'a disguise to incite a nationwide strike of all workers',[135] which, in its view, inherently threatened public order and national security.

The HRC found in favour of the complainant, stating that the state party's 'reference to the general nature of the labour movement' did not 'specify the precise nature of the threat' posed by the complainant's actions.[136] The HRC apparently felt that the state party had failed to substantiate its allegations regarding the alleged incitement by the complainant of a national strike. Indeed, the possibility that the complainant wished to incite a national strike (the complainant did not confirm or deny this allegation) does not mean that there was any real danger that such a strike would eventuate. *Sohn* is a

---

[130] See also the judgments of the European Court of Human Rights in *Young, James and Webster v UK* (1982) 4 EHRR 38 and *Sigurjónsson v Iceland* (1993) 16 EHRR 462.

[131] Joseph, Schultz, and Castan (n 115) 583.

[132] See eg, *Weinberger v Uruguay* (1981) UN Doc Supp No 40 (A/36/40) 114, *Pietraroia v Uruguay* (1981) UN Doc Supp No 40 (A/36/40) 153, and *Lopez Burgos v Uruguay* (1981) UN Doc Supp No 40 (A/36/40) 176.

[133] *Sohn v Republic of Korea* CCPR/C/54/D/518/1992.

[134] Ibid [9.1] and [9.2].

[135] Ibid [9.3].

[136] Ibid [10.4].

useful case for the protection of the labour movement, as the HRC rejected the state party's generalised arguments about the danger posed by the alleged 'mischievous left-wing agenda' of trade unions. These arguments are commonly made by states such as South Korea which may genuinely face or at least fear a threat from advocates of communism given its history and its proximity to North Korea, but may also manipulate such fears to suppress workers' rights.

Forced Labour

The most meaningful consideration of the prohibition on forced labour in article 8(3) in an OP case arose in *Faure v Australia*.[137] The complaint related to provisions in Australian law requiring some recipients of unemployment benefits to undertake certain work as part of a 'Work for the Dole' scheme. Failure to perform such work will result in a reduction of unemployment benefit rates upon a second breach within two years and, upon a third breach, cancellation of unemployment benefit for a period of two months. The complainant committed at least three breaches and therefore lost two months' worth of her dole. She claimed that the Work for the Dole scheme amounted to forced labour in breach of article 8.

The HRC disagreed. It stated that 'forced or compulsory labour' covered labour imposed as a criminal punishment, 'particularly coercive, exploitative or otherwise egregious conditions' through to 'circumstances where punishment as a comparable sanction is threatened if the labour directed is not performed.[138] Of course, sanctions did arise for failure to comply with the Work for the Dole scheme, as such failure resulted in reduced dole payments. Article 8(c)(iv) distinguishes forced labour from 'normal civic obligations'. The HRC stated that work forming part of 'normal civic obligations' 'must, at a minimum, not be an exceptional measure; it must not possess a punitive purpose or effect; and it must be provided for by law in order to serve a legitimate purpose under the Covenant'.[139]

The HRC found that work performed under the scheme classified as 'normal civic obligations', though it offered no particular reasoning beyond noting an 'absence of a degrading or dehumanising aspect of the specific labour performed'.[140] Presumably, the HRC accepted the state party's extensive arguments regarding the 'concept of mutual obligation between

---

[137] *Faure v Australia* CCPR/C/85/D/1036/2001 (2005).
[138] Ibid [7.5].
[139] Ibid [7.5].
[140] Ibid [7.5].

an unemployed person and the community supporting him or her',[141] as well as the limited nature of the Work for the Dole scheme.[142]

Ms Ruth Wedgwood issued a separate opinion, which contained the following reprimand of the complainant:

> In a world that is still replete with problems of caste, customary systems of peonage and indentured labor, forced labor in remote areas under conditions that often mimic slavery, and the disgrace of sexual trafficking in persons, it demeans the significance of the International Covenant on Civil and Political Rights to suppose that a reasonable work and training requirement for participation in national unemployment benefits in a modern welfare state could amount to 'forced or compulsory labor' within the meaning of Article 8(3)(a).

Judith Bessant, writing in 2000, put forward a number of arguments against the Work for the Dole scheme, which were not iterated in the *Faure* submissions. She questioned the existence of truly reciprocal or 'mutual' obligations under the Work for the Dole scheme, noting that an unemployed person had an obligation to work under the scheme, while the Government had no corresponding domestic legal obligation to ensure that there was work available for all who sought it.[143] She also questioned the premise that the scheme prevents 'dole-bludgers' from taking advantage of the social security system; polls had indicated that most of those in receipt of dole payments genuinely wanted a job.[144] In her opinion, the scheme denied 'civil liberties' to the jobless, though she fell short of classifying work under the scheme as forced labour.[145]

Interestingly, the CESCR has expressed concern in Concluding Observations over the similar 'workfare' programmes in the Canadian provinces, whereby the recipients of certain social security benefits are required to accept certain work commitments in return for those benefits. The CESCR noted in 1998 that 'these [workfare] programmes constitute work without the protection of fundamental labour rights and labour standards legislation', and it implies that the scheme undermines the 'right to choose freely what type of work [one] wish[es] to do'.[146] While schemes

---

[141] Ibid [4.15].

[142] Ibid [4.16]: participants only work for six months at a time and for six months per year in work that is 'suitable and reasonable', the state pays for relevant insurance costs, and 'a fortnightly supplement is paid' to cover extra costs.

[143] Bessant, J, 'Civil Conscription or Reciprocal Obligation: the Ethics of "Work for the Dole"' (2000) 35 *Australian Journal of Social Issues* 15, 24. Indeed, no federal Australian government since 1975 has committed to the goal of full employment.

[144] Bessant, 'Civil Conscription or Reciprocal Obligation' (2000) 26, citing *Youth Bureau Report on Youth Consultations* (Canberra, DEET, 1995) 2, cited in Youth Affairs Council of Victoria (YACvic), 'Submission to Senate Community Affairs Committee Inquiry into the Proposed Social Security Legislation Amendment (Work for the Dole)' (April 1997).

[145] Bessant (n 143) 30.

[146] CESCR, 'Concluding Observations on Canada' (1998) UN Doc E/1999/22 para 405; see also para 430.

such as 'workfare' in Canada or 'work for the dole' in Australia do not breach the right to be free from forced labour in article 8 of the ICCPR, they might therefore breach the right to work in article 6 of the ICESCR. It may be noted however that the CESCR did not take the opportunity to clarify its position on such schemes in General Comment 18. Nor did CESCR criticise the Work for the Dole scheme in 2000, when it issued Concluding Observations on Australia.[147]

Prison Labour

Prison labour is permitted under article 8(3)(b) and (c)(i). In *Wolf v Panama*,[148] the HRC inferred that this exception cannot apply unless the relevant labourer has been convicted and sentenced.

In *Radosevic v Germany*,[149] the complaint concerned the poor remuneration of the labour he performed in prison, which he claimed was discriminatory. The complainant failed however to give details of the remuneration of equivalent workers outside prison, or indeed information on whether equivalent workers existed outside prison. In the absence of a relevant comparator, the complaint regarding article 26 discrimination was not substantiated.

The complainant also argued that the poor wages breached article 10(3) of the ICCPR, which requires that the 'essential aim' of the treatment of prisoners be 'their reformation and social rehabilitation'. Indeed, the Federal Constitutional Court of Germany agreed that adequate remuneration was an essential aspect of prisoner 'resocialisation' (provided for in the German Constitution).[150] In 1998, that Court found that the existing prison wage breached this principle. However, it permitted a transitional period of 30 months, which terminated on 31 December 2000, for the Government to amend relevant legislation and to calculate an appropriate rise in prison wages. The *Radosevic* complaint related to wages payable before that date. The HRC dealt with this point weakly, noting that 'States may themselves choose the modalities for ensuring [appropriate] treatment of prisoners, including any work or service normally required of them.'[151] In this respect, the HRC deferred to the Constitutional Court's decision to permit a transition period for amendment of the law.[152] The HRC does not adequately explain why a delay in implementation of a decision,

---

[147] Similarly, no mention of the scheme was made in the latest Concluding Observations on Australia from 2009.
[148] *Wolf v Panama* CCPR/C/44/D/289/1988, 80 (1992).
[149] *Radosevic v Germany* CCPR/C/84/D/1292/2004 (2005).
[150] Ibid [2.4].
[151] Ibid [7.3].
[152] Ibid [7.3].

which strongly indicated that the existing wages were incompatible with article 10(3),[153] should be permitted. While it may have taken time for the Government to calculate an appropriate wage rise, that rise could have been backdated to at least the date of the Constitutional Court's decision. The HRC decision seems to be permitting a progressive obligation given the resource implications of wage rises, despite the clear immediacy of ICCPR obligations dictated by article 2(1). Alternatively, it may be that, regardless of the position in German constitutional law, the HRC does not believe that adequate prison wages are necessary to implement article 10(3), in which case it should have said so explicitly. At the very least, the issue should have been examined on the merits rather than dismissed at the admissibility stage.

On the issue of prison labour, it may be noted that under the ICESCR, prisoners cannot be required to work for private companies without their explicit prior consent,[154] and that the conditions of such work 'must be close to those of a free employment relationship'.[155] These rules echo the requirements of ILO Convention No 29 concerning Forced or Compulsory Labour.[156]

Discrimination Regarding Employment Rights

The labour market must be accessible to all without discrimination in accordance with article 2(2) of the ICESCR and article 26 of the ICCPR. In General Comment 18, the CESCR outlined prohibited grounds of employment discrimination that are not enumerated in article 2(2), namely health (including HIV-AIDS) status, sexual orientation, disability, or 'civil, political social or other status' such as caste.[157]

In General Comment 18, the CESCR addresses issues regarding employment of specific groups. For example, regarding women, states must take steps to combat traditional cultures which impede the employment prospects of women.[158] Regarding young people, states should invest in vocational training to give young people the necessary skills to gain jobs.[159]

---

[153] Though the decision was based on German constitutional law, the German requirement of prisoner re-socialisation seems very similar to the obligation in art 10(3).

[154] See eg, 'Concluding Observations of the Committee on Economic Social and Cultural Rights on Germany' (2001) UN Doc E/2002/22 97, para 663.

[155] See eg 'Concluding Observations of the Committee on Economic Social and Cultural Rights on Luxembourg' (2003) UN Doc E/2004/22 24, paras 81 and 93.

[156] See also Fenwick, C, 'Private Use of Prisoners' Labour: Paradoxes of International Human Rights Law' (2005) 27 *Human Rights Quarterly* 249.

[157] General Comment 18 (n 20) para 12(b)(i).

[158] Ibid para 13.

[159] Ibid para 14.

The CESCR adopted General Comment 5 on 'Persons with Disabilities' on 9 December 1994. In General Comment 5, the CESCR noted that unemployment amongst disabled persons was 'two to three times higher' than for other persons.[160] Furthermore, they are often employed in low-paying and menial jobs 'with little social and legal security', and 'segregated from the mainstream of the labour market'.[161] In that respect, states should focus on integrating disabled persons into 'the regular labour market'.[162] Of course, truly equal access by disabled persons to work will require states to adopt legislation to enhance the physical accessibility of workplaces, via, for example, ramps, elevators, specially designed workspaces, and modification of transport facilities.[163]

Love et al v Australia[164] concerned a complaint of age discrimination contrary to article 26 of the ICCPR by four pilots who were forced to retire at the age of 60. Distinctions are justifiable under the ICCPR if they are deemed to be 'reasonable and objective'.[165] The HRC noted that 'systems of mandatory retirement age may include a dimension of workers' protection by limiting the life-long working time, in particular when there are comprehensive social security schemes that secure the subsistence of persons who have reached such an age'.[166] Furthermore, the HRC noted the ILO's failure to prohibit mandatory retirement ages. Regarding the facts of *Love*, the HRC agreed with the state party's argument that 'the aim of maximising safety to passengers, crew and persons otherwise affected by flight travel was a legitimate aim under the Covenant'.[167] Furthermore, there was a widespread global practice within the airline industry of imposing a retirement age of 60.[168] All of these considerations led the HRC to find that the mandatory retirement age was reasonable and objective, and therefore did not constitute a breach of article 26.

Hinostroza Solís v Peru[169] concerned a public servant who was made redundant during a restructuring of the public service. Redundancies were based on age and time in service. As the complainant was over 60 years of age, and had only served for 11 years, his employment was terminated. He claimed that his termination constituted discrimination contrary to article 25(c) of the ICCPR, which guarantees access to the public service on

---

[160] General Comment 5: Persons with Disabilities (11th session 1994) para 20.
[161] Ibid para 20.
[162] Ibid para 20.
[163] Ibid paras 22, 23. See also Convention on the Rights of Persons with Disabilities 2006.
[164] *Love et al v Australia* CCPR/C/77/D/983/2001.
[165] General Comment 18 (n 20): Non-discrimination at para 13.
[166] *Love* CCPR/C/77/D/983/2001 [8.2].
[167] Ibid [8.3].
[168] Ibid [4.12], citing the International Civil Aviation Organisation (ICAO) Convention on International Civil Aviation (Chicago Convention) Doc No 7300.
[169] *Hinostroza Solís v Peru* CCPR/C/86/D/1016/2001 (2006).

general terms of equality. The HRC ultimately found that 'the age limit ... for continued post occupancy was an objective distinguishing criterion and that its implementation in the context of a general plan for the restructuring of the civil service was not unreasonable'.[170] Therefore, no violation was found. Four HRC members dissented, and noted that the HRC's reasoning departed from that in *Love*. Whereas the HRC in *Love* examined whether, in the circumstances, the mandatory retirement age was reasonable, the HRC in *Hinostroza Solís* seemed to assume that the use of age as a criterion for choosing redundancies was per se reasonable. In contrast, the dissenters found that the state party had failed to show that age was an objective criterion upon which to base decisions regarding dismissal.[171]

The CESCR issued General Comment 6 on 'The Economic Social and Cultural Rights of Older Persons' of 8 December 1995, where it called for expedition of the elimination of mandatory retirement ages.[172] Efforts should also be made to prepare older workers for their retirement, including information about their rights and obligations, and techniques to cope with this major change in lifestyle.[173] It therefore appears that there is dissonance between the non-discrimination provisions of the ICESCR and the ICCPR regarding age discrimination at work. It is also an area where the ICESCR seems more progressive than the ILO.

CONCLUSION

The contribution of the CESCR and the HRC to labour rights jurisprudence has not been auspicious. Many important areas of labour rights, such as the right to collectively bargain, have not been meaningfully addressed. Other important areas, such as the right to strike, have been the subject of unsatisfactory jurisprudence such as *JB v Canada*, a case which might have deterred trade unionists from seeking redress for labour rights abuses under the Covenants. On a number of occasions, the relevant Committee has missed an opportunity to clarify important issues. For example, it is a shame that the HRC failed to expand upon the distinction between forced labour and normal civic obligations in *Faure v Australia*. CESCR's General Comment 18, whilst it is probably the greatest contribution by the treaty bodies to the field of labour rights, suffers from an over-abundance of unsophisticated generalised motherhood statements. In contrast, the reasoning in *Love v Australia* regarding age discrimination was sound. It is a shame

---

[170] Ibid [6.4]. The non-discrimination provision in art 25 has been interpreted similarly to that in art 26.

[171] Ibid, dissenting opinion of Messrs O'Flaherty, Kälin, Johnson, and Solari-Yrigoyen.

[172] General Comment 6: The Economic, Social and Cultural Rights of Older Persons, contained in UN doc. E/1996/22, 8 December 1995 [12].

[173] Ibid [24].

that the good work in that case was somewhat undone in the more recent case of *Hinostroza Solís v Peru*.

Most importantly, the treaty bodies, particularly the CESCR, should address the impact of globalisation upon labour rights more coherently and strategically, taking advantage of the serious cracks in the edifice of the Washington Consensus. Thus far, the treaty bodies' approach has been to point out the negative human rights effects of globalisation. Whilst it is important to note such consequences, the treaty bodies should also clarify when and how globalisation can be compatible with labour rights protection. That is, some detailed positive solutions should be mixed in with the criticism. The current approach of apparently sitting on the sidelines and criticising the globalisation juggernaut jeopardises the perceived relevance and worth of the treaty bodies' labour rights jurisprudence.

12

Taking Social Rights Seriously: Is there a Case for Institutional Reform of the ILO?*

JILL MURRAY

INTRODUCTION

THE OVERARCHING THEME of this volume is workers' human rights. This chapter takes as its starting point the idea that the emergence of a 'rights discourse' concerning International Labour Organization (ILO) institutions, actions and output needs to be mapped on to our understanding of the ILO, rather than simply assumed to be a complete and natural emanation of its activities. There is nothing new in this approach, as ILO officials and academic commentators have discussed the nature of the interface and overlap between ILO work and 'rights' for many years.[1] In 1968, for example, the International Labour Conference passed a resolution on human rights which identified a core group of labour standards and asked the Governing Body to seek their immediate ratification.[2] In this chapter, I consider the latest evolution in the relationship by considering the impact of 'core labour standards', as crystallised in the 1998 Declaration on Fundamental Principles and Rights at Work on one aspect of the ILO's functions, its rule-making function. By 'rule-making' I mean the creation of the conventions and recommendations, as explained in the Note on Terminology (below). I identify a 'core/rights' position, a bundle of ideas about international labour standards or rules which tends

---

* I would like to thank the participants in the Onati Workshop, the editors of this volume and the anonymous referees for their comments on an earlier draft of this chapter. Any remaining errors are my sole responsibility.

[1] See, eg International Labour Organization (ILO), *Human Rights: A Common Responsibility*, Report of the Director-General to the International Labour Conference (Geneva 1988) 46. See generally Murray, J, *Transnational Labour Regulation: the ILO and EU Compared* (The Hague, Kluwer Law International, 2001). This chapter discusses ILO instruments as at December 2007.

[2] Murray, *Transnational Labour Regulation: the ILO and EU Compared* (2001) 121–24.

to de-emphasise non-core rules and rule-making[3] and, it is argued, hampers the progressive evolution of the core itself. The dominance of the core/rights approach narrows the scope for ILO rule-making and rule-elaboration because it tends to be hostile to international labour standards which are 'aspirational', substantive, detailed, contingent and not immediately linked to a core/rights basis.

An argument built around only the rule-making function of the ILO is, of course, fundamentally incomplete. The ILO is a complex, multifaceted organisation in which direct and facilitative action to achieve ILO goals (often called technical co-operation within the ILO) has coexisted with standard setting and enforcement for many years. However, those programmes of technical cooperation do not exist in an organisational vacuum. To a marked extent, the status and nature of the ILO rules regime has been integral to debates about the ILO's technical cooperation function. From the 1950s onwards, arguments about the proper balance between making rules and making things happen through direct interventions or facilitations were based on the perceived need to de-centre rule-making and focus instead efforts to improve employment generation, reduce poverty, encourage education and development and so on.

Even today, the debates about the future of technical cooperation are expressed in terms of participants' views of the rule-making function of the ILO. The ideological divide between those who see technical cooperation primarily as the engagement of market forces to achieve economic and social outcomes, and those who see technical co-operation primarily in terms of ensuring adherence to ILO standards within the national realm was evident in the 2006 deliberations of the Committee on Technical Co-operation.[4]

So, while a discussion of the ILO which focuses only on rule-making and evolution does not do justice to the enormously complex sweep of ILO activities in the world, it goes to the heart of the ideological, practical and institutional arguments which are current today.

This chapter argues that the core/rights position or tendency, as it is identified here, is not natural or inevitable. The ILO's constitutional and policy goals are consistent with a broader conception of social rights.[5] Such a

---

[3] This point is powerfully made in Alston, P, '"Core Labour Standards" and the Transformation of the International Labour Rights Regime' (2004) 15(3) *European Journal of International Law* 457. But see the robust response to Alston's argument in Langille, B, 'Core Labour Rights—the True Story (Reply to Alston)' (2005) 16(3) *European Journal of International Law* 409.

[4] The employer representatives adopted the 'market forces' view, and the worker representatives the 'standards-based' view of technical cooperation. ILO, International Labour Conference (95th Session): Report of the Committee on Technical Co-operation (ILC95-PR19-166-En.doc), (Geneva 2006).

[5] I am drawing here on the work of Sandra Fredman, Ruth Ben-Israel, Simon Deakin and Frank Wilkinson, Keith Ewing, Amartya Sen, Bob Hepple and Guy Standing amongst others.

conception is encompassed in the current Director-General's sophisticated, multifaceted concept of 'decent work'.[6] I will use 'decent work' throughout this chapter to refer to the suite of values embodied in social rights which underpin the ILO and its activities. If we adopt this broader conception of rights, then there is a strong case for a *renewal of international rule-making and rule-elaboration tasks* as an urgent response to the changing world of work in the twenty-first century. The broader outlook of a social rights perspective further invites a creative approach to elaboration of the core standards themselves. I will discuss the opportunities for regulatory innovation in the core area of freedom of association and the 'non-core' field of working time.

It is further argued that the ILO has not fully 'constitutionalised' decent work. The ILO can become trapped in political gridlock where the tripartite parties are unable to agree on an agenda for rule-making, even though it is clear that new international rules would help to achieve decent work. Working time is a good example of such an issue, because despite recognition in the 1990s that new rules were needed, it has not been possible to gain the political support necessary for the creation of a new convention.[7] Further, the content of ILO rules is itself the product of vigorous contestation and negotiation. The International Labour Office, the international independent organisational unit within the ILO, does not have the power to veto rules that subvert decent work. Nor does it have the power to insist on the regulatory evolution necessary to achieve decent work.

There are no easy answers to these problems. The political gridlock around rule-making is likely to intensify in the face of any internal reform agenda aimed at unblocking it. The current process of contestation and bargaining over the agenda for rule-fixing and the content of the rules themselves is necessary to the legitimacy and authority of those rules. It is an essential part of the process by which rules made by the International Labour Conference become available for ratification, leading to the creation of binding legal obligations in the national spheres. However, regulation discourse, with its emphasis on 'de-centred' control,[8] suggests that there are other approaches which might serve some useful purpose. Several proposals are made in this chapter which suggests that a stronger role for the Office and a wider conception of the intended audience of ILO rules may assist in bringing the decent work agenda to fruition. Other regulatory clients—firms engaged in 'self-regulation', the international financial

---

[6] ILO, *Decent Work*, Report of the Director-General to the International Labour Conference (Geneva 1999).

[7] Servais, J-M, *International Labour Law* (The Hague, Kluwer Law International, 2005) 185.

[8] Black, J, 'Decentring Regulation: Understanding the Role of Regulation and Self-Regulation in a Post-Regulation World' (2001) 54 *Current Legal Problems* 103.

institutions and so on—could be more actively engaged in this process *provided* a clear view is maintained of their appropriate role in the regulatory system. Non-state actors cannot stand as states in relation to ILO obligations, and the limitations on their scope for action must be considered in any delegation of regulatory power to them, as I have argued elsewhere.[9]

The chapter is organised as follows. In the next section, the core/rights position and its implications for rule-making and rule-elaboration by the ILO are analysed. It is argued that the sharp binary distinctions between standards and rights upon which the core/rights position is based is artificial, and fails to recognise the actual nature of the ILO's regulatory functions. Then, an alternative vision involving a concept of broadly-based social rights is considered. It is argued that rule-making should evolve to give full effect to 'decent work' in response to the changed conditions experienced by workers around the world, and in response to innovations in regulation and social learning about its impact. In the next section, the current capacity of the ILO to initiate and develop new rules, and undertake the elaboration of existing ones is considered. It is noted that in some respects, the horse-trading and bargaining that is associated with ILO rule-making exposes the Organisation to charges that it may not always progress, or even comply with its own underlying values. Finally, I consider some possible institutional reforms which may provide a basis to progress a vigorous and targeted agenda of decent work. The problems with even these modest proposals are then analysed in the concluding section.

A Note on Terminology

Throughout this chapter I refer to ILO rules and rule-making. By this I mean the conventions and recommendations adopted by the International Labour Conference which form the heart of the ILO's regulatory interaction with states. I have deliberately avoided a detailed discussion of the question of the legal force of conventions, because this chapter seeks to highlight the possibilities which lie beyond a narrow focus only on the legally binding status (or otherwise) of such rules. This is not intended to minimise the potential *legal* impact of ILO rules in national settings. On the contrary, it is argued here that despite the current focus on enshrined rights, new rules (which includes direct and clear 'messages to law' in the national sphere) are needed in order for the ILO to fulfil its objectives. Rather, I hope to show that national labour law reform to attain decent work may come about through a multiplicity of ways, only one of which is state ratification.

---

[9] Murray, J, 'The Sound of One Hand Clapping: the "Ratcheting Labour Standards" Thesis and International Labour Law' (2001) 14 *Australian Journal of Labour Law* 306.

THE CORE/RIGHTS POSITION

In 1998, the ILO produced its Declaration on Fundamental Rights and Principles at Work. The Declaration contains what are known today as the core labour standards, a small set of labour rights and principles around which the ILO has been restructured, and to which special priority and processes have been accorded. The content of the Declaration is considered elsewhere in this volume. The Declaration can be seen as the ILO's response to intense yet disparate pressures to reform itself in response to globalisation and to intensifying criticism of its operations.[10] Of these various intellectual, political and pragmatic critiques of the ILO, a rights discourse played a part. In the human rights literature, which had paid scant regard to the ILO, there was a revitalised interest in the ILO and its place in a human rights schema.[11] Calls for the ILO to focus on a small number of core areas to prove its continuing relevance came to be associated with the language of rights in some quarters. For example, in 1994, Alston wrote that the ILO should select a core of conventions from its corpus of rules, and disseminate these widely. He argued that 'a clear ideological position in favour of basic human rights can be the Organisation's only viable *raison d'etre*'.[12]

Claims for the primacy of a small core of labour rights could only be made if a workable boundary were drawn between the core and the other labour standards. In the following Table 1, I set out various elements of the core/rights position which have been used to construct and justify this boundary. The table sets out a range of descriptive and normative elements, and each of these aspects is addressed in more detail in the next section. It should be noted that the core/rights position as posited here are an amalgam of views which is arguably coherent and at times is evident in the actual debates within and about the ILO. I do not intend to imply that the individual authors who are mentioned in connection with the table necessarily adopt the core/rights position as it is set out, nor would they necessarily support the binary poles posited below. The purpose of the table is to set up a paradigm position which is then assessed in terms of its descriptive power and normative force.

---

[10] See for example, Cordova, E, 'Some Reflections on the Over-Production of International Labour Standards' (1993) 14 *Comparative Labor Law Journal* 138.

[11] Leary, VA, 'The Paradox of Workers' Rights as Human Rights' in LA Compa and SF Diamond (eds), *Human Rights, Labour Rights and International Trade* (Philadelphia, University of Pennsylvania Press, 1996); Marks, S and Clapham, A, *International Human Rights Lexicon* (Oxford, Oxford University Press, 2005) 431–48.

[12] Alston, P, 'Post-post-modernism and International Labour Standards: The Quest for a New Complexity' in W Sengenberger and D Campbell (eds), *International Labour Standards and Economic Interdependence* (Geneva, International Institute for Labour Studies, 1994) 102. In his 2004 work, Alston argued that the Declaration amounted to a dilution of the ILO regime, because *all* ILO standards should be regarded as statements of rights not just the core, Alston, '"Core Labour Standards"' (2004).

Table 1: The Core/rights Position and the Boundary between Core and Non-Core International Labour Rules

Column 1 The Core	Column 2 The Non-Core
ILO rules that take the form of rights, with particular focus on civil and political rights.[13]	Aspirational standards.[14]
Rules that give expression to rights that are fundamental and are of the highest priority. Status as 'human rights' evidence of this.[15]	Rules about less important matters, not of the greatest priority.[16]
Permanent. Fixed.	Evolving. Contingent.[17]
Procedural.	Substantive.
Global or universal.[18]	Local, in the nature of short-term policy goals.[19]
Apply irrespective of economic level of development.[20]	Application depends on level of economic development.
Won't distort international trade, provided limited to rights that 'increase freedom of choice and freedom of contract'.[21]	'Costly' therefore suitable only for developed world.[22]
Corpus of rules is small and therefore manageable. Easier to implement and monitor.[23]	Corpus of other rules is large with voluminous rules and sometimes inconsistent provisions. Hard to implement and monitor. Rules of this kind inherently ineffective if not counterproductive, given the unknowable diversity of the world.[24]
Capable of attracting broad consensus amongst states.[25]	No consensus likely because of the 'need for cultural and political homogeneity' for such rules.[26]
These matters are amenable to clear expression in legally binding form at the national level.	Rules that require more nuanced national interpretation and are not amenable to an internationally determined 'one size fits all' approach;[27] or potentially ineffective 'command and control'[28] regulation (centrally determined legally binding rules) unsuited to such matters as pay, working time, health and safety and so on.

[13] Alston concludes that the selection of labour standards for the 1998 Declaration was based on the view that 'the international community cannot productively worry about specific social outcomes. Rather, its role is to ensure that workers enjoy certain basic civil and political freedoms'. Alston (n 3) 487.

[14] For example, Cooney welcomes the focus on the 'worst form' of child labour as a shift to rights away from aspirational standards in ILO rule-making: Cooney, S, 'Testing Time

The Descriptive Force of the Core/Rights Position

Two Kinds of Rules?

Do the two columns set out above establish a satisfactory schema for describing ILO rules? It is possible to argue that the boundary between the

for the ILO: Institutional Reform for the New International Political Economy' (1999) 20 *Comparative Labor Law and Policy Journal* 365.

[15] Alston points out that this is the claim made for the core labour standards: Alston (n 3)

[16] For example, Böhning argues of the right to work, to social security and just conditions of employment that 'their aura of important human rights seems to have evaporated ...': Böhning, WR, *Labour Rights in Crisis: Measuring the Achievement of Human Rights in the World of Work* (Houndsmill, Basingstoke, Palgrave Macmillan, 2005) 3.

[17] For some commentators, standards which need to evolve in line with shifting real world conditions are not suitable for legal regulation. An early expression of this view is that of TH Marshall, who argued that social rights existed in a sphere 'largely beyond the reach of juridical mechanisms', quoted in Deakin, S and Wilkinson, F, *The Law of the Labour Market: Industrialisation, Employment and Legal Evolution* (Oxford, Oxford University Press, 2005) 343.

[18] For a discussion of the interaction of international rules and trade, see McCrudden, C and Davies, A, 'A Perspective on Trade and Labour Rights' (2000) 3(1) *Journal of International Economic Law* 43, 51.

[19] Hepple argues that we should distinguish between global and local issues. Only the former need to be regulated internationally in line with the theory of 'subsidiarity': Hepple, B, 'Equality: A Global Labour Standard' in W Sengenberger and D Campbell (eds), *International Labour Standards and Economic Interdependence* (Geneva, International Institute for Labour Studies, 1994) 123.

[20] This binary opposition is put, for example, by Böhning, *Labour Rights in Crisis* (2005).

[21] Such rules may aid productivity and would not distort trade, McCrudden and Davies, A Perspective on Trade and Labour Rights' (2000) 51.

[22] McCrudden and Davies (n 18) 50.

[23] Cooney, 'Testing Time for the ILO' (1999) presents a compelling picture of the kind of regulatory burden an over-production of standards can place on states.

[24] There is a large literature on the topic this topic. Generally, see Ogus, A, 'New Techniques for Social Regulation: Decentralisation, and Diversity' in H Collins, P Davies and R Rideout (eds), *Legal Regulation of the Employment Relationship* (London and Dordrecht, Kluwer Law International, 2000) 88ff. A broad range of political philosophies underpins some of the theory about complexity and its challenge to law. See for example, Hayek's liberal position which argued that laws should be abstract and negative in character: Touchie, JCW, *Hayek and Human Rights: Foundations for a Minimalist Approach to Law* (Cheltenham, Edward Elgar, 2005) 10. Alternatively see Dorf, MC and Sabel, CF, 'A Constitution of Democratic Experimentalism' (1998) 98 *Columbia Law Review* 267, 270 which proposes communitarian participation in iterative rule-making processes to overcome the impossibility making effective laws from a central perspective.

[25] Valticos also argues that there is a 'universal consciousness' of importance of human rights: Valticos, N, 'International Labor Standards and Human Rights: Approaching the Year 2000' (1998) 137(2) *International Labor Review* 135, 144.

[26] Collins, H, 'Justifications and techniques of Legal Regulation of the Employment Relationship' in Collins et al, *Legal Regulation of the Employment Relationship* (2000) 15.

[27] See for example Wisskirchen, A, 'The Standard-setting and Monitoring Activity of the ILO: Legal Questions and Practical Experience' (2005) 114(3) *International Labor Review* 253.

[28] Fung, A, O'Rourke, D and Sabel, C, 'Realising Labor Standards' (2001) 26 *Boston Review* 1.

kinds of rules described in Columns 1 and 2 is more fluid than is recognised in the core/rights position. As Jenks noted in 1960, some ILO conventions do take the clear and classic form of a right: these standards are directions to ratifying states to refrain from infringing against the civil liberties or freedoms of workers in the areas of freedom of association, forced labour and discrimination in employment.[29] But is this the sum total of the ILO's 'human rights' output? At that time, Jenks identified a comparatively large number of ILO rules (26 conventions plus many recommendations) which he said were 'human rights' standards, suggesting, in his view, that the first column above should contain much more than is covered by the 1998 Declaration.[30] In addition, he argued that many other ILO standards, 'have a bearing on human rights', suggesting a relationship between the kinds of rules in Column 1 and Column 2 above.[31]

It is further evident that the classic rights formulation does not adequately capture the actual character of ILO rules said by the core/rights position to belong in Column 1. The most recent Convention on Child Labour, covered by the 1998 Declaration, does not take the classic rights form. The Convention takes the form of blunt directives to ratifying states, which must take 'immediate and effective measures to' prohibit and eliminate slavery, child prostitution and pornography, child drug trafficking and so on, rather than the classic rights construction of the definition of a liberty not to be infringed by the state.[32] It is not a statement of the human rights of the child at work. Indeed, it is notable that the Convention does not aim to *fully* guarantee the human rights of the child as they might be infringed through work, because of its specific focus and scope on particular gross abuses only.

Is there really a bright line boundary between these rules and the rest of the ILO conventions? I think the answer is no. This is because many non-core standards are constitutive of the principles/values/rights of the core. For example, many conventions permit the devolution of decision-making about the final nature of the standard to the processes of collective bargaining in the national realm. These conventions are not properly described as insulated from the core, but rather have a seamless connection to it via the fundamental right to freedom of association.

It is also relevant that, as Alston points out, the ILO core conventions on freedom of association must be 'read' in the light of the jurisprudence of the

---

[29] Jenks argued that the ILO rules on freedom of association, forced labour and discrimination are 'more closely akin to civil liberties than other economic and social rights which are in the nature of aspirations or general principles of economic and social policy'. Jenks, CW, *Human Rights and Labour Standards* (London, Stevens and Sons Ltd 1960) 9.

[30] Ibid xv.

[31] Jenks, *Human Rights and Labour Standards* (1960) 8.

[32] Convention No 182, Worst Forms of Child Labour Convention (1999) arts 1 and 3.

supervisory bodies.[33] Although Column 1 insists on the clarity and simplicity of the rights approach, the elaboration of the core right to freedom of association is complex, voluminous, attuned to a myriad of different national arrangements and circumstances. Taking the rule and its elaboration as a whole, it meets many of the characteristics ascribed to rules in Column 2.

The Nature of ILO Rules

Much of the characterisation of the rules in Column 2 seems to be misplaced because the core/rights position fails to recognise the sophisticated, calibrated, multi-faceted nature of the ILO rules.[34] The ILO Constitution provides guidance on the making of the kind of rules characterised in column 2 as inflexible and 'centrist'. The ILO must ensure that conventions are framed having regard to

> those countries in which climatic conditions, the imperfect development of industrial organisation, or other circumstances, make the industrial conditions substantially different and [the Convention] shall suggest any modifications, if any, which it considers may be required to meet the case of such countries.

Hence we see the widespread use of options for derogation by ratifying states, having regard to local economic conditions and the national government's superior knowledge of how to regulate them.

The structural flexibility of many ILO conventions is a complete answer to some of the Column 2 characterisations, especially the notion of imposition of developed world conditions on less developed states, and the charge that a 'single labour template' is being forced on disparate states. The nature of ILO rules is also part of an answer to the charge that labour standards on non-core subjects require homogeneity of national conditions to support widespread adoption.

Many examples could be given. Let us look at the ILO Convention No 138 on Minimum Age for Admission to Employment (1973), which has as its key provision:

> Each Member [State] for which this Convention is in force undertakes to pursue a national policy designed to ensure the effective abolition of child labour and to raise progressively the minimum age for admission to employment or work to a level consistent with the fullest physical and mental development of young persons.[35]

Other provisions in the Convention give more specific content to the ages which states may wish to consider unsuitable for their child workers: it refers to the various circumstances in which the minimum age for employment

---

[33] Alston (n 3) 491.
[34] The following section is based on Murray, 'The Sound of One Hand Clapping' (2001) 311.
[35] ILO Convention No 138 art 1.

may be set at 13, 14, 15, 16 and 18 years of age, as well as adopting a broader standard of 'the age of completion of compulsory schooling' which permits states to calibrate their standards to suit national economic and social need.

This Convention does not sit comfortably with much of the rhetoric of the core/rights framework. It does not look much like a negatively framed right of the kind promoted in Column 1. Of course, the abolition of child labour gives expression to various human rights as expressed in the international bill of rights and other instruments. Yet the actual Convention contains the kind of flexible detail associated with Column 2, without committing any of the 'sins' identified with those kinds of standards in the core/rights discourse.

NORMATIVE IMPLICATIONS OF THE CORE/RIGHTS POSITION

The implication of the core/rights position is that the ILO *should* limit its rule-setting to the kinds of rules envisioned in Column 1. It is argued here that the core/rights position fails to give expression to the broad range of rule-making and rule-elaboration tasks which the ILO should be performing if it wishes to do everything it can in relation to the attainment of decent work around the world.

Why does limiting the ILO to the core/rights position not fit with the goal of decent work? First, there are imperfections in the core labour rights as they are currently expressed. For example, in 1992 Compa pointed to inadequacies in Convention No 111 on Discrimination in connection with gender discrimination.[36] The capacity for the core rights to evolve to meet emerging social needs is by no means clear. A corollary of this is that the core rights may ossify and lose meaning in the face of these new conditions.[37] This issue is considered further in the following section.

Secondly, the core rights are necessary but not sufficient for the attainment of decent work. Legal rights to join a union and collectively bargain, while critical, are not a guarantee of the reality of collective voice and the uplift of working conditions. Legal protection creates some of the foundational conditions within which such processes and activities could occur, but social and economic conditions may slow or even stymie such

---

[36] Compa, LA, 'International Labour Standards and Instruments of Recourse for Working Women' (1992) 17 *Yale Journal of International Law* 151.

[37] See for example, Vosko, L, 'Gender, Precarious Work, and the International Labour Code: the Ghost in the ILO Closet' in J Fudge and R Owens (eds), *Precarious Work, Women and the New Economy: The Challenges to Legal Norms* (Oxford and Portland Oregon, Hart Publishing, 2006).

practices. Even where unions exist and function well, the interests of some workers may not be furthered through these processes. Women's social rights to decent work have not always been at the forefront of union claims. For example, in relation to Australia, Baird argues that the 'maleness' of the Australian trade union movement accounts for the fact that paid maternity leave was never seriously pursued through the (at the time) powerful mechanisms of national and sectoral collective bargaining in that country.[38]

A third issue is that the core rights may only provide a 'weak signal' to law and policy-makers in national jurisdictions as they deal with the plethora of matters covered by Column 2. Say, for example, a national government was puzzling over how best to devise strategies to ensure that workers could combine paid employment with domestic care, in order to meet a national need for increased birth rates, or increase women's labour market participation, or increase productivity, etc. If the international labour obligations of that country were limited to the core rights, then there is little information in the relevant ILO convention[39] about what steps would be consistent with the attainment of decent work, and very little (if any) indication of the kinds of regulatory innovation from which states could select an appropriate regulatory approach. That is, despite the claims of some experts that the core labour rights such as the right to work free from discrimination have a *positive* legal content,[40] little has been done to explicate and publicise this content in ways that could be used in national jurisdictions.

Most significantly, of course, is the fact that a limitation on the ILO's rule-making may have the effect (or create the impression) of leaving rule-making beyond the core 'ungoverned' at the international level. That is, other norm-creators—states, regional bodies, other international organisations, multinational enterprises or individual companies within national jurisdictions, individuals, un-mediated economic and social forces and so on—may be seen to be, or are, left to determine matters for themselves. While it is certainly not the intention of many advocates of the core/rights position, the core/rights position can therefore be comfortably aligned with neo-liberal philosophy, which advocates minimal regulation based around

---

[38] Baird, M, 'Parental Leave in Australia: The Role of the Industrial Relations System' in J Murray (ed), *Work, Family and the Law* (Sydney, Federation Press 2005) 45.

[39] Convention No 156 concerning Equal Opportunities and Equal Treatment for Men and Women Workers: Workers with Family Responsibilities (1981), art 4 of which requires ratifying states to take 'all measures compatible with national conditions' to help workers reconcile work and care, but does not specify legal or policy options/models.

[40] Hepple, B, 'Equality and Empowerment for Decent Work' (2000) 139(2) *International Labor Review* 5. For a more detailed account, see Hepple B, *Labour Law and Global Trade* (Oxford and New York, Hart Publishing, 2005).

individual choice with 'unregulated' markets determining substantive outcomes.[41]

AN ALTERNATIVE TO THE CORE/RIGHTS POSITION

The Idea of Broadly Conceived Social Rights

Many critiques of the core/rights position can be found in the literature on the ILO,[42] and can be derived from commentary on the role of human rights in labour matters in regional settings, such as the European Union (EU), and national settings themselves.

In relation to EU law, Fredman argues that human rights per se may cast an individualistic light on labour matters, and that a broader concept of social rights is to be preferred.[43] She argues that such rights should be capable of teleological evolution, having regard to their constitutionally defined foundation purpose. Although the technologies of regulation in the EU are very different to those of the ILO, the broad based focus Fredman recommends for the EU resonates with the social rights goals of the ILO. She argues for law which furthers the fundamental principle of equality by ensuring that workers are conceptualised by regulators as living within the network of responsibilities and bonds which characterise family and community life.[44]

Deakin and Wilkinson deconstruct the neo-liberal notion of the unregulated market by arguing that the satisfactory operation of markets requires legal protection of social rights and minimum standards in order to secure equality of opportunity in labour market participation. Interestingly for this chapter, they adopt a completely non-prescriptive approach to the content of the minimum rules they say are necessary to ensure that markets are adapted to enable people to exercise their capabilities within them. If Deakin and Wilkinson's argument for minimum rules to secure decent work is accepted, then surely it is the responsibility of the ILO to play a major international role in shaping the development of national legal rules and processes to achieve this end.

---

[41] Alston (n 3) explains the link between the Declaration and neo-liberalism, at 483ff. An apparent example of such advocacy in found in Wisskirchen, A, 'The Standard-setting and Monitoring Activity of the ILO: Legal Questions and Practical Experience' (2005) 114(3) *International Labor Review* 253.

[42] See for example Mundlak, G, 'The Transformative Weakness of Core Labour Standards Rights in Changing Welfare Regimes', in E Benvenisti and G Nolte (eds), *The Welfare State, Globalisation and International Law* (Berlin, Springer, 2004).

[43] Fredman, S, 'Discrimination Law in the EU: Labour Market Regulation or Fundamental Rights?' in H Collins, P Davies and R Rideout (eds), *Legal Regulation of the Employment Relationship* (London and Dordrecht, Kluwer Law International, 2000) 183.

[44] Fredman, 'Discrimination Law in the EU' (2000) 184.

In relation to the ILO itself, for example, Sen argues for a vision of rights which is compatible with aspirational standards. He argues that rights shouldn't be taken only to have a fixed meaning that is set for all time. There is therefore a role for the concept of 'aspiration'—the setting of standards at a level that is higher than the one that can be possibly obtained in a particular setting. The value of the 'rights claim' in this context is the moral and political weight it gives to those advocating for the higher standards. Systems should permit credit to be given for attempts to attain rights, even when they fall short.[45] Ben-Israel makes a strong case for the use of a broader social rights approach when describing what the ILO has done and when considering pathways for future action.[46]

Implications for ILO Rule-making of the Alternative Approach

If we accept the view that ILO rule-making exists to give effect to the goal of decent work or broadly defined social rights, what role should there be for ILO rule-making in the twenty-first century? As Cordova has shown, it is not rational to simply posit a real-world problem then mindlessly make a convention dealing with it.[47] The ILO's international character means that its rules have a particular role in what is a multi-level governance system. The ILO is in a 'regulatory conversation'[48] with states: they are the bodies which decide whether or not to ratify conventions, and thereafter what steps (if any) are taken to ensure compliance. The European idea of subsidiarity is relevant here: *ILO rules are useful to the extent that they further the attainment of social rights by adding to this regulatory conversation with states.*

This is not to say that the ILO can only have a legitimate field of activity in relation to rules which countries are prepared to ratify and adopt in law. This would be a way of internalising a global race to the bottom within the ILO, with only the most anodyne standards acceptable to all being promulgated. However, the states with whom the ILO engages are not monolithic entities which robotically agree (or reject) new ILO rules as they come off the production line. The behaviours which the ILO seeks to influence in making rules is broad, and includes that of legislators, ministers with policy or fiscal responsibilities, public agencies bound to adhere to ILO norms, lobby groups and others in civil society and even individual employers and firms. Within national regimes, many 'within State' and transnational

[45] Sen, A, 'Work and Rights' (2000) 139 *International Labor Review* 119.

[46] Ben-Israel, R, 'The Rise, Fall and Resurrection of Social Rights' in R Blanpain (ed), *Labour Law, Human Rights and Social Justice*, Liber Amicorum in Honour of Ruth Ben-Israel (The Hague, Kluwer Law International, 2001) 2.

[47] Cordova, 'Some Reflections on the Over-Production of International Labour Standards' (1993).

[48] I am using Julia Black's phrase.

actors and processes are capable of pressuring states to adopt or respond to a particular attitude to ILO rules.

Therefore, while the ILO system of legal enforcement revolves around its relationship with state entities addressed in conventions, in practical terms, the ILO speaks to a much wider audience. One of the key capacities of the ILO to influence national behaviour, then, is not only through the production, ratification and monitoring of standards and the publication of reports on compliance: it is through the informing and empowering of civil society about matters including what the role of law should be in response to common barriers to decent work. This observation informs some of the recommendations for institutional reform made in the final section of this chapter.

What are the tasks for rule-creation and rule-making? It is argued, far from rule-making becoming redundant now that the core labour standards are identified and enshrined in the Declaration, the goal of decent work requires new rules in response to important changes in the world of work. Before turning to possible instances of such rules, it is useful to return to the core/rights position to consider the issue of 'complexity'. It will be recalled that the core/rights position contains a tendency to argue that the world is too complex or too diverse for any internationally devised rule on a non-core topic to be of much use or legitimacy. It is commonly said, for example, that international conventions on working time or annual leave fall clearly into Column 2 for this reason. It will also be recalled that voluminous rules, or a corpus of many different rules was seen as inimical to the ILO's core mission, and therefore to be avoided.

However, are these arguments really valid? There are good reasons to adopt the opposite overall conclusion from that reached in the core/rights debates. Complexity and diversity in the real world (and its evolution over time) may call for multiple rules addressed to particular areas or elements of the ILO constituencies. A good example of the effectiveness of such specific, detailed and targeted rule-making is ILO Convention No 180 on Seafarers' Hours of Work and the Manning of Ships (1996). This Convention has been adopted without amendment as a European Community Directive, giving it legally binding effect within the Member States of the EU.[49] It is therefore arguably one of the most successful of ILO rules in terms of actual legal scope, despite the fact that it looks nothing like the brief, pure expressions of fundamental rights envisaged in Column 1 above. Of course, the fact that Convention No 180 deals with a relatively homogenous global industry, the maritime sector, might explain the ease with which it has been translated into EU law.

In the next subsections, I briefly discuss two areas where the attainment of decent work calls for the revision, renewal or re-elaboration of ILO standards.

---

[49] Council Directive (EC) 1999/63 Concerning the Agreement on the organisation of working time of seafarers concluded by the European Community Shipowners' Association (ECSA) and the Federation of Transport Workers' Unions in the European Union (FST) [1999] OJ L 167/33.

Challenges for Freedom of Association: the Need for Elaboration

In recent years, increasing attention has been paid to the concept of work itself.[50] Two burgeoning forms of work have evolved in isolation from the conceptualisation of work which led to the principal conventions on freedom of association and the right to collectively bargain. The first of these is what is known as the informal sector.[51] In developing countries, but not only there, this sector provides much of the available opportunities for work. Work in the informal sector is usually outside the legal regulation of work as it is traditionally conceptualised, and is often undertaken without the traditional formalities of the employment relationship. In some occupations, sectors, regions and countries such 'non-standard' work is in fact that norm. Informal sector workers may have no employer, no workplace as such and no legal security or protection whatsoever. The second development is the fragmentation of the employment relationship into other forms of work—self-employment, franchising, sub-contracting and so on, often as part of a deliberate employer policy to outsource risks of work to an employment agency, a contractor or to the worker themselves.[52] Despite their apparent legal independence, many people who work under such conditions are vulnerable to the abuse of economic power by others. However, what characterises such work in both the informal and fragmented sectors is its diversity, and the very different problems confronting those who perform the work. We can think, for example, of the different regulatory requirements of people who make a living 'gleaning' in urban settings compared with care workers whose formerly secure employment has been outsourced to the workers' own individual 'companies'.

The ILO has dealt with some of these issues in its deliberations on the employment relationship, which led to the creation of a Recommendation on this subject in 2005.[53] However, the challenges presented to decent work by both informal work and these non-traditional employment forms are many, and call for creative elaboration of both core and non-core conventions relevant to contemporary economic conditions.[54] Just as subordinate

---

[50] Supiot, A et al, *Beyond Employment: Changes in Work and the Future of Labour Law in Europe* (London, Oxford University Press, 2001).

[51] For a discussion of recent ILO activity in this area, see Trebilcock, A, 'Using Development Approaches to Address the Challenge of the Informal Economy for Labour Law' in G Davidov and B Langille, *Boundaries and Frontiers of Labour Law* (Oxford and Portland Oregon, Hart Publishing, 2006).

[52] Fredman, S, 'Women at Work: the Broken Promise of Flexicurity' (2004) 33 *Industrial Law Journal* 299; Fudge and Owens *Precarious Work, Women and the New Economy* (2006).

[53] ILO Recommendation 198 concerning the Employment Relationship (2006).

[54] See for example Fudge, J, 'Self-Employment, Women and Precarious Work: the Scope of Labour Protection' in Fudge and Owens (n 37) 201.

workers in traditional employment relationships needed to gather together to overcome their power imbalance with their employer, there are good reasons for the principles of freedom of association to be actively applied to work performed under informal and non-employment conditions. Just what form these new kinds of collectivity would take, and the shape of any 'bargaining' role, will depend on the actual circumstances of particular groups. This could only be done if the fundamentals of freedom of association are perceived to extend to such employment modes, which calls for creative elaboration of the conventions in ILO policies and public information. This is precisely what a recent study of organising amongst the self-employed called for: '[I]t is necessary to provide legislative support for alternative institutional arrangements to accommodate a diversity of employment situations and the changing boundaries of employment'.[55]

If national governments are to respond to calls such as this, there is little at the international level in the ILO rules as they are often understood to assist. What is needed is a careful, rigorous investigation of the proper boundaries of the idea of freedom of association, then the modelling of possible measures. As the ILO has shown in its Column 2 work over the decades, it has the capacity to create sophisticated proposals targeted at particular needs, selecting from a wide range of possible regulatory techniques including instructions to ratifying states to adopt hard law, soft law, policy, institution-building and so on. As Cranford et al say, new ideas about freedom of association may well lead to a 'plurality of representational forms',[56] not the clean minimalism of Column 1. Where possible, the voices of those engaged in these forms of work should be heard in the ILO discussions, as was the case to some extent with the creation of the ILO's Homeworkers Convention.

Working Time

Working time is the leading instance in the core/rights discourse of a matter the ILO should not regulate any further, if at all. From the core/rights perspective, rules dealing with working time are said to clearly belong in Column 2 (despite the presence of working time guarantees within the International Bill of Rights). In the ILO context, this view seems to hinge on the (mis)perception that any ILO rule, if adopted, would have the effect of increasing labour costs, presumably because commentators believe that ILO rules are *necessarily* going to alter the balance between work and 'not work' in favour of workers to the detriment of economic competitiveness in

---

[55] Cranford, CJ, Fudge, J, Tucker, E and Vosko, L, *Self-Employed Workers' Organising: Law, Policy and Unions* (Montreal and Kingston, McGill-Queen's University Press 2005) 184.
[56] Ibid 183.

ratifying states.[57] Working time is also a Column 2 matter because it invites the argument that a 'one size fits all rule' set at the international level has no hope of capturing the myriad of rich regulatory needs in the real world. Yet despite these arguments, the ILO has gathered compelling evidence that its current ILO working rules are out of date. There is a need for the circulation of ideas from the international realm about how best to achieve modern working time systems in national jurisdictions.

There is a paradigmatic view of working time evident within the existing ILO conventions, which is echoed in the human rights instruments themselves. This is the view that working time regulation involves adjudication between workers who want more leisure (at the same wage) and employers who want to extend working hours is reflected in the international bill of rights and the regional human rights instruments.[58] As Hall points out, policy paradigms are a framework of ideas that specify not only goals and instruments to attain them, but also carry with them a vision of the problem that the policy is designed to address.[59] The ILO's working time paradigm developed alongside the concept of the standard worker, a gendered entity who was presumed to work 'full-time' (itself a social construct with a particular, contestable meaning) over the life course, and for whom time away from work was leisure.[60]

The important rule-creating work which the ILO needs to undertake to give effect to social rights in the twenty-first century is the development of new working time paradigms. One element of a new working time paradigm should recognise the need to make work permeable to domestic care responsibilities, an issue which is poorly dealt with in the existing ILO conventions and which should be at the heart of the attainment of decent work. McCann has suggested a new way of conceptualising work, as 'time out of life', which creates a complete starting point from which such rules could be developed.[61] The ILO's new working time rule should also convey to state

[57] See Charny, D, 'Regulatory Competitiveness and the Global Co-ordination of Labor Standards' (2000) 3(2) *Journal of International Economic Law* 281 for a more nuanced discussion of the different economic effects of certain standards. Even Charny appears to place working time regulation in the 'static', not 'dynamic' category, ie it represents a 'tax on labor'.

[58] The Universal Declaration of Human Rights (UDHR) sets out a right to 'just and favourable conditions of work' (art 23(1)), and a right to 'rest and leisure, including reasonable limitations of working hours and periodic holidays with pay' (art 24). These provisions are restated in the International Covenant on Economic, Social and Cultural Rights (ICESCR) pt IIIk, art 7.

[59] Hall, PA, 'Policy Paradigms, Social Learning and the State: the Case of Economic Policymaking in Britain' (1993) 25(3) *Comparative Policy* 275.

[60] Murray, J, 'The International Regulation of Maternity: Still Waiting for the Reconciliation of Work and Family' (2001) 17(1) *International Journal of Comparative Labour Law and Industrial Relations* 25.

[61] McCann, D, 'The Role of Work/Family Discourse in Strengthening Traditional Working Time Laws: Some Lessons from the On-Call Debates' in J Murray (ed), *Work, Family and the Law* (Sydney, Federation Press, 2005).

governments and other non-state actors the plethora of regulatory innovation which has assisted workers and employers in modernising working time, while maintaining levels of employment and productivity.

It is not appropriate to regard such a rule as *necessarily* detrimental to developing nations, as Column 2 implies. To assert this is to argue that such countries should be encouraged to adopt and implement nineteenth and early twentieth century paradigms of work, including the male breadwinner model that has been the source of such disadvantage to working women in developed states. No costs necessarily flow from the paradigm shift as it is proposed. Indeed, there is a strong business case for such regulation. *The test of good international regulation should be whether or not it can convey a useful message of messages to the national realm which will alter behaviour (of the state and/or other actors) in ways which further decent work.*

ILO'S REGULATORY CAPACITY TO FURTHER SOCIAL RIGHTS/DECENT WORK

The ILO's institutional architecture is not as well adapted to serving the international agenda of attaining decent work as it might be. The role assigned to the International Labour Office by the ILO's Constitution, and the active involvement of the International Labour Conference's Legal Adviser in ensuring that particular conventions are permissible under the terms of the Constitution, are meant to ensure that rule-making is not suborned to deal-making and horse-trading in such a way that fundamental principles are neglected. I believe these processes need to be strengthened and made more transparent. For example, I have argued that in the case of Convention No 175 on Part-Time Work (1999), the Convention permits derogation from the core labour rights such as freedom of association in the case of part-time workers. This is despite the fact that the core convention on freedom of association does not itself permit this kind of derogation.[62] Perhaps a more muscular institutional framework would be useful in such cases: the Office could be given an explicit power of veto, or the less dramatic power to remove a draft convention from the consideration of the Conference for re-consideration at a later time. Such extraordinary powers would of course be linked to the need to preserve the integrity of the fundamental principles of the ILO, as understood in the era of 'decent work'.

The second serious issue is that the ILO itself does not have the independent power to shape the rule-making agenda. This means that it is possible for an issue to be of vital real world importance, as I would argue is the

---

[62] Murray, J, 'Social Justice for Women? The ILO Convention on Part-time Work' (1999) 15 *International Journal of Comparative Labour Law and Industrial Relations* 3.

case in relation to the working time revision discussed above, yet not be able to act because of the lack of political consensus to deal with the issue. For many years, the International Labour Office argued that the conventions which prohibited women's work at night were contrary to the ILO's own Convention on Discrimination in Employment. However, it could not engineer the necessary support to deal with the matter despite this being brought to the tripartite parties' attention.[63] The question of general working time revision has been gridlocked since the 1990s. Despite much activity in 2005 and this year,[64] the ILO Governing Body has announced that the only option for future regulation of working time is

> the holding of a tripartite meeting of experts on working time with a view to preparing a guidance document, opening up the possibility of placing the question of a general discussion on the agenda of a future session of the Conference.[65]

The ideological divisions, especially between the employer and worker groups, are stark. The employers have adopted the core/rights position:

> [The employers group] pointed out that work today was by nature very diverse and that therefore a 'one-size-fits-all' approach to working hours was simply not practical ... workers and employers should have considerable discretion to negotiate working time arrangements in a decentralised manner, although general rules were needed to structure this process to enforce minimum standards (eg health and safety).[66]

POSSIBLE REFORMS OF THE ILO TO PROTECT AND PROMOTE SOCIAL RIGHTS/DECENT WORK

A Reform of the Permanent Organs of the ILO

One of the strengths of a permanent organisation is that it has the institutional capacity to build up expertise and skills across the breadth of its activities. The International Labour Office is the independent arm of the ILO, and more should be done to exploit the resources of the Office to ensure that the work done in the ILO bureaucratic divisions is fully integrated into the political, rule-making process. The Office should be given a more explicit and transparent power to require the International Labour

---

[63] Murray (n 1). In 1990 a new ILO Night Work Convention (Convention No 171) was created which essentially 'leveled down' in equalising the position for men and women. Work at night is conceptualised as basically acceptable for all workers, irrespective of gender, subject to health and safety considerations.

[64] See ILO, *Hours of Work—From Fixed to Flexible?* International Labour Conference (93rd Session), 2005, Report III (Part 1B).

[65] ILO Document GB.294/LILS/7/1.

[66] ILO Document GB.294/LILS/7/1 para 10.

Conference to ensure that rules are 'constitution-compliant'. All ILO proposals for action, agenda setting, allocation of resources and so on should pass through the Office to ensure that the action proposes furthers, not undermines, the goals of the Organisation.

If it were conceptualised as a 'guardian' of the ILO Constitution, the Office could usefully be empowered to make independent proposals for new rules. Further, it could aid the development of constitutionally sound rules by preparing model rules on all topics before the Conference, and disseminating these amongst a broad sweep of the ILO's clients (see below for further comment on this notion). Of course, at the moment the Office plays a very significant role akin to this in drafting new conventions and recommendations, by providing the Conference organs with starting points for their negotiations. What is envisaged here is a more formal process, and one which is less attuned to the bargaining demands and real politic of the negotiating parties. That is, the Office's model rule should be a 'best' option based on a deep understanding of the demands of decent work, rather than a strategic instrument.

This modelling would serve two purposes. First, it would give the Office the chance to access into the Organisation's deep expertise in order to propose regulatory strategies unclouded, as it were, by the politics of the negotiation process. Although these model rules would not have formal status for ratification, they may serve a significant purpose in shaping the Conference debates about a topic. Ideally, the Conference would be 'bargaining in the shadow' of the model rule, which could be a default convention which is deemed to have been accepted if the Conference fails to agree an alternative constitution-compliant instrument on that topic. Secondly, provided the active role of the Office was strengthened in the ways suggested, the model rule itself may ultimately be able to play an important role in diffusing innovation around the world even if it is not ultimately adopted as a convention available for ratification. This could be achieved more readily if the following suggestion is adopted.

Widening the ILO's Regulatory Conversation/s:[67] The Force of Ideas

One of the claims made for rules emanating from Column 1 in the core/rights discourse was that such ILO rules provided a clear 'message to law' in the state realm. That is, ratifying states were obliged to secure fully known ends through legal means in their jurisdiction. This view of ILO rules means that

---

[67] I have used the phrase 'regulatory conversation' which I first heard when Julia Black mentioned it in her speech to the Australian Society of Legal Philosophy Conference at the Australian National University in Canberra in 2003.

the core/rights position starts from a traditionally narrow understanding of ILO rule-making, with ratification by states the key product to secure success. However, as briefly argued above, many different agents within the national and international social world may make use of rules made by the ILO to built support for regulatory change in one or another (or all) jurisdictions in the world. It is this decentred view of decision-making, based on a more complicated view of the state than is evident in much of the core/rights literature, which informs this section of the chapter.

Given the gridlock in formal rule-making under pressure from the core/rights position, the ILO's permanent bureaucracy should continue to strengthen its 'regulatory conversations' with the widest possible range of groups. In doing so, it should adopt as broad a view of ILO 'products' (a phrase now used within the Organisation to describe its output). This gives rise to the possibility of utilising rules such as the ILO Recommendation on Employment Relationships to foster debate and legal change within national realms without the traditional instrument of the convention as the centrepiece of the conversation. Such an approach should recognise that an important regulatory mechanism at both national and international levels is the force of ideas.[68] It is possible for ideas about, say, the reconciliation of work and family to circulate around the world and bring about change within jurisdictions in the absence of any legally binding compulsion to adopt new ideas. For example, in 2005, the Australian Industrial Relations Commission specifically acknowledged that it had adopted a version of the United Kingdom's 'right to request' laws (which enable workers to request changed hours of place of work, and simply require employers to consider the requests) in the very different context of the Australian system of conciliation and arbitration.[69] Of course, new ideas only take root if the circumstances are right, and so this method could never replace the creation of authoritative instruments that have the capacity to bind states in international law. In the absence of the political will to develop the necessary instruments, however, a strategy based around ramping up the diffusion of regulatory options is a 'least worst' alternative.

The literature on how and why 'states' change their minds about important policy issues suggests that different actors might be engaged at different times.[70] Coalitions may form and dissolve. As Black et al put it, 'our analysis has highlighted the importance of moving beyond broad stereotypes of "institutional matter" toward a close study of what types of mechanisms

---

[68] Baldwin, R and Cave, M, *Understanding Regulation: Theory, Strategy and Practice* (Oxford, Oxford University Press, 1999) 18.

[69] Murray, J, 'The AIRC's Test Case on Work and Family Provisions: the End of Dynamic Regulatory Change at the Federal Level?' (2005) 18(3) *Australian Journal of Labour Law* 325.

[70] Black, J, Lodge, M and Thatcher, M, *Regulatory Innovation: A Comparative Analysis* (Cheltenham, Edward Elgar, 2005).

and processes are underlying regulatory innovation and how different elements of regulatory regimes interact'.[71]

A full analysis of these issues from an ILO perspective has not, to my knowledge, been undertaken. However, as Braithwaite and Drahos have shown, the ILO is comparatively well-placed to engage with groups, 'ideas entrepreneurs', various 'epistemic communities' (such as the academics at this conference) and local communities because of its system of regional offices around the world.[72]

Hall's work suggests that the media in some historical settings is a very important influence on changes in government policy.[73] Like everything it does, the ILO's media interface with the world is complex and difficult to characterise. But at least in some respects its use of modern media techniques including 'spin' is not as effective as it could be, albeit that it has vastly improved in recent years. For example, the Director-General could usefully play a more prominent role in global and national media debates about labour issues. The tools of advertising and modern media management could prove powerful in the hands of the ILO. As Hall argues, sometimes even a simple metaphor like 'the war on drugs' can carry ideas around the world and lead to real changes in behaviour at the national level. Yet to date the phrase 'decent work', despite its widespread acceptance within international and regulation governance structures including the UN generally and the EU, in my experience within Australia scarcely resonates beyond its own commonsense meaning. Other participants at the Workshop which preceded this book took a different view, so no doubt the reality is more complex than I have experienced it from an Australian, English-language perspective. However, I doubt if anyone would disagree with the idea that the ILO could do more to improve public awareness of its mission and standards.

Pressing the ILO's Regulatory Advantage in Relation to Corporate Self-Regulation

Much has been written about the complex network of institutions and instruments which seek to promote the ILO core labour standards through the processes of voluntary corporate self-regulation.[74] Yet insofar as the ILO core standards take the form of negative civil liberties, adoption by

---

[71] Ibid 190.

[72] Braithwaite, J and Drahos, P, *Global Business Regulation* (Melbourne, Cambridge University Press, 2000).

[73] Hall, PA, 'Policy Paradigms, Social Learning and the State: the Case of Economic Policymaking in Britain' (1993) 25(3) *Comparative Policy* 275.

[74] These are discussed in Murray, J, 'Corporate Social Responsibility' (2004) 4(2) *Global Social Policy* 171.

companies requires a complex act of translation. The instruction to the state must be put into terms which a company is capable of applying. For example, it makes little sense for a company to say that it will respect freedom of association unless it actually has a policy which deals with right of entry, processes for information, consultation and bargaining. Core labour standards need to be brought to life by positive programmes of action, not just passive acceptance of principles.[75]

The task of elaborating and reviving the core standards could be furthered in this context, if the ILO were able to prepare codes which set out the meaningful corporate steps to compliance. The same is true of the non-core standards. For example, the ILO's chief Work and Family Convention has, as its main provision, a requirement that ratifying states adopt a national policy on this subject. It is meaningless for *companies* to make this undertaking (indeed they are not in a position to make any undertakings in relation to national policy, other than to support it once made). Yet, to date, the ILO has not explicated what steps firms should take to give effect to the spirit of this and the anti-discrimination conventions. It would be appropriate for the ILO to explicate the positive aspects of the Discrimination in Employment Convention, for example, in order to create specific provisions at the firm level. To date, these tasks have not been performed, probably because of political resistance from employer groups and their state supporters to anything that would lead to more accountability in the self-regulatory schemas. However, if the role of the Office could be strengthened and made even more central to ILO policy formation as suggested above, then the organisational space may be available for this work to be performed.

CONCLUSION

This chapter has identified a core/rights position, a bundle of attitudes to the ILO's body of rules which seeks to place great emphasis on the core labour standards, especially their status as fundamental human rights. The core/rights position suggests that other kinds of ILO rules (the non-core kind) should no longer be pursued, and that existing rules on non-core topics are inherently less important than the core. The dominance of the core/rights position is associated with a hostile environment for rule-making and elaboration within the ILO. Yet the need for such work is clear.

This chapter has argued that if there is a rights discourse it should start with the confluence of broadly defined social rights and the ILO's own concept of decent work. Then, a rights discourse could energise an extensive programme of rules revision, renewal and new rule-making by the

[75] Ibid 180.

Organisation. However, the current organisational structure and powers of the ILO mean that it is not able to guarantee the social rights already created, nor to ensure that all future actions are consistent with a goal of achieving these rights. Some modest proposals to further the agenda for decent work were outlined above.

There are difficulties with even these proposals. The key problem is that of legitimacy. Model 'rules' made by the International Labour Office would not be ILO conventions, would not be open for ratification and would not be part of the implementation and monitoring procedures. Any further empowerment of the Office as suggested above would have the capacity to threaten the transparency and participatory features of the ILO system as it exists now. An unaccountable bureaucracy might be prey to 'capture' by one group or another, or become victim to an institutional goal of self-preservation or simple inertia. Without direct participation from the social partners and national government representatives, the feedback loops in the system as it currently stands may shut down.

And, of course, the kind of measures outlined above would only lead to *legal* change if there was some happy conjunction of circumstances which aligned political decision-making in the national realm with the Office's model proposals. Further, in some important areas even though there is an extant ILO convention, its 'message to law' in the national realm is vague or weak, as discussed above in relation to the Convention on Workers with Family Responsibilities. The ILO must not abandon its traditional role of showing the way to national labour law through the creation of conventions which instruct ratifying states as to national minimum *legal* standards. Without legal rules, the disadvantages of private ordering for those who combine work and care will continue without impetus for change at the international level.

Finally, it is not entirely clear that the decent work concept, even if placed in the framework of social rights in the ways suggested by Ben-Israel and others, can bear the weight that is being placed on it here. For example, its normative content is rather vague, and tends to be discussed primarily in the context of the core labour standards. Perhaps the first step to constitutionalising social rights within the ILO has to be a rigorous programme of work to clarify in authoritative terms the key components of decent work. I imagine that even this task would be extremely controversial. However, this work is necessary to ensure that the contemporary language of core/rights is mobilised in a constructive way to help the ILO continue its important task of fostering social justice for the world's workers.

13

The ILO, Freedom of Association and Belarus*

LISA TORTELL

INTRODUCTION

DEVELOPMENTS IN THE International Labour Organisation's (ILO) approach in the past decade are emblematic of wider changes in labour law theory and practice internationally. The ILO has, from its inception, utilised the language of human rights and social justice to explain the nature of its task. The preamble to the ILO's 1919 Constitution refers to the necessity of achieving social justice as part of a universal and lasting peace, and the 1944 Philadelphia Declaration, setting out the Organisation's aims and purposes, unambiguously affirmed that individuals 'have the right to pursue both their material well-being and their spiritual development in conditions of freedom and dignity, of economic security and equal opportunity'.[1]

In recent years, the Organisation has increased its emphasis on the human rights aspect of workers' rights. This can be seen particularly in relation to the 1998 Declaration on Fundamental Principles and Rights at Work which reformulates certain of the Organisation's traditional standards and principles in the modern language of rights, creating four 'core labour standards': freedom of association and collective bargaining; elimination of forced labour; abolition of child labour; and elimination of discrimination in employment.[2] The 'cornerstone' of the Declaration is '[h]uman rights at work'.[3]

* The author gratefully acknowledges the financial support of the Portuguese Fundação para a Ciências e a Tecnologia, and the perceptive comments of Karen Curtis and Oksana Wolfson on an earlier version of this chapter. The views expressed here are solely those of the author.

[1] International Labour Organisation (ILO), 'Declaration of Philadelphia, Concerning the Aims and Purposes of the International Labour Organisation' (1944) art III.

[2] Note that the language used within the text of the Declaration is of 'core labour standards' and not 'labour rights': see eg Alston, P, '"Core Labour Standards" and the Transformation of the International Labour Regime' (2004) 15 *European Journal of International Law (EJIL)* 457. Nevertheless, its full title refers to 'fundamental principles and rights'.

[3] N'Diaye, M, 'The Annual Review and the Promotion of the 1998 ILO Declaration on Fundamental Principles and Rights at Work: Developments and Initial Assessment' in J Javillier et al (eds), *Les Norms Internationales du Travail: Un Patrimoine pour l'avenir. Melanges en l'honneur de Nicolas Valticos* (Geneva, International Labour Office, 2004) 411.

In 1999, the Director-General introduced 'decent work' as a unifying framework for the Organisation's work.[4] It is, simply put, a re-packaging of the Organisation's work as '[i]t has greater resonance with the public than the conventional way of formulating the organisation's central objectives'.[5] Another example of the modern emphasis on 'rights-talk' in the ILO is the 2004 Report of the World Commission on the Social Dimension of Globalisation, in relation to which the Director-General stated that the ILO was 'positioning [itself] for the future'.[6] The 2008 ILO Declaration on Social Justice for a Fair Globalisation continues the emphasis on rights at work, positioning the discussion within the debate on the labour standards and trade nexus.

One consequence of this re-branding of the ILO's goals has been a vigorous debate concerning the desirability of developing core labour rights, potentially relegating the rest of the ILO's work to a second-tier of urgency, reducing the potency of the conventions, and depriving workers of access to recourse.[7] This debate has become a defining feature of analyses of the ILO's work.[8]

In that context, this chapter focuses on the potential of the ILO to impact upon workers' lives by examining the observance of freedom of association in Belarus. The chapter attempts to assess the impact of the ILO's regulatory bodies on workers in Belarus in relation to the country's observance of freedom of association, one of the core rights. It begins by outlining the nature of the relevant legal mechanisms. Following a survey of the way in which those mechanisms have addressed the question of freedom of association in Belarus, it discusses the effectiveness of traditional ILO mechanisms.

THE ILO AND BELARUS

Supervisory Mechanisms

Traditionally, the key ILO mechanisms to protect workers' rights are its conventions and recommendations. The Committee of Experts on the

---

[4] International Labour Organisation (ILO) (87th Session) Decent Work, Report to the Director General, International Labour Conference (Geneva, 1999).

[5] Ghai, D, 'Decent Work: Concepts, Models and Indicators' (Discussion Paper 139/2002, Geneva, International Institute for Labour Studies (IILS), 2002).

[6] International Labour Conference (92nd Session) Record of Proceedings, Provisional Record 25 (Geneva, 2004) 1.

[7] See eg Alston, '"Core Labour Standards" and the Transformation of the International Labour Regime' (2004); Alston, P, 'Facing Up to the Complexities of the ILO's Core Labour Standards Agenda' (2005) 16 (3) *EJIL* 467; Langille, B, 'Core Labour Rights—The True Story (Reply to Alston)' (2005) 16 (3) *EJIL* 409; Maupain, F, 'Revitalisation Not Retreat: The Real Potential of the 1998 ILO Declaration for the Universal Protection of Workers' Rights' (2005) 16 (3) *EJIL* 439; and Murray, J, in chapter twelve.

[8] See especially, Macklem, P, 'The Right to Bargain Collectively in International Law: Workers' Right, Human Right, International Right?' in P Alston (ed), *Labour Rights as Human Rights* (Oxford, Oxford University Press, 2005) 82.

Application of Conventions and Recommendations (CEACR) considers government reports in relation to ratified conventions, providing technical supervision. The 'more difficult cases' are referred to the tripartite Conference Committee on the Application of Standards, a standing committee of the International Labour Conference.[9] The Conference Committee 'provides an opportunity for direct dialogue between governments, employers and workers' and considers in detail individual countries called to appear before it.[10] While the Committee of Experts 'conducts a technical and impartial examination of the cases', the Conference Committee 'contributes the political weight'.[11]

In contradistinction to the other core labour rights, the right to freedom of association is subject to a further supervisory mechanism. The Committee on Freedom of Association (CFA) is a tripartite body comprising members of the ILO Governing Body that examines complaints submitted by governments or workers' and employers' organisations concerning violations of trade union rights by states, regardless of whether or not the state in question has ratified either of the freedom of association conventions. It then recommends action to governments through the Governing Body.

Further, articles 26–29 and 31–34 of the ILO Constitution allow for complaints of non-compliance with ratified conventions to be heard by an ad hoc Commission of Inquiry, set up for each case by the Governing Body. The Commission will examine the complaint and produce a report including recommendations. In the case of a failure to carry out recommendations within the time frame, pursuant to article 33, the Governing Body may itself recommend 'such action as it may deem wise and expedient to secure compliance therewith'.

The Commission of Inquiry is reserved for the more serious cases.[12] It has the potential to be an important human rights supervisory body given the usual high standing of its members,[13] the considerable resources at its disposal, and its power to make recommendations sculpted to the particular circumstances, with time limits and subject to the scrutiny of the

---

[9] Swepston, L, 'Human Rights Law and Freedom of Association: Development through ILO Supervision' (1998) 137(2) *International Labour Review* 169, 174.

[10] ILO, *ILO Law on Freedom of Association: Standards and Procedures* (Geneva, ILO, 1995) 166.

[11] Ibid 166.

[12] Only 12 Commissions have been established: in relation to complaints against Portugal (1961), Liberia (1962), Haiti and the Dominican Republic (1968), Nicaragua (1973), Chile (1974), Poland (1982), the former German Democratic Republic (1985), Romania (1990), Myanmar (1996), Nigeria (1998), and Belarus (2003) and Zimbabwe (2008).

[13] Valticos, N, 'Les commissions d'enquête de l'Organisation internationale du Traveail' (1987) 3 *Revue Générale de Droit International Public*, 847, 856 noted that the members of the first seven Commissions were 'de hauts magistrats nationaux ou internationaux, des professeurs d'université, quelques anciens chefs d'Etat ou de gouvernement ou d'anciens ambassadeurs ou hauts fonctionnaires'. This equally sums up the membership of the following Commissions.

world's governments through the Governing Body and Conference. The first Commission of Inquiry, established in 1960 in relation to Portugal's observance of the forced labour convention in its African territories, stressed three basic considerations: the Commission's procedure is of a judicial nature; its functions are quasi-inquisitorial; and there is a need for rapidity.[14] Finally, 'coordination of the response by the supervisory system mainly falls on the Governing Body'.[15]

The Republic of Belarus, then the Byelorussian Soviet Socialist Republic and a member of the Soviet Union, has been a member of the ILO since 1954 and ratified both the Freedom of Association and Protection of the Right to Organise Convention 1948 (No 87) and the Right to Organise and Collective Bargaining Convention 1949 (No 98) in 1956. Accordingly, Belarus submits periodic reports to the Office in relation to legislative aspects of freedom of association in the country pursuant to article 22 of the ILO Constitution. The Committee of Experts has commented on Belarus' legislative implementation of the conventions, and the country has been called before the Conference Committee. Simply by membership of the Organisation, Belarus is subject to the scrutiny of the CFA in relation to cases submitted against it. In response to an article 26 complaint alleging breach by Belarus of its obligations towards freedom of association, the Governing Body established a Commission of Inquiry. In addition, the country has received technical assistance from the ILO, including a number of on-the-spot and direct contacts missions by ILO officials to Belarus, during this time.

Freedom of Association in Belarus: The Committee of Experts, the Conference Committee and the CFA 1995–2003

Belarus, a member of the ILO for a number of years, only became truly independent in 1991 with the break-up of the Soviet Union. Following the establishment of a sovereign Belarus, the Committee of Experts had noted with satisfaction[16] that it appeared that the country's legislation allowed

---

[14] ILO, Report of the Commission Appointed under Art 26 of the Constitution of the International Labour Organisation to Examine the Complaint Filed by the Government of Ghana concerning the Observance by the Government of Portugal of the Abolition of Forced Labour Convention 1957 (No 105) (1962) OB XLV(2) II, 271 para 15. See further Wolfson, O, Tortell, L and Pimenta, C, 'Colonialism, Forced Labour and the International Labour Organization: Portugal and the first ILO Commission of Inquiry' (ILO Century Project Working Paper, 2008).

[15] ILO, Improvements in the standards-related activities of the ILO: Improving the coherence, integration and effectiveness of the supervisory system through a better understanding of its dynamics (further study from a substantive and practical standpoint) (GB.303/LILS/4/2, 303rd Session, Geneva November 2008) para 11.

[16] Observations of satisfaction are used when a government has taken the steps called for by the Committee of Expert's earlier comments: *Handbook of procedures relating to international*

for a genuine system of trade union pluralism.[17] This was not, however, to continue. Although the Belarusian Constitution and legislation appears to provide for an independent trade union movement, with voluntary membership, freedom to organise and carry out actions in defence of workers' rights, and trade union pluralism, it has been the subject of considerable concern by various organs of the ILO.

In essence, Belarus' problems in relation to freedom of association and collective bargaining are typical of those that post-communist states have experienced in the early stages of transition.[18] Allegations of breach of freedom of association in Belarus concern the independent trade unions, as opposed to those with connections to governmental authorities. Although the allegations often overlap and cross between those relating to legislative issues and those relating to factual issues, they fall roughly into four groups, involving restrictions on the right to strike, protest, and receive foreign financial aid; obstacles to trade union activity; governmental interference in trade unions; and harassment and discrimination.

Right to Strike, Protest and Receive Foreign Gratuitous Aid[19]

The first issue to be raised was strike, the subject of consideration by the CFA, the Committee of Experts and the Conference Committee. It was at the basis of a case against Belarus filed in the CFA in 1995 by a group of national and international trade unions, alleging restrictions on the right to strike, the suspension of unions, anti-union discrimination, governmental interference in trade union affairs and the arrest and detention of

---

labour Conventions and Recommendations, endnote 8(iii) available at www.ilo.org/ilolex/english/manualq.htm. In comparison, when the Committee of Experts notes 'with interest', it is indicative of a lower form of approval: Böhning, R, Gaps in Basic Workers Rights: Measuring International Adherence To and Implementation of the Organisation's Values with Public ILO Data (Declaration Working Paper 13/2003, Geneva, 2003) 23.

[17] International Labour Conference (79th Session) Report III (Pt 1A): Report of the Committee of Experts (Geneva 1991); International Labour Conference (81st Session) Report III (Pt 1A): Report of the Committee of Experts (Geneva 1993).

[18] The 2004 Commission of Inquiry report observed that 'the industrial relations system in Belarus and the practice of trade unions still retain many of the characteristics of the Soviet period': 'Trade Union Rights in Belarus', Report of the Commission of Inquiry appointed under Art 26 of the Constitution of the International Labour Organisation to examine the Observance by the Government of Belarus of the Freedom of Association and Protection of the Right to Organise Convention 1948 (No 87) and Right to Organise and Collective Bargaining Convention 1949 (No 98) (Geneva, 2004) para 631.

[19] Although the right to strike is not explicitly set out in any ILO Convention, the Committee on Freedom of Association (CFA) considers it to be 'one of the essential means through which workers and their organisations may promote and defend their economic and social interests': ILO, *Digest of Decisions and Principles of the Freedom of Association Committee of the Governing Body of the ILO*, 5th (revised) edn (Geneva, International Labour Office, 2006) para 475.

trade unionists.[20] The case concerned matters that arose in the context of measures taken by the public authorities against industrial action taken at Minsk metro and the Gomyel trolleybus system.

The CFA found severe violations of Convention No 87. In particular, Presidential Ordinance No 336, suspending the activities of the Belarussian Free Trade Union (BFTU) and the Minsk metro local union organisation, violated the Convention and the dismissal of workers for taking part in legitimate strike action constituted anti-union discrimination. Although the Belarussian Constitutional Court had declared Ordinance No 336 to be unconstitutional, it seemed that it was being enforced and there were no steps to repeal it.

The CFA urged the Government to implement the Court's decision in relation to Ordinance No 336 and requested modification of Ministerial Edict No 158, restricting the right to strike in a large number of sectors and enterprises, and reinstatement of all workers dismissed in connection with the strikes. The CFA further requested the Government to refrain from using police force in relation to future legitimate strikes, and from imprisoning trade unionists.

Despite numerous reconsiderations of the case by the CFA,[21] an advisory mission from the Office and indications of some positive legislative amendments particularly in relation to the restrictions on the right to strike, by 2001 the CFA noted that many of the workers dismissed for taking part in the strikes were still not reinstated, nor compensated for loss of wages. In light of the fact that six years had elapsed since the workers were dismissed, the CFA could

> only once again request the Government to take the necessary measures, as a matter of urgency, to ensure a satisfactory solution for the situation of the remaining unemployed workers, including full compensation for the lost wages of all those dismissed.[22]

The same facts were considered in the context of article 22 supervision by the Committee of Experts and the Conference Committee. In its observations of 1996, the CEACR noted the Ordinance and Edict 'with concern' and 'ask[ed]' the Government to 're-establish freedom of association in law and in practice'.[23]

In 1997, Belarus was called before the Conference Committee in relation to its application of Convention No 87. The Government, in its address to the Committee, stressed that it was in the early stages of transition and

---

[20] *Name (Case No 1849)* (date?) Report No 324 (Vol LXXXIV 2001 Series B No 1).

[21] The effect given to the Committee's recommendations was considered 15 times between 1996 and 2001.

[22] Case No 1849 (n 20) at para 20.

[23] International Labour Conference (84th Session) Report III (Ptt 1A): Report of the Committee of Experts (Geneva 1996).

that it was committed to conforming with international law. It requested technical assistance from the ILO. The Committee of Experts, in its observations for 1997, noted 'with interest' the existence of a draft law concerning the right to strike, but noted 'with regret' that the Presidential Ordinance suspending the trade unions was still being implemented despite the Constitutional Court's earlier declaration of its unconstitutionality.[24] In 1998, the Committee of Experts noted 'with satisfaction' the repeal of the Presidential Ordinance that the union was registered and functioning, and that new legislation concerning strike had been passed.[25]

Nevertheless, the issue of strike arose again albeit concerning different matters. In 2000, while noting 'with satisfaction' that the new Labour Code had entered force, the Committee of Experts noted that restrictions on the right to strike were still possible.[26] The Committee requested the Government to ensure that unions in Belarus were able to benefit from foreign gratuitous financial aid for strikes despite legislative provisions appearing to limit this right. In 2001 and 2002, the Committee of Experts requested a copy of legislation purportedly concerning strike and, noted 'with regret' that the Government had not replied concerning the prohibition on trade unions receiving foreign gratuitous aid for strikes.[27]

Obstacles to Trade Union Activity—Registration, Check-off, and Other Financial Interference

In 2000, a new set of legislative problems arose in relation to Presidential Decree No 2 that required trade unions to be re-registered. Trade unions were obliged to provide a legal address and comply with a 10 per cent minimum requirement. In the absence of compliance with either of these two requirements, trade unions could not be registered, in which case the Decree provided for their dissolution. These requirements constituted a major obstacle to trade union activities. Other alleged obstacles to trade union activities involved the withdrawal of check-off facilities and interference with other financial matters.

In 2000, the Committee of Experts 'request[ed] the Government to consider amending' the Decree.[28] In 2001, Belarus was once again called before the

---

[24] International Labour Conference (85th Session) Report III (Pt 1A): Report of the Committee of Experts (Geneva 1997).

[25] International Labour Conference (86th Session) Report III (Pt 1A): Report of the Committee of Experts (Geneva 1998).

[26] International Labour Conference (88th Session) Report III (Pt 1A): Report of the Committee of Experts (Geneva 2000).

[27] International Labour Conference (89th Session) Report III (Pt 1A): Report of the Committee of Experts (Geneva 2001); International Labour Conference (90th Session) Report III (Pt 1A): Report of the Committee of Experts (Geneva 2002).

[28] International Labour Conference (88th Session) (n 26).

Conference Committee, where its representative provided some explanation of the requirements for re-registration of trade unions by Decree No 2. Despite the Government's indication that amendments to ensure that problems would not continue were being drafted, the Conference Committee placed its conclusions regarding Belarus in a 'special paragraph' to its report, an action akin to its highest sanction.[29]

Later in 2001, the Committee of Experts noted the indications that the Presidential Decree was to be amended in relation to the requirements of a legal address and the 10 per cent minimum requirement, and requested copies of that draft legislation.[30] The Committee of Experts 'once again' requested amendment of the provisions of Decree No 2 which allowed for the dissolution of non-registered trade unions. In its 2002 consideration of Belarus, the Committee of Experts was advised that a tripartite group was being set up to consider its comments.[31] It 'hoped' that the necessary measures would be taken. In 2003, the Government emphasised before the Conference Committee that Belarus understood the need to undertake further legislative action in relation to registration.[32] Noting that the Government had been referring to the need for legislative change for many years, the Conference Committee included its conclusions in a special paragraph of its report, mentioning it as a case of continued failure to implement the Convention.

External Interference in Trade Union Elections and Activities

At the same time, concerns began to be raised in relation to external interference in trade union activities. This principally involved the existence of presidential orders to interfere in trade union elections, and allegations that there had been consequential interference by governmental authorities and employers in the activities of various trade unions. In 2000, the Committee of Experts 'requested' the Government to ensure that there was no interference in the elections of trade union officials despite the existence of written Presidential Instructions directing authorities to so interfere.[33]

In 2002, the Credentials Committee of the International Labour Conference heard a complaint that the workers' delegation from Belarus was

---

[29] International Labour Conference (89th Session) Record of Proceedings: Report of the Committee on the Application of Standards (Geneva 2001) Pt 2/19.

[30] International Labour Conference (89th Session) Report III (Pt 1A): Report of the Committee of Experts (Geneva 2001).

[31] International Labour Conference (90th Session) Report III (Pt 1A): Report of the Committee of Experts (Geneva 2002).

[32] International Labour Conference (91st Session) Record of Proceedings: Provisional Record 24 (Geneva 2003).

[33] International Labour Conference (88th Session) (n 26).

not in fact representative of the workers in the country.[34] The Committee considered that there was indeed a breach of the ILO's Constitution as the largest trade union in the country, the Federation of Trade Unions of Belarus (FPB), was not represented in the Belarussian workers' delegation. The Government had, instead, nominated representatives of small, indus-try-specific trade unions. The usual sanction of invalidating the credentials of the delegation was irrelevant, however, as the Belarussian delegation chose to absent itself from the Conference that year. The absence of a dele-gation further meant that Belarus was not discussed in the 2002 Conference Committee.

Allegedly, when the governmental efforts to weaken the FPB failed, the Government changed its strategy to 'aiming to change its leadership to one that was supportive of the Government'.[35] As a result, union elections were the subject of allegations of governmental interference and intimida-tion. In the end, individuals associated with the Government were elected to FPB office, most notably the former Deputy Head of the Presidential Administration was elected to the leadership of the FPB.

At the 2003 Conference Committee,[36] the Government stated that recent trade union elections had been carried out fairly and that it did not interfere in the internal workings of unions. Nevertheless, the Credentials Committee remained concerned at the serious doubts surrounding the independence of the workers' delegation from Belarus—although this year the FPB was included in the delegation, it was a significantly different trade union from previously.[37]

This factor was considered in great detail in the CFA, in Case No 2090, discussed in the next section below.

Harassment, Retaliatory Acts, Arrests and Dismissals

Allegations concerning harassment, retaliatory acts, arrests and dismissals were principally dealt with by two CFA cases. Case No 1885, presented to the CFA in 1996, concerned the serving of a court summons on lead-ers from an independent trade union on account of their attendance at a union gathering, and the continued threat of implementation of the ban on the union's activities and its dissolution. The facts of the case arose in the context of a visit by a trade union delegation from Poland when its mem-bers were arrested and expelled from Belarus. As the Government did not

---

[34] International Labour Conference (90th Session) Record of Proceedings: Provisional Record 5 (Rev) Third Report of the Credentials Committee (Geneva 2002).

[35] 'Trade Union Rights in Belarus' (2004) para 437.

[36] International Labour Conference (91st Session) Record of Proceedings: Provisional Record 24 (Geneva 2003).

[37] International Labour Conference (91st Session) Record of Proceedings: Provisional Record 5 (Rev) Second Report of the Credentials Committee (Geneva 2003).

respond to the allegations, the CFA examined the case without the benefit of the Government's arguments.

The CFA requested the immediate withdrawal of the charges against the Belarussian union officials, future observance of the proper procedure in relation to visiting union delegations, and urged the immediate revocation of the Ordinance banning the BFTU.[38] Later in the year, the CFA reiterated its wish for the Government to keep it informed in relation to developments in the case.[39]

In 2000, Case No 2090, covering almost all allegations concerning freedom of association in Belarus, was filed in the CFA. Between March 2001 and November 2003, the CFA examined the case on eight occasions, and two on-the-spot missions were carried out. The case principally concerned allegations of governmental interference, prompted by presidential instruction, in trade union elections and their internal activities; and both the requirements of Presidential Decree No 2 on registration of trade unions, and its provisions allowing for the banning and dissolution of non-registered organisations.

In 2001, in its first report on the case,[40] the CFA noted that free trade unions had become virtually non-existent at the local level as a result of the minimum membership requirement of the registration procedure. Further, the legal address requirement had resulted in great problems for a large number of organisations. The CFA requested the Government to exclude trade unions from Decree No 2 or at least from the most excessive restrictions in relation to registration. In relation to the allegations concerning governmental interference, the CFA requested the Government to consider revoking presidential instructions to interfere in the elections of the free trade unions, and establish independent investigations into the allegations of anti-union discrimination and interference. The CFA also requested the reinstatement of a trade union official who had been dismissed.

Later in the year, the CFA again considered the case following the receipt of further information.[41] The Committee once again urged the removal of obstacles to registration, and a stop to governmental interference in union matters. The CFA requested independent investigations into various matters relating to governmental interference, and urged steps to be taken to ensure foreign gratuitous aid could be used by trade unions in Belarus. The CFA once again requested the reinstatement of named officials who had been dismissed.

---

[38] *Name (Case No 1885)* (date) Report No 306 (Vol LXXX 1997 Series B No 1) paras 121–41.

[39] *(Case No 1885)* Report No 307 (Vol LXXX 1997 Series B No 2) para 44.

[40] *(Case No 2090)* Report No 324 (Vol LXXXIV 2001 Series B No 1) paras 133–218.

[41] *(Case No 2090)* Report No 325 (Vol LXXXIV 2001 Series B No 2) paras 111–81.

In its final session of 2001, the CFA included the case as a serious and urgent case to which it drew the special attention of the Governing Body.[42] The CFA again requested the Government to institute a 'truly independent investigation' into the allegations of interference and intimidation; urged legislative amendments to allow foreign gratuitous aid, to eliminate obstacles to registration and restrictions on pickets. It requested information on the 'measures taken in accordance with its previous recommendations to ensure the reinstatement' of two union officials'.[43]

In 2002, the CFA once again considered Belarus to be a special and urgent case.[44] Further allegations considered at this time concerned the change in the leadership of the FPB, Belarus' largest trade union centre, as well as that of other regional trade unions, so that the majority of trade union posts were filled by former government officials.[45] In conclusion, the CFA noted 'with deep alarm' that since the complaint had been submitted in 2000, 'a serious deterioration in the respect of trade union rights has occurred in the country'.[46] The CFA's conclusions 'condemned' the manipulation of the trade union movement. It regretted that no information had been provided about the independent investigations that it had requested previously and repeated many of its earlier recommendations, requesting information of any measures taken, including in relation to the reinstatement of dismissed trade unionists.

In 2003, allegations were made concerning further efforts to destroy the independent trade union movement in Belarus and the CFA included the case as one that it considered serious and urgent in all three sessions of that year.[47] In its first session of the year, the CFA urged the Government to take steps to implement its previous recommendations.[48] At its second session, the CFA observed 'with deep regret' that the Government had not replied fully to the substance of the allegations, and 'deeply deplored the persistent failure of the Government to implement the Committee's recommendations'.[49]

In its final consideration of Case No 2090 in 2003, the CFA was 'regrettably obliged to conclude that the Government has had no real intention to take the necessary measures to have these extremely serious allegations investigated'.[50] The Committee was not 'able to observe any steps on the

---

[42] (*Case No 2090*) Report No 326 (Vol LXXXIV 2001 Series B No 3).
[43] Ibid.
[44] (*Case No 2090*) Report No 329 (Vol LXXXV 2002 Series B No 3) para 11.
[45] (*Case No 2090*) Report No 329 (Vol LXXXV 2002 Series B No 3).
[46] Ibid para 280.
[47] (*Case No 2090*) Report No 330 (Vol LXXXVI 2003 Series B No 1) para 10; (*Case No 2090*) Report No 331 (Vol LXXXVI 2003 Series B No 2) para 10; (*Case No 2090*) Report No 332 (Vol LXXXVI 2003 Series B No 3) para 4.
[48] (*Case No 2090*) Report No 330 (Vol LXXXVI 2003 Series B No 1) para 238.
[49] (*Case No 2090*) Report No 331 (Vol LXXXVI 2003 Series B No 2) paras 157 and 160.
[50] (*Case No 2090*) Report No 332 (Vol LXXXVI 2003 Series B No 3) para 351.

part of the Government to implement its recommendations'.[51] It noted with 'deep concern' and 'regret' the continued interference, obstacles to registration, administrative detention of trade unionists, continued legislative obstacles to the use of foreign gratuitous aid by unions and restrictions on picketing, and the lack of action taken in relation to the reinstatement of dismissed officials. The CFA recommended that a Commission of Inquiry be established.[52]

ILO Commission of Inquiry into Belarus: 2003–04

In 2003, various workers' representatives to the International Labour Conference filed a complaint under article 26 of the Constitution alleging non-observance of the freedom of association Convention by Belarus. In November 2003, the Governing Body referred the article 26 allegations of breach of freedom of association and collective bargaining and the pending allegations in CFA Case No 2090 to a Commission of Inquiry. As in the previous Commissions of Inquiry, the Commission was composed of three members. Professor Budislav Vukas, a Croatian professor of international law, Vice-President of the International Tribunal for the Law of the Sea, and member of the Permanent Court of Arbitration and the ILO Committee of Experts, was its chair. Its two members were Professor Niklas Bruun, a professor of business and labour law from Sweden, and Justice Mary Gaudron, a former Australian judge and current judge of the ILO Administrative Tribunal.

The Commission began its work in January 2004 and its report was received by the Governing Body at the end of the year. In accordance with the usual practice, the Committee of Experts suspended its normal supervision of Belarus during the pendency of the Commission from its appointment in November 2003. The Commission operated with the cooperation of the Government despite its objection to the procedure being established and heard witnesses both in Minsk and Geneva. This can be contrasted with the Commissions of Inquiry in relation to forced labour in Myanmar,[53] and in relation to freedom of association in Poland[54] which had not been

---

[51] Ibid paras 360–61.

[52] Ibid paras 360–61.

[53] 'Forced Labour in Myanmar (Burma)' Report of the Commission of Inquiry appointed under Art 26 of the Constitution of the International Labour Organisation to examine the observance by Myanmar of the Forced Labour Convention 1930 (No 29) (Geneva 1998).

[54] Report of the Commission instituted under Art 26 of the Constitution of the International Labour Organisation to examine the complaint on the observance by Poland of the Freedom of Association and Protection of the Right to Organise Convention 1948 (No 87), and the Right to Organise and Collective Bargaining Convention 1949 (No 98), presented by delegates at the 68th Session of the International Labour Conference (Geneva 1984).

allowed entry to the countries under consideration. The Commission into Belarus followed the same formula as previous Commissions in terms of procedure and the nature of its report.

The Commission of Inquiry reached the conclusion that the rights of independent trade unions in Belarus had been compromised. First, the Presidential Decree requiring trade unions to register impeded the free formation of trade union organisations, and impacted uniquely on independent trade unions.[55] Secondly, the trade union movement was the subject of significant interference by governmental authorities.[56] Thirdly, the Government failed to protect the rights of trade unionists and, in particular, to protect them from discrimination on the basis of their trade union membership and activities.[57] Fourthly, various pieces of legislation were contrary to the Convention.[58] Finally, it concluded that there were significant deficits in collective bargaining and social dialogue.[59]

Accordingly, the Commission made a number of recommendations.[60] In relation to the issue of registration, it recommended the Government to immediately register all the trade unions listed in the complaint, regardless of the legislative obstacles; amend the law to eliminate the obstacles; and ensure that all future registrations were a matter of mere administrative formality. The Commission recommended that all its conclusions and recommendations be made public, that the Government declare publicly that acts of interference in trade unions were unacceptable, and that instructions were issued to ensure complaints of interference were thoroughly investigated. It recommended that organisations that had suffered interference should be guaranteed protection to carry out their activities freely and that where enterprise managers were trade union members, they should be instructed not to take part in trade union decision making.

The Commission recommended that independent investigations should be carried out into outstanding complaints of anti-union discrimination and that effective procedures for protection against anti-union discrimination be instituted, including implementation of the recommendations of the UN Special Rapporteur on the independence of judges and lawyers. It recommended amendment of legislation concerning foreign gratuitous aid and 'mass activities' and recommended that the national level independent trade union that has a seat on the national consultative body be allowed to participate. Finally, it recommended that the Government undertake a thorough review of its industrial relations system with the aim of ensuring a

---

[55] 'Trade Union Rights in Belarus' (n 18) para 598.
[56] Ibid para 614.
[57] Ibid para 621.
[58] Ibid para 627.
[59] Ibid para 629.
[60] Ibid para 634.

clear distinction between the role of the Government and that of the social partners, and of promoting clearly independent structures of workers' and employers' organisations.

The Commission of Inquiry was 'of the opinion' that its recommendations could and should be carried out without delay and provided a time limit by which a certain number of them should be implemented.[61] Its concluding observations noted the Government's insistence on the need to take into account the historical and socio-economic realities characteristic of the country, but emphasised that the promotion of an independent trade union movement would benefit Belarussian society as a whole and that this relied upon the full respect of basic civil liberties of trade union members and leaders.[62]

Follow-Up to the Commission of Inquiry 2004–08

With the publication of its report in 2004, the Commission of Inquiry concerning Belarus completed its work. It had considered that it was important that the implementation of its recommendations be followed up by the CFA and observed that the Committee of Experts would continue to examine the legislative aspects involved within the framework of its regular supervision.[63] The Governing Body, at its 291st session in November 2004, took note of the Commission of Inquiry's Report and the Government's reply.[64]

As many of the Commission's recommendations had a deadline of June 2005 for implementation, in March 2005 the CFA asked the Government to transmit its observations and information relating to the measures taken to implement the recommendations as soon as possible.[65] At its next meeting, in May 2005, the CFA noted that the Government had sent only partial observations, and urged it to send additional observations and information to ensure a proper consideration of the matter at its next meeting.[66] During the International Labour Conference in June 2005, Belarus was once again discussed at the Conference Committee, having been expected to fully report on the implementation of recommendations. The partial nature of the Government's response was noted by many of the speakers. The employers' representative indicated that 'they remained somewhat sceptical of the Government's will to give full effect to the Convention at any time in the future'.[67] The Conference Committee

---

[61] Ibid para 635.
[62] Ibid para 637–40.
[63] Ibid para 636.
[64] Sixth Item on the Agenda GB.291/6 (Geneva 2004).
[65] (*Case No 2090*) Report No 336 (Vol LXXXVIII 2005 Series B No 1) para 13.
[66] (*Case No 2090*) Report No 337 (Vol LXXXVIII 2005 Series B No 2) para 15.
[67] International Labour Conference (93rd Session) Record of Proceedings: Provisional Record 22 (Geneva 2005) Pt 2/23.

deplored that no real and concrete measures had been taken to implement the recommendations of the Commission and Belarus was once again included in a special paragraph.

The CFA considered, in substance, the measures taken by the Government of Belarus to implement the Commission of Inquiry's recommendations during its November 2005 meeting.[68] The Committee noted that it had received allegations 'enumerating in detail' continuing violation of trade union rights in Belarus, while the Government had 'only communicated a plan of action'; the CFA 'deeply deplore[d]' that 'no concrete and tangible steps' appeared to have been taken.[69] In fact, the CFA noted in relation to suggested changes to the trade union legislation in the country that it could 'only be understood as an attempt to eliminate any independent voices within the trade union movement in Belarus'.[70] The CFA noted continuing problems with registration, including the de-registration of one independent trade union, and threats, harassment and the blacklisting of trade unionists and in particular those who spoke to the Commission.[71] It substantially repeated the recommendations of the Commission.

In 2005, in the first Committee of Experts following the Commission of Inquiry, the Committee recalled that it had been making comments on many of the same points as the Commission for many years.[72] It once again urged the Government to take the appropriate steps regarding registration, strikes and mass activities. The Committee of Experts noted 'with deep concern' draft amendments to the trade union legislation which appeared to worsen matters, which it urged the Government to withdraw. In the light of all the information, the Committee of Experts considered that there existed 'serious discrepancies with the provisions of the Convention such that the survival of any form of an independent trade union movement in Belarus is truly at risk'.

In its second consideration of the Government's implementation of the recommendations, in March 2006, the CFA had information from a mission undertaken earlier in the year. The Committee felt

> obliged to sound the alarm that, rather than making good faith efforts to imple-
> ment the recommendations of the Commission of Inquiry, the Government is
> on a path to eliminating all remnants of an independent trade union in Belarus,
> apparently hoping that in this way there in effect will be no further sources of
> complaint.[73]

---

[68] (*Case No 2090*) Report No 339 (Vol LXXXVIII 2005 Series B No 3).
[69] Ibid para 70.
[70] Ibid para 89.
[71] Ibid.
[72] International Labour Conference (92nd Session) Report III (Pt 1A): Report of the Committee of Experts (Geneva 2004).
[73] 341st Report, 2006, paras 51 and 53(a).

The CFA reiterated its previous recommendations and urged the Government 'in the strongest of terms' to take concrete measures to ensure that workers may form and join independent organisations freely and without pressure or intimidation.[74] In June 2006, the CFA noted that it was awaiting the Government's reply in this regard.[75]

Belarus was again called before the Conference Committee in June 2006,[76] when the Committee also called for 'concrete steps' to be taken by the Government so that 'real and tangible progress could be noted' by the November 2006 session of the Governing Body. In the case that no progress would be noted, 'the Committee trusted that the Governing Body would begin to consider, at that time, whether further measures under the ILO Constitution should be considered', impliedly threatening the application of article 33 and so sanctions by ILO Members. Its conclusions concerning Belarus were included in a special paragraph and Belarus was mentioned as a case of continued failure to implement the Convention.[77]

In November 2006, when the Governing Body again considered the matter, it noted that a high-level mission from Belarus had visited Geneva to discuss a plan for implementation with the Office, and that there were indications of progress. In that context, no further discussion of article 33 was necessary.[78] Later that year, the Committee of Experts noted with deep regret that no steps had been taken to implement the Commission's recommendations.[79] It feared that a new draft trade union law 'may result in the elimination of any remnants of an independent trade union movement in Belarus'.

In March 2007, while noting some positive steps taken by the Government, the CFA nevertheless regretted that 'the current situation in Belarus remains far from ensuring full respect for freedom of association and that several recommendations of the Commission of Inquiry are still not implemented'.[80] The positive steps taken by the Government included the disbandment of the Republican Registration Commission, the publication of the Commission's recommendations in a widely disseminated national newspaper, and an indication that the Chairperson of one of the independent trade unions had a seat in the National Council on Labour and Social Issues.[81]

---

[74] Ibid para 51.
[75] 342nd Report, 2006, para 12.
[76] International Labour Conference (94th Session) Record of Proceedings: Provisional Record 24 (Geneva 2006) Pt 2.
[77] Ibid Pt 2/24.
[78] Minutes of the 297th Session of the Governing Body (GB.297/PV) para 166.
[79] International Labour Conference (94th Session) Report III (Pt 1A): Report of the Committee of Experts (Geneva 2006).
[80] 345th Report para 97.
[81] 345th Report (Vol XC 2007 No 1) paras 88–89.

Nevertheless, the CFA deeply regretted that the primary-level trade union organisations mentioned in the complaint remained unregistered and new allegations of non-registration had been made.[82] It also noted the draft trade union law that would, according to the Committee of Experts, result in a worsening of the situation, and new allegations of interference in trade union internal affairs, anti-union pressure and anti-union discrimination at two enterprises. It had received information concerning only one of the workers who apparently had 'suffered consequences for cooperating with the Commission of Inquiry'; he had been reinstated. The Conference Committee and Governing Body similarly noted some progress, expressed their concern at the draft law, and recommended consultation between the social partners in the country.[83]

In 2007, the Committee of Experts considered a new version of the draft trade union law, as amended following consultation with the social partners and the Office, and took into account two further missions to the country. Despite important progress, concerns still remained with the draft law, particularly in relation to the issue of registration. During the Governing Body's November 2007 consideration of the matter, some Government Members suggested removing consideration of Belarus' observance of the Conventions from the Governing Body's agenda on account of the positive developments. Following interventions from both the Employer and Worker Vice-Chairpersons indicating that it was the Governing Body's responsibility to continue monitoring the situation, it undertook to review developments at its 2008 sessions.[84]

In March 2008, the Governing Body considered the Government's information concerning steps it had taken that it was confident 'would lay the foundations needed to ensure full implementation of the recommendations made by the Commission of Inquiry'.[85] The Workers' Group was aware of all manner of violations of trade union rights in the country; the Government's progress 'was so slow as to seem more like stagnation'.[86] The Governing Body deeply regretted the lack of specific progress.

At the same time, the CFA once again noted with regret continuing problems in relation to registration of trade unions, and further allegations of interference and anti-union pressure, and arrest and detention of workers. However, it also noted the Government's indication that it had 'held back' the proposed draft trade union law and that a new draft would be developed in consultation with the social partners.[87] Once again, despite some positive

---

[82] 345th Report paras 90–91.
[83] Minutes of the Governing Body (298th Session March 2007) GB.298/PV para 159.
[84] Minutes of the Governing Body (300th Session November 2007) GB.300/PV paras 220–39.
[85] Minutes of the Governing Body (301st Session March 2008) GB.301/PV para 290.
[86] Ibid para 292.
[87] 352nd Report (Vol XCI 2008 No 3) para 67.

steps taken by the Government, the current situation in Belarus remained far from ensuring full respect for freedom of association and that several recommendations of the Commission of Inquiry had still not been implemented.[88]

During the 2008 Conference Committee, a change in the attitude of the Belarussian Government was noted by many speakers. The Employer members stated that while in 2005–06 the Government had taken the approach that the Commission's recommendations had to be adapted to national circumstances, in 2008 the Government appeared to accept the need to implement the recommendations without reservation. The Worker members considered the situation 'to be encouraging', seeing 'some positive steps', but stressed that they would 'remain vigilant'. The Committee welcomed the fact that the draft law had been held back and the indications of improved social dialogue, but remained concerned at new allegations of harassment of independent trade unions and that the key recommendations of the Commission of Inquiry had not been implemented.[89]

In November 2008, the Committee of Experts regretted that full implementation had still not taken place, but noted the Government's indication that it would continue to cooperate with the ILO and to that effect, a tripartite seminar on the implementation of the recommendations of the Commission of Inquiry was under preparation. The Committee welcomed this initiative and expressed the firm hope that concrete and tangible steps would be taken in the near future so as to ensure the full implementation of the recommendations of the Commission of Inquiry without delay.

THE INTERPLAY OF WORKERS' RIGHTS AND HUMAN RIGHTS

This survey of the ILO's response to freedom of association in Belarus illustrates the multi-faceted interplay of freedom of association and human rights in the ILO context. Clearly, the issue of human rights is one that is of intrinsic importance to the debate surrounding trade union rights in the ILO context.

The most obvious point is that freedom of association is 'an integral part of basic human rights' and the jurisprudence of the CFA is couched in the language of rights.[90] Trade union rights should be respected no matter what the level of development of the country concerned,[91] and facts imputable to individuals incur the responsibility of states because of their obligation to remain vigilant and take action to prevent violations of human rights.[92] As there is very little basis upon which a case may be determined

---

[88] Ibid para 74.
[89] Conference Committee re Convention No 87, 97th Session of the International Labour Conference (2008).
[90] International Labour Conference (81st Session) (1993) at 2.
[91] ILO, *Digest of Decisions* (2006) para 19.
[92] Ibid paras 17–18.

to be irreceivable, it is clear that the ILO considers all complaints concerning freedom of association to be of particular importance and worthy of the attention of this special supervisory mechanism.[93]

At the same time, 'respect for civil and political rights is necessary for the exercise of trade union rights',[94] and 'violations of human rights and civil liberties affecting trade union rights largely depend ... on whether the country concerned has an authoritarian regime'.[95] The jurisprudence of the CFA emphasises the importance of ensuring respect for human rights and civil liberties in general, to enable the proper respect for workers' rights.[96] The repression of trade unions in Belarus is portrayed by the ILO supervisory mechanisms as part of wider human rights abuses and, in particular, the stifling of political dissension. As the Commission of Inquiry remarked in its concluding observations:

> The Commission stresses the importance of ensuring full respect for the basic civil liberties of trade union members and leaders. Without such respect, independent trade unions cannot survive. ... If these basic freedoms are not guaranteed and protected by an independent judiciary, then there is little prospect for the full realisation of trade union rights.[97]

The opposite is also true: freedom of association is a tool to achieve human rights and democracy in practice. Trade unions 'have been to the fore in the democratic advances of recent years' in which the ILO has been involved, opening 'the way to the exercise of basic freedoms'.[98] There is a clear link between freedom of association rights and democracy: 'gains in freedom of association represent, unequivocally, advances for democracy'.[99] It is perhaps for this reason that authoritarian or undemocratic governments will often target the trade union movement.

AN EFFECTIVE MECHANISM FOR PROTECTING WORKERS' RIGHTS?

In the first place, this overview illustrates the great commitment that the ILO has directed towards Belarus. A commendable desire to take an active role in

---

[93] See eg *Georgia* (*Case No 2144*) Report No 330 (Vol LXXXVI 2003 Series B No 1) paras 692–720.

[94] Swepston, 'Human Rights Law and Freedom of Association' (1998) 176.

[95] von Potobsky, G, 'Freedom of Association: The Impact of Convention No. 87 and ILO Action' (1998) 137(2) *International Labour Review* 195.

[96] ILO, *Digest of Decisions* (n 19) paras 30–41.

[97] 'Trade Union Rights in Belarus' (n 18) para 639.

[98] Dunning, H, 'The Origins of Convention No. 87 on Freedom of Association and the Right to Organise' (1998) 137(2) *International Labour Review* 149.

[99] Curtis, K, 'Democracy, Freedom of Association and the ILO' in J Javillier et al (eds), *Les Norms Internationales du Travail: Un Patrimoine pour l'avenir. Melanges en l'honneur de Nicolas Valticos* (Geneva, International Labour Office, 2004) 106.

protecting and improving the rights of workers in the country is evident: all the possible mechanisms of the Organisation have been deployed, excepting article 33 of the ILO Constitution which was threatened but not implemented.[100] This is an example of where 'the persistence and perseverance of the supervisory bodies are an extremely powerful weapon in the ILO's armoury'.[101] The coordination responsibility the Governing Body assigned itself is an important aspect in ensuring this persistent—and insistent—response. Both the Committee of Experts and the Conference Committee emphasised similarities between the Commission's conclusions and statements that the two standing committees had been making for many years in relation to implementation of the Conventions.[102] The high-standing of the Commission and its position at the culmination of a long period of sustained criticism by ILO supervisory mechanisms give the body its potential influence to support the work of the other components of the ILO system.

Secondly, this process illustrates an admirable dialogue between the ILO and the Government of Belarus. The Belarussian Government has been an active part of the procedure, responding to requests and participating in the various parts of the process. Missions to the country continue, and technical assistance is still requested and provided. The Government has never questioned the need for freedom of association in the country; it has scarcely questioned the legitimacy of the ILO intervening in its domestic affairs; and it has not disputed the content of the Commission of Inquiry's recommendations nor the necessity of implementing them. This dialogue is remarkable: the ILO has succeeded in retaining relations with the Government of Belarus at the same time as producing stinging criticisms of it. Thus, it seems that even a government considered to be a persistent violator of freedom of association considers it to be an indisputable and predominant right.

Interestingly, this seems to be the case in relation to most Commissions of Inquiry.[103] An important power that the Commissions of Inquiry seem to enjoy, therefore, is that of compelling governments to engage in the discussion surrounding the implementation of the recommendations, if not

---

[100] Article 33 allows, in the case of failure of a Member State to carry out the recommendations of a Commission of Inquiry, the Governing Body to recommend to the International Labour Conference 'such action as it may deem wise and expedient to secure compliance therewith'. To date, the article has only been used in relation to Myanmar.

[101] von Potobsky, 'Freedom of Association: The Impact of Convention No. 87 and ILO Action' (1998).

[102] International Labour Conference (92nd Session) Report III (Pt 1A): Report of the Committee of Experts (Geneva, 2004). Note similar statements in relation to Myanmar: International Labour Conference (87th Session) Report III (Pt 1A): Report of the Committee of Experts (Geneva, 1999).

[103] Valticos, 'Les commissions d'enquête de l'Organisation internationale du Traveail' (1987) 870; this point is clear in relation to the first COI concerning Portugal: see Wolfson et al, 'Colonialism, Forced Labour and the International Labour Organization' (2008).

in the process as a whole. The largely consensual, rather than combative, approach that ILO supervision takes to cases of non-observance of its conventions, therefore, can be seen as allowing transgressing governments to continue to work with the Organisation without losing face.

Thirdly, to the Belarussian trade union movement, the ILO appears to have been seen as a lifeline. Faced with repression by governmental authorities, a judicial system criticised as lacking independence,[104] and a censored media,[105] the trade union movement looked outside national boundaries for the enforcement of its rights. With the support of international federations and confederations of trade unions, the case of interference, intimidation and near annihilation of the free trade unions has been heard in almost all possible ILO procedures.[106] In this way, and in particular through the CFA and Commission of Inquiry, individual Belarussian workers have had a voice within the international community, and the question of Belarus' observance of freedom of association has become a matter of international concern.[107] While the Government of Belarus has been characterised as being on an isolationist path,[108] the independent trade union movement has positioned itself within the international mainstream.

Fourthly, the powerful rhetoric associated with human rights and the symbolic nature of much of the process may have some practical importance. Violations of human rights will spark 'a reaction in public opinion similar to that produced by a criminal act or infringement of a moral or legal code'.[109] To say that a person has labour rights accords greater urgency than saying that a person should enjoy labour standards. The importance of this as a rhetorical tool to show commitment to the trade union movement and to individual workers is important to those workers and their organisations. If nothing else, the absence of rights language for trade unions and their members would create a gaping hole for workers. It is key, in this respect, that the Commission of Inquiry on Belarus chose

[104] See UN Special Rapporteur on the Independence of Judges and Lawyers (2001): Civil and Political Rights, including questions of: Independence of the Judiciary, Administration of Justice, Impunity, document to the United Nations Economic and Social Council E/CN.4/2001/65/Add.1.

[105] See Freedom House Report 2006, available at: www.freedomhouse.org/template. cfm?page=22&year=2006&country=6920.

[106] See eg, in the procedure before the Commission of Inquiry, the independent trade unions of Belarus were represented by the International Confederation of Free Trade Unions: 'Trade Union Rights in Belarus' (n 18) para 57.

[107] The European Union imposed sanctions against Belarus in response to breach of trade union rights.

[108] The Declaration by the Presidency on behalf of the European Union on recent events in Belarus issued on 14 June 2005 in response to the arrest of opposition candidates, including trade unionists, refers to 'Belarus' isolationist tendencies' available at: www.eu2005.lu/en/ actualites/pesc/2005/06/14belarus/index.html.

[109] Valticos, N 'International Labour Standards and Human Rights: Approaching the Year 2000' (1998) 137 (2) *International Labour Review* 135, 144.

not to use the language of 'international labour standards' in the title to its report, calling it 'Trade Union Rights in Belarus'.

Nevertheless, despite the great significance of those four factors, the ILO supervisory mechanisms have not achieved wholesale protection of workers' rights in Belarus in the 13 years since the first case was submitted. In fact, in some respects, matters progressed from bad to worse during the ILO's involvement, before recent indications of a possible improvement. For example, the several individuals who had been dismissed and whose reinstatement had been sought by the Committee of Experts and the CFA have still not been, at this point in time, compensated for the unlawful loss of their jobs and only one of the individuals allegedly dismissed for cooperating with the Commission of Inquiry has since been re-hired. Additionally, the independent trade union movement that the ILO first sought to protect in 1995 was almost non-existent by the time of the Commission of Inquiry's report in 2005; in the first years of the follow-up period, the only indications of change suggested a continued progression in the same, negative, direction. The Committee of Experts in 2006 talked of 'remnants of an independent trade union movement' remaining in the country.[110] It is only more recently that it appears that the Government has taken some steps towards including independent trade unions in institutionalised social dialogue and halting unfavourable legislative changes.

In one instance it appears that, rather than being an impetus to improve matters, the ILO involvement may have affected the pattern of governmental interference in a less satisfactory way. In 2002, ILO bodies expressed deep concern at the way in which the Belarussian Government appeared to be sidelining the FPB—the largest trade union in the country—notably by not including it in its delegation to the International Labour Conference and allegedly harassing it in relation to its financial affairs.[111] The following year, however, the union was included in the Belarussian delegation and it ceased complaining of harassment. In fact, in the intervening months, the leadership of the federation had changed almost entirely to be composed of people with close links to the Government. The independent trade union movement indicated that it considered the federation to no longer be independent, but to have become an arm of the state following a change in the Government's policy from attempting to destroy the FPB by sidelining and harassing it, to controlling it by managing a takeover of its functions.[112] The Government, on the other hand, indicated that it had followed the ILO's advice to restore links with the largest trade union centre in the country and to include it within the Belarussian delegation to the Conference.

---

[110] International Labour Conference (94th Session) (2006).
[111] See above.
[112] 'Trade Union Rights in Belarus' (n 18) para 443.

Such indicators suggest that the concerted efforts of the supervisory bodies of the ILO had little impact on the rights of workers in the face of governmental intransigence, at least for the first 10 years that the ILO directed efforts at the resolution of these concerns. This rather depressing observation mirrors earlier conclusions:

> It would be agreeable ... to be able to conclude that the existence of the Convention, and the elaborate machinery created to ensure its application ... have led to a universal improvement in respect for trade union rights. Unfortunately, this is not the case.[113]

While in the first two years following the Commission of Inquiry's report the Government appeared to argue that the recommendations of the Commission needed to be moulded to national circumstances, the approach more recently has increasingly been one of acceptance that they should be implemented in full. Accordingly, certain of the Commission of Inquiry's recommendations have been implemented and an objectionable draft law— that was first mooted following the Commission of Inquiry report—was withdrawn and submitted to consultation with the social partners, including the independent trade unions. Why this change? It is at least arguable that the EU's withdrawal of trade preferences in its GSP system in June 2007 had a significant effect on the Government's approach, particularly when combined with the ILO's own apparent threat of application of article 33 sanctions by its extensive membership. The 'impetus' provided by EU sanctions, explicitly premised on Belarus' breach of core labour standards, is an interesting correlative to the persuasiveness of the ILO's consensual dialogue approach.

Of course, ILO supervisory bodies 'must work ceaselessly and over the long term' to achieve success in individual cases,[114] and it would seem sensible that assessments should be made in the same way. In relation to Commissions of Inquiry in particular, it has been stated that while '[r]esults are not usually immediately forthcoming because of resistance from vested interests, ... they do eventually occur'.[115] In this regard, it has been noted that in the first four Commissions of Inquiry concerned with freedom of association, progress was eventually recorded by the Committee of Experts in all cases.[116]

This could be the case for Belarus, most particularly in light of the recent encouraging steps by the Government. A continuing dialogue both with

---

[113] Dunning, 'The Origins of Convention No. 87 on Freedom of Association and the Right to Organise' (1998) 165. Although, note that this writer concludes that the Convention and the work of the CFA 'have proved invaluable defences against social injustice' in the most severe cases.

[114] von Potobsky (n 95).

[115] Ibid.

[116] Ibid.

the ILO and with the social partners within the country, combined with the Government's acceptance of the need for the Commission's recommendations to be implemented, would ensure future change. Should these most recent moves by the Government prove to be the beginning of a new strategy within Belarus? The Belarussian case would be an illustration of the success of the ILO's supervisory mechanisms through a consistent and patient approach.

For these reasons, a conclusion questioning the ILO's success in attaining improved trade union rights for individual trade unionists in Belarus may be rather hastily reached. What would the situation have been 'if the ILO had never existed'?[117] Would the situation in Belarus have been worse if the ILO had not been involved? Intuition demands the answer that it may, indeed, have been worse for individual workers and trade unions if the country had not been, and did not continue to be, subject to the continued scrutiny of the ILO. In particular, this might be so in relation to individuals' experience of repression. While many Belarussian trade union members and officials were detained and imprisoned, for example, they have not been, unlike some representatives of political parties and the media, kept in prison indefinitely nor have trade unionists disappeared.[118] This may or may not be linked with the Government's continued interaction with the ILO.

CONCLUSION

While the CFA and Commission of Inquiry are potentially powerful tools for workers and their organisations, allowing complaints to be brought to international fora within which trade union rights are accorded primacy, the lack of enforcement procedures beyond voluntary compliance means that in cases in which the Government's attitude and bona fides is at issue, solutions will be sparse until the root reasons for the non-observance of the particular convention are changed. Such a considerable amount of time appears to be needed for trade union rights to be improved that there may be little impact on the aspirations of individual trade unionists. This is, of course, not unique to the ILO, but relates equally to other international and regional organisations.

While the ILO supervisory mechanisms may not have succeeded, up to this point in time, in solving Belarus' breach of the freedom of association conventions, the ILO's great success has been in maintaining a dialogue that

---

[117] Maupain, F, 'Is the ILO Effective in Upholding Workers' Rights?: Reflections on the Myanmar Experience' in P Alston (ed), *Labour Rights as Human Rights* (Oxford, Oxford University Press, 2005) 142.

[118] The Freedom House 2006 Report (n 105) documents the deaths of two journalists and the abduction of another.

will allow improvements to occur, should the political will in the country change. The traditional supervisory mechanisms of the ILO have evolved a jurisprudence in which freedom of association was accorded the status of a fundamental human right, and in a complex entanglement of mutually reinforcing functions, have had the effect of placing such concerns at centre-stage in the supervisory system.

In relation to Belarus, it can be seen that the fact that freedom of association is a basic human right has meant that its importance is not disputed, the Government's obligations in relation to it are not doubted, and the dialogue concerns the manner of implementation. An assessment that ignored the importance of the ILO supervisory mechanisms to trade unions in countries such as Belarus, where workers' rights have been systematically denied, would be to ignore the reality of the situation for the very subjects of the Conventions. Whether this categorisation gives 'teeth' to the ILO in relation to its protection of freedom of association is an open question.[119] The interplay of workers' rights and human rights suggests that until human rights and democracy are fully protected in Belarus, implementation of the spirit of the Commission of Inquiry's recommendations involving freedom of association will not be possible.

---

[119] Maupain, 'Is the ILO Effective in Upholding Workers' Rights?' (2005) 86, describes the ILO as an 'old lady' born without teeth who 'seemed to be growing them exactly as she passed her 80th year with respect to Myanmar'.

14

Protection of Workers under Regional Human Rights Systems: An Assessment of Evolving and Divergent Practices

TONIA NOVITZ

INTRODUCTION

THIS CHAPTER* INVESTIGATES how regional human rights systems may be utilised by workers and their organisations for protection of their interests. Its focus is on three regional mechanisms: the Council of Europe (CoE), the Organisation of American States (OAS), and the African Union (AU).

It should be admitted, at the outset, that comparison between these discrete systems is far from straightforward. Each system has emerged at a different historical juncture and developed at a different rate depending on the concerns of the region in question, as well as key state and non-state actors within that region. Awareness of these differences and their significance underlies the analysis provided below. Nevertheless, it can also be observed that both officials and academic commentators are actively seeking to make comparisons between regional systems,[1] such that we see, for example, former officials in the Inter-American system commenting on the viability of an African Court of Human Rights,[2] the Inter-American Court of Human Rights referring to jurisprudence of the European Court of Human Rights,[3] and at least one UK academic commentator reminding

* The author is very grateful to her colleague, Rachel Murray, who provided advice and assistance early in the drafting of this chapter and to Colin Fenwick who provided subsequent comments on the paper delivered in Oñati. All errors and omissions are the author's own.
[1] Eg Heyns, C, Strasser, W and Padilla, D, 'A Schematic Comparison of Human Rights Systems' (2003) 3 *African Human Rights Law Journal* 76, 79.
[2] Padilla, D, 'An African Human Rights Court: Reflections from the Perspective of the Inter-American System' (2002) 2 *African Human Rights Law Journal* 185, 190.
[3] Inter-American Court of Human Rights, 'Advisory Opinion OC-18/03 of September 17 2003, Requested by the United Mexican States' available at: www.oas.org, para 143.

us of what can be learnt by European human rights specialists from the operation of the African system.[4] This suggests that, while simplistic generalisations may not be appropriate, a comparative analysis may be able to provide us with a useful overview.

It is suggested here that it is possible to detect two overarching trends. First, we are witnessing the gradual evolution of normative and supervisory structures at the regional level, which have the capacity to provide enhanced protection for workers' rights. Secondly, despite this jurisprudential shift, cases relating to workers' rights are very much in the minority of those addressed by regional human rights mechanisms.

To varying degrees, all three organisations have recognised that workers' claims against governments and employers can have the status of 'human rights'. As was observed in chapter 1, there is scope for this to be achieved in two divergent, but potentially complementary ways. The first is the recognition of the socio-economic circumstances of workers within a human rights instrument, such that particular provision is made for their treatment in the workplace, specifying entitlements which would promote their welfare, such as collective bargaining, industrial action, safe working conditions, fair and equal pay, maternity pay, holidays and time off for dependants. The second is for workers' claims to be understood in terms of civil and political rights, which apply as much in the context of the workplace as they would elsewhere, such as freedom from forced labour, freedom of speech, freedom of association, freedom from discrimination, the right to privacy, and freedom of conscience and religious belief. The first option has the advantage of providing specific protection for workers' needs, which is appropriate to their collective circumstances. However, as we shall see, supervisory mechanisms for the enforcement of socio-economic rights under regional human rights mechanisms tend to suffer by comparison with civil and political rights.

A civil and political rights approach is of particular interest when we consider the case of freedom of association, which is linked to rights to form and join trade unions, to participate in trade union activities, to engage in collective bargaining and to take industrial action. Given difficulties associated with protection of trade union rights as socio-economic rights, their potential characterisation as civil and political rights has considerable significance. It has the capacity to provide workers' organisations with the means to resist anti-trade union laws adopted in developed countries, such as the United Kingdom, aimed at promoting deregulatory competition[5] and

---

[4] Murray, R, 'International Human Rights: Neglect of Perspectives from African Institutions' (2006) 55 *ICLQ* 193, 198–99.

[5] See on the activities of UK Conservative governments in this regard, Davies, P and Freedland, M, *Labour Legislation and Public Policy* (Oxford, Clarendon Law Series, 1993) ch 9; and for the current direction of UK policy, see Pollert, A, 'The Unorganised Worker: The Decline in Collectivism and New Hurdles to Individual Employment Rights' (2005) 34 *Industrial Law Journal* 217.

those measures taken in developing countries aimed at boosting foreign direct investment and promotion of new industries.[6] However, this chapter suggests that such benefits need also to be weighed against what may be the costs of an approach oriented around conventional understandings of civil and political rights, which may require an unduly individualistic and legalistic approach to the protection of trade union rights and may not take into account the realities of the industrial relations context in which they are to be exercised.

This chapter considers the pros and cons of each approach, and how through integrated protection under either the same instrument or inter-related supervisory mechanisms, they could be combined to foster protection of workers' rights as human rights at the regional level. It is also suggested that, by reference to jurisprudence established within the International Labour Organisation (ILO), regional organisations may more readily achieve this mode of integration.

However, this jurisprudential analysis does not seem to be sufficient, for it does not of itself explain why, where regional mechanisms attempt to transcend traditional divisions between civil, political and socio-economic rights, so few cases come to address workers' rights, especially those concerning trade unions. It is suggested that further attention has to be paid not only to jurisprudential constructs, but also the practical aspects of the operation of different regional human rights systems and the discrete political context within which each operates.

RECOGNITION OF WORKERS' RIGHTS UNDER REGIONAL HUMAN RIGHTS INSTRUMENTS

There are three regional human rights systems which have achieved prominence to date.[7] These have arisen within three systems of regional governance, the CoE established in 1948, the OAS founded the same year, and the Organisation of African Unity (OAU) created in 1963, which was replaced by the AU in 2002. The CoE currently has 47 members, the OAS has 35 members and the AU has 53 members. Together, they account for a significant number of the states in the international community.

---

[6] See eg, Governing Body Committee on Employment and Social Policy, 'Employment and Social Policy in Respect of Export Processing Zones (EPZs)' GB.286/ESP/3 (286th Session Geneva, ILO, 2003); and Report Of Global Unions Panel on 'Sustainable Trade, Social Development And Decent Work' (Geneva, 16 June 2003), available at: http://72.14.203.104/search?q=cache:09qxAmGTI_UJ:www.wto.org/English/tratop_e/dda_e/symp03_icftu_report_e.doc+trade+unions+in+developing+countries&hl=en&gl=uk&ct=clnk&cd=12.

[7] For the potential creation of a human rights mechanism under the auspices of the Association of Southeast Asian Nations (ASEAN) and the working group set up for this purpose, see materials available at: www.aseanhrmech.org/.

Within both the CoE and the OAS, established in the wake of World War II, peace and political stability were at the forefront of their founders' ambitions. There was also consensus in both organisations that, following wartime atrocities, immediate steps should be taken to secure the protection of human rights.[8]

The founding members of the OAU also sought to promote peace and stability, but their joint endeavour can also be understood in terms of resistance to colonialism and its residual manifestations in Africa.[9] While the OAU Charter acknowledged the respect due to human rights protection, OAU activities initially centred on other facets of policy co-ordination, and it was not until 1981 that the African Charter on Human and Peoples' Rights (ACHPR) was adopted.[10]

Despite the longstanding link between these regional organisations and the protection of human rights, it was not initially clear to what extent, if any, workers' rights and those of their organisations would receive protection under their auspices. One difficulty which arose, particularly within the CoE and OAS, was that rights associated with the interests of workers were designated socio-economic rather than civil and political, as they were thought to promote material welfare rather than human freedom or political participation. There was little appreciation of the potential for integrated protection of both species of rights. Nevertheless, the overall picture of protection of workers' rights within regional organisations is one of slow and incremental change, whereby workers' human rights have only gradually come to be recognised as having not only socio-economic but also civil and political dimensions, and thereby as worthy of receiving enhanced protection under regional supervisory mechanisms.

The Council of Europe (CoE)

The CoE was designed to foster inter-governmental co-operation to resist the reoccurrence of fascism and totalitarianism in Europe. It was to set common standards for the conduct of governments and the scope of

---

[8] See the American Declaration of the Rights and Duties of Man 1948; and *Congress of Europe: The Hague—May 1948 Resolutions* (London, European Movement, 1948) 5–7 and 12–14.

[9] Murray, R, *Human Rights in Africa: From the OAU to the African Union* (Cambridge, Cambridge University Press, 2004) 7.

[10] It was preceded, for example, by the Organisation of African Unity (OAU) Convention Governing the Specific Aspects of the Refugee Problem in African 1969, thought to be a long-standing legacy of colonialism in the African continent. Note that issues of refugee status and workers' rights arise simultaneously in jurisprudence developed under the African Charter on Human and Peoples' Rights (ACHPR); in respect of which, see n 121 below.

their common action on various matters, including the maintenance and realisation of human rights.[11]

This entity must at the outset be distinguished from another organisation now flourishing in Europe, the European Union (EU), which emerged later, with a more economic orientation and a very different legal regime. Given its market influence, not only within Europe but globally, it is not unusual for the EU to be more widely recognised than its counterpart, the CoE, and there is often confusion even in European media as to the relative scope of their influence. However, while the EU has recognised the significance of human rights protection through its adoption of the EU Charter of Fundamental Rights in 2000, this instrument would appear to have only declaratory effect and the priority of the Union would seem to remain the preservation of market freedoms under the European Community (EC) Treaty, which have particular status in the legal systems of EU Member States.[12] Protection of workers' rights as human rights within the EU arises through the general principles jurisprudence of the European Court of Justice, but only as an exception to key tenets of EC law, such as free movement of goods, services and establishment.[13] Within the EU legal framework there is no free-standing right of workers to bring a claim for protection of their human rights other than insofar as these are given legislative effect by virtue of EC directives adopted in the field of social policy.[14]

The Statute of the Council of Europe drew no distinction between civil, political and socio-economic rights, but the reference to 'individual freedom' in the Preamble did not bode well for the inclusion of workers' claims which might be exercised collectively. In debates over the content of the European Convention on Human Rights (ECHR), it became evident that unanimous endorsement in the Committee of Ministers necessary for the adoption of that instrument would not be achieved were socio-economic rights included in that instrument.[15] It was considered 'necessary to begin at the beginning and to guarantee political democracy in the European Union and

[11] Statute of the Council of Europe 1949 art 1; and see also Council of Europe, *The Union of Europe: Its Progress, Problems and Prospects, and Place in the Western World* (Strasbourg, Council of Europe, 1951).

[12] See for an exceptionally useful analysis of the dominant economic and market-led aspirations of the EU in the field of social policy, Kenner, J, *EU Employment Law: From Rome to Amsterdam and Beyond* (Oxford, Hart Publishing, 2003).

[13] See chapter 16.

[14] See Ryan, B, 'The Private Enforcement of European Union Labour Laws' in C Kilpatrick, T Novitz, and P Skidmore (eds), *The Future of Remedies in Europe* (Oxford, Hart Publishing, 2000).

[15] *European Convention on Human Rights (ECHR) Travaux Preparatoires* (Strasbourg Council of Europe, 1949–50) vol I, Preparatory Commission of the Council of Europe, Committee of Ministers, Consultative Assembly, 11.05.49–8.09.49 (The Hague, 1975) vol I (Sir David Maxwell-Fyfe (UK)) 116.

then to co-ordinate our economies, before undertaking the generalisation of social democracy'.[16]

Freedoms of direct relevance to workers were included in the ECHR of 1950, such as article 4 which prohibited slavery and forced labour, and article 11 which provided for freedom of association, including 'the right to form and join trade unions'. The latter provision was adopted on the explicit understanding that it would not cover the negative freedom to disassociate, but would provide only for the positive right to form and join trade unions and other associations.[17] Other entitlements also of considerable practical significance to workers included the right to a fair trial (under article 6), the right to respect for private and family life (under article 8), and prohibition of discrimination in respect of Convention rights (under article 14). However, socio-economic rights received explicit recognition only under the European Social Charter of 1961 (ESC). Part I of the ESC sets out a long list of aims for contracting parties, which then have the choice to select from Part II a minimum number of provisions by which they will be bound (under article 20). These include an extensive list of workers' rights,[18] supplemented by an Additional Protocol of 1988,[19] and the Revised European Social Charter of 1996.[20]

The determination to distinguish civil and political rights from socio-economic rights in this fashion has been linked to the emergence of the division between Eastern and Western Europe during the 'Cold War'. There was a palpable tension between socialist states, which emphasised the importance of social and economic claims of groups collectively as well as persons individually, and the western liberal democracies which stressed the value of individual freedom and democratic forms of political participation. Nevertheless, it has also been observed that, at this point in history, there had not previously been so extensive a 'welfare State' provision as emerged

---

[16] *ECHR Travaux Preparatoires* (1949–50) vol I, 194, para 5.

[17] Ibid vol IV, 262.

[18] Such as the right to work (art 1), the right to just conditions of work (art 2), the right to safe and healthy working conditions (art 3), the right to a fair remuneration (art 4), the right to organise (art 5), the right to bargain collectively (art 6), the right of children and young persons to protection in employment (art 7), the right of employed women to protection (art 8), the right to vocational guidance (art 9) and vocational training (art 10).

[19] See the right to equal opportunities and equal treatment in matters of employment and occupations without discrimination on grounds of sex (art 1), the right to information and consultation (art 2) and the right to take part in the determination and improvement of the working conditions and working environment (art 3).

[20] See the right to protection in cases of termination of employment (art 24), the right of workers to the protection of their claims in the event of insolvency of their employer (art 25), the right to dignity at work (art 26), the right of workers with family responsibilities to equal opportunities and equal treatment (art 27), the right of workers' representatives to protection in the undertaking and facilities to be afforded to them (art 28) and the right to information and consultation in collective redundancy procedures (art 29).

in western European countries after 1950.[21] At the end of the Cold War, despite speeches reverting to the rhetoric of indivisibility of rights,[22] and various proposals to integrate the protection of human rights within the Council of Europe,[23] the status quo has by and large been maintained. Any blurring of the distinction between civil liberties and socio-economic rights has occurred through the intervention of the European Court of Human Rights rather than the Member States.[24]

The ECHR is remarkable for having introduced an innovative supervisory mechanism, namely a means by which individuals could bring a petition against a state before competent judges, who would provide a final judgment on legal principles and, where necessary, award compensation to the victim.[25] This was in its time so radical as to be unpalatable to many contracting parties, with the result that a compromise was reached, whereby states had the option to accept individual petition or accede to the jurisdiction of the Court by a declaration under articles 25 and 46 of the ECHR respectively. It took time for there to be a critical mass of declarations, so that the European Court of Human Rights only began sitting in 1959, its role in the scrutiny of complaints being preceded by the establishment of a European Commission on Human Rights.

Today all state parties accept the right of individual petition and the jurisdiction of a single permanent Court by virtue of Protocol 11,[26] which entered into force on 1 November 1998. Since 1999, there is no longer a European Commission on Human Rights; its role in 'friendly settlement' and in scrutinising the admissibility of applications is now performed by the Committees and Chambers of the Court. A judgment of the Court cannot 'annul, repeal or modify any legislation or individual decision of a competent State', but can give a legally binding judgment determining whether a domestic administrative act, court decision or law is in breach of

---

[21] Indeed, this is often thought of as the 'classic period' in its history, see for example Lowe, R, *The Welfare State in Britain since 1945* (Basingstoke, Palgrave Macmillan, 2005) pt 2.

[22] See the Vienna Declaration on Human Rights (1993) UN Doc A/CONF.157/24. Another example is the Declaration on the Occasion of the 50th Anniversary of the Universal Declaration of Human Rights, adopted by the Council of Europe Committee of Ministers on 10 December 1998, para 4: civil, political and socio-economic rights are 'universal, indivisible, interdependent and interrelated'.

[23] See text accompanying nn 39–41 below.

[24] See Mantouvalou, V, 'Work and Private Life: Sidabras and Dziautas v Lithuania' (2005) 30(4) *European Law Review* 573; Mantouvalou, V, 'Servitude and Forced Labour in the 21st Century: The Human Rights of Domestic Workers' (2006) 35 *Industrial Law Journal* 395; and in this volume below.

[25] See Robertson, AH, 'The European Convention for the Protection of Human Rights' (1950) 27 *British Yearbook of International Law* 145.

[26] See for a summary of the content of Protocol 11, Drzemczewski, A, 'A Major Overhaul of the European Human Rights Convention Control Mechanism: Protocol 11' (1995) VI(2) *Collected Courses of the Academy of European Law: The Protection of Human Rights in Europe* 206; and Schermers, HG, 'The Eleventh Protocol to the European Convention on Human Rights' (1994) 19 *ELRev* 367.

the ECHR and, in giving reasons, specify the obligations incumbent upon the state concerned, including compensation to an injured party.[27] The Court also has the capacity to give advisory opinions.[28] This supervisory system has been remarkable in its achievement of a public profile, the status of the judgments delivered and the media attention it has received, but is also hugely overburdened with applications, prompting attention to further reform.[29]

There were initial suggestions that enforcement of the European Social Charter be linked to that of the ECHR, by involving the European Commission on Human Rights in the supervisory process.[30] This would have been more consistent with the notion that civil, political and socio-economic rights are indivisible, but the proposal was rejected.[31] Instead, a convoluted system of reporting was put in place,[32] whereby reports from states (potentially supplemented by the views of national trade unions and employers' organisations) would be submitted for legal assessment by a Committee of Independent Experts (CIE), then a Governmental Committee (consisting of ministerial representatives who tended to reject the findings of the CIE), then the Parliamentary Assembly, and finally the Committee of Ministers, with the latter having the capacity to issue recommendations to the state concerned.[33] The result of this complex and lengthy process was that, for 30 years, no recommendation was directed to a state by the Committee of Ministers.[34] In comparison with the Convention, the Charter was 'little known, rarely referred to and often ignored in practice'.[35]

At the end of the Cold War, with the prospect of reunification of Europe ahead, members of the CoE became acutely aware of the inadequacy of

[27] ECHR post amendment by Protocol 11, arts 41–46.

[28] Previously under Protocol No 2 and now, post amendment by Protocol 11, arts 47–49 of the ECHR.

[29] Discussed in Janis, M, Kay, R and Bradley, A, *European Human Rights Law* (Oxford, Oxford University Press, 1995) 70; and Greer, S, *The European Convention on Human Rights: Achievements, Problems and Prospects* (Cambridge, Cambridge University Press, 2006) 55–59. Note also in 2009, the opening of provisional Protocol No 14bis for signature, available at: http://conventions.coe.int/Treaty/Commun/QueVoulezVous.asp?NT=204&CM=2&DF=5/30/2009&CL=ENG.

[30] Consultative Assembly, 'European Social Charter and European Economic and Social Council Draft Recommendation' (1955) Doc 403. European Social Charter, *Collected Travaux Preparatoires* (provisional edition) (1955) vol II, s II.

[31] *Cf* Consultative Assembly, 'Economic Social Charter and European Economic and Social Conference, Draft Recommendations and Reports, presented on behalf of the Committee on Social Questions' (1956) Doc 488 22. European Social Charter, *Collected Travaux Preparatoires* (provisional edition) (1956) vol III, s IV.

[32] See European Social Charter (ESC) 1961 arts 21–23.

[33] Ibid arts 26–29.

[34] See Betten, L, 'Committee of Ministers of the Council of Europe Call for Contracting States to Account for Violations of the European Social Charter' (1994) 10 *International Journal of Comparative Labour Law and Industrial Relations* 147.

[35] Hepple, B, '25 Years of the European Social Charter' (1989) 10 *Comparative Labor Law Journal* 460.

the supervisory process attached to the ESC and set reform in motion.[36] The supervisory process was streamlined by the Turin Protocol 1991, the crucial features of which were brought into effect by a decision of the Committee of Ministers. The result was that the CIE interpretation of the ESC was acknowledged as being authoritative (so as to prevent their findings being opposed by the Governmental Committee), that the Assembly was removed from direct participation in the supervisory process (so as to alleviate the problem of delay), and that the Committee of Ministers was given greater power to make recommendations. A further initiative was the Collective Complaints Protocol (CCP) adopted in 1995, which came into force in 1998, and makes provision for complaints relating to non-compliance with the ESC to be heard by the CIE, that body having since been renamed the European Committee of Social Rights (ECSR). While this new system of complaints has the capacity to highlight breaches of the ESC, it suffers from a variety of limitations. Only collective entities can lodge complaints which relate to 'non-compliance' rather than 'violation' of the Charter.[37] There is also no possibility of awarding just satisfaction to a victim and it is highly doubtful that any recommendations made by the ECSR or the Committee of Ministers will be regarded as having the binding status of judgments issued by the European Court of Human Rights.[38]

The CoE Parliamentary Assembly has adopted two Recommendations calling for further amendment of ESC, creating either a 'parallel European Court of Social Rights' or enforcement of certain social rights through the European Court of Human Rights.[39] The first initiative had the provisional support of the ECSR,[40] but both were ultimately rejected by the

[36] In the informal Rome Conference of 1990, the Committee for the European Social Charter (known as 'Charte-Rel') was created to investigate and suggest appropriate reforms. See Council of Europe, *The Social Charter of the 21st Century: Colloquy Organised by the Secretariat of the Council of Europe 14–16 May 1997* (Strasbourg, Council of Europe Publishing, 1998) 43–49, 71.

[37] See the recommendations made to this effect by Chapman, A, 'A "Violations Approach" to Monitoring Economic, Social and Cultural Rights' (1996) 18 *Human Rights Quarterly* 23.

[38] For further detail relating to its operation, see Novitz, T, 'Are Social Rights Necessarily Collective Rights? A Critical Analysis of the Collective Complaints Protocol to the European Social Charter' (2002) 1 *European Human Rights Law Review* 50; and Churchill, R and Khaliq, U, 'The Collective Complaints System of the European Social Charter—An Effective Mechanism for Ensuring Compliance with Economic and Social Rights?' (2004) 15(3) *European Journal of International Law* 417.

[39] Council of Europe (CoE) Parliamentary Assembly: Recommendation No 1354 on the Future of the European Social Charter (1998) para 18; and CoE Parliamentary Assembly: Recommendation No 1415 on An Additional Protocol to the European Convention on Human Rights Concerning Fundamental Rights (1999).

[40] Conclusions of the European Committee of Social Rights (ECSR) XIV-1 ((Strasbourg, Council of Europe, 1998) 26–27; and Conclusions XIV(2) ((Strasbourg, Council of Europe, 1998) 28–29.

Committee of Ministers.[41] The result is that the supervisory processes for the implementation of civil and political rights under the ECHR and socio-economic rights under the Charter carry on in tandem, sometimes with similar cases arising under each, especially, for example, in the context of trade union rights.

The Organisation of American States (OAS)

In 1948, the OAS Charter stated the intention of its members to promote 'their economic, social, and cultural development'.[42] The American Declaration of the Rights and Duties of Man, which was adopted simultaneously, recognised certain socio-economic rights alongside civil and political rights. These included in chapter one 'the right to associate with others', for instance in respect 'of a labor union' (under article XXII), as well as the right to work and to fair remuneration (under article XIV) and the right to leisure time (under article XV). Chapter two made the more unusual provision for duties, including the 'duty of every person to work, as far as his capacity and possibilities permit in order to obtain the means of livelihood or to benefit his community' (under article XXXVII). This may be linked to the general concern after World War II to achieve full employment which would assist economic recovery.[43] However, as its name suggests, this is primarily a 'declaratory' instrument, although it has since been accepted that this instrument may be relevant in the interpretation of binding instruments such as the OAS Charter and the American Convention on Human Rights of 1969 (ACHR).[44]

It has been suggested that adoption of the ACHR became imperative in the light of extreme repression which occurred in the Americas over the Cold War period. This was an era notable for the emergence of military regimes and civilian dictators who detained, assassinated and tortured those who opposed them.[45] In this context, the ACHR was drafted to focus

---

[41] Decision of the Committee of Ministers (Deputies): Future of the European Social Charter and Additional Protocol to the European Convention on Human Rights Concerning Fundamental Social Rights—Parliamentary Assembly Recommendations 1354 (1998) and 1415 (1999) CM/Del/Dec(98)645/4/4 and (99)677b/3.1 (75th meeting, 18 April 2001), 'Appendix to the Reply' para 23 I, ii.

[42] Charter of the Organisation of American States 1948 art 2(f).

[43] See for example the International Labour Organisation (ILO) Declaration of Philadelphia 1944 art 3(a).

[44] Interpretation of the American Declaration of the Rights and Duties of Man within the Framework of art 64 of the American Convention on Human Rights (ACHR) Advisory Opinion No 10 I/A Court HR Series A No 10 Appendix IV 109, 11 *HRLJ* 118; and Statute of the Inter-American Commission approved by Resolution 447 of the OAS General Assembly 1979 art 1(2).

[45] Buergenthal, T, 'Remembering the Early Years of the Inter-American Court of Human Rights' (2005) 37 *International Law and Politics* 259, 259.

primarily on protection of civil and political rights in chapter II of that instrument, self-consciously following the example set by the CoE.[46]

Once again, many of the entitlements set out in the Convention are of interest to workers in their relations with both their employer and the state, such as freedom from slavery and involuntary servitude (in article 6), the right to a fair trial (under article 8), the right to privacy (under article 11), and freedom of association for 'labor' among other purposes (under article 16). The only specific recognition of economic, social and cultural rights arises in article 26 in chapter III, which provides that the state parties:

> undertake to adopt measures, both internally and through international coopera-
> tion, especially those of an economic and technical nature, with a view to achiev-
> ing progressively, by legislation or other appropriate means, the full realisation
> of the rights implicit in the economic social, educational, scientific and cultural
> standards set forth in the Charter [of the OAS].

This provision has been described as a 'disappointment', for it gives little apparent scope to supervisory bodies to receive complaints relating to viola-tion of socio-economic rights.[47]

The work of the Inter-American Commission on Human Rights began in 1960 and therefore significantly precedes both the adoption of the ACHR in 1969 and its entry into force in 1979. Provision was made for the Commission's activities in the ACHR, but the Commission still regards its role to be to promote human rights generally, with reference to the OAS Charter and the Declaration (including socio-economic rights set out in the latter instrument). By this means the Commission claims jurisdiction not only over parties to the ACHR but in respect of all members of the OAS.[48] The Commission has a variety of functions,[49] but in practice its seven members have tended to focus upon two tasks: 'the preparation of country reports on the general State of human rights in a country, normally follow-ing an *in loco* visit, and the examination of individual petitions'.[50]

---

[46] Cabra, M, 'Rights and Duties Established by the American Convention on Human Rights' (1980) 30 *American Universities Law Review* 21, 60.

[47] Craven, M, 'The Protection of Economic, Social and Cultural Rights under the Inter-American System of Human Rights' in DJ Harris and S Livingstone (eds), *The Inter-American System of Human Rights* (Oxford, Clarendon Press, reprinted 2004) 299–301. The scope of art 26 of the ACHR was raised by petitioners before the Inter-American Court of Human Rights in *Case of Acevedo-Jaramillo et al v Peru*, Judgment of February 7 2006 [282]–[285], but the Court declined to analyse the potential for violation of this provision, given other serious violations in respect of the Convention already established under arts 25 and 8 of the ACHR regarding art 1(1), namely right to judicial protection and a fair trial.

[48] Cerna, C, 'The Inter-American Commission on Human Rights: its Organisation and Examination of Petitions and Communications' in Harris and Livingstone, *The Inter-American System of Human Rights* (2004) 69; and Craven, 'The Protection of Economic, Social and Cultural Rights under the Inter-American System of Human Rights' (2004) 305.

[49] See art 41 of the ACHR.

[50] Harris, D, 'Regional Protection of Human Rights: The Inter-American Achievement' in Harris and Livingstone (n 47) 19–20.

The Inter-American Court of Human Rights came into being in the same year that the ACHR came into force. This is a judicial body which can issue advisory opinions[51] and deliver binding judgments on contentious cases referred by the Commission. There has been tension between the Commission and the Court, partly due to the early reluctance of the Commission to refer cases,[52] but also due to the more legalistic approach taken by the Court to admissibility and violations.[53] The focus of the Court is predominantly on the Convention rather than the Declaration, given that it is to this instrument that it owes its very existence.[54]

One key question is whether the failure of the ACHR to address socio-economic rights and the consequent limited jurisdiction of the Inter-American Court has been rectified by the Protocol on Economic, Social and Cultural Rights (commonly known as the San Salvador Protocol) which was adopted in 1988 and entered into force on receiving 11 ratifications in 1999. The text of this instrument bears 'remarkable similarities in form and terminology' to the International Covenant on Economic, Social and Cultural Rights 1966, making provision for such entitlements as the right to work (under article 6), the right to just, equitable and satisfactory conditions of work (under article 7), and trade union rights (under article 8).[55] However, the implications of this supplementary instrument for the protection of workers will be dependent on the actual scope of its application by supervisory bodies, alongside and integrated with those operating under the ACHR.

The Protocol of San Salvador, like the ESC, is to be enforced predominantly by a system of reporting. This reporting system was finally agreed in 2007. Reports are to be submitted to the Secretary-General of the OAS which will transmit them to the Inter-American Council for Integral Development (CIDI) for examination.[56] In June 2007, the OAS General Assembly meeting agreed the composition and functioning of the working group within the CIDI that would perform this function,[57] but in 2008 the American Commission was still considering the progress indicators which would be

---

[51] See Pasqualucci, J, 'Advisory Practice of the Inter-American Court of Human Rights: Contributing to the Evolution of International Human Rights Law' (2002) 38 *Stanford Journal of International Law* 241.

[52] Buergenthal, 'Remembering the Early Years of the Inter-American Court of Human Rights' (2005) 269–70.

[53] See eg, the *Cayara case*, Preliminary Objections, I/A Court HR Series C No 14 (1993), discussed by Gomez, V, 'The Interaction Between the Political Actors of the OAS, the Commission and the Court' in Harris and Livingstone (n 47) 184–85.

[54] See c VIII of the ACHR.

[55] Craven (n 47) 309.

[56] Art 19 of the San Salvador Protocol refers to the Inter-American Economic and Social Council and to the Inter-American Council for Education, but these two bodies were merged in 1996 to form the Inter-American Council for Integral Development (CIDI).

[57] Protocol of San Salvador: Composition and Functioning of the Working Group to Examine the Periodic Reports of the States Parties (adopted at the Fourth Plenary Session, held on June 5, 2007) Ag/Res. 2262 (Xxxvii-O/07).

appropriate for the evaluation of national reports.[58] It is anticipated that the CIDI will issue general recommendations and submit an annual report, with a view to its presentation to the OAS General Assembly. Copies of reports will also be sent to the Inter-American Commission on Human Rights.[59] This seems consistent with the Commission's existing jurisdiction over socio-economic rights recognised by the ADHR and its current reference to the Protocol in the course of its other activities. The Commission will then formulate observations and recommendations, which it may also include in an annual or special report to the OAS General Assembly. This may allow the Commission to integrate further its expertise on protection of civil liberties and political rights with that of socio-economic rights, and could have relevance for workers whose interests bridge this artificial divide.

Individual petition to the Commission and the Court (otherwise available under the ACHR) will apply where there is a violation of article 8(a) or article 13 of the San Salvador Protocol.[60] Article 8(a) concerns the right to form and join trade unions and article 13 relates to the right to education. This is a highly selective approach to integration of the enforcement of civil liberties and socio-economic rights. It has also led to certain individual petitions being treated as inadmissible by the Inter-American Commission on Human Rights where these are based on provisions set out in the San Salvador Protocol other than articles 8(a) and 13, and where the Commission cannot characterise the complaint as relating to possible violations of human rights protected by the American Convention.[61] Nevertheless, the albeit limited scope for individual petition offers a glimmer of hope that trade union freedoms will receive reinforced protection, given the guarantee of freedom of association already set out in article 16 of the ACHR. Indeed, in some instances the Commission has countered state objections to admissibility (raised in reliance on the limitations of the San Salvador Protocol) by finding that the circumstances relating to workers raise issues in relation to rights guaranteed under the ACHR, rather than just under the Protocol.[62]

---

[58] Protocol of San Salvador: Composition and Functioning of the Working Group to Examine the Periodic Reports of the States Parties (Adopted at the fourth plenary session, held on June 3, 2008) AG/RES. 2430 (XXXVIII-O/08).

[59] Protocol of San Salvador: Composition and Functioning of the Working Group to Examine the Periodic Reports of the States Parties (Adopted at the fourth plenary session, held on June 4, 2009) AG/RES. 2506 (XXXIX-O/09).

[60] See art 19(6) of the San Salvador Protocol, discussed by Craven (n 47) 311. For admission of admissibility of a complaint on the basis of art 8(a), see Report No 23/06, Petition 71-03, Admissibility, *Unions of Ministry of Education Workers (ATRAMEC) v El Salvador* (2 March 2006).

[61] For eg, Inter-American Commission on Human Rights, Report No 44/04, Petition 2582/02, Inadmissibility, *Laura Tena Colunga et al v Mexico* (13 October 2004).

[62] For eg, Inter-American Commission on Human Rights, Report No 84/06, Petition 1068-03, Admissibility, *Nuesa dos Santos Nascimento and Gise Ena Ferreira v Brazil* (21 October 2006). For the state's objection, see para 31; and for the Commission's response, see paras 54 and 55.

The African Union (AU)

The original OAU Charter stated that 'freedom, equality, justice and dignity' were to be regarded as essential for 'the achievement of the legitimate aspirations of the African Peoples'. The ACHPR takes as its inspiration the Universal Declaration of Human Rights 1948 (UDHR), but also appreciated 'the virtues of their historical tradition and the values of African civilisation which should inspire and characterise their reflection on the concept of human and Peoples' rights'. Additionally, the ACHPR links its aspirations to the 'total liberation of Africa' from colonialism and other forms of subjection.

The ACHPR makes more direct provision for workers' rights than either the European or American Conventions on Human Rights, arguably thereby integrating protection of civil, political and socio-economic rights. While it provides for protection of such liberties as freedom from slavery (under article 5) and free association (under article 10), the African Charter additionally makes specific reference in article 15 to the right of every individual 'to work under equitable and satisfactory conditions' and 'to receive equal pay for equal work'. Other entitlements arising under the ACHPR, which may also prove useful to workers, are protections from discrimination (under articles 2 and 19), equality before the law (under article 3), the right to have one's cause heard (under article 7), the right to receive information and express one's opinions (under article 9), and the right to free assembly (under article 11). The ACHPR also follows a precedent set by the OAS Charter, in that chapter II sets out the duties owed by every individual, including 'to serve his national community by placing his physical and intellectual abilities at its service' and 'to work to the best of his abilities and competence' (under article 29).

The ACHPR has since been supplemented by other instruments. The most relevant of these, in substantive terms, for the purpose of the protection of workers' rights are the African Charter on the Rights and Welfare of the Child 1990 (ACRWC) and the Additional Protocol on the Rights of Women in Africa (APRWA), adopted in 2003. The former provides potentially useful protections against child labour (under article 15) and sale, trafficking and abduction (under article 29), as well as making provision for the entitlement of children to protection from discrimination (under article 3) and freedom of association (under article 8). The subject matter of the APRWA is not restricted to violence against women,[63] but covers women's entitlements to resist discrimination in a range of fields, including the workplace (under article 13).[64]

---

[63] *Cf* The Inter-American Convention on the Prevention, Punishment and Eradication of Violence Against Women adopted by the OAS in 1994.

[64] For a useful outline of its content and potential ramifications, see Baderin, MA, 'Recent Developments in the African Regional Human Rights System' (2005) 5 *Human Rights Law Review* 117, 118–24.

The ACHPR entered into force in 1986 and utilises a system of both reports and complaints. The African Commission on Human Rights established in 1987 receives reports from states on the extent of their compliance with ACHPR provisions (under article 62) and has the capacity to make decisions on alleged violations of Charter rights made by complainants (under articles 47–59). Reports are submitted by signatory states, but communications may be submitted by individuals, non-governmental organisations (NGOs) or other states (under articles 47–59). Such communications may relate to socio-economic as well as civil and political rights, as both species of human right are protected under the ACHPR. Indeed, Guidelines for National Periodic Reports include 'General Guidelines Regarding the Form and Contents of Reports on Economic and Social Rights' contemplating reports on, inter alia, 'the right to work, just and favourable conditions of work; right to form and belong to free and independent trade unions', etc.[65] Having the same systems of supervision in place for both civil liberties and socio-economic rights may enable the Commission to recognise the extent to which they are inter-related. It should be noted that article 26 of the African Women's Protocol (the APRWA) provides for an almost identical method of supervision.

Additionally, a Protocol on the Establishment of an African Court on Human and Peoples' Rights was adopted in 1998 and came into force in 2004.[66] As many commentators have observed, the existence of a Court could considerably enhance effective supervision of the Charter's implementation, for it will be able to deliver legally binding judgments rather than the recommendations issued by the Commission.[67] The 11 judges of the Court were only elected in January 2006 and held their first meeting in July 2006, but their ability to entertain cases was prevented by a realisation that the AU lacked the resources to maintain two judicial institutions, such that the functions of the African Court of Justice and the African Court of Human Rights should be merged. Finally, in July 2008, a 'Protocol on the Statute of the African Court of Justice and Human Rights' (the single

---

[65] R Murray and M Evans (eds), *Documents of the African Commission on Human and Peoples' Rights* (Oxford, Hart Publishing, 2001) 53. For detailed requirements of reporting on laws relating to trade union rights, the right to form and join trade unions, rights of trade unions to federate, rights of trade unions to function freely, and the right to strike, see paras 10–16.

[66] For list of ratifications, see www.africa-union.org/Official_documents/Treaties_% 20Conventions_%20Protocols/List/Protocol%20on%20the%20African%20Court%20on% 20Human%20and%20Peoples%20Rights.pdf.

[67] See, for example, Murray, R, 'A Comparison Between the African and European Courts of Human Rights' (2002) 2 *African Human Rights Law Journal* 195; and van der Linde, M and Louw, L, 'Considering the Interpretation and Implementation of Art 24 of the African Charter on Human and Peoples' Rights in the light of the SERAC Communication' (2003) 3 *African Human Rights Law Journal* 167, 180.

Protocol) was adopted by the AU Summit.[68] For these reasons, the impact of a Court on the African regional human rights system can only be the subject of conjecture for the purpose of this chapter. At best, one can say that it is indicative of the ongoing evolution of regional human rights protection in Africa and may yet have significant implications for the protection of workers' rights as human rights once it comes into operation. However, lessons learnt from Europe and America suggest that much may depend on the manner in which a court operates.

THE OPERATION OF REGIONAL SUPERVISORY
MECHANISMS IN THE CONTEXT OF
FREEDOM OF ASSOCIATION

The effective protection of workers' rights as human rights relies on the practical application of regional human rights instruments by the relevant supervisory body (or bodies). This section investigates the efficacy of their work, with particular reference to workers' entitlement to freedom of association, manifested in trade union rights. It examines, in this respect, both the scale of their activity evident from the number of complaints they handle and the principles they disseminate on hearing the complaint.

Of the three regional human rights organisations, there is little doubt that the CoE is by far the most active. The collective complaints procedure under the ESC remains relatively modest, having received only 59 complaints between 1998 and 2009. By contrast, the demands on the European Court of Human Rights are much more extensive. In 2008, almost 50,000 applications were made for judicial intervention and 1,543 judgments were delivered by the Court in that year.[69]

In comparison, during 2008, the Inter-American Commission approved a total of 49 admissibility reports, 10 inadmissibility reports, and four friendly settlements. It published seven merits reports, as well as held 93 hearings and 70 working meetings.[70] Nine cases were presented to the Inter-American Court in 2008.[71] It was estimated in 2003 that the African Commission hears approximately 10 complaints per year,[72] but that number seems to have escalated swiftly with 80 communications tabled between

---

[68] See www.africa-union.org/root/au/Documents/Treaties/text/Protocol%20on%20the%20Merged%20Court%20-%20EN.pdf. As at 7 July 2009, only one country, Libya, had ratified the 2008 instrument. See www.africa-union.org/root/au/Documents/Treaties/list/Protocol%20on%20Statute%20of%20the%20African%20Court%20of%20Justice%20and%20HR.pdf.

[69] European Court of Human Rights, 'Annual Report 2008' (2009) 5.

[70] Annual Report of the Inter-American Commission on Human Rights 2008 (25 February 2009) OEA/Ser.L/V/II.134 Doc 5 rev 1 ch II.

[71] Ibid ch III.

[72] Heyns et al, 'A Schematic Comparison of Human Rights Systems' (2003) 79.

December 2008 and May 2009, although it would seem that only two are currently being investigated in depth.[73]

However, the more salient point may be that within these three regional human rights systems only a very small minority of complaints come from workers or, perhaps more significantly, their organisations. For example, under the ECHR, only six cases relating to trade unions were decided out of the 1,560 judgments otherwise delivered in 2006[74] and in 2008 only one, albeit one of considerable significance, was decided.[75] Most cases relating to violation of freedom of association within the Inter-American system tend to be linked to the assassination, detention or other ill-treatment of human rights protestors, trade union leaders or other activists,[76] with few recent judgments having considered in any respect the scope of trade union rights. Moreover, despite considerable numbers of complaints made by African trade unions to the ILO Committee on Freedom of Association,[77] the African Commission receives few communications directly relating to trade unions rights and none which it has found to be admissible.[78]

There would seem to be a number of explanations. The first is that failure to fully integrate protection of civil, political and socio-economic rights within a regional human rights system can lead to relative neglect of workers' trade union rights. A second is that workers will only bring forward complaints in a regional forum, if they consider that international jurisprudence which respects their interests, such as that which has developed within the ILO, will guide the findings of regional supervisory systems. A final explanation may be that there is potential for serious systemic failings

[73] 26th Activity Report of the African Commission on Human and Peoples' Rights (ACHPR) submitted in accordance with Art 54 of The African Charter on Human and Peoples' Rights, Ex.Cl/529(XV), Presented To The Executive Council, Fifteenth Ordinary Session (24–30 June 2009, Sirte, Libya) para 136.

[74] European Court of Human Rights, 'Survey of Activities 2006' (2007) 19.

[75] See reference to *Demir and Baykara v Turkey* (App No 34503/97) in European Court of Human Rights, 'Annual Report 2008' (2009) 101.

[76] For recent examples, see Inter-American Court of Human Rights, Case of *Kawas-Fernández v Honduras*, Judgment of 3 April 2009 and Inter-American Court of Human Rights, Case of *Valle Jaramillo et al v Colombia*, Judgment of 27 November 2008. Both available at: www.oas.org.

[77] Since the ACHPR came into force, the ILO Committee on Freedom of Association has heard a considerable volume of complaints made by trade union organisations from contracting parties to the Charter. These can be found at: www.ilo.org/ilolex/english/caseframeE.htm.

[78] There does not appear to be any change in this trend, as is indicated in the absence of reference to trade unions in any of the communications outlined in 26th Activity Report of the African Commission on Human and Peoples' Rights (ACHPR) (n73). For an example of treatment of trade union activity, see Communication 204/97—*Mouvement Burkinabé des Droits de l'Homme et des Peuples/Burkina Faso*, Fourteenth Annual Activity Report, it was alleged that there was dismissal of many workers on account of a strike, but the Commission commented that the information provided to the Commission did not allow it to establish in any certain manner that there was violation of art 13(2) (para 48). This does however suggest that the Commission considers that protection of the right to strike comes within their jurisdiction.

within regional human rights organisations, which have to be addressed if workers' human rights are to be adequately protected. This analysis is necessarily speculative, in the absence of detailed empirical research, but reasons may include the scope for delays, the status of findings made, the remedies available, and the degree of compliance with recommendations made by supervisory bodies. A further underlying factor may be the amount of funding supplied by the relevant regional system. These last possibilities are examined in greater detail at the end of this section.

Council of Europe (CoE)

A substantial body of jurisprudence relating to the appropriate scope of protection of workers' human rights has developed under the auspices of the ESC within the CoE. This has emerged from CIE (now the European Committee on Social Rights) and Governing Body observations on state reports, as well as the decisions reached by the former since the collective complaints system came into operation.[79]

An applicant cannot directly rely on Charter rights in an application to the Court, but the European Court of Human Rights has ventured into the arena of social rights in the course of interpretation of provisions contained in the ECHR.[80] In *Airey v Ireland*, the Court found that:

> the mere fact that an interpretation of the Convention may extend into the sphere of social and economic rights should not be a decisive factor against such an interpretation; there is no watertight division separating that sphere from the field covered by the Convention.[81]

In that case, access to a 'fair and public hearing' under article 6 of the Convention was found to be dependent on the provision of free legal assistance. Protection of article 6(1) has since been applied in the context of claims for social security benefits.[82] In this manner, the Court would appear to have accepted that civil liberties and socio-economic rights are interconnected. The Court has gone on to state that the exercise of

---

[79] Summarised, inter alia, by Samuel, L, *Fundamental Social Rights: Case Law of the European Social Charter,* 2nd edn (Strasbourg, Council of Europe, 2002).

[80] Parliamentary Assembly, 'Additional Protocol to the European Convention on Human Rights Concerning Fundamental Social Rights' (23 March 1999) Doc 8357, Explanatory Memorandum at paras 48–49.

[81] *Airey v Ireland* (1980) 2 EHRR 305, cited in Flinterman, C, 'Economic, Social and Cultural Rights and the European Convention on Human rights' in R Lawson and M de Blois (eds), *The Dynamics of the Protection of Human Rights in Europe: Essays in Honour of Henry G. Schermers* (Dordrecht, Nijhoff, 1994) 173.

[82] See for example *Feldbrugge v the Netherlands*, judgment of 29 May 1986, A/99 and *Salesi v Italy*, judgment of 26 February 1993 A/257-E, discussed extensively in Schleinin, M, 'Economic and Social Rights as Legal Rights' in A Eide, C Krause, and A Rosas (eds), *Economic, Social and Cultural Rights: A Textbook* (Dordrecht, Martinus Nijhoff, 1995).

fundamental human rights, such as privacy, is vital both within and outside the workplace.[83]

However, the Court was at least initially more reluctant to find that socio-economic rights were connected with civil and political rights in the context of freedom of association. In two key cases decided in 1979, the Court found that article 11 of the ECHR did not require trade unions to be consulted or give rise to a right to engage in collective bargaining or take industrial action.[84] The reason given in both instances was that these entitlements were also set out in the ESC. Since contracting parties to the ESC are not obliged to accept as binding all ESC provisions, the Court thought it unreasonable to impose a Charter obligation on a state under article 11 of the ECHR. This was done despite the existence of ILO jurisprudence that definitively stated that these trade union rights were an important facet of freedom of association.[85] The lack of substantive and supervisory integration between the ESC and ECHR arguably lends itself to such an interpretation. To some extent the Court has corrected this anomaly by accepting that the ability of an employer to offer incentives to opt out of collective bargaining can constitute a violation of article 11,[86] and that the right to strike could be a potentially legitimate exception to the exercise of other civil liberties.[87] However, for some time it remained unclear to what extent the Court will deviate from its earlier findings on this issue.[88]

One difficulty with the restrictive approach taken by the Court in the 1970s is that the findings of the Court have greater authority than those of the ECSR, for they are 'judgments' binding on states. Should the Court decide tangentially on an issue relating to the scope of a Charter right, the Court's judgment is likely to prevail, rather than the pre-existing jurisprudence developed under the Charter supervisory procedure. An example was the determination of the Court, despite evidence in the *travaux preparatoires* to the contrary, that the guarantee of freedom of association under article 11 includes the individual entitlement to refuse to be a member of a trade union or 'negative' freedom of association.[89] This could be because

---

[83] See *Halford v UK* (1997) 24 EHRR 523 and *Smith and Grady v UK* (1999) 29 EHRR 493.

[84] *National Union of Belgian Police v Belgium* (1979) 1 EHRR 578. See also *Swedish Engine-Drivers' Union Case* (1979) 1 EHRR 617, 628.

[85] ILO, *Digest of Decisions of the Committee on Freedom of Association* (Geneva, ILO, 1972).

[86] *Wilson and the NUJ v UK* (2002) 35 EHRR 20, although it should also be noted that in that case compensation was awarded only to the individual complainants concerned and not the union affected (at [62]–[64]).

[87] *Gustafsson v Sweden* (1996) 22 EHRR 409. See Novitz, T, 'Negative Freedom of Association' (1997) 26 *Industrial Law Journal* 79.

[88] See eg, *UNISON v UK* (2002) IRLR 497.

[89] *Young, James and Webster v UK* (1982) 4 EHRR 38; confirmed in *Sørensen v Denmark and Rasmussen v Denmark* (App nos 52562/99 and 52620/99) judgment of the European Court of Human Rights, 11 January 2006.

an individualistic approach to the protection of civil liberties, although not essential, fits more readily within an established liberal jurisprudential tradition.[90] Prior to this judgment, the then CIE (now the ECSR) had ruled that governments could not impose compulsory trade unionism, but that it was permissible for workers themselves to negotiate a 'closed shop' with their employers.[91] However, the CIE changed their position after the matter had been decided by the Court.[92] Such shifts in the jurisprudence on collective socio-economic rights in response to findings on the more individualistic dimensions of civil and political rights have the potential to make a mockery of ESC supervisory machinery and jurisprudence.

A more positive development is the recent willingness of the European Court of Human Rights to acknowledge and even be guided by the views expressed by the ECSR and ILO supervisory bodies. For example, in the 2007 judgment issued in respect of *ASLEF v UK*, the Court set out the opinion of the ECSR on UK compliance with article 5 of the ESC,[93] and later applied the findings of ESCR as the basis for its conclusions.[94] Also, although the view of ILO supervisory bodies were not cited in *ASLEF*, in *Wilson and the NUJ v UK* there was specific mention of the findings of the ILO Committee on Freedom of Association that the United Kingdom was in breach of ILO Convention No 98, which again appears to have influenced the Court's findings.[95]

Perhaps more significant, in terms of citation of ILO sources, was the 2008 judgment delivered by the Grand Chamber in *Demir & Baykara v Turkey*.[96] The case concerned the requirement that workers repay wages paid under a collective agreement which was subsequently determined invalid due to Constitutional and legal reform. The Turkish Government responded to the complaint by arguing that it has been established in the jurisprudence of the European Court of Human Rights that no right to collective bargaining arose by virtue of article 11 of the ECHR. Moreover, as Turkey was not a party to article 5 (the right to organise) or article 6 (the right to bargain collectively) of the ESC, it would be improper to interpret article 11 to hold Turkey accountable for failing to protect these

---

[90] See in this respect the dissenting opinion of Judge Martens joined by Judge Maatscher in *Gustafsson* (1996) 22 EHRR 409.

[91] See 'Conclusions of the Committee of Independent Experts IV' (Strasbourg, Council of Europe, 1978), 47.

[92] See 'Conclusions of the Committee of Independent Experts XIV-1 (Strasbourg, Council of Europe, 1998) and XV-1 (Strasbourg, Council of Europe, 2001)' in respect of Denmark.

[93] *Case of Associated Society of Locomotive Engineers & Firemen (ASLEF) v United Kingdom* (App no 11002/05) unreported judgment of the European Court of Human Rights, 27 February 2007, [23].

[94] Ibid [24].

[95] Ibid [37] and especially [48] and *Wilson and the NUJ v UK* (2002) 35 EHRR 20.

[96] *Demir and Baykara v Turkey* (App no 34503/97) Grand Chamber Judgment of 12 November 2008.

entitlements in respect of civil servants. However, the Grand Chamber chose to reflect on Turkey's ratification of ILO Convention Nos 98 and 151.[97] The Court also referred to article 28 of the EU Charter of Fundamental Rights 2000 which provides that 'workers and employers, or their respective organisations, have, in accordance with Community law and national laws and practices, the right to negotiate and conclude collective agreements at the appropriate levels'.[98] As a result, the Grand Chamber concluded that:

> In the light of these developments, the Court considers that its case-law to the effect that the right to bargain collectively and to enter into collective agreements does not constitute an inherent element of Article 11 ... should be reconsidered, so as to take account of the perceptible evolution in such matters, in both international law and domestic legal systems. While it is in the interests of legal certainty, foreseeability and equality before the law that the Court should not depart, without good reason, from precedents established in previous cases, a failure by the Court to maintain a dynamic and evolutive approach would risk rendering it a bar to reform or improvement ....
>
> Consequently, the Court considers that, having regard to the developments in labour law, both international and national, and to the practice of Contracting States in such matters, the right to bargain collectively with the employer has, in principle, become one of the essential elements of the 'right to form and to join trade unions for the protection of [one's] interests' set forth in Article 11 of the Convention, it being understood that States remain free to organise their system so as, if appropriate, to grant special status to representative trade unions. Like other workers, civil servants, except in very specific cases, should enjoy such rights, but without prejudice to the effects of any 'lawful restrictions' that may have to be imposed on 'members of the administration of the State' within the meaning of Article 11 § 2—a category to which the applicants in the present case do not, however, belong.[99]

Potentially significant decisions have also been made regarding the connection between freedom of association and the right to strike, so that the latter also merits protection under article 11. In the case of *Affaire Dilek et Autres v Turquie* (also known as the *Satilmis* case),[100] a Chamber of the Court concluded that the right to strike is so significant an aspect of the defence of workers' interests, that any interference with this right has to be assessed in terms of whether it comes within the defence provided in article 11(2), namely whether that interference is 'prescribed by law' and is 'necessary in a democratic society for the protection of the rights and

---

[97] Ibid [147]–[148].

[98] Ibid [150]. The practice of other European states and their willingness to allow collective bargaining by civil servants was also acknowledged at [151].

[99] Ibid [153]–[154].

[100] *Affaire Dilek et Autres v Turquie* (App nos 74611/01, 26876/02 et 27628/0) Judgment of 17 July 2007 (available only in French).

freedoms of others or for the protection of public interest, national security, public health, or morals'. More recently, in the case of *Enerji Yapi-Yol Sen v Turkey*,[101] a Chamber of the Court gave an even more firm indication that industrial action could arise as an entitlement under article 11. This case concerned another civil servants' union, whose members were subjected to sanctions due to a national one day strike constituting peaceful action aimed at securing a collective agreement, despite prohibition of the event by the Government. The Court accepted that the right to strike was not absolute and could be subject to certain conditions and restrictions, but expressed concern that the sanctions imposed were such as to discourage trade union members and other persons from acting upon a legitimate wish to take part in such a day of strike action or other forms of action aimed at defending their affiliates' interests.[102] There had been disproportionate interference with the applicant union's rights and therefore been a violation of article 11. In this respect, the findings of the Court are consonant with ILO jurisprudence on the connection between freedom of association and the right to strike.

If the Court is prepared to seek to integrate its jurisprudence with the findings of those supervisory bodies that have specialist expertise in socio-economic rights or international labour law,[103] then the influence of its jurisdiction in respect of freedom of association may seem less objectionable. It can be seen, rather, as a way in which to give force to findings that otherwise have less immediate impact upon domestic law.

Organisation of American States (OAS)

The Inter-American Commission on Human Rights has stressed the importance of workers' rights in its reports. For example, in a report on Venezuela published in 2003, the Commission commented critically on treatment of trade union rights, citing both article 16 of the ACHR and article 8 of the Protocol of San Salvador. Reference was also made to the comments of ILO supervisory bodies on compliance with the right to freedom of association.[104] In the 'Annual Report of the Inter-American Commission on Human Rights 2004', the Commission recorded precautionary measures taken for the protection of trade unions leaders who had become military targets,

---

[101] *Enerji Yapi-Yol Sen v Turkey* (App no 68959/01) Judgment of 21 April 2009 (available only in French).

[102] Ibid [35].

[103] For continuation of this trend, see *Danilenkov v Russia* (App no 67336/01) Judgment of 30 July 2009.

[104] For a recent example, see Inter-American Commission on Human Rights, 'Report on the Situation of Human Rights in Venezuela' (29 December 2003) OEA/Ser.L/V/II.118 Doc 4 rev 2 ch VII.

and also recommendations concerning the need for additional protection of trade union rights in Colombia and Cuba, again with reference to ILO standards.[105]

However, it is the Inter-American Court which has the capacity to issue authoritative judgments and opinions on workers' rights. The Court also treats workers' rights as human rights worthy of protection under the ACHR. For example, in Advisory Opinion OC 18/03, delivered at the request of the United Mexican States challenging US laws and practices, the Court asserted that migrant workers were fully entitled to the protection of key labour rights, such as freedom from forced labour, elimination of discrimination, abolition of child labour, trade union rights, rest and holidays, as well as health and security in the workplace, and should be given the means of exercising their rights.[106] The Court concluded that:

> A person who enters a State and assumes an employment relationship acquires his labor human rights in the State of employment, irrespective of his migrant status, because respect and guarantee of the enjoyment and exercise of those rights must be made without discrimination.[107]

There is no obligation to offer migrants work, but once they have gained employment, 'they immediately become possessors of the labor rights corresponding to workers',[108] and the state 'should not allow private employers to violate the rights of workers, or the contractual relationship to violate minimum international standards'.[109] In this context, the Inter-American Court referred explicitly to the findings of the European Court of Human Rights, as a guide.[110] Even more significantly, the Court reached the conclusion that:

> since there are many legal instruments that regulate labor rights at the domestic and international level, these regulations must be interpreted according to the principle of the application of the norm that best protects the individual, in this case, the worker.[111]

However, there was little information in this Opinion as to how the United States was expected to apply such guidance in concrete terms, for example, what precise legislative reform was required.

---

[105] 'Annual Report of the Inter-American Commission on Human Rights 2004' (23 February 2005) OEA/Ser.L/V/II.122 Doc 5 rev 1 chs III and IV.

[106] Inter-American Court of Human Rights, 'Advisory Opinion OC-18/03 of September 17 2003, Requested by the United Mexican States' paras 157–60, available at: www.oas.org.

[107] Ibid para 133.

[108] Ibid para 136.

[109] Ibid para 148.

[110] Ibid para 143. For specific reference to ILO standards, see also Reasoned Concurring Opinion of Judge Sergio García Ramírez in relation to Advisory Opinion Oc-18/03 on Legal Status and Rights of Undocumented Migrants of September 17, 2003.

[111] Ibid para 156. In particular, the Court stressed that this was of great importance, for differences between norms should not be allowed to prejudice the workers.

Most commonly, when the Inter-American Court has considered the issue of trade union rights, it is either in conjunction with failure of the state to comply with judgments issued by domestic courts,[112] or in the context of stark violation of other fundamental human rights. One example of the latter circumstance was the *Huilca Tesce* case brought against Peru in 2005. This concerned the assassination of a trade unionist, which was found to violate inter alia article 16 of the ACHR. The Court made extensive provision for reparations, requiring the state to establish a course on human rights and labour law to be called the 'Cátedra Pedro Huilca', to 'recall and praise the work of Pedro Huilca Tesce in favour of the trade union movement in Peru during the official celebrations of May 1 (Labor Day)' and to erect a bust in his memory.[113] The extremity of the fate suffered by the trade unionist in this case indicates, as David Harris has observed, that:

> human rights issues in the Americas have often concerned gross, as opposed to ordinary violations of human rights [being] more to do with forced disappearance, killing, torture and arbitrary detention of political opponents ... than with particular issues ... that are the stock in trade of the European ... Court.[114]

This has perhaps led the Inter-American Court's jurisprudence on freedom of association to be less detailed than that emerging within the CoE. The sole exception would seem to be the findings of the Court in the *Baena Ricardo (270 Workers v Panama)* case, which received judgment on its merits in 2001.

This was a case which concerned the actions of the Government of Panama in 1990. What had occurred was that a national trade union federation had presented certain petitions concerning labour-related issues to the Government, which were rejected. The federation's response was to call a march and a 24-hour work stoppage. The march took place, but the stoppage did not, on hearing the news that a political opponent of the Government had escaped from prison on the evening before it was due to commence. The Government asserted (mistakenly) that there was a link between the escape and the action taken by the trade union federation and took immediate action against affiliated trade unions and their leaders, subsequently endorsing the legality of their conduct by retrospective legislation. In 2001, the Court upheld the claim of 270 workers to redress, finding

---

[112] Inter-American Court of Human Rights, Case of *Acevedo-Jaramillo et al v Peru*, Judgment of February 7 2006 [282]–[285].

[113] Inter-American Court of Human Rights, Case of *Huilca-Tecse v Peru*, Judgment of 3 March 2005, *(Merits, Reparations and Costs),* discussed in 'Inter-American Court of Human Rights Annual Report 2005' 8.

[114] Harris, 'Regional Protection of Human Rights: The Inter-American Achievement' (2004) 2.

that there had been inter alia a violation of article 16 of the ACHR.[115] The Court had already determined that it was not precluded from considering the case by reason of previous conclusions reached by the ILO Committee on Freedom of Association,[116] and indeed referred to those conclusions in its judgment, making the point that it alone had supervisory powers to award substantial relief to those affected.[117] What was, however, peculiar in the judgment, was that despite its lack of relevance to the present case, the Court made overt reference to negative freedom of association, and the right not to join a trade union. The reason is unclear but this may have been an attempt to stress the status of freedom of association as an individual human right. This was, interestingly, the only context in which the Court referred to article 8 of the San Salvador Protocol.[118] For the reader familiar with the case law of the European Court of Human Rights, such an approach rings warning bells. One wonders whether this indicates that the familiar individualistic rhetoric associated with human rights could take thereby precedence over the protection of collective action by workers.

African Union (AU)

Under the ACHPR, violations of workers' rights have been dealt with in conjunction with other breaches of civil liberties.[119] An example was the case of *Annette Pagnoulle (on behalf of Abdoulaye Mazou)/Cameroon*,[120] in which the Commission found that the Government of Cameroon had violated Mr Mazou's right to work under article 15 of the ACHPR by not restoring him to his former position as a magistrate after his unlawful detention. A similar issue has also been raised in relation to illegal expulsions.[121] There has also been recent confirmation in the case of *SERAC/CESR* that the Commission is prepared to find there to be breach of economic, social and cultural rights

---

[115] *Baena Ricardo (270 Workers v Panama)*, Judgment of 2 February 2001, available at: www.oas.org.

[116] *Baena Ricardo (270 Workers v Panama)*, Judgment of 18 November 1999, available at: www.oas.org.

[117] *Baena Ricardo (270 Workers v Panama)*, Judgment of 2 February 2001 [162]–[165].

[118] Ibid [159].

[119] Bekker, G, 'The Social and Economic Rights Action Center and the Center for Economic and Social Rights/Nigeria' (2003) *Journal of African Law* 126, 126.

[120] Communication 39/90 *Annette Pagnoulle (on behalf of Abdoulaye Mazou)/Cameroon*, Tenth Annual Activity Report (1996–7).

[121] Communication 159/96 *Union Inter Africaine des Droits de l'Homme, Federation Internale des Ligues des Droits de l'homme, Recontre Africaine des Droits de l'Homme, Organisation Nationale des Droits de l'Homme au Sénégal and Association Malienne des Droits de l'Homme au Angola*, Eleventh Activity Report (see para 17). For detailed analysis of the overlap between the rights of refugees within the AU and human rights protections, see Murray, *Human Rights in Africa* (2004) ch 7.

even in the absence of a breach of civil and political rights,[122] which may yet be significant in terms of its implications for the protection of workers' rights, even if these were not at issue in the case in question.

Article 10(1) of the ACHPR guarantees every individual the right to free association provided that 'he abides by the law'. The African Commission elaborated on the meaning of this provision in the 1992 Resolution on the Right to Freedom of Association, stating that competent authorities, in their use of law, 'should not override constitutional provisions or undermine fundamental rights guaranteed by the constitution and international standards' and 'should not enact provisions which would limit the exercise of this freedom' and thereby extends the remit of the Commission's jurisdiction.[123] However, this principle has yet to be applied to the specific circumstances of workers, having been applied primarily in the context of political association, including freedom of assembly for the purpose of free expression,[124] and the formation of political parties.[125] There have been passing references by the Commission to the social role of trade unions. For example, in the Commission's report on its Mission to Mauritania, the Government was asked to take additional measures to promote the participation of former slaves in civil society organisations, such as trade unions;[126] also, in the Commission's report on its Mission to Botswana, queries were made relating to the scope of collective bargaining.[127] However, this is as far as the Commission's jurisprudence extends at present.

A last potentially significant development was the Commission's 2004 Pretoria Resolution on Economic, Social and Cultural Rights in Africa, which observes that 'despite the consensus on the indivisibility of human rights, economic, social and cultural rights remain marginalised in their

---

[122] Communication 155/96, *The Social and Economic Rights Action Centre (SERAC) and another v Nigeria*, Fifteenth Annual Activity Report, discussed inter alia in Bekker, 'The Social and Economic Rights Action Center and the Center for Economic and Social Rights/Nigeria' (2003); and van der Linde and Louw, 'Considering the Interpretation and Implementation of Art 24 of the African Charter on Human and Peoples' Rights in the light of the SERAC Communication' (2003) 182.

[123] ACHPR Res 5(XI) 92.

[124] Communication 228/99 *The Law Office of Ghazi Suleiman*, Sixteenth Annual Activity Report paras 44 and 56.

[125] In the Commission's most recent Eighteenth Annual Activity Report, adopted in 2005, the Commission considered Communication 251/2002 *Lawyers for Human Rights/Swaziland*, in which a human rights non-governmental organisation (NGO) challenged the Swazi King's proclamation which abolished all political parties on the basis that inter alia this decree violated the right to freedom of association. Again, the Commission referred to its entitlement to scrutinise the content of legislative measures under the 1992 Resolution (in paras 34, 60).

[126] Tenth Annual Activity Report (1996–7) 47. See also the *Suleiman* case (n 124), in which the Commission noted that freedom of expression could be regarded as 'a *condition sine qua non* for the development of' such entities as political parties, scientific and cultural societies and also notably trade unions (para 49).

[127] ACHPR, 'Mission Report to the Republic of Botswana' (14–18 February 2005), available at: www.achpr.org/english/_info/reports_en.html.

implementation'. In the 2004 Resolution, the Commission urges 'its members, its Special Rapporteurs and Working Groups to pay particular attention to such rights in their missions and the discharge of other duties'. This Resolution also records the decision to establish a working group composed of members of the Commission and NGOs to develop and propose to the Commission a draft 'Principles and Guidelines on Economic, Social and Cultural Rights' and develop revised draft guidelines for state reporting. This working group is also undertaking studies and research on specific economic, social and cultural rights and making progress reports to the Commission.[128] It may be that further elaboration on the status of workers' rights as human rights will come out of this process. However, there is no indication as at 2009 that this working group has reached any conclusions which can be put into practice.[129]

One is left wondering why freedom of association has not been at issue in the African system, given the plentiful complaints from African trade unions placed before the ILO Committee on Freedom of Association.[130] Some attraction may lie in the potential exposure of difficulties faced by national trade unions to an audience that goes beyond Africa and the ability to call on global (as opposed to regional condemnation). However, the same appeal might be expected to arise in respect of European or American trade unions.

Differences in the level of complaints activity cannot simply be attributed to admissibility requirements, for these are very similar, if not more relaxed, in the case of the African Commission which does not impose the 'victim' requirement found in the ECHR.[131] One reason for the reluctance to bring complaints could be delay, but we know that this has also been at issue in the Inter-American[132] and European human rights systems.[133] It is more likely that the attractiveness of the forum can be linked to the relative authority of the findings of supervisory bodies. In this respect, it may be

---

[128] ACHPR Res 73(XXXVI) 04.

[129] For the status quo, namely the continuation of the work of the working group in 2007 for a further two years, see: www.achpr.org/english/resolutions/resolution124_en.htm.

[130] A current list of complaints is available at: www.ilo.org/ilolex/english/caseframeE.htm. More than 20 cases are currently outstanding.

[131] Murray, R, 'International Human Rights: Neglect of Perspectives from African Institutions' (2006) 55 *ICLQ* 193, 198–99.

[132] See the preliminary judgment on admissibility of 18 November 1999, *Baena Ricardo (270 Workers v Panama)*, Judgment of 18 November 1999, available at: www.oas.org, which took place some seven years after the case had been the subject of recommendations made by the ILO Committee on Freedom of Association (CFA). See 'Complaints against the Government of Panama presented by the International Confederation of Free Trade Unions (ICFTU), the Trade Union of Water and Electricity Board Workers (SITIRHE) and the Trade Union of National Telecommunications Board Workers (SITINTEL)' (1992) Report No 281 Case No 1569 LXXV Series B No 1.

[133] On planned further reform of the ECHR supervisory system for, in part, this reason, see Greer, S, 'Protocol 14 And The Future Of The European Court Of Human' [2005] *Public Law* 83; and Greer, *The European Convention on Human Rights* (2006) 38–47.

significant that contracting parties to the ECHR 'undertake to abide by the final judgment of the Court in any case to which they are parties',[134] and that the CoE Committee of Ministers has the political will to follow up on and secure execution of judgments.[135]

By contrast, the African Commission sees the aim of the communications procedure under the ACHPR to be 'to initiate a positive dialogue, resulting in an amicable resolution, which remedies the prejudice complained of. A prerequisite for amicable remedying violations of the Charter is the good faith of the parties concerned, including their willingness to participate in dialogue'.[136] It has been observed that the efficacy of the Commission's recommendations then depends very much on the willingness of a state to co-operate. In this respect, it seems to be helpful if local human rights agencies also place pressure on the government concerned. However, where there is no political will to comply with recommendations, nothing seems to be achieved, even with the concerted effort of NGOs.[137] This may be remedied by the introduction of judicial proceedings, since parties to the protocol on the establishment of a Court have undertaken to 'comply with the judgment in any case to which they are parties within the time stipulated by the Court and to guarantee its execution'.[138]

Finally, although this is perhaps a more speculative and controversial observation, the efficacy of supervisory mechanisms may also depend on resources placed at their disposal. In this respect, it may be useful to compare what the size of the budget is for each regional organisation and the percentage spent on human rights protection. Here, the CoE emerges as the best endowed, with an annual budget of approximately €205 million (or US $303 million), of which it has been estimated approximately €57 million (or US $84 million) is spent on the enforcement of the ECHR in the European Court of Human Rights. By way of contrast, only €2,380,000 (or US $3,530,000) is devoted to the ESC directorate.[139] The annual budget of

---

[134] ECHR post amendment by Protocol 11 art 46(1).

[135] See art 46(2) Rules of the European Court of Human Rights. Although note that there still remain significant barriers to achieving full compliance even with judgments of this Court, as observed by Greer (29) 279–82.

[136] See Communications 25/89, 47/90, 56/91 and 100/83 joined, cited in Naldi, G, 'Future Trends in Human Rights in Africa: The Increased Role of the OAU?' in M Evans and R Murray (eds), *The African Charter on Human and Peoples' Rights: The System in Practice, 1986–2000* (Cambridge, Cambridge University Press, 2002) 10.

[137] See the comments of van der Linde and Louw (n 67) 183, on the respective enforcement of recommendations made in decisions of the Commission on Communication 97/93 *Modise v Botswana*, Fouteenth Annual Activity Report and Communications 54/91, 61/91, 98/93, 164/97 and Communication 210/98 *Malawi African Association v Mauritania*, Thirteenth Annual Activity Report.

[138] See art 30 of the Protocol on the African Court of Human Rights.

[139] For the current annual budget, see www.coe.int/T/e/Com/about_coe/facts_en.asp and the budget of the European Court of Human Rights, see www.echr.coe.int/ECHR/EN/Header/The+Court/The+Budget/Budget/. See also Heyns (n 1) 84.

the OAS is US $90 million of which approximately US $5.5 million is spent directly on human rights protection.[140] The annual budget of the AU is US $164 million,[141] but the ACHPR's 2009 budget was cut to almost half of the budget allocated to it in 2008 (from US $6,003,000.00 in 2008 to US $3,671,000 for 2009).[142]

Budgets affect the work of the secretariat in terms of processing complaints, assisting complainants, collecting submissions, maintaining library resources, engaging in research, and disseminating findings; and thereby the perception of their importance and relevance. David Padilla, a former Assistant Executive Secretary to the Inter-American Commission on Human Rights, has commented that:

> In order for a future African Court to be successful, it will require adequate financial and human resources. It will need proper quarters and a well-trained staff, modern office equipment and the support of competent administrative personnel. It will also need a fund that will permit the African Court to provide legal aid to indigent petitioners ...[143]

CONCLUSION: ASSESSMENT BY WORKERS AND THEIR ORGANISATIONS?

There are obvious differences between the three regional organisations considered in this chapter. They have adopted their own unique human rights instruments and established diverse supervisory mechanisms from which there has emerged their own distinctive jurisprudence. What they do appear to have in common is the gradual and incremental extension in the scope of human rights protection, such that they are able to offer ever-improving protection of workers' rights.

One aspect of this evolutionary process has been the eventual explicit recognition of the specific socio-economic concerns of workers in human rights instruments. Another has been the protection of certain rights of workers as civil and political rights, in particular trade union rights under the head of freedom of association. There has also been increasing

[140] 2009 Program Budget of the Organization Approved by the General Assembly XXXVI Special Session September 2008 AG/Res 1 (XXXVI-E/08). See www.oas.org/budget/2009/Budget%20Approved%202009%20English.pdf.

[141] Decision on the Budget for the African Union for the 2009 Financial Year Doc EX.CL/455 (XIV), Assembly of the African Union, Twelfth Ordinary Session, 1–3 February 2009, Addis Ababa, Ethiopia *cf* outdated estimates from Heyns (n 1) 84; and for comment of the impact of funding, see Murray, R, *The African Commission on Human and Peoples' Rights and International Law* (Oxford, Hart Publishing, 2000) 12.

[142] 26th Activity Report of the African Commission on Human and Peoples' Rights (ACHPR) (n 73) para 125.

[143] Padilla, 'An African Human Rights Court: Reflections from the Perspective of the Inter-American System' (2002) 190.

cross-referencing, in particular within the Council of Europe and OAS supervisory systems to ILO standards. With these developments has come the gradual improvement of conditions under which regional human rights systems operate and awareness of their activities. In all cases, however, the progress has been slow.

If this process of evolution is to continue in a direction favourable to workers, more will need to be done. There has been occasional deference by regional Courts (which deal primarily with civil and political rights) to the findings of specialist ILO and other bodies (which have specialist expertise in the field of workers' rights). Nevertheless, this may not always be sufficient to ensure that the collective dimension of workers' rights is recognised as opposed to negative freedoms, such as that *not* to associate. This suggests that, first, there is a case for integration of substantive guarantees of civil liberties, political rights and socio-economic rights within human rights instruments, which is complemented by an integrated supervisory process. Secondly, attention must be paid to the practical impediments to claims under these human rights systems, with a focus on removing these for potential complainants. It will also be necessary to ensure that findings of supervisory bodies are regarded as authoritative and that adequate relief is provided to successful complainants. This may perhaps require greater funding of human rights institutions and more targeted funding for assistance in workers' rights cases, especially within the AU.

In the absence of these proposed changes, it seems that workers and their representatives will continue to be hesitant to utilise regional systems for the protection of human rights. Already, workers' organisations seem to be assessing carefully whether they wish to spend their often limited funds on pursuing litigious strategies and, if so, where they wish to pursue these. Some evidently take the view that it is preferable to focus on mobilisation of workers behind a cause in a domestic context than to pursue legal remedies within a constitutional setting or within regional institutions, which they know are unlikely to prompt action by a recalcitrant government already in breach of regional human rights norms. Others, such as trade union organisations in African countries, have clearly decided that the ILO offers a preferable avenue for highlighting violations of freedom of association. This suggests that, although regional human rights have the potential to offer a useful route for workers and their organisations to bolster claims against governments and employers, this potential has yet to be realised.

15

Is There a Human Right Not to Be a Trade Union Member? Labour Rights under the European Convention on Human Rights

VIRGINIA MANTOUVALOU

INTRODUCTION*

COURTS DEALING WITH labour rights in human rights treaties have had to address complex questions, for reasons that involve the perceived nature of this group of entitlements, either as social entitlements or as collective claims. A labour right that illustrates the issue, included in both civil and political and socio-economic rights documents, is freedom of association. This is often specifically worded as a right to form and join trade unions.[1] 'Freedom of organisation', Kahn-Freund wrote:

> has two social and therefore two legal functions. It is a civil liberty, a human right, an aspect of freedom of association ... its existence and adequate guarantees for its exercise, are, however, also indispensable conditions for the operation of collective labour relations.[2]

* The author is grateful to all Workshop participants and particularly to the organisers and editors of the present collection, Colin Fenwick and Tonia Novitz. The author also wishes to thank Hugh Collins, Ruth Dukes, George Letsas, Bob Simpson, Charlie Webb and two anonymous reviewers for valuable comments on a draft. The author has benefited from discussions with Conor Gearty, Margot Salomon and participants of the London School of Economics Human Rights Centre PhD Affiliation Programme, and the Law Department PhD seminar. The author's attendance at the Oñati Workshop was supported by the London School of Economics.
[1] See art 11 of the European Convention on Human Rights (ECHR), art 16 of the American Convention on Human Rights, art 22 of the International Covenant on Civil and Political Rights, art 10 of the African Charter of Human and Peoples' Rights.
[2] Cited in Wedderburn, Lord, 'Freedom of Association or Right to Organise? The Common Law and International Sources' in Wedderburn, Lord (ed), *Employment Rights in Britain and Europe* (London, Lawrence and Wishart, 1991) 142.

A problem that often appears to obstruct the effective protection of freedom of association in human rights documents is the apparent tension between these two aspects of the right. This can be otherwise described as a conflict between the individual character of human rights and the collective interests of labour. Could this tension be resolved?

The example of closed shop agreements provides an excellent illustration of the interplay between the individual and the collective aspects of the right to associate. Closed shops are agreements between one or more employers and one or more workers' organisations, according to which an individual can only be employed or retain her job upon condition of membership to a specific union.[3] Trade unions favour closed shop arrangements, for they lead to increased union membership. Powerful unions can negotiate the terms and conditions of employment with the employer more effectively. In addition, compulsory union membership is seen as a solution to the problem of 'free riding', namely the enjoyment of benefits earned through union struggles by those who did not contribute to the relevant burdens.

Compulsory membership, though, might not always be compatible with individual rights, because trade unions have the ability to exercise power on the individual, similar to the coercive power of the state.[4] Human rights treaties generally protect voluntary association. Associations are usually formed by individuals who share some ideas or beliefs and who come together in order to promote these ideas and beliefs. People are free to choose if they will join an association or not. Compelling an individual to relate with others with whom she deeply disagrees, in order to achieve some other purpose—however valuable that purpose may be—appears unacceptable at first glance. People should be free from such a compulsion, and this is an important principle in modern liberal societies. Is compelled union membership as a condition in order to get a job or remain employed compatible with human rights law?

In order to explore closed shops and their compatibility with human rights law, the present chapter looks at the European system for the protection of human rights.[5] It contributes to the debates on closed shops and

---

[3] The first type of agreement is a pre-entry closed shop agreement, while the second is a post-entry closed shop. For an analysis of closed shops in the UK and the US, see Leader, S, *Freedom of Association* (New Haven and London, Yale University Press, 1992) ch 9. In the US the question is put in terms of a right to work against the trade union. On this see Hepple, B, 'A Right to Work?' (1981) 10 *Industrial Law Journal* 65, 78. For further discussion of relevant US legislation see Delaney, JT, 'Redefining the Right-to-Work Debate: Unions and the Dilemma of Free Choice' (1998) XIX *Journal of Labor Research* 425 and, for a brief comparison between the US, the UK and Canada, see Miller, K, 'Union Exclusivity Arrangements: A Comparative Overview' (2000) 16 *International Journal of Comparative Labour Law and Industrial Relations* 387, 403 ff.

[4] For analysis, see Summers, C, 'Trade Unions and their Members' in L Gostin (ed), *Civil Liberties in Conflict* (London and New York, Routledge, 1988) 65.

[5] For a presentation of the European system, see Novitz, ch 16, in this volume.

human rights in two ways. First, it presents a new interpretive method of the European Convention on Human Rights (ECHR or Convention) that the European Court of Human Rights (ECtHR or Court) increasingly follows when it examines work-related complaints, and assesses how it affects the regulation of compulsory union membership. It suggests that this interpretive method, at least the way it has evolved to date, cannot provide a definite answer to the complex questions of closed shops and human rights. For this reason, the chapter takes a different route. It attempts to resolve the tension between the individual character of human rights and the collective interests of labour, reflected in closed shop arrangements, looking at the underlying values of the ECHR that shed light on its object and purpose. In this part of the analysis, the chapter relies heavily on an insightful essay by Stuart White on the compatibility of trade unionism with liberal values.[6] I argue that there are indeed important challenges that the employment relation in general and closed shops in particular pose to human rights law; concerns about the tension between the individual and the collective are not necessarily misplaced. Yet, they are overstated. Analysis of the underlying values of the ECHR reveals that if certain conditions are satisfied, closed shop arrangements will have to be regarded as compatible with human rights law.

THE ECHR AND LABOUR RIGHTS

The ECtHR and the European Commission of Human Rights (EComHR or Commission)[7] were traditionally reluctant when looking at the impact of the ECHR on labour rights. Influenced by Cold War prejudice and a belief that social and labour rights are by definition non-justiciable, the Court and the Commission usually decided to protect them only minimally. They found, for instance, that the right to associate does not necessarily encompass a right to consultation[8] or a right to strike.[9] In doing so, they allowed wide discretion to national governments and placed special weight on the fact that these rights were set down in the counterpart of the ECHR in the area of social and labour rights, the European Social Charter (ESC). When an alleged component of a Convention right was protected in the ESC, it was ruled to fall outside the material scope of the Convention.[10]

---

[6] White, S, 'Trade Unionism in a Liberal State' in A Gutmann (ed), *Freedom of Association* (Princeton, Princeton University Press, 1998) 330.

[7] The European Commission of Human Rights (EComHR) was abolished in 1998 with the entry into force of Protocol 11 to the ECHR ETS 155.

[8] *National Union of Belgian Police v Belgium* (App no 4464/70) Judgment of 27 October 1975.

[9] *Schmidt and Dahlstrom v Sweden* (App no 5589/72) Judgment of 6 February 1976.

[10] See, among others, *National Union of Belgian Police* (App no 4464/70) Judgment of 27 October 1975 [38].

Human rights and labour law scholars were critical of this approach. Craig Scott, for instance, suggested that the ECtHR opted for what he called 'negative textual inferentialism' or a 'ceiling effect', which:

> is created when an institution ... refers to human rights commitments found in a legal instrument other than its own as a reason to *limit* the meaning, and thus the scope of protection, given to a right in that institution's own instrument.[11]

Labour lawyers expressed concern that human rights and labour law are competitive areas by definition. The goals served by the two bodies of rules are incompatible, as the case law of the Court clearly indicated by denying any actual advantage to trade unions and their members.[12] Article 11 case law, which examined the components of the right to associate, was also criticised for not treating the relevant provisions of the ESC 'as a more detailed map of the rights sketched out by the Convention'.[13] The stance of the Court and the Commission led to characterisations of the case law as disappointing,[14] 'individual and formalistic',[15] and Novitz argued that 'the Court has limited enthusiasm for the protection of trade union rights', while it has shown 'a greater interest on the defence of individual autonomy than collective solidarity'.[16]

An Integrated Approach to Interpretation

Yet, a recent development gave reasons for optimism to labour law scholars. A new method of interpretation emerged in post-2002 case law. Following the so-called 'integrated approach'[17] to interpretation, the Court referred to social rights materials of the International Labour Organisation (ILO) and the European Committee of Social Rights (ECSR), the monitoring body of the ESC,[18] so as to widen the scope of the rights protected in

---

[11] Scott, C, 'Reaching Beyond (Without Abandoning) the Category of "Economic, Social and Cultural Rights"' (1999) 21 *Human Rights Quarterly* 633, 638–39.

[12] Ewing, KD, 'The Charter and Labour: The Limits of Constitutional Rights' in G Anderson (ed), *Rights and Democracy, Comparative Essays in UK/Canadian Constitutionalism* (London, Blackstone Press, 1999) 79–80.

[13] Hendy, J, 'The Human Rights Act, Article 11 and the Right to Strike' (1998) *European Human Rights Law Review* 582, 588.

[14] Ewing, KD, 'The Human Rights Act and Labour Law' (1998) 27 *Industrial Law Journal* 275. See also Novitz, ch 16 in this volume.

[15] Wedderburn, 'Freedom of Association or Right to Organise?' (1991) 144.

[16] Novitz, T, *International and European Protection of the Right to Strike* (Oxford, Oxford University Press, 2003) 238.

[17] For analysis see Mantouvalou, V, 'Work and Private Life: *Sidabras and Dziautas v Lithuania*' (2005) 30 *European Law Review* 573. The term was used by Scheinin, M, 'Economic and Social Rights as Legal Rights' in A Eide, C Krause and A Rosas (eds), *Economic, Social and Cultural Rights*, 2nd edn (Dordrecht, Kluwer, 2002) 32. See also Koch, IE, 'The Justiciability of Indivisible Rights' (2003) 72 *Nordic Journal of International Law* 3.

[18] See Novitz, ch 16 in this volume.

the Convention. A number of cases can usefully illustrate this interpretive method. In 2002, for instance, in *Zehnalova and Zehnal v the Czech Republic*,[19] when the disabled applicants alleged that they had suffered a violation of certain ECHR rights, but also articles 12 and 13 of the ESC (right to social security and social and medical assistance), the Court, declaring the ESC part of their complaint inadmissible *rationa materiae*, stated:

> ... it is not [the Court's] task to review governments' compliance with instruments other than the European Convention on Human Rights and its Protocols, even if, like other international treaties, the European Social Charter (which, like the Convention itself, was drawn up within the Council of Europe) *may provide it with a source of inspiration.*[20]

Three landmark labour-related cases where the Court adopted the integrated approach to interpretation were *Wilson, National Union of Journalists and Others v UK*,[21] *Sidabras and Dziautas v Lithuania*[22] and *Siliadin v France*.[23] In *Wilson*, the ECtHR referred to ILO materials as relevant to the interpretation of the right to form and join a trade union, and added that the Committee of Independent Experts (renamed to ECSR) and the ILO's Committee on Freedom of Association had criticised the UK legislation under scrutiny. In this way, contrary to its past stance, the Court took cognisance of these materials in order to maximise rather than limit the coverage of the Convention.[24] *Wilson* was, therefore, the first decision to show 'how social rights can have indirect legal effect by influencing the interpretation of legally enforceable rights', as Collins argued.[25]

In *Sidabras*, the Court examined the alleged violation of article 8 of the ECHR that guarantees the right to private life, in conjunction with article 14 that prohibits discrimination. Following a similar approach to that adopted in *Wilson*, the ECtHR stated:

> ... having regard in particular to the notions currently prevailing in democratic states, the Court considers that a far-reaching ban on taking up private-sector employment does affect 'private life'. It attaches particular weight in this respect to the text of Article 1 § 2 of the European Social Charter and the interpretation

---

[19] *Zehnalova and Zehnal v the Czech Republic* (App no 38621/97) Admissibility decision of 14 May 2002.

[20] Emphasis added. See also *Mihailov v Bulgaria* (App no 52367/99) Judgment of 21 July 2005 [33].

[21] *Wilson, National Union of Journalists and Others v UK* (App nos 30668/96, 30671/96 and 30678/96) Judgment of 2 July 2002.

[22] *Sidabras and Dziautas v Lithuania* (App nos 55480/00 and 59330/00) Judgment of 27 July 2004.

[23] *Siliadin v France* (App no 73316/01) Judgment of 26 July 2005.

[24] Ewing, KD, 'The Implications of *Wilson and Palmer*' (2003) 32 *Industrial Law Journal* 1, 16.

[25] Collins, H, *Employment Law* (Oxford, Oxford University Press, 2003) 235.

given by the European Committee of Social Rights ... and to the texts adopted by the ILO.[26]

In *Siliadin*, finally, the Court looked at the prohibition of slavery, servitude and forced or compulsory labour under article 4 of the ECHR.[27] Here, in examining a complaint of a former domestic worker who had been living and working in conditions of 'modern slavery', the Court made reference to ILO instruments, in order to determine the content of states' positive obligations and to analyse the material scope of article 4, one of the most underexplored provisions of the ECHR.[28] Relying on these social and labour rights materials, the Court classified the applicant's situation as 'servitude', and ruled that France violated the Convention, for it did not have in place effective criminal legislation to prosecute her employers.

In the post-2002 case law presented above, in other words, and contrary to its usual practice before *Wilson*, the Court did not approach the alleged social components of the Convention with its usual past hostility. To the contrary, it referred to the views and materials of monitoring bodies of the ILO and the ESC, so as to broaden, rather than minimise, the material coverage of the Convention.

The ECHR: A System 'in Constant Dialogue'

Interestingly, the adoption of the integrated approach in the examination of socio-economic claims under the ECHR can be better understood if it is put in the broader picture of materials that are not part of the Convention, but which are used in the exploration of its values and evolving material scope. This 'dialogue' between the ECtHR and other bodies has become a technique commonly employed in recent years. The Court repeatedly and increasingly takes note of non-Convention materials in cases that involve controversial social and political issues, or when it seeks support to reverse its past case law. The Convention system, Judge Rozakis suggested in this context, is 'in constant dialogue with other legal systems',[29] namely the European legal order, the international legal order and other national legal orders.[30] The ECtHR and its judges 'do not operate in the splendid isolation of an ivory tower built with materials originating solely from the ECHR's interpretative inventions or those of the States party to the Convention'.

---

[26] *Sidabras* (App nos 55480/00 and 59330/00) Judgment of 27 July 2004 [47]. On this see Mantouvalou, 'Work and Private Life: *Sidabras and Dziautas v Lithuania*' (2005).

[27] See Mantouvalou, V, 'Servitude and Forced Labour in the 21st Century: The Human Rights of Domestic Workers' (2006) 35 *Industrial Law Journal* 395.

[28] *Siliadin* (App no 73316/01) Judgment of 26 July 2005 [51], [85]–[86].

[29] Rozakis, CL, 'The European Judge as Comparatist' (2005) 80 *Tulane Law Review* 257, 268.

[30] Ibid 269–70.

Other bodies' materials have gained weight in the case law and '[t]his is a good sign for the founders of a court of law protecting values which by their nature are inherently indivisible and global'.[31]

There are several decisions that exemplify the interaction between the case law of the Court and relevant materials of other national and supranational legal orders. The cases *Goodwin v UK*[32] and *Mamatkulov and Askarov v Turkey*[33] can usefully illustrate this point. In *Goodwin*, the Court examined the right to private life and the right to marry, invoked by a claimant who had changed sex. In this context and before departing from its previous case law, the ECtHR considered European developments on the matter, noting particularly the stance of the European Union Charter of Fundamental Rights and the European Court of Justice. Similarly in *Mamatkulov* the Court assessed whether the respondent state should comply with a request for interim measures adopted by the ECtHR, although the provision on interim measures is only found in the internal rules of the Court and not in the text of the Convention. The Court examined whether interim measures are generally binding in international law and took note of various international legal materials, such as decisions of the United Nations (UN) Human Rights Committee, the UN Committee against Torture, the International Court of Justice and the Inter-American Commission and Court.

The general trend to have recourse to non-Convention materials is not hard to explain, for looking at these documents enhances the legitimacy of judicial decisions. The Court sometimes needs support when reaching judgments on controversial issues, and reliance on materials adopted by democratically elected and accountable bodies is useful for this purpose. By establishing some kind of general consensus, the Court avoids criticisms that its views are arbitrary. In addition, this interpretive technique addresses the standard concern that courts lack expertise and are, therefore, not competent to adjudicate on technical matters. Finally, looking at materials of other international bodies has the additional positive effect that it promotes coherence in supranational adjudication.

In the area of labour rights in particular, the cross-fertilisation between the Court and other expert bodies enhances the legitimacy of the decisions, and leads to outcomes friendlier to the interests of labour. The adoption of the integrated approach also enriches the material scope of the Convention, for the case law becomes more open to the inherent socio-economic components of labour rights.

---

[31] Ibid 278–79.

[32] *Goodwin v UK* (App no 28957/95) Judgment of 11 July 2002.

[33] *Mamatkulov and Askarov v Turkey* (App nos 46827/99 and 46951/99) Judgment of 4 February 2005. The cases of *Goodwin* and *Mamatkulov* are discussed by Rozakis, 'The European Judge as Comparatist' (2005) 265–67.

CLOSED SHOPS UNDER THE ECHR

The integrated approach to interpretation was generally welcomed with optimism by labour lawyers. It was regarded as a positive first step, with potential to address the complex questions that labour law poses to human rights law. *Wilson*, for instance, was described by Ewing as a decision that would 'restore confidence in Article 11 of the Convention',[34] while Collins suggested that 'it is important to appreciate that recent years have revealed a profound reorientation in the ECHR's interpretation of Convention rights in the context of the workplace and employment relations'.[35] But the expressed optimism about the potential of this interpretive method was not bound to be long-lasting. The issue of closed shops showed that the integrated approach, at least the way it has evolved to date, cannot address the most difficult problems that arise in the interplay between human rights and labour law. The present section first briefly presents how the ECtHR dealt with closed shops in the past, before turning to a recent decision that addressed the matter.

Past Case Law

The first judgment that explored closed shop arrangements was *Young, James and Webster v UK*.[36] The applicants were dismissed because they refused to join the trade unions with which their employer, British Rail, signed a closed shop agreement when they were already employed. They alleged, among other things, that article 11 of the ECHR was violated, arguing that the negative aspect of the right to associate is an inherent aspect of the provision. Article 11 provides as follows:

1. Everyone has the right to freedom of peaceful assembly and to freedom of association with others, including the right to form and to join trade unions for the protection of his interests.

2. No restrictions shall be placed on the exercise of these rights other than such as are prescribed by law and are necessary in a democratic society in the interests of national security or public safety, for the prevention of disorder or crime, for the protection of health or morals or for the protection of the rights and freedoms of others. This Article shall not prevent the imposition of lawful restrictions on the exercise of these rights by members of the armed forces, of the police or of the administration of the State.

---

[34] Ewing, 'The Implications of *Wilson and Palmer*' (2003) 5.

[35] Collins, H, 'The Protection of Civil Liberties in the Workplace' (2006) 69 *Modern Law Review* 619, 627.

[36] *Young, James and Webster v UK* (App nos 7601/76, 7806/77) Judgment of 13 August 1981.

The ECtHR ruled that setting no limitations to compelled association, would strike at the very substance of Article 11, because 'a threat of dismissal involving loss of livelihood is a most serious form of compulsion'.[37] The majority of the Grand Chamber found that the limitation imposed upon negative freedom of association here was disproportionate to the aims pursued and, therefore, in breach of the ECHR.

Closed shops were later examined in *Sibson v UK*[38] and *Sigurjonsson v Iceland*.[39] The applicant in *Sibson* would have had to move to another depot should he decide not to join a particular trade union. The facts differed from *Young, James and Webster* in a number of respects. First, the fact that Sibson used to be a member of the specific union (TGWU) before it signed a closed shop agreement with his employer, but resigned from it following a personal dispute, and that he was willing to rejoin the union if he received a public apology, indicated that he was not opposed to rejoining TGWU 'on account of any specific convictions'.[40] Secondly, the closed shop agreement was not in force when the applicant resigned. Thirdly, and '[a]bove all', according to the Court, 'the applicants in the earlier case were faced with a threat of dismissal involving loss of livelihood ... whereas Mr Sibson was in a rather different position'. Mr Sibson had the option to move to a nearby depot, where he would have no obligation to join TGWU, and where his working conditions would not be much different than before. The majority of the ECtHR decided that there had been no violation of article 11 of the ECHR.

Sigurjonsson, finally, had to become a member of a specific association, Frami, in order to retain a taxi driver's licence, which would be revoked if he left the association. The obligation to join a union was imposed on the applicant by national legislation. The majority of the Court held that Iceland could promote Frami's aims in some other way; imposing a duty of membership contrary to the applicant's convictions was a disproportionate interference with article 11 of the Convention.

Sorensen and Rasmussen v Denmark

The 2006 judgment of the Grand Chamber in *Sorensen and Rasmussen v Denmark*[41] is of great importance for a number of reasons. Not only is it the most recent decision that examined the complex question of closed shop

---

[37] *Young, James and Webster* (App nos 7601/76, 7806/77) Judgment of 13 August 1981 [55]. Of particular importance, here, was the fact that British Rail was a nationalised industry.

[38] *Sibson v UK* (App No 14327/88) Judgment of 20 April 1993.

[39] *Sigurdur Sigurjonsson v Iceland* (App No 16130/90) Judgment of 30 June 1993.

[40] *Sibson* (App No 14327/88) Judgment of 20 April 1993 [29].

[41] *Sorensen and Rasmussen v Denmark* (App nos 52562/99 and 52620/99) Judgment of 11 January 2006.

agreements, but it also illustrated the integrated approach as an interpretive method, opening up new questions and avenues for research.

The first applicant, Mr Sorensen, was born in 1975. Before commencing his studies at university, he applied for the post of holiday-relief worker. The company had a closed shop agreement with a trade union called SID. Having been informed that he would not have full SID membership, because he was a holiday-relief worker, the applicant told his employer that he no longer wanted to be a member of the union. He was immediately dismissed with no notice or compensation. The second applicant, Mr Rasmussen, was born in 1959. He was a gardener and a member of SID for some years before he ceased his membership, because he disagreed with the union's political affiliations. He became a member of the Christian Trade Union. Having been unemployed for a few years, he then got a job at a nursery. Membership of SID was a condition of his new job. Mr Rasmussen, as a result, rejoined SID and took up his new post. Both applicants claimed before the ECtHR that Danish legislation, which permitted the existence of closed shop agreements, breached the negative aspect of the right to associate under article 11 of the ECHR. They further argued that they disagreed with the political views of SID and that they wished to join a different union.

The Court stated that article 11 of the ECHR encompasses a negative right not to associate next to its positive right to form and join an association. While compulsion to join a union does not always breach article 11, it went on to say, it may do so when it strikes at the very substance of the provision. The fact that this case involved a pre-entry closed shop agreement, while past case law had only examined post-entry agreements, did not alter the decision. There are important similarities between the two types of arrangements—had [the applicants] refused they would not have been recruited. 'In this connection', it went on to say, 'the Court can accept that individuals applying for employment often find themselves in a vulnerable situation and are only too eager to comply with the terms of employment offered'.[42]

The Court accepted the Government's argument that the applicants could seek employment with an employer that was not covered by a union shop arrangement. It stated, though, that it would still have to look at the impact of the arrangement on each individual applicant. Looking at Mr Sorensen first, the Court said that the fact that he was dismissed without notice, in spite of his young age and of the fact that he would only take up the job 10 weeks before going to university, constituted a significant restriction on his freedom of choice. Mr Rasmussen, on the other hand, had been unemployed for some time before taking up his job at the nursery. Should he resign SID membership, he would be dismissed with no right to reinstatement or compensation.

---

[42] Ibid [59].

Additionally, the sector of horticulture was covered by closed shop agreements to a large extent. Equally to Mr Sorensen, in this sense, his freedom of choice was extremely limited. In response to the argument that both applicants objected to union membership for political reasons, the Danish Government claimed that they had an option of 'non-political membership' of SID. Yet the ECtHR stated that this possibility was in reality non-existent, because first, the membership fee would not be reduced, and secondly, the union might support political parties indirectly, through funds raised from other activities. The duty to become a member of SID was therefore considered to strike at the very substance of article 11 in the circumstances of the case.

Did the Government strike the right balance between the individuals' interests and the need of trade unions to operate effectively? To answer this question the Court first considered recent developments in Denmark and other Council of Europe States, which pointed towards a tendency to limit closed shop agreements, as they are no longer seen as indispensable for the effective protection of workers' rights. Here, the Court turned to the relevant case law of the ECSR to adopt an integrated approach to the interpretation of the ECHR. It referred to the Conclusions of the Committee, which had repeatedly found that the Danish legislation on closed shops was contrary to article 5 of the ESC on the right to organise.[43] It also mentioned the 1989 EC Charter of the Fundamental Rights of Workers, which guarantees a right to join or not to join a trade union, and then made reference to the 2000 EU Charter of Fundamental Rights, which protects freedom of association and further states that nothing in it can be interpreted as restricting rights that are already protected in existing treaties and agreements. All these materials, the Court stated, suggested that there is increasing consensus that closed shop arrangements are not necessary for the effective protection of the interests of labour. Article 11 of the ECHR, the majority therefore concluded, had been breached in respect of both applicants.

Five judges dissented from the decision of the majority, demonstrating in their opinions the tensions and the complexity of the issue. Of special interest is the partly dissenting opinion of Judges Rozakis, Bratza and Vajic, who drew a distinction between the two applicants based on the degree of compulsion that each of them faced. If Mr Rasmussen resigned from SID, he would be dismissed without compensation and with no real prospect of finding a job as a gardener, an area covered to a large extent by closed shop agreements. On the judges' view, '[t]he threat of dismissal and the potential loss of livelihood which would result, amounted [...] to a serious form of compulsion which struck at the very substance of the right guaranteed by Article 11'.[44] For Mr Sorensen, on the other hand, it would be relatively

---

[43] Ibid [72].
[44] Ibid (Dissenting Opinion) [5].

uncomplicated to find a similar job with an employer that was not covered by a closed shop. For this reason, the degree of compulsion that he faced did not amount to a violation of his right to associate.

The other two Judges who dissented focused on different aspects of the compatibility of closed shops with human rights law. Judge Zupancic put his emphasis on the problem of free riders. Judge Lorenzen, on the other hand, stressed the sensitive socio-political character of closed shops, which should lead to the recognition of a wide margin of appreciation to Member States of the Convention. Moreover, he argued that individuals looking for a job are often compelled to accept terms that they disagree with and which may interfere with their personal life. He concluded that, on his view, neither of the applicants was significantly affected by closed shops, as they both had the possibility to find a job with another employer.

IN SEARCH OF A SOLUTION

The decision in *Sorensen and Rasmussen* was disappointing to proponents of closed shop arrangements, for it appeared that there is little scope for union security clauses that are compatible with the ECHR. Indeed, following this latest judgment of the Grand Chamber, it is difficult to envisage a situation where a closed shop agreement will not violate human rights law. Yet, this section will argue that this is not necessarily correct. In order to examine the compatibility of closed shop arrangements with the ECHR, I will look at three alternative solutions that emerge from the case law. I will first consider whether the integrated approach to interpretation can provide a satisfactory answer. I will then discuss the proposition of Judges Rozakis, Bratza and Vajic that the crucial factor to focus on is the degree of compulsion that an employee faces when there is a closed shop in place. Finally, I will explore the character, the object and purpose of the Convention, to determine whether negative freedom of association should always and by definition be regarded as more weighty when it conflicts with the positive aspect of the right.

The Integrated Approach

Closed shops revealed the shortcomings of the integrated approach as it has evolved to date. In most past case law, as explained earlier in this chapter, the ECtHR was unwilling to take into account ESC materials, when it had to decide whether the right to strike is an aspect of freedom of association, for instance. In refusing to do so, it stated that these issues are covered in the ESC and are, therefore, for its own machinery to regulate. Contrary to this negative textual inferentialism, the Court's stance on closed shops was different. From early on in its jurisprudence, in *Sigurjonsson*, the Court was keen to refer to the case law of the Committee of Independent Experts (current ECSR), which examined negative freedom of association and found that it is protected under article 5 of the ESC that protects the right to organise.[45] In a similar fashion it made mention of the ILO's findings, according to which closed shops imposed by law are in breach of Convention No 87 on Freedom of Association and Protection of the Right to Organise and Convention No 98 on the Right to Organise and Collective Bargaining. In the same way, Judges Sorensen, Vilhjalmsson and Lagergren, dissenting in *Young, James and Webster*, pointed at the stance of the ILO and the ESC,[46] which had expressed the view that union security arrangements should be regulated at national level.[47] In other words, although in the examination of other labour-related matters the Court showed deference to bodies, which were said to be more competent to decide the issues, when it looked at union security clauses, it relied on these bodies' findings from early on in its jurisprudence, in order to reach a decision itself.

In addition, some further complications make the analysis of the compatibility of closed shops with human rights law less straightforward than other labour-related matters. In recent case law where the Court adopted the integrated approach to interpretation, the ILO and the ESC had taken a similar view on the matters under consideration. The ECtHR, then, based its own findings on this common stance, this consensus of the expert bodies. Yet things were different with closed shops. This is because while both the ILO and the ECSR have looked into them, they have adopted a different position towards their regulation. The ILO has refrained from interference with the matter.[48] Article 2 of Convention No 87 provides that '[w]orkers and employers, without distinction whatsoever, shall have the right to establish and, subject only to the rules of the organisation concerned, to join organisations of their own choosing without previous authorisation'. The ILO Committee on Freedom of Association has said that:

> it leaves it to the practice and regulations of each State to decide whether it is appropriate to guarantee the right of workers not to join an occupational organisation, or on the other hand, to authorise and, where necessary to regulate the use of union security clauses in practice.[49]

---

[45] *Sigurjonsson* (App No 16130/90) Judgment of 30 June 1993 [35].

[46] The Committee's findings on the European Social Charter (ESC) changed later on.

[47] A similar stance is to be found in *Gustafsson v Sweden* (1996) 22 EHRR 409, where Judges Martens and Matscher discuss both ESC and International Labour Organisation (ILO) provisions and jurisprudence.

[48] *Sorensen and Rasmussen* (App nos 52562/99 and 52620/99) Judgment of 11 January 2006 [38].

[49] International Labour Conference (43rd Session) (1959) RCE Report III (Part IV) para 36. See also the 1994 General Survey on Freedom of Association and Collective Bargaining: Right of Workers and Employers to Establish and Join Organisations para 100.

Only union security clauses that were imposed by law would result in union monopoly and would, as a result, be found contrary to Convention Nos 87 and 98.[50]

The ESC, on the other hand, has been much less deferential to national authorities than the ILO. It is interesting to note here that while most research to date has focused on the impact of materials of other expert bodies on the case law of the ECtHR, closed shops illustrate another aspect of the integrated approach—an integration which took place initially in the opposite direction.[51] Article 5 of the ESC, which guarantees the right to organise, says that:

> [w]ith a view to ensuring or promoting the freedom of workers and employers to form local, national or international organisations for the protection of their economic and social interests and to join those organisations, the Contracting Parties undertake that national law shall not be such as to impair, nor shall it be so applied as to impair, this freedom.

In the past, the Committee had stated that it would not rule on the compatibility of union security clauses with the ESC.[52] Following *Young, James and Webster*, though, the Committee reassessed its stance.[53] It found that only state-imposed closed shops were contrary to the ESC, and also took a step further to hold that the state has a duty under the ESC to protect individuals positively from such arrangements.[54] For this reason, Novitz therefore rightly drew attention to the fact that:

> the ECSR has become a more staunch opponent of the closed shop than the European Court of Human Rights ever dared to be, but it seems that the origin of its enthusiasm lies with the sentiments of the Court rather than its own initiative.[55]

While the ILO, to sum up, has repeatedly held that closed shop arrangements should be left to the national authorities to regulate, the ECSR has taken a more robust view, ruling that these arrangements violate the right to associate under the ESC. Which of the two expert bodies should the ECtHR follow, adopting an integrated approach to interpretation? Should it opt for the ILO's deferential stance or should it follow the ESC's more

---

[50] See Complaint against the Government of New Zealand presented by the New Zealand Employers' Federation, *Case No 1385*, 259th Report para 551. See also Committee on Freedom of Association, 'Digest of Decisions' (1996) para 321.

[51] For an overview of the evolution of the Committee's stance towards closed shops, see *The Right to Organise and Bargain Collectively*, Social Charter Monographs—No. 5, 2nd edn (Council of Europe Publishing, 2001) 23–29. See also Samuel, L, *Fundamental Social Rights—Case Law of the European Social Charter* (Strasbourg, Council of Europe Publishing, 2002) 112–18.

[52] European Committee of Social Rights, Conclusions I, 31.

[53] European Committee of Social Rights, Conclusions VII, 3233.

[54] See, for instance, European Committee of Social Rights Conclusions IX-1, 47. Danish legislation has been repeatedly found in breach of this obligation. See, for instance, Conclusions XI-1, 77, Conclusions XII-1, 110, Conclusions XIII-1, 130.

[55] Novitz, *International and European Protection of the Right to Strike* (2003) 242.

intrusive case law? This is a question that the integrated approach, the way it has evolved to date, leaves unanswered.

Degree of Compulsion

In *Sorensen and Rasmussen*, Judges Rozakis, Bratza and Vajic argued that the degree of compulsion that each individual employee faces should carry most weight in determining the compatibility of closed shops with article 11 of the Convention. The crucial question, on this view, is whether the employee has an option to work for another employer, before she alleges that her human rights have been violated, or whether she is really deprived of almost all alternatives. Individuals are not free to either accept a job and union membership or to turn to another employer.[56] To put it in the Court's words from *Young, James and Webster,* '[a]n individual does not enjoy the right to freedom of association if in reality the freedom of action or choice which remains available to him is either non-existent or so reduced as to be of no practical value.'[57]

The dissenting Judges' argument appears attractive at first. It is understandable, for instance, that the burden placed upon the applicants in *Young, James and Webster*, who would be dismissed if they did not join the trade union, with which their employer signed an agreement while they were already employed, constitutes real compulsion and strikes at the very substance of their right to associate. Turning to *Sorensen and Rasmussen*, it is probably uncontroversial that the latter of the applicants, who had already been unemployed and had very few alternative options open to him, faced real and strong compulsion because of the closed shop agreement. The situation of Sorensen, though, is not as straightforward. Did he really have freedom of choice or was the restriction of his choices such, as to say that his Convention rights were infringed?

While Judges Rozakis, Bratza and Vajic illuminate an important aspect of the problem, it will be hard to measure the actual compulsion that each individual faces when seeking employment or if dismissed. There is a danger of arbitrariness in the assessment of whether someone really needs a particular job or not, as even a temporary job that a student takes up during her summer vacation, for instance, may be extremely valuable to her: the income may contribute to the continuation of her studies and the working experience may be crucial for her future work prospects. It is hard to extract clear principles focusing solely on the element of compulsion, when examining the regulation of closed shop agreements under the ECHR.

---

[56] This was Iceland's argument in *Sigurjonsson* (App No 16130/90) Judgment of 30 June 1993 [33].

[57] *Young, James and Webster* (App nos 7601/76, 7806/77) Judgment of 13 August 1981 [56].

The Object and Purpose of the Convention: A Libertarian Bill of Rights?

Judge Martens joined by Judge Matscher, dissenting in *Gustafsson v Sweden*, claimed that when the negative and positive aspect of the right to associate are in conflict, the former should in principle prevail. This is due to the character of the ECHR. 'The Convention', they argued, 'purports to lay down fundamental rights of the individual and to furnish the individual an effective protection against interferences with these rights'.[58] The right to dissociate, being a right of the individual, should therefore carry more weight when it conflicts with the right to associate, which is, on this reading of the ECHR, a positive right.

The correctness of the above suggestion is questionable. Its first problem lies in that it views positive freedom of association as a collective right, unlike its negative aspect. This is a false assumption. The right to associate is an individual right, like all other human rights, which can nonetheless only be exercised collectively, in association with others. There is nothing in the nature of the entitlement, therefore, that makes it less weighty than negative freedom of association, when the two aspects of article 11 are in conflict. Secondly, and more generally, the above suggestion of the dissenting Judges implies that the ECHR is a libertarian bill of rights and that its interpretation should be guided by libertarian principles that really reflect its object and purpose.[59] Libertarians oppose union security clauses because they limit employees' and employers' freedom of choice, and may also have an impact on economic efficiency.[60] If the ECHR is regarded as a libertarian document, it will be hard to reconcile its underlying values with closed shops arrangements.

However, the ECHR should not be viewed as a libertarian bill of rights. Nothing in its character, in its object and purpose, suggests that negative freedom of association is to be given priority over the positive aspect of the right. The Convention should more accurately be described as an egalitarian document, a point that can be supported with several arguments. First of all, the ECHR contains an anti-discrimination provision. Article 14 is not a free-standing equality clause, but only prohibits discrimination in the enjoyment of other ECHR rights.[61] The construction of the clause is

---

[58] *Gustafsson* (1996) 22 EHRR 409 [8] (Dissenting opinion of Judges Martens and Matscher).

[59] Article 31 of the Vienna Convention on the Law of Treaties provides in its first paragraph: 'A treaty shall be interpreted in good faith in accordance with the ordinary meaning to be given to the terms of the treaty in their context and in the light of its object and purpose.'

[60] On libertarian approaches to compelled association, see Cohen, J and Rogers, J, 'Associations and Democracy' in EO Wright (ed), *Associations and Democracy* (London, Verso, 1995) 15 and for a liberal egalitarian response see 18–21.

[61] Article 14 of the ECHR provides that '[t]he enjoyment of the rights and freedoms set forth in this Convention shall be secured without discrimination on any ground such as sex, race, colour, language, religion, political or other opinion, national or social origin, association with a national minority, property, birth or other status'.

narrow, at first glance, and leaves little scope for the protection against unequal treatment in the enjoyment of all human rights. The evolving egalitarian character of the Convention, however, has led to decisions, where the Court looked at other substantive provisions of the ECHR in conjunction with article 14 and opted for a wide interpretation. It found that a complaint may 'fall within the ambit' of the relevant right, without holding that there has been a breach of the substantive provision alone.[62] In this way, the ECtHR gave the anti-discrimination provision a somewhat autonomous meaning of a free-standing equality clause.

Moreover, importantly for present purposes and increasingly over the last few years, the Court reads social components in the material scope of the Convention when a substantive provision is examined together with the anti-discrimination clause—components that it would have otherwise been reluctant to protect.[63] Through article 14, and in particular when it was read in conjunction with the right to property, the ECtHR often adopted an integrated approach to the interpretation on a variety of matters, reading socio-economic rights in the Convention.[64] A particularly interesting example here is *Koua Poirrez v France*.[65] The decision involved discrimination in the enjoyment of social benefits on the basis of nationality. The Court found that a non-contributory right could give rise to a pecuniary right which falls within the ambit of article 1 of the 1st Additional Protocol of the Convention on private property. In the examination of the complaint, it adopted an integrated approach to the interpretation of the ECHR, taking note of a relevant decision of the ECSR on the issue.[66] The construction of the non-discrimination provision, in other words, has led the Court to opt for a wide reading of other Convention rights, showing how the instrument has taken on an egalitarian meaning containing social elements, which were probably not envisaged by its drafters.

A further development, finally, which serves as evidence that equality is a central value of the Convention system, is the entry into force of Additional Protocol 12, in April 2005. This Protocol sets out a free-standing equality clause,[67] while its Explanatory Report stresses the central role of equality and non-discrimination for international human rights law

---

[62] See, among others, *Abdulaziz, Cabales and Balkandali v the UK* (App nos 9214/80, 9473/81 and 9474/81) Judgment of 28 May 1985 [71] and *Inze v Austria* (App no 8695/79) Judgment of 28 October 1987 [36].

[63] Examples include the *Sidabras* (App nos 55480/00 and 59330/00) Judgment of 27 July 2004.

[64] See eg, *Gaygusuz v Austria* (App no 17371/90) Judgment of 16 September 1996.

[65] *Koua-Poirrez v France* (App no 40892/98) Judgment of 30 September 2003.

[66] Ibid [29].

[67] Additional Protocol 12 article 1—General prohibition of discrimination.

'1. The enjoyment of any right set forth by law shall be secured without discrimination on any ground such as sex, race, colour, language, religion, political or other opinion, national or social origin, association with a national minority, property, birth or other status.

in general. The 12th Protocol will unavoidably open up the Strasbourg machinery to more individual applications involving social rights, and this may explain why some governments have not ratified it yet.[68]

The ECHR should not be viewed as a libertarian document, contrary to what Judges Martens and Matscher suggested, for its object and purpose reflect egalitarian values. The notion of equality that the Convention promotes, moreover, is not a narrow notion. The ECHR and the Court endorse a rich understanding of equality, which is open to elements of social equality. The very existence of labour rights in articles 4 and 11 of the Convention, for instance, suggests that there is no firm distinction between the Convention and socio-economic rights, as the Court put it in *Airey v Ireland*.[69] At the same time, the case *Koua Poirrez*, which was presented above, shows that the understanding of the prohibition of discrimination in the enjoyment of other Convention rights is not narrow.

The best evidence perhaps of a rich approach to socio-economic aspects of the Convention are decisions such as *Sidabras*, *Wilson* and *Siliadin*, presented earlier in this chapter, where the Court adopted an integrated approach to interpretation. These judgments, particularly if considered in juxtaposition to past case law, demonstrate an increased interest in the social aspects of civil and political rights. In this spirit, it was observed in an analysis of the Council of Europe on social cohesion that:

> [t]he European Convention on Human Rights, the most famous normative instrument of the Council of Europe, does not contain social rights properly speaking, but concentrates on civil and political rights ... On this basis the European Court of Human Rights has developed interpretations to all the rights contained in the convention, a jurisprudence that can be compared to the jurisprudence of national constitutional courts.

The analysis continued and then recognised that '*[t]he jurisprudence of the Court has also repercussions on the interpretation of the social rights* (emphasis added), e.g. when certain social security benefits are understood as property'.[70]

In a similar fashion, the Court has protected the right to healthcare and the right to housing in the context of art 8 of the Convention.[71] In all

2. No one shall be discriminated against by any public authority on any ground such as those mentioned in paragraph 1.'

[68] On this see Grief, N, 'Non-Discrimination under the European Convention on Human Rights: A Critique of the United Kingdom Government's Refusal to Sign and Ratify Protocol 12' (2002) 27 *European Law Review—Human Rights Survey* 3, 11–12.

[69] *Airey v Ireland* (App no 6289/73) Judgment of 9 October 1979 [26].

[70] See Battaini-Dragoni, G and Dominioni, S, 'The Council of Europe's Strategy for Social Cohesion' (Conference on Social Cohesion, November 2003) 11, fn 9, available at: www.hku.hk/socsc/cosc/Full%20paper/BATTAINI-DRAGONI%20Gabriella%2025.11.pdf.

[71] On the right to health, see, among others, *Lopez Ostra v Spain* (App No 16798/90) Judgment of 9 December 1994. On the right to housing see *Selcuk and Asker v Turkey*

these instances, the ECtHR examined complaints that the drafters of the document never envisaged, and underlined that the Convention is a living instrument with a constantly evolving object and purpose. Certain social elements have already been read in the document, in a line of cases that reflect a more holistic understanding of the rights guaranteed therein and reveals its changing nature. A treaty that was once adopted as a bulwark to totalitarianism has come to reflect egalitarian ideas and to constitute a forum that safeguards to a certain extent social and labour rights.

The ECHR, to conclude, does not reflect libertarian values, contrary to the view expressed by Judges Martens and Matscher. It can better be described as a liberal egalitarian bill of rights that encompasses social elements. Can this analysis of the object and purpose of the Convention illuminate us on the question of the compatibility of closed shops with human rights law?

IS THERE A HUMAN RIGHT NOT TO BE
A TRADE UNION MEMBER?

The solution to the conflict between individual and collective interests, which is reflected in the closed shops debate in human rights law, cannot be found in the integrated approach to interpretation, which has taken the form of mere reliance on experts' views. This is partly because expert bodies do not always agree on the regulation of social and labour matters. The degree of compulsion that each individual employee faces, moreover, does not provide adequate guidance to the Court, which may reach arbitrary decisions when measuring the importance of a job to an individual's wellbeing. The nature, the object and purpose of the Convention and its underlying values, on the other hand, could lead to some clear guiding principles, which can enlighten our understanding of the problem. Unionisation is protected under the Convention, and the Court has frequently held that some kind of participation in the workplace is essential, so as to advance workers' claims against their employers. It offers to them the possibility to play a role in the decisions that affect their lives and promotes their feelings of dignity and self-respect. Union shops, at the same time, are not by definition contrary to liberal/egalitarian values reflected in the document. They should not necessarily be banned, but could be protected by the Court, subject to certain conditions that will be explored later on.

Yet, there are two objections to the compatibility of closed shops with the ECHR that need to be dealt with at this point. First, it could be suggested

(App nos 23184/94 and 23185/94) Judgment of 24 April 1998. For a more detailed list of the relevant case law, see Koch, IE, 'Dichotomies, Trichotomies or Waves of Duties?' (2005) 5 *Human Rights Law Review* 81, fn 39.

that trade unions are associations that promote a specific ideal of the good life and are, therefore, incompatible with a liberal bill of rights. Secondly, it could be said that empowering a group of individuals—employees in this context—would be contrary to equality, which is also a central value of the Convention. Both objections can be rebutted.

Neutrality

Stuart White, in an insightful essay on trade unionism in a liberal state, answered the question of whether an effective right to trade union membership is compatible with liberalism in the affirmative. Having drawn a useful distinction between *expressive* associations and *instrumental* associations, White showed that state protection and promotion of trade unionism can be compatible with liberal values, similar to the ones that the ECHR enshrines. He suggested that '[a]n expressive association is a community whose members are united by sharing a distinctive set of religious or ideological beliefs'.[72] There are, however, other associations, which are purely instrumental, and which the state may have a duty to promote. An instrumental association is:

> an association whose primary purpose is to secure for its members improved access to strategic goods, such as income and wealth, the possession of which is important from the standpoint of more or less any conception of the good life. The goals of such an association are independent of any particular conception of the good life or controversial ideology, and participation in such an association cannot be said, therefore, necessarily to express commitment to any particular conception of the good life or controversial ideology ....[73]

While in practice it will not always be easy to distinguish which association is of the one and which is of the other kind, in principle 'the primary purposes of a trade union, qua trade union, are essentially instrumental in kind: to increase members' access to certain all-purpose goods such as employment and income'.

Of course, trade unions will always be related to the political process. Yet this does not imply that they will support a specific view of a good life. Neutrality is here understood as ethical neutrality and not as political neutrality. As White put it:

> a trade union may often articulate its instrumental ambitions by reference to an overarching set of ideas about distributive justice and democratic citizenship. Indeed, from a liberal standpoint, it is highly desirable that it should. But this does not necessarily make the union an expressive association, in the above sense, if the

---

[72] White, 'Trade Unionism in a Liberal State' (1998) 334–35. For another interesting discussion of the issue, see Davies in chapter 6.
[73] Ibid 334–35.

values to which it is appealing are, as they may well be, part of the shared public moral vocabulary of a liberal society.[74]

A trade union, according to this analysis, may be regarded as neutral, for it does not necessarily promote a specific ideal of the good life. This happens when it has as its primary function the promotion of workers' rights and their participation in decisions that affect their lives.

Equality

Looking at the second possible objection, namely the position that promoting unionism and employees' rights would be contrary to equality, White's analysis is again useful. White argued that it is not adequate for a state to be neutral towards trade unions. A liberal state should adopt a 'power-adjusted conception of neutrality',[75] which will balance the inequality of bargaining powers that commonly characterises the employment relation. An approach that takes into account this power-adjusted conception of neutrality would be in line with the character of the ECHR as an egalitarian document. This approach implies that the Court should not be reluctant, when having to interfere with the regulation of labour matters. However, in doing so, it should keep in mind the inequality of power that characterises the employment relation, on the one hand, and the importance of employee workplace participation, on the other.

Closed Shops and Human Rights

Closed shops are compatible with neutrality and equality—both ideals that the ECHR reflects. While these values leave scope for union security clauses, it is important to appreciate the potential conflict of compelled association with other rights. Closed shop arrangements may have an impact on individual liberties, such as negative freedom of association and freedom of expression, more generally. Of course workers, both individually and in association with others, have the power to act to promote their interests, and human rights law provides some minimum guarantees that their voice be heard through their unions. At the same time, though, the effective protection of human rights should not permit trade unions to set arbitrary restrictions on individual freedom.

The imposition of membership to an association with which someone fundamentally disagrees infringes individual autonomy, running contrary to

[74] Ibid 335.
[75] Ibid 337.

central values of the Convention. The general principle is that an individual should not be compelled to join an association, if its purposes are incompatible with the person's beliefs. This principle is instantiated in a case where the ECtHR examined compulsion to join a hunters' association. Analysing disagreement with the aims of an association on ethical grounds, the Court held that compulsion to join such an association was in breach of article 11.[76]

Certain conditions ought to be met, so as to avoid illiberal outcomes in the regulation of closed shops. In order to identify the more concrete principles that are applicable here, I will take White's analysis as a starting point. Looking at the Court's decisions and dissenting opinions in the relevant case law, it emerges that we can envisage such arrangements that do not breach the ECHR and that are compatible with its values.

Closed shop agreements are compatible with the Convention when either of the following two conditions is met. First, that a trade union is of a neutral, instrumental character, and does not support specific political parties; secondly, when a trade union does have political affiliations, that an option for non-political membership be offered. The first possibility would perhaps be rare in Europe, where trade unions are usually connected to left-wing politics. Yet, examples of unions that are non-political are not an unknown phenomenon globally.[77] In the second and more common alternative, namely that of unions with political affiliations, an option of non-political membership would meet the requirements of the Convention. This option should not be merely theoretical, as was the case with Danish legislation in *Sorensen and Rasmussen*. It should be effectively guaranteed in practice. This would imply that, unlike the Danish case, the membership fee should be reduced for employees who do not support the political activities of the union. The US example, where closed shops are allowed but the contributions are whittled down to the financial core, can serve to illustrate this position. Additionally, there should be a clear policy to ensure that fees paid by employees, who have opted for non-political membership, are spent to promote members' workplace interests, and not in support of a political party.

The idea that an individual should not be compelled to associate with others, who hold political views that clash with her own, was confirmed by the Court in another labour-related case, *Associated Society of Locomotive Engineers and Firemen (ASLEF) v UK*.[78] *ASLEF* involved negative freedom

---

[76] *Chassagnou v France* (App nos 25088/94, 28331/95 and 28443/95) Judgment of 29 April 1999 [117]. See also, *Sorensen and Rasmussen* (App nos 52562/99 and 52620/99) Judgment of 11 January 2006 [63].

[77] A country where there are non-political, instrumental, trade unions is India. See Gopalakrishnan in chapter 7.

[78] *Associated Society of Locomotive Engineers and Firemen (ASLEF) v UK* (App no 11002/05) Judgment of 27 February 2007. For analysis, see Ewing, KD, 'The Implications

of association, but not from the viewpoint of the individual employee who was unwilling to associate, but from the viewpoint of the trade union that wished to exclude an employee from membership.[79] ASLEF, the applicant union, is a socialist labour association. Mr Lee, a train driver and member of a political party of the far-right, the British National Party (BNP), was a member of ASLEF. He was expelled from the union when its officers were informed of his membership of the BNP and some of his activities, such as handing out anti-Islamic leaflets and engaging in serious harassment of anti-Nazi demonstrators. In its letter to Mr Lee, the union stated that his membership of the BNP was contrary to its aims, and potentially harmful to its reputation. Mr Lee brought proceedings before UK employment tribunals on the basis of section 174 of the Trade Union and Labour Relations (Consolidation) Act 1992, which bans expulsion from a union on the grounds of membership to a political party. UK tribunals found in favour of Mr Lee and imposed on ASLEF an obligation to readmit him as a member. Before the ECtHR, ASLEF complained that it had not been allowed to exclude from membership an individual who holds views contrary to its own, a situation that was in breach of article 11 of the Convention. The Court stated that a union should have a right to choose with whom it will associate in a way similar to individual employees. This is because '[w]here associations are formed by people, who, espousing particular values or ideals, intend to pursue common goals, it would run counter to the very effectiveness of the freedom at stake if they had no control over their membership'.[80]

Yet, the Court implied that in the case of trade unions, the balancing test between the right to associate and freedom of expression may be more complex than when looking at other types of associations. This is because of the special role that unions may be afforded in representing the interests of employees before the employer. In such circumstances, when an association promotes what can be described as a public purpose, compulsion to associate may be justified, even if there is a clash of political views.[81] Here, nonetheless, the Court found that UK employment tribunals did not strike the right balance between Mr Lee's right to belong to a political party and the right of ASLEF to disassociate with him. The right of the union to choose its members was not given adequate attention. Mr Lee's exclusion from membership had not been abusive, and the tribunals had erred in imposing

---

of the ASLEF Case' (2007) 36 *Industrial Law Journal* 425. For a discussion before the decision of the European Court of Human Rights (ECtHR), see Hendy, J and Ewing, KD, 'Trade Unions, Human Rights and the BNP' (2005) 34 *Industrial Law Journal* 197.

[79] This can otherwise be seen as a right of individual members of a union with political affiliations not to associate with individuals who hold political views diametrically contrary to their own.

[80] *ASLEF* (App no 11002/05) Judgment of 27 February 2007 [39].

[81] Ibid [40].

upon the union an obligation to accept him as a member.[82] Expulsion would not be detrimental to him, for there was no closed shop agreement in place, while the union represented all employees in the collective bargaining process, irrespective of membership.

The Court held in ASLEF that placing restrictions on the right of the union to choose with whom it will associate, notwithstanding the fact that the individual had political views that conflicted with its own, constituted an illegitimate interference with the Convention. Trade unions are often affiliated to political parties, and imposition of a duty to associate with someone who holds views contrary to their own, was ruled to be in breach of negative freedom of association.

CONCLUSION

The ECHR, a civil and political rights instrument, includes a right to form and join a trade union and can provide broad protection for the labour right to organise, one of the most fundamental entitlements that the ILO and the ESC also promote. The Convention can usefully serve the collective interests of labour. Even the imposition of compulsory union membership may be compatible with its provisions, if its underlying objectives are properly understood and the obligation to associate is accordingly construed.

The example of closed shops that the present chapter discussed shows that human rights and labour law share important values. The collective interests of labour are not irreconcilable with human rights law. The protection of freedom of association and closed shop agreements shed light on two different aspects of the issue. On the one hand, workers, both individually and in association with others, have the power to act to promote their interests; human rights law provides some minimum guarantees that their voice be heard through the protection of the right to form and join trade unions. At the same time, though, the protection of human rights does not permit unions to impose excessive restrictions on other individual freedoms in an arbitrary manner. The ECtHR, as it emerged from the above discussion, has not explored thoroughly the conditions under which union security clauses are compatible with the ECHR. Careful exploration of the evolving object and purpose of the document, however, can shed light on the interplay between the individual and the collective, and offer guiding principles, on which the Court can rely. To conclude, a close analysis of the compatibility of closed shops with human rights law suggests that the rights of workers and their unions cannot be harmed; they can only be enhanced through an effective and principled human rights regime.

---

[82] For the conditions in which exclusion from union membership may be abusive, see ibid[43].

16

Giving with the One Hand and Taking with the Other: Protection of Workers' Human Rights in the European Union

TONIA NOVITZ AND PHIL SYRPIS

INTRODUCTION

T HE EUROPEAN UNION (EU) has long recognised certain economic entitlements, notably the freedom for employers to establish themselves in any Member State and to supply goods and services across national boundaries. This chapter examines what happens when these 'fundamental freedoms', as they have come to be known, are in conflict with human rights claimed by workers and their organisations. Four crucial cases decided in 2007 and 2008 indicate that precedence will systematically be given to the former rather than the latter.

This is not to say that the EU does not recognise the human rights of workers. Its foundational treaties, the Treaty Establishing the European Community (or EC Treaty) and the Treaty on European Union (or EU Treaty) do so, as do key declaratory human rights instruments, such as the Community Charter on the Fundamental Social Rights of Workers 1989 and the EU Charter of Fundamental Rights (EUCFR) 2000. Protection of human rights, including the protection of workers' rights, is also a key aspect of the general principles jurisprudence of the European Court of Justice (ECJ).

Nevertheless, where the EU does not have competence to adopt Community legislation on workers' entitlements, such as in relation to freedom of association or the right to strike, these enter the Court's frame of reference as a potentially legitimate exception to other tenets of EU law, such as an employer's economic freedom of movement. Where this occurs, the judgments delivered in the cases of *International Transport Workers'*

Federation (ITF) and Finnish Seamen's Union (FSU) v Viking Line[1] and *Laval un Partneri v Svenska Byggnadsarbetareförbundet*[2] demonstrate that industrial action protected under national labour law will only be regarded as lawful under EU law to the extent that it comes within the narrowly circumscribed definition of a 'right to strike' for 'the protection of workers' adopted by the Court. Moreover, such industrial action will only be defensible to the extent that it is strictly 'proportionate'; that is to the extent that it is necessary and does not interfere with an employer's freedom of movement more than is strictly required to defend the interests of the workers concerned. This chapter examines the implications of such an approach.

Laval, and the later cases of *Rüffert v Land Niedersachsen* and *Commission v Luxembourg*,[3] also indicate that the ECJ construes Community legislation, on the extent to which an EU Member State may impose its own labour law rules on workers who are 'posted' there temporarily by an employer based in another EU Member State, very narrowly. The result is that, unless host states remain strictly within the ambit of the Posted Workers Directive,[4] the imposition of local terms and conditions of employment may be deemed illegal under EU law.[5]

Finally, this chapter considers, briefly, the potential implications of changes introduced by the Treaty of Lisbon, in particular those in the new article 6 EU. We argue that the incorporation of the EUCFR into EU law would have little effect, but that the contemplated accession of the EU to the European Convention on Human Rights 1950 (ECHR) could be more significant, given that accession would change the way in which compliance with human rights would be regarded. Under this new arrangement, EU law might be regarded not as the rule, but as an exception to human rights principles,

---

[1] Case C-438/05 *International Transport Workers' Federation (ITF) and Finnish Seamen's Union (FSU) v Viking Line* [2007] ECR I-10779; [2008] All E.R. (EC) 127; [2008] IRLR 143 (hereafter *Viking*). See Novitz, T, 'Resistance to Re-flagging: A Restricted Right to Strike: ITF v Viking' (2008) *Maritime and Commercial Law Quarterly* 66.

[2] Case C-341/05 *Laval un Partneri v Svenska Byggnadsarbetareförbundet* [2007] ECR I-11767; [2008] All E.R. (EC) 166; [2008] IRLR 160 (hereafter *Laval*). Both cases are discussed in Davies, A, 'One Step Forward, Two Steps Back? The *Viking* and *Laval* Cases in the ECJ' (2008) 37 *Industrial Law Journal (ILJ)* 126; and Syrpis, P and Novitz, T, 'Economic and Social Rights in Conflict: Political and Judicial Approaches to their Reconciliation' (2008) 33 *European Law Review* 411.

[3] Case C-346/06 *Rüffert v Land Niedersachsen* [2008] ECR I-1989 (hereafter *Rüffert*); and Case C-319/06 *Commission v Luxembourg* [2008] ECR I-4323 (hereafter *Luxembourg*). For discussion, see Davies, P, 'Case note on *Rüffert*' (2008) 37 *ILJ* 293 and Kilpatrick, C, 'The ECJ and Labour Law: A 2008 Retrospective' (2009) 38 *ILJ* 180, 194–205.

[4] Directive 96/71/EC of the European Parliament and of the Council of 16 December 1996 concerning the posting of workers in the framework of the provision of services [1997] OJ L18/1 (henceforth 'Posted Workers Directive 96/71'). For discussion, see Davies, P, 'Posted Workers: Single Market or Protection of National Labour Law Systems?' (1997) 34 *Common Market Law Review (CMLRev)* 571.

[5] See further Barnard, C, 'The UK and Posted Workers: The Effect of *Commission v Luxembourg* on the Territorial Application of British Labour Law' (2009) 38 *ILJ* 122.

so that it is an employer's exercise of free movement rights (and not workers' right to strike) which would have to be shown to be legitimate, necessary and proportionate.

THE ECONOMIC ORIENTATION OF THE EUROPEAN UNION

The capacity of the EU to protect workers' rights has to be understood in terms of its origins as primarily an economic institution. Its orientation has been towards economic integration of the markets of European Member States, as was reflected in the titles of its foundational institutions, the European Coal and Steel Community founded in 1951 and the European Economic Community (EEC) created in 1957.[6] Under the EC Treaty, a substantially amended and renumbered version of the Treaty of Rome which established the EEC, there is no doubting the prominence of what have come to be known as 'the four fundamental freedoms', namely rights of workers to move freely throughout the EU for employment purposes without discrimination on grounds of nationality, and the entitlements largely relied upon by commercial entities to free movement of goods, services and establishment across the borders of the Member States.[7] Moreover, the conditions under which goods and services are supplied are subject to extensive regulation under competition law.[8]

Free movement of workers is one crucial entitlement available to EU workers that is not found elsewhere in regional or international human rights instruments; although it should be noted that in the process of EU enlargement from 15 to 27 Member States, transitional arrangements imposed severe restrictions on this freedom.[9]

The other highly significant specific provision made for workers' rights under the EC Treaty stems from article 141,[10] which states 'the principle of equal pay for male and female workers for equal work'. This entitlement

---

[6] See Davies, P, 'The Emergence of European Labour Law' in W McCarthy (ed), *Legal Intervention in Industrial Relations: Gains and Losses* (Oxford, Oxford University Press, 1992); and Barnard, C, 'EC "Social Policy"' in P Craig and G de Búrca (eds), *The Evolution of EU Law* (Oxford, Oxford University Press, 1999).

[7] Treaty Establishing the European Community (EC Treaty) Title III arts 39–69. For an excellent exposition on the implications of these provisions, see Barnard, C, *The Substantive Law of the EU: The Four Freedoms*, 2nd edn (Oxford, Oxford University Press, 2007).

[8] See Jones, A and Sufrin, B, *EC Competition Law*, 3rd edn (Oxford, Oxford University Press, 2007); Monti, G, *EC Competition Law* (Cambridge, Cambridge University Press, 2007); and Odudu, O, *The Boundaries of EC Competition Law: The Scope of Article 81* (Oxford, Oxford University Press, 2006).

[9] Discussed in Ryan, B (ed), *Labour Migration and Employment Rights* (London, Institute of Employment Rights, 2005). For an example of those restrictions applicable in the UK, see also Ryan, B, 'The Accession (Immigration and Worker Authorisation) Regulations 2006' (2008) 37 *ILJ* 75.

[10] This provision is derived from what was art 119 of the Treaty of Rome 1957.

to protection from discrimination on grounds of sex was initially included on the insistence of France on grounds of fair market competition,[11] but has since spawned several EC directives,[12] and an extensive jurisprudence,[13] concerning gender equality. Gender equality, as a source of economic growth and prosperity, is also promoted through the 'open method of co-ordination' under the Lisbon strategy.[14] Other forms of social equality and protection from discrimination have more recently been addressed, such as discrimination on grounds of race, sexual orientation, disability, religious belief and age.[15]

Notwithstanding the above, the competence for EC institutions to adopt legislation in other fields of social policy and for European-level representatives of management and labour to adopt binding collective agreements on social standards is restricted.[16] The EC Treaty refers to such instruments as the Council of Europe European Social Charter of 1961 (ESC) and the

[11] Kenner, J, *EU Employment Law: From Rome to Amsterdam* (Oxford, Hart Publishing, 2003) 4.

[12] Such as Council Directive 75/117/EEC of 10 February 1975 on the approximation of the laws of the Member States relating to the application of the principle of equal pay for men and women 75/117/EEC [1975] OJ L 45/19; Council Directive 76/207/EEC of 9 February 1976 on the implementation of the principle of equal treatment for men and women as regards access to employment, vocational training and promotion, and working conditions [1976] OJ L 39/40; Council Directive 92/85/EEC of 19 October 1992 concerning the implementation of measures to encourage improvements in the safety and health of pregnant workers, workers who have recently given birth and women who are breastfeeding (Tenth individual Directive within the meaning of Article 16(1) of Directive 89/391/EEC) [1992] OJ L 348/1; Council Directive 97/80/EC of 15 December 1997 on the burden of proof in cases of discrimination based on sex [1998] OJ L 14/6; Directive 2002/73/EC of the European Parliament and of the Council of 23 September 2002 amending Council Directive 76/207/EEC on the implementation of the principle of equal treatment for men and women as regards access to employment, vocational training and promotion, and working conditions [2002] OJ L 269/15; and Directive 2006/54/EC of the European Parliament and of the Council of 5 July 2006 on the implementation of the principle of equal opportunities and equal treatment of men and women in matters of employment and occupation (recast) OJ L204/23.

[13] See Costello, C and Davies, G, 'The Case Law of the Court of Justice in the Field of Sex Equality Since 2000' (2006) 43 *Common Market Law Review* 1567.

[14] For a thorough recent study of the aims of this mechanism and its operation, see Ashiagbor, D, *The European Employment Strategy: Labour Market Regulation and New Governance* (Oxford, Oxford University Press, 2005). See also as regards concerns generated by an approach focussed on economic targets, Fagan, C, Grimshaw, D and Rubery, J, 'The Subordination of the Gender Equality Objective: The National Reform Programmes and 'Making Work Pay' Policies' (2006) 37 *Industrial Relations Journal* 571.

[15] EC Treaty art 13; Council Directive 2000/43/EC of 29 June 2000 implementing the principle of equal treatment between persons irrespective of racial or ethnic origin [2000] OJ L 180/22; and Council Directive 2000/78 of 27 November 2000 establishing a general framework for equal treatment in employment and occupation [2000] OJ L 303/16 which made further provision for protection from discrimination on grounds of sexual orientation, disability, religious belief and age. See further Bell, M, *Anti-Discrimination Law and the European Union* (Oxford, Oxford University Press, 2002).

[16] See EC Treaty Title XI c I arts 137–39. For a discussion of the evolution of these provisions, see Syrpis, P, *EU Intervention in Domestic Labour Law* (Oxford, Oxford University Press, 2007) 61–67.

1989 Community Charter on the Fundamental Social Rights of Workers.[17] Nevertheless, competence does not extend to 'pay, the right of association, the right to strike or the right to impose lock-outs'.[18] The EC does not therefore possess standard-setting competence in respect of the entire spectrum of workers' rights recognised in European or other human rights instruments.

It should also be noted that the tasks of the EC are to include 'a high level of employment and of social protection' as well as 'equality between men and women',[19] and that the EU 'is founded on ... respect for human rights and fundamental freedoms'.[20] In particular, the EU is obliged to 'respect fundamental rights', guaranteed by the ECHR and 'the constitutional traditions common to the Member States', as general principles of EC law.[21] This statement is a reflection of case law developed by the ECJ relating to human rights protection since 1970.[22] There remain, however, considerable difficulties pertaining to the protection of workers' rights through this medium.

First, in the EU context, human rights act as a 'shield' rather than as a 'sword', and thus tend to be invoked to protect a Member State or private party from the consequences of what would otherwise be regarded as a breach of EC law.

Secondly, the articulation and definition of human rights by the ECJ has been oriented almost entirely around the provisions of the ECHR as opposed to the ESC, and is therefore heavily dependent on the views of the European Court of Human Rights.[23] Traditionally, the European Court of Human Rights has been reluctant to regard collective labour rights such as collective bargaining or the right to strike as a necessary aspect of freedom of association, and this has had implications for the approach taken by the ECJ.[24] It will be interesting to see whether the ECJ changes the approach

---

[17] In what is effectively the Preamble to Title XI c I of the EC Treaty, art 136. The Community Charter was a declaratory instrument adopted in 1989 by 11 of the then 12 Member States, the dissenting state being the UK. Both of these instruments also receive specific recognition in the Preamble to the Treaty on European Union (EU Treaty).

[18] EC Treaty art 137(5); for comment see Ryan, B, 'Pay, Trade Union Rights and European Community Law' (1997) 13 *International Journal of Comparative Labour Law and Industrial Relations* 305. For an analysis of the implications of this exclusion, see Case C-268/06 *Impact v Minister of Agriculture and Food and others*, judgment of 15 April 2008, especially [122]–[129].

[19] EC Treaty art 2.

[20] EU Treaty art 6(1).

[21] Ibid art 6(2).

[22] See Case 11/70 *Internationale Handelsgesellschaft v Einführ- und Vorratsstelle Getreide* [1970] ECR 1125; Case 4/73 *Nold KG v Commission* [1974] ECR 491 [13]. See endorsement by the European Parliament, the Council and Commission in a 'Common Declaration' of 5 April 1977 [1977] OJ C103/1.

[23] See Chapters 14 and 15 in this volume above.

[24] Case C-499/04 *Werhof v Freeway Traffic Systems GmbH & Co KG* [2006] ECR I-2397 [33] states that the principle of negative freedom of association established by the European Court of Human Rights requires that, after a transfer of an undertaking, an employer should

it has taken in cases concerning labour law, following the judgment of the Grand Chamber of the European Court of Human Rights in *Demir and Baykara v Turkey*, which makes it clear that:

> the right to bargain collectively with the employer has, in principle, become one of the essential elements of the 'right to form and to join trade unions for the protection of [one's] interests' set forth in Article 11 of the Convention.[25]

Moreover, we have yet to see whether the ECJ will acknowledge the view taken in two recent cases decided by a Chamber of the European Court of Human Rights which indicate that interference with the right to strike needs to be justified with reference to article 11(2) of the ECHR.[26] The 'common constitutional traditions of Member States' is an alternative source of norms, but is likely to prove controversial given the diversity of industrial relations systems, especially now within the current 27 EU Member States.[27]

The EUCFR, which was drafted after an extensive deliberative process,[28] subsequently solemnly proclaimed by the Council, and approved by both the Parliament and the Commission, has now begun to be cited as a point of reference by the Court.[29] The EUCFR has gained legal status through incorporation into the EC and EU Treaties (the former being renamed the Treaty on the Functioning of the European Union) following implementation of the Lisbon Reform Treaty. This is significant insofar as this instrument allows greater scope for social and economic rights than was hitherto contemplated within the EU. For example, reference is made explicitly to a right to collective bargaining and a right to strike under article 28.

We propose to consider the extent to which, in this peculiar legal context, the EU protects workers' collective rights. We suggest that the outcome of the cases is indicative of the limitations of both legislative and judicial

---

not be bound by the terms of any subsequently negotiated collective agreement or be obliged to maintain bargaining arrangements. In *Viking* [2007] ECR I-10779 [86], the ECJ cited the view of the European Court of Human Rights that 'collective action, like collective negotiations and collective agreements may, in the particular circumstances of a case, be one of the main ways in which trade unions protect the interests of their members', but is not the only way. This meant that any exercise of collective action which was a disproportionate interference with EC market freedoms could be deemed to be in violation of EC law.

[25] *Demir and Baykara v Turkey* (App no 34503/97) Grand Chamber Judgment of 12 November 2008 [153]–[154]. For comment, see Ewing, K and Hendy, J, 'The Dramatic Implications of *Demir and Baykara*' (2010) 39 *Industrial Law Journal* 2.

[26] *Affaire Dilek et Autres v Turquie* (App nos 74611/01, 26876/02 et 27628/0) Judgment of 17 July 2007 (available only in French); and *Enerji Yapi-Yol Sen v Turkey* (App no 68959/01) Judgment of 21 April 2009 (available only in French).

[27] On the divergence in the enlarged EU, see Majone, G, 'Legitimacy and Effectiveness: A Response to Professor Michael Dougan's Review Article on Dilemmas of European Integration (2007) 32 *European Law Review* 70.

[28] de Búrca, G, 'The Drafting of the European Union Charter of Fundamental Rights' (2001) 26 *European Law Review* 126.

[29] Case C-303/05 *European Parliament v Council* [2006] ECR. I-5769 [38].

treatment of such entitlements. We then investigate the potential for the Treaty of Lisbon to change the status quo through its treatment of the EUCFR and accession to the ECHR. Our view is that while change is possible, current indications are not encouraging.

THE CIRCUMSTANCES IN WHICH RECENT LITIGATION ON COLLECTIVE RIGHTS AROSE

One concern arising from EU enlargement was that there would be increased competition for jobs in the more prosperous pre-accession EU Member States. Indeed, the failure of national referenda to endorse a new EU Constitution was attributed to a fear of cheap labour caricatured as the 'Polish plumber';[30] as has been (at least in part) the recent failure of the Irish referendum on the Treaty of Lisbon.[31] The political response was the restriction on the free movement of workers from accession states,[32] but there emerged 'an asymmetry' between restricted movement of labour and unrestricted movement of services and establishment.[33] The latter operate unhindered by the transitional arrangements governing accession and are indeed promoted through the Services Directive 2006.[34]

In the *Laval* case, it was on the basis of freedom to provide services that a Latvian employer resisted engagement in negotiations with Swedish trade unions in respect of workers posted to perform a building contract in Sweden. In the *Viking* case, it was on the basis of freedom of establishment

[30] For media coverage of the issue, see Asthana, A, 'The Polish Plumber Who Fixed The Vote' *The Observer* (29 May 2005); and Arnold, M, 'Polish Plumber Symbolic of All French Fear about Constitution' *Financial Times* (28 May 2005). For academic comment, see Pijpers, R, '"Help! The Poles are Coming": Narrating a Contemporary Moral Panic' (2006) 88B.1 *Geografiska Annaler* 91, 99–100; and Majone, G, 'Legitimacy and Effectiveness: A Response to Professor Michael Dougan's Review Article on Dilemmas of European Integration (2007) 32 *European Law Review* 70, 74.

[31] See Milne, S, 'Today Ireland has a chance to change Europe's direction', *The Guardian* (12 June 2008).

[32] The three notable exceptions to the adoption of transitional measures relating to free movement in 2004 were Ireland, Sweden and the United Kingdom (UK). Note that the UK has, however, decided to apply transitional measures in respect to workers from Bulgaria and Romania. See 'Free Movement for Workers After Enlargement' available at http://europa.eu/scadplus/leg/en/cha/c10524.htm and advice available at http://ec.europa.eu/eures/main.jsp?acro=free&lang=en&countryId=UK&accessing=0&content=1&restrictions=1&step=1; and for comment, Carrera, S, 'What Does Free Movement Mean in Theory and Practice in an Enlarged EU?' (2005) 11 *European Law Journal* 699.

[33] Editorial, 'Mobility of Services and Posting of Workers in the Enlarged Europe— Challenges for Labour Market Regulation' (2006) 12(2) *Transfer* 137, 138.

[34] Directive 2006/123/EC of the European Parliament and of the Council of 12 December 2006 on services in the internal market [2006] OJ L376/36 (henceforth 'Services Directive 2006/123'); see also Woolfson, C and Sommers, J, 'Labour Mobility in Construction: European Implications of the Laval un Partneri Dispute with Swedish Labour' (2006) 12(1) *European Journal of Industrial Relations* 49, 50–51.

that a Finnish employer sought to replace its existing workforce with cheaper labour by 're-flagging' a vessel in Estonia. The facts of these cases merit further elaboration.

Laval un Partneri Ltd was a Latvian company, which hired out Latvian workers to a Swedish company, L & P Baltic Bygg AB (Baltic), for building work to be completed in Sweden. Laval concluded an agreement with a Latvian building workers' union in respect of the Latvian workers which entailed lower terms and conditions than those applicable had a collective agreement been concluded with the Swedish Building Workers' union, Byggnads. Laval and Baltic were owned by the same person, who represented both companies.[35] Swedish trade unions responded by taking industrial action, including secondary action boycotting the plant (which was described by the ECJ as a 'blockade')[36] in order to persuade Laval to sign a collective agreement with Byggnads and thereby to prevent Latvian labour undercutting the cost of Swedish labour. Laval brought an action in the Swedish courts in order to obtain a declaration that this action was unlawful, and orders that such action should cease and that compensation be paid. Laval also argued that certain aspects of the Swedish law directly discriminated against foreign undertakings.[37] Questions were then referred to the ECJ concerning the scope of the right to take industrial action in potential breach of free movement of services under article 49 of the EC Treaty,[38] and the relevant piece of EC legislation, the Posted Workers Directive.

Viking Line APB, a Finnish company, had sought to sell a vessel to its Estonian subsidiary, thereby justifying 're-flagging' and enabling replacement of a Finnish crew with a less costly Estonian crew.[39] The Finnish Seamen's Union (FSU), in accordance with the rules of its membership of the International Transport Workers' Federation (ITF) and with its support in the form of an ITF circular sent to all members, had previously taken industrial action to prevent Viking doing exactly this. The FSU would most

[35] Ahlberg, K, Bruun, N and Malmberg, J, 'The *Vaxholm* case from a Swedish and European Perspective' (2006) 12(2) *Transfer* 155, 159. See also Deakin, S, 'Regulatory Competition after *Laval*' in C Barnard (ed) *Cambridge Yearbook of European Legal Studies Volume 10* 2007–08 (Oxford, Hart Publishing, 2008) 711.

[36] See, for analysis of this distinction, Comments by Advocat Ulf Öberg, counsel for Byggnads and Elektrikerförbundet before the ECJ, 'Implications of the Preliminary Rules in the Laval Case (C-341/05) and the Viking Line Case (C-438/05)' (ERA-Conference, Recent Developments in European Labour Law, Trier, 4–5 April 2008).

[37] This aspect of the case relates to the so-called Lex Britannia, a 1991 amendment to the Swedish Co-determination Act 1976 s 42(3). See Woolfson and Sommers, 'Labour Mobility in Construction' (2006) 58–59.

[38] EC Treaty art 49.

[39] Discussed by Davies, A, 'The Right to Strike versus Freedom of Establishment in EU Law: The Battle commences' (2006) 35 *Industrial Law Journal* 76; and Novitz, T, 'The Right to Strike and Re-flagging in the European Union: Free Movement Provisions and Human Rights' (2006) 2 *Lloyd's Maritime and Commercial Law Quarterly* 242.

probably have done so again upon the expiry of the collective agreement, had such action not been anticipated by the employer, Viking, and been subjected to legal challenge, given Estonia's recent admission to the EU. Viking brought an action in the High Court in the United Kingdom, on the basis that the ITF had its headquarters in London, requesting an injunction preventing further industrial action which was alleged to be contrary to the right to free establishment protected under article 43 of the EC Treaty.[40] Judgment was initially given in Viking's favour,[41] but on appeal, the Court of Appeal lifted the injunction referring a series of questions to the Court of Justice.[42]

Both *Viking* and *Laval* concern the legitimacy of collective action taken by trade unions to prevent any diminution in terms and conditions of employment for their own members and to seek equivalent terms and conditions for other workers. *Rüffert* and *Luxembourg* were different.

Rüffert related to the attempt by local government, in its capacity as a model employer, to seek to protect terms and conditions of employment agreed under collective agreements otherwise applicable to a sector of employment, by requiring both domestic and foreign service providers to undertake that they would abide by those terms when making a tender for a public works contract.

The *Rüffert* reference concerned a provincial law applicable in Land Niedersachsen (the Land of Lower Saxony), which provided that:

> Contracts for building services shall be awarded only to undertakings which, when lodging a tender, undertake in writing to pay their employees, when performing those services, at least the remuneration prescribed by the collective agreement at the place where those services are performed and at the time prescribed by the collective agreement.[43]

The argument made by the employer was that this requirement went beyond the minimal terms and conditions which could be imposed by the state or by a collective agreement (declared universally applicable) on the provider of posted workers under the Posted Workers Directive and was in breach of article 49 of the EC Treaty. This was the legal issue referred by the Oberlandesgericht Celle (Germany) to the ECJ.

The *Luxembourg* case was brought by the Commission against the Grand Duchy of Luxembourg in relation to a law of 2002, through which the Grand Duchy sought to impose obligations on undertakings which post workers on its territory which went beyond those laid down in article 3(1)

---

[40] EC Treaty art 43.

[41] *Viking Line ABP v International Transport Workers' Federation* [2005] EWHC 1222; *Times* (22 June 2005) (QBD Commercial Court, 16 June 2005).

[42] *Viking Line ABP v International Transport Workers' Federation* [2005] EWCA Civ. 1299; [2006] 1 Lloyd's Rep. 303; [2006] IRLR 58; [2005] All E.R. (D) 47 (Nov).

[43] Para 3(1) of the Landesvergabegesetz, cited in *Rüffert* [2008] ECR I-1989 [6].

of the Posted Workers Directive. Luxembourg sought to rely on article 3(10) of the Directive, which expressly permits the imposition of extra obligations on service providers; but only 'in the case of public policy provisions'. The Court viewed article 3(10) as 'a derogation from the fundamental principle of freedom to provide services which must be interpreted strictly', adding that its scope 'cannot be determined unilaterally by the Member States'.[44] Following *Jean-Claude Arblade, Arblade & Fils SARL and Bernard Leloup, Serge Leloup, Sofrage SARL*[45] a case with a very different criminal law context, it held that:

> the classification of national provisions by a Member State as public-order legislation applies to national provisions compliance with which has been deemed to be so crucial for the protection of the political, social or economic order in the Member State concerned as to require compliance therewith by all persons present on the national territory of that Member State and all legal relationships within that State.[46]

Given this outlook, it was no surprise that it held that various aspects of the law of 2002 which imposed restrictions on the freedom to provide services could not be saved by article 3(10) of the Posted Workers Directive.

THE TREATMENT OF COLLECTIVE LABOUR RIGHTS AS HUMAN RIGHTS

In both the *Viking* and *Laval* judgments, delivered on 11 and 18 December 2007 respectively, the ECJ affirmed that the activities of the EC were to be taken 'to include not only an "internal market characterised by the abolition, as between Member States, of obstacles to the free movement of goods, persons, services and capital", but also "a policy in the social sphere"'. They observed that article 2 of the EC Treaty states that the Community is to have as its task, inter alia, the promotion of 'a harmonious, balanced and sustainable development of economic activities' and 'a high level of employment and of social protection'.[47]

Even more significantly, notwithstanding the submissions of the United Kingdom, both judgments contained the first explicit recognition by the ECJ that 'the right to take collective action for the protection of workers', including the right to strike, must 'be recognised as a fundamental right which forms an integral part of the general principles of Community

---

[44] *Luxembourg* [2008] ECR I-4323 [30].
[45] Joined Cases C-369/96 and C-376/96 *Jean-Claude Arblade, Arblade & Fils SARL and Bernard Leloup, Serge Leloup, Sofrage SARL* [1999] ECR I-8453 [30].
[46] *Luxembourg* [2008] ECR I-4323 [29].
[47] *Viking* [2007] ECR I-10779 [78]–[79]; and *Laval* [2007] ECR I-11767 [104]–[105].

law the observance of which the Court ensures'.[48] Notably, that view was opposed by the UK Government,[49] and the Court's conclusion was reached in defiance of UK submissions. In *Laval*, the principle was stated that the right of workers and their organisations to take industrial action includes action, not only aimed at improving terms and conditions for Latvian workers, but also at protection of Swedish workers from 'social dumping'.[50] Moreover, it extends beyond primary action to sympathetic action, such as 'a blockade'.[51]

It remains, however, unclear whether the ECJ would also be prepared to recognise a right to engage in collective bargaining.[52] At various junctures, the *Viking* judgment relied upon various connections between collective action, collective agreements and collective bargaining to explain the Court's reasoning.[53] However, in *Laval*, the Court viewed it as troubling that the employer 'may be forced, by way of collective action, into negotiations with the trade unions of unspecified duration at the place at which the services in question are to be provided'.[54] Moreover, the failure to mention any right to engage in collective bargaining in *Rüffert* suggests that recognition of such a right is not at present contemplated by the Court. There may yet be speculation that collective bargaining is a 'principle' to which Member States are to aspire, rather than a right protected by the Court.[55]

In the *Rüffert* case, the Advocate-General advising the ECJ noted article 136 of the EC Treaty, which states that:

> [t]he Community and the Member States, having in mind fundamental social rights ..., shall have as their objectives ... improved living and working conditions, so as to make possible their harmonisation while the improvement is being maintained, [and] dialogue between management and labour.[56]

However, the judgment of the ECJ made no reference at all to workers' rights. Instead, the Court found that the Posted Workers' Directive, inter-

---

[48] *Viking* [2007] ECR I-10779 [42]–[44]; and *Laval* [2007] ECR I-11767 [89]–[91].

[49] Written Observations of the UK in Case 438/05 *International Transport Workers' Federation (ITF) and Finnish Seamen's Union (FSU) v Viking Line* [2007] ECR I-10779, 10–20. See also Bercusson, B, 'The Trade Union Movement and the European Union: Judgment Day' (2007) 13 *European Law Journal* 279, 298–300.

[50] *Laval* [2007] ECR I-11767 [102]–[103].

[51] Ibid [107].

[52] Cf Case C-67/96 *Albany International* [1999] E.C.R. I-5751 at [159] (Opinion of AG Jacobs).

[53] See *Viking* [2007] ECR I-10779 [82]; and the link made between collective action and collective agreements in [54]–[55].

[54] *Laval* [2007] ECR I-11767 [100].

[55] See above the analysis of the distinction between principles and rights which has arisen in the discourse of protection of socio-economic rights in an ILO context, chapter 1. See also, this chapter, below.

[56] *Rüffert* [2008] ECR I-198920 September 2007 [121] (Opinion of AG Bot).

preted in the light of article 49 of the EC Treaty, precludes a public authority from adopting a legislative measure:

> requiring the contracting authority to designate as contractors for public works contracts only those undertakings which, when submitting their tenders, agree in writing to pay their employees ... at least the remuneration prescribed by the collective agreement in force at the place where those services are performed.[57]

This curious conclusion was reached despite a clear inconsistency with International Labour Organisation (ILO) Convention No 94 (the Labour Clauses (Public Contracts) Convention), which was adopted in 1949 by the ILO and has since been ratified by 10 EU Member States. The Court's failure to address the significance of ILO Convention No 94 would seem to be due to the decision taken by Germany not to ratify this Convention.[58]

Recognition of the right to collective action was not determinative of the outcome of either the *Viking* or the *Laval* cases. Indeed, the Court rejected arguments that industrial action be excluded from scrutiny under articles 43 or 49 of the EC Treaty, which had been made by analogy with the treatment of collective agreements under competition law.[59] Instead, the ECJ cited other cases where the exercise of fundamental rights were at issue, such as concerning freedom of expression and freedom of assembly,[60] in which the Court held that the exercise of such rights did not fall outside the scope of EC Treaty provisions regarding free movement, but could be justified insofar as their exercise was proportionate.[61] It is in the process of assessing whether collective action can be justified as proportionate that difficulties are likely to arise for trade unions.

JUSTIFYING BREACH OF AN EMPLOYERS' FREEDOM OF MOVEMENT BY COLLECTIVE ACTION

Earlier cases which considered whether the exercise of human rights constituted, in the circumstances, a justifiable exception to what would otherwise amount to a breach of free movement rights, had required the EU Member State in question to justify its laws and administrative actions.[62]

---

[57] *Rüffert* [2008] ECR I-1989 [43].

[58] See answer by the EU Commission of 8 September 2008 to written question by Sahra Wagenknecht, tabled on 7 July 2008 available at: www.sahra-wagenknecht.de/en/article/401. effects_of_the_european_court_of_justice_judgment_in_the_ruffert_case.html.

[59] Case C-67/96 *Albany International BV v Stichting Bedrijfsfonds Textielindustrie* [1999] ECR I-5751 [59]–[60].

[60] Case C-112/00 *Eugen Schmidberger, Internationale Transporte und Planzüge v Republik Österreich* [2003] ECR I-5659; Case C-36/02 *Omega Spielhallen- und Automatenaufstellungs-GmbH v Oberbürgermeisterin der Bundesstadt Bonn* [2004] ECR I-9609.

[61] See *Viking* [2007] ECR I-10779 [45]–[46]; and *Laval* [2007] ECR I-11767 [93]–[94].

[62] Case C-112/00 *Schmidberger* [2003] ECR I-5659; Case C-36/02 *Omega* [2004] ECR I-9609 [for full references see n 60 above].

By way of contrast, in *Viking* and *Laval*, the ECJ called upon *trade unions* to demonstrate that their actions could be justified, an extension of principles of direct horizontal effect, which has caused controversy.[63] Two crucial criteria, usually applicable to the defence of the conduct of Member States, were then stated. First, trade unions had to demonstrate that they were pursuing 'a legitimate aim' compatible with the EC Treaty and justified by 'overriding reasons of public interest'. Secondly, the unions had to satisfy the requirement of proportionality, demonstrating that their actions were 'suitable for securing the attainment of the objective pursued' and did not 'go beyond what is necessary in order to attain it'.[64] Both of these requirements were applied by the ECJ in a way which seems likely to pose significant difficulties for trade unions seeking to call industrial action in the future.

A Legitimate Aim: Protection of Workers

In both *Viking* and *Laval*, the ECJ recognised that collective action was a fundamental right and had a legitimate aim, insofar as this was for the 'protection of workers'. Under ILO jurisprudence, trade unions are entitled to:

> use strike action to support their position in the search for solutions to problems posed by major social and economic policy trends which have a direct impact on their members and on workers in general, in particular as regards employment, social protection and standards of living.[65]

On this basis, the ILO Governing Body Committee on Freedom of Association criticised the attempts made by the Greek Government to end a strike called by seafarers' unions, which was directed at opposing proposed legislation relating to seafarers, as well as changes to systems of vessel registration (that is, 'flagging'), employment, taxation and pensions.[66] One might therefore expect that the requirement 'protection of workers' would be generously construed by the ECJ, but this was not the case in *Viking* or *Laval*.

In *Viking*, the actions of the FSU were treated by the ECJ as justifiable only if they could be linked to the protection of the jobs and conditions of members of their union. If the employer were to make an undertaking, which was enforceable under national law, 'that statutory provisions would be complied with and the terms of the collective agreement governing their

---

[63] For further elaboration on this point, see Syrpis and Novitz, 'Economic and Social Rights in Conflict: Political and Judicial Approaches to their Reconciliation' (2008) 420–22.

[64] See *Viking* [2007] ECR I-10779 [75] and *Laval* [2007] ECR I-11767 [101].

[65] International Labour Organisation (ILO), *Freedom of Association: Digest of Decisions of the Freedom of Association Committee of the ILO Governing Body*, 5th Revised edn (Geneva, ILO, 2006) para 527.

[66] *(Case No 2506)* Report of the Committee on Freedom of Association No. 346, Vol. XC, 2007, Series B, No. 2) available at: www.ilo.org/ilolex/english/caseframeE.htm.

working relationship maintained', then the protection of workers would not be at issue.[67] The terms and conditions of the future Estonian workforce are not apparently considered to be a relevant consideration for the FSU, even if these were in the future likely to undercut those of Finnish seafarers and prevent future jobs arising for their members. As regards the ITF 'flags of convenience' policy, the ECJ expressed concern that the:

> ITF is required, when asked by one of its members, to initiate solidarity action against the beneficial owner of a vessel which is registered in a State other than that of which that owner is a national, irrespective of whether or not that owner's exercise of its right of freedom of establishment is liable to have a harmful effect on the work or conditions of employment of its employees.[68]

The argument of the Court was that if re-flagging did not have harmful effects on a particular group of workers, the ITF could not logically rely on the protection of workers justification to take collective action opposing all re-flagging. The Court did not consider the argument that flags of convenience are a means by which ship owners have progressively eroded seafarers' terms and conditions of employment, since ship owners can cut costs by re-flagging in a state where labour laws are less stringent or less well-enforced. Moreover, where the ship owner has no link with the jurisdiction, the assets to compensate seafarers for any breach of their rights may not be available.[69] The private settlement of the *Viking* litigation on 5 March 2008[70] meant that these arguments were not considered by the UK Court of Appeal (to which final determination of the case was remitted).

In *Laval*, the Court conceded that 'in principle, blockading action by a trade union of the host Member State which is aimed at ensuring that workers posted in the framework of a transnational provision of services have their terms and conditions fixed at a certain level, falls within the objective of protecting workers',[71] as did prevention of 'possible social dumping'.[72] However, on the facts of the case, the Court considered that a 'blockade' designed to 'force' an employer to enter into negotiations on rates of pay could not be justified on public interest grounds,[73] since the negotiations formed 'part of a national context' characterised by a lack of 'sufficiently precise and accessible' provisions, which rendered it 'impossible or excessively difficult in practice' for the employer to determine the obligations with which it was required to comply as regards minimum pay.[74] This narrow construction of the 'protection

---

[67] *Viking* [2007] ECR I-10779 [81]–[85].
[68] Ibid [89].
[69] See Couper, A, 'Historical Perspectives on Seafarers and the Law' and Churchill, R, Fitzpatrick, D and Khaliq, U, 'Seafarers' Rights at the National Level' in D Fitzpatrick and M Anderson (eds), *Seafarers' Rights* (Oxford, Oxford University Press, 2005).
[70] Available at: www.itfglobal.org/news-online/index.cfm/newsdetail/1842.
[71] *Laval* [2007] ECR I-11767 [107].
[72] Ibid [103].
[73] Ibid [111].
[74] Ibid [110].

of workers' and the emphasis placed on certainty of employer obligations is consistent with the Court's interpretation of the Posted Workers Directive as being intended to render the obligations of foreign service providers clear and readily accessible, thereby facilitating access to markets of other EU Member States.[75] Priority is apparently given to their interests.

The *Rüffert* and *Luxembourg* judgments also took a limited view of potential justifications arising in respect of free movement of services, again with reference to the Posted Workers Directive.[76] The reasons given for the Court's conclusion in *Rüffert*, namely that the local law requiring that a foreign tenderer for a public works contract undertaken to comply with the terms set by a regionally applicable collective agreement in respect of construction workers was in breach of the freedom to provide services was twofold. The first reason was that the collective agreement, which was at issue in the case, applied only to part of the construction sector within a particular geographical area and only to public contracts. It had not been declared universally applicable as required under the terms of the Posted Workers Directive. Its lack of universal application indicated, secondly, that it was not a matter of overriding public interest and 'also cannot be considered to be justified by the objective of ensuring independence in the organisation of working life by trade unions'.[77]

The European Trade Union Confederation (ETUC) has stated its objection to these findings of the Court, since the judgments allow for only the most minimal protection for posted workers, and effectively make no provision for them to engage in collective bargaining or participate within existing collective bargaining structures within a host country. The result is that the wage costs for posted workers are likely to significantly undercut those of domestic labour, especially in light of the stark differences between rates of pay in the different EU Member States following enlargement. The ETUC is asking for equal pay for home and posted workers, and recognises that not doing so risks hostility towards posted workers and the kind of xenophobia, which was for example directed towards Polish workers during the referendums on the EU constitution.[78]

Proportionality

Proportionality acts as a further filter. The guidance given by the Court to national courts when assessing proportionality was that it was necessary:

> for the national court to examine, in particular, on the one hand, whether, under the national rules and collective agreement law applicable to that action, [the union] did not have other means at its disposal which were less restrictive of freedom

---

[75] *Rüffert* [2008] ECR I-1989 [64]–[88].

[76] On the relationship between the Posted Workers Directive 96/71 and art 49 EC, see Kilpatrick, 'The ECJ and Labour Law: A 2008 Retrospective' (2009) 199–201.

[77] *Rüffert* [2008] ECR I-1989 [41].

[78] See www.etuc.org/r/846.

of establishment in order to bring to a successful conclusion the collective negotiations ... and, on the other, whether that trade union had exhausted those means
before initiating such action.[79]

In an earlier case concerning freedom of speech and freedom of assembly,
the Austrian Government was found to have acted in a proportionate manner when permitting an environmental protest, which blocked a motorway
and affected free movement of goods. In this context, it was relevant that
the protest was lawful, relatively small in scale and that the authorities
had sought to avoid disruption as much as possible, by taking steps to
warn those potentially affected.[80] Applying such a test to the actions of
the Finnish Government in *Viking*, it might not be difficult to find that the
legislation and system of industrial relations it supported was defensible
under Community law. Should the objectives of the Finnish law, which
provided for trade unions to have access to industrial action at the expiry of a
collective agreement, come within the rather restrictive 'protection of workers' test identified above, then it would seem that the Finnish Government
had done everything possible to mitigate the potential harms of industrial
action. For example, the Finnish Government provided industrial dispute
mediation services in order to minimise industrial disruption and inconvenience to employers, and there seemed to be appropriate procedures for
notice in place.[81]

It is more difficult to apply a proportionality test to the actions of a trade
union. 'It is in the very nature of negotiations that both parties set demands
at their highest and through negotiation over time seek a compromise ...'[82]
Indeed, industrial action is intended to cause sufficient disruption to extract
concessions from an employer. *Viking* seems to require that unions be more
moderate in their demands or take initiatives in conciliation not required
under national law, for it is evident that they cannot rely upon the latter
for their protection.

The judgment in *Viking* also invites national courts, responsible for
implementing EU law, to examine the proportionality of trade unions'
actions. This means that unions' liability will turn on whether particular
judges decide that it would have been possible to achieve their objectives in
a way which was, perhaps marginally, less restrictive of the free movement
rights of, in many cases, the very enterprise with which they are in dispute;

---

[79] *Viking* [2007] ECR I-10779 [87]. Note the reliance placed on pre-existing ECHR jurisprudence, insofar as the European Court of Justice (ECJ) also cited the earlier view of the
European Court of Human Rights that collective action was not a necessary aspect of freedom
of association, discussed above at n 24.

[80] Case C-112/00 *Schmidberger* [2003] ECR I-5659 [86]–[89].

[81] *Viking* [2007] ECR I-10779 [16].

[82] Bercusson, 'The Trade Union Movement and the European Union: Judgment Day'
(2007) 304.

the problem being that courts have seldom been regarded as the most sympathetic locus for hearing trade union evidence on labour disputes.[83]

The result may be that, in the EU, trade unions are less willing to risk legal liability by taking industrial action, and that, in the exceptional cir cumstances in which they do so, employers will be swift to bring opportunistic applications for interlocutory injunctions.[84] This state of affairs does not seem conducive to the balance between 'the rights under the provisions of the Treaty on the free movement of goods, persons, services and capital' and 'the objectives pursued by social policy' which the Court acknowledged in both *Laval* and *Viking*.[85] What has been given with one hand—the right to take collective action—has been so circumscribed as to be taken away with the other. The next section investigates whether the Treaty of Lisbon, which came into force on 1 December 2009, will result in any change to the current judicial position.

THE IMPLICATIONS OF THE TREATY
OF LISBON FOR WORKERS' RIGHTS

After the 'no' vote in the Irish referendum held in June 2008, the European Council responded to the concerns of the Irish people, including in relation to workers' rights and social policy.[86] This paved the way for the Irish to be consulted again on the text of the Treaty; and for the result of the 2008 referendum to be reversed in October 2009. The formalities of ratification were then completed in the Czech Republic, Germany and Poland, and the Treaty came into force before the end of 2009.[87]

First, it should be observed that the Lisbon Treaty does not substantially extend the social competence of the EU. The Treaty on the Functioning of the EU (TFEU) makes new provision for recognition and promotion

---

[83] Lord Wedderburn, 'Labour Law 2008: 40 Years On' (2007) 36 *Industrial Law Journal* 397, 422.

[84] For an example of circumstances in which this was threatened, see *Application by the British Air Line Pilots Association to the International Labour Organisation Committee of Experts on the Application of Conventions and Recommendations against the United Kingdom for breach of ILO Convention No. 87* drafted by John Hendy QC, available at: www.balpa.org/Document-Library/Industrial-Issues/BALPA-ILO-Application-2009-01-26.aspx. See further Apps, K, Damages Claims against Trade Unions after *Viking* and *Laval*' (2009) 34 *European Law Review* 141.

[85] *Viking* [2007] ECR I-10779 [79]; *Laval* [2007] ECR I-11767 [105].

[86] See European Council Presidency Conclusions, Brussels, 18/19 June 2008, in particular at 2–3 and Annex II.

[87] See also Syrpis, P, 'The Treaty of Lisbon: Much Ado... But About What?' (2008) 37 *ILJ* 219. For a thorough overview of the Lisbon Reform Treaty, see Dougan, M, 'The Treaty of Lisbon 2007: Winning Minds, Not Hearts' (2008) 45 *Common Market Law Review* 617.

of 'the role of the social partners' at EU level,[88] but does not make provision for their activities at the domestic level. There are elaborate powers of monitoring in respect of such matters as the right of association and collective bargaining between employers and workers, including studies, opinions, consultations, setting guidelines and indicators, and the organisation of 'exchange of best practice'.[89] This seems consistent with the 'soft law' approach of the open method of coordination, but does not add to the legislative powers of the EU. Instead, it seems most likely that if any change is to occur at the EU level which is significant in terms of protection of workers' rights it is likely to occur through the revision made to article 6 of the EU Treaty.

The first paragraph of this provision states that:

> The Union recognises the rights, freedoms and principles set out in the Charter of Fundamental Rights of the European Union of 7 December 2000, as adapted at Strasbourg, on 12 December 2007, which shall have the same legal value as the Treaties. The provisions of the Charter shall not extend in any way the competences of the Union as defined in the Treaties. The rights, freedoms and principles in the Charter shall be interpreted in accordance with the general provisions in Title VII of the Charter governing its interpretation and application and with due regard to the explanations referred to in the Charter, that set out the sources of those provisions.

Such recognition remains subject to a Protocol which limits its application in Poland and the United Kingdom, due to the feared effects of the rights to collective bargaining and industrial action set out in chapter IV, namely that without their objections, these provisions would create justiciable rights, something which both countries deem inappropriate as regards, in particular, a right to collective action.[90]

However, a closer look at the wording of the EUCFR suggests that the fears expressed by Poland and the United Kingdom are misplaced. For example, the EUCFR gives privileged treatment to the right of the individual worker to join or refuse to join an association.[91] By way of contrast, rights to negotiate, conclude collective agreements and engage in collective action are made explicitly subject to national laws and practice and even Community law.[92] Article 28, set out in part IV of the EUCFR, which relates to collective bargaining and collective action, thereby does not so much allow scope

---

[88]   Treaty on the Functioning of the EU (TFEU) art 152.

[89]   Ibid art 156.

[90]   See Lisbon Treaty, Protocol on the Application of the Charter of Fundamental Rights of the European Union to Poland and to the United Kingdom, which states, inter alia, 'for the avoidance of doubt, nothing in Title IV—Solidarity of the Charter creates justiciable rights applicable to Poland and the United Kingdom except in so far as Poland and the United Kingdom has provided for such rights in its national law'.

[91]   EU Charter of Fundamental Rights (EUCFR) 2000 art 12.

[92]   Ibid art 28.

for exceptional protection of the right to strike, but rather suggests that entitlements under national law may be struck down by the ECJ to the extent that they are inconsistent with EC market freedoms. It is not so very surprising that, in both the *Viking* and *Laval* judgments, reference was made to article 28 in the context of stressing the priority to be given, ultimately, to the employers' entitlement to free movement.[93] As the House of Lords European Union Committee has observed: 'Interestingly, the Charter was used to introduce the limitation to the right to strike, and thus seemed to be employed by the Court more as a brake than an accelerator in these cases.'[94]

The House of Lords Committee has also observed that they 'expect the effect of the change in the Charter's status to be limited'.[95] Courts at the national and EU level may more frequently refer to the Charter when interpreting and applying EU law, but the rights contained therein broadly reflect the existing commitments of EU Member States under other international human rights instruments and will not, in any case, apply to domestic law unrelated to the implementation of EU law. They also consider that the Polish and UK Protocol may temper the enthusiasm of the ECJ in any expansion of its human rights jurisprudence in reliance on the Charter.[96] It may well be that the Protocol does not so much have a legal as a political 'chilling' effect.

More significant may be the second paragraph of the revised article 6, which provides that 'the Union shall accede to the European Convention for the Protection of Human Rights' (ECHR), even though this is subject to the proviso that 'such accession shall not affect the Union's competencies as defined in the Treaties'.

The mechanisms for accession have yet to be determined. There are indications that the Parliamentary Assembly of the Council of Europe would like this process to be expedited.[97] However, for some time, the process was obstructed by the fact that Protocol 14 to the ECHR had not yet entered into force, Article 17 of which amends article 59 of the ECHR so as to make specific provision for the European Union to accede to the Convention. Russian ratification of Protocol 14 finally occurred in January 2010 and we can expect further elaboration of the modalities of accession to follow shortly.[98]

---

[93] *Viking* [2007] ECR I-10779 [44]; and *Laval* [2007] ECR I-11767 [91].

[94] House of Lords, European Union Committee, 10th Report of Session 2007–8, 'The Treaty of Lisbon: An Impact Assessment' Vol 1 Report, 92, para 5.35.

[95] Ibid 101, para 5.80.

[96] Ibid 107, para 5.109.

[97] Parliamentary Assembly, The accession of the European Union/European Community to the European Convention on Human Rights, Resolution 1610 (2008) (Assembly debate, 17 April 2008).

[98] See EU Declaration on Russian Federation's ratification of Protocol 14 to the European Convention on Human Rights (2010) available at: http://www.europa-eu-un.org/articles/fr/article_9465_fr.htm.

Thus far, the European Court of Human Rights has sought to avoid conflict with the ECJ, deferring to its competence to 'secure' Convention rights,[99] considering the protection of fundamental rights by EC law to be 'equivalent to that of the Convention system'.[100] However, accession would reserve the right of the former to intervene in the latter where it perceived clear cases of abuse of rights or non-implementation. The consequence is that it may be possible for those disappointed by the Court of Justice's interpretation of the Treaty in cases involving human rights to argue before the Strasbourg Court that the EU has, in some way, infringed Convention rights.

In the light of the recent case law of the European Court of Human Rights concerning collective bargaining and collective action identified above,[101] it may be possible to identify a prima facie infringement of a Convention right by the EU institutions in the labour law arena. If so, the burden would then shift to the EU, which would have to explain that the any restriction on Convention rights, imposed in order to further the goal of free movement, is proportionate. Given the deference which the European Court of Human Rights has showed towards the EU to date, it is unlikely that the EU would be subject to the same level of scrutiny which the Court of Justice tends to direct towards Member States and trade unions whose actions restrict free movement rights.

Nevertheless, the reversal of the proportionality principle may yet turn out to be significant.[102] In EU law, the Court of Justice takes the economic goal of free movement as its starting point, and then assesses the proportionality of any restrictions on free movement. Under the ECHR regime, the European Court of Human Rights takes Convention rights as its starting point, and assesses the proportionality of restrictions to those rights. The status of the economic and the social could thereby, in effect, be reversed.

Article 6(2) of the Treaty on European Union endeavours to ensure that 'accession shall not affect the Union's competences as defined in the

---

[99] *Matthews v UK* (1999) 28 EHRR 361 [32].

[100] *Bosphorus Hava Yollari Turzim ve Ticaret Anonim Sirketi v Ireland*, judgment of the European Court of Human Rights 30 June 2005, at [165]; see also *Coopérative Laitière Maine-Anjou v France*, admissibility decision of 10 October 2006. Both cited in van Dijk, P, 'Comments on the Accession of the European Union/European Community to the European Convention on Human Rights' (European Commission for Democracy through Law (Venice Commission) Council of Europe, 12 October 2007, CDL(2007)096). See also Costello, C, 'The Bosphorus Ruling of the ECtHR: Fundamental Rights and Blurred Boundaries in Europe' (2006) 6 *Human Rights Law Review* 87.

[101] See *Demir and Baykara v Turkey* (App no 34503/97) Grand Chamber Judgment of 12 November 2008 [153]–[154]; *Affaire Dilek et Autres v Turquie* (App nos 74611/01, 26876/02 et 27628/0) Judgment of 17 July 2007 (available only in French); and *Enerji Yapi-Yol Sen v Turkey* (App no 68959/01) Judgment of 21 April 2009 (available only in French).

[102] Syrpis, 'The Treaty of Lisbon: Much Ado ... But About What?' (2008) 234.

Treaties'.[103] The European Court of Human Rights may well maintain a deferential stance, such that the Court of Justice's interpretation of the dictates of the internal market is not challenged in Strasbourg. However, the dialogue between the two courts[104] may be such that the European Court of Justice is more eager to see its rulings on the scope of economic and social rights become, and remain, closely aligned. The consequence may well be that the Court of Justice arrives at a rather different balance between the economic freedoms of employers and the human rights of workers.

Thus, the EU's accession to the European Convention on Human Rights, rather than the incorporation of the EU Charter of Fundamental Rights, offers the opportunity for greater protection for the human rights of workers within the EU. Without such a change, it seems that we are left with the so-called 'balance' achieved in the labour law cases discussed herein, which leaves the Court of Justice and national courts with the difficult task of assessing whether restrictions on the exercise of free movement rights by Member States and trade unions acting to protect the interests of workers are justifiable and proportionate. To date, there is little evidence that the courts accord sufficient weight to the protection of workers' human rights.

---

[103] There is also a Protocol relating to art 6(2) of the Treaty on European Union (TEU), and a Declaration attached to the Treaty, both of which seek to protect the specific characteristics and features of Union law.

[104] The Declaration on art 6(2) of the TEU states that the regular dialogue between the Court of Justice and the European Court of Human Rights 'could be reinforced' when the Union accedes to the Convention.

Part III

Regulatory Possibilities

17

Core Labour Standards in the GSP Regime of the European Union: Overshadowed by other Considerations

JAN ORBIE AND FERDI DE VILLE

S HOULD CORE LABOUR standards (CLS) as human rights be integrated into trade relations? In the course of the 1990s, in parallel with the rise of globalisation and the establishment of the World Trade Organisation (WTO), the debate on a social clause resurfaced at the top of the international trade agenda. Yet this issue quickly reached a total deadlock within the multilateral trade regime because of suspicions of hidden protectionism and the concomitant resistance by developing countries.

This chapter takes a particular angle to this topic, focussing on the integration of CLS in the Generalised System of Preferences (GSP) of the European Union (EU). It is assumed that the GSP system, which allows developed countries to unilaterally condition market access on the observance of CLS, may help to increase the legitimacy of a social clause. On the basis of a process-tracing analysis and a study of literature, and with reference to the broader EU trade policy agenda, we attempt to answer the question whether Europe's social GSP has been applied in a way that suspicions of hidden protectionism and the resulting impasse at the WTO level can be removed.

The conclusion reads that the EU's social GSP system has not served protectionist goals, but neither has it substantially enhanced the legitimacy of a social clause. This critical evaluation partly stems from the ambiguity in EU decision-making on CLS conditionality and more fundamentally from its limited generosity in supporting CLS through market access, compared with other foreign policy and trade-related objectives. After all, the EU's limited role in the external promotion of CLS seems to reflect its incomplete internal capacity to act in the very same CLS vis-à-vis the Member States.

LINKING LABOUR STANDARDS AND TRADE

The Debate on a Social Clause

Whereas the promotion of CLS as human rights is widely considered as a legitimate goal in international relations, the potential contribution of trade politics has been the subject of much debate among academics and policy-makers. Neo-liberal economists are highly critical towards the idea of linking labour standards and trade rules.[1] Policy-makers cannot be trusted with such a discretionary power in trade policy. Developed countries will use social clauses as veiled protectionist instruments, undoing the comparative advantage of developing countries in international trade.

According to mainstream neoliberal thinking, other instruments should be employed to achieve this objective. Some point to the role of development aid budgets, but usually the emphasis lays on soft governance mechanisms such as corporate social responsibility, private codes of conduct for multi-nationals, and social labelling. The indirect influence of the International Labour Organisation (ILO) is equally highlighted.

Proponents of a social clause do not question the ILO's contribution, or the relevance of development aid. Nevertheless they argue that 'fair' trade rules should somehow allow for interventionist trade measures favouring CLS, while at the same time providing enough guarantees against protectionist abuse. Advocates of a social clause refer to moral arguments and to the legitimacy of the trading regime. The free trade system may be efficient, but it also needs to be seen as legitimate by the public at large. One implication of this reasoning may be that the incorporation of labour standards in the world trade regime is necessary to preserve the legitimacy of the liberal international trading system,

Although this 'free versus fair trade' debate has been going on for decades, it became a hot international trade issue only in 1993–94. During the final stage of the General Agreement on Tariffs and Trade (GATT) Uruguay Round, a growing body of opinion expressed itself in favour of a social clause. The United States and France were particularly enthusiastic about including labour standard provisions in the world trade system. They argued for a working group on the social dimension of trade liberalisation under the umbrella of the new-established WTO. This was fiercely resisted by developing countries, especially Malaysia, India, and Pakistan, but countries such as the United Kingdom and Germany were equally reluctant. A last-minute compromise provided that the issue could be put on the WTO agenda at a later stage.

---

[1] *Cf* Lee, E, 'Globalisation and Labour Standards: A Review of Issues' (1997) 2 *International Labour Review* 136.

During the coming years the debate on a social clause continued to be highly politicised, culminating in the WTO Singapore Conference in 1996. The Singapore Declaration de facto puts the issue on the sidelines, referring to the ILO as the competent organisation to deal with international labour standards, thereby consolidating the idea that social issues are not to be dealt with in the multilateral trade regime.[2] EU and US attempts to put this on the agenda of the WTO Millennium Round failed with the debacle of Seattle, partly because of the growing assertiveness of the developing countries, which strongly rejected US President Clinton's suggestion to introduce a punitive social clause. When a new trade round was finally launched in Doha (2001), the agenda simply referred to the Singapore text. Henceforth, labour standards are excluded from multilateral trade negotiations. The impasse at the WTO track provided the ILO with the opportunity to present itself as the appropriate international forum on labour standards.

This brief sketch illustrates the resistance against the idea of a social clause, for fear of veiled protectionism; and the deadlock in the WTO, due to developing country opposition. The next section explains why the GSP of the EU may address both related problems.

Focussing on the GSP of the European Union

In the 1970s the GATT established the GSP system as a temporary exception to the Most Favoured Nations (MFN) principle in the context of developing countries' demands for a New International Economic Order. Under the 1979 Enabling Clause, industrial countries are allowed to grant more favourable and non-reciprocal tariff preferences to developing country imports. Each developed country can unilaterally design its own GSP scheme, determining the product coverage and the extent of liberalisation. Differentiation among developing countries is also possible; for example, the EU's 'Everything But Arms' (EBA) initiative of 2001 constitutes a special GSP, granting more favourable tariff preferences to the group of least-developed countries (LDCs).[3]

Equally, developed countries may differentiate based on developing countries' compliance with CLS. There are two dimensions to such a 'labour GSP clause': on the one hand, additional tariff reductions can be granted to countries observing CLS, on the other, GSP preferences may be withdrawn in the case of serious violations of these standards. The 'carrot' implies that

[2] Wilkinson, R, 'The WTO in Crisis: Exploring the Dimensions of Institutional Inertia' (2001) 3 *Journal of World Trade* 35, 409.

[3] Council Regulation (EC) No 416/2001 of 28 February 2001 amending Regulation (EC) No 2820/98 applying a multiannual scheme of generalised tariff preferences for the period 1 July 1999 to 31 December 2001 so as to extend duty-free access without any quantitative restrictions to products originating in the least developed countries, OJ L 60, 1.3.2001, p.43–50.

developing countries can export to western markets at tariffs that are more generous than the standard GSP rate, whereas the 'stick' reverts the level of market access back to the regular MFN level.

Until recently the WTO compatibility of such labour GSP conditionality remained unclear. Under what conditions is discrimination among developing countries allowed under the GATT Enabling Clause? Following Europe's inclusion of Pakistan in the GSP drug arrangement in 2001 (see below), India decided to bring this question to the WTO dispute settlement mechanism. Although India chose to limit its formal complaint to the drugs incentives after consultations with the EU,[4] it was feared that a conviction of the drug regime would also undermine the legitimacy of the labour arrangements.[5] But in contrast with the more restrictive Panel Report,[6] in 2004 the WTO Appellate Body basically ruled that discrimination is allowed under the Enabling Clause provided that the selection is based on objective and transparent criteria.[7] Although the drug arrangement was found illegal, objective and transparent labour incentive provisions in Europe's GSP regimes continue to be legitimate.[8]

This is an important finding, since labour GSP clauses may help to solve the double problem identified above as the major obstacle at the multilateral level: avoiding protectionist misuse of and overcoming developing country opposition against a social clause. Although a much more ambitious trade and aid package would be needed to integrate labour standards in trade relations without raising legitimate fears of hidden protectionism with developing countries, we argue that the integration of labour standards in the GSP trade system potentially constitutes a first symbolical step.

First, the GSP system is by nature incentive-based rather than punitive. In itself the GSP already provides more favourable market access, and the special labour incentives are even more beneficial. Moreover, the sanction clause is limited compared with article XX of the WTO: developing countries that

---

[4] Thailand's earlier request for consultations never led to the establishment of a World Trade Organisation (WTO) panel.

[5] Cole, A, 'Labor Standards and the Generalised System of Preferences: the European Labor Incentives' (2003) *Michigan Journal of International Law* 25; Howse, R, 'India's WTO Challenge to Drug Enforcement Conditions in the European Community GSP: a Little Known Case with Major Repercussions for "Political" Conditionality in US Trade Policy' (2003) 2 *Chicago Journal of International Law* 4.

[6] European Communities—Conditions for the Granting of Tariff Preferences to Developing Countries—Report of the Panel, WT/DS246/R, 1.3.2003.

[7] European Communities—Conditions for the Granting of Tariff Preferences to Developing Countries—Report of the Panel, WT/DS246/AB/R, 7.4.2004.

[8] However, Bartels doubts whether the sanction clause is still permitted under WTO rules: Bartels, L, 'The WTO Ruling on EC—Tariff Preferences to Developing Countries and its Implications for Conditionality in GSP Programs' in T Cottier, J Pauwelyn and E Bürgi (eds), *Human Rights and International Trade* (Oxford, Oxford University Press, 2005); *cf* Charnovitz, S, Bartels, L, Howse, R and Bradley, J, 'The Appellate Body's GSP Decision' (2004) 2 *World Trade Review* 3.

violate CLS risk sliding back into the regular MFN rate instead of the normal GSP, but their imports are not banned. They are still allowed to export albeit at a higher tariff. Ultimately, the legitimacy of the sanctioning and the stimulating clauses depends on the objectivity and transparency of the decision-making process, on the consistency of GSP applications with the ILO findings, and on the generosity of labour incentive schemes. If these three conditions are fulfilled, a social GSP clause can barely be considered as a protectionist tool.

Secondly, this would also enhance the legitimacy of incorporating labour standards in the WTO regime. A successful application of the unilateral labour GSP clause may help to overcome the current deadlock in the multilateral trade negotiations. Experiences with the GSP labour system could provide a concrete basis for discussions on a social clause and pave the way for similar schemes in the WTO. From this perspective the GSP labour clause is largely symbolic: it enhances the legitimacy of the idea of a social clause, even though the potential economic benefits are limited given the ongoing phenomenon of tariff erosion.

Indeed, the difference between the internationally-agreed MFN and zero tariffs—which is precisely the maximum scope for GSP concessions—has strongly decreased in the past decades, and with it the leeway for labour conditionality. Nevertheless, the available preferential margin is still relatively large. Precisely those sectors where developing countries have a competitive advantage, viz. agriculture and textiles, continue to be characterised by high tariff peaks. Thus, there is still much room for tariff reductions under the GSP, especially for sensitive products.[9]

Yet to what extent and how has this preferential margin been used? This chapter addresses this question, focusing on the GSP of the EU. Through the unilateral use of its GSP system—in fact a trade regulation based on article 133 of the EC Treaty—the EU has a considerable discretion to attach (positive or negative) conditionality with regard to CLS. The conditioning of access to the prosperous European market is one of the Union's most powerful trade and even foreign policy instruments.[10]

Delineating our research to the EU's policy on a social clause in the GSP, and not in bilateral or multilateral trade issues, has the advantage that there are no third countries involved. The absence of a third (international)

---

[9] The Generalised System of Preferences (GSP) tariff margin may even increase, since WTO concessions often involve the 'tariffication' of previous non-tariff barriers. This is certainly also the case for the EU. India's challenge before the WTO illustrates that the labour GSP preferences make a difference for Indian textile exporters to the EU compared with their Pakistani competitors. Also, the EU's scapegoat role in the WTO negotiations on agricultural market access show that—despite Everything But Arms' (EBA) treatment for the least-developed countries (LDCs)—there is still room for tariff reductions vis-a-vis other developing countries.

[10] Smith, M and Woolcock, S, 'European Commercial Policy: A Leadership Role in the New Millennium?' (1999) 4 *European Foreign Affairs Review* 451.

negotiating level in EU trade policy-making analysis solves one of the main obstacles to determining Europe's commitment to a social clause. Previous research has suggested that labour standards have not been an EU priority in the past decade.[11] Member States have long been divided on the issue of a social clause, implying that at the crucial Singapore Conference the Council Presidency could not even bring up an 'EU' position. Moreover, Europe's commitment to other trade-related issues such as competition and investment prevailed, whereas the issue of labour standards was abandoned even months before Doha. However, it remains difficult to assess the 'EU factor' in the multilateral setting of the WTO, since the impasse is usually explained by the mere reference to developing country resistance—without further questioning the actual EU commitment on labour standards in WTO negotiations. Being entirely designed by EU policy-makers, the GSP provides a better way to distil the 'EU factor', analysing whether Europe's discourse about CLS in trade corresponds with its actual policy practise.

The following sections describe the development and application of labour standards in the EU GSP through the 1990s. On the basis of a process-tracing analysis and a study of literature, and with reference to the broader EU trade policy agenda, we attempt to answer the question whether Europe's social GSP has been applied in a way that suspicions of hidden protectionism and the resulting impasse at the WTO level can be removed.

A SOCIAL CLAUSE IN EUROPE'S GSP: DEVELOPMENT AND APPLICATION

The First Social GSP Clause: the Stick before the Carrot

Proposals for a social clause in EC trade relations had already been tabled at the end of the 1970s,[12] but these quickly sank into oblivion.[13] Even the

---

[11] For similarly critical views on Europe's commitment within the WTO, see Novitz, T, 'Promoting Core Labour Standards and Improving Global Social Governance: an Assessment of EU Competence to Implement Commission Proposals' (2002) *EUI Working Papers* 59, 7–8; and Van den Hoven, A, 'Assuming Leadership in Multilateral Economic Institutions: The EU's 'Development Round' Discourse and Strategy' (2004) 2 *West European Politics* 265–67. Other analyses, in contrast, consider the EU as 'the most aggressive proponent': Young, AR, 'The EU and World Trade: Doha and Beyond' in M Green Cowles and D Dinan (eds), *Developments in the European Union* 2 (Basingstoke, Palgrave Macmillan, 2004); or as a 'leader': Johnson, A, *European Welfare States and Supranational Governance of Social Policy* (Houndmills, Palgrave, 2005) 178 in promoting a social clause within the WTO; Orbie, J, Vos, H and Taverniers, L, 'EU Trade Policy and a Social Clause: a Question of Competences?' (2005) *Politique Européenne* 17.

[12] Alston, P, 'Linking trade and human rights' in J Delbrück, W Fiedler and W Ewening (eds), *German Yearbook of International Law* (Berlin, Duncker & Humblot, 1980) 141; Hansson, G, 'Social Clauses and International Trade. An Economic Analysis of Labour Standards in Trade Policy' (1981) *Lund Economic Studies* 25.

[13] Arts, K, *Integrating Human Rights into Development Cooperation. The Case of the Lomé Convention* (Den Haag, Kluwer Law International) 125.

Commission's comprehensive proposal for a 10-year GSP reform in 1990[14] contained no reference whatsoever to labour standards. In the context of the debate during the last months of the Uruguay Round, proposals for a social clause quite suddenly reappeared on the EU agenda at the instigation of France, Belgium, and the European Parliament. Although initially reluctant, Trade Commissioner Sir Leon Brittan also showed himself in favour of this idea. His suggestion to include labour standards in the reformed GSP[15] system was followed by consultations with the Member States and by an official Commission proposal.[16] A few months later the Council gave its approval to the first European GSP regulation with provisions on labour standards.[17] Although the principle of a social clause was supported by a broad majority within the Council of Ministers,[18] two Member States remained reluctant. The desirability of linking labour standards and trade was questioned by the Conservative governments in Germany and especially in the United Kingdom, which abstained from voting on the final GSP regulation.[19]

Developing countries needed to adopt the substance of the relevant ILO conventions in their legislation and they had to effectively apply (but not ratify) them. The ILO was in no respect involved in the supervision procedure, but the Commission had a central role in the suspension procedure in case of violations of the relevant labour standards. Brandtner and Rosas observe that the Commission has a relatively large margin of appreciation (assessing the 'interest' of the complaining party, deciding whether or not to initiate and terminate an investigation, and proposing the withdrawal of preferences) although the final responsibility lies with the Council of Ministers, acting by qualified majority.[20]

---

[14] AE Documents 3 August 1990.

[15] Communication from the Commission (EC) to the Council and the European Parliament integration of developing countries in the international trading system, Role of the GSP 1995–2004 COM (1994) 212 final, 1.7.1994.

[16] Proposal for a Council Regulation (EC) applying a three-year scheme of generalized tariff preferences (1995–97) in respect of certain industrial products originating in developing countries, COM (1994) 337, OJ C 333, 29.11.1994, p.9

[17] Council Regulation (EC) No 3281/94 of 19 December 1994 Applying a four-year scheme of generalized tariff preferences (1995 to 1998) in respect of certain industrial products originating in developing countries, OJ L 348, 31.12.1994.

[18] For a general overview of the decision-making process behind this GSP reform, see Waer, P and Driessen, B, 'The new European Union Generalised System of Preferences. A Workable Compromise in the EU—But a Better Deal for Developing Countries?' (1995) 6 *Journal of World Trade* 29; for a more general analysis of the EU debate, see Waer, P, 'Social Clauses in International Trade. The Debate in the European Union' (1996) 4 *Journal of World Trade* 30; and Barnard, C, 'The External Dimension of Community Social Policy: the Ugly Duckling of External Relations' in N Emiliou and D O'Keeffe (eds), *The European Union and World Trade Law After the Gatt Uruguay Round* (United Kingdom, John Wiley & Sons, 1996).

[19] 1820th Council Meeting, Draft minutes, 19–20 December 1994, 11982/94, PV/CONS 92.

[20] Under the 'temporary withdrawal' procedure (art 10–12), Member States or 'any natural or legal persons, or associations not endowed with legal personality which can show an interest in such withdrawal', could bring violations to the Commission's attention. This may lead

Another notable characteristic of the first social GSP clause is the emphasis on the punitive dimension (Title III of the Regulation), whereas the decision on the possible introduction of an incentive regime (Title II) was postponed. The original Commission document of April 1994 did make a distinction between the 'carrot'[21] and the 'stick'.[22] But the final Council Regulation provided that the suspension clause could be applied from 1995 onwards, whereas the possible introduction of the carrot was postponed.

This decision somewhat contradicted Europe's discourse on the multilateral trade front. Despite divergent opinions on the desirability of a social clause, there was a broad EU consensus on the need for positive (non coercive) measures. The reason for this inconsistency of course lies in the different economic effects of the stick versus the carrot. While the first option can only benefit EU producers (and in case trade sanctions did hurt EU producers, special measures were foreseen), the carrot implied larger trade concessions. This explanation fits in with the general observation that the new GSP system was on the whole more restrictive than the previous one.[23]

Intra-European competence conflicts also emerged. EU Member States' susceptibility to cede competences to the EU in these domains also characterised the political debate about a social GSP clause. Several Member States such as Germany, the United Kingdom and the Netherlands, but also proponents of a social clause such as France and Denmark attached a declaration to the Council minutes, stressing that the references to labour standards in ILO Conventions 'do not imply any Community competence in respect of the matter contained'.[24] They apparently fear that external Community competences to promote labour standards could bring a 'boomerang effect' on *intra*-European relations.

The Regulation soon resulted in two complaints by the international trade union movement against alleged abuses of labour rights. In the case of Burma (Myanmar), the Commission and the GSP Committee decided to investigate practices of forced labour. The Commission held hearings with

---

to consultations in the GSP Committee with Member State representatives and chaired by a Commission representative. Based on this, the Commission could decide to initiate an investigation. During this investigation the Commission may hear the interested parties and it may 'dispatch its own experts to establish on the spot the truth of the allegations'. If it concludes that withdrawal is necessary, it makes a submission to the Council, which decides by qualified majority voting. Brandtner, B and Rosas, A, 'Trade Preferences and Human Rights' in P Alston (ed), *The EU and Human Rights* (New York, Oxford University Press, 1999) 715.

[21] Internation Labour Organisation (ILO) Conventions No 87 and No 98 on freedom of association and the right to organise; No 138 on minimum age for employment.

[22] In case of forced labour as defined in ILO Conventions No 29 and No 105.

[23] *Cf* Waer and Driessen 'The New European Union Generalised System of Preferences' (1995) 124.

[24] 1820th Council Meeting, Draft minutes, 19–20 December 1994, Statement by the UK, Denmark, Germany, France and the Netherlands.

several parties, but the Burmese State Law and Order Restoration Council (SLORC) regime refused the entry of a European fact-finding team into the country. In 1997 the Council approved the Commission's conclusion that Burma's tariff preferences had to be withdrawn on the basis of Title III of the GSP Regulation.[25]

Another complaint against child labour in Pakistan, however, never resulted in an investigation. Some suggest that Member States feared 'retaliation and cancellation of contracts' in Pakistan.[26] The Commission advances legal arguments: at that time the social GSP clause allowed for a suspension on the basis of forced labour or prison labour, not child labour as such.[27] Some discern a distinction between child labour as an instance of forced labour and child labour as an economic contribution to the survival of their families. Others notice a new approach to improving CLS, favouring incentive to punitive measures. In contrast to the Burmese case, the Pakistani authorities were willing to cooperate and to deal with the problem of child labour.[28] Apart from substantial considerations, the Pakistan case shows that the transparency of the decision-making procedure leaves much to be desired: 'the whole procedure has been conducted not only away from public accountability, but in deep secrecy'.[29] Instead of being excluded from EU preferences, Pakistan would move up on Europe's 'preferential pyramid' through the GSP drugs incentives.

The GSP Incentive Scheme: not Just about Labour Rights

In May 1998, the Council finally approved a social incentive scheme[30] based on Commission documents in May, June and October 1997.[31] The

---

[25] Fierro, E, *The EU's Approach to Human Rights Conditionality in Practice* (The Hague/London/New York, Martinus Nijhoff Publishers, 2003) 371–74.

[26] Tsogas, G, 'Labour Standards in the Generalised Systems of Preferences of the European Union and the United States' (2000) 3 *European Journal of Industrial Relations* 6, 362.

[27] Fierro, *The EU's Approach to Human Rights Conditionality in Practice* (2003) 375–76.

[28] Dispersyn, M, 'La Dimension Sociale Dans le Système des Préférences Généralisées (SPG) de l'Union Européenne' (2001) *Revue du Droit ULB* 23, 109; Brandtner and Rosas, 'Trade Preferences and Human Rights' (1999) 717–18.

[29] Tsogas, 'Labour Standards in the Generalised Systems of Preferences of the European Union and the United States' (2000) 364.

[30] Council Regulation (EC) No 1154/98 of 25 May 1998 applying the special incentive arrangements concerning labour rights and environmental protection provided for in Articles 7 and 8 of Regulations (EC) No 1256/96 applying multiannual schemes of generalised tariff preferences in respect of certain industrial and agricultural products originating in developing countries, OJ L160, 4.6.1998, p.1–10.

[31] AE 6976 17 May 1997; Commission Report to the Council pursuant to Article 7(2) of Council Regulations Nos 3281/94 and 1256/96 on the scheme of generalized preferences—Summary of work conducted within the OECD, ILO and WTO on the link between international trade and social standards COM (1997) 260, 2.6.1997; Commission Report to the Council pursuant to Article 8(2) of Council Regulations Nos 3281/94 and 1256/96 on the

Commission proposal basically reflected the previous one in 1994: additional tariff preferences for countries that incorporate ILO Conventions Nos 87, 98 and 138 in their legislation and take effective measures to implement and control these labour rights. Developing countries requesting to benefit from this arrangement need to supply all necessary information to the Commission, which makes an inquiry into the eligibility of the country involved. The Commission can carry out on-site inspections, assisted by the country's authorities and possibly also by EU Member States. After consulting with the GSP Committee, the Commission decides whether the preferential margin will be granted.[32]

Again there is no ratification requirement: potential beneficiaries have to adopt the contents of the relevant ILO conventions. Dispersyn doubts whether the Commission has the means and expertise to make such evaluations and to carry out fact-finding missions.[33] He also observes that, once the incentive tariff has been granted, the monitoring of labour rights largely depends on Europe's confidence in and cooperation with the beneficiary country's authorities.[34]

Looking at the political debate, the most remarkable evolution is the consensus within the Council about the principle of a social clause. This reflects the growing dominance of centre-left governments within the Council and in particular the electoral victory of New Labour in the United Kingdom. Ironically, traditional sceptics of a social clause (the United Kingdom and the Netherlands) at that time favour a more generous incentive scheme, whereas advocates of this idea (Spain, Portugal, Greece) want smaller tariff reduction for countries complying with CLS.[35] The objective to promote CLS seems to be overshadowed by economic considerations, basically reflecting the familiar trade policy debate in the EU between the 'Northern liberals' and the 'Southern Club Med'.

About half a year later, the different GSP systems were merged into one single GSP regulation. The Northern Member States used this occasion to voice criticism about the incentive arrangement, arguing that 'the preferences should have been more substantial than those now adopted in order

---

scheme of generalized preferences—Summary of work conducted within the ITTO, OECD and WTO on the link between international trade and the environment, COM (1997) 260, 2.6.1997, Proposal for a Council Regulation (EC) applying the special incentive arrangements concerning labour rights and environmental protection provided for in Articles 7 and 8 of Council Regulations (EC) Nos 3281/94 and 1256/96 applying the scheme of generalized tariff preferences in respect of certain industrial and agricultural products originating in developing countries, COM (1997) 534 final, OJ C 360, 26.11.1997.

[32] Dispersyn, M, 'Régulation et Dimension Sociale Dans le Système des Préférences Généralisées (SPG) de l'Union Européenne' in C Euzéby, F Carluer et al (eds), *Mondialisation et Régulation Sociale. Tome 1* (Paris, L'Harmattan, 2003) 457.

[33] Ibid 103.

[34] Ibid.

[35] AE 7200 14–15 April 1998; AE 7207 24 April 1998.

to create real incentives for the developing countries. We wonder where the basic aim of the system can be achieved under these premises'.[36]

European importers also accused the Southern Member States of being 'primarily concerned with the frightening prospect of increased imports', rather than engaging in a coherent strategy for improving labour standards throughout the world.[37]

Another point of criticism concerns the adoption of 'double standards', viz. the differences in the sets of labour standards chosen for the incentive and the punitive regimes. Tsogas denounces that '[I]t seems that, according to this peculiar EU "carrot and stick" approach, exploiting children and organising death squads against trade unionists are less serious breaches of human rights than running forced labour camps!'.[38] He castigates the dual character of the EU system, because it goes against the universality of the ILO fundamental rights. Given that the 1998 GSP reforms coincided with the ILO Declaration on Fundamental Principles and Rights at Work, the EU could have chosen to use all eight fundamental labour conventions as a basis for both the incentive and the punitive clause. Although some Member States made suggestions for such a consistency with the ILO Declaration,[39] it took another three years before this materialised.

Thus, although the social incentive clause had been envisaged since 1994, one year elapsed between the first Commission document (May 1997) and the final Council Decision (May 1998) on the new GSP. This timing is important because, during the very same period, the EU approved other GSP regulations that have an impact on the effectiveness of the new-established social incentive clause. First, there is the graduation of Hong Kong, Singapore and South Korea from the GSP regime, implying that they no longer qualify for the labour incentive scheme.[40] Secondly, the Union enlarged its market access for products originating from LDCs since 1 January 1998.[41] This forerunner of EBA stems from a Council agreement in June 1997. It grants non-African, Caribbean and Pacific LDCs equivalent market access as their ACP counterparts under the Lomé regime. Although in principle this initiative does not affect the social incentive clause, it

---

[36] GSP Working Party, Document to Coreper/Council, 14166/1/98 REV 1, 21 December 1998.

[37] Von Schöppenthau, P, 'Social Clause: Effective Tool or Social Fig Leaf?' (1998) *European Retail Digest* 20, 44.

[38] Tsogas (n 26) 363–64.

[39] Ibid.

[40] Council Regulation (EC) No 2623/97 of 19 December 1997 applying Article 6 of Regulations (EC) No 3281/94 and (EC) No 1256/96 on multiannual generalized tariff preferences schemes in respects of certain industrial and agricultural products originating in developing countries, OJ L 354, 30.12.1997, p.9–10.

[41] Council Regulation (EC) No 602/98 of 9 March 1998 extending the coverage of Regulations (EC) No 3281/94 and No 1256/96 concerning community schemes of generalised tariff preferences for the benefit of the least-developed countries OJ L 80, 18.3.1998, p.1–16.

essentially reduces the attractiveness for LDCs to request additional trade preferences based on CLS.

A similar logic, thirdly, applies to the Latin American countries that benefit from the GSP drug arrangement. Since 1990 members of the Andean Community (Bolivia, Colombia, Ecuador, Peru and Venezuela) had benefited from a GSP arrangement that granted additional market access to countries that fight against drug trafficking and production.[42] In 1998 the EU wanted to extend this drug arrangement to members of the Central American Common Market (CACM): Costa Rica, Guatemala, Honduras, Nicaragua, El Salvador and Panama. However, the Commission proposal also suggested that the Andean Community and CACM beneficiaries of the drug arrangements would henceforth have to comply with the labour incentive arrangement as well. In other words, their (continued) benefits from the GSP tariff reduction would also depend on their compliance with the relevant CLS. Otherwise the new social incentive scheme would be almost superfluous for these Latin American countries.

This linkage between drugs and social provisions provoked considerable debate. The Colombian president of the Andean Community started a lobby campaign in the European capitals. At the instigation of Spain, Italy and the United Kingdom,[43] the Council kept the drugs and labour incentive arrangements separate, arguing that a linkage between both regimes would run counter to the incentive-based character of the GSP.[44] Former beneficiaries from the Andean Community would indeed face higher tariffs if they fail to comply with the labour requirements. The European Parliament[45] and the international trade union movement strongly criticised this decision, pointing to the assassination of nearly 1,500 trade union activists in Colombia:

> the one time there is a courageous proposal emanating from Europe, one that respects human rights and allows for real pressure on the political leaders of Latin America, it is not supported by our countries. Incomprehensible. [...] The one time the EU had an instrument for putting pressure on the oligarchies in these countries, the political debate was eclipsed. It is crushing.[46]

---

[42] Council Regulation (EEC) No 3835/90 of 20 December 1990 amending Regulations (EEC) No 3831/90, (EEC) No 3832/90 and (EEC) No 3833/90 in respect of the system of generalized tariff preferences applied to certain products originating in Bolivia, Colombia, Ecuador and Peru OJ L 370, 31.12.1990, p.126–132.

[43] AE 7348 23–24 November 1998.

[44] AE 7357 5 December 1998.

[45] Resolution on the Communication from the Commission to the Council on the trading system and internationally recognised labour standards (COM(96)0402—C4-0488/96), European Parliament, A4-0423/98, OJ C104, 13.1.1999.

[46] AE 7357 5 December 1998.

The 2001 Reform of the GSP: Limited Applications, Larger Role for the ILO

The point of departure in the subsequent 2001 reform was the unsuccessful application of the social GSP clause. Moldova became the first beneficiary of the labour incentive regime in November 2000.[47] Burma and Moldova were for a long time the only (respectively negative and positive) applications of labour arrangements in Europe's GSP scheme. In its proposal for GSP reform, the Commission admitted that 'the special incentive arrangements did not encounter the success that was hoped for at the time they were adopted'.[48]

This unsuccessfulness clearly relates to the limited number of *potential* beneficiaries. Although legally eligible for the incentive clause, many developing countries already enjoy additional access to the European market through other trade arrangements. ACP countries benefit from the relatively favourable provisions under the Lomé/Cotonou Agreements. The EBA Regulation of February 2001 basically abolished tariff duties for ACP and non-ACP LDCs. There are also the abovementioned Latin American beneficiaries of the drug arrangement.

However, also potential beneficiaries were reluctant to take up the available labour incentive arrangement. Although the Commission shortly mentions that this may be due to 'the relatively small margin of preferences available under those arrangements', it put much more emphasis on the 'extremely complicated calculation of the additional preferences that beneficiaries might get on top of the normal ones—which are already sufficiently difficult to calculate'.[49] The Commission therefore proposed some rather technical simplifications of the social incentive procedures.

Some developing countries, such as India and Pakistan, still resisted any linkage of trade relations with labour standards as a matter of principle.[50] They also criticised the Commission's authority to carry out on-site inspections of the implementation of CLS as an infringement on their national sovereignty.[51] Anyhow, apart from the incentive arrangement's complexity,

---

[47] Commission Regulation (EC) No 1649/2000 of 25 July 2000 granting the Republic of Moldova the benefit of the special incentive arrangements concerning labour rights, OJ L189, 27.7.2000, p.13.

[48] Proposal for a Council Regulation applying a scheme of generalised tariff preferences for the period 1 January 2002 to 31 December 2004, COM (2001) 293, OJ C 270E, 25.9.2001, p.24–76; Council Regulation (EC) No 2501/2001 of 10 December 2001 applying a scheme of generalised tariff preferences for the period from 1 January 2002 to 31 December 2004—Statements on a Council Regulation applying a scheme of generalised tariff preferences for the period from 1 January 2002 to 31 December 2004, OJ L346, 31.12.2001, p.1–60.

[49] Ibid.

[50] AE 7233 2–3 June 1998.

[51] Dispersyn, 'La Dimension Sociale Dans le Système des Préférences Généralisées (SPG) de l'Union Européenne' (2001) 109–10.

the additional tariff margin for developing countries turns out to be too small to entail the abandonment of their fundamental objections to the idea of a social clause.

The Commission also proposed an extension of the relevant ILO labour standards. Referring to the 1998 Declaration on Fundamental Principles and Rights at Work, the national legislation of beneficiaries of the incentive regime has to incorporate the substance of the standards laid down in *all eight* fundamental ILO Conventions. In the previous GSP regulations, only Convention Nos 87, 98 and 138 were referred to. Similarly, the withdrawal of GSP benefits will be based on 'serious and systematic violation' of ILO Convention Nos 87, 98, 29, 105, 138, 182, 100 or 111. The Council's approval of this extended legal basis was undoubtedly facilitated by the fact that it could not harm EU economic interests.

But it also illustrates the emerging European consensus about the ILO as the competent organisation to deal with CLS—even though formal ratification of the relevant ILO conventions is not required. The key reference is to the relevant conventions rather than the principles in the 1998 Declaration.[52] An even more remarkable indication of the ILO's increasing relevance is that from now on this organisation's proceedings will be taken into account during the GSP decision-making process:

> The available assessments, comments, decisions, recommendations and conclusions of the various supervisory bodies of the ILO, including in particular Article 33 procedures, should serve as the point of departure for the examination of requests for the special incentive arrangements for the protection of labour rights, as well as for the investigation as to whether temporary withdrawal is justified on the grounds of violations of ILO Conventions.[53]

The new regulation also cautiously hints to a possible future linkage of drugs preferences with labour standards. But the 2004 WTO dispute would necessitate a much more radical reorganisation of Europe's incentive regimes.

The Difference between GSP and GSP+

The 2001 reforms were not very helpful in stimulating the use of the GSP social clause. In 2004 Sri Lanka became the second beneficiary of the

[52] Alston, P, ' "Core Labour Standards" and the Transformation of the International Labour Regime' (2004) 3 *European Journal of International Law* 15, 492.
[53] Council Regulation (EC) No 2501/2001 of 10 December 2001 applying a scheme of generalised tariff preferences for the period from 1 January 2002 to 31 December 2004— Statements on a Council Regulation applying a scheme of generalised tariff preferences for the period from 1 January 2002 to 31 December 2004, OJ L 346, 31.12.2001, p.1–60.

incentive scheme[54] but there was no decision on the requests by the Ukraine, Uzbekistan, Georgia and Mongolia;[55] and the Commission initiated an investigation to alleged violations of the freedom of association in Belarus. In addition, the legality of the labour standards in Europe's GSP was contested by India before the WTO. In November 2001, the EU included Pakistan in the list of beneficiary countries of the drug arrangement. It explicitly situated this measure in the context of the events of 11 September and the international community's acknowledgement of Pakistan's serious problems. The proposal adds that Pakistan's 'campaign to eradicate the production and transit of drugs' should be supported and that Pakistan faces similar problems as the Andean Community and the CACM countries.[56] Within the Council, only Portugal voted against the resolution, arguing that Pakistan did not satisfy the criteria of the drugs arrangement and it may not be compatible with WTO law.[57]

As explained above, the decision was indeed challenged before the WTO. Although the Appellate Body's ruling did not undermine the social GSP clause as such, it suggested that Europe's attempts to promote labour standards through its GSP regulations needed to be made more objective and transparent. Therefore the EU reviewed its incentive schemes, abandoning the separate social, environmental and drugs clauses and incorporating these into a broader 'sustainable and good governance' regime.[58] To be eligible for the incentives under this 'GSP+' system, requesting countries have to 'ratify and effectively implement' several international conventions that are listed in Annex III. More specifically, it concerns all the conventions of Part A (including the eight ILO fundamental conventions, but also, for example, the Convention Against Torture) and at least seven of Part B (for example, the Kyoto Protocol, the United Nations (UN) Convention against Corruption), with a commitment to overall ratification and implementation by the end of 2008.

This time the EU took a somewhat different approach to stimulate requests for the incentive regime. In the new GSP Regulation, 14 developing countries were provisionally listed as GSP+ beneficiaries. They received GSP preferences since July 2005, but in order to continue to benefit from these ex ante incentives, they had to make an application within

---

[54] Commission Regulation (EC) No 2342/2003 of 29 December 2003 granting the Democratic Socialist Republic of Sri Lanka the benefit of the special incentive arrangements for the protection of labour rights, OJ L 346, 31.12.2003, p.34–35.

[55] Russia also applied but requested to postpone the decision in 2002. Georgia and Mongolia benefit from the GSP+ scheme from 2006 (see below).

[56] Amended Proposal for a Council Regulation applying a scheme of generalised tariff preferences for the period 1 January 2002 to 31 December 2004, COM (2001) 688, OJ C 075 E, 26.03.2002, p.51–103.

[57] General Affairs Council, Draft minutes, 10 December 2001.

[58] Council Regulation (EC) No 980/2005 of 27 June 2005 applying a scheme of generalised tariff preferences OJ L 169, 30.6.2005, p.1–43.

three months. The Commission then examined the requests, taking into account the findings of the relevant international organisations, implying that the beneficiary countries' compliance with the CLS should be monitored, making use of the findings of the relevant ILO bodies. On that basis, the Commission would confirm whether the preferences would be continued. For the 14 listed countries, not applying for the GSP+ preferences thus implied a higher tariff barrier to the EU market.

GSP+ beneficiaries henceforth have to *ratify* the eight ILO Conventions,[59] which again illustrates the ILO's growing relevance. Moreover, Europe's emphasis remains on trade incentives—although the punitive regime continues to exist in case of 'serious and systematic violations' of the ILO CLS. Pascal Lamy announced the new Regulation as a clear example of Europe's 'soft power' and as a 'step towards better global governance'.[60] However, only 'vulnerable countries' are eligible for GSP+ preferences.[61] This means that countries such as China and India no longer qualify for the incentive scheme—including its provisions about labour standards. The list of eligible countries[62] reveals that most GSP+ beneficiaries are former beneficiaries of the drugs arrangement. Since 1 January 2006, the following 15 countries have benefitted from GSP+ incentives: Bolivia, Colombia, Costa Rica, Ecuador, Georgia, Guatemala, Honduras, Sri Lanka, Republic of Moldova, Mongolia, Nicaragua, Panama, Peru, El Salvador and Venezuela. This means that *all* former drugs beneficiaries from the Andean Community and the CACM successfully switched over to the GSP+ incentives. Among non-drugs beneficiaries are the two former beneficiaries of the labour incentives (Moldova and Sri Lanka) as well as Georgia and Mongolia. All countries that provisionally (before the approval of their application) received the preferences turned out to benefit from the incentive scheme.[63] It is difficult to escape the impression that the GSP+ regime basically boils down to an objectively legitimised recycling of the former drugs GSP—excluding Pakistan.

It is thus not surprising that the international labour movement[64] condemned the granting of special trade preferences 'to some of the

[59] Ibid.

[60] Lamy, P, *Financial Times* (17 January 2004).

[61] Article 9(3) of the Council Regulation (EC) No 980/2005 of 27 June 2005 applying a scheme of generalised tariff preferences, OJ L 169, 30.6.2005, pp. 1–43 defines a vulnerable country based on World Bank classifications and import figures to the EU market.

[62] Commission Decision of 21 December 2005 on the list of the beneficiary countries which qualify for the special incentive arrangement for sustainable development and good governance, provided for by Article 26(e) of Council Regulation (EC) No 980/2005 applying a scheme of generalised tariff preferences, OJ L 337, 22.12.2005, p.50.

[63] Moldova is the only country that was not listed among the provisional beneficiaries in the Council Regulation, but receives GSP+ preferences since 1 January 2006.

[64] India has also expressed some doubts as to whether the new GSP+ faithfully implemented the WTO ruling, and it made clear that it may return to this matter in the future.

world's worst violators of trade union rights'. The European Trade Union Confederation (ETUC) stated that each of the 15 beneficiaries has been criticised by the ILO.[65] On the other hand, Trade Commissioner Mandelson declared that:

> According to the ILO supervisory committees, most of the applicant countries have made substantial changes to their legal systems in order to comply fully with the rights enshrined in the ILO conventions, in particular regarding the freedom of association and the right to collective bargaining.[66]

However, recent research has indicated that several countries have received GSP+ preferences, despite being seriously criticised by the ILO for their flawed implementation of the relevant conventions.[67] Moreover, the EU GSP+ scheme has neither led to an overall improvement in labour standards implementation in those countries.

Conditionality provisions in the latest GSP amendment, of July 2008, are identical to the system sketched above.[68] Also, the list of beneficiaries remains largely unchanged.[69] However, the EU has recently started investigations against violations of the GSP+ conventions in El Salvador[70] and Sri Lanka.[71] This will be a test for the willingness of the EU to withdraw GSP+ preferences.

THE BALANCE SHEET: CORE LABOUR STANDARDS DROWNING AMONG OTHER OBJECTIVES

Have labour standards in the EU's GSP system been used as a veiled protectionist instrument? If not, could Europe's unilateral practice in this domain pave the way for a more constructive dialogue on a social clause at the multilateral trade level? The answer to both questions is negative. Although the EU has not engaged in hidden protectionism through its social

---

[65] European Trade Union Confederation (ETUC) (Press Release, 21 December 2005).

[66] European Parliament, H-1052/05, 15 December 2005.

[67] Orbie, J and Tortell, L (2009) 'The New GSP-Plus Beneficiaries: Ticking the Box or Truly Consistent with ILO Findings?', European Foreign Affairs Review, 3 (forthcoming).

[68] Council Regulation (EC) No 732/2008 of 22 July 2008 applying a scheme of generalised tariff preferences for the period from 1 January 2009 to 31 December 2011 and amending Regulations (EC) No 552/97, (EC) No 1933/2006 and Commission Regulations (EC) No 1100/2006 and (EC) No 964/2007 OJ L 211, 6.8.2008, p.1–39.

[69] Panama and Moldova have disappeared but not for political reasons, while Paraguay, Armenia and Azerbaijan have been added.

[70] Commission Decision of 31 March 2008 providing for the initiation of an investigation pursuant to Article 18(2) of Council Regulation (EC) No 980/2005 with respect to the protection of the freedom of association and the right to organise in El Salvador OJ L 108, 18.4.2008, p.29.

[71] Commission Decision of 14 October 2008 providing for the initiation of an investigation pursuant to Article 18(2) of Council Regulation (EC) No 980/2005 with respect to the effective implementation of certain human rights conventions in Sri Lanka OJ L 277, 18.10.2008, p.34.

GSP clauses, the process-tracing analysis reveals that three crucial criteria for a legitimate application of a social clause (objectivity and transparency, consistency with the ILO, and generosity in tariff reductions) have only partly been met.

To be sure, the ILO has become increasingly important in the EU's GSP[72]—basically reflecting Europe's broader attitude towards a social clause since 2001. Whereas the decision-making procedures in the 1994 and 1998 regulations made no reference to the ILO, from 2001 onwards the Union declares its intention to use the available ILO assessments, comments, decisions, recommendations and conclusions. At the same time the legal basis of the incentive and punitive clauses was extended, removing the implicit hierarchy among 'fundamental' labour standards and embedding the social GSP regime into the international consensus about the eight ILO CLS. The GSP+ Regulation further upgrades the relevance of the ILO CLS: beneficiaries have to effectively implement *and* also ratify the relevant conventions.

However, this evolution was partly prompted by external events: the WTO case following Pakistan's doubtful inclusion in the GSP drugs arrangement. In addition, the granting of GSP+ incentives to a number of Latin American countries has been found conflicting with ILO evaluations. Notwithstanding increased emphasis on ILO consistency in the GSP+ Regulation, the 'special incentive arrangement for sustainable development and good governance' has not amounted to much more than a recycling of the previous GSP drugs preferences—plus Georgia, Mongolia, Sri Lanka and Moldova, and minus Pakistan. Also, the most recent GSP amendment and the newest list of GSP+ beneficiaries confirms this conclusion.

In addition, the intra-European skirmishing around the application of the sanction clause to Belarus has put the legitimacy of the social GSP clause and the alleged consistency with the ILO into perspective. In 2005 the Commission concluded that ILO Convention Nos 87 and 98 were seriously and systematically violated.[73] Since Belarus showed no commitment to improve this situation in the following months—which was confirmed by strong criticism from the ILO—the Commission proposed the withdrawal of GSP preferences. However, contrary to expectations, the Council did not give its approval instantly. The official reason for the delay that the complaint brought before the ILO would be resolved after meeting the Belarus deputy prime minister, barely hides the fact that the rejection of

---

[72] *Cf* Clapham, A and Martignoni, JB, 'Are We There Yet? In Search of a Coherent EU Strategy on Labour Rights and External Trade' in VA Leary and D Warner (eds), *Social Issues, Globalisation and International Institutions* (Leiden, Martinus Nijhoff Publishers, 2006) 286.

[73] Commission Decision of 17 August 2005 on the monitoring and evaluation of the labour rights situation in Belarus for temporary withdrawal of trade preferences OJ L 213, 18.8.2005, p.16.

the mini-sanctions against Belarus was linked with other EU trade dossiers such as anti-dumping measures against Chinese shoes.[74] At the end of 2006, the Council of Ministers finally agreed on trade sanctions, which have been implemented since 21 July 2007.[75]

Ambiguous decision-making on granting and withdrawing GSP labour preferences weakens the legitimacy of the system. But this does not necessarily imply that the social GSP clause has served as a protectionist tool. On the contrary, in line with general findings on Europe's international role,[76] EU discourse and policy practice has increasingly emphasised the carrot instead of the stick. Although in 1995 a punitive social clause was established, whereas the possible introduction of labour incentives was postponed, Europe has 'moved from a "carrot and stick" to a "more carrots" approach' since 1998.[77] The EU propagated the social incentive scheme as a model for the multilateral trading system.[78] Up to today the punitive clause has only been used with regard to Burma and Belarus, where there is a wide international consensus that trade sanctions are legitimate, and reflected in an unambiguous statement by ILO bodies that a serious breach has occurred persistently.[79]

It is thus safe to conclude that the social GSP clause has not been a protectionist wolf in social clothing. It is not the protectionist use of GSP labour provisions that provoked political debate, but rather the *absence* of trade measures against trading partners such as Pakistan, China, Colombia and Belarus. One could cynically conclude that the EU missed an opportunity to legitimately engage in protectionist behaviour vis-à-vis relatively competitive developing countries in Latin America and Asia.

The more fundamental issue is that since the 1990s, the EU has relatively generously granted trade preferences albeit in pursuit of other foreign policy objectives than the promotion of CLS. What is more, these other initiatives have basically undermined the relevance of a social GSP clause. Although the preferential scope of its GSP is relatively limited, Europe has extensively used its available margin to achieve a number of foreign policy and trade-related

---

[74] Rettman, A, 2006, 'Belarus Sanctions Farce Sheds Light on EU Machine'. In: *EUObserver*, 12.10.2006.

[75] Council Regulation (EC) No 1933/2006 of 21 December 2006 temporarily withdrawing access to the generalised tariff preferences from the Republic of Belarus OJ L 405, 30.12.2006 p.35.

[76] Smith, KE, *European Union Foreign Policy in a Changing World* (Cambridge, Polity, 2003) 199.

[77] Brandtner and Rosas (n 20) 714.

[78] Von Schöppenthau, P, 'Trade and Labour Standards: Harnessing Globalisation?' in KG Deutsch and B Speyer (eds), *The World Trade Organisation Millennium Round. Freer Trade in the Twenty-First Century* (London/New York, Routledge, 2001) 226.

[79] Orbie and Tortell (2009) 'The New GSP-Plus Beneficiaries: Ticking the Box or Truly Consistent with ILO Findings?'.

objectives, and the pursuit of fundamental labour standards has not taken priority among these goals.

Three instances substantiate this point. First, the EU elaborated a separate GSP policy vis-à-vis the LDCs. Shortly before the introduction of the social incentive clause in 1998, LDCs received more favourable access to the EU market. This was extended in 2001 when free access for (almost) all LDC imports was granted under EBA. There is no linkage between EBA eligibility and CLS. Thus, half a year before the extension of Europe's social incentive regime, it had in fact become irrelevant for 50 LDCs. Whatever the reasons for these generous LDC initiatives since 1998,[80] it is remarkable to note that there has not been a European political debate on its consequences for the social GSP clause.

While most LDCs are situated in Africa and Asia, the second point relates to trade preferences for Latin American countries. The Council's 1998 decision to unlink the drugs and labour GSP systems was extended in 2001. As in the case of LDCs, this GSP system made the labour incentive scheme essentially superfluous. As explained above, it is very questionable whether the new GSP+ system is a step forward in this respect. Moreover, the application of the new Regulation's social incentive clause is henceforth limited to 'vulnerable countries'—largely defined in terms of (limited) export to the EU market. This means that additional tariff preferences can no longer be used as a carrot to stimulate the observance of CLS with important trading partners—and potential violators of these standards—such as the United Arab Emirates, Argentina, Brazil, Chile, China, Egypt, Indonesia, India, Morocco, Mexico, the Philippines, Pakistan, Russia, Saudi Arabia, South Africa, Thailand, Ukraine, Uruguay and Uzbekistan.

Lastly, some of the potential GSP+ beneficiaries have concluded or are in the process of negotiating bilateral free trade agreements (FTAs) with the EU,[81] which then replace the GSP preferences. This brings us to the third instance: these so-called FTA+ or WTO+ agreements provide for reciprocal liberalisation in goods and agriculture, as well as regulatory issues in areas such as services, intellectual property rights, investment, competition, government procurement, and geographical indications. The question to what extent has the EU managed to integrate CLS in these new-established bilateral

---

[80] See Orbie, J, 'The Development of EBA' in G Faber and J Orbie (eds), *European Union Trade Politics and Developing Countries: Everything but Arms Unravelled* (London/New York, Routledge, 2007).

[81] For eg, the FTA+ agreements with Mexico (signed in 1997), South Africa (1999), Chile (2002), and some Southern Mediterranean countries. Similar agreements are being negotiated with Mercosur, the Gulf Cooperation Council, and with five ACP regions, the EU-Cariforum Economic Partnership Agreement already being concluded. The EU has, following the Commission's Global Europe communication of 2006, also started FTA+ negotiations with South Korea, India and ASEAN. In the context of the European Neighbourhood Policy the EU has recently also started negotiations with Ukraine.

agreements is beyond the scope of this chapter, but a cursory reading of existing FTAs learns that ILO labour standards are at best marginally referred to.

Limiting our focus to the unilateral GSP, our conclusion reads that Europe's pursuit of CLS in trade was overshadowed by a commitment to other objectives. In parallel with EU negotiations on a social GSP clause since 1995, Europe's available preferential margin has been used for *other* objectives. Geopolitical concerns (Latin America and drugs regime, including Pakistan), as well as multilateral and bilateral trade policy agendas (the instrumentality of the LDC initiatives in launching a WTO round and in reforming the ACP regime; the pursuit of reciprocal FTA+ agreements with larger developing countries; linkage between Belarus sanctions and other trade issues) took priority over the advancement of CLS through trade.

The point of this discussion is thus not so much that the EU has lacked the generosity to grant extra trade preferences—let alone that it has been protectionist—but rather that EU policy-makers showed a *selective* generosity targeted to other international goals than CLS. This inconsistency also explains why the decision-making process on the application of the GSP labour incentives and sanctions remains ambiguous. A more transparent, objective and generous commitment to CLS through the GSP system would be required in order to gain confidence with developing countries and resuscitate the issue of a social clause at the WTO level. Developing countries may now be reassured that the EU is not intent to use labour standards as a convenient barrier against their imports, but the social GSP case also illustrates Europe's limited ambition to advance CLS through trade.

This links up with the internal dimension of EU politics, where the role of the European Community in promoting CLS is also relatively modest.[82] Tonia Novitz' research shows that the capacity of the EU in the ratification,[83] coordination, implementation and control of some ILO fundamental

---

[82] For a legal analysis of competence issues between the EU, its Member States and the ILO, see also: Novitz, T, '"A Human Face" For the Union or More Cosmetic Surgery? EU Competence in Global Social Governance and Promotion of Core Labour Standards' (2002) 3 *Maastricht Journal of European and Comparative Law* 9; Cavicchioli, L, 'The Relations Between the EC and the International Labour Organisation' in E Cannizzaro (ed), *The European Union as an Actor in International Relations* (The Hague/London/New York, Kluwer Law International, 2002); Picard, L, 'L'Union Européenne et l'Action des Nations Unies dans le Domaine des Droits de l'Homme' in D Dormoy (ed), *L'Union Européenne et les Organisations Internationales* (Bruxelles, Editions Bruylant, Réseau Vitoria, 1997); and Clapham and Martignoni, 'Are We There Yet? In Search of a Coherent EU Strategy on Labour Rights and External Trade' (2006). For a political science analysis about competence issues in the EU position on a social clause, see Johnson, *European Welfare States and Supranational Governance of Social Policy* (2005) and Orbie et al, 'EU Trade Policy and a Social Clause: a Question of Competences?' (2005).

[83] One indication is the number of ratifications within the EU. By the end of the 1990s the EU-15 had ratified the eight ILO core conventions, but the picture again became incomplete with the accession of Estonia, the Czech Republic, and Latvia. Since 2007, these Member States have also ratified all fundamental conventions.

conventions (eg freedom of association) leaves much to be desired.[84] She also criticises the EU's incoherence: the 'laudable external policies' in Europe's social GSP clause do not correspond with its incomplete internal competences regarding the very same CLS.[85] This chapter adds that, after all, these external policies may not be all that laudable. From this perspective, the EU's internal and external commitments to labour standards seem to be coherent. The prioritisation of political and trade objectives over CLS basically reflects the intra-European integration project.

[84] Novitz, T, 'The European Union and International Labour Standards: the Dynamics of Dialogue between the EU and the ILO' in P Alston (ed), *Labour Rights as Human Rights* (Oxford, Oxford University Press, 2005).

[85] Alston, P, 'Labour Rights as Human Rights: The Not So Happy State of the Art' in P Alston (ed), *Labour Rights as Human Rights* (Oxford, Oxford University Press, 2005) 19; *cf* Novitz, 'The European Union and International Labour Standards' (2005) 234.

18

Decent Working Hours as a Human Right: Intersections in the Regulation of Working Time

DEIRDRE McCANN

INTRODUCTION*

ORKING LIFE ACROSS the world continues to involve working hours that are long, unpredictable or performed during periods that workers would expect to devote to their families or other elements of their lives. The failure of labour law to protect these workers persists, and is even intensifying as responses to the pressures of globalisation embrace a paradigm of flexibility that valorises unhealthy and antisocial hours.[1] It has long been apparent that labour law must be strengthened if it is to play an effective role among strategies to remedy the downside of work in the globalised economy, and efforts to identify, reinforce and reinvigorate methods of protecting workers are now intense. These endeavours, whether to highlight new or overlooked policy objectives, find ways of reinforcing existing labour laws or identify techniques to complement or replace traditional approaches, embrace an attentiveness to the potential of recognising the status of labour rights as human rights, and of recourse to the forums and techniques of human rights law.

* The author is grateful to the editors for their comments, the Oñati workshop participants, in particular Jill Murray, and Sangheon Lee for their comments on an earlier draft. This chapter is current as of 1 May 2009.

[1] On industrialised countries, see Golden, L and Figart, DM, *Working Time: International Trends, Theory and Policy Perspectives* (London, Routledge, 2000); Houesman, S and Nakamura, A (eds), *Working Time in Comparative Perspective* (Kalamazoo, Mich., WE Upjohn Institute for Employment Research, 2001); Messenger, JC (ed), *Working Time and Workers' Preferences in Industrialised Countries: Finding the Balance* (London, Routledge, 2004). For a review of working time policies and practice in developing and transition countries, see Lee, S, McCann, D and Messenger, J, *Working Time Around the World* (Geneva, International Labour Organization (ILO), 2007).

The debates about how to advance and reinforce labour law through human rights law, however, are not usually directed towards improving working conditions, despite the prominence of conditions of work in the widespread unease about the impact of globalisation. The subjects of this chapter, working time protections, have been central to labour law since its inception and can claim a secure position in human rights instruments. Yet, the interrelationship between the treatment of working time in the labour law and human rights traditions is rarely discussed in either of their literatures. This chapter attempts to take a first step towards evaluating the potential of the human rights dimension of working time regulation to come to the aid of workers in the global economy. The goal is not to present a wide-ranging review of all of the points at which labour law and human rights law intersect in the regulation of working time or to craft any definitive conclusions about the relative merits of the two regimes. Instead, given that this has been an under-examined interaction, the aim is to focus on a number of the concerns shared by labour law and human rights regimes, identify overlaps in certain of the subjects they regulate and techniques they deploy, and suggest some ways in which they can enrich and reinforce each other.

The chapter first examines the status of working time rights as human rights at the international level, including in the International Labour Organisation (ILO) standards. It next highlights the renewed interest in the role of working time rights as among a set of minimum entitlements envisaged for workers across the world, in particular by the ILO's Committee of Experts on the Application of Conventions and Recommendations (CEACR), and assesses the strength of one element of this 'social floor,' namely limits on weekly working hours. The chapter then explores key areas in which the intersections between the fields of labour law and human rights law are currently significant in the area of working time, focusing on trends in the regulation of mandatory overtime work and measures that allow individual workers to adapt their work schedules in line with their needs.

THE LIMITATION OF WORKING HOURS AS A HUMAN RIGHT

If the nature of the right to limitation of working hours is assessed solely by its presence in international human rights texts, its status is apparent. The Universal Declaration of Human Rights (UDHR) recognises that: 'Everyone has the right to rest and leisure, including reasonable limitation of working hours and periodic holidays with pay.'[2]

---

[2] Universal Declaration of Human Rights (UDHR) art 24.

The International Covenant on Economic, Social and Cultural Rights (ICESCR), while shifting the focus slightly from preserving time outside of work by configuring working time protections as elements of a right to 'just and favourable' working conditions, reiterates the protections of the UDHR and adds a right to remuneration for public holidays.[3]

Working time rights are also recognised at the regional level. The Revised European Social Charter 1996 (RevESC),[4] Charter of Fundamental Rights of the European Union (the EU Charter)[5] and Additional Protocol to the American Convention on Human Rights in the Area of Economic, Social and Cultural Rights 1988 (the Protocol of San Salvador),[6] all contain rights to daily and weekly hours limits, weekly rest periods and annual leave. Indeed, the RevESC and Protocol of San Salvador build on the international instruments, in that they are more extensive and certain of their rights are elaborated in more detail. Moreover, working time rights, in the shape of specific daily and weekly hours limits or broader entitlements to maximum hours and rest, are protected as constitutional rights in a number of countries, an approach that is particularly prominent in Latin America,[7] and in Central and Eastern Europe.[8]

There has been some debate, however, as to whether the International Labour Organisation (ILO) standards can be conceived of as protecting or advancing human rights. Indeed, the status of the working time instruments in particular is necessarily complex. The early standards on daily and weekly hours limits[9] and weekly rest[10] preceded the post-War evolution of international human rights law, rendering the nature of their protections difficult to classify. It is well known, for example, that the instrumental goal of protecting existing domestic regulations has been among the rationales for ILO standards.[11] Indeed, this objective can be seen as an element of the

---

[3] International Covenant on Economic, Social and Cultural Rights (ICESCR) art 7(d).

[4] The Revised European Social Charter 1996 (RevESC) art 2.

[5] Charter of Fundamental Rights of the European Union (the EU Charter) art 31(2).

[6] Additional Protocol to the American Convention on Human Rights in the Area of Economic, Social and Cultural Rights 1988 (the Protocol of San Salvador) art 7.

[7] Eg Argentina, Costa Rica, Cuba, El Salvador, Guatemala, Mexico, Nicaragua, Panama, Paraguay, Peru and Venezuela.

[8] Eg Bulgaria, Latvia, Lithuania, the Slovak Republic. On the constiutionalisation of social rights see Estlund, CL, 'An American Perspective on Fundamental Labour Rights' and Araki, T, 'The Impact of Fundamental Social Rights on Japanese Law' in B Hepple (ed), *Social and Labour Rights in a Global Context: International and Comparative Perspectives* (Cambridge, Cambridge University Press, 2002) 192 and 215.

[9] Hours of Work (Industry) Convention 1919 (No 1); Hours of Work (Commerce and Offices) Convention 1930 (No 30); Forty-Hour Week Convention 1935 (No 47).

[10] Weekly Rest (Industry) Convention 1921 (No 14); Weekly Rest (Commerce) Recommendation 1921 (No 18).

[11] See, eg Murray, J, *Transnational Labour Regulation: The ILO and EC Compared* (The Hague, Kluwer, 2001) 16–25 and Macklem, P, 'The Right to Bargain Collectively in International Law: Workers' Right, Human Right, International Right?' in P Alston (ed), *Labour Rights as Human Rights* (Oxford, Oxford University Press, 2005).

warning in the ILO Constitution that 'the failure of any nation to adopt humane conditions of labour is an obstacle in the way of other nations which desire to improve the conditions in their own countries'.[12]

In contrast, as Macklem has pointed out, human rights instruments are conceptualised as protecting 'universal elements of what it means to be a human being', rather than defending the domestic rights of workers against international competition.[13]

This desire to avert destructive regulatory competition, however, has been accompanied by another rationale for international standards, which is encapsulated in the Constitution's opening statement that 'universal and lasting peace can be established only if it is based upon social justice'.[14] This statement is followed in the Constitution by a recognition of the existence of unacceptable working conditions and a call for urgent improvements, including through the regulation of working hours;[15] the warning of the potential for a race-to-the-bottom in labour standards is situated after these concerns and phrased as in addition to them.[16] The social justice objective, then, can convincingly be interpreted as an 'over-arching goal' of ILO standards,[17] and is also in line with the imperative on which human rights instruments are grounded, that certain rights must be considered universal.[18] Moreover, the pursuit of social justice appears to have been the dominant goal of the earliest set of ILO standards adopted in 1919, which included the first working time instrument, the Hours of Work (Industry) Convention 1919 (No 1).[19]

The social justice objective was not prominent in the debates around the later working hours standard, the Forty-Hour Week Convention 1935 (No 47), attention having shifted during the depression towards the potential for working time reductions to create jobs. Subsequently, however, the ILO reinforced this orientation in the Declaration of Philadelphia of 1944, which

[12] ILO Constitution Preamble, third recital.
[13] Macklem, 'The Right to Bargain Collectively in International Law: Workers' Right, Human Right, International Right?' (2005) 70.
[14] ILO Constitution Preamble, first recital.
[15] Ibid Preamble, second recital.
[16] Ibid Preamble, third recital.
[17] Murray, *Transnational Labour Regulation: The ILO and EC Compared* (2001) 28. See also Leary, VA, 'The Paradox of Workers' Rights as Human Rights' in LA Compa and SF Diamond (eds), *Human Rights, Labor Rights, and International Trade* (Philadelphia, University of Pennsylvania, 1996).
[18] Murray suggests that the concept of universalism is undercut by articles in the Constitution that qualified the ILO's powers in order to protect national differences in labour conditions, Murray (n 11) 37 and 39.
[19] See, eg Murray (n 11) 42–43. The other Conventions adopted in 1919 were the Unemployment Convention 1919 (No 2); Maternity Protection Convention 1919 (No 3); Night Work (Women) Convention 1919 (No 4); Minimum Age (Industry) Convention 1919 (No 5); and Night Work of Young Persons (Industry) Convention 1919 (No 6).

stresses that labour is not a commodity[20] and reiterates the goal of social justice, envisaged to entail that all human beings 'have the right to pursue both their material well-being and their spiritual development in conditions of freedom and dignity, of economic security and equal opportunity'.[21]

The Declaration, then, embodies 'a view of the inherent value of social rights in enabling true liberty, self-fulfilment and well-being to be realised'.[22] Subsequently, the ILO has emphasised this vision of its role, and the intersections between labour rights and human rights, in various elements of its work.[23] Although the centrality of this approach has varied, in recent years it has been a prominent strand of the Organisation's 'decent work agenda',[24] which outlines a role for the ILO that is grounded in the social justice objectives of the Declaration of Philadelphia[25] and stresses the Organisation's contribution to the promotion of human rights.[26] The intersection of labour rights and human rights has also recently been stressed specifically with respect to the working time standards, as is discussed below.

It is possible, then, for the ILO's working time standards to be read as advancing human rights protections. Indeed, when viewed in this light, these conventions and recommendations can be seen as expressing as specific standards the broader working time rights enumerated in the international and regional human rights instruments.[27] Thus, rights to reasonable limitations of working hours, for example, have been embodied in the ILO regime initially as an eight-hour day and 48-hour week,[28] and later as a 40-hour week;[29] the right to weekly rest is in the form of the right to at least 24 hours to be taken in principle on the traditional or customary rest day;[30] the entitlement to a paid holiday is pinned down as a right to paid leave of at least three weeks;[31] and the call for measures to protect night

---

[20] Declaration of Philadelphia of 1944 s I(a).

[21] Declaration of Philadelphia of 1944 s II(a).

[22] Hunt, J, 'Fair and Just Working Conditions' in T Hervey and J Kenner (eds), *Economic and Social Rights Under the EU Charter of Fundamental Rights—A Legal Perspective* (Oxford, Hart Publishing, 2003) 50.

[23] Leary, 'The Paradox of Workers' Rights as Human Rights' (1996) 26.

[24] International Labour Conference (87th Session) *Decent Work*: Report of the Director-General (Geneva, International Labour Office, 1999).

[25] The primary goal of the ILO has been identified as 'promot[ing] opportunities for women and men to obtain decent and productive work, in conditions of freedom, equity, security and human dignity.' Decent Work report (n 24) 3.

[26] Decent Work report (n 24) 14.

[27] Valticos, N, 'International Labour Standards and Human Rights: Approaching the Year 2000' (1998) 137 *International Labour Review* 135.

[28] Hours of Work (Industry) Convention 1919 (No 1); Hours of Work (Commerce and Offices) Convention 1930 (No 30).

[29] Forty-Hour Week Convention 1935 (No 47).

[30] Weekly Rest (Industry) Convention 1921 (No 14); Weekly Rest (Commerce and Offices) Convention 1957 (No 106).

[31] Holidays with Pay Convention (Revised) 1970 (No 132).

workers has been responded to most recently in the elaboration of a range of protections from regular health assessments to the provision of alternative schedules for pregnant workers and new mothers and compensation that recognises the nature of night work.[32] Among their other roles, then, the ILO standards on working time can be viewed as concrete expressions of the broader prescriptions of human rights documents, embodying the spirit of these instruments and advancing their goals by translating them into more specific entitlements. It is in this capacity that they have become prominent in the debate on the role of social rights in the global economy.

GLOBALISATION AND SOCIAL RIGHTS: WORKING HOURS LIMITS IN THE 'SOCIAL FLOOR'

In recent years, the role of social rights as a set of entitlements recognised at the international level that should be reflected as a minimum in domestic legal regimes has been given new life, as part of the quest to address the mistreatment of workers in the globalised economy.[33] This development has been observed to entail a shift within international human rights law, from being conceptualised as protecting the individual against the power of the state to being relied on to police the international legal order.[34] With respect to international labour law, however, the revived role for social rights can be seen as a persistence of the dual function ascribed to the ILO standards, as both fundamental human rights and a brake on any downward spiralling of labour protections.[35] Moreover, it implies that the working time rights reflected in the international standards, and the domestic laws that embody them, are available to form part of the envisaged 'social floor' for the global economy.

A parallel trend over the last decade, however, has been towards differentiating social rights and designating some, although not those on working conditions, as 'fundamental'. Hunt has observed this dynamic in the drafting of the EU Charter, during which it was contended that working conditions and unfair dismissal rights were not sufficiently fundamental to be included.[36] With respect to the international standards, this distinction emerged with the adoption of the ILO Declaration on Fundamental Principles and Rights at Work in 1998, which designated a 'core' set of standards, on freedom of association and collective bargaining, forced

---

[32] Night Work Convention 1990 (No 171).

[33] See, eg Hepple, B, 'Introduction' in Hepple, *Social and Labour Rights in a Global Context* (2002).

[34] Macklem (n 11) 84.

[35] For an alternative account of the role of international labour law, see Langille, BA (2009) 'What is International Labor Law For?' 2009 (3) 1 *Law & Ethics of Human Rights* Article 3.

[36] Hunt, 'Fair and Just Working Conditions' (2003) 48–49.

labour, child labour, and discrimination. The response to the Declaration has been in part a promising degree of acceptance of the fundamental principles and their recognition in laws and collective agreements, codes of practice and transnational instruments.[37] The risk, as Alston and Heenan have pointed out, is that the measures required by the core standards could be perceived as the necessary elements of labour market regulation, rather than as an absolute minimum of protection;[38] and consequently that the other protections in the international labour code, including those on working time, could be viewed as peripheral.[39]

The ILO's Committee of Experts on the Application of Conventions and Recommendations (CEACR or Committee), however, has recently offered a counterweight to the signs of the fading significance of working time rights, in its General Survey on the original working hours standards, Convention Nos 1 and 30. While identifying certain elements of these instruments it considered outdated, the CEACR strongly asserted the vision of working hours limits as human rights. It referred to the rights to limitations of working hours and to rest found in the international and regional human rights instruments, citing both the UDHR and the ICESCR.[40] Further, the Committee explicitly identified a 'human rights perspective' on working time regulation, which embraces its primary rationales of preserving health and safety and ensuring adequate time for social and family life.[41] The Committee concluded that Convention Nos 1 and 30 'have set forth principles which have been widely followed and have become part of the list of the fundamental rights of human beings and their dignity'.[42]

The CEACR also captured the universality inherent in the human rights dimension of working time law, by affirming one of the rationales for internationally designated working time rights, that every worker in the global economy is entitled to limits on their working hours and minimum rest periods, 'regardless of where she or he happens to be born or to live'.[43]

---

[37] See, eg Hepple, B, 'A Race to the Top? International Investment Guidelines and Corporate Codes of Conduct' (1999) 20(3) *Comparative Labor Law and Policy Journal* 347.

[38] Alston, P and Heenan, J, 'Shrinking the International Labor Code: An Unintended Consequence of the 1998 ILO Declaration on Fundamental Principles and Rights at Work?' (2004) 36 *New York University School of Law Journal of International Law and Politics* 221. See also Hunt (n 22) 48–49.

[39] This risk may be to some degree averted by the adoption in 2008 of the Declaration on Social Justice for a Fair Globalization, which stresses the breadth of the ILO's 'strategic objectives'—employment promotion, social protection, social dialogue and tripartism, and the fundamental rights and principles—and asserts that these goals are 'interrelated, inseparable and mutually supportive'. Section IB.

[40] International Labour Office *Hours of Work: From Fixed to Flexible?*: Report of the Committee of Experts on the Application of Conventions and Recommendations (Geneva, International Labour Office, 2005) para 318. (ILO *Hours of Work*).

[41] Ibid para 317.

[42] Ibid para 319.

[43] Ibid para 317.

Given this renewed focus on working time protections, then, a compelling question is the extent to which they currently fulfil the role envisaged for them. If this question is addressed by taking into account the ratification of the international standards, the influence of the rights they contain does not appear to be substantial. The working hours conventions that prescribe an eight-hour day and 48-hour week, Nos 1 and 30,[44] have been ratified by a total of 50 Member States; and the Forty-Hour Week Convention 1935 (No 47) by only 14. However, although ratification of the international conventions is a significant element in advancing the proposed social floor, by ensuring a visible, and supervised, commitment to social rights at the international level, the related domestic measures are also significant, since it is plausible that the international instruments, and in particular the primary standards they contain, are influential even in the absence of ratification.[45]

Indeed, domestic laws offer a healthier picture of progress towards a 'social floor', at least with respect to working time rights. Taking as an example one of the most fundamental elements of working time regulation, limits on normal weekly hours, a recent review of domestic standards in more than 100 countries found almost all to have generally-applicable limits.[46] In these countries, the 40-hour week called for by Convention No 47 is the most prevalent standard: around half have a 40-hour or lower limit. Moreover, the trend has been towards reductions in hours limits since the late 1960s, including over the last decade. An examination of national-level standards, then, reveals weekly hours limits to remain vigorous in domestic law, to an extent that is perhaps surprising when compared to the ratification rates of the international standards. Indeed, there is a broad international consensus in favour of the limit found in the least-ratified standard, the 40-hour week.[47]

A consideration of domestic laws, then, lends substance to the quest for a floor of working time protections by offering evidence of their already significant presence. This suggests that a primary task for future research

---

[44] Hours of Work (Industry) Convention 1919 (No 1); Hours of Work (Commerce and Offices) Convention 1930 (No 30).

[45] The ILO's Committee of Experts on the Application of Conventions and Recommendations (CEACR) has suggested that the impact of ILO conventions should not be measured exclusively by the number of ratifications. ILO *Hours of Work* (n 40) para 327. See also Lee, S and McCann, D, 'Measuring Working Time Laws: Texts, Observance and Effective Regulation' in D Kucera and J Berg (eds), *In Defence of Labour Market Institutions: Cultivating Justice in the Developing World* (ILO and Palgrave Macmillan, 2008).

[46] This section is derived from a comparison of legislation in 102 countries in Lee, McCann and Messenger, *Working Time Around the World* (2007).

[47] This is also the CEACR's preferred limit. In the 2005 General Survey, it offered suggestions for any future international instrument on working time, including that the objective of the 40-hour week should be retained, coupled with 48 hours as a maximum limit on total hours, including overtime: para 332(g).

is to analyse in more detail the factors that contribute towards deviation from the enacted standards, in particular in developing countries, in order to gauge which policies would enable the legal protections to be more closely reflected in actual working hours.[48] It also highlights the merits of an analysis of social rights that takes into account not only the relationship between international labour standards and human rights instruments, but also the role of domestic laws. When national measures are conceptualised as enforcement mechanisms that give life to social rights in domestic legal regimes, it highlights their role and thereby the strength of many elements of the social floor, and thus avoids understating the degree of resistance at the national level for calls for these rights to be removed.[49] This kind of consideration of the interaction between different forms and levels of regulation is also useful in examining the relationship between one of the ILO's fundamental principles, the elimination of forced labour, and domestic laws on working time, which is explored in the following section.

REGULATING MANDATORY OVERTIME WORK

Despite the concerns outlined above about the partitioning of the international labour code, working time is not entirely exiled from the realm of the fundamental principles. One of the subjects of modern working time law, mandatory overtime work, has in recent years emerged as a concern under the international standards on forced labour. This form of overtime, rather than being voluntarily chosen or agreed to, is required by the employer; the worker is, explicitly or implicitly, subject to a sanction for refusing to work beyond normal hours, which can range from being assigned to a less desirable task or shift or missing out on promotion to being dismissed.[50]

The ILO's Forced Labour Convention 1930 (No 29) and Abolition of Forced Labour Convention 1957 (No 105) prohibit 'forced or compulsory labour', defined as 'all work or service which is exacted from any person under the menace of any penalty and for which the said person has not offered himself voluntarily'.[51]

The forms of forced labour addressed under these instruments have included longstanding and egregious abuses such as chattel slavery, abduction,

---

[48] See also Lee and McCann, 'Measuring Working Time Laws' (2008).

[49] Deregulatory approaches to working time laws have been particularly strongly advanced in recent years by the World Bank in its 'Doing Business' project. See, for example, World Bank, *Doing Business 2009* (Washington DC, World Bank, 2008).

[50] For a discussion of mandatory overtime in the context of an industrialized economy, see Golden, L and Jorgensen, H, 'Time After Time? Mandatory Overtime in the US Economy' (2002) 1 *Economic Policy Institute Briefing Paper*, January 2002, available at www.epinet. org/content.cfm/ accessed 30 April 2009; Golden, L and Wiens-Tuers, B, 'Mandatory Overtime Work in the United States: Who, Where, and What?' (2005) 30 *Labor Studies Journal* 1.

[51] Forced Labour Convention 1930 (No 29) art 2(1).

bonded labour and other work performed subject to threats of violence or imprisonment.[52] In 1997, however, the CEACR addressed compulsory overtime in response to a question raised by the governments of Canada and Turkey as to its compatibility with Convention No 29, pronouncing the requirement to work overtime to be compatible with the Convention 'so long as it is within the limits permitted by ... national legislation or collective agreements'.[53] The Committee has since built on this terse statement to indicate some of the circumstances in which it considers mandatory overtime to constitute forced labour.[54] This development has been particularly pronounced in its investigation of complaints from Guatemala about unpaid overtime required under threat of dismissal or through production targets that compel workers to work extra hours in order to earn the minimum wage.[55] In this context, the CEACR has concentrated on the element of compulsion:

> The Committee notes the vulnerability of workers who in theory have the choice of not working beyond normal working hours, but for whom in practice the choice is not a real one in view of their need to earn at least the minimum wage and retain employment. This then results in the performance of unpaid work or services. The Committee considers that in such cases the work or service is imposed through the exploitation of the worker's vulnerability, under the threat of a penalty, namely dismissal or remuneration below the minimum wage rate.[56]

The CEACR, then, has interpreted the penalty facet of the definition of forced labour in the ILO standards to embrace the sanctions that can be used to require overtime work. In doing so, the Committee is forging a concept of forced labour that is capable of capturing certain aspects of its evolution over recent decades. The ILO's 2005 *Global Report* on forced labour has traced the emergence of these newer forms, often found alongside the 'traditional' versions, in which the element of coercion takes the form of financial penalties.[57] It highlights widespread reports from South Asia, for

[52] See International Labour Office 'A Global Alliance Against Forced Labour. Global Report Under the Follow-up to the ILO Declaration on Fundamental Principles and Rights at Work 2005'. (Report of the Director-General International Labour Conference (93rd Session) 2005 Report I(b) (Geneva 2005) paras 32–35 (International Labour Office 'A Global Alliance').

[53] International Labour Office 'Report of the Committee of Experts on the Application of Conventions and Recommendations' International Labour Conference (86th Session) 1998 Report III (Part 1A), (Geneva, International Labour Office, 1998) para 107.

[54] See generally International Labour Office *Eradication of Forced Labour*: Report of the Committee of Experts on the Application of Conventions and Recommendations (Geneva, International Labour Office, 2007) paras 132–34, 206.

[55] Individual Observations concerning Convention No 29, Forced Labour, 1930 Guatemala (ratification: 1989) Published: 2004, 2005, 2008. See also Individual Observations concerning Forced Labour Convention 1930 (No 29) El Salvador (ratification: 1995) Published: 2004, 2006, available from www.ilo.org/ilolex/english/iloquery.htm accessed 30 April 2009.

[56] Individual Observation concerning Convention No 29, Forced Labour, 1930 Guatemala (ratification: 1989) 2004.

[57] International Labour Office 'A Global Alliance' paras 14 and 32–33.

example, of assembly plants in export processing zones where overtime is often required without additional pay under the threat of penalties that include dismissal.[58] Similar concerns have also emerged in the *maquiladora* assembly industries in the export processing zones of Central American and Andean countries;[59] in Africa;[60] and among migrant workers in Russia.[61]

Besides strengthening the reach of the international standards, these developments also highlight an intersection between the regulation of forced labour and working time, namely their shared concern about mandatory overtime. For by recognising certain forms of compulsory overtime as illegitimate, the CEACR has tapped into a broader unease about its nature and import. In developing countries, as has been seen, the dominant concern is about workers who are compelled to work very long hours, often without additional pay, to avoid losing the jobs that keep them out of poverty. In industrialised countries, the concerns tend to be those long associated with all forms of overtime and long hours work: their impact on worker health and safety;[62] public safety;[63] and productivity.[64] Mandatory overtime is also relevant to the more recent policy objective of ensuring that working time arrangements do not inhibit workers in combining their jobs with other elements of their lives. Indeed, it can be expected to have a particularly deleterious impact on the reconciliation of paid labour and life beyond work, given that the workers involved, by definition, do not choose these hours, and therefore might face difficulties in synchronising them with the myriad of other responsibilities in their lives.

For parents in particular, being required to work beyond normal hours, especially at short notice, can involve considerable disruption. They may, for example, have to arrange for alternative childcare or transport for their children, with the related inconvenience and financial outlay. It is not surprising, then, that workers whose overtime is mandatory have been found to be more likely to report that work interferes with their family lives.[65] The impact of compulsory overtime, however, is not confined to workers with family responsibilities. It can restrict the involvement of all workers

---

[58] Ibid para 136.

[59] Ibid para 178.

[60] Ibid para 216, citing the *Séminaire Sur les Normes Internationales du Travail et les Procédures Constitutionnelles* (29 November–1 December 2004).

[61] Ibid 230, citing Tyuryukanova, E, 'Forced Labour in the Russian Federation Today' (ILO Moscow and SAP-FL, unpublished, 2004).

[62] See Spurgeon, A, *Working Time: Its Impact on Safety and Health* (Geneva, International Labour Office and Korea Occupational Safety and Health Agency, 2003).

[63] See, eg Schuster, M, 'The Impact of Overtime Work on Industrial Accident Rates' (1985) 24 *Industrial Relations* 234.

[64] Eg Shephard, E and Clifton, T, 'Are Longer Hours Reducing Productivity in Manufacturing?' (2000) 21 *International Journal of Manpower* 540.

[65] Golden and Wiens-Tuers, 'Mandatory Overtime Work in the United States: Who, Where, and What?' (2005) 9 and Table 7.

in any social, community or educational activity that needs to be planned in advance.[66] Moreover, the available evidence, from the United States, is that the incidence of mandatory overtime work is increasing. A recent analysis of data from the 2002 General Social Survey found it to be noticeably more prevalent than 25 years ago, involving slightly over a quarter of those surveyed.[67]

In response to these kinds of concerns, mandatory overtime has begun to be addressed by working time laws.[68] In addition to the traditional techniques of overtime regulation (criteria for overtime work, minimum wage premia, hours limits), in some jurisdictions, legislation and collective agreements offer individual workers a right to refuse to work overtime hours. The strongest version of this right, exemplified by the Finnish working time legislation, entitles all workers to refuse any work beyond their normal hours.[69] In other regimes, rights to refuse to work overtime are available to specific groups, such as pregnant women, young workers or individuals who are experiencing health problems.[70] Also prominent among these measures are laws that require consent for overtime hours by workers who have caring obligations.[71] Moreover, in some jurisdictions these kinds of refusal rights represent the only bulwark against long hours. This is the case in the United States, where, although the absence of maximum hours limits means that unlimited overtime can be required subject only to the payment of a wage premium,[72] rights to refuse at least some overtime hours have been enacted in a number of states over the last 15 years, primarily due to the efforts of nurses' associations and unions.[73]

The treatment of mandatory overtime, then, highlights the intersections between the regulatory fields of working time and forced labour, most

---

[66] Ibid 4.

[67] Ibid 9–10 and Table 7. The GSS survey question is 'When you work overtime, is it mandatory (required by your employer)?' About 26% of those surveyed faced the prospect of mandatory overtime, including about 28% of full-time workers.

[68] See further McCann, D, 'Temporal Autonomy and the Protective Individualisation of Working-Time Law: The Case of Overtime Work' (2007) 17(3) *Labour and Industry* 29.

[69] *Työaikalaki* No 605/1996 (Working Hours Act) s 18.

[70] These kinds of rights recall the suggestion in ILO's Workers with Family Recommendation 1981 (No 165) that consideration be taken in arranging overtime by young, pregnant, breast-feeding and disabled workers (para 18).

[71] These include the Estonian Working and Rest Time Act, with respect to workers who care for children under 12 years of age, disabled children or invalids (§ 8(2)); and the Swiss *Loi sur le travail*, which requires consent from workers responsible for children until the age of 15 (art 36(2)).

[72] Under the federal legislation, the overtime premium is 50% of the ordinary wage. Fair Labor Standards Act of 1938, 19 USC §§ 207(a)(1) (2000).

[73] These include California, Connecticut, Maine, Maryland and West Virginia. These refusal rights are confined to the health sector, except in Maine, where the first universally applicable mandatory overtime law in the US permits all workers to refuse to work more than 80 hours of overtime in any two-week period (26 MRSA § 603). Lung, S, 'Overwork and Overtime' (2005) 39 *Indiana Law Review* 51.

obviously in that they share an understanding of this form of overtime as potentially abusive and worthy of regulation. This may raise a degree of concern, to the extent that the application of forced labour standards to mandatory overtime could be considered a dilution of the concept of forced labour, by extending it to work situations insufficiently coercive to compare to the problems traditionally captured by the human rights instruments.[74] Within the field of labour law, however, it has the distinct advantage of tying working time protections to another right widely viewed as more central to the pantheon of human rights and designated as fundamental within the ILO regime, thus reinforcing the national and international standards on long hours and overtime by bringing the weight of the forced labour regime behind them. This discussion has also highlighted, however, the potential of working time laws alone creatively to respond to evolving concerns about working life, in this case through rights to refuse to work beyond normal hours, which are intended to ensure that overtime is voluntary and thus to sidestep the problems that can arise when it is required. Moreover, these rights draw on a newly prominent theme in working time regulation, the notion that individual workers should be entitled to a degree of choice over their working hours, which is being pursued from a number of directions and is the subject of the following section.

RIGHTS TO INFLUENCE WORKING HOURS: A CONVERGENCE OF REGULATORY TECHNIQUES

A further intersection between human rights and working time regimes is that both can be a source of rights for individual workers to influence the scheduling of their working hours. In contrast to the concerns about mandatory overtime discussed above, however, it has been in legal fields more commonly classified as part of human rights law that the notion that individuals should be able to change their work schedules first found legal expression. It is well-known that sex discrimination laws have been interpreted to permit mothers to change their working hours, primarily to enable them to work on a part-time basis. This development has been highly visible in UK sex discrimination law.[75]

---

[74] For a discussion of the interpretation of forced labour under the International Covenant on Civil and Political Rights, see chapter 11.

[75] For a discussion of the development of the right to adjust working hours under sex discrimination law in the UK, see Conaghan, J, 'The Family-Friendly Workplace in Labour Law Discourse: Some Reflections on *London Underground Ltd v Edwards*' in H Collins, P Davies and R Rideout (eds), *Legal Regulation of the Employment Relation* (London, Kluwer Law International, 2000).

Less often recognised in the labour law literature, however, are the intersections between working time measures on individual choice and human rights laws that protect freedom of religion or prohibit discrimination on religious grounds. In a number of jurisdictions, workers have resorted to these human rights measures, with varying degrees of success, to argue that they are entitled to time-off to take part in religious services or to ensure that their weekly rest or leave periods coincide with the holy days recognised by their religious traditions. These kinds of arguments have been made under article 9 of the European Convention for the Protection of Human Rights and Fundamental Freedoms (ECHR), for example, which embodies a right to freedom of religion, including to 'manifest [the] religion or belief, in worship, teaching, practice or observance'.[76] In other regimes, claims have been more likely to emerge under laws that prohibit workplace discrimination on religious grounds, as has been the case in Canada under human rights legislation.[77] Irrespective of their genre, however, the contention is that these rights encompass an obligation on employers to accommodate religious observance by permitting work schedules to be adapted, which can be achieved in a number of ways, ranging from permitting reductions in lunch breaks in exchange for early departures, to arranging flexitime, shift swaps or lateral transfers.[78]

These developments in human rights regimes have been more recently paralleled by an evolving concern within working time law that individual workers should be able to influence their working time arrangements. The outcome, particularly over the last decade, has been the introduction in both collective agreements and legislation of entitlements for individuals to change their working hours.[79] A number of these measures embody a negative approach, in that they contain rights to refuse certain working time arrangements such as overtime, night work or work on weekly rest days. Others offer positive rights to influence work schedules more substantially including, most prominently, in the shape of entitlements that are available to parents. Parental leave schemes, for example, can grant rights to change working hours by permitting the leave to be taken in the form of reduced hours. In some countries, these entitlements are available over much longer periods. In Sweden, parents have a right to work part-time until their

---

[76] *Ahmad v the United Kingdom* (App no 8160/78) 22 Eur. Comm'n H.R. Dec. & Rep. 27 (1981); *Konttinen v Finland* (App no 249/49/94) (3 December 1996); *Stedman v UK* (App no 29107/95) 89-A Eur. Comm'n H.R. Dec. & Rep. 104, 107–8 (1997)).

[77] *Ontario Human Rights Commission v Simpsons-Sears* [1985] 2 SCR 536; *Alberta Human Rights Commission v Central Alberta Dairy Pool* [1990] 2 SCR 489.

[78] These are among the suggestions offered by the US Equal Employment Opportunity Commission, 29 CFR 1605 (1980).

[79] For more details on these measures, see Lee and McCann (n 45). See also Collins, H, 'The Right to Flexibility' in J Conaghan and K Rittich (eds), *Labour Law, Work, and Family: Critical and Comparative Perspectives* (Oxford, Oxford University Press, 2005).

children are eight years old;[80] and a right to request 'flexible working', which encompasses both reduced hours and working from home, has been available in the United Kingdom since 2003 and now extends to parents of children under 16 and carers of adults.[81]

This trend towards legislated rights to working time adjustments has culminated in the enactment of laws that extend not only to specified groups, but to all workers. One version entitles full-timers to priority in applying for part-time vacancies in their employers' firms, and vice versa; others offer workers the right to alter their hours while remaining in their current posts. These latter measures were pioneered in Dutch collective agreements and introduced in legislation in the Netherlands in 2000[82] and in Germany the following year.[83] More recently, this shift towards facilitating forms of working time flexibility primarily intended to benefit employees has been recognised and encouraged by the ILO's CEACR. In its 2005 General Survey, the Commission identified certain factors that could be taken into account in any revised instrument on working time, including permitting individual workers to exercise a degree of choice over their working hours.[84]

These rights to adjust working hours, then, mirror those offered under freedom of religion and discrimination laws, to the extent that both require adjustments in working hours. The working time laws are more direct, however, in that their primary purpose is to enable employees to alter their schedules. They thereby sidestep any question of whether such accommodation is required, which can arise under religious rights and has been highlighted by the failure to have working hours adjustments recognised under the ECHR. The European Commission on Human Rights rebuffed the argument that article 9 protects workers dismissed for refusing to work in schedules that conflict with their religious beliefs, citing the freedom of these individuals to resign from their jobs, an act characterised in its decision in *Konttinen v Finland* as the 'ultimate guarantee' of the right to freedom of religion.[85]

When this initial hurdle is overcome, however, a number of similarities emerge between claims for hours adjustments that are framed as religious rights and those brought under working time laws. Most obviously, the central question in both is the extent to which employers should be required to accommodate workers' preferences. The legislative formulae that circumscribe this obligation vary, but in both kinds of regimes tend to take the

---

[80] *Föräldraledighetslag* (Parental Leave Act) s 7.
[81] Employment Rights Act 1996 pt VIIIA.
[82] *Wet op de aanpassing van de arbeidsduur* (Act on the Adaptation of Working Time).
[83] *Gesetz über Teilzeitarbeit und befristete Arbeitsverträge* (Act on Part-Time Work and Fixed Term Contracts).
[84] ILO *Hours of Work* (n 40) paras 327 and 332(i).
[85] *Konttinen* (App no 249/49/94) (3 December 1996).

form of a broadly-worded statement of what is expected of the employer and an indication of the limits of this requirement. Thus, under human rights legislation in both the United States and Canada, reasonable accommodation of employees' religious beliefs is required, provided it would not result in 'undue hardship' for the employer.[86] Similarly, most of the working time laws that provide for rights to adjust working hours mandate that employers must grant workers' requests for changes in their working hours, subject to a right to refuse on grounds identified in the legislation. One of the most strongly worded, for example, is the Dutch Act on the Adaptation of Working Time, which permits only 'serious business reasons' to trump requests to adapt working hours.[87]

Decisions under both regimes, then, hinge on how these obligations are interpreted in specific cases, and the ways in which the interests of employers and employees are balanced in this endeavour. Although the courts are guided by the legislative texts, beyond these broad parameters the success of both kinds of claim depends to a substantial extent on whether courts are prepared carefully to scrutinise and evaluate the reasons offered by employers for persevering with the current schedule; and whether they view these arrangements as inherent in the job, or recognise that there may be alternatives. Given these similarities, the human rights and working time instruments and jurisprudence have the potential to inform each other, and the more highly developed working time laws are available as a model for future freedom of religion and anti-discrimination measures and to aid in the interpretation of the existing ones. In some jurisdictions, working time laws can also be accessed directly to advance religious rights, where workers are able to have recourse to universal entitlements to secure time for religious observance.

Moreover, working time and human rights laws on accommodation and the approach they represent may also share a common future, in that they are likely to become increasingly significant in the context of current global economic trends. Among the developments associated with the globalising economy is that many employers are responding to increased competitive pressures by changing the organisation of working time, accompanied by pressures to establish a regulatory framework that permits work schedules to extend across all seven days of the week. These developments are generating tension in a number of the vast majority of jurisdictions in which a communal weekly rest period is designated by law and rest day work

---

[86] This terminology is drawn from the US Civil Rights Act of 1964, Title VII (US) 42 USC § 2000e(j) (1994). A similar standard was adopted by the Supreme Court of Canada in *Simpsons-Sears* [1985] 2 SCR 536.

[87] Dutch Act on the Adaptation of Working Time art 2, ss 4 and 5, translation by SD Burri, HC Opitz and AG Veldman, 'Work-Family Policies on Working Time in Practice. A Comparison of Dutch and German Case Law on Working-Time Adjustment' (2003) 19 *International Journal of Comparative Law and Industrial Relations* 321, 322.

reserved for a limited number of sectors or occupations (certain industrial facilities, hospitals, the emergency services, tourism etc.).[88] In recent years, for example, the liberalisation of restrictions on rest day work has been the subject of controversy in countries as diverse as Chile, Hungary and Jamaica.[89]

So far, the most prominent claims under religious rights have been initiated by workers whose holy days diverge from the customary or legally mandated rests days and public holidays. A prominent case under the ECHR, for example, involved a Muslim worker in the United Kingdom who had requested time-off to attend his mosque on Fridays;[90] and the claims that have reached the Supreme Courts of both the United States and Canada were brought by members of the Seventh-Day Adventist Church and the World Wide Church of God seeking weekly rest on Saturdays or leave on their religious holidays.[91] However, clashes between workers' holy days and their work schedules are not confined to these groups, and, given the logic of the trends outlined above, may arise more frequently among workers whose holy days coincide with the established or customary rest day. Indeed, a recent case before the UK Court of Appeal may prove to be a bellwether for future developments. In *Copsey v WWB Devon Clays Ltd*,[92] a worker who objected to being required to work on a Sunday and was subsequently fired brought a claim that included an alleged breach of article 9 of the ECHR.[93] Most significantly for present purposes, his predicament was precipitated by the introduction of a shift pattern that extended the operating hours of his employer's firm by substituting a Monday to Friday shift pattern with a seven-day schedule. As this case suggests, rights to influence working hours may become an increasingly visible element of the regulatory landscape in countries in which they represent one of the few available defences against being required to work on a customary rest day.

---

[88] See also Lee, McCann and Messenger (n 1).

[89] Ibid.

[90] *Ahmad v the United Kingdom* (App no 8160/78) 22 Eur. Comm'n H.R. Dec. & Rep. 27 (1981).

[91] *Trans World Airlines Inc v Hardison* 432 US 63 (1977) and *Ansonia Board of Education v Philbrook* 479 US 60 (1986) (US); *Simpsons-Sears* [1985] 2 SCR 536 and *Alberta Dairy Pool* [1990] 2 SCR 489. The application before the European Commission on Human Rights in *Konttinen* (App no 249/49/94) (3 December 1996) was also brought by a member of the Seventh-Day Adventist Church.

[92] *Copsey v WWB Devon Clays Ltd* [2005] IRLR 811.

[93] Such claims can now also be brought under the UK religious discrimination legislation, the Employment Equality (Religion or Belief) Regulations 2003 and a number of others have been successful: see *Williams-Drabble v Pathway Care Solutions Ltd* [2005] ET/2601718/04; *Edge v Visual Security Services Ltd* [2006] ET/1301365/06; *Estorninho v Zoran Jokic t/a Zorans Delicatessen* [2006] ET/2600981/06.

CONCLUSION

The above discussion has sought to contribute to the ongoing evaluation of the potential of the human rights tradition to strengthen labour law by examining the interaction between these legal spheres with respect to one set of rights, those that entitle workers to decent working hours. By confining the analysis to this element of labour law, the objective has been to elicit more detail than is so far available on the interaction of the discourses and techniques of labour law and human rights law in this field. Moreover, this detail has been drawn from a subject, working time law, which is situated beyond what has come to be designated as labour law's 'core' and therefore concerns rights that tend to be wallflowers in the debates about the relevance of human rights approaches. This analysis has revealed a substantial degree of overlap between the fields of human rights and labour law in the regulation of working hours, and made it possible tentatively to suggest a number of benefits for working time law, and perhaps by extension for labour law as a whole, from engaging more strongly with its human rights dimension. It is also possible to suggest certain lessons that human rights law can derive from the techniques and approaches of labour law and express some reservations about its contribution towards ensuring the viability of labour law in its current state of siege.

The faith invested by the ILO's CEACR in the status of working time protections as human rights reflects an intensification of this vision of labour rights in labour law discourse more generally, albeit in the shape of a relatively rare foray into the field of working time. There would be cause for concern were this approach entirely to displace equally compelling accounts of the role of working time laws, including those that stress their contribution to constructing economies that generate quality jobs. However, it can clearly be of benefit to working time law, as to other labour law entitlements, to recall the compelling narrative offered by the human rights tradition, particularly when asserting the fundamentality of working time standards in the face of calls for them to be dismantled; an avenue that is not offered by discourses preoccupied with instrumental goals for labour regulation. Moreover, viewing working conditions rights, including those on working hours, through a human rights prism may have an additional potential, to avert, at least to some degree, the risk of marginalisation threatened by too strong a preoccupation with core rights.

The intersection of the fields of forced labour and working time found in their parallel initiatives to address mandatory overtime also suggests the value of harnessing the rhetorical force of human rights discourse to working time protections. The recourse to the forced labour standards to backstop working hours limits is valuable, in part, simply because it serves to expose one of the most severe and widespread abuses in the global economy, of workers who are compelled to work hours that can destroy their health and undermine the familial and social bonds that shape their lives. The recognition that mandatory overtime can constitute a form of forced labour, as well as offering this problem a more visible platform than available through working time law alone, also embodies a technical advance. It ushers in a joint approach whereby working time and forced labour instruments operate on the same problem, in this case by prohibiting long hours in domestic law while addressing at the international level the flouting of the domestic limits through required overtime.

The case of working time also reinforces the insight that rights that are not designated as fundamental or situated in human rights regimes can be the most effective. As Estlund has noted,

> sometimes leaving the development of employee rights to lower and more local sources of legal authority yields rather ambitious and durable employee rights. Perhaps there is some trade-off between the aspiration to universality and the creativity and scope of legal rights—some tension between these two dimensions of 'fundamentality' in the nature of employee rights.[94]

This observation is drawn from the US experience, but nevertheless illuminates the present discussion simply as a reminder of the significance of domestic labour laws, including their role, among others, as the primary enforcement mechanism for many human rights. Domestic working time measures in particular are a testament to the resilience of national labour law regimes, which have sustained, so far, a widespread floor of working hours standards in the face of profound and intensifying pressures to abandon them.

Also apparent, but perhaps worth stressing, is that even where both regimes offer avenues of recourse, it is often labour law, rather than human rights law, that embodies the most sophisticated mechanisms for protecting workers' interests. As has been pointed out in other contexts, human rights forums and techniques can be less responsive to the needs of workers than their labour law equivalents. This is illustrated in the working time arena by rights to adapt working hours, which appear to hold more promise for individuals who are unable to observe the practices of their religion than rights to freedom of religion or against religious discrimination, the directness and specificity of the labour law rights being their virtues. It is also clear that it is entitlements beyond the realm of the fundamental that are the most obvious means of preventing mandatory overtime, in the shape of rights to refuse to work beyond normal hours. Indeed, the experience in addressing both of these problems suggests a need for attentiveness to the advances made by labour law, so that its preoccupations, traditions and techniques can be drawn on to refocus and strengthen human rights law.

---

[94] Estlund, 'An American Perspective on Fundamental Labour Rights' (2002).

Finally, working time law is not immune to the concern that the integration of human rights discourses into labour law could threaten to undermine the latter's collective values and institutions.[95] The emerging individual rights with respect to overtime and scheduling can be seen as informed by one element of human rights discourse, the conviction that individuals, as autonomous beings, are entitled to exercise choice in shaping their lives; in this case, by transferring a degree of control over working hours to individual workers.[96] These laws are of value where 'collective' protections applicable in the same way to all workers, such as limits on overtime work or communal weekly rest days, do not adequately respond to individual needs. Caution should be exercised, however, as has been explored in more detail elsewhere, about the manner in which individual-choice rights are integrated into domestic regimes.[97] In particular, it is necessary to consider how these rights can reinforce and benefit from both laws that embody substantive protections and collective institutions, and to prevent individual rights from becoming accepted as a primary defence against long hours.

---

[95] Ibid.
[96] Lung, 'Overwork and Overtime' (2005) 83.
[97] See Lee and McCann (n 45).

19

Justice without the Rule of Law? The Challenge of Rights-Based Industrial Relations in Contemporary Cambodia

DANIEL ADLER AND MICHAEL WOOLCOCK

Our starting assumption was that a globalization of rules without a globalization of enforcement would *not* be a process of great consequence. Empirically we found this assumption to be false ...[1]

INTRODUCTION*

GLOBALISING LABOUR RULES has long been a goal of international labour movements and organisations. In contemporary developing country contexts like Cambodia, such globalisation offers the prospect of bringing labour conditions and wages into alignment with international norms: a great advance on local labour isolation under sweatshop conditions. One significant problem with globalisation from a labour rights perspective is that the key advances in terms of labour protection achieved during the twentieth century were structured around the regulatory strength of the nation state. Over the past 20 years, with the rise of systems of production, investment and trade that allow capital much greater freedom in terms of where it will locate production, the cost of

* Thanks are due to David Craig, Adrian Di Giovanni, Colin Fenwick, Stephane Guimbert, Caroline Hughes, Richard Messick, Doug Porter, Jamele Rigolini, John Ritchotte and Caroline Sage who gave vital input to the development of this chapter. Earlier (truncated) drafts of parts of this chapter appeared in *Informalizing the Formal: Labor Relations in Cambodia* (Justice for the Poor Briefing Note, Issue 3, 2007), available at: www.worldbank.org/justiceforthepoor, and *Sharing Growth: Equity and Development in Cambodia* (Phnom Penh, The World Bank, 2007). The views expressed in this chapter are those of the authors and should not be attributed to the World Bank, its executive directors or the countries they represent.
[1] Braithwaite, J and Drahos, P, *Global Business Regulation* (Cambridge, Cambridge University Press, 2000) 10.

labour becomes a major point of competition between nations, and as such there arises a continuing pressure to allow the market to determine labour conditions. This is especially the case in the developing world.

But even in today's relatively deregulated international contexts, capital and global markets are not all powerful vis-à-vis labour. Rather, in Cambodia (as elsewhere), international markets exist in a tension with local regulatory and other factors, all of which offer the prospect of what Karl Polanyi described as the 're-embedding' of labour market relations in a range of social, cultural and regulatory contexts.[2] This chapter attempts to delineate some key dimensions of the way such re-embedding might foster the emergence of labour rights. It is based theoretically on a reconsideration of the nature of contemporary local-international regulatory arrangements, and empirically on an analysis of recent Cambodian case studies.

Writing in 1944, Polanyi argued that an unregulated market 'could not exist for any length of time without annihilating the human and natural substance of its society'.[3] That society had not been 'annihilated' as part of the industrial revolution was, in Polanyi's view, due to the fact that 'markets and societies always existed in a lurching relationship and struggle which progressed unevenly as, in a two stage "double movement", markets disembedded themselves from social constraint, and were then re-embedded and thereby secured and sustained' by movements of 'enlightened reaction'.[4] Although Polanyi's thinking developed as an attempt to explain the social and economic transformations which occurred in early modern Europe, its relevance to questions of globalisation and labour rights is apparent. If the past three decades have been characterised by a process of markets breaking out from and disrupting the social norms of a previous era, the question becomes, in Polanyi's terms, whether and how a double movement can be supported with a view to 're-embedding' markets in the social, governmental and regulatory contexts which, while constraining them, also lead to their long term viability. Particularly for this chapter, important questions remain as to (1) the sorts of re-embedding which might be expected in a context like Cambodia's, and (2) which mechanisms might support such processes.

Regulatory re-embedding, especially in today's global market environment, will clearly be a complex process and one about which we should be appropriately cautious in terms of our ability to engineer. Local social and territorial governance modes, like local labour, must engage international capital and compete with other countries' labour. At the same time, however, just as there were in earlier periods of labour market regulation in, for example, Europe, there are international opportunities, both for those

---

[2] Polanyi, K, *The Great Transformation* (New York, Rinehart and Co, 1944).
[3] Ibid 3.
[4] Craig, D and Porter, D, *Development Beyond Neoliberalism?: Governance, Poverty Reduction and Political Economy* (London, Routledge, 2006) 3.

organising labour and for those seeking models and support for labour market regulation. As Ronaldo Munck notes, labour and labour practices can now be conceived of as being socially constructed and embedded along multi-scalar lines: there are local, national and international dimensions to this construction, each interpenetrating the others. As Munck describes, a focus on the interpenetration of these 'scales' of human activity can 'open up labor analysis and strategizing in ways that recognize the complexity and fluidity of the world we now live in'.[5]

John Braithwaite's socio-legal perspectives, in effect, describe the legal dimensions of these kinds of internationally uneven, multi-tiered regulatory arrangements. Braithwaite's work on the development and reach of international regulatory frameworks has thrown light on the processes by which these are embedded in local and social contexts of 'enlightened reaction', which he describes as in part 'self regulatory'. Such arrangements, he argues, can have effects even where, as in Cambodia, there is a relative absence of the formal rule of law. For example, he argues that:

> [g]lobalized rules and principles can be of consequence even if utterly detached from enforcement mechanisms. Rules or principles do not have to be incorporated into state law or international law to have significance. Modelling of self regulatory principles and the rules of private justice systems of corporations are crucial to understanding how the globalization of regulation happens.[6]

Braithwaite's regulatory new institutionalism is particularly interested in the kinds of deliberative, negotiated possibilities for regulation that emerge where what otherwise might be conflictual contexts can be turned into *institutionalised* negotiations. In relation to developing countries he claims, for example, potential for 'networked regulation', a situation whereby 'weaker actors [state or non-state] can become stronger by networking with weaker actors' and 'enrol the power of one strong actor against another'.[7] Without overemphasising either the importance of local strategy, or the limits of the kinds of self-regulatory and dialog-based frameworks Braithwaite pursues, this chapter is concerned to investigate the possibilities presented by what it calls an 'interim institutional approach' to the divide between law and politics in the emergence of labour rights.

In part 1, this chapter commences with a description of the social and economic circumstances which define labour relations in contemporary Cambodia. It then provides an overview of the legal framework for industrial relations both in terms of national and international law. In part 2, it examines two contemporary attempts to achieve enhanced labour rights, with

---

[5] Munck, R, 'Globalization, Labor and the "Polanyi Problem"' (2004) 45(3) *Labor History* 251, 258.

[6] Braithwaite and Drahos, *Global Business Regulation* (2000) 10.

[7] Braithwaite, J, 'Responsive Regulation and Developing Economies' (2006) 34(5) *World Development* 884, 892.

a view to providing an empirical basis for a discussion of how workplace justice might be advanced in the absence of the rule of law, and in part 3, it reflects on lessons emerging from these cases—in particular on the role of law in the emergence of labour rights and on the consequences of these cases for our thinking on law and development more generally.

PART I: THE COUNTRY CONTEXT

To establish the context for this discussion, it is useful to recount briefly the key debates around development in Cambodia.

Representing an early post-cold war attempt by the international community to engage in the process of peace building, Cambodia was to be a showcase for development—an example of how the new global consensus around markets and liberal democracies could be used to put a small, conflict-ridden country on the road to recovery. The extent to which this vision has been brought to fruition is the subject of significant debate. However, there is one thing that Cambo-optimists and Cambo-pessimists can agree on—the country represents an interesting test of the orthodoxies of development at the beginning of the 21st century. It is in this context that Cambodia offers us a valuable case study in the theory and practice of the struggle for labour rights in the global south.

Put schematically, Cambo-optimists see a country which has achieved a remarkable transition since the economic and social meltdown of the Khmer Rouge era (1975–79) and the debilitating civil war which ensued which was not finally brought to a close until 1998. They see a country which has entered into an unprecedented era of peace, stability and economic growth. They see Cambodia as a poor country—with a per capita Gross Domestic Product (GDP) of US $2,100 (PPP) in 2008 it was still one of the poorest countries in Asia—but as one which has achieved widespread poverty reduction. The national poverty rate fell from an estimated 47 per cent in 1993/94 to 35 per cent in 2004.[8] While acknowledging that governance is still weak, the optimists would point to the durability of the 1993 Constitution which established Cambodia as a liberal democracy with commitments to the rule of law and the key international human rights instruments. They might also point to:

— the staging of periodic national elections in 1993, 1998 and 2003 and 2008;
— progress that has been made in developing more participatory forms of governance at the local level;

[8] The World Bank, *Cambodia: Halving Poverty by 2015?* (Washington, World Bank, 2006).

— the country's accession to the World Trade Organisation (WTO); and
— the Government's ability to steadily increase tax revenue as a percentage of GDP.

Finally, they would highlight progress in terms of human development. A feared HIV/AIDS epidemic appears to have been contained, with prevalence rates declining steadily from three per cent in 1997 to 1.9 per cent in 2003, and net primary school enrolment has increased even among the poorest quintile of the population.[9] For the optimists then, Cambodia is undergoing an impressive, if gradual, post-conflict transition and will likely continue to do well out of its increased participation in a regional economy, that, despite the current downturn, in the long run is likely to be a driver of global growth.

Without necessarily contradicting any of the above data, Cambo-pessimists paint a different picture. They argue that while achieving double digit annual economic growth, the country has nonetheless under-performed in terms of poverty reduction. The reasons for this are manifold. First, the past decade has seen significant population growth. Secondly, improvements in GDP have been accompanied by a rapid increase in inequality. Accordingly, development has disproportionately favoured the wealthy. Importantly for the current study, Cambodia's growth has been driven by a few key industries, particularly tourism and garment manufacture, which have primarily created jobs in and around the urban centres. These industries have international connections of very particular kinds, which have been crucial to enabling labour rights, but which do not exist to similar extents in other industries. By way of contrast, the vast majority of Cambodia's population, particularly the poor, live in rural areas, and are dependent on agricultural production and the exploitation of common pool natural resources for livelihoods. The pessimist would point out that the past decade has seen the widespread depletion or privatisation of many of these resources in a process which has impacted particularly heavily on the poor.

This brings us to the question of governance, wider institutional arrangements and capacity. For the pessimists, this is the key problem in Cambodia. Despite the formal establishment of a range of liberal democratic institutions, the pessimists would remind us that real power continues to be exercised through entrenched patronage networks which have developed around the ruling Cambodian People's Party (CPP). Such power structures leave little room for a functional system of checks and balances on government power, and as such lend themselves to large scale corruption and rent seeking. In these circumstances, any discussion of rights becomes somewhat

[9] The World Bank, *Cambodia: Sharing Growth—Equity and Development Report 2007* (Washington, World Bank, 2007).

theoretical, as the existing elite have little interest in the emergence of independent courts or other systems of accountability which might challenge their grip on power. Middle class interests, which have been vital to the strengthening of a range of rights and rule of law agendas in other contexts are, in Cambodia, yet to emerge as a significant bloc. For the pessimists then, Cambodia's wealth is being channelled for the benefits of local elites and their associates, while existing systems of patronage and political structures are both dynamic and (at a fundamental level) durable. To the extent that benefits have flowed to the poor, this has largely been the result of a one off 'peace dividend' which is unlikely to produce sustained benefits to Cambodia's poor over the next decade.

Labour Relations in Cambodia

The size of Cambodia's workforce has grown significantly over the past 10 years, particularly in the garment and tourism sectors. In 1998 the garment industry employed 80,000 workers; by 2008 this figure had grown to over 350,000. The tourism sector has experienced similar rates of growth, with employment now estimated at 100,000 workers, up from 10,000 in 1994. Despite growth in these sectors, the lack of formal employment opportunities is without doubt the central issue in the Cambodian labour market. Having experienced a baby boom in the 1980s, more than 250,000 young Cambodians now enter the labour market each year. There is no current prospect for the absorption of these job-seekers in the formal labour market, particularly in the context of a global economic downturn. Instead they are finding work in the informal sector, primarily in agriculture, but also in trade, construction and services.[10]

The formal labour market, defined for current purposes as those enterprises registered with the labour inspectorate as required by law, represents an estimated 10 per cent of the entire workforce. Within this group of enterprises some attempts are made at compliance with the labour law. Nevertheless, enforcement is patchy and issues remain with regard to wages, working hours, leave, forced overtime and anti-union discrimination. Outside the formal labour market there is little expectation of compliance with even the most basic labour standards. Seven day working weeks are common, as are 12 to 14-hour days. Child labour is prevalent, with an estimated 27 per cent of children between the ages of 10 and 14 in the

---

[10] Mysliwiec, E, *Youth, Volunteering and Social Capital in Cambodia: Results of a Feasibility Study Conducted for a Cambodian Youth Service Program* (Phnom Penh, Youth Star, 2005); World Bank, *Cambodia at the Crossroads: Strengthening Accountability to Reduce Poverty* (Phnom Penh, The World Bank, 2004) 72.

labour force.[11] The majority of these children are engaged in agriculture. More pernicious forms of child labour are also in evidence, including minors working in dangerous conditions in brick-making, mining, and on rubber plantations, salt farms, and fish processing plants. In urban areas, children engage in a variety of income generating activities, from scavenging to shoe polishing. Children, particularly girls, are engaged in domestic and sex work. The trafficking of children for the purposes of sexual exploitation and various forms of work, including forced labour and begging, is a significant issue.[12]

Cambodia's shortcomings in terms of labour rights do not derive primarily from weaknesses in its labour or anti-trafficking laws. Rather, the problem lies with poverty, poor governance and the gap between the law in the books and the law in action. This situation is hardly unheard of in the developing world. Writing about the application of land law in Africa, Wardell describes how formal law provides only part of the picture—a state of affairs which could equally apply in Cambodia:

> ... practice often differ[s] significantly from what the law (-makers) could be held to expect. Law is not implemented or enacted unscathed by everyday negotiations or more dramatic circumvention, by manipulation or outright non-observance. Thus the meaning and affect of law in a particular place depend on the history, the social setting, the power structure, and the actual configuration of opportunities. This does not mean that laws and regulations do not have an effect. In fact they constitute significant, though not exclusive, reference points for actors and politico-legal institutions in the negotiations of access and rights—even if they are not enforced.[13]

It is in this context, as a 'significant though not exclusive' reference point around which negotiations over labour rights occur, that a brief description of Cambodia's legal framework is required.

Labour and other Law in Cambodia

The current Constitution of the Kingdom of Cambodia has been in place since 1993. It was adopted by a Constitutional Assembly at the end of the United Nations Transitional Administration for Cambodia (UNTAC), which established the Kingdom of Cambodia as a constitutional monarchy to be

---

[11] World Bank, *Cambodia at the Crossroads* (2004) 136.

[12] International Labor Affairs Bureau (ILAB), 'Foreign Labor Trends—Cambodia' (2005), available at: www.dol.gov/ILAB/media/ reports/flt.

[13] Wardell, DA and Lund, C, 'Governing Access to Forests in Northern Ghana: Micro-Politics and the Rents of Non-Enforcement' (2006) 34(11) *World Development* 1887, 1887–1906.

governed according to the principles of 'liberal democracy and pluralism' (article 1).

Of particular importance for the current study is chapter III of the Constitution (articles 31–50), titled 'Rights and Duties of Khmer Citizens'. These articles include broad-ranging protections of human rights, including a number of provisions of relevance to industrial relations.

International labour law thus has at least formal relevance to Cambodia labour contexts. The cornerstone of chapter III of the Constitution is paragraph 1 of article 31, which provides that:

> The Kingdom of Cambodia shall recognize and respect human rights as stipulated in the United Nations Charter, The Universal Declaration of Human Rights, the covenants and conventions related to human rights, women's rights and children's rights.

This provision requires the state, in all its manifestations, to respect all of the major UN human rights instruments that were in effect at the time the Constitution was adopted. Whether this provision would extend to the fundamental ILO conventions, to all of which Cambodia is now a signatory, is not clear.

To give an example relating to labour rights: article 22 (1) of the International Convention on Civil and Political Rights (ICCPR) provides that 'everyone shall have the right to freedom of association with others, including the right to form and join trade unions for the protection of his interests'. Accordingly, any act of the Cambodian state that impinges upon freedom of association could be challenged under the Constitution on the basis that it violates article 22 (1) of the ICCPR.

Other substantive rights relevant to work are included in the following articles of the Constitution:

— The right to strike and to conduct non-violent demonstrations 'within the framework of the law' (article 37).
— The right to participate actively in the political, economic, social and cultural life of the nation, regardless of sex (article 35 (1)).
— The right to choose any employment according to their ability and to the needs of the society (article 36 (1)).
— The right to receive equal pay for equal work regardless of sex (article 36 (2)).
— The right to form and to be member of trade unions (article 36 (5)).

The Constitution further prohibits discrimination against women (article 45), guarantees maternity leave (article 46 (1)), provides that the state must give 'opportunities to women, especially to those living in rural areas without adequate social support, so they can get employment (...) and have decent living conditions' (article 46(2)). With regard to children, the Constitution obliges the state to ensure that they are not employed in ways that 'affect their education and schooling, or that are detrimental to their health and welfare' (article 48 (2)).

Of course such provisions are largely unrealised at present. As with other dimensions of Cambodia's legal system, it is important to recall that the Constitution is only weakly embedded in the various institutional, political and cultural settings which might lend it stronger normative power.

Similar considerations apply to the primary piece of legislation governing employment in Cambodia—the Labour Law of 1997. This law was drafted with assistance from the International Labour Organisation (ILO) and the US union movement.[14] It is a hybrid piece of legislation which draws on a number of sources including: most significantly, Cambodia's post-colonial (and heavily French influenced) 1972 labour code; international labour standards; and the immediate post-socialist Cambodian labour code of 1992.

The 1997 law is similar to earlier Cambodian labour laws in that it provides a detailed framework for the regulation of most private sector employment relationships. The only significant category of private sector employees which is excluded from the labour law is domestic servants. Major topics covered by the law are: wages and benefits (although establishment of a minimum wage is left to the executive or through collective bargaining); working hours; leave; health and safety; discipline and dismissals. The areas in which the law contained major innovations vis-à-vis the 1992 code related to the ILO's key labour rights norms, namely:

— the establishment of a system for the resolution of labour disputes;
— the inclusion of the right for workers to form, and be members of, unions;
— the elaboration of the right to bargain collectively; and
— the protection of the right to strike (according to mandated procedures).

In examining the process whereby international standards permeated into local legislation, it is noteworthy that the passage of the 1997 labour law preceded Cambodia's ratification of the ILO's conventions on freedom of association (No 87) and collective bargaining (No 98) which occurred in 1999, but followed its ratification of the ICCPR and the *International Covenant on Economic, Social and Cultural Rights* (ICESCR) which occurred in 1992 while the country was under de facto administration by the United National Transitional Authority in Cambodia (UNTAC). Emerging from this period as a heavily donor-dependent country seeking reintegration in the international community, Cambodia's openness to the formal adoption of international human rights instruments has been a

---

[14] Bronstein, A, 'The Role of the International Labour Office in the Framing of the Labor Law' (2004–5) 26 *Comparative Labor Law and Policy Journal* 339.

hallmark of its post conflict transition. Law reform has, however, by no means automatically lead to changes in labour relations. A combination of existing practices and systems of incentives in workplaces, the labour market and the institutions of state charged with upholding and enforcing the law ensure that this is not the case. In these circumstances the practical attainment of human rights with regard to work is not a project which relates primarily to law. Rather, it is one which is the subject of political contests played out at multiple levels, both legal and non-legal.[15]

PART II: LABOUR REFORMS IN CAMBODIA

Two practical examples serve to illustrate this point. The first relates to efforts to improve working conditions in Cambodia's garment factories (the working conditions improvement project) and the second to labour dispute resolution, the establishment of the labour arbitration council and, in particular, a dispute which occurred in the hotel industry in 2003/04.

Case Study 1: Garment Factory Monitoring

Cambodia emerged as a garment exporter in the mid 1990s, not so much because of the natural advantages the country has as a site for garment manufacture but because of its cheap labour, increased political stability and the restrictions placed on major exporters, particularly China, as part of the Multi-Fibre Arrangement (MFA) which regulated international trade in textiles until its expiry in December 2004. Following a rapid expansion of the industry between 1995 and 1998, the US Government sought to impose quotas on Cambodia's textile exports.

At the same time, labour conditions in Cambodia's factories developed as a major issue. Responding both to issues of national politics and the growth of the garment sector, local unions became more active, the number of strikes increased and international labour rights groups drew attention to working conditions in Cambodia's factories.[16] This combination of factors informed the negotiation of a bilateral trade agreement between the United States and Cambodia which was concluded in January 1999. In short, the agreement imposed quotas on a range of Cambodia's garment exports. However, building on similar clauses in other bilateral trade deals driven by the United States, the agreement provided

---

[15] Cf de Sousa Santos, B and Rodríguez-Garavito, C (eds), *Law and Globalisation from Below: Towards a Cosmopolitan Legality* (Cambridge, Cambridge University Press, 2005).
[16] Hall, JA, 'Human Rights and the Garment Industry in Contemporary Cambodia' (2000) 36 *Stanford Journal of International Law* 199.

that Cambodia would support the implementation of 'a program to improve working conditions in the textile and apparel sector, *including internationally recognized core labour standards*, through the application of Cambodian labour law'.[17]

In order to provide an incentive for such improvements, the agreement also established a system whereby quotas would be increased by 14 per cent per year[18] if the United States determined that 'working conditions in the Cambodia textile and apparel sector substantially comply with such labour law and standards'. The agreement created an immediate commercial incentive for improved implementation of the labour law for all stakeholders—employers, unions, and government as a whole, which auctioned the quotas to manufacturers. Crucially, it also provided opportunities for high ranking government officials, for whom rent seeking is widely held to exist in the allocation of quotas.[19] The question remained, however, how the labour standards clause would be implemented given the absence of credible country systems for monitoring and enforcing the law.

After some negotiations, this question was answered by the establishment of an ILO Project (funded primarily by the United States)[20] which would 'operate an independent system to monitor working conditions in garment factories'.[21] Under this system, all garment exporters would be subject to inspection by the ILO and the United States would make its decisions on the quota increase based on the ILO's findings. This was a novel development in two senses: it involved the ILO in the monitoring compliance with a national labour law, and it established linkages between monitoring and quotas.

The ILO working conditions improvement project produced its first 'Synthesis Report' on working conditions in 30 garment factories in November 2001. In terms of international labour standards it found no evidence of child labour or forced labour, but did find significant limitations on freedom of association. Other findings focused on breaches of the Cambodian labour law, primarily related to wages and overtime. Later

---

[17] Cambodia Bilateral Textile Agreement (1999) available at: http://cambodia.usembassy.gov/uploads/images/M9rzdrzMKGi6Ajf0SIuJRA/uskh_texttile.pdf.For further analysis of the trade agreement see: Polaski, S, 'Cambodia Blazes a New Path to Economic Growth and Job Creation' (2004) 51 *Carnegie Papers*; Kolben, K, 'Trade, Monitoring, and the ILO: Working To Improve Conditions in Cambodia's Garment Factories' (2004) 7 *Yale Human Rights and Development Law Journal* 79, 79–107; Abrami, R, *Worker Rights and Global Trade: The US-Cambodia Bilateral Textile Trade Agreement* (Harvard Business School Case Study, 2004).

[18] A figure which was increased to 18% when the agreement was extended in 2001.

[19] Kolben, 'Trade, Monitoring, and the ILO: Working to Improve Conditions in Cambodia's Garment Factories' (2004) 86.

[20] Financial contributions from the Royal Government of Cambodia and the Garment Manufacturers Association were also received.

[21] International Labour Organisation (ILO), 'Synthesis Reports on Working Conditions in Cambodia's Garment Sector' (2001).

reports identified findings for individual enterprises and assessed whether these were remedied or not. The ILO synthesis reports, for example, indicate that progress is being made in terms of overall compliance:

> In most of the factories, significant progress has been made in improving working conditions, but obstacles still persist. A substantial number of factories continue to implement suggestions, while a small number of factories made little effort to improve.[22]

Progress in terms of international labour standards is not necessarily easy to measure. In Cambodia, however, at least in relation to the garment industry, we have a rich source of data from the ILO monitoring reports.[23] This data is supplemented by annual US State Department Human Rights Reports which include a chapter on labour rights, as well as findings from interviews with unionists and others involved in labour rights issues.

Based on the above sources, it appears that the initial years after the signing of the bilateral trade agreement (2000–2003) showed a marked improvement in terms of freedom of association. Though accurate figures are hard to ascertain, US Embassy estimates were that approximately 12 per cent of Cambodia's 150,000 to 170,000 garment workers were unionised in the year 2000.[24] This figure increased to 25 per cent, 30 per cent in 2001 and by 2005 it was estimated that 40–50 per cent of the approximately 280,000 garment and footwear workers were union members.[25] Surveys of garment workers conducted for the Asian Development Bank (ADB)[26] and the ILO/World Bank[27] suggest union membership at similar levels with the latter study, suggesting that membership is strongest among unions that are considered to be independent of the ruling CPP. The past five years have also seen fundamental improvements in terms of the registration of unions. Up until 2002 independent or opposition-aligned unions often reported difficulty in registering with the Ministry of Labour.[28] Since 2003, this issue

[22] ILO, 'Synthesis Reports on Working Conditions in Cambodia's Garment Sector' (2006) 57.

[23] Though the methodology for monitoring factories has evolved over the years, it is nevertheless possible to conduct some longitudinal analysis of data contained in the synthesis reports.

[24] Bureau of Democracy, Human Rights, and Labour, 'Cambodia 2001: Country Reports on Human Rights Practices' (4 March 2002) s 6a, available at: www.state.gov/g/drl/rls/hrrpt/2001/eap/8283.htm; 2000 estimate from 'Foreign Labor Trends—Cambodia' (2003).

[25] Bureau of Democracy, Human Rights, and Labour, 'Cambodia 2005: Country Reports on Human Rights Practices' (8 March 2006) s 6a, available at: www.state.gov/g/drl/rls/hrrpt/2005/61604.htm.

[26] Asian Development Bank (ADB) (2004).

[27] Makin, J, 'Cambodia: Women and Work in the Garment Industry' (Phnom Penh, ILO and World Bank, 2006), available atwww.popline.org/docs/1760/319262.html.

[28] Bureau of Democracy, Human Rights, and Labour, 'Cambodia 2001' (2002) s 6a; Bureau of Democracy, Human Rights, and Labor, 'Cambodia 2002: Country Reports on Human Rights Practices' (31 March 2003) s 6a, available at: www.state.gov/g/drl/rls/hrrpt/2002/18238.htm.

has been substantially addressed, and recent years have seen a proliferation of new union registrations.[29]

However, in the period since 2004 there exist indications of a resurgence of anti-union activities. 2004 was marked by the murder of two union leaders associated with the opposition-affiliated Free Trade Union and a series of major disputes around the unionisation of the hotels sector. A longitudinal analysis of the ILO synthesis reports also reveals a marked upturn in the number of factories cited for anti-union discrimination and other freedom of association issues starting in mid-2004 (see Figure 1). While the causes of any fluctuations in the enabling environment for freedom of association are no doubt complex, and the ILO's methods for collecting the data on which this analysis is based have not been fully consistent, local union activists point out that the final round of quota increases under the US Cambodia trade agreements was assessed in July 2004 and that, absent the prospect of further compliance-related increases in market access, the incentives for employers to engage positively with unions may have been reduced.

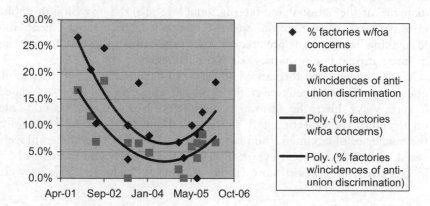

Figure 1: Overall trends in issues related to Freedom of Association and Anti-Union Discrimination[30]

---

[29] Though there are still complaints about delays in the registration process. See for example: Bureau of Democracy, Human Rights, and Labour, 'Cambodia 2005' (2006) s 6a; Bureau of Democracy, Human Rights, and Labor, 'Cambodia 2004: Country Reports on Human Rights Practices' (28 February 2005) s 6a, available at: www.state.gov/g/drl/rls/hrrpt/2004/41638.htm; Bureau of Democracy, Human Rights, and Labor, 'Cambodia 2003 Country Reports on Human Rights Practices' (25 February 2004) s 6a, available at: www.state.gov/g/drl/rls/hrrpt/2003/27766.htm.

[30] Source: Authors' calculation based on ILO reports. Data taken from ILO, *Synthesis Reports on Working Conditions in Cambodia's Garment Sector* (2001–06) vols 1–16.

While the garment sector in Cambodia remains at one level 'essentially no different from the industry in other parts of the world'[31] in terms of its fundamental outcomes and the constellations of power by which it is framed, the consensus seems to be that it has seen a significant though uneven improvement in compliance with the labour law and international labour rights standards since 2001.[32] A number of factors have influenced this outcome.

Primary among these was the role which the US–Cambodia trade agreement had in creating the immediate financial incentives necessary for the system to work. Looking behind the agreement, it is important to acknowledge the political interests which led the United States to push the labour standards clause. These included protectionist elements in the United States (including unions and apparel manufacturers) and increased consumer sensitivity of international labour standards driven by US labour rights activists, the media and union movements in the developing world.

It is also important to consider the impact of a number of changes to the conditions under which the new arrangements worked. Once operational, the ILO project promoted labour rights by relying on (a) processes of 'social dialogue' at the national and international level; (b) the provision of public information; (c) 'remediation' efforts targeted at factory management; and (d) making links to trade preferences, rather than direct recourse to national or international law or more grass roots strategies.

While improved performance had financial benefits at the industry level, one might have expected free-riding at the enterprise level. This was avoided in three ways. First, the granting of export licenses was made conditional on an enterprise subjecting itself to the ILO monitoring system.[33] Secondly, the ministries of commerce and labour set up a system whereby employers could be deprived of their export licenses if they were found to be involved in continued breaches of core labour standards.[34] Thirdly, benefits were

---

[31] Miller, D, Nuon, V, Aprill, C and Certeza, R, '"Business–as Usual?" Governing the Supply Chain in Clothing—Post MFA Phase Out. The Case of Cambodia' (GURN 2007) 22, available at: <http://library.fes.de/pdf-files/gurn/00268.pdf.

[32] Foreign Investment Advisory Service, 'Cambodia–Corporate Social Responsibility & the Apparel Sector Buyer Survey Results' (2004); Polaski, 'Cambodia Blazes a New Path to Economic Growth and Job Creation' (2004); Wells, D, 'Best Practice in the Regulation of International Labor Standards: Lessons from the U.S.—Cambodia Textile Agreement' (2006) 27 *Comparative Labor Law and Policy Journal* 357.

[33] This ensured maximum participation in the project. Nevertheless, cases of participating enterprises outsourcing production to non-participating manufacturers were reported. It is estimated that such off-site manufacturing accounts for approximately 10% of the industry.

[34] Joint Prakas 2588/00 ('on The Enforcement of the Labour Law in the Kingdom of Cambodia', July 25, 2000) set up an inter-ministerial committee to monitor the implementation of the Labour Law in the garment industry. This committee had the right to receive complaints and conduct investigations into suspected violations of the Labour Law with the result that

focussed and free riding lessened by publishing information on individual factories; in this way, the system generated pressure for improved 'corporate citizenship' both from other members of the garment manufacturing community and their brand name buyers in the United States.[35] Though it is difficult to assess the relative importance of these factors, the willingness of both the Cambodian Government and the employers to continue with the monitoring after the end of the expiry of the MFA, and thus of the quota system, suggests that the financial incentives established by the trade agreement, while instrumental in the establishment of the system, were only part of the story in terms of its long term attractiveness.

Whether monitoring and associated processes can generate the necessary incentives to drive long term improvements in terms of core labour rights, absent the direct carrot and stick effect of access to US markets, remains to be seen. The extent to which improvements in the garment sector will extend to broader labour conditions such as pay and working hours or have positive flow on effects for industrial relations generally is more questionable.

In relation to these broader issues the ILO has attracted criticism, most notably from political scientist Caroline Hughes who argues that the working conditions improvement project is typical of an approach to development that 'channels participation into atomizing problem solving' by divorcing 'the issues of pay and conditions from wider questions regarding power relations between workers, their employers, and the state' and thus undercuts 'any agenda of collective representation' of workers.[36] Put briefly, Hughes' position is that the focus of the project on compliance with existing rights and its method centred around negotiations at the national and international level was fundamentally disempowering. These factors, she argues, undermine unions' ability to mobilise workers on more fundamental issues from pay increases and reform of the labour law, to anti-corruption and greater social justice.

In support of her argument, Hughes cites increases in the minimum wage following strikes in 1997 (to US $40) and 2000 (to US $45), the disappointing trajectory of real wages since then, and the involvement of the

---

serious offenders could have their export licenses revoked. Though this sanction was never invoked, in November 2002 the Ministry of Commerce issued a warning to 28 factories ordering them to refute within 48 hours accusations that they had been involved in anti-union activities. The warning threatened to restrict these factories' access to export licenses if they could not provide an adequate explanation.

[35] A survey of major brands conducted in 2004 found that labour conditions and cost were the two most important factors in determining where garments were sourced. See Foreign Investment Advisory Service, 'Cambodia—Corporate Social Responsibility & the Apparel Sector Buyer Survey Results' (2004).

[36] Hughes, C, 'Transnational Networks, International Organizations and Political Participation in Cambodia: Human Rights, Labour Rights and Common Rights' (2007) 14(5) *Democratization* 834.

opposition-aligned Free Trade Union in the political tumult of the late 1990s as indicators of the early potential of collective action among Cambodia's garment workers.

The contrary argument would point to the rapid growth of the union movement from 25–30 per cent membership (circa 50,000 members) in 2001 to 40–50 per cent membership (circa 150,000 members) in 2006 and the continued prominence of the Free Trade Union which Hughes singles out as the union most disadvantaged by the new regime.[37] It would also point to a spike in strikes, followed by collectively bargained wage increases in 2006 and 2008 and inherent limitations on wage growth based on the Cambodian industry's productivity and position *vis-à-vis* its regional competitors.[38]

In the view of the current authors, Hughes probably overestimates both the transformative potential of Cambodia's nascent union movement in the late 1990s, as well as the negative impact of the ILO project on that potential. To a significant extent, however, we accept her argument about the tendency of international actors to promote forms of participation that are both individualising and heavily policed, and it is here that our second case study—with its focus on collective action—contributes to the discussion.

Case Study 2: Labour Dispute Resolution

Our second example, relating to labour dispute resolution, emerges from the same context as the working conditions improvement project. The initial ILO proposal to United States Department of Labor (USDOL) for work in relation to the trade agreement, entitled 'Labour Law Implementation in the Textile and Apparel Industry of Cambodia', focused more on building the capacity of national institutions of labour relations and less on direct factory monitoring.[39] This was in effect an acknowledgement that, beyond any monitoring system, effective tripartism is founded in institutions wherein potentially conflictive relations between unions, companies and government can be turned into processes of legally framed and enforced deliberation and negotiation.

---

[37] Makin, *Cambodia: Women and Work in the Garment Industry* (2006) 25.

[38] In this regard a 2005 United States Agency for International Development (USAID) study on the competitiveness of Cambodia's garment industry noted that: 'The range of products currently produced emphasizes basic construction and design, with very little added value. This forces Cambodian producers to compete directly with other low-wage countries.' Nathan Associates, 'Measuring Competitiveness and Labor Productivity in Cambodia's Garment Industry' (USAID, 2005) 31, available at: www.eicambodia.org/downloads/download. php?unumber=88.

[39] Kolben (n 17) 91–92.

A significant component of the project was to be on strengthening mechanisms that fostered 'closer cooperation in preventing disputes, settling quickly and fairly those disputes that do arise, and generally contributing to the development of an industrial relations system that encourages harmony and cooperation rather than confrontation and conflict'.[40] As the garment sector working conditions improvement project moved to focus on direct factory monitoring by the ILO, the industrial relations component of the earlier proposal was hived off in a separate labour dispute resolution project. This project was to provide technical assistance to the Ministry of Labour in consultation with the union movement and employers associations to establish and implement 'transparent, fair and expeditious dispute procedures'.[41] Activities were anticipated at the enterprise level, with the Ministry's conciliators, through the establishment of an arbitration tribunal, and in relation to the establishment of a labour court.

The working conditions improvement project described above stressed, at least in its initial phases, the need for reliable monitoring of working conditions in the garment sector. By contrast, the labour dispute resolution project was an attempt at an engagement with the question of how labour rights and equitable industrial relations could be promoted using national systems. The core problem in this respect was the lack of credible institutions for law enforcement and dispute resolution.

When the project was established in 2002 there were basically three ways to deal with labour disputes: (1) negotiated outcomes could be sought at the enterprise level, with or without recourse to industrial action; (2) the issue could be referred to the Ministry of Labour for conciliation or enforcement proceedings; or (3) rights disputes could be dealt with by the courts.

Each of these methods of dispute resolution had significant drawbacks. Systems of grievance-handling at the factory level were under-developed and the failure to manage conflict was leading to increasing levels of (often violent) industrial action. The labour inspectorate, responsible for both the conciliation of labour disputes and the enforcement of the law, suffered from all of the deficiencies of the Cambodian public service. Capacity was limited and at around US $40 per month, official wages were well below that required to support a family. In these circumstances, labour inspectors developed reliance upon informal payments from industry to support their livelihoods, and as such their credibility as neutral conciliators or enforcers of the law was heavily undermined.

---

[40] Ibid 92.
[41] As cited in Adler, D et al (eds), *The Arbitration Council and the Process for Labour Dispute Resolution in Cambodia: Law and Commentary* (Phnom Penh, Cambodia, Community Legal Education Center, 2004) 6.

The courts suffered from similar problems. The UN Special Representative for Human Rights in Cambodia summarised these as follows:

> The issue of impunity lies at the centre of problems in the administration of justice and continues to be compounded by the lack of neutrality and independence in the judicial and law enforcement systems, as well as by a low level of professionalism in those bodies. Inadequate funds are allocated to the administration of justice. The judiciary is subject to executive interference and open to corruption from interested parties. Judges have concerns about their personal security (…). Law enforcement officials often fail to enforce court orders and judgements, and sometimes act in open defiance of their terms.[42]

There existed a range of possible responses to these circumstances. A provision for a labour court existed in the labour law and a rights-based approach to industrial relations could have led to a focus on the judiciary, with the argument that equitable institutions for the enforcement of law are the *sine qua non* of rights. However, the ILO, represented by its Chief Technical Advisor (CTA) (a Dutchman who had prior experience working on legal and judicial reform in Cambodia and thus brought with him a particular *habitus*),[43] came to the conclusion that it is very difficult to get classical institutions of the rule of law (those which are both independent and have the power to make binding decisions) to work in settings where government is dominated by a strong neo-patrimonial executive.[44] Observing previous attempts at legal and judicial reform in Cambodia, the CTA anticipated that the result of pursuing the rule of law directly would be either that: (a) the process of setting up a new labour court would be stalled or (b) the new institution would be immediately captured by powerful government and private sector interests. As a result, a choice was made to focus on the establishment of a new arbitration tribunal called the Arbitration Council, a body which was also provided for in the 1997 law, but had never been operationalised.[45]

---

[42] Situation of Human Rights in Cambodia [A/58/317], Third Report of the Special Representative for Human Rights in Cambodia, Peter Leuprecht to the UN General Assembly, dated 22 August 2003, para 25. Available at cambodia.ohchr.org/download.aspx?ep_id=98.

[43] The term is used in Bourdieu's sense whereby *habitus* can be thought of as a system of lasting and transposable dispositions (ie a matrix of , perceptions, appreciations and actions) that colour 'the kinds of problems that are posed, the kinds of explanations that are offered and the kinds instruments that are employed' in any given context (Brubaker, R, 'Social Theory as Habitus' in C Calhoun et al (eds), *Bordieu: Critical Perspectives* (Chicago, University of Chicago Press, 1993) 213.

[44] *Cf* Keang, who posits that Cambodia is a 'state dominated by networks of patron-clientelism [and] sustained by corruption' and that this state of affairs fundamentally 'inhibits the development of an independent judicial system'. See Kheang, U, 'Democratization without Consolidation: The Case of Cambodia 1993–2004' (PhD Dissertation, Canberra, Australia, Australian National University, 2004) 5.

[45] Although there is no indication that is was ever operational, an Arbitration Council is also provided for in the 1972 Labour Law. The origins of the institution are not clear, though French (or ILO) influence is indicated as similar provisions exist in the Labour Code of the Cameroon.

Articles 309 to 317 of the Cambodian Labour Law set out a framework for the arbitration of collective labour disputes which cannot be resolved by conciliation. The body to conduct these arbitrations, the Arbitration Council, was established by Prakas (Ministerial Proclamation) 338 of 2002 and the first cohort of 21 arbitrators began their terms of office on 1 May 2003.[46] The Arbitration Council, then, is a tripartite body composed of members nominated by unions, employer organisations and the Government. Despite this composition, the Arbitration Council also has aspirations to independence in that its members are not considered representatives of the stakeholder groups which nominated them. Rather, they are required to approach each case on its merits. In order to enhance the independence of the newly established institution, the ILO coordinated the selection of the first cohort of arbitrators and ensured that no major stakeholder group had objections to any of the appointments.[47]

Each case which is referred to the Arbitration Council is decided by a panel of three. Of these three arbitrators, one is chosen by each of the parties to the dispute, while the third arbitrator (the chairperson of the panel) is chosen by the two arbitrators already selected by the parties. This panel is responsible for hearing the dispute, and making orders with a view to settling the dispute between the parties. In making such orders the panel is free to grant any civil remedy or relief which it deems just and fair in the circumstances.

Though arbitration is a mandatory part of the process for the resolution of collective labour disputes under Cambodian law, the parties choose whether the decisions or awards of the Arbitration Council are *binding* or *non-binding*; in over 90 per cent of cases, one or both parties will choose non-binding. An award will be enforceable immediately (a) if the parties have agreed in writing to be bound by the award or (b) if the parties are bound by a collective agreement which provides for binding arbitration. In all other cases, a party who does not wish to be bound by an award may file an opposition within eight days of receiving notification of the award, with the effect that the award is without legal effect. On the other hand, if neither party files an opposition to the award within the time permitted, the award becomes enforceable. Technically, enforcement would require one party to commence proceedings with the court, in which case the court should issue an order for the execution of the award unless there were clear reasons to set the award aside.[48] To date, however, the authors are not

[46] Prakas (Ministerial Proclamation) 38 of 2002 (Pr 38/2002).

[47] The Arbitration Council is often held up as a rare Cambodian example of a clean institution. Thus, in a speech to a national industrial relations conference, the US Ambassador to Cambodia described the Council as 'a highly functioning, [and] transparent [body] that is a model for dispute resolution ...'

[48] As provided for in Pr 38/2002 (superseded by Pr 99/2004).

aware of any cases in which this has occurred. Practically, it is not expected that enforcement would be feasible due to (a) the high costs and delays involved in court proceedings in Cambodia;[49] and (b) the susceptibility of the courts to bribery, which would most likely result in one or other party to the dispute having the case heard *de novo*.[50] Fully reasoned decisions of the Council are published both in hard copy and via the internet—a novelty for a country where courts have not generally published reasoned decisions.[51]

As a tripartite body that generally issues non-binding and practically unenforceable awards, the Arbitration Council is something of a hybrid between an institution of the rule of law and a forum for social dialogue between organised labour and management. Yet it would appear from the Cambodian experience that this sort of institution can be used as a tool for focussing and legitimating collective action with a view to the enhancement of workers' rights.

According to its own statistics, the Arbitration Council's case load has increased sharply since its inception in May 2003. From 31 in the first year, it rose to 158 cases in 2008. The success rate has remained steady; of the 575 cases received through September 2008, 68 per cent were reported as resolved successfully, 37 per cent because the parties reached an agreement prior to the issuance of an award, 25 per cent because the parties fully or substantially implemented an award, and seven per cent because the parties reached a post award settlement.

To a significant extent these disputes have dealt with details of compliance with the minimum standards set out in the local Labour Law. However, there have been a number of instances in which the Council has engaged with key human rights issues. These have arisen in cases related to anti-union discrimination, freedom of association and the right to bargain collectively.

A series of cases relating to disputes in the Raffles hotels in Siem Reap and Phnom Penh serves to illustrate both the ways in which international labour rights are penetrating Cambodian workplaces and the limited scope of such rights in the local context.

The Raffles dispute arose in late 2003 as a newly established hospitality sector union mobilised workers in the five star Raffles le Royal (Phnom

---

[49] See for example World Bank, 'Doing Business Indicators' (2009), available at www. doingbusiness.org which rate the cost of enforcing a standard commercial contract at 102.7% of the value of the contract.

[50] A recent corruption perception survey reported that bribes are paid in all or nearly all court cases: Center for Social Development (CSD), 'Corruption and Cambodian Households: A Household Survey, Phnom Penh: Center for Social Development' (2004).

[51] Awards are available at: www.arbitrationcouncil.org. For an analysis of the impact of the publication of these decisions online, see Adler, D, 'Access to Legal Information in Cambodia: Initial Steps, Future Possibilities' (2005) 2-3 *The Journal of Information, Law and Technology*, available at: www2.warwick.ac.uk/fac/soc/law/elj/jilt/2005_2-3/adler/.

Penh), and the Raffles Grande Hotel d'Ankor (Siem Reap) to engage in collective bargaining for the first time. Negotiations foundered around the issue of service charges (mandatory tips included on clients' bills) and how these should be distributed to workers. The legal basis for this discussion is set out in article 134 of the Labour Law, which provides that monies collected as a mandatory 'service charge' added to bills in hotels and similar establishments must be 'paid in full to staff who have contact with the clientele'. In practice, the Raffles hotels had been collecting a service charge from clients for a number of years and although management argued that the amount collected had been distributed in full to workers through a combination of wages, bonuses and other benefits, neither of the hotels had established a transparent or agreed method which showed how the service charge was being distributed. The breakdown in negotiations led to lengthy strikes in both hotels and the dispute became one which focussed on issues of core labour rights when management moved to dismiss the remaining strikers (some 97 workers in Phnom Penh and 220 in Siem Reap) in mid April 2004. In response, the strikers brought cases for reinstatement to the Arbitration Council.

In its awards, the Arbitration Council found that the workers should be reinstated and that:

> the employer party has shown a flagrant disregard for the right to freedom of association and the right to bargain collectively, as provided for by the Constitution and laws of the Kingdom of Cambodia, not to mention ILO Conventions on *Freedom of Association and Protection of the Right to Organise* (C87) and the *Right to Organise and Collective Bargaining* (C98) both of which Cambodia has ratified.[52]

While the Arbitration Council makes clear reference to both national and international law in its decisions, its decision, being non-binding, meant that the Raffles group had the option of filing objections. Having done this within the prescribed time limits, the awards became unenforceable. Nevertheless, the unions involved, with support from their international partners, continued to advocate for the reinstatement of their members. The strategies used were multi-pronged, targeting the international clientele of the Raffles Hotel chain both in Cambodia and internationally. Using methods seen in the footwear and textile sectors, the union initiated campaigns to boycott the Raffles chain internationally. The International Republican Institute was prominent in this boycott, which was also supported in Cambodia by the US Embassy, and even raised as an issue in the House of Representatives by Congressman George Miller, who called on all major international organisations to boycott Raffles. Through their

---

[52] *Raffles Hotel le Royal v Union of Raffles Hotel le Royal* (AC Case 24/04), 07 June 2004.

affiliations with the American Center for International Labor Solidarity, the Raffles unions were also able to tap into the resources of the international union movement. Activists picketed the Raffles' New York and London properties. The dispute was very costly to the Raffles brand. As a Singaporean diplomat observed at the time, 'It is our biggest investment in Cambodia. It is so sad ... Raffles Le Royale is bleeding'.[53]

While such approaches to advocacy are primarily political, rather than legal, the use of law (ILO conventions, Cambodian law and the awards of the Arbitration Council) to legitimate these campaigns is notable. Union press releases on the dispute cited the ILO conventions as applied by the Arbitration Council in support of workers' claims for reinstatement, and this despite the fact that the Council's awards had no legal effect. There is a something of a paradox in this situation. Put schematically, the hotels—which had sought and received decisions from Cambodia's courts declaring the strikes illegal—were limited in the extent to which they were able to rely on these decisions at least partially due to the widespread acknowledgement of the corrupt nature of Cambodia's judiciary. The unions, on the other hand, were able to prevail politically (an agreement to reinstate the dismissed workers was struck in September 2004) on the basis of a campaign constructed around a set of practically unenforceable international norms as applied in an arbitral award without legal effect.

In these circumstances, human rights law becomes a powerful tool because it reflects certain pre-negotiated and internationally legitimate understandings about what is just. Markets, or at least the market for beds in five star hotels (just like the market for branded garments), are somewhat embedded in this set of norms; as such, we observe the consequence of the process of developing rules even without enforcement, a process that Braithwaite alludes to in the quotation with which this chapter opens. In Wardell's terms, we see an illustration of how laws can be 'significant, though not exclusive, reference points for actors and politico-legal institutions in the negotiations of access and rights—even if they are not enforced'.

Taking this line of thinking to its logical conclusion, one could argue that it is the extent to which these rules are embedded in social and political contexts that counts, rather than their formal enforceability. The ideal of the rule of law is then merely the expression of a sociological fact—a state of affairs which can be approached when dealing with rules (or at least rules for rule-making) and institutions for their enforcement which are well embedded in particular social contexts.

---

[53] Quoted in 'Boycott Hits Cambodian Hotels' *Far Eastern Economic Review* (8 July 2004), available at: www.asianfoodworker.net/cambodia/040706raffles.htm.

PART III: LESSONS LEARNED: POLITICS, LABOUR
AND THE RULE OF LAW IN CAMBODIA

In the liberal ideal, law on the books is enforced through administrative
and judicial mechanisms which monitor compliance systematically and/or
respond to grievances from claim holders. Though actually enforced in few
cases, the anticipation of such enforcement gives the law a more general
normative effect. In the context of the Cambodian workplace, however,
these enforcement mechanisms were perceived as not being viable due to
high transaction costs, perceptions of bias, and corruption. Absent the
anticipation of systematic enforcement, legislation is just one of many sets
of norms competing for legitimacy and ascendancy in how decisions are
made. This means that working conditions are determined at the enterprise level with reference to the market and the particular constellations of
culture and power which emerge in particular employment relationships.
While the law is not absent from the workplace, other norms play a defining role: for example, those emerging from the managerial culture of (often
foreign) employers; corporate codes of conduct imposed by global buyers,
and the culture of rapidly escalating (and sometimes violent) collective
action which emerges in a context where socially marginal migrant workers
encounter difficult working conditions; and freedom from systems of social
control based around kinship and patronage that dominate rural Cambodia
and a volatile union movement.[54]

The basis for somewhat more equitable labour relations began to emerge
in the late 1990s. The extent to which these efforts have been successful, it
is argued here, rests on the willingness and ability of key players to engage
with the inherently contested nature by which rights are attained. Thus,
rather than investing primarily in more detailed regulation, administrative
or judicial capacity, a number of alternative initiatives were undertaken.
Both of the initiatives described above contain the implicit recognition that
there may be advantages in supporting the emergence of rights through
ongoing processes of contestation and negotiation—where issues of power
are at once more overt and more fluid—before trying to fix them in formal legal and enforcement frameworks.[55] The work on labour dispute
resolution in particular promotes collective action as a crucial part of such
processes.

[54] Derks, A, *Khmer Women on the Move: Migration and Urban Experiences in Cambodia*
(Dutch University Press, 2005) 93ff.

[55] For a similar argument from Indonesia drawing on Habermasian social theory to stress
the importance of enhancing the 'capacity to engage' of marginalised groups in public spaces
through the forging of alternative modes of dialogue and deliberative contestation, see Gibson,
C and Woolcock, M, 'Empowerment, Deliberative Development and Local Level Politics in
Indonesia: Participatory Projects as a Source of Countervailing Power' (2008) 43(2) *Studies in
Comparative International Development* 151.

In these circumstances, this chapter argues that the Labour Law's main (equity enhancing) effects have been establishing: (i) a set of (more or less) agreed standards regarding working conditions, which even though not formally enforced, can, in certain circumstances, be drawn upon to legitimate an argument as to what working conditions should be; and (ii) a framework for collective action which includes a structure under which the constitutional right to strike and form unions could be realised and a system of tripartite dispute resolution procedures.

The cases outlined above illustrate how a more equitable regulatory context can emerge incrementally, but it also shows some clear limitations of this approach. First, we almost only see law being drawn upon in enterprises (primarily garment factories and hotels) that are accountable to an international public through their branding. Secondly, it must be acknowledged that the systems referred to above operate primarily at the level of the collectivity. In practice, the current regulatory system neither protects workers rights as individuals, nor does it extend to the most vulnerable workers, such as those in small and medium sized enterprises producing for local markets. Thirdly, it should be noted that while steps are being taking to improve compliance with national law, the systems alluded to above do little to address the fundamental international inequities which are played out in Cambodian workplaces.

Despite these limitations and specificities, it would appear that the examples cited above provide some food for thought about the process of the development of law more generally. As such, this chapter concludes with some reflections on the question of how rights emerge and how different types of law get embedded in social relationships.

As law and development practitioners, our normative agenda often drives us to leap to the end game—a discussion about model rules and model institutions for their enforcement. To the extent that these are absent, we try to fix the situation by drafting better rules and trying to build modern judicial and bureaucratic institutions to enforce them. In doing this we implicitly assume that there are technical shortcuts which lead to the rule of law.

The Cambodian experience of garment sector monitoring and that of labour dispute resolution recounted above follow a different path. They remind us that politics matter in the realisation of rights and that 'the law is not so central'.[56] This seems to be a crucial insight. As the discussion above illustrates, rights may be best pursued in the realms of the non-legal, semi-legal, or even the illegal. This finding echoes Braithwaite's insights

---

[56] This turn of phrase is owed to Professor Daniel Nina who used it in the context of a discussion of legal pluralism (and its relationship to Bladerunner) at a graduate seminar in Oñati in 2004.

into the inaccessibility of coercive systems to the weak and his preference for building law from the bottom up in circumstances of significant power imbalance: 'Dialogue builds concern and commitment first; when there is shared concern, a regime can move on to agreement on principles, then to agreement on rules, then to commitment to enforce rules.'[57]

A similar concept is advanced (albeit from quite a different political perspective) by Santos and Rodriguez,[58] who stress that political mobilisation (at the local and international level) will be a necessary precursor to effective rights-based strategies for the disenfranchised of the global south. In the absence of (a) lawmaking processes which reflect the interests of marginalised groups or (b) systems (judicial or bureaucratic) that can be relied upon to uphold the law in an impartial manner, it will be naïve to suggest that the poor put too much stock in overly legal conceptions of rights. In these circumstances, systems that facilitate more political contests over rights may be preferable to those that institutionalise unfair legal contests.

This said, the law is clearly important to the development of rights; indeed the law may be more central than we think. Neither the garment sector monitoring project nor the initiatives around labour dispute resolution described above neglect the law. Rather they acknowledge that the law is not formally enforceable and instead of ploughing on merrily as though it were, they treat it instead as a set of norms around which to structure dialogue (in the case of the working conditions improvement project) or more overt contestation (in case of labour dispute resolution). The methods for doing this are quite different. The working conditions improvement project conducts regular inspections of garment factories based on an agreed list of criteria derived from the law,[59] publishing these for a primarily international audience. The labour dispute resolution project has focused on the establishment of a new national tribunal which arbitrates collective labour disputes, but because of its non-binding nature allows both the political and legal aspects of these contests to emerge. A number of principles behind the two projects, however, are very similar. Both are driven by tripartism and the provision of institutional spaces for the playing out of structural conflict between capital and labour.

Searching for an operational synthesis of these two perspectives—on the importance and marginality of law—leads to a description of the sorts of cases described here in terms of what we have called elsewhere an

---

[57] Braithwaite and Drahos (n 1) 553–54.

[58] de Sousa Santos and Rodríguez-Garavito, *Law and Globalisation from Below: Towards a Cosmopolitan Legality* (2005).

[59] And interestingly also, the Arbitration Council's interpretation of the law. See Adler, D et al (eds), 'Better Factories–Guide to Cambodian Labor Law for the Garment Industry' (ILO, 2005). Available at: www.betterfactories.org.

'interim institutional approach'.[60] This can be thought of as an attempt to understand the 'how' in the contemporary expression of Polanyi's challenge with regard to the re-embedding of market relations in socialising regulatory frameworks.[61] Acknowledging that the nature of state-society relations in the countries where we practice development limits the effectiveness of both law and politics as drivers of more equitable governance, the interim institutional approach is based on the argument that:

> (a) equitable, rule-based systems for allocating resources and resolving disputes— i.e., the very content and legitimacy of modern institutions of government— emerge and continue to develop because they are subject to ongoing social contest; and (b) because equitable institutional arrangements for social regulation must emerge through social contest, there will be limits to the extent to which they can be designed *ex ante* on the basis of technical knowledge (i.e., by governance 'experts').[62]

The operational consequence of this approach is a shift in focus from the adoption of 'pre-packaged' legal/institutional forms (or reforms) deemed effective elsewhere to the location—in a particular political economy—of opportunities for the institutionalisation of what we call 'good struggles'.[63]

The test then for the above cases is the extent to which they have (in the Cambodian context) generated more equitable (thus 'good') struggles out of the dynamic of local unions, the legitimation of collective action and international trade. While this will be open to debate, the argument presented here is that a modest but useful engagement has occurred in the grey area between law and politics. Yet even in these circumstances law is seen only as providing a framework for framing more equitable contestation— and not as a technology for securing rights. The situation described is then neither the nostalgic 'justice without law' about which authors such as Auerbach[64] and Nader[65] are properly sceptical, nor Ellickson's more sanguine 'order without law'[66]—but rather a form of legally infused social dialogue—and thus perhaps a little more justice without (or at least in advance of) the rule of law.

---

[60] See Adler, D, Sage, C and Woolcock, M, 'Interim Institutions and the Development Process: Opening Spaces for Reform in Cambodia and Indonesia' (Brooks World Poverty Institute Working Paper 86/2009) available at www.bwpi.manchester.ac.uk/resources/Working-Papers/index.html and Adler, D, Porter, D and Woolcock, M, *Legal Pluralism and the Role of Interim Institutions: Challenges and Opportunities for Equity in Cambodia* (Mimeo, World Bank, 2007).

[61] Polanyi, *The Great Transformation* (1944).

[62] Adler, Porter and Woolcock, 'Interim Institutions and the Development Process' (2009).

[63] Ibid.

[64] Auerback, J, *Justice without Law* (Oxford, Oxford University Press, 1984).

[65] Nader, L, 'Disputing without the Force of Law' (1979) 88(5) *Yale Law Journal* 998–1021.

[66] Ellickson, RC, *Order Without Law: How Neighbors Settle Disputes* (Boston, Harvard University Press, 1991).

20

Australian Textile Clothing and Footwear Supply Chain Regulation

SHELLEY MARSHALL

INTRODUCTION*

A MAJOR CRISIS in labour regulation has arisen in recent years due to growing 'gaps' in the reach of regulation, leaving a significant proportion of workers unprotected by labour standards in many countries. These gaps are caused by a range of overlapping factors: the limited scope of the employment relationship;[1] regulatory failure on behalf of nation-states leading to an inability to enforce existing laws;[2] significant informal or semi-informal economies;[3] labour market deregulation;[4] and also by labour market re-structuring resulting from the vertical disintegration of businesses and the privatisation of state corporations.[5] There is

---

* The author would like to thank Adam Bandt and Kathryn Fawcett for their helpful insights.

[1] See International Labour Conference (ILC) (95th Session) Report V(1): The Employment Relationship (2005) and the International Labour Organisation (ILO) Employment Relationship Recommendation (No 198), subsequently adopted at the ILC 95th Session, 2006, Provisional Record available at: www.ilo.org/public/english/standards/relm/ilc/ilc95/records.htm.

[2] Fenwick, C, Howe, J, Marshall, S and Landau, I, 'Labour and Labour-related Laws in Micro- and Small Enterprises: Innovative Regulatory Approaches' (Global Issues Paper, ILO, Geneva), forthcoming, ch III.

[3] ILC (90th Session) Report VI: Decent Work and the Informal Economy (2002) 2; Maldonado, C, 'The Informal Sector: Legalization or Laissez-Faire?' (1995) 134 *International Labour Review* 705, 727.

[4] Deregulation is more accurately described as 're-regulation': a changing of the rules and institutions that constitute a labour market. In Australia, the number and complexity of labour laws has increased in recent years: Marshall, S and Mitchell, R, 'Enterprise Bargaining, Managerial Prerogative and the Protection of Workers' Rights: An Argument on the Role of Law and Regulatory Strategy in Australia under the Workplace Relations Act 1996 (Cth)' (2006) 22/3 *The International Journal of Comparative Labour Law and Industrial Relations* 299, also available at http://cclsr.law.unimelb.edu.au/index.cfm?objectid=E3D38F25-B0D0-AB80-E2F1BF648C87997F; See also Howe, J, '"Deregulothon" of Labour Relations in Australia: Toward Command and Control' (Working Paper No 34, Melbourne, Centre for Employment and Labour Relations Law, University of Melbourne, 2005).

[5] Davies, P and Freedland, M, 'The Disintegration of the Employing Enterprise and its Significance for the Personal Scope of Employment Law' (Paper presented at The Scope of

mounting concern that a failure to provide some form of protection for workers who are disenfranchised from labour regulation is a breach of basic human rights. This has been accompanied by resurgence in the appeal of the idea of 'industrial citizenship'—a concept that extends beyond the traditional conception of the rights resulting from the employment relationship and may form the basis for a new suite of social human rights.[6]

The aim of many recent international and national regulatory innovations has been to close growing regulatory gaps and extend industrial citizenship to a greater range of workers: to re-enfranchise disenfranchised workers. Many of the mechanisms (proposed or realised) for closing regulatory gaps are 'soft' in nature and involve non-state regulators due to an acceptance that governments will not reverse the trend towards the retraction of traditional labour protections or are incapable of enforcing existing 'command and control' labour laws. To say that they are soft law initiatives simply denotes that they lack the force of punitive sanctions. Examples of such mechanisms include ISO14001, Rugmark and SA8000. There has also been a proliferation of Corporate Codes of Conduct, many of which are generated by companies themselves, whilst some have resulted from the efforts of trade associations, unions, universities or other stakeholders.[7] Perhaps the best-known and influential example of an academic proposal for a soft law mechanism is Sabel et al's 'Ratcheting Labour Standards' proposal.[8]

More recently, there appears to be growing interest in combining state and non-state-based (soft) regulation in order to both lend greater 'reflexivity' to state-based regulation and give non-state based regulation more teeth.[9] Reflexive regulation is also sometimes called 'responsive' regulation. Proponents of 'reflexive' regulation see non-state actors as

Employment Law: Re-drawing the Boundaries of Protection Conference, Bellagio, 23–27 May 2005).

[6] For a comprehensive review of the concept of industrial citizenship, see Fudge, J, 'After Industrial Citizenship: Market Citizenship or Citizenship at Work' (2005) 60 *Industrial Relations* 1; see also Johnston, P, 'The Resurgence of Labor as Citizenship Movement in the New Labor Relations Environment' (2000) 26 *Critical Sociology* 139.

[7] Ferguson, C, 'A Review of UK Company Codes of Conduct' (Social Development Division, Department for International Development, 1998); Jenkins, R, 'Corporate Codes of Conduct, Self Regulation in a Global Economy' (Technology, Business and Society Programme Paper No 2, United Nations Research Institute for Social Development, 2001). See also, Jenkins, RO, Pearson, R and Seyfang, G, *Corporate Responsibility and Labour Rights: Codes of Conduct in the Global Economy* (London, Earthscan, 2002).

[8] Fung, A, O'Rourke, D, *et al*, Ratcheting Labor Standards: Regulation for Continuous Improvement in the Global Workplace. *Work Bank Social Protection Discussion Paper* (2000); Fung, A, O'Rourke, D, *et al*, 'Realizing Labor Standards: How Transparency, Competition and Sanctions Could Improve Working Conditions Worldwide' (2001) *Boston Review* 26.

[9] See for example, Kuruvilla, J and Verma, A, 'International Labour Standards, Soft Regulation, and National Government Roles' (2006) 48 *Journal of Industrial Relations* 41. See also various chapters in Macdonald, K and Marshall, S (eds), *Fair Trade, Corporate Accountability and Beyond: Experiments in Global Justice Governance Mechanisms* (London, Ashgate, forthcoming) and McBarnet, D, Voiculescu, A and Campbell, T (eds),

responsible and empowered participants through all stages of the regulatory process, rather than being the resistant subjects of oppositional forms of top down regulation. This view regards regulation as more likely to be effective if used in a manner that is responsive to and draws upon existing distributions of power and resources among economic and social actors.[10] According to this view, the challenge for government is to determine how best to try and facilitate the active involvement of private actors in public action. Businesses are offered opportunities to engage in organisational learning, and to design corporate responsibility methods that are appropriate to their own business cultures. The role of government changes from (only) regulator and controller to (also) facilitator and coordinator. Law becomes a process of shared problem solving rather than purely an ordering activity.[11]

This chapter aims to contribute to the literature concerning reflexive and extra-state regulatory mechanisms which might close the regulatory gap caused by de-regulation and vertical disintegration by examining an example of a partially soft-law mechanism which is operational in Australia. The chapter critically assesses 'Supply Chain Regulation' in the textile, clothing and footwear (TCF) industry in Australia, using regulatory theory as a tool to examine the extent to which the laws extend outworkers' industrial citizenship and protects their human rights as workers.

The case study of TCF supply chain regulations examines the operation of three interlocking regulatory mechanisms which govern the rights and conditions of outworkers until mid-2006.[12] In this chapter the terms 'outworker' and 'homeworker' are used interchangeably. The term outworker is used colloquially to denote the idea that people are working outside of factories—in small workshops or in their homes. Whilst the term 'homeworker' would seem to include only those people who are working in their homes, it is defined in International Labour Organisation (ILO) Convention No 177 article 1, as work carried out by a person in his or home or in other premises of his or her choice, other than the workplace of the employer for remuneration which results in a product or service as specified by the employer, irrespective of who provides the equipment, materials or other inputs used. This legal definition is very close to the colloquial use of 'outworker', then. The term 'sweatshop' is also in common colloquial use.

The New Corporate Accountability: Corporate Social Responsibility and the Law Cambridge (Cambridge, Cambridge University Press, 2007).

[10] McBarnet, D, 'Corporate Social Responsibility Beyond Law, Through Law, For Law: the New Corporate Accountability' in McBarnet et al, *The New Corporate Accountability* (2007).

[11] Parker, C, *The Open Corporation: Effective Self-regulation and Democracy* (Cambridge, Cambridge University Press, 2002).

[12] The discussion in this chapter is only accurate to mid-2006 and does not include developments after this date.

The workers in sweatshops are most often, but not always, homeworkers, in accordance with the Convention No 177 definition.

The Australian Homeworkers' Code of Practice is often invoked as an example of best practice in 'soft law' initiatives, without recognising its relationship with state-based regulation. It is difficult to consider one of these mechanisms in isolation to the others. They include the following:

    i. *Industrial awards* which govern the minimum conditions TCF workers, including outworkers, should enjoy and are set by industrial tribunals in a tripartite setting. These might be termed 'hard' laws, because they are enforceable by sanction, although the way they are created is 'reflexive'.

    ii. *The Homeworkers' Code of Practice* also regulates the supply chain and aims to bolster the award by requiring further transparency and information sharing along the supply chain. This is a soft law which lacks enforceability but which sets up an incentive structure in the form of a labelling system and consumer preferencing. It is currently being codified by state legislatures. As a result, it will be mandatory, but remain in the soft zone in the sense that it does not contain punitive sanctions.

    iii. *State-based supply chain legislation* also allows outworkers to make claims for unpaid entitlements against another party higher up in the supply chain, even where they are not deemed employees under the award or state 'deeming' acts. This is a form of hard law.[13]

The primary aim of these interlocking regulations is that outworkers receive the same pay and conditions as workers who toil within factories. They aim to regulate an informal sector in which labour conditions experienced by workers are markedly lower than the formal sector: a third world within the first. These regulations are consistent with the ILO's Decent Work agenda,[14] the ILO's Core Labour Rights, ILO Home Worker Convention No 177 1996 and Recommendation No 184 1996, which seek to ensure that all workers, whether covered by a traditional contract of employment or not, enjoy decent work. The regulations also aim to enforce the rights of the child by reducing incentives for the use of child labour.

The chapter is divided into four parts. The first part outlines the key theoretical concepts used in the chapter, including industrial citizenship and regulatory theory. Part two describes the three supply chain regulatory mechanisms. The third part of the chapter conducts an analysis of the regulations, assessing to what extent they extend the industrial citizenship of the target population. The final part of the chapter concludes by placing Australian TCF supply chain regulation in a broader regulatory context.

---

[13] In this chapter these three regulatory mechanisms are jointly referred to as 'supply chain regulation', whereas the state acts are referred to as 'supply chain legislation'.

[14] ILC (87th Session) Decent Work, Report of the Director General, International Labour Conference (ILO, Geneva 1999); and ILC (90th Session) Report VI: Decent Work and the Informal Economy.

A thesis underlying many extra-legislative or soft law initiatives is that the problem of non-adherence of labour standards is due to not enough regulation or the failure of national governments to adequately enforce their own legislation. An analysis of the broader regulatory context leads us to question whether additional regulation, soft or hard, will be sufficient to ensure adherence to international labour standards.

KEY THEORETICAL CONCEPTS

Industrial Citizenship

The idea of industrial citizenship may usefully provide the basis for a subset of human rights to govern work relations or be used as a standard against which to measure existing labour rights regimes. Industrial citizenship is used here in both a normative and aspirational sense. It is normative because the idea of industrial citizenship entails a claim that workers should not lack rights or fail to be offered protection simply because of an historical anomaly which has resulted in rights and protections being linked to the employment contract. Understanding workers' rights to be a consequence of industrial citizenship rather than a contract of employment thus involves a reframing of the basis of those rights. It is aspirational because, whilst the subject of citizenship has received a resurgence of interest across a wide range of disciplines, as Judy Fudge puts it: 'the citizenship regimes that were institutionalised in liberal democracies after World War II are confronting fundamental economic and political challenges from the forces of globalisation and neoliberalism'.[15] This chapter is particularly concerned with the challenge to industrial citizenship for workers in the TCF industry posed by vertical disintegration and the labour market restructuring which has resulted from market penetration following tariff reductions. Yet, it is not clear that the *range* of rights, which might be a consequence of industrial citizenship, have ever been realised in liberal democracies.

Put in the simplest terms, industrial citizenship can be defined as a status limiting commodification and conferring rights to influence terms and conditions of work.[16] The rights which might be said to flow from industrial citizenship are imbued in individuals primarily by virtue of engaging in work or productive activity, regardless of place of work. Secondary justifications might include the presence of some level of 'subordination' or 'control', although the level might not be sufficient to locate the worker within the protective prism of the employment relationship. Providing sufficient

---

[15] Fudge, 'After Industrial Citizenship: Market Citizenship or Citizenship at Work' (2005) 1.
[16] Ibid 6.

protection to allow smoother transitions in a flexible workforce is also a social policy objective of extending industrial citizenship to a greater number and range of workers.[17] This conception of the basis of rights replaces the paradigm of employment with a broad conception of socially necessary labour, including caring for family members, as a contribution to the community, and covers 'people from the cradle to grave ... in both periods of inactivity proper and periods of training, employment, self-employment and work outside the labour market'.[18]

The Supiot Report to the European Commission provides the most detailed recent outline of the content of citizenship rights at work, which were conceived as 'social drawing rights'. The suit of rights the state would guarantee according to this vision would include:[19]

> non-discrimination, minimum wage, collective rights, etc; guarantees of equal access to ongoing, high quality public services (not conceived merely in terms of minimum universal standards); and freedom of profession, understood to be a specific freedom that involves not employment but work, and the concomitant right to information.

This range of rights is wider than those which might normally be conceived of as employment rights.

However, the core rights associated with employment rights are no less crucial to the expanded domain of industrial citizenship. Collective rights and the right to participate in decision making over matters central to working life are vital elements of industrial citizenship, just as the right to vote and the right to freely associate are crucial to the exercise of political citizenship and civil and political human rights.[20] Industrial democracy is an *end* in itself. Moral arguments for industrial democracy make appeals to the ideas of justice or freedom.[21]

Industrial democracy, either in the form of collective rights or other participatory 'voice mechanisms', is also a *means* for distributing power within the enterprise, the industry and the economy more equally, and handling conflicts of interests by democratic procedures. It is a means of adapting the operation of an enterprise or the nature of work to the needs of those who

[17] Supiot, A et al, 'A European Perspective in the Transformation of Work and the Future of Labour Law' (1999) *Comparative Law and Policy Journal* 20(6).
[18] Supiot, A, *Beyond Employment: Changes in Work and the Future of Labour Law in Europe* (Oxford, Oxford University Press, 2001) 54.
[19] Supiot, 'A European Perspective in the Transformation of Work and the Future of Labour Law' (1999) 633.
[20] Crouch, C, 'The Globalised Economy: An End to the Age of Industrial Citizenship?' in T Whilthagen (ed), *Advanced Theory in Labor Law and Industrial Relations in a Global Context* (Amsterdam, North-Holland, 1998).
[21] See for example Horvat, B, 'Ethical Foundations of Self-Government' (1980) 1(1) *Economic and Industrial Democracy* 1, who seeks a non-utilitarian basis for participation, which he finds in a modified version of John Rawls' theory of justice.

work in it or those in society at large.[22] The right to collective bargaining is based on the recognition of the unequal power between the parties involved in market exchanges. Collective bargaining modifies the units entering the exchange so that associations or combinations of workers, rather than individual workers, enter into agreements over wages and conditions with employers. Thus, while we can say that the rights associated with industrial citizenship entail an acceptance of market exchange, these rights intrude into the private sphere and place positive obligations on state and private actors in a way that civil and political human rights do not.[23]

Regulatory Theory

It might be said that industrial citizenship provides the 'what' or the content of human rights for workers, and regulatory theory provides the 'how'. The term 'regulation' includes, but is not limited to, the use of legal rules and sanctions as a mechanism for setting and enforcing behavioural norms. For Braithwaite, regulation is conceived of as that subset of governance that is about steering the flow of events, as opposed to providing and distributing.[24] Regulatory theory recognises that the state is not the only actor with power to influence the actions of others.[25] State regulation co-exists, supplements and often collides with co-regulation and self-regulation within a given 'regulatory space'.[26] This chapter takes a broad view of labour market regulation and considers the effects not only of labour law, but also of other protective measures offered by the nation-state when exploring the regulatory context.

Regulatory theory suggests that designing and applying regulation according to a number of principles assists in making it more effective and responsive.[27] First, regulation is likely to be more effective when regulators have a number of different options available to them in ensuring compliance, including punitive mechanisms of enforcement and more reflexive mechanisms of encouragement and regulatory learning. These principles

---

[22] Bowles, S and Gintis, H, 'Is the Demand for Workplace Democracy Redundant in a Liberal Economy?' in U Pagono and R Rowthorn (eds), *Democracy and Efficiency in the Economic Enterprise* (London, Routledge, 1996) 82–97.

[23] Fudge (n 6) 6.

[24] Braithwaite, J, 'Neoliberalism or Regulatory Capitalism' (Occasional Paper 5, Regulatory Institutions Network, Research School of Social Sciences, Australian National University, Canberra, 2005) 1.

[25] Black, J, 'Critical Reflections on Regulation' (2002) 27 *Australian Journal of Legal Philosophy* 1, 7.

[26] Howe, '"Deregulation" of Labour Relations in Australia' (2005).

[27] These principles have been adapted from Fenwick, Howe, Marshall and Landau, 'Labour and Labour-related Laws in Micro- and Small Enterprises: Innovative Regulatory Approaches' (forthcoming).

are encapsulated within the 'labour regulation pyramid', shown in Figure 1, which is a tool that can be used in the design and assessment of responsive labour regulation.[28] Secondly, both regulatory design and implementation should be participatory. This is both a *means* to greater effectiveness and *end* in itself in franchising industrial citizens.

The Labour Regulation Pyramid

The 'regulation pyramid' graphically depicts the range of options available to regulators in enforcing regulations. The existence of legal rules and norms enshrining labour or human rights and standards as non-negotiable behavioural minimums, with non-compliance subject to non-discretionary punishment, are at the apex of the pyramid. They serve as a goal, guide, and ultimately as a source of sanction. This is because in the absence of the apex, regulators will have far less capacity to apply any leverage against businesses unwilling to comply with regulation. However, frequently the

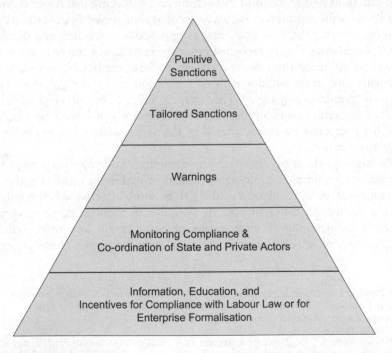

Figure 1: Pyramid of Regulation Strategies

[28] This concept is based on the idea of an 'enforcement pyramid', developed in Ayres, I and Braithwaite, J, *Responsive Regulation: Transcending the Deregulation Debate* (New York, Oxford University Press, 1992) 38–41. The discussion in the third part of the chapter draws extensively on their work.

most effective way for governments to achieve behavioural change is if businesses themselves *choose* to comply with relevant rights and standards, *without* the application of sanctions. The pyramid therefore contemplates other regulatory strategies that the state might use, often in collaboration with other regulatory actors, to achieve the desired change in a manner that is responsive to the circumstances of businesses. A central principle of this approach is that responsive regulation would be best designed in a way that utilised different elements of the pyramid in interlinked ways depending upon a range of particular circumstances.

The regulatory pyramid is used as an analytical tool in the third part of the chapter to assess the likely effectiveness of Australian supply chain regulation in re-enfranchising outworkers as industrial citizens.

CASE STUDY OF SUPPLY CHAIN REGULATION IN THE AUSTRALIAN TCF INDUSTRY

Impetus for Regulatory Innovation

For the greater part of the last century, the standard worker in the TCF industry in Australia was assumed to be working in a factory under a contract of employment, the terms of which were bolstered by multi-employer industrial agreements called awards and, in the latter part of the century, enterprise agreements. However, outworkers have always existed, and their numbers have ebbed and flowed with waves of immigration and other economic trends such as levels of protection.[29] The TCF industries in Australia, particularly clothing manufacture, were traditionally protected by high tariffs and/or import quotas. The early emphasis was on tariffs. In 1974, as part of the process of meeting the requirements of the General Agreement on Tariffs and Trade (GATT) Multifibre Agreement, tariffs were reduced and replaced with import quotas.[30]

Further reductions in protection occurred between 1988 and 1995 under the Button Plan, with the eventual effect of reducing the maximum tariff on TCF products to 25 per cent in 2000.[31] Core businesses in the Australian TCF industry—retailers, fashion houses and brand names—responded by

---

[29] For a historical analysis of outwork in Australia see Peck, J, 'Outwork and Restructuring Processes in the Australian Clothing Industry' (1990) 3 *Labour and Industry* 302.

[30] This section draws on the Department of Industry, Science and Resources, 'Textile, Clothing, Footwear and Leather Industries: Action Agendas: A Discussion Paper' (Commonwealth of Australia, 7–8 March 1999), available at: http://apecenergy.org.au/content/itrinternet/cmscontent.cfm?objectid=BCCB4B2B-4877-4C71-A76CB89E1A77BE3B&indexPages=/content/sitemap.cfm?objectid=48A5B076-20E0-68D8-EDDA6165C0953D2F.

[31] Department of Industry Tourism and Resources, 'Review of the Textile, Clothing and Footwear Strategic Investment Program Scheme—Report' (Commonwealth of Australia, September 2002).

'vertically disintegrating'. They outsourced many of the activities that were previously performed inside the company. Some of these functions were outsourced offshore, whilst other functions were outsourced into homes and sweatshops in Australia. Figure 2 provides an example of a typical supply chain in the clothing industry. The supply chain may be more complicated in practice than the system shown in the diagram. For example, there may be an additional agent between the factory and the outworker who outsources the sewing (the outworker boss). There may also be multiple interlinked supply chains related to service providers (shown as Service

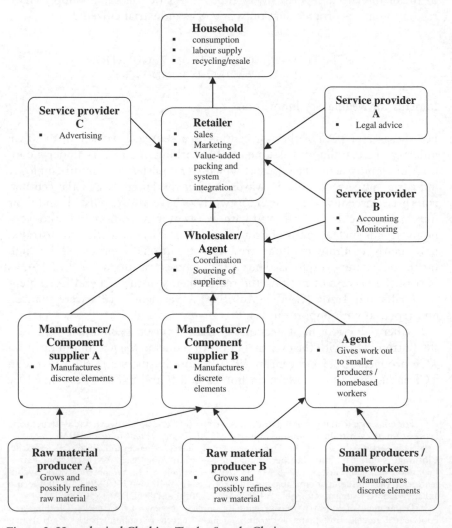

Figure 2: Hypothetical Clothing Trades Supply Chain

Provider A, B and C) or component suppliers. Each of the businesses in this diagram is likely to employ a number of workers. The supply chain is multipolar and the parties are linked in complicated ways.

The result of vertical disintegration was a further contraction in formal employment in the industry.[32] By the mid-1990s, the number of outworkers working in the TCF industry in Australia numbered anywhere between 23,650[33] and 329,000,[34] depending on the source of the estimate. Figures are likely to be unreliable due to the informal, sporadic and seasonal nature of outworker employment. The Textile, Clothing and Footwear Union of Australia (the Union or the TCFUA) estimated that outworkers outnumbered factory workers by 12 to 1 by 1994.[35] A study of pay and conditions suggested that outworkers, on average, receive around $0.50 to $5.00 an hour for their work—less than half the legal minimum—once piece rates are converted to hourly rates.[36] Around 62 per cent of the workers who responded to one survey worked seven days a week and 95 per cent of respondents did not receive holiday leave, sick leave or public holiday pay.[37] Another study comparing the occupational health and safety (OHS) experience of factory-based workers and outworkers in the clothing industry found that outworkers suffered three times the level of injuries experienced by factory-based workers. The two main reasons for the differences in injury rates were the use of a piecework payment system and the long hours worked by outworkers.[38]

Since the mid-1980s, trade unions and community groups have campaigned for the extension of formal entitlements to outworkers. The response to such pressure by governmental authorities has been incremental: first, the federal industrial tribunal adopted award provisions designed to permit regulatory agencies to supervise the contracting process and to extend minimum entitlements to outworkers. In the mid-1990s,

---

[32] Peck, 'Outwork and Restructuring Processes in the Australian Clothing Industry' (1990) 308.

[33] Industry Commission Enquiry, 'The Textile, Clothing and Footwear Industries, Report No. 59', (Commonwealth of Australia, 1997).

[34] Textile, Clothing and Footwear Union of Australia (TCFUA), *The Hidden Cost of Fashion* (Sydney, TCFUA, 1995).

[35] Ibid.

[36] Cregan, C, 'Home Sweat Home' (Department of Management, University of Melbourne, 2002), available at: www.nosweatshoplabel.com/Downloads/HomeSweatHome.pdf; see also, Marshall, S, 'Report on the National Phone Advice Service for Outworkers, 13 November–2nd December 2000' (2001), available at: www.nosweatshoplabel.com/report.htm.

[37] Cregan, 'Home Sweat Home' (2002).

[38] Mayhew, C and Quinlan, M, *Outsourcing and Occupational Health and Safety: A Comparative Study of Factory-based and Outworkers in the Australian TCF Industry* (Sydney, Industrial Relations Research Centre, University of New South Wales, 1998). See also, Nossar, I, Johnstone, R and Quinlan, M, 'Regulating Supply-Chains to Address the Occupational Health and Safety Problems Associated with Precarious Employment: The Case of Home-Based Clothing Workers in Australia' (2004) 17 *Australian Journal of Labour Law* 137, 146.

further pressure by community groups led to the adoption of voluntary codes of practice by retailers and manufacturer employers intended to secure formal entitlements for employees. The limitations of these two approaches, however, have led to the development and adoption of a more comprehensive and innovative regulatory strategy.

Award Regulation

In 1987, the Deputy President of the Australian Industrial Relations Commission (then known as the Conciliation and Arbitration Commission), Joe Riordan, made a determination that '[t]he evidence in this case points to the conclusion that many of the persons engaged as outworkers are engaged in an employer-employee relationship'.[39] This resulted in a variation to the Clothing Trades Award. The key conditions of outworkers are now regulated by the federal Clothing Trades Award *1999* (the Award), which is mirrored by state awards.[40] This multi-employer industrial agreement sets out the minimum conditions under which employees in the clothing industry can be employed. This section of the chapter first outlines the process by which the Award was set, and secondly the conditions which it establishes for workers. Thirdly, it considers how successful the Award has been in regulating the conditions of outworkers and what barriers exist to compliance with the Award.

The process through which awards are established in Australia is significant because it resembles the tripartite system which is recommended by many of the advocates of both reflexive and soft regulatory mechanisms.[41] Awards are set in a tripartite and decentralised system by industrial tribunals. The tribunal acts as the state's regulatory agent within the system, operating through a regulatory model based on dispute resolution. During applications to tribunals to set or vary awards, employer representatives and industry bodies make representations to the tribunal, as do unions. The parties are encouraged to come to an agreement on the terms of the award

---

[39] Australian Conciliation and Arbitration Court, *In the Matter of an Application by the Clothing and Allied Trades Union of Australia to Vary the Clothing Trades Award 1982 in Relation to Contract Work* (Print G6996, Melbourne, 1987) 31.

[40] Other sources of lawful entitlements for outworkers include the Workplace Relations Act 1996, the Long Service Leave Act 1992 (Victoria (Vic)) and equivalent acts in other states, the Occupational Health and Safety Act 1985 (Vic) and equivalent acts in other states, Public Holidays Act 1993 (Vic) and equivalent acts in other states, as well as private contracts.

[41] See, for example, Kuruvilla and Verma, 'International Labour Standards, Soft Regulation, and National Government Roles' (2006) 55 who advocate such a model. For a further description of the Australian system see Howe, J, '"Deregulation" of labour relations in Australia: Towards a More "Centered" Command and Control Model' in C Arup et al (eds), *Labour Law and Labour Market Regulation: Essays in the Construction, Constitution, and Regulation of Labour Markets and Work Relationships* (Sydney, Federation Press, 2006).

through mediation or 'conciliation', and if this is not possible, the tribunal arbitrates, making a decision which reflects the views of all parties.

The awards and enterprise agreements resultant from this process have traditionally also been enforced in a decentralised manner. Although legal sanctions for breaches of awards have always been a part of the formal system, the formal state institutions of the industrial relations system, such as the Arbitration Inspectorate, have never been particularly effective or active in enforcing these sanctions. It has rather been the case that trade unions have been most active in enforcing the terms of awards and agreements. Enforcement of the outworker provisions of the Clothing Trades Award 1999, such as it has been, has primarily fallen upon the TCFUA, although some state inspectorates have been more active than others. In recent years, the Union has begun issuing batches of complaints for breaches of the outworker provisions in the Federal Court against up to 30 companies at a time.

Under the federal Clothing Trades Award 1999 and its state equivalents, outworkers are entitled to:

— regular work as either full-time or part-time workers;
— overtime pay;
— paid public holidays, annual and long-service leave;
— superannuation; and
— the right to skill assessment and payment according to the level of skill exercised.

The Award provides that employers pay outworkers and contract workers at a specified piece-rate. This rate is calculated using a formula based on the standard factory rate. The Award provides that outworkers are to be given 38 hours worth of work per week or pay for that amount of work. Any overtime is to be paid at time and a half.

The Award also provides for detailed reporting obligations for respondents regardless of whether outworkers are directly employed or are employed through an agent or intermediary. Under the Award, these details are to be given to the outworker when each batch is delivered. Employers of outworkers must be registered with a tripartite Board of Reference representing the Union, an employer representative and the Australian Industrial Registrar.

Sadly, there has never been widespread compliance with the outworker provisions of the Award or the parallel state awards. In 1996, a Senate Committee noted that '[t]he practice of non-compliance with the award wages and conditions is so widespread that it is considered to be the norm'.[42] There are a number of reasons for this which the chapter now

---

[42] Senate Economics Reference Committee, *Outworkers in the Garment Industry* (Parliament of the Commonwealth of Australia, December, 1996) 28.

briefly examines. Part of the problem arises from the structure of labour law which assumes the existence of a clearly defined 'employee' and 'employer'. The complex chain of production shown in Figure 2 sees work passed from retailer to manufacturer to contractor to subcontractor to outworkers, with strong market control wielded by retailers or other core businesses. Within this system, the exact employer is difficult to define. This complexity allows all parties in the chain above the outworker to avoid meeting their legal obligations. Other reasons for non-compliance are a consequence of outworker misinformation and fear. These barriers to compliance also have implications for other regulatory mechanisms.

A preliminary barrier to enforcement arises from the fact that awards only cover 'employees' under the Workplace Relations Act 1996 and its predecessor, the Industrial Relations Act 1988. This has given rise to an 'entitlement' gap between those workers who are formally entitled to legal protection and those who are not and perverse incentives for employers to avoid compliance through choosing advantageous legal forms.[43] Employers and intermediaries often pressure outworkers to establish themselves as separate business enterprises and thus become, by definition, self-employed contractors.[44] Workers who are considered employees under the Award, and those who were not, may have been working in the same supply chain, carrying out the same work for the same intermediary, but because one was registered as a 'business' they were not entitled to the same conditions as those who were not.

Secondly, there have traditionally been too few legal obligations under the Award on major retailers, who wield high levels of effective control over the supply chains. The Award was varied to stretch its reach downward from manufacturers to the intermediaries who directly employ outworkers. The problem with this, from a regulatory perspective, is that the direct employers, known as 'outworker bosses' in the TCF industry, may not have very much discretion in determining the wages (piece rates), hours (largely determined by volume of work) or other conditions under which outworkers toil. Parties above them in the supply chain, such as manufacturers, wholesalers and retailers, may, in fact, have far greater control over these factors. As has been demonstrated elsewhere,[45] supply chains in the TCF industry are hierarchical markets in which 'core businesses' (retailers, fashion houses and brand names) wield strong control over the other parties in the supply chain in order to reduce risk and increase profits. They are able

---

[43] These deficiencies are identified and discussed in Nossar et al, 'Regulating Supply-Chains to Address the Occupational Health and Safety Problems Associated with Precarious Employment' (2004).

[44] Senate Economics Reference Committee (1996) 29.

[45] Marshall, S, 'An Exploration of Control in the Context of Vertical Disintegration, and Regulatory Responses' in C Arup et al, *Labour Law and Labour Market Regulation* (2006).

to do so by virtue of their high market concentration and buying power in contrast to the growing number of suppliers who compete for their work. As a consequence, regulations targeting manufacturers and suppliers may be an inadequate counterforce to 'private regulation' from core businesses. Suppliers competing for rare contracts with retailers may be willing to risk non-compliance with the Award in order to comply with demands for low prices from core businesses upon whom they are dependent for survival. The sanctions available under the Award (the largest penalty awarded to date has been AUS $100,000) are insignificant compared with the sanction of being dropped as a supplier by a major retailer.

Putting aside these problems with the structure of the Award, even where workers have formal entitlements, mechanisms for enforcement are often weak due to low levels of legal literacy and mistrust of institutions of the state. Outworkers are often actively misinformed of their rights by intermediaries. Language and cultural barriers further cloud knowledge of legal entitlements. Most workers have recently immigrated to Australia from China, Vietnam, Cambodia, Laos, the Middle East and the Horn of Africa. (Chinese and Vietnamese workers make up the majority.) Immigrants who have fled state oppression are reticent to access the systems of enforcement available to them. They are often suspicious towards unions, who may have been an apparatus of a state party in their country of origin. They are often in receipt of welfare benefits, and fear that they will be punished for cheating the welfare system upon making a claim. Significantly, also, they are reluctant to enforce their rights due to a (not unfounded) belief that they will not attract further employment in the industry after initiating a legal dispute. All of these factors result in an environment in which, even armed with adequate knowledge of their entitlements, outworkers are significantly disenfranchised as industrial citizens.

All of these factors combine to make the outworker provisions of the Award difficult to enforce. This is despite the fact that it has arisen from a reflexive, tripartite regulatory system and is an example of significant regulatory innovation in the area of labour law in that it seeks to extend the regulatory reach of the Award beyond the standard 'employee'.

Homeworkers' Code of Practice

In the mid-1990s the TCFUA, together with an alliance of community groups which came together under the banner of 'FairWear', developed a soft-law mechanism in light of repeated government refusal to take further legislative action to close the 'entitlement gaps'. Codes were initially negotiated with key manufacturers and 'brand names'. These early experiments were deeds signed between the Union and an individual company. Next, the Union negotiated a standard agreement with industry representatives of both manufacturers (the

Council of Textile and Fashion Industries of Australia (TFIA)) and retailers (the Retail Traders Association of Australia, now the AiG and ABL)). This Code (the Code) provides for different responsibilities for retailers (companies that *buy* their goods from suppliers) and manufacturers (companies which *organise* production from suppliers). This difference in responsibility reflects the disparity in power between these parties. The retailers' association resisted involvement in the Code for some time. Their confidence was bolstered by assurances from the Conservative Government that it was committed to industry self-regulation and saw no role for government intervention in the marketplace of supplier relations. Both retailers and manufacturers sign the Code as an initial step, demonstrating their 'commitment' to ethical production. However, manufacturers who sign are expected to go through a more rigorous accreditation in due course. The Code has six aspects which are worthy of comment from a regulatory perspective.

First, although the Code is voluntary it may not be accurate to describe it as entirely 'soft' in nature due to its symbiotic relationship with hard law. The Code builds on the outworker provisions of the Award and uses the conditions set in the Award as its base. Its aim is to enhance the operation of the Award through the elements described in this section of the chapter. Secondly, the Code provides a mechanism by which outworkers are provided with information about their legal entitlements. Once the contractor has established the rate per piece, this information is to be combined with other sewing instructions and standard information about the Award, the Union and how to make a complaint for underpayment. This, it is hoped, will assist in overcoming the chronic problem of misinformation in the industry concerning the employment status of outworkers.

Thirdly, as well as creating disincentives for non-compliance, the Code also creates incentives for compliance. Manufacturers which complete the accreditation process are licensed to display the 'No SweatShop' label in their goods. This will, it is hoped, attract consumer preferencing. FairWear publicises those companies which have adopted the Homeworkers' Code of Practice, as well as publicly 'shaming' those companies which have been found to be underpaying or who have failed to adopt the Code. Some government funding was provided to advertise the No SweatShop label. However, this funding was extremely limited and much more publicity is required if this incentive is to function effectively.

Fourthly, the Code enhances supply chain transparency because signatories must provide information about their suppliers. In order to become accredited, manufacturers must ensure that their suppliers are only sourcing ethically and provide lists of all suppliers and homeworkers to the Code Committee. Retailers or fashion houses also provide lists of all their suppliers and agree only to use suppliers that comply with employment laws and awards. This requirement extends supply chain transparency beyond that required under the Award, which only pertains to the relationship between manufacturers and outworkers. This extended transparency allows the union to trace the *entire* contracting chain to ensure compliance at every step in the supply chain. It also empowers the union to trigger the most powerful disincentive to non compliance available under the Code: the risk of losing contracts to supply major retailers.

Fifthly, the TCFUA is responsible for receiving complaints from outworkers and monitoring compliance with the Code. This includes identifying problems and providing details to the manufacturers/fashion houses/wholesaler or retailer. If the problem is not rectified within a reasonable period of time, the non-complying company risks losing its contract to supply the retailer or accredited manufacturer after the Code Committee considers the complaint. This is the most powerful sanction available under the Code. The Committee is also able to revoke a manufacturer's accreditation.

This aspect of the Code makes it a useful organising tool, in contrast to the technical monitoring by accounting firms common to many Codes of Conduct. When outworkers make a complaint to the Union they are contributing to a collective body of knowledge about the conditions of outworkers. They are informed of other services provided by the union, including English lessons and a Vietnamese language radio programme run by outworkers which was initiated by the union and FairWear. They can, in turn, inform their co-workers of the collective resources that are available to them and become part of a movement, as opposed to simply initiating a technical mechanism for enforcement. Furthermore, every successful complaint bolsters the power of the Union to insist upon compliance without having to trigger Award or Code-based enforcement mechanisms as industry knowledge of the risks of the non-compliance becomes widespread.

Sixthly, the Code established a Committee constituted by industry representatives to oversee the establishment and ongoing management of the Code. As a result, both its establishment and management is a multi-party affair, placing responsibility for enforcement of the Code on all major representatives in the industry.

How successful has the Code been in enhancing compliance with the Award? Around 50 retailers and fashion houses have signed part one of the Homeworkers' Code of Practice. This means that they are obliged to provide lists of their suppliers to the TCFUA on a quarterly basis. Whilst most retailers provided lists when they initially sign the Code, they have failed to update these lists. During the period of 1 November 2003 to 1 November 2004, five companies completed the annual accreditation process, four new companies were accredited and one company has become de-accredited as it no longer manufacturers in Australia.[46] There are around

[46] Ethical Clothing Trades Council of Victoria, '12 Month Report' (Parliament of Victoria, 2005).

50 companies pending accreditation. Whilst this is a major achievement, it only accounts for a miniscule proportion of production in Australia. The complaint mechanism has been under-utilised. However, when complaints have been made, companies have generally been quick to rectify problems. One complaint resulted in a supplier being dropped by a major retailer as a result of a failure by the non-complying supplier to rectify problems, suggesting that this mechanism could be more effectively utilised by the Union. Overall, it cannot be concluded that the Code has made a marked dent on mainstream practices within the industry, although it certainly has potential as a regulatory mechanism.

Supply Chain Legislation

Over the last five years, a number of state governments in Australia have enacted supply chain regulation in response to strong campaigns run by coalitions of unions, church and community organisations, organised under the auspices of the FairWear campaign.[47] In publicly lobbying the government for law reform, the FairWear campaign emphasised the link between control and responsibility: if a retailer or manufacturer can control the size, design, quantity and quality of a product, and can indirectly control the working conditions of outworkers, they should share ethical and legal responsibility for outworkers' pay and conditions.[48] State governments accepted these arguments and supply chain legislation is progressively becoming a generic model of regulation applicable to a wide range of outsourced work in hierarchically organised industries.[49]

Supply chain legislation imposes responsibility on all major players in the textile, clothing and footwear industry for the performance of work by outworkers, including manufacturers and retailers. The regulation involves two principle steps.[50]

First, the legislation extends the scope of labour law to cover work arrangements and contracts beyond the traditional employment relationship. The legislation 'deems' outworkers to be employees. 'Deeming' provisions overcome the limitations imposed by the conventional formulation of

---

[47] The Industrial Relations (Fair Work) Act 2005 (South Australia) amended the Industrial and Employee Relations Act 1994 (South Australia); Schedule 2 of the Industrial Relations (Ethical Clothing Trades) Act 2001 (New South Wales (NSW)) amended the Industrial Relations Act 1996 (NSW); the Outworkers (Improved Protection) Act 2003 (Vic); and the Industrial Relations and Other Acts Amendment Act 2005 (Queensland) amended the Industrial Relations Act 1999 (Queensland).

[48] See the FairWear website at www.fairwear.org.au/engine/php.

[49] Rawling, M, 'A Generic Model of Regulating Supply Chain Outsourcing' in C Arup et al (n 40).

[50] See Marshall, 'An Exploration of Control in the Context of Vertical Disintegration, and Regulatory Responses' (2006).

the contract of employment. In particular, such provisions seek to overcome the perverse incentives created by the limited scope of the employment contract, which has led intermediaries and manufacturers to ensure that outworkers work under a contract for service rather than an employment contract.

Secondly, the laws include provisions that permit workers who are not protected by the Federal or state Awards to recover lawful entitlements from parties. This right to recovery entitles outworkers to claim entitlements from parties who did not directly give the work to the outworker. These entitlements generally include annual and long service leave, commission and reimbursements, or compensation for expenses incurred. This right to recovery is based on the recognition that parties other than the person who directly provides the work may wield control over outworkers.

The legislation assigns enforcement tasks to a number of actors. The Outworkers (Improved Protection) Act 2003 (Victoria), for example, provides for the appointment of information services officers to disseminate information, and to monitor and enforce the laws. Importantly, it also assigns a number of rights to trade union officials, including a right of entry into workplaces and rights to appear in court and to bring legal proceedings on behalf of workers.

Advisory committees in each state have steered the legislative developments. These Advisory Committees are composed of the traditional tripartite parties—government, industry and trade union representatives—as well as community group representatives. They are responsible for overseeing the implementation of the legislation. The committees can make recommendations concerning ways to amend the legislation to make it more effective and simple and are required to make yearly reports to this end. The committees are also responsible for monitoring voluntary participation in, and compliance with, the National Homeworkers' Code of Practice and for making recommendations concerning the development of mandatory codes. In October 2004, one state released a Clothing Trades Mandatory Code of Practice that applies to retailers, suppliers and their contractors who are not compliant signatories to the voluntary Code.[51] Another state is in the process of drafting a Mandatory Code following a recommendation by its advisory committee.[52]

Supply chain legislation has been lauded as a significant regulatory innovation extending labour law rights and obligations to parties who were not previously covered by labour regulation.[53] Whist this is certainly true,

---

[51] NSW Ethical Clothing Trades Extended Responsibility Scheme, enacted under pt 3 of the Industrial Relations (Ethical Clothing Trades) Act 2001 (NSW).

[52] Ethical Clothing Trades Council of Victoria, '*12 Month Report*' (Parliament of Victoria, 2005) Recommendation 1.

[53] See Rawling, 'A Generic Model of Regulating Supply Chain Outsourcing' (2006).

the legislation does have some noteworthy limitations. It is important to distinguish the right to recovery available under these Acts from the broad enforcement of an employment contract, however. Enforcement is restricted to recovery of non-payment or under-payment. It does not provide for the enforcement of broader employment rights such as the right of specific performance in the event of a breach of the contract of employment or the right to bargain collectively. The rights available under supply chain legislation for workers who are not deemed employees are only 'labour law-like rights',[54] not full employment rights. This means that significant numbers of outworkers, who might have been 'employees' if it were not for the fact of labour market restructuring, do not enjoy full labour rights. Their formal industrial citizenship has been extended significantly by supply chain legislation, but not on parity with employees.[55]

ANALYSIS: STRENGTHS AND WEAKNESSES
OF INTERLOCKING TCF SUPPLY CHAIN REGULATION

Insights from Regulatory Theory

The second part of this chapter, titled 'Key Theoretical Concepts', provided a brief outline of regulatory theory and the idea of industrial citizenship. This section provides an analysis of supply chain regulation by using recent developments in regulatory theory as a means to assess the potential of supply chain regulation to bolster outworkers' industrial citizenship. The extended reach of the TCF supply chain regulation to workers who have not previously been considered employees, is what makes it an impressive regulatory experiment. It is self-evident; however, that industrial citizenship is more likely to be bolstered when regulation is effectively applied: when it reaches and affects its targets.

Assessment of Supply Chain Regulation: Using the Regulation Pyramid

As the following analysis assessment of the Australian TCF supply chain regulations show, a strength of the interlocking system of regulations is that the combination of voluntary mechanisms under the Code with the punitive options available under the Award and supply chain legislation results in an overall regulatory mechanism which contains most of the elements recommended by the Regulation Pyramid shown in Figure 1. It is the range

---

[54] Davies, P and Freedland, M, 'Employees, Workers, and the Autonomy of Labour law' in H Collins, P Davies and R Rideout (eds), *Legal Regulation of the Employment Relation*, (Kluwer Law International, London, 2000) 268.

[55] Whether or not full labour rights can be justified requires further discussion. See Marshall (n 44).

of options to encourage and enforce compliance available to state and non-state regulators that distinguishes it from many of the other mechanisms aimed at closing regulatory gaps.

The Apex

The Award supplies the content of the apex of the pyramid, entitled 'punitive sanctions'. As well as containing basic, non-negotiable, labour standards, it also provides for sanctions that can be applied for in court by either the labour inspectorate or unions. This element of the interlocking regulations gives it more 'teeth' than other 'soft law' approaches. However, penalties available under the Workplace Relations Act 1996 (Cth) have, until recently, been low. Companies may thus have assumed the risk of sanctions in preference to the risk of losing contracts with major suppliers by increasing labour costs.

Warnings and Tailored Sanctions

Regulatory theorists recognise that whilst it is important for regulators to impose sanctions on businesses for non-compliance with labour law, they should do so in a manner that is accommodative to their context. The Award and the Workplace Relations Act 1996 (Cth) do not provide for warnings or sanctions that are tailored to the size or nature of the enterprise. In formal terms, there is a one size fits all approach. One of the strengths of the Homeworkers' Code of Practice, therefore, is the fact that signatory companies and their suppliers which are found to be noncomplying must be given an opportunity to correct the problem. It is a term of the Code that the Union will not prosecute under the Award until companies have had a reasonable time to comply after a complaint is made. This means that small companies, which might have difficulty sustaining the cost of representation in court or bearing penalties, are provided with a means to correct their behaviour before the union enters into the formal system of sanctions.

A further aspect of tailoring arises from the 'party jumping' aspects of both the Award and the supply chain legislation. The right to recovery clauses entitle outworkers to claim entitlements from parties who did not directly give the work to the outworker. This right to recovery is based on the recognition that parties other than the person who directly provides the work may wield control over outworkers. It is also a practical solution to the transitory nature of many businesses in the informal economy in which outworkers work. A frequent problem for outworkers wishing to make claims in the past was the fact that the business that contracted them to conduct the work had often folded or wound up prior to a claim being made. Alternatively, the business was simply impossible to find. Without the ability to make claims against a party higher up in the supply chain, outworkers were left without any ability to recover lost payments in an informal and slippery economy. The party jumping aspects of the regulation thus provide a flexible regulatory answer to the seasonal and transitory nature of the industry that may act as a model for regulators of other informal and hierarchical markets.

Information, Education and Incentives for Formalisation

Regulatory scholars recognise that a low level of legal literacy is a key obstacle to the application of labour law: for many businesses and their workers, non-compliance with labour laws is a result of ignorance of the regulatory requirements. As was described earlier in the article, the Homeworkers' Code of Practice provides a means by which suppliers/ contractors are informed of their obligations and workers are informed of their rights under the Code and the Award. The Code therefore fills an important gap in the 'hard law' process. Nevertheless, far more is required in this respect.

Entrepreneurs make strategic choices about conforming to labour laws, and they may perceive labour regulation to be a constraint on enterprise growth. The Homeworkers' Code of Practice provides an incentive in the form of labelling which it is hoped will lead companies being rewarded by consumer preferencing. The Code also provides a significant disincentive to non-compliance which may prove more important than the punitive sanctions available under the Award or the threat of recovery of unpaid entitlements under supply chain legislation. Both accredited manufacturers and signatory retailers must stop using suppliers if they do not comply with the Award after they have been given an opportunity to rectify problems. This aspect of the Code takes advantage of the hierarchical nature of the supply chain described in part two of this chapter.

Design and Implementation Should be Participatory

A second major principle, recognised by regulatory theorists, is that both regulatory design and implementation should be participatory. The right participation, understood through the prism of industrial citizenship, is understood as a positive right. Whilst the right to freedom of association and the right to bargain collectively might potentially be satisfied by the absence of legal impediments to the making of collective demands by workers on company management, this principle suggests that regulators must actively facilitate and encourage participation. This positive duty is all the more important in informal economies where traditional representative organisations often have little coverage or capacity to organise.

There are three elements to this principle. First, that those who will most be affected by regulation, or their representatives, should be involved in its design. Secondly, that representative organisations, especially trade unions, should be involved in monitoring and compliance. Thirdly, that representative organisations should be involved in periodic assessment of the regulatory programme.

The People Who Will be Affected by the Regulation, or Their Representatives, should be Involved in the Design of the Regulation

It is believed that optimal structuring of responsive regulation, which takes account of local conditions, is more likely to result from negotiations between governments, businesses, and other interested organisations.[56] Consultation during design also generates demand for regulatory programmes. Assessment of problems and joint generation of solutions allows project participants to develop a sense of ownership, awareness and respect of the programmes.[57] This is likely to foster cooperation with monitoring and enforcement of labour laws. Importantly, a transparent and well-designed consultative process can also assist in avoiding capture by dominant players or groups opposed to enforcement.

The involvement of representative organisations in design has been a major strength of Australian TCF supply chain regulation. However, analysis of the nature of the participation of the parties suggests that the 'power redistributive' aspects of traditional labour law have been eroded with each addition to the TCF supply chain regulation. The sources of power for the parties have shifted and participation has arguably become more technocratic over time.

Awards have traditionally been negotiated within a system in which the rights of trade unions in the bargaining process have been protected by legislation, including the right to freely associate and to conduct strikes under particular conditions. Beneficial minimum conditions contained in awards thus partially reflected the relative industrial strength of workers in negotiation processes, as well as the views of commissioners who presided over the cases. The variations to the Clothing Trades Award which resulted in the outworker provisions were generated through this adversarial process. Changes to labour laws by the Workplace Relations Act 1996 (Cth) and the more recent Work Choices legislation have eroded these bargaining rights

[56] Servais, JM, 'Working Conditions and Globalization' in R Blanpain and C Engels (eds), *Comparative Labour Law and Industrial Relations in Industrialized Market Economies*, 7th edn (The Hague; London, Kluwer Law International, 2001) 361.

[57] Rinehart, R, 'Designing Programmes to Improve Working and Employment Conditions in the Informal Economy: A Literature Review' (Conditions of Work and Employment Series No 10, ILO, Geneva, 2004) 11.

for unions, limiting this potential source of industrial strength within TCF supply chain regulation.[58]

The power of the Union to bring other parties to the negotiating table in the regulatory setting of the Code flowed not mainly from its industrial strength (as it has very little in this context), but from its ability to call on consumer power. The Union is largely powerless to call on outworkers to strike; however, it can work with consumer advocacy groups to bring a company into disrepute due to its poor labour practices. In relation to the design process, therefore, the labour rights of the respective parties mattered very little. The reliance on consumer advocacy marked a significant shift in the nature of the Union's role.

Supply chain legislation was designed through a traditional parliamentary process, following intense lobbying from interested parties, rather than an adversarial industrial relations process. Modifications to the design of legislation, such as making the Codes mandatory, will be the result of reports from advisory committees, which provide for representation by all significant parties, including community groups. This aspect of the legislation is impressive, and reflects the principle of participation in design and monitoring. However, the committee is a non-adversarial body whose power is limited to the making of representations which may or may not be accepted by state parliaments. This process does not incorporate any of the traditional industrial relations mechanisms for redressing the imbalance of power between parties, and is instead based on the principle that Parliament will act in the best interests of all parties. As was commented upon earlier, as well, the legislation itself does not extend the right to collective bargaining to outworkers who are not deemed employees. Supply chain legislation is not, therefore, a replacement for traditional labour law regulations.

The breadth of consultation—that is, the proportion of targeted population which will be subject to the regulation involved in the consultation process—is an additional factor in generating 'ownership' of regulatory processes. Whilst the participatory aspects of the supply chain regulations are impressive, there has never been a broad participatory process involving large numbers of outworkers, contractors or manufacturers in the design or assessment process. It may be fair to assume that representative organisations will carry out their own internal, consultative processes, and further industrial citizenship in this manner. However, the failure of the regulatory agencies responsible for regulatory design to carry out 'official', widespread consultation may limit the extent to which individuals feel franchised. In the context of an attempt to extend regulation into an informal sector

---

[58] See Marshall and Mitchell, 'Enterprise Bargaining, Managerial Prerogative and the Protection of Workers' Rights' (Cth)' (2006).

where individuals mistrust state agencies and are often unaware of the legal remedies available to them, it may be a mistake to entrust broader consultative processes to representative organisations.

Representative Organisations Should be Involved in Assessment of the Regulatory Programme

Another way that design of labour law can incorporate responsive regulation is by providing for periodic assessment of the regulatory framework that has been established. Award variations have traditionally acted as a mechanism through which monitoring of terms and structure of labour regulation can occur. Employer and worker representatives submit evidence concerning problems with the regulation, or needs which have arisen which must be responded to, and the award is varied accordingly. It was through this system that the outworker provisions of Clothing Trades Award 1982 were first enacted. Supply chain regulation in various states is also monitored by the committee which oversees it. It is this system of monitoring which has resulted in recommendations that the voluntary Homeworkers' Code of Practice become mandatory in certain states. The development of both the content, enforcement and publicising of the supply chain legislation is understood to be an iterative, learning process. By providing for the legislation to be overseen by various interested parties, the process both draws on the expertise of the parties and also contributes to the expertise of the parties. This creates a useful enforcement loop.

Representative Organisations, Especially Trade Unions, Must be Involved in Monitoring and Compliance

Ensuring that representative organisations are involved in the compliance process in informal economies is no simple task.[59] The significant role of the Union in monitoring and enforcing the Award, the Code and the supply chain legislation is both a strength and a weakness of the interlocking regulations. On the one hand, the Union's role in the regulation contributes to the collective strength of the union and the workers it represents. On the other hand, the Union is simply too under-resourced to be primarily responsible for enforcement. Unions rely on membership dues to resource activities. Because outworkers are a seasonal and informal workforce, only small numbers are members, leaving the union in a poor financial condition. Only a handful of union officials are available to work on monitoring and enforcing the Code. This results in the impressive regulatory system,

---

[59] See eg, ILC (90th Session) Resolution concerning Decent Work and the Informal Economy (ILO, Geneva 2000).

described in this chapter, being under-enforced. This fact alone may explain why compliance with the minimum standards remains low.

CONCLUSION

Assessed against key regulatory criteria, the Australian TCF supply chain regulation appears to be a model of regulatory design. It is responsive. It is participatory. It is multifaceted: it provides incentives for voluntary compliance as well as punitive sanctions. It provides mechanisms for workers who have traditionally been extruded from labour law protection to gain at least partial, if not full, rights compared with traditional workers. Yet, the regulations have made no evident difference to the conditions of outworkers in the time of their operation. In the close to 20 years since variations to the Award extended its reach to outworkers, and the 10 years since the Homeworkers' Code of Practice was agreed upon, the conditions of outworkers in Australia may have become worse, rather than better.[60] Outworkers remain disenfranchised as industrial citizens. Thus far this chapter has speculated that there are a number of likely reasons for this. An additional reason may be that regulation of this nature will simply never be sufficient to stem competitive pressures brought about by import penetration from countries with lower labour costs following reductions in tariffs and import quotas.

There is broad consensus that trade liberalisation and the resulting increase in import levels accelerated the process of job losses in the TCF industry due to outsourcing overseas and to the shifting ratio of outworkers to factory workers in order to drive down production costs.[61] Indeed, the rationale for tariff protection in Australia in the early part of the twentieth century was both to provide shelter for infant industries and also to foster decent work. The 1929 Brigden report stated that 'there is more to be said for protecting an industry because it employs labour at good wages than for any other reason'.[62] In 1986 the Australian Industry Assistance Commission predicted that there were natural barriers to the trend to overseas sourcing of the domestic clothing market following tariff reductions.[63] History has shown that the industry has responded to these natural

---

[60] See Ethical Clothes Trades Council of Victoria, '12 Month Report' (Parliament of Victoria, 2005).

[61] See Peck (n 28) 310; Tait, D and Gibson, K, 'Economic Restructuring: an Analysis of Migrant Labour in Sydney' (1987) *Journal of Intercultural Studies* 8. The dispute in the economic literature is over whether this is a bad thing.

[62] Samuelson, M, 'The Australian Case for Protection Re-examined' (1940) 54 *Quarterly Journal of Economics* 143.

[63] Industries Assistance Commission, 'The Textile, Clothing and Footwear Industries, IAC Report' (Commonwealth of Australia, 1986) 204.

barriers by outsourcing production to outworkers in Australia in order to exploit the cost savings resulting from reduced overheads, lower wages, and enhanced flexibility in production.

Regulations, no matter how effective, may not ever be effective in curtailing this trend. Other forms of governance available to states, such as the provision of services and subsidies, may be more likely to produce better results, but are unlikely to be utilised given the trend towards 'regulatory capitalism' which is reinforced by certain regional and multi-national agreements.[64] Braithwaite observes that states have become rather more preoccupied with the *regulation* part of governance and less with *providing*. Empirical work by Vogel has showed that far from there being less rules or 'deregulation' as a result of attempts to free up the market, there is ever more regulation; what he calls *Freer Markets, More Rules*, and also 'more capitalism, more regulation'.[65] This regulation is not only by the state of private actors. Non-state regulation has grown even more rapidly than state regulation. Regulation is 'delegated to business and professional self-regulation and to civil society, to intra- and international networks of regulatory experts, and increased regulation of state by the state, much of it regulation through and for competition'.[66] More and more so, the art of government 'consists in coordinating the functions of the various self-regulating bodies in different spheres of the economy'.[67]

Consistent with these observations, this case study has shown that the 'freeing up' of markets from tariffs and quotas in the TCF sector in Australia has resulted in an expanding number of regulations to counteract the negative effects on labour. More and more complex layers of state and non-state regulation have been added to the regulatory mix in response to the gaps created by labour market restructuring. Putting aside the debate concerning the efficacy of tariffs and quotas, the labour regulation system is now significantly over-burdened both by the complexity of regulations and also by responsibility. There may simply be limits to the amount that labour regulation can be expected to achieve in the absence of the adequate deployment of alternative governance mechanisms aimed at protecting labour and bolstering industrial citizenship.

---

[64] Braithwaite, J, 'Neoliberalism or Regulatory Capitalism, Occasional Paper 5' (Canberra, Regulatory Institutions Network, Research School of Social Sciences, Australian National University, 2005); Levi-Faur, D, 'The Global Diffusion of Regulatory Capitalism' (2005) *Annuals of the American Academy for Political and Social Science*, cited in Braithwaite, ibid 11.

[65] Vogel, S, *Freer Markets, More Rules: Regulatory Reform in Advanced Industrial Societies* (Ithica and London, Cornell University Press, 1996) cited in Braithwaite, 'Neoliberalism or Regulatory Capitalism, Occasional Paper 5' (2005) ibid 11.

[66] Braithwaite (n 63) 11–12.

[67] Shepel, H, *The Constitution of Private Governance* (Oxford, Hart Publishing, 2005), cited in Braithwaite (n 63) 34.

Accepting, however, that labour regulation is the only governance mechanism likely to be employed to improve the conditions of outworkers, the assessment conducted in this chapter points to some clear reforms which may increase regulatory efficacy. At a minimum it is clear that if unions are to continue to be the main enforcers of supply chain regulation, their capacity to do so should be bolstered by additional funding to counteract the effects of a declining membership of formal employees as a result of vertical disintegration. It would be desirable for state inspectorates, who currently have the power to enforce state Awards and state labour laws, to be better equipped to conduct this role, also, with the threat of increased penalties to augment the power of both enforcement parties.

Simplicity of regulatory techniques is also desirable. A uniform national approach to supply chain regulation, or federal legislation would reduce transaction costs for businesses and increase the chances of compliance. The reform of South Australian labour law to incorporate supply chain regulation could act as the best model for national legislative reform. Whilst other states have enacted supply chain legislation in separate statutes to labour law, South Australian supply chain legislation is located within the main labour statute. In enacting its amendment, the South Australian legislature avoided the language of employment law altogether. The amendment significantly extends the scope of the industrial statute to deal with work arrangements and contracts beyond the traditional employment relationship.[68] It is thus most consistent with the broad concept of industrial citizenship introduced in this chapter, not only because it covers a wider range of workers than normal labour legislation, but also because it covers a wider range of 'employers'. The language of the legislation extends its scope to enterprises which organise work and exercise some control over worker conditions, but might not resemble a traditional employer. It may, at times, extend to retailers, if they have played a sufficient role in organising work.

It would seem desirable, also, for the South Australian model to be added to and for a mandatory code of conduct which covers manufacturers and retailers to be incorporated into this legislation to further extend its scope. It may be that because the Homeworkers' Code of Practice was negotiated through an extra-state, non-parliamentary process, significant innovation was possible. This innovation should now be adopted by state regulators. Effective regulation must make use of the hierarchical nature of the supply chain. The strongest penalty for non-compliance with labour standards for a manufacturer—loss of a contract to supply a core business—ought to be given legal force instead of being left to voluntary compliance.

---

[68] The South Australian legislation uses the language of the 'responsible contractor' who is defined as any person in a contracting chain who organises or gives out work: s 99B(1) of the Fair Work Act 1994 (South Australia).

This chapter has shown that, despite clever regulatory design, outworkers are falling through regulatory gaps caused by the difficulties for state and non-state regulators in enforcing supply chain regulation and wilful non-compliance by all parties in the supply chain. Together the Award, supply chain legislation and the Homeworkers' Code of Conduct contain many of the elements of good regulatory design, including penalties for non-compliance, warnings and tailored sanctions and incentives for compliance. Despite these important elements, outworkers are being deprived of fundamental human rights as workers. This provides a clear impetus for further review and redesign of the regulatory terrain in order to ensure that all workers enjoy full rights as industrial citizens.

21

Conclusion: Regulating to Protect Workers' Human Rights

COLIN FENWICK AND TONIA NOVITZ

INTRODUCTION

There is a long intellectual tradition of arguing that workers—that is, those who depend upon their labour for their living—have fundamental entitlements, or rights, which inhere in them by virtue of their status as workers.[1] Various debates within this tradition about the true nature and extent of workers' entitlements are reflected in the differences between countries in their treatment of labour rights, whether in constitutional instruments or domestic legislation. Despite such differences, the fundamental idea that workers have basic entitlements is reflected in key international instruments which proclaim and protect fundamental human rights. One of the first international instruments to do so was the Constitution of the International Labour Organisation (ILO), adopted in 1919. Subsequent constitutional developments in the ILO have further oriented the Organisation toward a concept of workers' basic, or core rights.[2] The Universal Declaration of Human Rights (adopted in 1948) enshrines certain rights for workers, as do the key United Nations (UN) covenants that elaborate upon its content: the International Covenant on Civil and Political Rights and the International Covenant on Economic, Social and Cultural Rights, both adopted in 1966. Labour rights are also protected in other international human rights instruments, in regional human rights instruments, and in international trade and aid instruments.[3]

---

[1] See chapter one, above.

[2] On the shift in orientation from 1919 to 1944 and, in particular, the emergence of fundamental human rights as a clear part of the ILO mission from the adoption of the Declaration of Philadelphia and through the 1998 Declaration on Fundamental Principles and Rights at Work, see Novitz, T, *International and European Protection of the Right to Strike* (Oxford, Oxford University Press, 2003) 95–106.

[3] See, for different views of the potential for further developments in this respect, Kaufmann, C, *Globalisation and Labour Rights: The Conflict Between Core Labour Standards and International Economic Law* (Oxford, Hart Publishing, 2007); Hepple, B, *Labour Laws*

One of the aims of this collection of essays has been to investigate how current legal forms, institutions and practices, whether national, regional or international, reflect or have been shaped by long-standing traditions and patterns of thought about the rights of labour. Each chapter in this book alone sheds some further light on the relationships between employment, industrial relations and human rights, as they are presently understood and protected in law. But at a deeper level we hope this collection facilitates inter-related national and international comparisons. Not only can we compare aspects of different national systems with each other (India as compared with the United States of America; or Brazil as compared with Nigeria), we can also compare approaches taken by national systems with the approaches taken in regional and/or international systems (mechanisms for protection of civil liberties within the United States as compared with those available under the European Convention on Human Rights; or the jurisprudence adopted under the Canadian Charter with the interpretation and understanding of UN human rights instruments). We can also consider the interaction of these systems with domestic legal systems and developments (the impact of the European Convention on Human Rights on the United Kingdom; or the impact of ILO standards in Nigeria or South Africa), and we can compare different international systems of human rights law and how they conceptualise and implement norms relating to workers' rights (the African, Inter-American and European human rights systems; or the regulation of working time in ILO instruments as compared with its regulation in other international norms).

These different comparisons are further enhanced by the several chapters that explore the efforts of those who strive *in practice* to make good on the promise of human rights law to workers, together with those that are concerned with how we can think about and improve the way we use the law to achieve that goal. Thus, we can compare litigation seeking protection of trade union autonomy (such as the *ASLEF v United Kingdom* case brought before the European Court of Human Rights)[4] with innovative legal and regulatory strategies (regulating the textile, clothing and footwear industry in Australia), and an analysis of the way that law has played a role in promoting workers' rights in Cambodia. Moreover, we are able to consider a proposal for quite significant reform of the ILO (by changes to the focus of its work and the role of the International Labour Office) in the light of a detailed examination

---

and Global Trade (Oxford, Hart Publishing, 2005); and Hepple, B, 'The WTO as a Mechanism for Labour Regulation' in B Bercusson and C Estlund (eds), *Regulating Labour in the Wake of Globalisation: New Challenges, New Institutions* (Oxford, Hart Publishing, 2008).

[4] *ASLEF v United Kingdom* (App no 11002/05) [2007] IRLR 361. See chapter 6 and chapter 15 above. Also, Ewing, K, 'The Implications of the *ASLEF* Case' (2007) 36 *Industrial Law Journal* 425.

of how the ILO's systems for supervision of compliance with human rights obligations currently operate (the Commission of Inquiry concerning freedom of association in Belarus).

We hope then that this volume will serve, first and foremost, as a future resource for scholars and practitioners in the discipline. It follows that we do not pretend in this, our last chapter, to have exhausted the full wealth of potential analysis that this collection of essays might offer. Nevertheless, we do believe that some initial conclusions can be drawn from the study.

Philip Alston, in the preface to his edited collection on *Labour Rights as Human Rights*, quoted from a description of the ways in which globalisation has affected working conditions. Penned by Archon Fung, Dara O'Rourke and Charles Sabel, it referred in particular to 'child labor, punishingly long work days, harsh discipline, hazardous working conditions, sexual predation, and suppression of the freedom to associate and organize'.[5] Alston's point was that it is relatively easy to identify and to describe these problems, but that there is significant disagreement about how to respond to them.[6] Indeed he suggests that 'the key question remains whether the response is optimally, *or even usefully*, formulated in terms of labour rights'.[7]

The contributions to this volume demonstrate that, in practice, workers and their organisations have frequently pursued their efforts 'to promote and secure decent working conditions for all',[8] as a category of rights, within the broader framework of human rights. In other words, they have deployed the rhetoric of human rights, and they have presented their claims for protection of those rights within the institutional, legal structures established for the protection of human rights. Although these claims have been presented in diverse ways, there appears at least to be consensus amongst workers and their organisations, at the national, regional and international levels, that they *must* present their claims in terms of human rights—even if not exclusively so. The imperative to present their claims as human rights comes from the desire to utilise the potentially powerful legal methods of securing advantage to pursue their claims, and also from the perceived

---

[5] Fung, A, O'Rourke, D and Sabel, C, 'Realizing Labor Standards' (2001) 26 *Boston Review* 1.

[6] Indeed, Fung, O'Rourke and Sabel's 'Ratcheting Labour Standards' proposal has been one of the more controversial. For critiques, see for example Murray, J, 'The Sound of One Hand Clapping? The "Ratcheting Labour Standards" Proposal and International Labour Law' (2001) 14 *Australian Journal of Labour Law* 306; and Owens, A, 'Testing the Ratcheting Labor Standards Proposal: Indonesia and the Shangri-La Workers' (2004) 5 *Melbourne Journal of International Law* 169.

[7] Alston, P, 'Labour Rights as Human Rights: The Not So Happy State of the Art' in P Alston (ed), *Labour Rights as Human Rights* (Oxford, Oxford University Press, 2005) 2 (emphasis added). For a recent reflection on this issue in the United States context, see Kolben, K 'Labor Rights as Human Rights' (2010) 50 *Virginia Journal of International Law* 449.

[8] Ibid 1.

need to respond to employers' willingness to use these arguments and tools themselves. In that sense, Alston's question whether labour's claims are *usefully* pursued as human rights is easily answered. At the same time, however, much of the evidence in this volume suggests that the legal avenues presented to pursue workers' claims—by constructing them as human rights—do not always lead to *optimal* outcomes for workers and their organisations. On the contrary: the results have been decidedly mixed.

We suggest here that one reason for this may be the very breadth and diversity of human rights that might be called in aid of pursuing workers' claims. As we noted in our introduction, some workers' claims can be considered civil and political rights, some economic and social rights, and others (like freedom of association for trade union purposes) are protected in international instruments as both. Moreover, some institutions, particularly the ILO, do not confine themselves to these categories in their work to oversee states' compliance with their obligations. This breadth and diversity presents both opportunity and challenge for those seeking to frame workers' claims in terms of human rights law. A related issue is that courts seem to prefer the protection of some rights (and some interpretations of the scope of those rights) to others. In particular, we find differences between the treatment of what have been traditionally regarded as civil and political rights, on the one hand, and economic, social and cultural rights on the other. Courts, and even various regional and international supervisory bodies, also seem to prefer the protection of individual liberties to collective assertions of rights and assertions of collective rights. An emphasis on more easily identifiable civil and political rights is also apparent in the cases brought under the Alien Tort Claims Act, in which courts have expressed views about the meaning of the concept of 'the law of nations' that is focused solely on civil and political rights.[9]

It strikes us, however, that the construction of workers' rights as human rights poses other questions about the range of regulatory techniques that might be used to promote workers' interests, and their relationship to each other. A key issue is that taking a human rights approach raises the possibility that long-standing methods and institutions for resolving disputes between workers, their organisations and employers might be neglected, albeit if not completely abandoned. While pursuing labour rights as human rights may hold out the possibility of stringent enforcement through constitutional and other domestic courts, this raises starkly the long-standing issue of whether the general law is apt to the task of resolving industrial and employment-related disputes. Not surprisingly in view of the tensions to which they point, some of the authors in this collection (Chioma Agomo, writing on Nigeria in chapter eight, and Stefan van Eck on South Africa in chapter nine) do express misgivings about the consequences of

---

[9] See Joseph, S *Corporations and Transnational Human Rights Litigation* (Oxford, Hart Publishing, 2004).

labour law becoming an aspect of a broader trend toward constitutionalism. Historically, the emergence of special regimes governing labour was a response to the inadequate treatment of labour issues by the ordinary courts, but today we encounter a curious reverse trend towards the dominance of human rights jurisprudence in which the more concrete, practical concerns of working people may be secondary.

Conversely, the pronouncements of various regional and international supervisory bodies on human rights are attractive not because they may have any concrete legal effect, but rather because of their perceived potential to influence public policy and national legislation. Several contributors have identified the potential of supra-national human rights supervision to play a significant role in promoting labour standards. Beyond this core of international human rights supervision is a vast array of what might be thought of as promotional strategies for the protection of workers' interests, which have in common their insistence upon the proposition that labour rights are human rights. These include trade and aid conditionality (Generalised System of Preferences (GSP) programmes, for example), deployment of resources to assist programmatic reform (capacity-building work, whether delivered by the international trade union movement or other actors), and contract compliance (supply-chain regulation), although each may pose particular challenges for developing countries. In addition to promotional strategies there is the approach of direct action to enforce legal obligations in national courts, as in the case of suits under the Alien Tort Claims Act. Whether workers' claims can usefully (much less optimally) be constructed in terms of human rights may therefore also depend upon the institutional machinery—that is, the regulatory architecture—that can be deployed to pursue such claims. As Adler and Woolcock's examination of legal institutions in Cambodia in chapter nineteen shows, it may also depend upon the capacity of those institutions that exist. One of the things that this collection does, then, is to offer the opportunity to compare different modes of human rights regulation, their inter-relation, and how they might be changed so as to contribute better to the goal of promoting and securing decent working conditions for all.

VIEWING WORKERS' RIGHTS AS HUMAN RIGHTS: REASONS FOR DIVERGENT REGULATORY APPROACHES

The contributions to this volume illustrate at length and in depth that the pursuit of secure and decent working conditions—the promotion of labour standards—can be constructed in terms of human rights protection. There are very many instances of human rights discourse connecting with various aspects of what might otherwise be thought of as labour law. Examples include the response of the Supreme Court of India to the constitutional claims of workers (Ramapriya Gopalakrishnan in chapter seven), the treatment by the English courts of actions brought by employees on the basis of rights set out in the Human Rights Act of 1988 (as discussed by Anne Davies in chapter six), the right to work under the UN human rights covenants of 1966 (Sarah Joseph in chapter eleven), protection from discrimination under the Canadian Charter (Christian Brunelle in chapter four), the treatment of freedom of association by the European Court of Human Rights (Tonia Novitz, and Virginia Mantouvalou in chapters fourteen and fifteen respectively) and treatment of the right to strike by the European Court of Justice (Tonia Novitz and Phil Syrpis in chapter sixteen). Deirdre McCann in chapter eighteen points to the conditions under which ILO supervisory bodies may regard excessive working time as a form of forced labour. These examples illustrate the diverse and significant potential for the application of human rights discourse in the employment context. It is only further highlighted by Joseph, in chapter eleven, in her treatment of the potential breadth of human rights coverage for workers under international human rights instruments.

However, these examples also suggest that the ways in which human rights approaches can be adopted by workers and their organisations are far from settled. On the contrary: we identify a discursive process taking place, within which there is no straightforward or fixed meaning for many aspects of constitutionally-respected civil liberties, or international human rights. The point we are making is that conceptions of rights, and the uses to which they may be put, appear not to be fixed—despite the fact that there have been declarations that international human rights law protects rights that are universal, indeed indivisible.[10] This perhaps follows from our suggestion in the introductory chapter that there is no one true conception of rights, but rather divergent strands of a liberal tradition (and we do not pretend to have successfully traversed all other traditions) which tend in different directions, and which have seemingly led particular legislative bodies, courts and international and regional supervisory bodies to adopt divergent positions on identical questions. In other words, the form that institutions take does affect protection of rights.

It is evident that different human rights claims are treated very differently by national courts. This is perhaps illustrated by contrasting the approaches of the Indian and Canadian Supreme Courts. In chapter seven, Gopalakrishnan recognises that the judgments of the Indian Supreme Court reflect the compelling desire to protect children, and to prevent forced labour. However, the Supreme Court has prioritised these entitlements ahead of other identified 'core labour standards', which are usually understood

---

[10] See the 1993 Vienna Declaration on Human Rights UN Doc A/CONF.157/24. Another example commonly cited is the Declaration on the Occasion of the 50th Anniversary of the Universal Declaration of Human Rights, adopted by the Council of Europe Committee of Ministers on 10 December 1998 para 4: civil, political and socio-economic rights are 'universal, indivisible, interdependent and interrelated'.

in terms of human rights, including freedom of association and the right to collective bargaining. Arguably, this approach has the potential to marginalise the role of trade unions. However, this need not inevitably be the case. Indeed, we see in the Supreme Court of Canada an attempt to make collective agreements subject to other human rights law claims, thereby potentially *enhancing* the role of unions in pursuit of protection of their members' human rights, although as Brunelle notes in chapter four, this also poses significant challenges.

The more classic case is the confusion as to the borderline between civil and political rights, on the one hand, and economic, social and cultural rights on the other, a distinction which we highlighted in our introduction. The ramifications of the attempts to make such a distinction, and the confusion about boundaries which can follow, are evident from many of the chapters. Christian Brunelle notes that the Canadian Charter 'chooses to overlook economic, social and cultural rights found in the major international instruments'; while in chapter six, Anne Davies observes that 'the most worrying feature of English law's greater emphasis on human rights is its exclusive focus on civil and political rights'. The same is true in Australia, where entrenched legislative protection for fundamental human rights is only now beginning to emerge, and so far only at the sub-national level. Although there is no necessary reason for these jurisdictions to have done so, they looked to the English, or Commonwealth model of implementing human rights obligations, with its emphasis on civil and political rights, and also its deference to parliamentary sovereignty. These systems are reluctant to empower judges to do more than to make declarations of inconsistency with human rights obligations, leaving the responsibility to remedy such cases in the hands of the executive—and with it also the power not to do so.

In chapter seven, Gopalakrishnan recognises that the approach of the Indian Supreme Court cannot be reduced to this dichotomy, but also appreciates that it is the apparent economic expense involved in protecting certain socio-economic rights that appears to make them off-putting. As she observes, 'issues that could have significant financial implications for the state and other employers' are approached with caution. By way of contrast, van Eck's contribution to this volume in chapter nine demonstrates, as many others have also observed, that South Africa's experience of justiciable economic, social and cultural rights has fallen well short of bringing the country to a halt. The Constitutional Court has taken slightly different approaches in *Government of South Africa v Grootboom*[11] and *Minister of Health v Treatment Action Campaign*,[12] but each has been within the

[11] *Government of South Africa v Grootboom* 2001 (1) SA 46 (CC).
[12] *Minister of Health v Treatment Action Campaign* (2002) (5) SA 721 (CC).

bounds of the constitution and has not unduly affected the stability of the South African legal system.

At the international level the primary method of supervision is by analysis of government reports. But this is supplemented by a wide array of possible complaint procedures, both individual and collective. The European Social Charter, for example, provides for collective complaints, and this is perhaps a fair description of the ILO procedures that allow representative organisations to bring matters before its supervisory bodies. The Optional Protocol to the International Covenant on Civil and Political Rights, however, establishes an individual right of complaint, as does the European Convention on Human Rights—although in both cases subject to the requirement first to exhaust domestic remedies. These two procedures differ, however, when it comes to the body that is created and empowered to deal with the complaint: the UN Human Rights Committee is not a court. (Nor are the ILO's supervisory bodies, and neither are those with competence under the European Social Charter, although courts are established in the Inter-American and African human rights systems). Obviously enough this goes to the question of the type of remedy that might be ordered in a case where a complaint is upheld.

The adoption in 2008 of an optional protocol to the International Covenant on Economic, Social and Cultural Rights—under which nationals of states parties might have a right of individual petition to an international body after the fashion of the first optional protocol to the International Covenant on Civil and Political Rights—indicates the potential for justiciability of this second generation of rights. However, we have yet to see what the rate of ratifications will be. In Europe, there have been relatively few ratifications of the Collective Complaints Protocol to the European Social Charter. The United Kingdom, for example, is not amongst those which have undertaken to be subject to that procedure. Moreover, even for those states subject to the collective complaints procedure, the European Committee of Social Rights cannot issue a legally binding ruling in the same way as the European Court of Human Rights.[13]

The case of the ILO's complex supervision procedures has strong similarities to supervision under the European Social Charter.[14] In particular, it provides many avenues for workers' organisations to participate on behalf

[13] For an overview of the European Social Charter mechanisms see, for example, Alston, P, 'Assessing the Strengths and Weaknesses of the European Social Charter's Supervisory System' (Center For Human Rights And Global Justice Working Paper, Economic, Social And Cultural Rights Series, Number 6, 2005), available at: www.chrgj.org/publications/docs/wp/Alston%20Assessing%20the%20Strengths%20and%20Weaknesses%20of%20the%20European%20Social%20Charter's%20Supervisory%20System.pdf.
[14] On the supervision architecture, see Novitz, *International and European Protection of the Right to Strike* (2003) ch 8; also Tortell in chapter thirteen in this volume.

of their members, or even on behalf of other groups.[15] Both workers' and employers' organisations might also make comment on government reports, or supply information directly to the ILO for the attention of the Committee of Experts, which will consider it. And, of course, representatives of these social partners participate in all forums of the organisation, including its annual conference, which has a special committee whose purpose is to consider more serious cases of non-compliance with ratified instruments. All of this suggests an orientation toward economic and social rights, yet ILO instruments cannot so easily be confined.

Moreover the apparent emphasis on collective—or, better, representative—participation in supervision needs to be seen in light of the operation of article 26 of the ILO Constitution. As Lisa Tortell has shown in this volume, in chapter thirteen, the establishment of a Commission of Inquiry by the ILO under this provision is a highly unusual procedure in the pantheon of international human rights supervision. Indeed, it has no analogue. It might be thought passing strange then that the procedure can be initiated by a single delegate to the ILO Conference. Perhaps the resolution of this seeming paradox lies in the knowledge that ILO Conference non-governmental delegates come, in theory at least (and in most cases in practice) from representative organisations of workers and employers. Certainly the procedure is not one that facilitates complaints about individual cases (although allegations can refer to what has happened to particular individuals).

However, the ILO and its Commissions of Inquiry aside, economic, social and cultural rights continue to be seen widely as attended by significant obstacles to their implementation as fundamental human rights. They are often regarded as potentially costly (see Gopalakrishnan in chapter seven above), aspirational as opposed to capable of immediate realisation (as identified by Jill Murray in chapter twelve), relative to social and economic circumstances, and non-justiciable. As others have shown, some of these perceptions are inaccurate in both law and in fact. Many obligations under the International Covenant on Economic, Social and Cultural Rights, for example, are capable of immediate implementation, and on a proper reading of the instrument, states are *obliged* to implement them immediately.[16]

---

[15] Many of the representations brought under art 24 of the International Labour Organisation (ILO) Constitution concerning non-compliance with Convention No 169 on Indigenous and Tribal Peoples have been brought by unions on behalf of groups of indigenous and tribal peoples: see Fenwick, C, 'The International Labour Organisation: An Integrated Approach to Economic and Social Rights' in M Langford and S Liebenberg (eds), *Socio-Economic Rights Jurisprudence: Emerging Trends in Comparative and International Law* (Cambridge, Cambridge University Press, 2008).

[16] For a discussion of these misconceptions, see Van Hoof, GJH, 'The Legal Nature of Economic, Social and Cultural Rights: A Rebuttal of Some Traditional Views' in P Alston and K Tomasevski (eds), *The Right to Food* (Utrecht, Martinus Nijhoff, 1984); and P Alston and G Quinn, 'The Nature and Scope of States Parties' Obligations under the International Covenant on Economic, Social and Cultural Rights' (1987) 9 *Human Rights Q.* 156. See also

As we observed in the introduction to this volume, and as is clear from the contributions of Joseph and Novitz, in chapters eleven and fourteen respectively, worker's entitlements even to the accepted core labour standards may be taken to fall on either or both sides of the supposed boundary, depending on the specific content attributed to the right, or the particular claim that calls it in aid. When considering the scope of the legal protection of an individual's right of association, it always seems difficult to decide the relationship of the individual (civil and political) freedom, to the goals that might be pursued by an association formed in the exercise of the right. Courts and other bodies interpreting legal protections of human rights find it particularly hard to resolve whether (and if so, how far) the right includes a right to bargain collectively, or a right to strike.

It remains unclear, for example, to what extent article 22 of the International Covenant on Civil and Political Rights might extend to or include a right for workers to strike. The majority of the Human Rights Committee in the case of *JB et al v Canada*[17] dismissed as inadmissible a communication concerning a prohibition on the right to strike, on the grounds that the *travaux préparatoires* to the instrument did not support the necessary inference of the right from the text of the article itself. On the other hand, in the case of *Sohn v Republic of Korea*,[18] the committee received and upheld a complaint contained in a communication that concerned a trade union leader having been convicted of a crime for advocating a national strike. At least it is now clear that article 11 of the European Convention on Human Rights extends to a right to engage in collective bargaining. It was always difficult to reconcile the finding of the European Court of Human Rights that collective bargaining is not an essential aspect of freedom of association under article 11 (*Gustafsson v Sweden*),[19] with its ruling that a state fails in its obligation to protect the exercise of the same right, if its national law permits the use of financial incentives to workers to forego collective bargaining (*Wilson and the NUJ v UK*).[20]

Magdalena Sepúlveda, M, *The Nature of Obligations under the International Covenant on Economic, Social and Cultural Rights* (Utrecht, Intersentia, 2003); and the powerful critique presented by Fredman, S in *Human Rights Transformed: Positive Rights and Positive Duties* (Oxford, Oxford University Press, 2008).

[17] *JB et al v Canada* Communication No 118/1982 UN Doc Supp No 40 (A/41/40) 151 (1986).

[18] *Jong-Kyu Sohn v Republic of Korea* Communication No 518/1992 UN Doc. CCPR/C/54/D/518/1992 (1995).

[19] *Gustafsson v Sweden* (1996) 22 EHRR 409; Novitz, T, 'Negative Freedom of Association' (1997) 26 *Industrial Law Journal* 79.

[20] *Wilson and the NUJ v UK* (2002) 35 EHRR 20. *Cf Demir and Baykara v Turkey* (App. no. 34503/97) Grand Chamber, Judgment of 12 Nov 2008.

In this, however, we come up against another of the challenges of using human rights law to pursue workers' claims: arguably the pursuit of collective bargaining as something central to the exercise of workers' freedom of association requires much more than a mere right of representation, useful though it may be. Merely being able to appoint a nominal representative, for example in a staff association, is very different from being heard or consulted, much less negotiated or bargained with (collectively).[21] There would seem to be little point in pursuing the right in law if that which were delivered were so much less than what was sought.

The European Court has not been alone, however, in its uncertainty about the scope of the individual's freedom of association. As Christian Brunelle observes, the Canadian Supreme Court has decided two key cases on these issues in recent years—*Dunmore v Ontario*[22] and the *Health Services and Support-Facilities Subsector Bargaining Association v British Columbia (HSS)* case[23]—which have overturned important, and previously well-established interpretations of art 2(c) of the Charter. Since 2007, the law in Canada extends to the proposition that the right to bargain collectively with an employer is protected as part of the freedom of association, on the ground that it 'enhances the human dignity, liberty and autonomy of workers by giving them the opportunity to influence the establishment of workplace rules and thereby gain some control over a major aspect of their lives'.[24] This is a potentially significant departure from the decisions in the so-called 'trilogy' of labour cases, in which the Supreme Court held that the freedom of association extended neither to a right to strike, nor to a right to engage in collective bargaining. Indeed, in those cases the Court limited the scope of the right's protection for an association to little more than the activities that its individual members might otherwise lawfully pursue.[25]

For their part, the district courts of the United States have issued decisions in cases brought under the Alien Tort Claims Act which are also attended by a quality of normative dissonance. Perhaps the key area of difficulty for our present purposes is that the Alien Tort Claims Act uses, but does not define,

---

[21] Cf Hendy, J, *Every Worker Shall Have A Right to be Represented at Work* (London, Institute of Employment Rights, 1998) who considers that the right to be represented has extensive implications, including access to meaningful negotiation through collective bargaining. See also Hendy, J and Walton, M, 'An Individual Right to Union Representation in International Law' (1997) 26 *Industrial Law Journal* 205.

[22] *Dunmore v Ontario (AG)* [2001] 3 SCR 1016.

[23] *Health Services and Support-Facilities Subsector Bargaining Association (HSS) v British Columbia* 2007 SCC 27. See also Fudge, J, 'The Supreme Court of Canada and the Right to Bargain Collectively: The Implications of the *Health Services and Support* case in Canada and Beyond' (2008) 37 *Industrial Law Journal* 25.

[24] *HSS v British Columbia* [2007] SCC 27 [82].

[25] The Trilogy: *Reference re Public Service Employee Relations Act (Alberta)* [1987] 1 SCR 313; *Retail, Wholesale and Department Store Union, Locals 544, 496, 635 and 955 v Government of Saskatchewan* [1987] 1 SCR 460, and *Public Service Alliance of in Canada v Canada* [1987] 1 SCR 424.

the expression 'the law of nations'. Neither is there any legislative history that would enable a court to determine satisfactorily what Congress intended by the term when the Act was passed in 1789. The United States Supreme Court has held that the concept covers international norms that are 'specific, universal and obligatory', and cases have established that this includes (unsurprisingly) genocide, torture, and extra-judicial killing, among other breaches of human rights. It also includes being subjected to forced labour. But this still leaves the question whether 'the law of nations' might be capable of comprehending first, the other co-called 'core' labour standards (and in particular the freedom of association) and secondly, 'non-core' rights at work including provisions relating to working time, wages and occupational health and safety.

Such normative inconsistency, even dissonance, may in part be attributed to the simple fact that there are differences between the international, regional and national instruments and institutions that protect the human rights of workers that are on occasion subtle, but always potentially profound. First, there are differences between the terms of the instruments that protect rights. Where freedom of association is concerned, for example, one key difference is whether the freedom specifically extends to the formation of trade unions. They are mentioned in article 11 of the European Convention on Human Rights and in article 8 of the International Covenant on Economic, Social and Cultural Rights. Trade unions are not mentioned in article 2 of the Canadian Charter, however, which makes it something of a paradox that the Canadian Supreme Court went so far in its understanding of the importance of collective bargaining in facilitating the individual freedom of association.

Even those instruments that do protect the specific example of the formation of trade unions generally do not confer any particular rights upon the unions themselves. By contrast, ILO Convention No 87 goes to great lengths to do so. It is not surprising, then, that ILO jurisprudence around the rights of workers to associate, and the rights of the associations that they form, is by far the most extensive in the international arena. It reflects not only the ILO's particular institutional competence, but the different normative basis for its work. And so of course it is possible to arrive at different results in different systems in relation to the same case. A well-known example is the English case involving workers at Government Communication Headquarters (GCHQ) in the 1980s. The Government had banned GCHQ workers from forming a union that might engage in bargaining—although not a representative staff association. The ILO's Committee on Freedom of Association considered this to be in breach of ILO principles, and the ILO's Committee of Experts on the Application of Conventions and Recommendations considered it to be inconsistent with the United Kingdom's obligations under Convention No 87.[26]

---

[26] See Novitz, T, 'International Promises and Domestic Pragmatism: To What Extent will the Employment Relations Act 1999 Implement International Labour Standards Relating to Freedom of Association' (2000) 63 *Modern Law Review* 379, 384.

By contrast, the then European Commission on Human Rights did not consider there to have been a breach of article 11 of the European Convention on Human Rights, and the Committee of Independent Experts under the European Social Charter subsequently deferred to the opinion of the Commission.[27]

At the national level, complaints about violations of workers' human rights will almost always be heard in courts properly so-called, but that does not exclude the possibility of institutional difference: in many instances these cases will come before constitutional courts, but traditionally many issues relating to the rights of workers might have been dealt with in specialist labour courts or dispute settlement institutions. As we have seen, both Chioma Agomo and Stefan van Eck in chapters eight and nine respectively have a clear preference for the specialist jurisdictions. Nor are all courts with jurisdiction in respect of fundamental human rights similarly empowered. Constitutional courts in South Africa and Canada (for example) have the capacity to issue orders declaring laws or practices invalid for inconsistency with fundamental human rights. The UK Human Rights Act of 1998, however, gives no such power to a court, and nor do the Bills of Rights adopted in the Australian Capital Territory and the State of Victoria. Finally, it might be noted that the case of China also illustrates that it is not only courts that are or that might be empowered in important ways in respect of basic rights.

Nor is it only the institutions that differ at national level: so too do the norms themselves, and also the types of laws by which they are protected. Whereas constitutions protect basic rights in, for example, Brazil, Canada and South Africa, in England rights are protected in entrenched legislation, and in Australia any protection derives only from statute.

Moreover, it would appear that among the different countries considered here we can see that there are different local legal structures, traditions and capacities. Weakness of legal institutions in Cambodia, for example, acts as a significant dampener on the effective implementation of workers' basic rights. The differences between local legal structures and traditions can also have surprising outcomes. Australia, for example, has neither constitutional nor entrenched legislative protection of human rights, whether for workers or otherwise. The United States, on the other hand, has a strong bill of rights including protection of freedom of association. Yet the outcome is relatively similar: in each case domestic legislation, and the way that it has been interpreted by the courts, has facilitated significant limitations on the exercise of freedom of association, in ways that are clearly incompatible with international standards.

---

[27] See *Council of Civil Service Unions v United Kingdom* (App no 11603/85) (European Commission of Human Rights).

The similarity of outcome in these two different legal traditions sheds light, then, on Stefan van Eck's argument (in the case of South Africa) that the constitutionalisation of workers' rights is problematic for the continued operation of traditional labour law concepts and institutions. A final point that might be made about institutional and national differences in how rights are protected is that the allocation of legislative powers within federations (Australia, Canada, Nigeria, South Africa and the United States) may be significant. So too, as we have emphasised, will be the willingness of courts to play a role in the elaboration of principles and norms that are protective of workers' interests, as for example in India and, in more recent times at least, Canada.

In our view, these differences between both national and international systems further illustrate our argument that the differences we identified within the liberal tradition of human rights thinking continue to play a very important role in the construction and protection of the basic human rights of workers. Differences within the tradition have led to different ways of protecting rights, both in terms of legal instruments and the institutions established to oversee them. Those differences are also evident in both the arguments and the decisions that are made either for or against the use, application or scope of particular rights on behalf of workers. It stands to reason that the extent of the differences both within and between jurisdictions, and also the strength of their connection to unresolved theoretical differences of long-standing, are in turn likely to have a significant potential to perpetuate those very differences.

Nevertheless, we would agree with Patrick Macklem's suggestion that there may be ways to see labour rights, in particular, and economic and social rights, more broadly, as potentially central to the international economic order.[28] Indeed we are persuaded by many of the arguments that are presently being made in favour of exactly such a proposition, especially in the work of Deakin and Wilkinson,[29] and in the work of others, many of whom have been inspired in this direction by the writings of Amartya Sen.[30] What is striking about that work is that much of it is located *outside* the discourse of international human rights law. Nevertheless, in our view, on the evidence assembled in this volume, there is, at present in the outcomes of cases seeking to apply international human rights law, relatively little

[28] Macklem, P, 'The Right to Bargain Collectively in International Law: Workers' Right, Human Right, International Right?' in P Alston (ed), *Labour Rights as Human Rights* (Oxford, Oxford University Press, 2005) 84.
[29] Deakin, S and Wilkinson, F, 'Rights vs Efficiency? The Economic Case for Transnational Labour Standards' (1994) 23 *Industrial Law Journal* 289; and Deakin, S and Wilkinson, F, *The Law of the Labour Market: Industrialisation, Employment and Legal Evolution* (Oxford, Oxford University Press, 2005).
[30] Sen, S, *Development as Freedom* (Oxford, Oxford University Press, 1999).

support for some of the particular propositions that Macklem states. As to that of course, we must wait to see whether the reasoning of the Canadian Supreme Court in the *HSS* case has broader influence than in Canada alone.[31] We also observe that the disagreement both within and between jurisdictions reflects historical tensions in the human rights debate which have influenced political theory in such profound ways that it seems at best speculative to suggest that the majority of states have agreed or would be likely to agree upon it.

Looked at from another point of view, it may be that what we argue are artificial distinctions made in the international instruments between civil and political freedoms on one side and socio-economic and cultural rights on the other (notwithstanding the rhetoric of indivisibility) leads to a 'fudging' of issues and a failure to address rigorously the particular problems faced by workers within a human rights framework. Virginia Mantouvalou, in chapter fifteen, has suggested that the European Court of Human Rights might follow a more 'integrated' approach to its judicial task. That is, the Court might pay more thorough attention to the findings of other international supervisory bodies, such as the International Committee on Economic, Social and Cultural Rights, the ILO Committee on Freedom of Association and, in the European context, the European Committee on Economic and Social Rights.

There is another key difficulty that arises from the tendency to distinguish civil and political rights from economic, social and cultural rights. It is the common representation of civil and political rights as inherently individualistic in character, and economic and social rights as collective. (We have already touched on how this appears to influence the types of procedures established to supervise compliance with different types of rights.) The emphasis on a human right as civil and political, and therefore individual, can clearly have very negative potential. Lance Compa has cogently identified the negative consequences for union organisation in his contribution to this volume in chapter ten. It is also critical to recall that the rise of neoliberalism was accompanied by, indeed centred on, a significant emphasis on individual rights and liberties, and in particular on freeing them from the constraints of the nation (welfare) state. Hayek is perhaps the key thinker in that tradition for present purposes, but he has many followers, particularly among those who are in the business of promoting the advantages and benefits of economic globalisation.[32]

---

[31] See *HSS v British Columbia* [2007] SCC 27.

[32] Hayek, F, *Law, Legislation and Liberty: A New Statement of the Liberal Principles of Justice and Political Economy* (London, Routledge, 1980). See also the introduction to this collection, chapter one.

These arguments would appear already to have had a significant impact. The importance of individual rights was a key rhetorical tool underlying the Thatcher Government's breaking down of laws that had provided support for trade unions.[33] More recently, similar arguments were used in the mid 1990s in Australia for exactly the same purpose (see for example, Colin Fenwick in this volume in chapter two). Lance Compa also notes the fears of labour activists in the US context who are concerned by the individualistic emphasis of the neo-liberal approach to human rights. And as we have discussed in the introduction, Philip Alston has argued forcefully that insofar as freedom of association is part of a core of labour rights, the emphasis on civil and political rights—and the argument that the choice is sustainable because of the procedural or process nature of the rights—certainly has strong echoes of Hayek's insistence on the significance of individual human liberty. [34]

We do not suggest that all types of arguments about human rights, or even individual rights and liberties, are inevitably tainted with the consequences of these influences and trends. Indeed, in chapter thirteen, Lisa Tortell points to ILO attempts to protect labour rights by virtue of their fundamental importance to the reinstatement of civil liberties and free speech in Belarus in ways that few would find objectionable. What must be considered, however, is the extent to which these influences affect the weight of individual rights arguments when deployed for what are essentially collective purposes. Keith Ewing, in particular, was quick to question whether individual human rights concepts are suitable to the goal of promoting and protecting collective (that is, social) interests,[35] and indeed it may be timely to examine more thoroughly the ways in which these are balanced.[36]

This issue has been a cause of significant concern in relation to the jurisprudence of the European Court of Human Rights on the interpretation of

---

[33]   See eg Simpson, B, 'Freedom of Association and the Right to Organise: The Failure of an Individual Rights Strategy' (1995) 24 *Industrial Law Journal* 235. The author notes the importance of the negative freedom of association as both a rhetorical and a legal device for breaking down support for collective union activity. Note also his observations that a reason not to rely on individual rights is 'judicial conservatism' (commenting on the House of Lords in *Wilson v Associated Newspapers* [1995] IRLR 258, [1995] 2 All ER 100, [1995] 2 WLR 354—at 244), and his remarks on the prospect of using the individual right. Even if revitalised, he argues, there is a danger of it becoming a procedural right (compare Alston's concern about process rights): 'the law on the positive aspect of freedom of association could come to be seen to require no more of employers than to be able to show that decisions are taken as part of practices which ostensibly respect the individual right of workers to union membership and to be active in union affairs in their own time'.

[34]   See Alston, P, 'Facing Up to the Complexities of the ILO's Core Labour Standards Agenda' (2005) 16 *European Journal of International Law* 467, 477.

[35]   Ewing, KD, 'Social Rights and Constitutional Law' [1999] *Public Law* 105.

[36]   See for a superb starting point, McHarg, A, 'Reconciling Human Rights and the Public Interest: Conceptual Problems and Doctrinal Uncertainty in the Jurisprudence of the European Court of Human Rights' (1999) 62 *Modern Law Review* 671.

article 11 of the European Convention.[37] In particular, the Court appears to have shown a marked preference for the protection of the negative right of association, that is, an individual's right to disassociate from a collectivity, over the right to act collectively. At the same time, however, it appears that the strict formalism of rights and their influence on the rule of law[38] can, even in this context, operate to the benefit of trade unions. Thus, following the judgment of the European Court of Human Rights in *ASLEF v United Kingdom*,[39] it appears that a trade union can choose to disassociate itself from a potential member, a consequence investigated both by Davies and Mantouvalou in chapters six and fifteen respectively.

The *ASLEF* decision has the virtue of acknowledging the trade union itself as a bearer of fundamental rights. As noted, this is a characteristic in particular of ILO Convention No 87 on freedom of association and protection of the right to organise that distinguishes it from most other instruments. It is an explicit recognition of the need of the association, the collectivity, to be able to act on behalf of its members, in order to make good on their goals for associating in the first place. This sort of principle is, of course, missing from many of the decisions to which we have referred above, in which the individual freedom of association has been held not to extend to a right to collective bargaining, or to strike. Applying the idea that a union ought to be able to be effective on behalf of its members, it would seem to follow that in a case such as *ASLEF*, Convention No 87 would require that a union might exercise its right to develop its own rules, on behalf of its members, as a basis to determine who might or might not join, and subject to the general law, including of course any law on discrimination.

But that is quite a different basis upon which to reach the conclusion. Seen in this light then, the determination that a union has a right under article 11 to dissociate from a potential member is less an affirmation of the rights of the union *as representative of its members* than it is a further entrenchment of a neo-liberal, individualistic conception of human rights that is perhaps less likely in the long run to fulfil the goals of promoting social rights for workers. While Mantouvalou notes that, on a more principled basis, the Court's finding must be subject to exceptions, it appears that the Court's judgment adheres to a narrower parity of treatment principle, rather than one of contextual analysis.

As the comparison with how the *ASLEF* case might have been decided applying ILO freedom of association principles suggests, it may be the ILO

---

[37] Alston, 'Labour Rights as Human Rights' (2005) 20. See, in agreement Novitz above, in this volume in chapter fourteen and, for an alternative perspective, see also Mantouvalou in this volume in chapter fifteen above.

[38] *Cf* Thompson, EP, *Whigs and Hunters* (London, Allen Lane, 1975) who considers the rule of law, if not legal rights, to be an 'unqualified human good'.

[39] *ASLEF v United Kingdom* (App no 11002/05); [2007] IRLR 361. See Ewing, KD, 'The Implications of the *ASLEF* Case' (2007) 36 *Industrial Law Journal* 425.

which can supply the sort of context for which Mantouvalou calls. That is, the ILO might be better placed to give human rights an interpretation which reflects the reality of the industrial relations settings in which workers may wish to rely upon them. Teri Carraway has argued that the ILO is itself hostage to a liberal, market-led approach to freedom of association.[40] As Jill Murray observes in this volume, however, the current richness and breadth of jurisprudence on freedom of association from the ILO Governing Body Committee on Freedom of Association, and the Committee of Experts on the Application of Conventions and Recommendations would seem to indicate that this is not as reducible to a narrow neo-liberal agenda. Indeed, the ILO seems to be acting as a leader here, in terms of established supervisory mechanisms. Novitz has shown, for example, that unions frequently prefer to use the ILO supervision system over both the Inter-American and the African regional human rights systems. ILO condemnation had a significant influence on legislative reform in South Africa, as noted in this volume by van Eck in chapter nine.

The South African case also illustrates, however, the work the ILO did to provide direct assistance in the drafting of the country's new laws. Moreover, although it is not widely studied, that sort of approach continues to underpin much of the ILO's work directly with its Member States, especially its programmes to deliver technical cooperation to promote compliance with the 1998 Declaration. Indeed, between 1999 and 2007, the ILO's Programme on Promoting the Declaration ran over 90 projects in some 70 countries around the world, at a total cost of over US \$100 million. In Brazil, Indonesia and Morocco, for example, these projects focused, among other things, on assisting those countries' governments to reform key aspects of their labour laws.[41] The chapters in this volume also attest to the concrete effects that ILO work has had in affecting social conditions and legislative reform in Brazil, Cambodia and Nigeria. As we explore below, this suggests that a combination of hard and soft law approaches to the promotion of workers' basic human rights may offer greater potential than concentrating only on legal avenues to insist upon the protection of workers' human rights.

REGULATORY CHALLENGES AND INNOVATIONS

One of the primary goals of this book has been to explore the application of human rights law to the goal of promoting decent working

---

[40] Caraway, T, 'Freedom of Association: Battering Ram or Trojan Horse?' (2006) 13(2) *Review of International Political Economy* 210.

[41] Fenwick, C and Kring, T, *Rights at Work: An Assessment of the Declaration's Technical Cooperation in Select Countries* (Geneva, ILO, 2007).

conditions for all. As we have observed, the strategy of appealing to the idea of fundamental human rights as a way of pursuing that goal has two distinct, but related aspects. One is the moral or philosophical argument that those who work are thereby entitled to certain basic rights. As we have stressed, this is a line of argument with a long and varied intellectual history. The second limb of the human rights approach to protecting workers' rights has been the perceived practical utility of relying on 'real' or 'hard' law, and the possibility that it might be enforced in a meaningful way. As we have seen, in practice the results have been mixed. As we explore below, this perhaps both explains and justifies the variety of other means that have been used to promote the fundamental interests of workers.

An important question that arises is how best to understand both the limits and the possibilities of using human rights law in order to pursue workers' interests. Recent developments in the European Court of Human Rights and the Canadian Supreme Court notwithstanding, the outcomes of using human rights law have in many respects been less successful than might have been hoped for by those who have sought to rely upon it. The examples of Cambodia and China also suggest significant limits on using human rights law at the national level, even if for rather different reasons. And while there have been many cases brought in the United States under the Alien Tort Claims Act against corporations, they are hard fought, and to date only one—the litigation over Unocal's activities in Burma—has led to a settlement for the plaintiffs. Indeed, the only such case to be tried before a jury was decided for the defendant company, although at the time of writing a new trial was being sought as the plaintiffs argued that the trial judge improperly excluded key evidence.[42]

As we have discussed, the limits on the impact of using human rights law to promote workers' interests are, in our view, a product of the ongoing effects of long standing disagreements within the liberal tradition of theories about the rights of workers: these have affected both the institutions established and the decisions that they have made. On one view of things, then, pessimism about the utility of human rights law in the pursuit of workers' rights would be well justified. Inherent in such a view, however, are certain assumptions about the nature of 'hard' legal rules and their likely effects, that is, about the role of legal rules as methods of regulating to achieve particular economic and social policy outcomes.

In our view, insights from regulatory studies are useful in helping to understand the role and effects of human rights law, and the relationship between efforts to enforce those rights, and other strategies that have been developed to promote workers' interests.[43] 'Regulatory studies' is a broad

---

[42] See information available at www.iradvocates.org/drummondcase.html.

[43] Our overview of the key concepts of regulatory theory draws heavily on the work of John Howe (Melbourne Law School) and in particular his paper 'The Role of Regulation', presented

field of academic discourse that has sought to make sense of the role of the state and law in the context of changes to capitalist democracies.[44] One of the field's key concerns, then, is to examine the role of hard legal rules. Examination of the potential of regulatory theory for analysis of labour law, especially in the context of international regulatory regimes, has only recently begun,[45] although Jill Murray in chapter twelve in this collection marks a significant step in that direction, at least insofar as its application to the ILO is concerned.[46]

A key insight from regulatory theory is the analytical construct of 'regulatory space', and the related idea of a 'decentred' understanding of regulation. A 'decentred' approach is built upon a particular definition of regulation, as 'the intentional activity of attempting to control, order or influence the behaviour of others according to defined standards or purposes with the intention of producing a broadly identified outcome or outcomes', which may involve a variety of different regulatory mechanisms, techniques or instruments.[47] It can immediately be seen that this raises questions about the role of hard legal rules, and also other methods of pursuing the ends for which those rules might be enacted and deployed. At the heart of the idea of a 'decentred' approach to understanding regulation is an acknowledgement that any given 'regulatory space' (defined by the range of issues under investigation) is filled by contested policy objectives or rationales, a variety of regulators and regulated actors (with varying degrees of power) and a range of different regulatory techniques or systems. The idea of 'regulatory space' recognises that: 'Regulation is two-way, or three or four-way process,

at a Roundtable on International Labour Standards hosted by the Centre for Employment and Labour Relations Law in 2005. We are indebted to John for permission to draw on his work.

[44] For a comprehensive overview of the field, see Braithwaite, J and Parker, C, 'Regulation' in P Cane and M Tushnet (eds), *The Oxford Handbook of Legal Studies* (Oxford, Oxford University Press, 2003); Daintith, T, 'Regulation' in International Association of Legal Science, *International Encyclopaedia of Comparative Law*, vol XVII ch 10 (Tubingen, Germany, Mohr Siebeck, 1997) and Black, J, 'Critical Reflections on Regulation' (2002) 27 *Australian Journal of Legal Philosophy* 1.

[45] For a discussion of how regulatory studies may apply to labour law see Arup, C, 'Labour Law as Regulation: Promise and Pitfalls' (2001) 14 *Australian Journal of Labour Law* 229. For a more comprehensive attempt to think about labour law from the point of view of regulation theory, see Arup, C et al, *Labour Law and Labour Market Regulation* (Sydney, Federation Press, 2006). For the application of regulatory theory to international labour standards see Murray, 'The Sound of One Hand Clapping?' (2001).

[46] By contrast, there is a growing literature on the operation of compliance mechanisms in international law more broadly which, particularly in the area of human rights, acknowledges that enforcement is only a small part of the picture: Alston (n 7) 473, and see in particular the sources referred to in n 10.

[47] Black, J, 'Critical Reflections on Regulation' (2002) 27 *Australian Journal of Legal Philosophy* 1, 26.

between all those involved in the regulatory process, and particularly between regulator and regulated in the implementation of regulation.'[48]

It appears to us that these ideas from regulation theory might usefully offer our inquiry a way of thinking about the scope and the role of 'hard' human rights law, and about the relationship of that method of regulation to others. Thinking about human rights law from the perspective of a decentred approach to regulation takes us beyond a traditional concept of state (or international) regulation which is focused only or predominantly on legal rules that are backed by sanctions for non-compliance. Indeed, one of the principal concerns of regulation theory is to explore the weaknesses in practice of such a 'command and control' approach to regulation, and of how regulators might respond to those limits in innovative ways. Thus, there is now a very extensive literature identifying the weaknesses of hierarchical models of regulation in many contexts.[49]

It is important to emphasise, however, that insights from regulation theory do not dictate that a regulator ought to abandon any reliance on hard rules: we are certainly not arguing that regulation theory suggests that human rights *law* be abandoned. Rather, what regulation theory suggests is that the scope and the role of hard rules should be thought of and deployed in different ways than might traditionally be understood. In particular, they should be used as key elements of a broader approach to regulation and to regulatory enforcement, that is, one that deploys a wider range of regulatory techniques, but in all cases in the interests of pursuing the goals and interests that are enshrined in the hard rules themselves.

One way of thinking about this idea in regulatory scholarship is the notion of a 'regulatory pyramid', which helps to depict the concept graphically. The regulatory pyramid we present here is based on the idea of an enforcement pyramid developed by Ayres and Braithwaite.[50]

It is important to emphasise that while insights from regulatory theory suggest, and the pyramid helps to depict, the range of regulatory strategies that might be deployed, it does not mean that hard legal rules should be abandoned. On the contrary: it is the hard legal rules that serve as goal, guide, and potentially as a source of sanction. In the context of our

---

[48] Ibid 7.

[49] See eg, Ayres, I and Braithwaite, J, *Responsive Regulation: Transcending the Deregulation Debate* (New York, Oxford University Press, 1992); and Bardach, E and Kagan, R, *Going by the Book: The Problem of Regulatory Unreasonableness* (Philadelphia, Temple University Press, 1982).

[50] Ayres and Braithwaite, *Responsive Regulation: Transcending the Deregulation Debate* (1992); see also Marshall in chapter twenty on contract compliance in supply chains. In some regulatory scholarship, two 'enforcement pyramids' have been developed: in the area of environmental regulation, for example, Bridget Hutter used one pyramid for enforcement strategies, and another for sanctions: Hutter, B, *Compliance: Regulation and Environment* (Oxford, Clarendon Press, 1997) 229–30.

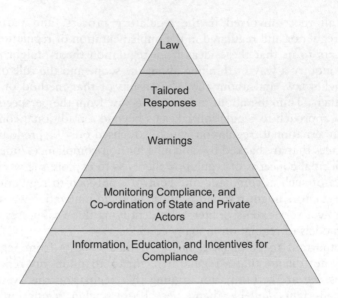

present inquiry, it is the rules that enshrine the fundamental rights of workers, to which they are entitled by virtue of their inherent human dignity. What regulation theory suggests, and what the pyramid is intended to depict, is that frequently the most effective way for a regulator to achieve its objective of behavioural change may be to *induce* compliance *without* the application of sanctions. The pyramid therefore contemplates other regulatory strategies that the regulator might use, often in collaboration with other regulatory actors, to achieve the desired change in a manner that is likely to promote the regulatory objectives, in this case, respecting the fundamental rights of workers.

A particular advantage of the regulatory pyramid is that it is flexible: it will not necessarily be the same for each situation in which it might be applied. Thus, it is not a concept of optimal regulation that might or must be applied in any social context. Rather, it is a way to conceptualise—and to depict graphically—a range of interlinked regulatory approaches that might be adopted, all of which reflect and promote key objectives by working *both toward and from* a basis in hard human rights law. Thus, an essential feature of each pyramid would be the 'apex' of substantive human rights law, and the institutions that are established to supervise and, in some cases, to enforce compliance with the obligations that these laws establish. This is because in the absence of these substantive legal rights (and any enforcement machinery sanctions), regulators will have far less capacity to apply any leverage against those unwilling to comply with the law. The rest of the pyramid shows that regulation can be tailored to particular circumstances. Thus, the vertical dimension of the pyramid does not dictate a linear progression through layers of regulatory action, but rather the options that are available.

There are certain weaknesses in using the idea of a regulatory pyramid for a universal or international issue, considered separately from a particular state, or regulatory regime or agency. On the other hand, there is significant potential to draw on the concept of the regulatory pyramid in considering the outcomes of efforts to protect workers' basic rights as human rights within particular jurisdictions. The contribution to this volume on developments in Cambodia provided by Adler and Woolcock in chapter nineteen illustrates the range of regulatory strategies that may need to be deployed in a given country in order to work toward making law effective in practice. Indeed, there is a case for the utilisation of multiple strategies.

There is also significant potential to draw on the concept of a regulatory pyramid as a way of thinking about the inter-relationship of the different regulatory modes and strategies that are available to the ILO, and to understand their relationship to each other. In particular, it has great potential to shape an understanding of the role of ILO standards, and the need for or desirability of different forms of ILO action. It could also shed light on how best to understand what may appear to be some of the significant weaknesses of the ILO system of standards supervision, and of how the various elements of that system are deployed from time to time.

One element of the regulatory pyramid that is of particular use in the broader context—that is, detached from any particular regime or agency—is its emphasis on the idea that there might be a range of regulatory actors and modes of regulation. This obviously has important links with the idea that, in any given 'regulatory space', there will be different actors, and with the idea of regulation as a process. In our view, these ideas may be useful in understanding the ways in which different approaches to promoting the human rights of workers might be related to each other, rather than seen as different from or alternative to each other, as Adler and Woolcock suggest. The idea of a regulatory space populated by different actors has the potential to bring together with some coherence the range of approaches to promoting the human rights of workers. In particular it can help in the development of a more coherent understanding of the inter-relationship of 'hard' and 'soft' means of regulation, and of approaches to the promotion of workers' human rights that may appear somewhat removed from enforcement of human rights law.

So-called hard law mechanisms are commonly associated with the domestic protection of human rights, which offers forms of constitutional protection in which rights are presented as a 'side constraint' on public policy.[51] We see the use of these mechanisms in the Canadian Charter of

---

[51] Classic examples include Nozick, R, *Anarchy State and Utopia* (New York, Basic Books, 1974) 30 et seq; and Dworkin, R, *Taking Rights Seriously* (Avon, Duckworth, The Bath Press, 1977) ch 7. See this collection, ch one above.

Rights and Freedoms, the UK Human Rights Act, and the US constitutional framework, as discussed by Brunelle, Davies, and Compa in chapters four, six and ten respectively. As we have seen, there are limits on what these 'hard' rules deliver. From the perspective of regulation theory, however, this does not mean that reliance on these rules should be abandoned: rather, those who seek to rely upon them should understand their limitations, and perhaps look to combine their operation with other regulatory modes.

At the international level, regional human rights instruments also create hard legal obligations, and they are from time to time the subject of enforcement action in courts of law. While Novitz has shown that there has been significantly more use of this option in the European regional system, it nevertheless exists in both the Inter-American and African systems of human rights. Novitz and Syrpis, in their analysis of key recent decisions of the European Court of Justice, have also shed light on the implications of how some types of hard law might do relatively little to protect workers' human rights, and might even contribute to the erosion of their protection.

At the international or multilateral level, it is more common to see a 'soft' law approach. The International Covenant on Civil and Political Rights and its counterpart, the International Covenant on Economic, Social and Cultural Rights create supervisory bodies whose findings and conclusions lack significant impact even if, strictly speaking, they do have legal effect. The same might be thought true of the machinery established to supervise obligations imposed on states by the European Social Charter. And to the frustration of some writers,[52] although the ILO has a long history of establishing international labour standards, it has no power to enforce compliance with the obligations that those standards create; indeed it is axiomatic that the ILO primarily operates by way of the 'mobilisation of shame'.

In this collection, Tortell's examination of ILO action in the case of Belarus in chapter thirteen serves in large measure to illustrate the limitations of the ILO's supervisory system, even when it deploys the full range of those mechanisms, which of course it does only in the most serious of cases. Another well-known example of the limitations of ILO supervision is the case of Burma, which has failed properly to implement the recommendations of an ILO Commission of Inquiry concerning its failure to comply with its obligations under the Forced Labour Convention 1929, which were delivered in 1997. While the case is well known—indeed Burma is notorious as a nation that routinely violates the full spectrum of its citizen's human rights in ways that are both gross and systematic—it has been the

---

[52] See, for example, Brown, D and McColgan, A, 'UK Employment Law and the International Labour Organisation: The Spirit of Cooperation' (1992) 21 *Industrial Law Journal* 265.

subject of relatively little academic writing. The principal exception to this is the work of Francis Maupain, a former legal advisor to the ILO who was closely involved for many years in its efforts to make progress in the case of Burma.[53]

Taken together with Tortell's chapter in this volume, and Murray's work both in chapter twelve and elsewhere, we see then something of the range of views on the proper role of the ILO. From one point of view, what these cases suggest is the need for hard law obligations that are accompanied by proper means of enforcement. The impact of ILO supervision might be contrasted with, for example, the effects of decisions of the European Court of Human Rights. From a regulatory point of view, as we have emphasised, hard legal rules have an essential role to play. What the cases also illustrate is an institutional weakness in using international human rights mechanisms to promote workers' rights: these mechanisms are fundamentally limited by states' unwillingness to limit their sovereignty by creating and submitting themselves to the jurisdiction of international organisations that might have real teeth. From this point of view, then, the ILO's efforts are not as ineffectual as they may first appear. It might be better to see the ILO as having deployed, and continuing to deploy, a wide range of regulatory strategies to engage with certain members of its regulated community, in a process that is intended to assist them in moving towards compliance.

A regulatory understanding of ILO supervision aside, the perceived weaknesses of ILO and other international supervision of workers' human rights have led others, (although not in this volume), to suggest that what is needed is more stringent international regulation. Indeed the idea of hard legal rules backed by real enforcements is the essence of arguments for some form of social clause to be included either in the framework of the World Trade Organisation (WTO), or in particular trade agreements.[54] Such a clause would be intended to restrict the opportunities to trade of those states which do not provide adequate protection of core labour standards. While the fierce opposition of developing states to such a provision

---

[53] Maupain, F, 'Is the ILO Effective in Upholding Workers' Rights? Reflections on the Myanmar Experience' in P Alston (ed), *Labour Rights as Human Rights* (Oxford, Oxford University Press, 2005).

[54] For debate on this issue, see for example, Addo, K, 'The Correlation between Labour Standards and International Trade' (2002) 36(2) *Journal of World Trade* 285; Bal, S, 'International Free Trade Agreements and Human Rights: Reinterpreting Article XX of the GATT' (2001) 10 *Minnesota Journal of Global Trade* 62; Blackett, A, 'Whither Social Clause? Human Rights, Trade Theory and Treaty Interpretation' (1999) 31 *Colum. Hm. Rts. L. Rev.* 1; and van Roozendaal, G, *Trade Unions and Global Governance: The Debate on a Social Clause* (London, Routledge, 2002). See also Kaufmann, *Globalisation and Labour Rights* (2007); and Hepple (both) n 3 above.

in WTO instruments has inhibited its development,[55] trade tariffs have been made provisional on compliance with core labour standards under the EU GSP. This regulatory strategy is, however, considered by Orbie and De Ville to be one more aligned with impression management than a determined effort to secure protection of labour rights as human rights through tariff preferences. Compa and others have elsewhere been similarly critical of the United States' GSP system,[56] and for that matter also of the labour side agreement to the North American Free Trade Agreement. For his part, Alston has been critical of the weaknesses he perceives in the labour clauses that have been included in bilateral trade agreements by the United States in recent years.[57]

Moreover, it is evident that where conditionality is utilised in aid arrangements by the International Finance Corporation (IFC) and the European Bank for Reconstruction and Development (EBRD), limited attention is paid to freedom of association. In both the IFC 2006 *Policy and Performance Standards on Social and Environmental Sustainability* and the EBRD 2008 *Environmental and Social Policy*, there is considerable deference to national limitations on the protection of workers' rights to organise. All that is required (under both policies, which have the same wording) is that: 'Where national law substantially restricts the establishment or functioning of workers' organisations, the client will enable means for workers to express their grievances and protect their rights regarding working conditions and terms of employment.'[58]

Leaving aside economic forms of conditionality, it is hard to believe that the collective organisation required to achieve and then to implement International Framework Agreements (IFAs) will be realised. The IFA is a mechanism used to promote ILO core labour standards through collective bargaining, rather than corporate social responsibility.[59] The aim is to create and foster bilateral dialogue, rather than one-sided implementation (and evaluation of implementation) of basic workers' rights. Current studies

---

[55] See Summers, C, 'The Battle in Seattle: Free Trade, Labor Rights, and Societal Values' (2001) 22 *University of Pennsylvania Journal of International Economic Law* 61.

[56] Compa, L and Vogt, JS, 'Labor Rights in the Generalized System of Preferences: A Twenty Year Review' 22 *Comparative Labor Law and Policy Journal* 199.

[57] Alston, P, 'Core Labour Standards and the Transformation of the International Labour Rights Regime' (2004) 15 *European Journal of International Law* 457.

[58] For the origins of this limited approach, see Novitz, T, 'Core Labour Standards Conditionalities: A Means by Which to Achieve Sustainable Development?' in Faundez, J and Tan, C, *International Economic Law, Globalization and Developing Countries* (London, Edward Elgar, 2010, forthcoming).

[59] Hammer, N, 'International Framework Agreements: Global Industrial Relations between Rights and Bargaining' (2005) 11(4) *Transfer* 511; Papadakis, K, 'Research on Transnational Social Dialogue and International Framework Agreements (IFAs)' (2008) *International Labour Review* 100; and Herrnstadt, O, 'Are International Framework Agreements a Path to Corporate Social Responsibility?' (2007–08) 10 *University of Pennsylvania Journal of Business and Employment Law* 187.

suggest partial success, but that more needs to be done to assist and foster collective bargaining in other ways than the over-arching framework provided by agreement between a multinational company and a Global Union Federation.[60]

In the end, the ideal regulatory mechanism may depend on what, as Brian Langille has argued, we consider to be the purpose of international labour law.[61] We agree that this is a vital question to raise and that it is not helpfully answered merely by attempting to construct labour rights in terms of human rights. After all, the human rights of workers are many and various, ranging from protection from slavery to privacy. There is a further question as to which rights claims should be prioritised within a legal framework and how workers can influence that process. Moreover, as observed in our introduction, the construction of workers' rights as human rights also leaves unanswered the relative weight of individual as versus collective rights. A purposive approach to labour law may suggest that it is the collective that should be the priority, given its instrumental importance in securing protection of labour standards.[62] However, this does not answer the question as to which blend of regulatory and enforcement mechanisms is appropriate.

Langille, in a very interesting way, has linked treatment of workers' rights as human rights under the ILO Declaration of Fundamental Principles and Rights at Work 1998 with soft law regulatory mechanisms. Moreover, he argues that this approach is appropriate. There is almost self-evidently a role for soft law on the international stage and, indeed, this has been the standard role of organisations like the ILO. Langille's views, however, are capable of challenge in a myriad ways, as many of the contributions to this volume demonstrate. Murray and McCann, for example, in chapters twelve and eighteen respectively, are insistent that labour law is not readily reducible

---

[60] Riisgard, L, 'International Framework Agreements: A New Model for Securing Workers Rights?' (2005) 44(4) *Industrial Relations* 707; Miller, D, 'Preparing for the Long Haul: Negotiating International Framework Agreements in the Global Textile, Garment and Footwear Sector' (2004) *Global Social Policy* 215; Wills, J, 'Bargaining for the Space to Organize in the Global Economy: A Review of the Accor-IUF Trade Union Rights Agreement' (2002) 9(4) *Review of International Political Economy* 675; and Bourque, R, 'International Framework Agreements and the Future of Collective Bargaining in Multinational Companies' (2008) 12 *Just Labour: A Canadian Journal of Work and Society* 30.

[61] Langille, B, *What is International Labour Law For?* (2009) 3 *Law and Ethics of Human Rights* 47. We are grateful to Brian Langille for presenting a version of this paper at the original Oñati workshop.

[62] See, for example, World Bank Report, *Unions and Collective Bargaining: Economic Effects in a Global Environment* (Washington, World Bank, 2003). This report found that: 'Countries with highly-coordinated collective bargaining tend to be associated with lower and less persistent unemployment, lower earnings inequality, and fewer and shorter strikes than uncoordinated ones. In particular, coordination among employers tends to produce low unemployment. In contrast, fragmented unionism and many different union confederations are often associated with higher inflation and unemployment.'

to human rights, and also question the idea of emphasising promotion rather than enforcement. We are inclined to agree, and in doing so to reiterate the point from regulatory theory, that hard rules and mechanisms for their enforcement must play a key role in any regulatory strategy. The analysis by Adler and Woolcock in chapter nineteen of the importance of a rules-based regime in Cambodia as a basis to develop a discourse around rights, illustrates the point in a different way. Likewise, many contributors to this volume advocate the use of litigation, but not as the only strategy to address human rights violations. We note that advocates of 'responsive' regulation do also emphasise the importance of retaining both institutional structures that regulate substantive ends, and sanctions for enforcing those ends as the apex of the regulatory (or enforcement pyramid). They play the key role in ensuring that other, more facilitative, or promotional techniques are effective.

One aspect of regulation by promotional means with which Langille does not engage at length—although it is apparent from national case studies in this volume relating to Brazil and Cambodia—is the significance of aid and technical co-operation provided to assist in the national implementation of the human rights set out in the 1998 Declaration.[63] Direct assistance to countries to revise their legal frameworks and to develop the institutional capacity to make their legal institutions effective in practice, can properly be understood as part of a broader regulatory approach that is neither inconsistent with nor derogatory of, international labour standards. Indeed, as Maupain has argued, and Fenwick and Kring have shown, international labour standards serve as the touchstone and the guide for the assistance that the ILO offers. From a different level of the regulatory pyramid, we can also see that the more direct condemnation of violations of workers' rights by ILO supervisory bodies is identified by Agomo and van Eck in chapters eight and nine as having played an important role in changing Nigerian and South African labour law, respectively.

In this we see support in both evidence and regulatory theory for McCann's arguments in chapter eighteen that a multi-faceted regulatory approach—such as that taken internationally and domestically in the regulation of working time—is the appropriate course. Some labour law is concerned with human rights and, indeed, working time and forced labour may be linked, but the force of the argument for regulation of working time does not only stem from human rights protection. Other sources of regulatory control, for example through collective bargaining, legislative controls and inspection regimes, may be as significant.

---

[63] See also, more generally, Fenwick and Kring, *Rights at Work: An Assessment of the Declaration's Technical Cooperation in Select Countries* (2007).

Other chapters in this volume also explore approaches to the promotion of workers' interests that are shaped by the content of hard rules protecting basic rights, but which do not take the form of direct enforcement of those rights. Adler and Woolcock in chapter nineteen, for example, illustrate the importance of capacity-building to make law effective in Cambodia. Shelley Marshall in chapter twenty illuminates the potential in using contract compliance as a mechanism for preventing sweated labour, highlighting the factors which are likely to make such a scheme successful. In her view, one of the key factors in making such an approach effective may be the participation of workers' organisations in the design and monitoring of the compliance system. That is, these schemes are more likely to be effective if they are 'responsive', in particular by enabling a range of actors in the regulatory space to participate in the design of the scheme.

We have been at pains to emphasise that the application of regulatory theory to the promotion and enforcement of human rights does not entail any derogation from the signal importance—and the key role—of hard legal norms. We reiterate that regulatory theory does not dictate, and we do not argue, that there should be a retreat to mere promotionalism in international legal regulation of the rights of workers. It is important to acknowledge this again, because there is often significant contestation over the place of standards and their enforcement where the interests of workers are concerned. Philip Alston has argued, for example, that the support of the United States for the adoption of the ILO Declaration of 1998 suited its own purpose of watering down existing hard international standards on workers' rights.[64] Jill Murray has touched on the role of employer organisations at the ILO, where they frequently argue against either the adoption or the enforcement of standards.[65]

Both in the ILO and beyond, there are, as we have noted, many governments in developing countries that stridently oppose the adoption of standards that are promoted in the interests of workers' rights but which they consider to be forms of disguised protectionism. The voting record of states at the ILO for the 1998 Declaration illustrates the division among states on these issues. Moreover, it cannot necessarily be assumed that all representatives of workers are in favour of hard standards and their enforcement, either generally or in particular cases.

The point we are making is not merely that there is division and contestation about rights and how they should be protected and enforced (if at all). So much is well known, and follows from the history of divisions within the liberal tradition to which we have pointed. Rather, our point is that there are clearly some actors with strong interests in opposing new

---

[64] Alston, 'Core Labour Standards and the Transformation of the International Labour Rights Regime' (2004) 491 and 519.
[65] See Murray in chapter twelve above.

regulation, and/or in watering down existing regulatory mechanisms. Multinational corporations, for example, fight hard in litigation under the Alien Tort Claims Act, and in their capacity as employers may not be well disposed to new forms of regulation in the ILO system. There is therefore significant potential danger in adopting a more diffuse approach to promoting rights than one that predominantly emphasises hard law and its enforcement. But on the other hand, regulation theory may have the potential to overcome some of these obstacles. In particular it may offer ways of understanding the inter-relationship of various modes of regulation, and the roles of different actors, as being consistent with each other, rather than in conflict. Moreover, it may offer ways of creating a space for some actors to participate in the debate over and the implementation of human rights regulation for workers that could help to overcome some of their present limitations.

That is, regulation theory might offer the opportunity to overcome some of the important power differentials that exist between and among the relevant actors; it may offer significant potential for weaker states, for example, to participate actively in a process of regulating to improve workers' human rights, rather than perceiving themselves as objects of various regulatory initiatives. Likewise, it offers ways to secure a role for trade unions to participate in regulation at the national level. These insights may therefore be of some value, as it is clear that the ways in which legal systems protect workers' rights (whether as human rights or not) are significantly affected by the interplay of political will and power, and by historical circumstances and conditions.

We might expect governments that do not operate within the bounds of liberal democratic constitutionalism to provide less than appropriate protection of workers' human rights. (Examples may, if controversially, include contemporary China or, in the not too distant past, Cambodia.) Yet this may also be true of governments that are unquestionably liberal, democratic and constitutional (Australia, Canada, the United States). Certain historical moments have presented opportunities to enhance the legal protection of workers' rights, and in some cases to entrench them constitutionally (Brazil, Nigeria, South Africa), although as noted, constitutional protection has not necessarily ensured significant benefits for workers. Historical moments and their impact on the legal protection of workers' rights appear to be situation specific, notwithstanding the overarching pressures of globalisation. Thus, at around the same time that South Africa entrenched protection for workers' rights in its Constitution, Australia implemented statutory reforms to its labour laws that significantly *restricted* the way they protected workers' rights. Developing a broader concept of regulating to promote workers' human rights may be one way of establishing a construct that may at once accommodate, and at the same time ameliorate, the more difficult effects of these phenomena.

A final theme that can be identified might be referred to as a strong feeling that work needs to be done to find ways to make law and legal institutions (including human rights law) more effective as means to promote and to protect workers' rights. This is certainly true of those contributions that have argued for reform and/or for reconceptualisation of the ILO (Murray). But it seems no less true of those authors who have addressed different methods of promoting or enforcing workers' rights, including litigation (as demonstrated by our national case studies), activism and advocacy combined with innovative legal regulation (Marshall in chapter twenty), and economic forces and institutions (Adler and Woolcock (chapter nineteen), as well as Orbie and De Ville (chapter seventeen)). We hope that many of the suggestions made here for enhancing forms of regulation will reach their audience, and that changes sensitive to the requirements of the employment relations context are made to human rights protection not only domestically, but regionally and internationally.

Index